Rendering Techniques '95

Proceedings of the Eurographics Workshop
in Dublin, Ireland, June 12–14, 1995

P. M. Hanrahan
W. Purgathofer (eds.)

Eurographics

SpringerWienNewYork

Prof. Dr. Patrick M. Hanrahan
Stanford University, Stanford, USA

Prof. Dr. Werner Purgathofer
Institut für Computergraphik, Technische Universität Wien,
Wien, Österreich

© 1995 Springer-Verlag/Wien

Typesetting: Camera ready by editors and authors

Graphic design: Ecke Bonk

Printed on acid-free and chlorine-free bleached paper

With 198 partly coloured Figures

ISSN 0946-2767
ISBN-13: 978-3-211-82733-8   e-ISBN-13: 978-3-7091-9430-0
DOI: 10.1007/978-3-7091-9430-0

Preface

This book contains the proceedings of the Eurographics Rendering Workshop 1995, which took place from 12th to 14th June, 1995, in Dublin, Ireland, and was hosted by Trinity College Dublin. Following five successful workshops in the previous five years, the Rendering Workshop is now well established as a major international forum and one of the most reputable events in the field of realistic image synthesis.

This year, 68 submissions were carefully evaluated by 22 program committee members and dozens of additional expert referees, all of whom are listed on page XI. Although many more papers received positive reviews, only the best 31 papers could be accepted and are included in this book. Their average quality is very high and many of the included contributions will certainly influence the scientific progress of the field. The book also contains two invited contributions by Jim Arvo and Alain Fournier.

Almost half of the book is concerned with new ideas on radiosity. Included are contributions on hierarchical radiosity, Monte Carlo radiosity, wavelet radiosity, non-diffuse radiosity, and radiosity performance improvements. Other papers deal with ray tracing, reconstruction techniques, volume rendering, illumination, user interface aspects, and importance sampling. As is the style of the Rendering Workshop, the contributions are mainly of algorithmic nature, often demonstrated by prototype implementations. From these implementations result numerous color images which are included as Appendix, in some papers without reference to this Appendix (so look there if you search for a missing image!).

The Rendering Workshop proceedings are certainly an obligatory piece of literature for all scientists working in the rendering field, but they are also very valuable for the practitioner involved in the implementation of state of the art rendering systems.

We want to thank all persons involved in the production of this book, in particular Mrs. Silvia Schilgerius from Springer-Verlag who was of invaluable help.

Patrick Hanrahan   Werner Purgathofer

May, 1995

Contents

International Program Committee

Anjyo, K. (Japan)
Bouatouch, K. (France)
Chalmers, A. (UK)
Cohen, M. (USA)
Feda, M. (Austria)
Glassner, A. (USA)
Green, S. (UK)
Jansen, F. (Netherlands)
Nakamae, E. (Japan)
Neumann, L. (Hungary)
Pattanaik, S. (India)

Puech, C. (France)
Pueyo, X. (Spain)
Rushmeier, H. (USA)
Sakas, G. (Germany)
Salesin, D. (USA)
Schlick, Ch. (France)
Shirley, P. (USA)
Sillion, F. (France)
Slusallek, Ph. (Germany)
de Sousa A. (Portugal)
Ward, G. (USA)

Referees

Aguas, M.
Arvo, J.
Baranoski, G.
Bastos, R.
Chiba, N.
Chiu, K.
Christensen, P.
Cross, R.
DeRose, T.
Drettakis, G.
Galla, Th.
Gershbein, R.
Gervautz, M.
Gortler, St.
Greiner, G.
Gröller, E.
Kolb, C.
Kopp, M.
Lacroute, P.
Lange, B.
Leitao, M.
Lischinski, D.
Löffelmann, H.
Mazuryk, T.
Navazo, I.
Neumann, A.
Nishita, T.
Peng, Q.

Pharr, M.
Rumpler, M.
Saito, T.
Schälls, A.
Schmalstieg, D.
Schröder, M.
Schröder, P.
Seidel, H-P.
Sharma, R.
Shinya, M.
Stamminger, M.
Stieglecker, P.
Stollnitz, E.
Stuttard, D.
Takahashi, T.
Tanaka, T.
Tastl, I.
Teller, S.
Tobler, R.
Tonnhofer, Th.
Traxler, Ch.
Wagner, R.
Westermann, R.
Wu, E.
Yamamoto, T.
Yokoi, Sh.
Zimmerman, K.

Pyramid Clipping for Efficient Ray Traversal

Maurice van der Zwaan, Erik Reinhard, Frederik W. Jansen

Faculty of Technical Mathematics and Informatics,
Delft University of Technology, Julianalaan 132,
2628BL Delft, The Netherlands

Abstract: Rays having the same origin and similar directions frequently appear in the form of viewing rays and shadow rays to area light sources in ray tracing, and in hemisphere shooting or gathering in radiosity algorithms. The coherence between these rays can be exploited by enclosing a bundle of these rays with a pyramid and by classifying objects with respect to this pyramid prior to tracing the rays. We present an implementation of this algorithm for a bintree spatial subdivision structure and compare the performance with a recursive bintree traversal and the standard grid traversal algorithm. In parallel implementations the technique can be used to create coherent intersection tasks, allowing demand-driven scheduling with low communication overheads.

1 Introduction

With high quality rendering becoming more and more widespread, the demand for shorter rendering times increases. Both ray tracing and ray tracing-based radiosity algorithms may satisfy the needs of users in terms of quality, but still lack behind when it comes to speed of execution. Spatial subdivision techniques have greatly improved the efficiency of ray tracing but further optimizations in that direction will be difficult to achieve.

Parallel processing offers an interesting alternative to further speed up the ray tracing process. A problem, however, occurs with object models that are too large to be replicated at each processor memory. Then object data will have to be communicated to the intersection tasks or the tasks will have to be brought to the data. In both cases severe communication overheads and/or load unbalances may be introduced. Efficient parallel rendering can only be achieved when enough data coherence is present in the handling of subsequent ray intersection tasks [1].

A way to create coherent ray intersection tasks is to bundle neighboring rays and to pre-select those objects that are likely to be intersected by this bundle of rays (see figure 1). In Shen et al. [2] such a technique is used to schedule ray tasks on a number of demand-driven intersection processors. Shooting a coherent bundle of rays is a powerful computing primitive that can be applied to tracing primary rays, tracing shadow rays for area light sources and in ray tracing based radiosity algorithms for shooting or gathering energy from one patch to another. Also with brdf-reflection models, incoming rays will spawn a large number of coherent reflection rays.

Earlier ray coherence methods exploiting the notion that rays with similar directions and origins, are likely to intersect the same objects, can be found

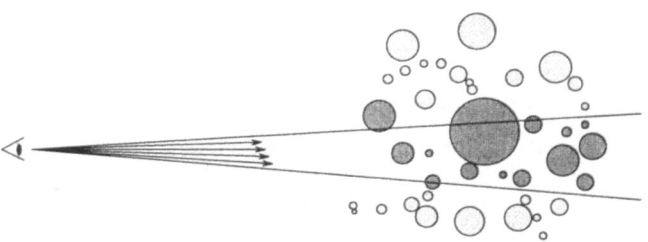

Fig. 1. Coherence between rays.

in [3, 4, 5]. Also shaft culling [6] is a method that classifies objects as in or outside of a shaft constructed, for instance, between a surface and a light source, or between a shooting patch and a receiving patch.

Recently, Greene published an algorithm for intersecting arbitrary convex polyhedrons with rectangular solids that can be used to efficiently cull polygons that are inside a viewing pyramid from an octree spatial subdivision structure [7]. The viewing pyramid is intersected with the octree and each (axis-aligned) cell of the octree is recursively tested for overlap with the pyramid. A maximum of three tests may be needed to conclude if the pyramid intersects with a cell. In the first test, the bounding box of the pyramid is tested against the cell. If some overlap is found, the second test is invoked, which tests on which side of each of the planes making up the pyramid the cell lies. If the cell is inside any of these planes, the third test is necessary. In this test, the cell and the pyramid are projected onto the three orthographic planes. If in all three views the projection of the cell is outside the projection of the pyramid, then the two do not intersect.

We have been experimenting with a similar algorithm that we originally gave the name of cone clipping [8] and recently renamed in pyra-clip, an abbreviation of pyramid clipping. Our method only differs from Greene's method in that a bintree is used instead of an octree, and for the second and third test a Cohen-Sutherland clipping test is used to determine whether the cell intersects the pyramid. Our version is explained in more detail in sections 2 and 3. In section 4 we compare the method with two regular single-ray traversal methods, one for a bintree and one for a grid. The results are discussed in the final section.

2 Pyramid - bintree intersection

The pyra-clip algorithm assumes the presence of a bintree structure. This structure is created in a preprocessing step. The pyra-clip algorithm itself consists of two parts. In the first part, a pyramid is created (this can, for instance, be the viewing pyramid or a subpart of it) that encloses a number of rays having the same origin and similar directions. This pyramid is intersected with the bintree structure. This results in an ordered list of bintree cells that are (partly) inside the pyramid. Then, in the second step, the individual rays that formed the pyramid are traced through the cells. The algorithm is done when for each ray an intersection is found. The first step is discussed in this section, while the ray traversal is discussed in section 3.

Central to the first step is the classification of each bintree cell to the pyramid. This classification uses a variant of the Cohen-Sutherland line clip algorithm. To this extent, the bintree is recursively tested for intersection with the pyramid. Each level requires at most two tests to determine whether an intersection occurs between a cell and the pyramid.

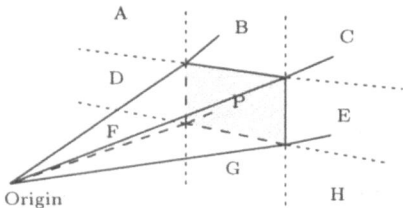

Fig. 2. The planes defining the pyramid generate nine subspaces.

The first test examines the position of the vertices of a cell with respect to the planes of the pyramid. The four planes of the pyramid define nine subspaces which may contain one or more of the vertices of the cell, see figure 2. The position of the vertices is derived from the distances of the vertices to the planes of the pyramid. The following cases now may occur:

- All distances are positive indicating that the vertices are inside sector P (see figure 2). This means that the cell is completely contained within the pyramid.
- Not all vertices are inside sector P. The cell will be partially inside the pyramid.
- The vertices are in three consecutive subspaces, excluding P (for example A-B-C or C-E-H). Now the cell will be completely outside the pyramid.
- The vertices are in both subspace B and G or in both D and E. Because of the convexity of the pyramid, the cell is partially inside the pyramid.
- The vertices are located in the subspace A, C, F and H. This means that the pyramid is contained within the cell.

These tests can be efficiently implemented with bitwise operations. For each vertex of the cell, a bitmask is set, indicating which of the subspaces it is in. The bitmasks for each vertex are OR-ed together, resulting in a bitmask indicating the position of the entire cell with respect to the pyramid.

All these tests are relatively simple and therefore fast. For bintree cells that are completely inside or completely outside, no further testing is needed. The cells that are partially inside require their descendants to be recursively tested. This test is expected to be conclusive for most situations, but there are exceptions. An example is if vertices are both in partly opposite subspaces (e.g. D and C). For these situations, a more conclusive second edge test is needed.

The second test explicitly classifies the edges of the bintree cell with respect to the pyramid. Because it is not necessary to know what exactly the shape of the intersecting volume is, no clipping in the true sense of the word is performed. The

4

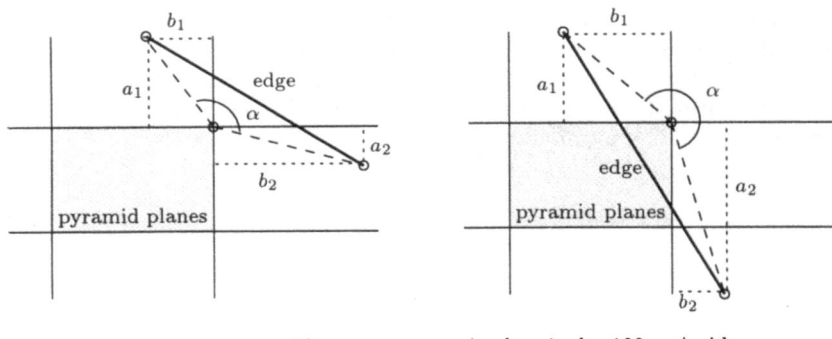

Angle $\alpha < \deg 180 \Rightarrow$ outside   Angle $\alpha \geq \deg 180 \Rightarrow$ inside

Fig. 3. Simplified clipping test.

following test is performed for each pair of vertices defining an edge. For each vertex of a bintree cell, the distance to each of the pyramid planes is known. Using these distances, we can easily compute whether an edge intersects the pyramid or not, see figure 3. In this example, the distances between the vertices and the pyramid planes are given by a_1, b_1 and a_2 and b_2 respectively. An edge intersects the plane if and only if

$$\frac{a_1}{b_1} \leq \frac{a_2}{b_2} \tag{1}$$

A special situation occurs if the vertices of an edge are in diagonally opposite sectors, as is depicted in figure 4 (left). In this case, two evaluations of equation 1 are necessary. If the first of these tests indicates that the edge does not intersect the pyramid, the second test can be omitted, otherwise the second one is conclusive.

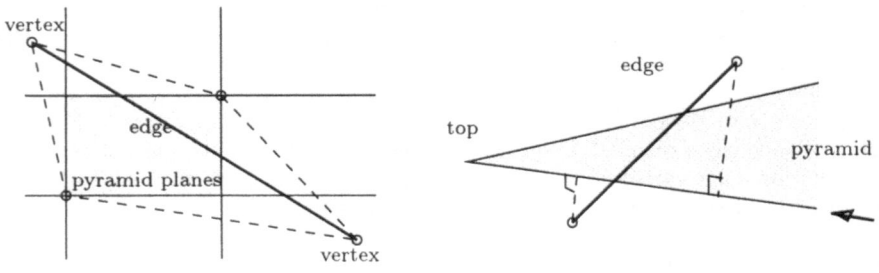

Edge vertices in opposite sectors   Side view of clipping test
require at most two tests

Fig. 4. Left: opposite sectors. Right: side view.

All edges are tested this way until an edge is found to intersect with the pyramid or until all twelve edges are tested. Then we can still have the case that no edge intersects the pyramid, but the cell completely surrounds the pyramid. In order to handle this case, for each edge a mask similar to the one in the first test, is updated. After each edge is tested, the orientation of the pyramid with respect to the cell is known and the intersection routine returns with the result.

In 3D, the distances that are used to classify an edge as inside or outside, are all with respect to the planes of the pyramid. Because for both vertices defining an edge, the distances to the same planes are used, the method is valid in 3D. Looking along the line indicated by the arrow in figure 4 (right), the image of figure 4 (left) would be seen.

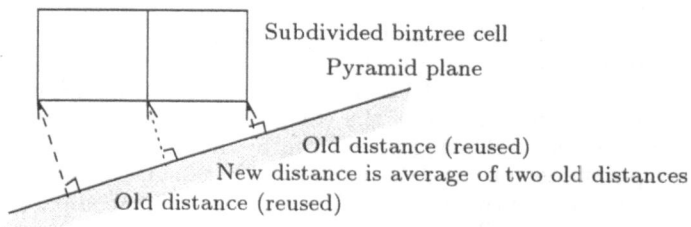

Fig. 5. Distances can be computed incrementally.

The distances are not computed for each vertex of each cell anew. Instead the regular structure of the bintree is used to efficiently calculate at each level of recursion the distances of the children nodes out of the distances of their parent node, see figure 5. Per subdivision only four new distances have to be computed, each by averaging two old distances. Eight old distances can be retained. Then, the pyramid - cell intersection routine can be called for the two new bintree cells.

The cell farthest from the view point is put on a stack and the cell nearest the view point is processed first. In this way, the first leaf cell reached is the one closed to the view point. All following leaf cells are automatically derived in the correct order.

The ordered cells are stored in a list, which is called the cliplist. Each pyramid thus generates its own cliplist during the traversal of the bintree that effectively contains all the cells that are traversed by at least one ray of the bundle and most likely by a majority of these rays (see figure 6). The six planes of each cell (x_{min}, x_{max}, y_{min}, y_{max}, z_{min}, z_{max}) are also copied to the cliplist. These are needed for the final ray traversal.

In addition, the objects in the cells may also be tested with respect to the pyramid planes and marked as in or out (excluding objects that will never be intersected by any of the rays).

3 Ray traversal

After the cliplist has been generated, the first step of the pyraclip algorithm is finished. The next step is to determine which objects intersect with the rays

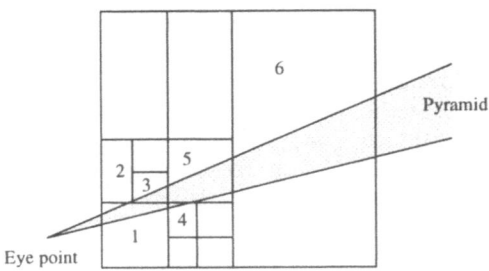

Fig. 6. Ray traversal generates cliplist (cells 1-6).

within the pyramid. The ray traversal traverses the cells in list order until an intersection is found. While examining a new cell from the cliplist, the ray parameter value of the exit point for that cell is calculated. The ray exit point is the closest intersection with one of the (three) backfacing cell planes. Which of the six planes are the backfacing planes can be determined from the ray direction. The ray parameter of the exit point is then calculated with three multiplications, three adds and two compare. With an additional compare, it is determined whether the ray actually intersects the cell. If the new ray parameter is smaller than the parameter of the previous exit point, then the cell is not intersected by the ray and can be skipped. For instance in figure 7, the exit point for cell 1 is p_1 (minimum of p_1 and p_2). The exit point for cell 2 is p_2 (minimum of p_2 and p_4). For cell 3 exit point p_1 would be selected again, which is closer to the origin of the ray than the exit point of the previous cell. Therefore, it is concluded that cell 3 can be skipped, after which p_3 is found to be the exit point of cell 4.

What we have obtained with this algorithm, is a traversal for an adaptive spatial subdivision but with a ray traversal cost comparable with the standard grid method.

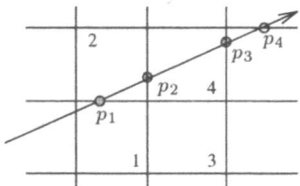

Fig. 7. Ray traversal.

4 Implementation and Evaluation

In order to have an idea how efficient the algorithm is, we have implemented it in Rayshade [9], a widely used public domain ray tracer. Earlier tests have shown that the grid traversal method in Rayshade is one of the fastest ray traversal methods [10, 11]. The grid traverseral in Rayshade is fast, because the standard

DDA algorithm is enhanced with raybox testing [12] and ray hit caching. In our tests we have also included a comparison with the recursive bintree traversal algorithm [13, 14], implemented in Rayshade by de Leeuw [15].

For the test we have only traced primary rays (no shadow and reflection rays). The screen is subdivided into a number of non-overlapping rectangular regions and for each region a pyramid is constructed with its top at the view point. The size (width) of the pyramids (number of rays) is an important parameter that will directly affect the performance. If there are too few rays in a pyramid, then the overhead induced by the clipping algorithm will be more than the gain in the reduction of ray object intersections. On the other hand, if the pyramids are too large, the number of cells tested as outside will reduce, resulting in more ray - object intersection tests per ray. Other parameters that will affect performance are the number of objects (polygons/balls), the maximum number of objects allowed in a cell and the maximum depth of the bintree

For the test we have used two models, balls and teapot, from the standard procedural database [16]. The models are depicted in figure 8. We chose these models because they do not distribute all objects uniformily over object space, which would give an unrealistic test result compared to models normally used in ray tracing and radiosity algorithms. We used the models in different resolutions.

Fig. 8. Standard Procedural Models (balls and teapot)

First we verified the optimum setting of the subdivision parameters. For the grid method (uniform spatial subdivision) the rule of thumb given by de Leeuw [15] was confirmed. The number of voxels should equal the number of objects, or stated otherwise the number of voxels in each direction should be approximately equal to $\sqrt[3]{N}$, where N is the number of objects in the model. In fact, we found $2 + \sqrt[3]{N}$ to be the optimal setting for the two models.

The bintree algorithms were less sensitive to different parameter settings. For both model ranges, a maximum of 12 (or 16) objects per cell proved to be optimal. The maximum number of subdivisions varied from 18 for the small models to 24 for the large models (a maximum subdivision level of 24 corresponds with a maximum resolution of $2^8 = 256$ in both x, y and z directions). For other parameter settings, the times are only a few seconds off.

Then the optimal size for the pyramids was tested. The image size is 512 by 512 pixels. For each of the models, images were computed with $2^2, 4^2, 8^2, \ldots, 128^2$ pyramids per image. The optimum size lies around 32x32 pyramids (16^2 rays per pyramid; see figure 9 (right)). The pyra-clip time to generate the cell list is about 1 second for 32x32 pyramids and 2 seconds for 64x64 pyramids (see figure 9 (left)). The preprocessing time is linear in the number of objects, see figure 10. We choose therefore the 32x32 pyramid subdivision.

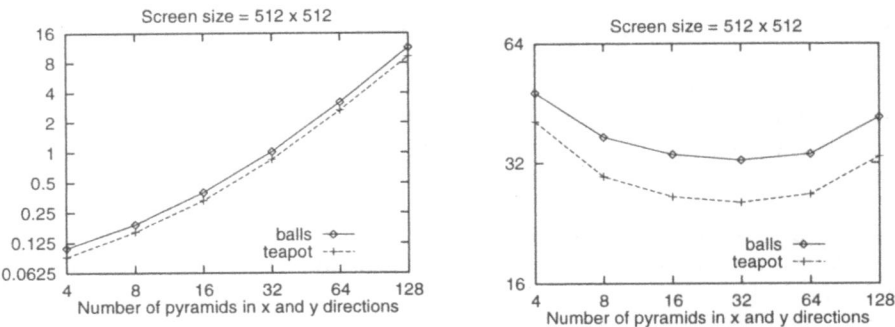

Fig. 9. Preprocessing time (left) and rendering time (right) as function of pyramid size (timing in seconds).

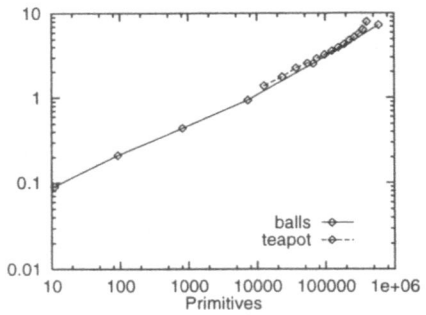

Fig. 10. Preprocessing time (in seconds) as function of the number of primitives.

Rendering times for the 16^2 rays per pyramid pyraclipping, the bintree recursive and the uniform grid algorithm, are shown in figure 11. The tests were done on a SGI Power Onyx with 256 Mb internal memory. The memory available prohibited testing larger models. The pyraclip numbers give the pure traversal time, without the overhead of the clipping and without tracing secondary rays.

The figures show that the grid performs linear with respect to the number of objects, while the recursive bintree is logarithmic and wins for larger N. A multi grid method would probably have shown a similar performance. In fact this is the first time that we are able to show that the performance of the recursive bintree traversal is $\log N$ for such large models. Unfortunately, the pyraclip traversal adheres more to the grid method than to the recursive bintree traversal and thus

looses in the end compared to the recursive ray traversal. The figures show that
there is no use for the pyraclip method for efficiency reasons only. All methods
perform equally well (within the tested range). We found this also to be true for
the other SPD models.

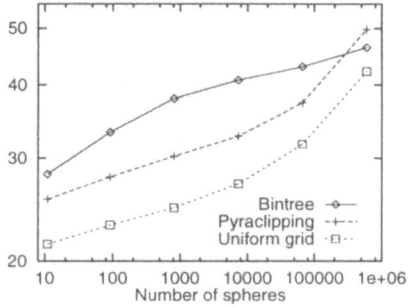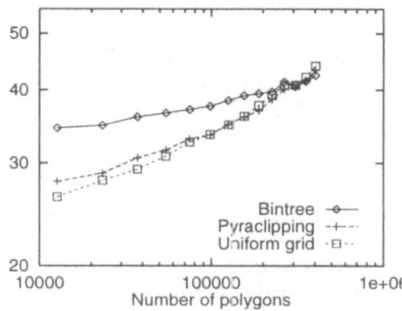

Fig. 11. Pyraclipping compared with uniform grid and bintree methods. Models used:
balls (left) and teapot (right); timing in seconds.

5 Conclusions and future work

The pyra-clip algorithm intersects a bundle of rays with a hierarchical spatial
subdivision structure. First an ordered list of bintree cells is generated using an
efficient pyramid - cell intersection method. Then the separate rays are traced
through the list of cells.

The tests showed that the pyraclip method is not faster than the standard
single ray traversal methods and thus for speed purposes only, the method as
such does not give any additional benefit. However, the method is ideal in that
it can generate with minor overhead coherent ray intersection tasks (a bundle
of rays and matching objects) that can be executed as fast as the fastest ray
traversal methods. We will therefore use this method to generate demand-driven
tasks in a parallel ray tracing and radiosity algorithm [17].

Each processor in such a parallel ray tracer would be capable of both performing data parallel tasks and demand driven tasks. The data parallel tasks
would provide a basic, though uneven load by tracing non-coherent secondary
rays, such as reflection and refraction rays. Primary rays are then handled in
demand driven manner and scheduled to processors with a low basic load. A
processor receiving a bundle of rays and a cliplist will do the intersection calculations using this data. Shadow rays that sample area light sources are handled in
a similar way. Such hybrid scheduling should both minimise data communication
and balance the workload, yielding an efficient and scalable algorithm [18].

References

1. Green, S. A., Paddon, D. J.: 'Exploiting coherence for multiprocessor ray tracing', *IEEE Computer Graphics and Applications* pp. 12–27. (1989)
2. Shen, L. S., Deprettere, E., Dewilde, P.: A new space partition technique to support a highly pipelined parallel architecture for the radiosity method, *in* Advances in Graphics Hardware V, proceedings Fifth Eurographics Workshop on Hardware, Springer-Verlag. (1990)
3. Speer, L. R., DeRose, T. D., Barsky, B. A.: A theoretical and empirical analysis of coherent ray-tracing, *in* Computer-Generated Images, Springer-Verlag, Tokyo, pp. 11–25. Proceedings Graphics Interface '85. (1985)
4. Hanrahan, P.: Using caching and breadth first search to speed up ray tracing, *in* Proceedings Graphics Interface '86, Canadian Information Processing Society, Toronto, pp. 55–61. (1986)
5. Glassner, A. S., ed.: *An Introduction to Ray Tracing*, Academic Press, San Diego. (1989)
6. Haines, E. A., Wallace, J. R.: Shaft culling for efficient ray-traced radiosity, *in* Photorealistic Rendering in Computer Graphics, proceedings Second Eurographics Workshop on Rendering, Springer-Verlag 1994, pp. 122–138. (1991)
7. Greene, N.: Detecting intersection of a rectangular solid and a convex polyhedron, *in* P. Heckbert, ed., Graphics Gems IV, Academic Press, Boston, pp. 74–82. (1994)
8. van der Wal, P. O.: De coneclip versnellingsmethode voor raytracing, Master's thesis, Delft University of Technology. (1994)
9. Kolb, C. E.: Rayshade User's Guide and Reference Manual, included in the Rayshade distribution, which is available by ftp from princeton.edu:pub/Graphics/rayshade.4.0. (1992)
10. Jansen, F. W., de Leeuw, W. C.: Recursive ray traversal. In Ray Tracing News, vol 5, no 1. (1992)
11. Jansen, F. W.: Comparison of ray traversal methods. In Ray Tracing News, vol 7, no 2. (1994)
12. Snyder, J., Barr, A.: Ray tracing complex models containing surface tessellations, *Computer Graphics* **21**(4), 119–128. (1987)
13. Jansen, F. W.: Data structures for ray tracing, *in* L. R. A. Kessener, F. J. Peters, M. L. P. Lierop, eds, Data Structures for Raster Graphics, Springer-Verlag, Berlin, pp. 57–73. (1985)
14. Sung, K., Shirley, P.: *Ray tracing with the BSP Tree*, Graphics Gems III, Academic Press, Boston, chapter 6, pp. 271–274. (1992)
15. de Leeuw, W. C.: Recursieve ray traversal, Master's thesis, Delft University of Technology. (1992)
16. Haines, E. A.: Standard procedural database, v3.1, 3D/Eye. (1992)
17. Jansen, F. W., Chalmers, A.: Realism in real time?, *in* 4th EG Workshop on Rendering, pp. 1–20. (1993)
18. Reinhard, E., Jansen, F. W.: Hybrid scheduling for efficient ray tracing of complex images. (1995) Accepted for the International Workshop on High Performance Computing for Computer Graphics and Visualisation, Swansea, United Kingdom, july 3-4, 1995.

A 5D Tree to Reduce the Variance
of Monte Carlo Ray Tracing

Eric P. Lafortune and Yves D. Willems

Department of Computer Science, Katholieke Universiteit Leuven
Celestijnenlaan 200A, 3001 Heverlee, Belgium
Eric.Lafortune@cs.kuleuven.ac.be

Abstract: In this paper we present a 5D tree structure to cache illumination information gained during Monte Carlo ray tracing. The structure is elegant and simple to use. It is adaptive and makes abstraction of the complexity of the input scene automatically.
We then show how the information in this structure can be used to reduce the variance of the Monte Carlo process. Unlike earlier approaches the techniques presented here do not introduce a bias in the results.

1 Introduction

Monte Carlo ray tracing is widely acknowledged as a general but slow technique for faithfully rendering scenes with global illumination effects. Its stochastic nature entails an uncertainty on the results, which is expressed by the variance of the process. In ray tracing it is visible as uncorrelated noise in the rendered images. Monte Carlo techniques typically reduce the variance by averaging the results from a large number of primary samples. The reduction of the variance is proportional to the number of samples, which means that the standard deviation is only reduced proportionally to the square root of the number of samples.

Most research on Monte Carlo techniques is therefore directed towards finding more efficient sampling schemes which yield a lower variance for the primary estimator. General optimisations [1, 2] can also be applied to the global illumination problem, on the basis of a concise mathematical description [3, 4, 5, 6, 7, 8, 9, 10].

Standard Monte Carlo ray tracing algorithms trace a large number of rays, all independently from one another. Only the eventual radiance values are averaged per pixel and stored. It seems wasteful to throw away all the information gained while tracing rays through the scene. Ward presented what seems the most successful caching scheme to date [11, 12]. He separates the calculations of indirect diffuse reflections from the calculations of the other components. Diffuse illumination is computed separately and cached in an octree. The cached values are interpolated whenever diffuse illumination values are required in their neighbourhoods. In this respect his technique is similar to various two-pass methods that work with an explicit discretisation of the surfaces in the scene; diffuse reflections are interpolated, extrapolated or averaged in some way. The correctness of the results largely depends on the granularity of the discretisations. From a Monte Carlo point of view the results are biased as the expected values of the results of the simulation are no longer the correct values.

In this contribution we propose techniques that do not introduce a bias. The first section presents a tree structure that subdivides the 5D space of positions and directions hierarchically. Computed values for incoming radiance are stored in this tree. The following section explains how these cached values can be used to improve importance sampling and control variates. We then present some results obtained using these optimisations.

2 The 5D tree

Various data structures to store information about the illumination in a scene have been proposed in the literature. Boundary element methods such as the radiosity method store information for each of the elements of the discretised surfaces. The information is usually restricted to the diffuse component of the illumination although extensions to store directional information as well have been proposed, e.g. by discretising the hemisphere [13] or by using spherical harmonics [14]. Ward [11, 12] uses an octree that is independent from the surfaces to store diffuse illumination along with information about the gradients. Finite element methods for rendering participating media discretise the space into regular grids [15, 16, 17] or hierarchical structures [18], mostly without storing directional information.

We propose a 5D tree which is a straightforward extension of the 1D binary tree, the 2D quadtree, the 3D octree, etc. The dimensions are the three regular spatial dimensions and two additional angular dimensions. For convenience a 5D point corresponding to a point (x, y, z) and a direction (θ, ϕ) is represented in coordinates that are normalised to lie between 0 and 1:

$$(x_n, y_n, z_n, s_n, t_n)$$

where:

$$x_n = (x - x_{min})/(x_{max} - x_{min}),$$
$$y_n = (y - y_{min})/(y_{max} - y_{min}),$$
$$z_n = (z - z_{min})/(z_{max} - z_{min}),$$
$$s_n = (\cos\theta + 1)/2,$$
$$t_n = \phi/(2\pi)$$

This parametrisation ensures a uniform subdivision: equally sized 5D volumes at any 5D position correspond to equal 3D volumes and equal spatial angles.

The branching factor of the tree is $2^5 = 32$. It may seem that this would give rise to an explosive growth of the storage requirements, but it is not a problem in practice as only nodes that are effectively needed to store values are created.

Which values are stored in the tree then? The ray tracing algorithm traces random walks through the scene. The process starts with a primary ray from the eye point through a pixel. At the closest intersection point the direct illumination is usually computed by sampling the light sources. Then a random direction is sampled for the reflected ray. The incoming radiance for this ray is estimated by repeating the tracing process recursively. These estimated radiance values for all the intersection points and the sampled directions are cached in the tree, in the nodes determined by their positions (Fig. 1). The values are averaged in the appropriate nodes at each level of the tree. Whenever the number of estimates averaged in a node exceeds a given maximum threshold the node is split; a new node is created if necessary. The building of the tree is in a sense importance-driven; more detailed representations are constructed in regions where more rays are traced.

The best averaged estimate for any point and direction can be retrieved from the tree at any time by descending to the lowest node corresponding to the given coordinates. We impose a minimum threshold on the number of averaged values for the estimate to be reliable. While the representation is not as accurate as representations that are specifically linked to each of the surfaces we now avoid any meshing problems. What is more, the tree automatically makes abstraction of the complexity of the scene. Large groups of small geometric and optical details (e.g. a desk cluttered with books, pencils and paper clips) are treated as a whole by storing only averaged incoming radiance values.

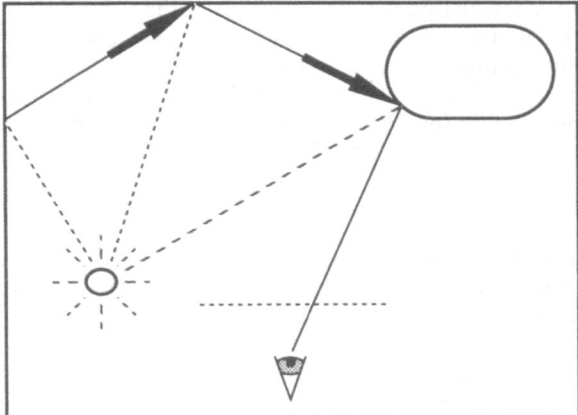

Fig. 1. During the Monte Carlo ray tracing process indirect illumination is estimated by casting reflected rays recursively. The computed estimates for incoming radiance (indicated by the arrows) are stored in the 5D tree.

3 Reduction of the Variance

The information stored in the 5D tree has to be put to good use. The first application is in adaptive importance sampling. This optimisation attempts to send more rays to bright regions in the scene. The second application is in constructing better control variates, approximations of the functions to be integrated that also help to reduce the variance.

3.1 Adaptive importance sampling

Importance sampling is an optimisation over uniform sampling [1, 2]. Rather than taking the random samples uniformly over the integration domain they are concentrated in regions where the integrand is large. For example, consider a one-dimensional function $f(x)$ that is to be integrated over the interval $[0, 1]$:

$$I = \int_0^1 f(x)dx = \int_0^1 p(x)f(x)/p(x)dx$$

If a random sample x is taken according to a uniform probability density function (PDF) the primary estimate for the integral is $f(x)$. If x is sampled according to the PDF $p(x)$ the estimate becomes $f(x)/p(x)$. The variance can be shown to go to 0 when the PDF is chosen proportional to the integrand. The function $p(x)$ must be normalised, and its cumulative function $P(x)$ has to be invertible. One can see that importance sampling in one parameter space corresponds to uniform sampling in another parameter space, by applying the transformation $x = P^{-1}(t)$, which yields:

$$I = \int_0^1 p(x)f(x)/p(x)dx = \int_0^1 f(P^{-1}(t))/p(P^{-1}(t))dt$$

In Monte Carlo ray tracing importance sampling is commonly used when sampling directions for reflected rays, to estimate indirect illumination [5, 7, 8]. The PDF, which is two-dimensional now, is usually chosen proportional to the bidirectional reflection distribution function (BRDF) times a cosine factor. This way more rays are sent in directions for which the incoming illumination is important. Formally, the outgoing radiance (or *surface radiance*) L_o is the integral over the incoming hemisphere Ω_i of the BRDF f_r times the incoming radiance (or *field radiance*) L_i times a cosine factor:

$$L_o(\Theta_o) = \int_{\Omega_i} f_r(\Theta_i, \Theta_0) L_i(\Theta_i) |\cos\theta_i| \, d\omega_i = \int_{\Omega_i} p(\Theta_i) L_i(\Theta_i) d\omega_i$$

Using the BRDF times the cosine factor as a subcritical PDF $p(\Theta_i)$ for sampling the direction Θ_i implicitly entails a transformation to a parameter space $(\xi_1, \xi_2) \in [0, 1] \times [0, 1]$ where ξ_1 and ξ_2 are sampled uniformly to obtain a $\Theta_i(\xi_1, \xi_2)$ [19]. The expression then becomes:

$$L_o(\Theta_o) = \int_0^1 \int_0^1 L_i(\Theta_i) d\xi_1 d\xi_2$$

This type of importance sampling already yields a major gain for specular surfaces. Most rays are reflected inside the specular cone rather than uniformly over the hemisphere. At diffuse surfaces however rays are only reflected according to a cosine distribution. A large number of samples are usually required to get a reliable estimate.

Additional information about the integrand may help to sample directions more intelligently. In our case the 5D tree structure contains information about the incoming radiance. In order not to loose the advantages of the importance sampling proportional to the BRDF we propose an additional importance sampling scheme in the (ξ_1, ξ_2) parameter space. For each reflection we first resample the stored incoming radiance values on a regular grid in this parameter space. We then construct a piece-wise constant PDF from this discrete representation by normalising the sampled values in the grid. A random pair (ξ_1, ξ_2) is now sampled on the basis of this PDF. As before the values map to a direction for the reflected ray. Figure 2 shows the 2D equivalent of this process schematically. Formally, if $\tilde{L}_i$ is the piece-wise constant approximation for the incoming radiance, with normalisation factor N:

$$L_o(\Theta_o) = \int_0^1 \int_0^1 \frac{\tilde{L}_i(\Theta_i)}{N} \frac{L_i(\Theta_i)}{\tilde{L}_i(\Theta_i)/N} d\xi_1 d\xi_2 = \int_0^1 \int_0^1 p'(\Theta_i) \frac{L_i(\Theta_i)}{p'(\Theta_i)} d\xi_1 d\xi_2$$

The net result is that we sample according to a PDF approximating the entire integrand of the original rendering equation. Both the BRDF with the cosine factor and the approximation of the incoming radiance are taken into account. As with any sampling process the selection of the PDF only influences the variance of the estimate and not its expected value. The expected value therefore remains correct, independent of the quality of the approximations.

3.2 Improved control variates

Control variates are another optimisation for Monte Carlo methods [1, 2, 20]. Consider the one-dimensional integral of $f(x)$ over $[0, 1]$ again. Suppose one knows a function $g(x)$ which approximates $f(x)$ and which can be integrated analytically. $g(x)$ can then be used as a control variate for $f(x)$:

$$I = \int_0^1 f(x)dx = \int_0^1 [f(x) - g(x)]dx + \int_0^1 g(x)dx = \int_0^1 [f(x) - g(x)]dx + J$$

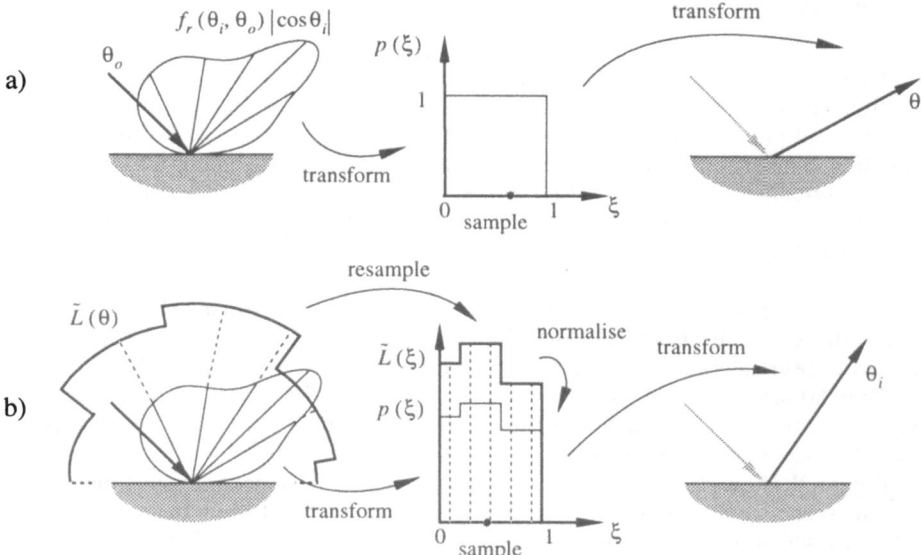

Fig. 2. (a) Importance sampling as it is commonly used with path tracing. For a given direction θ_o a reflected direction θ_i has to be sampled according to a PDF that is proportional to the BRDF times the cosine factor. This is implemented by taking a uniform random sample ξ in a parameter space for which the transformation can be computed analytically, and then transforming that sample to a direction θ_i.

(b) Adaptive importance sampling as presented here also uses the estimates for incoming radiance that are stored in the 5D tree. The estimates are resampled at regular intervals in the ξ parameter space. The resulting piece-wise constant approximation is normalised to obtain a PDF. The sample ξ is now taken according to this PDF and again transformed to a direction θ_i. As a result reflections will be sampled according to the BRDF but also preferentially in bright and thus important directions.

For a uniform sample x the primary estimate becomes $[f(x) - g(x)] + J$. If the function $g(x)$ approximates the function $f(x)$ closely enough this estimate will have a lower variance than the original estimate.

In an earlier paper we have already applied control variates to the rendering equation [21]. The incoming radiance could be approximated by a constant ambient radiance yielding a simple control variate. Thanks to the 5D tree we now have more detailed information about the incoming radiance. These estimates can be expected to be more effective. Formally, in the (ξ_1, ξ_2) parameter space where we have constructed the piece-wise constant approximation $\tilde{L}_i$:

$$L_o(\Theta_o) = \int_0^1 \int_0^1 (L_i(\Theta_i) - \tilde{L}_i(\Theta_i))d\xi_1 d\xi_2 + \int_0^1 \int_0^1 \tilde{L}_i(\Theta_i)d\xi_1 d\xi_2$$

The latter integral of the piece-wise constant approximation can easily be computed analytically. In fact, it comes for free with the importance sampling explained in the previous paragraph as it is the normalisation factor of the PDF.

4 Results

We have tested the proposed optimisations on an implementation of a path tracing algorithm which is already optimised by means of multi-dimensional stratified sampling and classical importance sampling of the BRDFs. Russian roulette is used to terminate a random walk. The BRDF model is a modified Phong model which is both reciprocal and energy-conserving [19]. For BRDF models such as this one which consist of a sum of a diffuse and a specular component the proposed importance sampling technique can be easily extended to select between specular and diffuse reflection in a more effective way.

Figure 3a shows a test scene which is mostly indirectly illuminated by lamp shades against the walls. This is a particularly difficult scene for stochastic ray tracing. Figure 4 shows images rendered without and with using the 5D tree respectively, at 100×100 pixels. Only 50 samples per pixel were used in order to clearly demonstrate the differences. Figure 5 shows more precisely how the optimisations reduce the RMS error (compared to a reference image). The reduction varies between 20 and 25%.

Figure 3b shows the same scene, now illuminated by light boxes against the ceiling. For this scene we have not used shadow rays to sample direct illumination separately, but rather added lighting contributions from the reflected rays only. This approach may be interesting for large or complex luminaires which cannot be sampled efficiently. The effect of the optimisations presented here will increase because they improve on the reflected rays. In this case they yield a reduction of the RMS error of about 30%.

a) b)

Fig. 3. The test scenes with different types of luminaires.

In the tests we have set the threshold for splitting nodes of the 5D tree proportional to the total number of primary samples. This resulted in about 11.000 nodes for the first test quickly levelling to about 86.000 nodes for the latter tests (requiring between 2 MBytes and 14 MBytes respectively). However, additional experiments have shown that the improvements are only affected slightly if the number of nodes is kept small. Figure 6 gives an impression of the radiance estimates stored in the 5D tree after rendering an image with 50 samples per pixel.

If the image is computed pixel per pixel the variance for the first pixels will be larger than the variance for the last pixels, as the data structure will have been refined in the meantime. Scanning over the image repeatedly, taking a single sample per pixel at a time removes this effect. Experiments have shown that the overall improvement is small though.

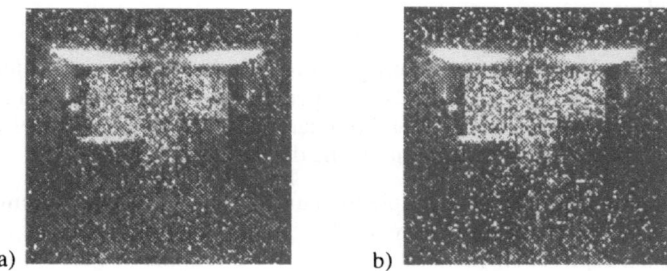

Fig. 4. The first test scene rendered with 50 samples per pixel, (a) without and (b) with the optimisation respectively.

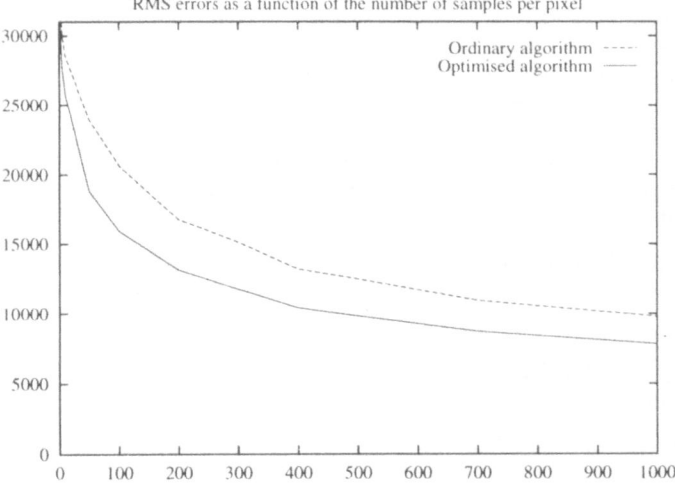

Fig. 5. The RMS error as a function of the number of samples per pixel N, for the first test scene. It decreases as $1/\sqrt{N}$, but for the optimised algorithm it is 20 to 25% smaller.

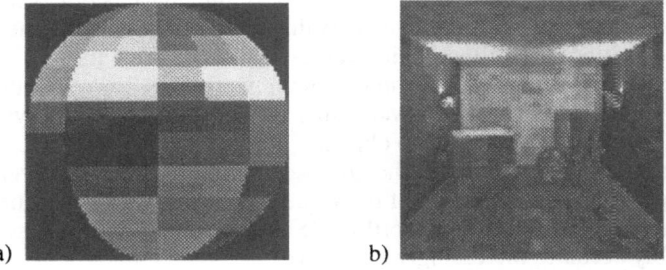

Fig. 6. An impression of the 5D tree structure after rendering the actual images with 50 samples per pixel. (a) A fish eye view of the radiance values stored at a point in the middle of the white wall. This image shows the directional subdivision of the 5D tree. (b) An image rendered with the stored radiance values integrated locally at each first intersection point. This image gives an idea of the spatial subdivision of the 5D tree. Note that the glossy reflections are a result of the directional information captured in the tree structure.

5 Conclusions

We have presented a 5D data structure to store information about incoming radiance for illumination simulations. The tree is independent from the surfaces in the scene and therefore somewhat less accurate than boundary element subdivisions of the surfaces. However, this spatial approach also has some distinct advantages:

- The structure is uniform and simple to maintain. All meshing problems inherent to boundary element methods are avoided.
- The tree is adaptive; only spatial and directional regions that are important for the simulation are refined. Empty spaces and uninteresting directions are not considered because no values are ever stored there.
- The top-down refinement automatically makes abstraction of the complexity of the scene. Because incoming radiance values are stored large sets of small objects can be grouped in an effective way, even if they have complex geometries or optical properties.
- The memory requirements are simple to control. More available memory allows for more detailed representations of the radiance function and faster convergence.
- The structure also seems to lend itself perfectly for use with participating media since it can store radiance values in the 3D space and not only at surfaces.
- We also intend to use it to store potential (or *importance*) for light tracing and bidirectional path tracing algorithms.

The 5D tree has the same kind of attractiveness that Monte Carlo methods have: while it is not overly efficient it is extremely general in its application.

We have then shown how the information stored in the 5D tree can be used to improve the efficiency of Monte Carlo ray tracing. More specifically indirect illumination can be computed more accurately thanks to two optimisations:

- An adaptive importance sampling scheme can send more reflected rays in bright directions.
- Better control variates can be constructed for the rendering equation on the basis of the information about incoming radiance.

The improved importance sampling scheme and control variates reduce the variance of the simulation. Practically, a lower RMS error of the image is obtained for the same number of samples per pixel. Moreover, they do not introduce a bias in the result, unlike most techniques that cache illumination values. This is of some theoretical importance and may be vital in practice when computing reference images to verify other techniques for instance. It comes at a cost however. Other methods like in Ward's system will produce better images if some bias is no object.

The computational overhead of the proposed optimisations is relatively large but it does not depend on the complexity of the scene. While the extra work does not pay off for simple scenes, it will become worthwhile as the complexity increases and tracing rays inevitably becomes increasingly expensive.

Compared to bidirectional path tracing [22, 8, 10, 23] this technique may offer an advantage if the sources of indirect illumination are relatively large and bright, or if there is a large number of light sources. In those cases seeking light starting from the eye will be more effective than distributing light starting from a random light source.

Elsewhere in these proceedings Dutré *et al.* [24] and Jensen [25] present similar adaptive importance sampling schemes, without the control variate optimisation. Dutré *et al.* apply it to light tracing, which is the dual algorithm of path tracing. They store approximated potential functions at discrete patches in the scene and sample the hemisphere without taking the BRDF into account. Jensen applies it to path tracing in virtually the same way as presented here. However, he uses information that is stored as a fixed set of reflected photons from a first light tracing pass. Our approach has the advantage that it does not require any extra rays and that computational effort and memory are only spent on regions of the scene that are important for the image.

6 Acknowledgements

The first author would like to acknowledge the financial support by a grant from the Flemish 'Institute for the promotion of Scientific and Technological Research in the Industry' (IWT #944045).

References

1. M. Kalos and P. Whitlock, *Monte Carlo Methods*. Wiley & Sons, 1986.
2. J. Hammersly and D. Handscomb, *Monte Carlo Methods*. Chapman and Hall, 1964.
3. M. Lee, R. Redner, and S. Uselton, "Statistically optimized sampling for distributed ray tracing," *Computer Graphics*, vol. 19, pp. 61–67, July 1985.
4. P. Shirley, *Physically Based Lighting Calculations for Computer Graphics*. PhD thesis, University of Illinois, Nov. 1990.
5. B. Lange, "The simulation of radiant light transfer with stochastic ray-tracing," in *Proceedings of the Second Eurographics Workshop on Rendering*, (Barcelona, Spain), May 1991.
6. G. Ward, "Adaptive shadow testing for ray tracing," in *Proceedings of the Second Eurographics Workshop on Rendering*, (Barcelona, Spain), May 1991.
7. S. Pattanaik, *Computational Methods for Global Illumination and Visualisation of Complex 3D Environments*. PhD thesis, Birla Institute of Technology & Science, Pilani, India, Feb. 1993.
8. E. Lafortune and Y. Willems, "A theoretical framework for physically based rendering," *Computer Graphics Forum*, vol. 13, pp. 97–107, June 1994.
9. P. Shirley, C. Wang, and K. Zimmerman, "Monte carlo techniques for direct lighting calculations," *ACM Transactions on Graphics*, to appear.
10. E. Lafortune and Y. Willems, "Reducing the number of shadow rays in bidirectional path tracing," in *Proceedings of WSCG 95*, (Pilsen, Czech Republic), pp. 384–392, Feb. 1995.
11. G. Ward, F. Rubinstein, and R. Clear, "A ray tracing solution for diffuse interreflection," *Computer Graphics*, vol. 22, pp. 85–92, July 1988.
12. G. Ward and P. Heckbert, "Irradiance gradients," in *Proceedings of the Third Eurographics Workshop on Rendering*, (Bristol, UK), pp. 85–98, May 1992.
13. D. Immel, M. Cohen, and D. Greenberg, "A radiosity method for non-diffuse environments," *Computer Graphics*, vol. 20, pp. 133–142, Aug. 1986.
14. F. Sillion, J. Arvo, S. Westin, and D. Greenberg, "A global illumination solution for general reflectance distributions," *Computer Graphics*, vol. 25, pp. 187–196, July 1991.

15. C. Patmore, "Illumination of dense foliage models," in *Proceedings of the Fourth Eurographics Workshop on Rendering*, (Paris, France), pp. 63–71, June 1993.
16. E. Languénou, K. Bouatouch, and M. Chelle, "Global illumination in presence of participating media with general properties," in *Proceedings of the Fifth Eurographics Workshop on Rendering*, (Darmstadt, Germany), pp. 69–85, June 1994.
17. N. Max, "Efficient light propagation for multiple anisotropic volume scattering," in *Proceedings of the Fifth Eurographics Workshop on Rendering*, (Darmstadt, Germany), pp. 87–104, June 1994.
18. F. Sillion, "Clustering and volume scattering for hierarchical radiosity calculations," in *Proceedings of the Fifth Eurographics Workshop on Rendering*, (Darmstadt, Germany), pp. 105–117, June 1994.
19. E. Lafortune and Y. Willems, "Using the modified phong brdf for physically based rendering," Technical Report CW197, Department of Computer Science, Katholieke Universiteit Leuven, Leuven, Belgium, Nov. 1994.
20. J. Halton, "On the relative merits of correlated and importance sampling for monte carlo integration," *Proceedings of the Cambridge Philisophical Society*, vol. 61, pp. 497–498, 1965.
21. E. Lafortune and Y. Willems, "The ambient term as a variance reducing technique for monte carlo ray tracing," in *Proceedings of the Fifth Eurographics Workshop on Rendering*, (Darmstadt, Germany), pp. 163–171, June 1994.
22. E. Lafortune and Y. Willems, "Bi-directional path tracing," in *Proceedings of CompuGraphics*, (Alvor, Portugal), pp. 145–153, Dec. 1993.
23. E. Veach and L. Guibas, "Bidirectional estimators for light transport," in *Proceedings of the Fifth Eurographics Workshop on Rendering*, (Darmstadt, Germany), pp. 147–162, June 1994.
24. Ph. Dutré and Y. Willems, "Potential-driven monte carlo particle tracing for diffuse environments with adaptive probability density functions," in *Proceedings of the Sixth Eurographics Workshop on Rendering*, (Dublin, Ireland), June 1995.
25. H. Jensen, "Importance driven path tracing using the photon map," in *Proceedings of the Sixth Eurographics Workshop on Rendering*, (Dublin, Ireland), June 1995.

Space Deformation using Ray Deflectors

Yair Kurzion and Roni Yagel

Department of Computer and Information Science
The Ohio State University

Abstract. In this paper we introduce a new approach to the deformation of surface and raster models in two and three dimensions. Rather then deforming the objects in the model, we deform the rays used to render the scene. The mechanism to specify the deformation, which we call a *deflector*, is a vector of gravity positioned in space. This gravity vector bends any ray that travels through its field of gravity in a view-independent fashion. Images generated by these curved rays give the impression of a deformed space. Unlike previous methods that deform all the objects in the scene, our approach deforms only those parts of the model that contribute to the final image. In addition, using deflectors, our approach can deform any object type that can be rendered by a ray casting algorithm, providing a unified solution to space deformation.

1 Introduction

When creating and animating complex models one commonly creates a base model and then modifies it by altering its physical attributes such as shape, position, or appearance. Thus we can express new models as functional derivatives of the base model. For example, constructive solid geometry (CSG) uses primitive geometric objects (solids) to hierarchically build more complex objects by recursively applying 3D boolean operators. Animation systems build a base model that consists of geometric objects augmented by some physical laws. Subsequent models are generated, for each time step, by repeatedly computing the behavior of the model under the influence of these laws. Finally, warping (and morphing) techniques gradually map a source model to a target model by incrementally computing a function that converges the shape (and color) of the source to the target [3,6,9,10,13].

Changing (deforming) the shape of an object is one of the most basic and widely used modeling tools. Existing methods for object deformation provide different algorithms for each object type (e.g., 2D polygon, 3D polymesh, 2D image, 3D volume). Although not all parts of the model participate in the generation of an image, the whole model has to go through the deformation phase. After surveying, in the next subsection, relevant previous related work, we turn to describe our approach which uses one deformation tool (the deflector) to deform any object that is ray tracable. Our approach, based on deforming rays rather then objects, invests computation effort only in those regions of the model that contribute to the final image.

1.1 Background

Targeted deformation where the input to the deformation algorithm is a source model and a target model, has gained much interest in recent years under names such as *warping, morphing, metamorphosis, shape interpolation,* and *shape blending.* Methods have been developed to deform various types of objects such as 2D polygons

[10], 3D polyhedral models [9], 2D rasters [3,13], and 3D rasters [5,6].

Functional deformations, where models are deformed according to some function, are much more basic and widely used. They can be as simple as the application of affine transformations or as complex as free form deformations. Functional deformations exist, in various forms, for each and every object type we can render. A few recent examples are, free form deformations of polymeshes and parametric surfaces, soft objects and hypertextures for implicit surfaces, space deformation [2] for parametric and implicit surfaces, and sculpting for 3D rasters. Our approach belongs to this category of functional deformations, however, it provides a uniform mechanism to deform all types of ray-tracable objects.

Some of the above deformations [2,3,13] can be thought of as *space deformation*. That is, a deformation operator deforms the 2D or 3D *space*, mapping every point to a new location. When a geometric model (e.g., a polymesh) is embedded in space, any control point in the model (e.g, a vertex) is mapped to a new position. After computing the mapping of all the control points, one is free to render the new model with the most appropriate rendering algorithm. For example, if one employs a ray casting (or ray tracing) algorithm [4], then a collection of rays is cast, from the eye, through each screen pixel, into the scene.

Traditionally one develops an algorithm to compute the deformation operation for each object type. Obviously, one cannot use a volume deformation algorithm [6], for example, to deform parametric surfaces.

The separation between the modeling phase and rendering phase requires one to deform the whole model — even those parts that do not contribute to the final image. Our approach is based on the idea of space deformation. We transform the rays emerging from the viewer's eye into curves according to the space deformation. Intersecting these curves with the scene objects creates an illusion of a deformed scene. The objects residing in the deformed space now appear to have changed their shape, although they have not been modified in any way. Barr [1] introduced the deformation of sight rays as a way to achieve the deformation of solid primitives. We discuss and compare his approach to ours in Section 5.

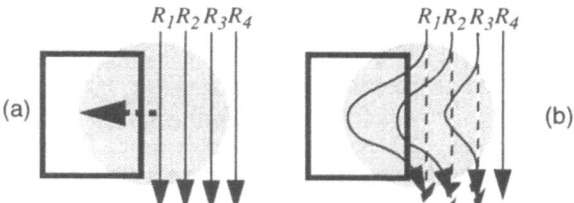

Fig. 1. (a) An object (box) and a deflector (shaded circle) being ray traced by the rays R_1 to R_4. The first three rays intersect the gravity field of the deflector that pulls them to the left (dashed arrow). (b) The rays (dashed) are bent and now go through the object. (solid lines).

1.2 Space Deformation with Ray Deflectors

In our approach, deformation is a part of the rendering process and therefore one is restricted to rendering by ray casting (or ray tracing). On the other hand, since computation is associated only with those regions that are visible in the final scene, no deformation computation is performed on hidden parts of the model. In addition, since we apply deformations to rays rather than to objects, one does not need to worry about the way to apply deformations to any specific type of object. Although we show only a few example object types, this approach can successfully deform polymeshes, implicit surfaces, algebraic surfaces (e.g., quadrics), volumes, parametric surfaces, and procedural surfaces (e.g., sweeps, CSG, fractals) [4].

Although existing methods for specifying object deformations (e.g., grids [13], vectors [3]) may be used to deform sight rays, we have chosen to introduce a new mechanism, called a *deflector*, that is specifically suited to our paradigm of deforming rays rather than objects. A *deflector* is simply a gravity vector, positioned in space, that bends all rays passing through its defined area of influence, as shown in Figure 1. We depict this area of influence, which we call *gravity field*, as a circle (sphere), however, it can have any user defined shape. The deflector affects rays only within a limited area — a feature that ensures operator locality and allows the intuitive modeling of spatial deformations.

In order to generate local deformations in space, we have to transform all sight rays in a direction *opposite* to that of the desired visual effect. For example, in order to create a bump facing right on a model of a box (see Figure 1), we must deflect all the sight rays passing along the right side of the box to the left. The four linear rays in Figure 1a do not intersect the box. When we transform them into curved rays, R_1 and R_2 intersect the box, while R_3 does not (Figure 1b). The ray R_4, as well as those parts of R_1, R_2 and R_3 which do not intersect the deflector's gravity field, are not affected. In the final image, the color of the box will show in the pixels where R_1 and R_2 emerged and not in the ones where R_3 and R_4 emerged. This is equivalent to deforming the box description by adding a bump, as shown in Color Figure 5 (See Appendix).

2 The Primitive Space Deflection Transform

We define A *deflector* by a 4-tuple $<C, G, R, T>$ where C is a point in space defining a *center of gravity*, G is the *gravity vector*, R is the radius of a sphere (or circle in 2D) centered at C. This sphere defines the *gravity field* of the deflector. Finally, T is the *primitive deflection transformation*. Our method for space deformation transforms sight rays into curves. These curves are later intersected with scene objects to generate the resulting image. Our transform T operates on sight rays as shown in Figure 2. In our discussion, we denote both the transform of a single point and of a line by T.

In order to make deflectors 'user-friendly' and intuitive, as well as view independent, we impose restrictions on the deflection transformation T. We say that T is *well behaved* if it meets the following intuitive requirements:

1. T is local to the deflector field of gravity. Points outside the deflector field of gravity are not affected. This will make T a local operator. Locality provides ease of use and intuitive control for modeling as well as simplicity and efficiency in implementation.

2. T takes points inside the field of gravity (the sphere of radius R centered at C) to other points inside it. Each point in the field of gravity is the image of a single point, also within the field of gravity. This will make T preserve line intersections. This requirement is important because it makes our deflectors view independent.

3. T preserves the C^1 continuity of all rays. This will preserve a degree of smoothness along the boundary of the deflector's gravity field.

4. T takes the center point C to the point $C+G$. When T is applied to any other point, the distance between the original point and the deformed one is smaller than the size of G. Controlling the transformation of the center point lets us create chains of deflectors. In these chains, each deflector deflects its center to the center of its successor. This will make modeling with deflectors easier (see Section 3).

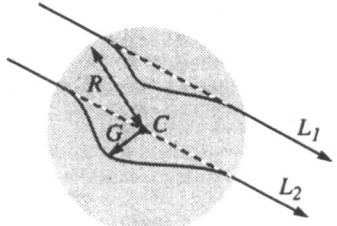 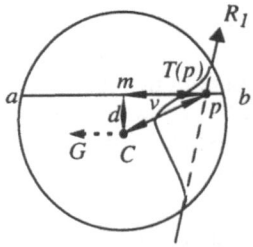

Fig. 2. Two rays, L_1, L_2 cross the gravity field of a deflector centered at C with radius R and gravity vector G. L_1 and L_2 are transformed into continuous curves (solid lines).

Fig. 3. A ray R_1 penetrates a deflector. The point p is mapped to $T(p)$ along $Chord(p)$ = ab. The distance between p and m, denoted by v, is defined along this chord.

These intuitive requirements translate into the following formal definition:

Given a deflector $D=<C, G, R, T>$, T is said to be *well behaved* if:

1. For any point p, at distance r from C, if $r>R$, then $T(p)=p$.

2. T is 1-1 and onto.

3. For any line L, $T(L)$ is a C^1 continuous curve.

4. $T(C) = C+G$, and for any $p \neq C$, $\|T(p) - p\| < \|G\|$.

There are infinitely many transforms satisfying the above requirements. We chose one such transform that is also fast to compute. Given a deflector $<C, G, R, T>$ and given a point p at distance r from C, we define the transform T of point p as:

$$T(p) = \begin{cases} p & , \text{if} \quad r > R \\ p + G \cdot \left(1 - \dfrac{r^2}{R^2}\right)^2 & , \text{if} \quad r \leq R \end{cases} \tag{1}$$

We now prove the following claim:

$$T(p) \text{ is well behaved for all } G \text{ s.t.} \quad 0 \leq \|G\| < \frac{3\sqrt{3}}{8} R \quad .$$

While following the proof it will also become clear how one can efficiently trace a deformed ray. We show that T meets all four requirements stated above.

Requirement 1: The locality of $T(p)$ results directly from its definition.

Requirement 2: Denote by $Chord(p)$ the sphere chord passing through the point p that is also parallel to the vector G (e.g. in Figure 3 $Chord(p)$ is the line ab). Note that T transforms every point p to another point on $Chord(p)$. By definition of T, it is C^1 continuous inside the sphere and thus it is also C^1 continuous along each sphere chord. Since the endpoints of each chord lie on the sphere surface, they are transformed to themselves. This proves that T is onto. For any sphere chord ab, parallel to G, located at distance d from C, let v denote the signed distance of a point p on ab from the chord midpoint m (see Figure 3). Define $D(v)$ to be the distance of $T(p)$ from m, that is, D is the projection of T into $\Re^1$:

$$D(v) = v + \|G\| \left(1 - \frac{v^2 + d^2}{R^2} \right)^2 \tag{2}$$

Note that a and b, the chord endpoints, are at distance $\sqrt{R^2-d^2}$ from m with opposite signs, and note that $D(\sqrt{R^2-d^2}) = \sqrt{R^2-d^2}$ and $D(-\sqrt{R^2-d^2}) = -\sqrt{R^2-d^2}$.

We now show that $D(v)$ is a monotone function and therefore 1-1. We show monotonicity by proving that the first derivative of D is greater than zero for all v. For the sake of simplicity, we use $|G| = kR$ for some $k \geq 0$.

$$D'(v) = 1 + 4\frac{kv^3}{R^3} + 4\frac{kv(d^2-R^2)}{R^3} \tag{3}$$

Since we need to show that $D'(v) > 0$ for all the possible d values, we have to check that even for the minimal d value, $D'(v) > 0$. The term d appears with a positive sign and by definition, d is always positive. Therefore, the minimal value of $D'(v)$ occurs when $d=0$. Geometrically, this means that the minimal derivative occurs on the sphere chord passing through C.

When we assign $d=0$, we get:

$$D'(v) = 1 + 4\frac{kv^3}{R^3} - 4\frac{kv}{R} > 0 \tag{4}$$

If we denote $u = v/R$, $u \in [-1, 1]$ and rearrange the terms (recall that $k \geq 0$), we get:

$$u(1-u^2) < \frac{1}{4k} \tag{5}$$

In the interval $[-1, 1]$ the function $u(1-u^2)$ has a maximum at $u = 2/(3\sqrt{3})$, and therefore setting $k < (3\sqrt{3})/8$ satisfies inequality (5). By the theorem condition, k meets this requirement and thus $D(v)$ is indeed monotone. Since $D(v)$ sends each segment's endpoint to itself, $D(v)$ is 1-1, and so is $T(p)$.

Requirement 3: Points on the sphere surface (where $r=R$) are transformed to themselves so C^0 continuity on the sphere surface is preserved. In order to show that rays are transformed into C^1 continuous curves, examine a ray crossing the deflector gravity field. Let this ray enter the gravity field at point P and exit at point Q. Examine:

$$S(r) = \left(1 - \frac{r^2}{R^2} \right)^2 \tag{6}$$

$S(r)$ is the scalar multiplying the gravity vector G in $T(p)$ where r is the distance between p and C. In order to examine the behavior of $S(r)$ along a chord PQ, we examine r values along the chord. Let

$$P = \left(X_0, Y_0, Z_0 \right), \quad Q = \left(X_1, Y_1, Z_1 \right), C = \left(C_x, C_y, C_z \right) \tag{7}$$

$$P_x = X_0 + t\left(X_1 - X_0 \right), \quad P_y = Y_0 + t\left(Y_1 - Y_0 \right), P_z = Z_0 + t\left(Z_1 - Z_0 \right) \tag{8}$$

where P_x, P_y, and P_z are the coordinates of points along the chord. The distance of points along the ray from C is now written as a quadratic function in t:

$$r^2 = \left(X_0 + t\left(X_1 - X_0\right) - C_x\right)^2 + \left(Y_0 + t\left(Y_1 - Y_0\right) - C_y\right)^2 + \left(Z_0 + t\left(Z_1 - Z_0\right) - C_z\right)^2 \quad (9)$$

If we replace r^2 in (6) by the expression in (9), we get a quadratic function of t which we denote by $P(t)$. For some scalars α, β, γ we get:

$$P(t) = \left(1 - \frac{\alpha t^2 + \beta t + \gamma}{R^2}\right)^2 \quad (10)$$

Observe that $\gamma = R^2$. Plugging R^2 we get:

$$P(t) = \left(\frac{\alpha t^2 + \beta t}{R^2}\right)^2 \quad (11)$$

The free variable in $P(t)$ is zero. Therefore, the derivative of $P(t)$ at $t=0$ is also zero. For reasons of symmetry this is also true for $t=1$. This shows that any ray crossing the deflector converts into a C^1 continuous curve.

The proof of requirement 3 suggests a fast method for traversing deflected rays. Equation (11) expresses the curved ray created by one deflector. Incrementing t we step along this ray. Of course it is not enough to make equidistant step along t as we want equidistant steps along the curved ray. In addition, we have not yet discussed what happens if multiple deflectors are involved. We devote some of Section 4 to the discussion of these and other implementation issues.

Requirement 4: At the deflector center $r=0$ and therefore $T(C)=C+G$. At any other point p located at distance r from C, the value of $\|T(p) - p\|$ is smaller than $\|G\|$ by a factor of $(1-r^2/R^2)^2$, which is always smaller than 1.

We have thus shown that the transformation $T(p)$ is a well behaved transformations.

3 Modeling with Multiple Deflectors

A single deflector introduces a round bump into space. In order to generate complex deformations we have to use multiple deflectors with various radii and gravity vectors. We must also impose ordering on the activation of the various deflectors on each ray. We do this by assigning each deflector an index number and transforming each ray by deflectors in increasing index order. For instance, in order to deform the side of a box into a long tubular curved arm we create a chain of deflectors d_0,..., d_n starting at the box face (d_0) and curving along some path leaving the box (up to d_n). Each deflector has a gravity vector sending its center point to the center point of its successor. Rays piercing the center of the outermost deflector d_0 are deflected along the gravity vectors of d_0, d_1,..., d_n and eventually sample data from the tip of the gravity vector of deflector d_n. It should be noted that the larger the deflector radius is, the more rays are deflected along the arm and the wider the resulting arm becomes.

4 Rendering in a Deformed Space

Depending on the nature of the data in space, we trace rays differently. When deforming geometric primitives, we compute the intersection of the deformed ray with the geometry as in traditional ray tracing [4], when deforming 2D rasters we sample at points along the deformed scan lines, and when deforming 3D rasters, we sample along rays as in traditional volume rendering [8].

4.1 Determining Ray Trajectory

When shooting rays we have to distinguish between two cases: either a ray does not intersect any field of gravity, or it intersects at least one such field of gravity. In the first case we need not transform the ray and can trace it as a traditional linear ray. We can do that because the transformation of points outside the field of gravity of any deflector is the identity transform. In the second case, we employ a ray-sphere intersection test to divide a ray into segments that lie inside or outside of a deflector's gravity field. The segments lying inside a deflector field of gravity are deflected into curves, while the segments lying outside any deflector field of gravity are traced as traditional linear rays. The locality of the deflection transform makes it valid to transform only those ray segments that pierce a deflector field of gravity.

4.2 Deforming Ray Segments

The proof of requirement 3 in Section 2 demonstrated how a ray segment is affected by a single deflector and how we can trace the path of a deflected ray by transforming all its points using a fourth degree polynomial. When the gravity field of deflectors intersect, we must enforce some order on the activation of each deflection transformation. We order the deflectors in a way that imitates the work of an artist sculpting a piece of material. We activate deflectors in their index order and accumulate their affect on each sight ray. Note that we number deflectors starting at the outermost one. An artist creating a tubular deformation (in Section 3) will start at deflector d_n working his way down to deflector d_0. We are deflecting sight rays instead of objects in space thus the order we impose on deflectors is the reverse of the one the artist picks.

When composing the effect of multiple deflectors on a ray segment we can not compute the curved ray path using a simple fourth degree polynomial. Composing the effect of two deflectors yields a polynomial of degree eight. For three deflectors we get a polynomial of degree sixteen, etc. Recall that the fourth degree polynomial resulted from plugging a linear segment equation into $T(p)$. We can use the fourth degree polynomial only for deflecting a linear segment. We compute further deflections by applying $T(p)$ directly to points along a sight ray.

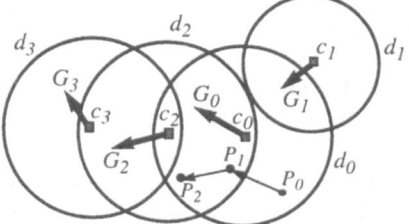

Fig. 4. Point P_0 is deflected by d_0 into point P_1. P_1 is in the gravity field of d_2 so P_1 is deflected by d_2 into P_2. P_2 is not in the gravity field of d_3 so it is not deflected any further.

For a point p, we define *Primary(p)* to be the smallest deflector index such that p is in its deflection field of gravity. Given a sight ray, we divide it into segments. For each segment S, all the points p in S have the same *Primary(p)*. For each segment, we transform the sight ray into a curve using the primary deflector. For each point along that curve, we activate deflectors with indices larger than that of the primary deflector in an increasing order of indices. Luckily, we do not have to check every point against every existing deflector. Requirement 2 on the deflection transform assures us that a point along the sight ray can only be deflected within the deflector's gravity field. Preprocessing all the deflectors in a scene, we maintain, for each deflector, a list of other deflectors with higher indices that intersect its gravity field. These are the only candidates for further deflecting a point p following its deflection by *Primary(p)*. For example, in Figure 4, a point P_0, deflected by deflector d_0 into a point P_1, has to be deflected by deflectors d_1, d_2 in that order because both intersect the gravity field of d_0. P_1 is only inside the gravity field of deflector d_2 so we deflect P_1 by deflector d_2 into P_2. Now we have to consider the deflector d_3, however, since P_2 is not in the gravity field of d_3, the final deflection of P_0 is P_2.

4.3 Sampling a Deflected Ray

When objects in space are polygons, we seek the first intersection along a ray. We first intersect each ray with the objects in space and with all the spheres defining the deflectors gravity fields. If an intersection with an object occurs along a ray before it enters any deflector field of gravity, we need not bother checking the rest of the ray. However, if the ray first intersects a deflector field of gravity, we start deflecting points along the ray and convert the ray into a polyline. We now look for intersections of space objects with segments along the ray. The first such intersection is the one we use for calculating the resulting color of the ray. We pick small enough steps along the original linear ray to ensure smooth evaluation of the resulting curved ray by line segments. This choice of a step size is similar to the choice of a sub-polygon size when breaking a polygon into a mesh of smaller polygons as done in traditional object deformation algorithms [9]. The smaller the pieces are, the smoother the resulting deformation is.

In volume graphics, we take equidistant steps along each sight ray and sample the volume contents at each step. When stepping along linear segments of a ray, we use standard volume ray tracing techniques. When we trace curved ray segments, we have to take equidistant steps along the resulting deflection curve. We do that by varying the linear distance along a ray segment such that the distance between every two consecutive samples of the volume is constant. Since we map long curved rays into the linear ray, we have to adjust the opacity of each sample to match the linear distance along the original ray. We do that by factoring each sample by the linear distance between two consecutive samples along the original ray.

4.4 Calculating the Normal Along Curved Rays

For every sample point $p = (x, y, z)$, we convert the point normal N to the deformed normal N' as follows: we take three new points $px = (x + \varepsilon, y, z)$, $py = (x, y + \varepsilon, z)$, and $pz = (x, y, z + \varepsilon)$, for some small distance ε. The three vectors $[px - p]$, $[py - p]$, and $[pz - p]$ form a basis B of the original 3D space at p. The three vectors $[T(px) - T(p)]$, $[T(py) - T(p)]$, and $[T(pz) - T(p)]$ are a basis of B' of the deformed 3D space at *T(p)*. We use these two basis to map tangent vectors and reconstruct N'.

5 Discussion

Barr [1] presented a deformation method for objects in space. Given some global space transform M, rays are transformed by the inverse of M. Barr [1] suggests expressing any local transforms as global ones. He accumulates the various transforms of space into a single analytical global transform. Clearly, sculpting space requires many localized modification of space. Converting such local sculpting operations into global analytic transforms results in very complex global transforms, and very slow rendering times. Our approach treats local transforms directly without converting into global ones. We compose the local transforms and accumulate their effect on the rays. This way we achieve practical rendering times and ease of modelling.

While traversing a sight ray within a deflector gravity field, we have to evaluate a fourth degree equation at each sample point. When the model is relatively small (e.g., a simple polymesh) it is cheaper to deform the model than to compute the sample points inside the deflectors gravity field. In addition, if one deforms an object once and then animates some global parameter such as camera position, lighting, object position and orientation (but not its shape), it is probably preferable to deform the model once and then repeatedly render it with a traditional renderer.

Another drawback in our approach is the lack of a simple inverse to the deflector transformation. The consecutive activation of two deflectors with identical gravity fields and opposite direction vectors does not result in an identity transform.

On the other hand, our approach exhibits attractive characteristics. When deforming polygons, traditional techniques break them down into a mesh of smaller polygons and deform their vertices [9]. Many of the smaller polygons may not contribute to the final image because they are hidden by other polygons in space. Moreover, polygons that lie farther away from the eye need not be subdivided into as many polygons as the closer polygons. In our technique, there is no need to subdivide the polygons at all. Nevertheless, we provide level of detail that is equivalent to the one achieved when a model is subdivided to the extent that each ray intersects a different polygon.

Techniques for volume deformations [5,6] deform and re-sample the entire volume every time the deformation changes. Our technique deforms only those parts of the volume that participate in the generation of the result image pixels. Parts of the data set that are hidden behind opaque voxels are neither deformed nor sampled.

In volume graphics, traditional deformation techniques involve re-sampling the volume. When a large area in a data set is deformed into a small one, either data is lost or a volume of a larger size is created. Our technique maintains all the original data with no re-sampling. Color Figure 6 (See Appendix) shows three examples of deforming an MRI dataset of a human head by multiple deflectors.

Since our method deforms rays rather then objects, we can deform any object that a ray can intersect, saving an implementation of a specific deformation procedure for each object type. In addition, our technique is dimension independent. It can be restricted to two dimensional images or extended to higher dimensions. In two dimensions we can use ray deflectors as a modeling primitive for image warping. Color Figure 7 (See Appendix) shows an example of a teapot modeled from a box (right) and a sphere (left) in a volumetric representation and a polymesh teapot with 256 polygons with deformations applied to it (center).

Unlike existing methods, deflector based deformation is much more intuitive as a modeling tool. Existing methods deform the space somewhat indirectly by moving grid points [13] or vectors [3], an extremely laborious operation in 3D. Our approach, on the other hand, simulates the process of creating a sculpture by deforming an initial set of objects in space using a sequence of local deformations.

Our technique makes it very easy to compose deformations. We can easily compose deformations of large portions of space onto deformation of small ones and vice versa.

In the future we plan to investigate deflectors with more complex shapes then spheres and different deflection operators such as higher order gravity functions. In volume graphics, we wish to improve our sampling technique by using a mip-mapped version of the volume [12]. Finally, the current technique forces smooth deformations and cannot be used to simulate cuts or cracks in objects. Adding continuity breakers such as three dimensional planes can help generate sharp cuts in objects.

6 Conclusions

We have introduced a new technique for modeling and rendering deformations in space. Our technique embeds the deformation transformation into the rendering process using ray tracing. It deforms space by changing the path of rays through space, and converting linear rays into curved ones. The technique operates locally, and so enables traditional ray tracing through undeformed parts of space. We demonstrated the application of this technique to spaces containing polygonal objects or volumes.

Acknowledgments

This work was partially supported by National Science Foundation Grant CCR-9211288, and by the Advanced Research Projects Agency Contract DABT63-C-0056. We thank Rick Parent, Joseph Reiss, and Ed Swan, for reading the manuscript and for their useful suggestions.

References

1. Barr A., "Global and Local Deformations of Solid Primitives", *Proceedings of SIGGRAPH '84, Computer Graphics*, 18(3):21-30, July 1984.

2. Barr A., "Ray Tracing Deformed Surfaces", *Proceedings of SIGGRAPH '86, Computer Graphics*, 20(4):287-296, August 1986.

3. Bier T. and Neely S., "Feature Based Image Metamorphosis", *Proceedings of SIGGRAPH '92, Computer Graphics*, 26(2):35-42, July 1992.

4. Glassner, A. S. (ed.), *An Introduction to Ray Tracing*, Academic Press, 1989.

5. He T., Wang S., and Kaufman A., "Wavelet-Based Volume Morphing", *Proceedings of Visualization'94*, IEEE Computer Society Press, 1994, pp. 85-92.

6. Hughes J.F., "Scheduled Fourier Volume Morphing", *Proceedings of SIGGRAPH '92, Computer Graphics*, 26(2):43-46, July 1992.

7. Isaacs P.M. and Cohen M.F., "Controlling Dynamic Simulation with Kinematic Constrains, Behavior Functions and Inverse Dynamics", *Proceedings of SIGGRAPH '87, Computer Graphics*, 21(4):215-224, July 1987.

8. Kaufman A. (ed.), *"Volume Visualization"*, IEEE Computer Society Press, 1990.

9. Kent J.R., Carlson W.E., and Parent R., "Shape Transformations for Polyhedral Objects", *Proceedings of SIGGRAPH '92, Computer Graphics*, 26(2):47-54, July 1992.

10. Sederberg, T.W. and Greenwood E., "A Physically Based Approach to 2-D Shape Blending", *Proceedings of SIGGRAPH '92, Computer Graphics*, 26(2):25-34, July 1992.

11. Terzopoulos D., Platt J., Barr A., and Fleischer K., "Elastically Deformable Models", *Proceedings of SIGGRAPH '87, Computer Graphics*, 21(4):205-214, July 1987.

12. Williams L., "Pyramidal Parametrics", *Proceedings of SIGGRAPH '83, Computer Graphics*, 17(3):1-10, July 1983.

13. Wolberg G., *"Digital Image Warping"*, IEEE Computer Society Press, 1990.

Editors' Note: see Appendix, p. 357 for colored figure of this paper

Bridging between surface rendering and volume rendering for multi-resolution display

T. Noma

Department of Artificial Intelligence, Kyushu Institute of Technology,
Iizuka, Fukuoka 820, JAPAN.

Abstract. This paper presents an approach to generating and rendering texels (3D volume textures) faithful to the geometry of a collection of surfaces, and thus to bridging an existing gap between surface rendering and volume/texel rendering. This approach enables us to render the identical collection of surfaces both in the far distance and close at hand. Experiments on clouds of spheres and trees/forests are reported.

1 Introduction

In conventional computer graphics, objects are modeled as a set of surfaces, and the surfaces are rendered depending on their reflection functions. This surface-based technique is called *surface rendering*. With this technique, any scene that is composed of surfaces can be rendered in principle. In case of complex scenes with a huge number of surfaces, however, traditional hidden-surface/visibility algorithms often take much time to render the scenes and/or cause severe aliasing artifacts. Greene et al.[6, 7] proposed algorithms that properly handle complex polygonal scenes. But their algorithms are still impractical if, for example, a distant forest is to be rendered considering the geometry of an enormous number of leaves.

To render a large collection of microscopic spherical particles, Blinn[2] presented a *volume density* algorithm for homogeneous media, and Kajiya and Von Herzen[9] extended his work to non-homogeneous media by ray tracing[1]. Furthermore, Kajiya and Kay[11] mixed volume densities with anisotropic reflection models[10] so that the volume cell called a *texel* represents a collection of microsurfaces, not spherical particles. Then they rendered fur independent of the geometric complexity of hairs of the fur.

In [11], Kajiya and Kay suggested that trees and bushes can be modeled as appropriate texels so that they are rendered as texels in the far distance, and are modeled as a collection of surfaces close at hand. Similar ideas on multi-resolution rendering are found in other literatures. For example, Westin et al.[15] proposed that BRDF's(Bidirectional Reflectance Distribution Functions), texels, texture/bump maps, and geometry should be chosen depending on the sizes of surface features and pixels. As pointed out in [8], however, such ideas have not been implemented yet in a general way. The existing methods on these lines are:

---

[1] The Blinn/Kajiya model was first developed for the synthesis of images with clouds, gases, and the rings of Saturn, but the model is now mainly and extensively used in medical imaging.

(1) generating BRDF's from geometry[3, 15], and (2) smoothing the transitions between BRDF's, bump mapping, and displacement mapping[1].

This paper presents an approach to generating and rendering texels consistent with an arbitrary collection of surfaces so that surface rendering and volume/texel rendering can be used to render the same collection of surfaces. To achieve this goal, we propose:

(1) a new texel model for making its area-averaged transparency and light intensity consistent with those of surface rendering,

(2) an algorithm that generates multi-resolution texels from arbitrary collection of surfaces, and

(3) an algorithm that renders both the texels and surfaces consistently.

Our new approach enables us, for example, to render distant forests as texels and nearby trees as polygons, and to make smooth transitions between the two rendering algorithms.

2   Kajiya's texel model and its problems

Suppose that a volume containing spherical particles with density $\rho(x, y, z)$ at each point is penetrated by a ray. Each point on the ray is parameterized as $(x(t), y(t), z(t))$. In [9], the transparency T along the ray (from t_0 to t_1) is:

$$T = \exp\left(-\tau \int_{t_0}^{t_1} \rho(x(s), y(s), z(s))ds\right) \qquad (1)$$

In Equation 1, τ is a coefficient that converts the density of particles into the degree of attenuation. Let $I_i(x, y, z)$ be the illumination at (x, y, z) from the light source i, and $p(\cos\theta_i)$ be a phase function (reflection function) where θ_i is an angle between the light direction and the eye direction. The brightness (intensity of light arriving at the eye) B is given as:

$$
\begin{aligned}
B \;=\;& \int_{t_{near}}^{t_{far}} e^{-\tau \int_{t_{near}}^{t} \rho(x(u),y(u),z(u))du} \\
\times\;& \left[\sum_i I_i(x(t), y(t), z(t))p(\cos\theta_i)\right] \\
\times\;& \rho(x(t), y(t), z(t))dt
\end{aligned}
\qquad (2)
$$

In Equation 2, the contribution of intensity is integrated along the ray.

In [11], Kajiya and Kay modified the above equations for rendering texels:

$$T = \exp\left(-\tau \sum_{s=t_{near}}^{t_{far}} \rho(x(s), y(s), z(s))\right) \qquad (3)$$

$$B = \sum_{t=t_{near}}^{t_{far}} e^{-\tau \sum_{u=t_{near}}^{t} \rho(x(u),y(u),z(u))}$$

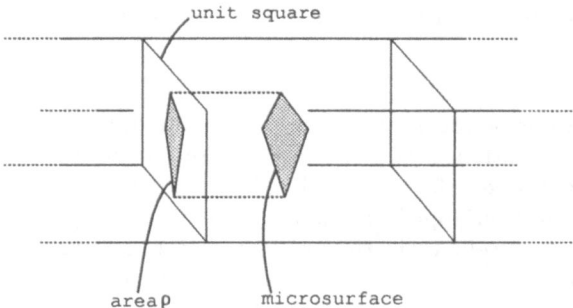

Fig. 1. A square beam and a microsurface.

$$\times \quad [\sum_i I_i(x(t), y(t), z(t))\Psi(x(t), y(t), z(t), \theta, \phi, \psi)]$$

$$\times \quad \rho(x(t), y(t), z(t)) \tag{4}$$

In Equations 3 and 4, ρ does not mean the density of particles but "how much of the projected unit area of a volume cell is covered by microsurfaces"[11] and then the line integrals are replaced by (formal) sums. $\Psi(x(t), y(t), z(t), \theta, \phi, \psi)$ is a BRDF that represents how much light is scattered from the light source to the eye by the microsurfaces around $(x(t), y(t), z(t))$.

Now let us try to turn geometry into texels in the above model. Suppose that a beam whose cross section is a unit square is partially blocked by a microsurface, and the projected area of the microsurface onto the cross section of the beam is ρ (Fig. 1). Obviously the transparency T of the beam is:

$$T = 1 - \rho \tag{5}$$

In Kajiya's model, however, T seems to be derived from Equation 3 as:

$$T = \exp(-\tau\rho) \tag{6}$$

The difference between Equations 5 and 6 arises from the fact that, in Equation 5, the actual geometry of the microsurface is considered, while Equation 6 is based on stochastic geometry, that is, *Poisson grain model*[14].

A *stationary Poisson point process* $\Phi = \{x_1, x_2, \ldots\}$ is a random point pattern where (1) the number of points of Φ in a bounded Borel set B has a Poisson distribution of mean $\lambda\nu_d(B)$ for some constant λ, and (2) the numbers of points of Φ in k disjoint Borel sets form k independent random variables. $\nu_d(Q)$ is a Lebesgue measure of Q in $\mathbf{R}^d$, and λ is the mean number of points to be found in a unit volume. Suppose that points are scattered in the plane perpendicular to the direction of the beam according to Φ. On each of these points, a projected microsurface is placed. If the mean projected area of the microsurfaces is $\bar{V}$, then the mean fraction of area occupied by these microsurfaces in a region of unit square is:

$$p = 1 - \exp(-\lambda\bar{V}) \tag{7}$$

Since the transparency is the fraction of area *not* occupied by the microsurfaces, then we have:

$$T = \exp(-\lambda \bar{V}) \tag{8}$$

Further discussions on stochastic geometry are found in [14].

Comparing Equations 3 and 8, ρ in Equations 3 and 4 should be interpreted as the density of microsurfaces multiplied by their mean projected area, and thus the elimination of overlapped area is not considered in the ρ. The exponent in Equation 3 *stochastically* takes the overlapping into account.

To obtain texels from the geometry of a collection of surfaces, we thus need to estimate the density and mean projected area of the surfaces. Such statistics are estimated well for large samples, and the resultant T and B from Equations 3 and 4 are applicable only to large volumes containing many surfaces.

This means that there is a wide gap in applicable resolution between surface rendering and stochastic texel rendering. In my view, this is the most serious reason why volume/texel rendering has not been integrated with surface rendering.

3   New texel model and rendering method

To bridge the gap between surface rendering and volume/texel rendering, we propose using sampled opacity, which is generated directly from the actual geometry of surfaces, instead of using statistics. The opacity $\rho(x, y, z, \theta, \phi, d)$ is a function of a sample point (x, y, z), a viewing direction (θ, ϕ), and a *diameter d* of the volume to be sampled. The last parameter d is a 3D version of the diameter in mip-mapping[16]. Note that the overlapped area of projected surfaces has already been taken into account in our ρ.

To calculate the transparency and the brightness from the above opacity, we suppose that microsurfaces in the beam are grouped into clusters of similar distance from the eye, and the clusters are sequentially numbered from the nearest cluster to the farthest one. If the parameter of the ray (axis of the beam) at the k-th cluster of microsurfaces is t_k, the transparency T is:

$$T = \prod_k (1 - \rho(x(t_k), y(t_k), z(t_k), \theta, \phi, d_k)) \tag{9}$$

d_k is the diameter at the k-th cluster. The diameter usually increases as the ray goes. For example, in case of an eye ray in ray tracing, d should be proportional to t if $t = 0$ at the eye (center of projection). Except for skipping empty volumes, $t_{k+1} - t_k$ should be equal to or less than d_k so as not to ignore some surfaces in the beam.

The brightness B is calculated by summing the brightness of all clusters along the beam(ray). The contribution of the k-th cluster, that is attenuated by $k - 1$ clusters, is:

$$[\prod_{j=1}^{k-1} (1 - \rho(x(t_j), y(t_j), z(t_j), \theta, \phi, d_j))]$$

$$\times \quad [\sum_i I_i(x(t_k), y(t_k), z(t_k))\Psi(x(t_k), y(t_k), z(t_k), \theta, \phi, \psi)]$$

$$\times \quad \rho(x(t_k), y(t_k), z(t_k), \theta, \phi, d_k)$$

Thus the brightness B is:

$$
\begin{aligned}
B \quad = \quad & \sum_k [[\prod_{j=1}^{k-1}(1 - \rho(x(t_j), y(t_j), z(t_j), \theta, \phi, d_j))] \\
\times \quad & [\sum_i I_i(x(t_k), y(t_k), z(t_k))\Psi(x(t_k), y(t_k), z(t_k), \theta, \phi, \psi)] \\
\times \quad & \rho(x(t_k), y(t_k), z(t_k), \theta, \phi, d_k)]
\end{aligned}
\tag{10}
$$

To support multi-resolution representation of the opacity ρ, we adopt a 3D version of mip-map[16] for storing ρ. The opacity ρ for an arbitrary d is obtained by linear interpolation as was in [16].

In [11], ρ is treated as a scalar independent of the viewing vector. In our model, however, it should take account of the viewing direction. How to treat direction-dependent ρ will be discussed in Section 5.

To render our new texels, we have only to follow Equation 10 by ray tracing. An outline of a basic algorithm[2] is:

```
for each pixel do
begin
    determine ray from center of projection through pixel;
    if ray does not intersect texel space then
    begin
        set pixel's color to background;
        continue
    end
    determine tnear and tfar as minimum and maximum t in texel space;
    trans := 1;  t := tmin;  b := 0;
    while ( trans > threshold ) and ( t < tfar ) do
    begin
        determine d;
        b := b + trans * lighting * rho(... ,d);
        trans := trans * (1 - rho(... ,d));
        t := t + d
    end;
    set pixel's color to b
end
```

In the following two sections, we will illustrate how to render surfaces/texels in a multi-resolution fashion with two examples: (1) clouds of spheres and (2) trees and forests.

---

[2]In practical algorithms, clusters should be subdivided if their ρ's are large, and ρ should be adjusted depending on the length of the sampled beam(ray) segment.

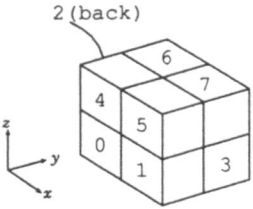

Fig. 2. Numbering children cells in a 3D pyramid.

4   Case 1: Clouds of spheres

This section discusses how to generate and render texels with a simplest example: clouds of spheres. The Blinn/Kajiya volume density model[2, 9] has been used for drawing clouds of spherical particles. To the best of my knowledge, however, volume densities and individual spheres have not been rendered consistently in a single image.

Calculating opacity. To render scenes containing both texels and individual spheres, we need to generate texels which are consistent with the geometry of the individual spheres. In case of spherical particles, the opacity ρ can be treated as a scalar independent of viewing vectors, and thus the texels can be treated as volume densities. As discussed in the previous section, ρ is stored as a 3D mip-map (completely balanced octree).

First, we calculate the opacities of the leaf cells in the octree. If the cell is a unit cube and it contains a sphere of radius r, the opacity ρ of the cell is:

$$\rho = \pi r^2 \tag{11}$$

Then ρ's of all the leaf cells are obtained[3].

Next, ρ's of the other (higher-level) cells are computed in a bottom-up fashion. Suppose that a cell has 8 children and their opacity are $\rho_0, \rho_1, \ldots, \rho_7$ (Fig. 2). Considering the overlapping of all the pairs of the children, the opacity of the parent cell is:

$$\rho = \frac{\sum_i \rho_i}{4} - \frac{\sum_{i<j} \rho_i \rho_j}{28} \tag{12}$$

Reflection functions. Suppose that each sphere reflects light according to the diffuse illumination equation of a diffuse reflection coefficient k_d. Integrating the brightness of the visible disk of a sphere for a given viewing direction yields[2]:

$$\Psi = \frac{2}{3\pi} k_d (\sin \theta + (\pi - \theta) \cos \theta) \tag{13}$$

---

[3]The opacities in other cases where, for example, two or more spheres are in a cell or a sphere is shared by neighboring cells, should be calculated accordingly.

Fig. 3. Cloud of spheres.

where θ is the angle between the light direction and the eye direction. Equation 10 is thus:

$$
\begin{aligned}
B \quad = \quad & \sum_k [[\prod_{j=1}^{k-1}(1 - \rho(x(t_j), y(t_j), z(t_j), \theta, \phi, d_j))] \\
\times \quad & [\sum_i I_i(x(t_k), y(t_k), z(t_k)) \frac{2}{3\pi} k_d(\sin\theta_i^j + (\pi - \theta_i^j)\cos\theta_i^j)] \\
\times \quad & \rho(x(t_k), y(t_k), z(t_k), \theta, \phi, d_k)]
\end{aligned}
\tag{14}
$$

Ray tracing algorithm integrating surface rendering and texel rendering. First, we examine whether each ray from the eye through a pixel intersects with nearby spheres. If it intersects with a sphere, then the color of the pixel is set to that of the sphere. Otherwise, the ray is traced in a texel space representing other distant spheres.

Experiments. Fig. 3 is an image of a flat cloud of spheres. The cloud is composed of $100 \times 100 \times 3$ cubic volumes, each of which contains 60 spheres. The eye (center of projection) is on the side of the planar cloud. The resolution of the image is 646 by 486. Neither shadowing nor antialiasing was done[4].

5 Case 2: Trees and forests

This section presents how texels are generated and rendered from complicated geometry of surfaces, botanical trees. Tree models are generated by AMAP on Macintosh[4].

---

[4] A single eye ray is traced per pixel.

Calculating opacity. The geometric models of trees generated by AMAP and other tree modelers are composed of surfaces representing trunks, branches, and leaves. We suppose that the major appearance of trees is determined by leaves, in particular, in the far distance, and thus calculate the opacities and reflection functions of texels only from the surfaces of leaves. To obtain the opacity ρ from the collection of surfaces, we sample opacities for some fixed directions, and then the opacity for an arbitrary direction is derived by interpolating ρ's sampled in advance. In our current implementation, we use three sampling direction, each of which is parallel to x-, y-, or z-axis.

First, we sample ρ's of the leaf cells for the three directions by projecting surfaces within the corresponding view volumes. We implemented this procedure by using a high-performance scan converter on a IRIS Crimson/VGXT.

Next, ρ's of the higher-level cells are computed in a bottom-up fashion. This bottom-up computation is performed independently for each direction. For example, in case of ρ's for the direction of x-axis, the opacity of a parent cell ρ^x is computed from those of its children cells $\rho^x_0, \ldots, \rho^x_7$ (Fig. 2) as:

$$\rho^x = \frac{\rho^x_0 + \rho^x_1 + \cdots + \rho^x_7}{4} - \frac{\rho^x_0 \rho^x_1 + \rho^x_2 \rho^x_3 + \rho^x_4 \rho^x_5 + \rho^x_6 \rho^x_7}{4} \tag{15}$$

Reflection functions. Suppose that each leaf of the tree reflects light according to the diffuse illumination equation of diffuse reflection coefficient k_d. The BRDF in Equation 10 for a collection of leaves is:

$$\Psi = k_d \frac{\sum s_i |\cos \theta_i|}{\sum s_i} = k_d \overline{|\cos \theta|} \tag{16}$$

where s_i is the projected area of the i-th leaf in the collection, and θ_i is the angle between its normal and the light direction. The symbol of an absolute value $|...|$ is used since both sides of leaves reflect light.

We obtain the averaged cosine $\overline{|\cos \theta|}$ for an arbitrary light direction in the following manner: First, for each cell, we calculate the averaged normal $\bar{n}$ of leaves in the cell. Next, we compute the averaged cosine α for directions at an angle of $\frac{\pi}{2}$ from $\bar{n}$, the averaged cosine β for directions at an angle of $\frac{\pi}{4}$ from $\bar{n}$, and the averaged cosine γ for $\bar{n}$. Then the averaged cosine for an arbitrary light direction is obtained by calculating the angle between the light direction and $\bar{n}$, and then interpolating it with α, β, and γ. Since a cosine curve is used for fitting α, β, and γ, $\overline{|\cos \theta|}$ coincides with $\cos \theta_i$ if only a single leaf exists in the cell.

Avoiding artifacts in algorithm switching. Switching rendering algorithms often cause artifacts in images. As suggested in [8], they are eliminated by smoothing the transitions using linear interpolation of colors.

Experiments. Fig. 4 (see Appendix) is an image of a collection of 80 × 3 cypress trees generated by AMAP[5] [4]. Each tree has about 5000 surfaces to be rendered. The resolution of the images is 440 by 320. In this image, shadowing was performed. Roughly speaking, large trees in the lower-left are drawn via

---

[5]The AMAP data is: Plant item: cypress1; Age: 30; Seed: 0; Simplification: 1.

distributed ray tracing[5] (3×3 rays/pixel), and small trees in the upper-right are rendered via our texel rendering (1 ray/pixel). Our experiments showed that both rendering algorithms are consistent in intensity for various lighting conditions.

Fig. 5 (see Appendix) compares the upper right corner of Fig. 4 with the same portion of two images generated by conventional surface rendering techniques. Compared with the images by Whitted-style ray tracing (left, 1 ray/pixel) and by distributed ray tracing (center, 3×3 rays/pixel), our texel rendering (right, 1 ray/pixel) properly represents the appearance of distant trees.

6   Discussions

We presented an approach to generating and rendering texels faithful to the actual geometry of a collection of surfaces, and thus to bridging the existing gap between surface rendering and volume/texel rendering. This approach enables us to render the identical collection of surfaces both in the far distance and close at hand.

Mixed representation combining surfaces and volumes has already been studied in illumination calculations. For example, Patmore[12] regarded a dense cluster of leaves as a volume, and thus approximated ambient illumination by the radiance interpolated from those at the grid points. Sillion[13] discussed the use of volumetric approximations of groups of surfaces in his hierarchical radiosity algorithm.

In our current implementation, there is much room for improvements in illumination models. In Figs. 3, 4 and 5, we used only a single point light source. The appearance of the images would be improved with more sophisticated illumination models taking account of sky light effects (e.g. [12]). In addition, we have not modeled specular reflections. In my view, it would be solved by introducing stochastic processes in rendering.

Determining the appropriate level of detail (the minimum size of the cells) of the hierarchical texel representation and the proper threshold of the diameter d for switching from surface rendering to volume/texel rendering and vice versa, is an open problem. Ideally, the texel representation should be in full detail so that surfaces and texels can be switched with no tricks. In our hierarchical texel representation, however, the required memory for the $(n+1)$-level representation is approximately eight times as much as that for n-level. Thus it would be desirable to minimize the number of levels of the hierarchical representation assuming the use of antialiasing techniques in surface rendering including distributed ray tracing[5] and error-bounded antialiased rendering of complex environments[7].

As seen from the above, one possible criticism to our approach would be on its huge memory requirements. In fact, if we straightforwardly model the whole environment by texels, the required memory would exceed the capacity of existing computer systems. But let us recall that Kajiya and Kay[11] rendered the whole furry surface of a teddy bear with a single texel. This suggests that realistic images can be generated within available memory by sharing, transforming, and perturbing texels. Such techniques should be further studied to make our texel model practical.

Acknowledgements

The author is grateful to Prof. Naoyuki Okada for his continuous support and encouragement.

References

1. Becker, B.G., Max, N.L.: Smooth transition between bump rendering algorithms. Proc. SIGGRAPH '93, 183–190 (1993).

2. Blinn, J.F.: Light reflection functions for simulation of clouds and dusty surfaces. Computer Graphics 16(3), 21–29 (1982).

3. Cabral, B., Max, N., Springmeyer, R.: Bidirectional reflection functions from surface bump maps. Computer Graphics 21(4), 273–281 (1987).

4. Unité de Modélisation du Cirad: AMAP user manual. 1994.

5. Cook, R.L., Porter, T., Carpenter, L.: Distributed ray tracing. Computer Graphics 18(3), 137–145 (1984).

6. Greene, N., Kass, M., Miller, G.: Hierarchical z-buffer visibility. Proc. SIGGRAPH '93, 231–238 (1993).

7. Greene, N., Kass, M.: Error-bounded antialiased rendering of complex environments. Proc. SIGGRAPH '94, 59–66 (1994).

8. Heckbert, P.S., Garland, M.: Multiresolution modeling for fast rendering. Proc. Graphics Interface '94, 43–50 (1994).

9. Kajiya, J.T., Von Herzen, B.P.: Ray tracing volume densities. Computer Graphics 18(3), 165–174 (1984).

10. Kajiya, J.T.: Anisotropic reflection model. Computer Graphics 19(3), 15–21 (1985).

11. Kajiya, J.T., Kay, T.L.: Rendering fur with three dimensional textures. Computer Graphics 23(3), 271–280 (1989).

12. Patmore, C.: Illumination of dense foliage models. Proc. 4th Eurographics Workshop on Rendering, 63–71 (1993).

13. Sillion, F.: Clustering and volume scattering for hierarchical radiosity calculations. Proc. 5th Eurographics Workshop on Rendering, 105–117 (1994).

14. Stoyan, D., Kendall, W.S., Mecke, J.: Stochastic geometry and its applications. John Wiley & Sons 1987.

15. Westin, S.H., Arvo, J.R., Torrance, K.E.: Predicting reflectance functions from complex surfaces. Computer Graphics 26(2), 255–264 (1992).

16. Williams, L.: Pyramidal parametrics. Computer Graphics 17(3), 1–11 (1983).

Editors' Note: see Appendix, p. 357 for colored figure of this paper

Multiple scattering as a diffusion process

Jos Stam

Department of Computer Science, University of Toronto
Toronto, Canada, M5S 1A4

Abstract. Multiple scattering in participating media is generally a complex phenomenon. In the limit of an optically thick medium, i.e., when the mean free path of each photon is much smaller than the medium size, the effects of multiple scattering can be approximated by a diffusion process. We introduce this approximation from the radiative transfer literature to the computer graphics community and propose several numerical methods for its solution. We implemented both a multi-grid finite differences scheme and a finite-element blob method.

1 Introduction

One of the principal aims of computer graphics is to accurately model the propagation of light. One challenge in this area is to model the propagation of light in the presence of a participating medium. Many natural environments contain participating media such as fog, steam, mist, clouds or dust. Typically in such environments each beam of light undergoes many changes as it interacts with the participating medium. The phenomenon of scattering, which changes the direction of propagation, makes this process particularly complicated. In rendering these effects, most researchers make the assumption that the light rays propagating through the medium encounter at most only one scatter event [3, 14]. To model the effects of multiple scattering, researchers either make simplifying assumptions about the participating medium or resort to expensive simulations. Rushmeier et al. assume a medium with isotropic scattering properties and derive a radiosity-style algorithm [13]. This method essentially models the interchange of energy between cubical elements (zones) of the environment. Anisotropic effects can also be modelled by discretizing the directions. These methods are known as *Discrete Ordinates* and have been applied to the rendering of participating media by Max and Languénou et al. [9, 8]. Other researchers have used direct Monte-Carlo techniques to simulate the paths of light particles in general environments [1, 11]. None of these models attempt to derive analytical models to account for the effects of multiple scattering. A notable exception is the work of Kajiya and Von Herzen [7]. They model the effects of multiple scattering by expanding the intensity field into a spherical harmonics basis. This method is known as the P_N-method in the transport theory literature, where N is the degree of the highest harmonic in the expansion [2]. Kajiya and Von Herzen derived the general method but used the P_1 expansion in their results as inferred from their statement: "We truncate the so-called "p-wave", viz. after the $l = 1$ term" [7]. In this situation, a diffusion-type equation is obtained for the scattered part of the illumination field. Unfortunately this characterization was obscured by the level of generality of their derivation. Also boundary conditions were not discussed in detail.

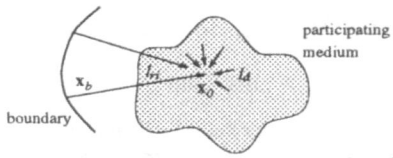

Fig. 1. Reduced Incident Intensity I_{ri} vs Diffuse Intensity I_d

The purpose of this paper is to present this *diffusion approximation* in greater detail to the computer graphics community. The approximation is valid when scattering events are frequent, i.e., in "optically thick" media. Under these exact conditions the effects of multiple scattering become apparent and the single scattering approximation is no longer valid. The effect of many scattering events is to smooth out the dependence of the intensity on its angular variable. Intuitively, in each region of the medium we find photons travelling in arbitrary directions.

The rest of the paper is organized as follows. Section 2 reviews the basic concepts and equations of transport theory. In Section 3 we show how the diffusion approximation is obtained from the transport equation. Section 4 presents numerical methods to solve diffusion equations. In Section 5 applications and results are given. Finally in Section 6 we state the conclusions and discuss future research.

2 Transport Theory

It is often convenient to separate the intensity field into two components: the *reduced incident intensity* I_{ri} and the *diffuse intensity* I_d [6]. The reduced incident intensity is that part of the intensity entering the participating medium which is attenuated by both scattering and absorption. The diffuse intensity, on the other hand, is created entirely within the medium through the phenomenon of scattering. Figure 1 illustrates the meaning of these two terms. Specifically, consider the ray $\mathbf{x}_u = \mathbf{x}_0 - u\,\mathbf{s}$ connecting a point $\mathbf{x}_b$ on one of the surfaces of the environment to a point $\mathbf{x}_0$ within the medium (again see Fig. 1). The reduced incident intensity is then the fraction of the intensity $I(\mathbf{x}_b, \mathbf{s})$ coming from the surface which is not scattered away or absorbed along the ray:

$$I_{ri}(\mathbf{x}_0, \mathbf{s}) = I(\mathbf{x}_b, \mathbf{s}) \exp\left(-\sigma_t \int_0^b \rho(\mathbf{x}_u)\, du\right),$$

where ρ is the *density* of the medium and σ_t is the *extinction cross-section* characterizing the scattering and absorptive properties of the medium. Indeed, it is the sum of a *scattering cross section* σ_s and an *absorption cross section* σ_a: $\sigma_t = \sigma_s + \sigma_a$. The *albedo* of the medium is the fraction of light that is scattered versus that which is absorbed: $\Omega = \sigma_s/\sigma_t$. Usually, there is no analytical closed form for the diffuse intensity. An equation for the diffuse intensity is obtained by equating the variation of the diffuse intensity along a given direction to the gain in intensity due to inscatter and emission minus losses caused by outscatter and absorption [6]:

$$\mathbf{s} \cdot \nabla I_d = -\sigma_t \rho (I_d + (1 - \Omega)Q + \Omega Q_{ri} + \Omega \mathcal{S}\{I_d\}), \tag{1}$$

where Q is the self-emission of the gas and $Q_{ri} = S\{I_{ri}\}$ is the intensity due to the first scatter of the reduced incident intensity. The functional S models the effect of a single scattering event and is equal to:

$$S\{I\}(\mathbf{x}, \mathbf{s}) = \frac{1}{4\pi} \int_{4\pi} p(\mathbf{s} \cdot \mathbf{s}') \, I(\mathbf{x}, \mathbf{s}') \, d\mathbf{s}', \tag{2}$$

where the *phase function* p gives the spherical distribution of light. The phase function is usually normalized such that its integral over all directions is 4π. A simple measure of the anisotropy of the participating medium is given by the *first moment* of the phase function defined by $\bar{\mu} = 3/2 \int_{-1}^{+1} \mu \, p(\mu) \, d\mu$. For negative $\bar{\mu}$ the phase function favours back scattering over forward scattering. The converse is true for positive $\bar{\mu}$. The reduced incident intensity is generally easy to calculate, since it involves only the integration of the density of the medium along a ray. A fast volume tracer can therefore be used [14, 17]. The diffuse intensity requires the solution of the transport equation and is usually more complicated to solve. In the next section we derive a diffusion equation for this intensity.

3 The Diffusion Approximation

As stated in the previous section, the diffused intensity is entirely created within the medium through the phenomenon of scattering. As the number of scattering events increases, the angular dependence tends to be smoothed out (see Appendix A). This is important since it shows that the diffuse intensity caused by many collision effects has only a weak dependence on direction. This motivates the main approximation made in the *diffusion approximation*, namely that the diffuse intensity can be expanded into the first two terms of its Taylor expansion in the directional component only:

$$I_d(\mathbf{x}, \mathbf{s}) = I_d^0(\mathbf{x}) + \mathbf{I}_d^1(\mathbf{x}) \cdot \mathbf{s}. \tag{3}$$

By substituting this reduced expansion of the diffuse intensity into Eq. 1 we obtain two equations by grouping terms that have the same order. Indeed, the left hand side of Eq. 1 becomes:

$$\mathbf{s} \cdot \nabla I_d = \mathbf{s} \cdot \nabla I_d^0 + \nabla \cdot \mathbf{I}_d^1.$$

The scattering term on the right hand side can be calculated likewise to be:[1]

$$\Omega S\{I_d\} = \frac{\Omega}{4\pi} \int_{4\pi} \left(1 + \bar{\mu}(\mathbf{s} \cdot \mathbf{s}') + \cdots\right) \left(I_d^0(\mathbf{x}) + \mathbf{I}_d^1(\mathbf{x}) \cdot \mathbf{s}'\right) \, d\mathbf{s}' = \Omega I_d^0 + \frac{\Omega \bar{\mu}}{3} \mathbf{I}_d^1 \cdot \mathbf{s}.$$

Using these relations and grouping terms that have the same order, we get two equations for the coefficients I_d^0 and $\mathbf{I}_d^1$:

$$\nabla \cdot \mathbf{I}_d^1 = -\rho \left(\sigma_a I_d^0 - \sigma_s Q_{ri}^0 - \sigma_a Q\right), \tag{4}$$

$$\nabla I_d^0 = -\rho \left(\sigma_{tr} \mathbf{I}_d^1 - \sigma_s \mathbf{Q}_{ri}^1\right), \tag{5}$$

---

[1] We use the following identities: $\int_{4\pi} \mathbf{s}' \, d\mathbf{s}' = 0$, $\int_{4\pi} \mathbf{s} \cdot \mathbf{s}' \, d\mathbf{s}' = 0$ and $\int_{4\pi} (\mathbf{s} \cdot \mathbf{s}') \mathbf{s}' \, d\mathbf{s}' = \frac{4\pi}{3} \mathbf{s}$.

where Q_{ri}^0 and $\mathbf{Q}_{ri}^1$ are the first two coefficients of Q_{ri} expanded in its angular variable. The *transport cross section* σ_{tr} is introduced as shorthand notation:

$$\sigma_{tr} = (1 - \Omega\bar{\mu}/3)\sigma_t = \sigma_s(1 - \bar{\mu}/3) + \sigma_a.$$

For constant phase functions, the flux $\mathbf{Q}_{ri}^1$ is equal to zero and the transport cross section equals the extinction cross section. These two functions, then, characterize the anisotropy of the diffuse intensity. Equations 4 and 5 are equivalent to the P_1 equations used by Kajiya and Von Herzen to render their clouds [7]. The diffusion aspect of these equations is, at this point, still hidden. We achieve a single equation for the average diffuse intensity as follows. The average flux can be extracted from the second equation and substituted into the first one to yield a diffusion equation for the average diffuse intensity:

$$\nabla \cdot \left(\kappa \nabla I_d^0\right) - \alpha I_d^0 + S = 0, \tag{6}$$

where we have used the following shorthand notations:

$$
\begin{aligned}
\kappa(\mathbf{x}) &= \left(\sigma_{tr}\rho(\mathbf{x})\right)^{-1}, \\
\alpha(\mathbf{x}) &= \sigma_a\rho(\mathbf{x}), \\
S(\mathbf{x}) &= \sigma_t\rho(\mathbf{x})Q_{ri}^0(\mathbf{x}) - \frac{\sigma_s}{\sigma_{tr}}\nabla \cdot \mathbf{Q}_{ri}^1(\mathbf{x}) + \sigma_a\rho(\mathbf{x})Q(\mathbf{x}).
\end{aligned}
$$

The boundary condition that no diffuse intensity can penetrate the medium at a surface cannot be satisfied exactly, because the diffuse intensity is approximated only by its first two moments. Instead, an approximate boundary condition that the total inward flux be zero is appropriate. The exact form of this condition is [6]:

$$I_d^0(\mathbf{x}_s) - 2\kappa(\mathbf{x}_s)\frac{\partial}{\partial\mathbf{n}}I_d^0(\mathbf{x}_s) + 2\frac{\sigma_s}{\sigma_{tr}}\mathbf{n} \cdot \mathbf{Q}_{ri}^1(\mathbf{x}_s) = 0, \tag{7}$$

for all points $\mathbf{x}_s$ lying on the boundary and $\mathbf{n}$ denotes the normal to the surface at point $\mathbf{x}_s$. Once the average diffuse intensity has been calculated, we can compute the average flux from Equation 5:

$$\mathbf{I}_d^1(\mathbf{x}) = \kappa(\mathbf{x})\left(-\nabla I_d^0(\mathbf{x}) + \sigma_s\rho(\mathbf{x})\mathbf{Q}_{ri}^1(\mathbf{x})\right). \tag{8}$$

In other words, the diffuse intensity is determined essentially by its first coefficient, since the flux $\mathbf{I}_d^1$ is proportional to the gradient of I_d^0.

The diffusion equation can also be obtained by expanding the intensity field into a perturbation series in the dimensionless ratio l/L_0, where $l = 1/\sigma_t\rho$ is the *mean free path* of the photons and L_0 is a characteristic length of the medium, e.g., $L_0 = 100$ km for clouds and $L_0 = 1$ m for steam rising from a kettle. When this ratio is small, local interactions dominate and the global transport equation collapses into a diffusion equation. The approximation is commonly considered valid when this ratio is smaller than $1/4$ [15].

From this diffusion equation, we can now make certain qualitative remarks concerning the phenomenon of multiple scattering. The basic effect is to smear out the initial source intensity S equal to the first scatter and the self-emission of the gas over time.

Fig. 2. The multi-grid method and a "v"-cycle

The effects of multiple scattering are most pronounced when the diffusion coefficient is high and the absorption rate is low. Specifically, the diffusion constant is higher for phase functions favouring forward scattering ($\bar{\mu} > 0$) versus backward scattering. The same is achieved when the albedo is close to unity. Chiefly, clouds have both a high albedo and a strong forward scattering. Multiple scattering is therefore an important phenomenon in clouds.

In the next section we will review some numerical techniques to solve the diffusion equation.

4 Numerical Solution of the Diffusion Equation

4.1 Multi-Grid Schemes

We obtain a straightforward numerical scheme for the diffusion equation when both the diffuse intensity and the source intensity are discretized on a three-dimensional grid of size N^3 and spacing h. The diffusion operator is then approximated using central differences:

$$\nabla \kappa \nabla I \approx \frac{\kappa_{i+1,j,k} I_{i+1,j,k} + \kappa_{i-1,j,k} I_{i-1,j,k} + \cdots + \kappa_{i,j,k-1} I_{i,j,k-1} - 6 I_{i,j,k}}{h^2},$$

where $\kappa_{i,j,k}$ is the sampled version of the diffusion constant. This discretization yields a system of equations for the interior points of the domain. For large N this system cannot be solved directly and is usually solved by relaxation [12]. After each relaxation step, we update the boundary by discretizing Equation 7. Let (i, j, k) be a point on the boundary. The variation along the normal is then approximated by:

$$\frac{\partial}{\partial \mathbf{n}} I_{i,j,k} \approx \frac{I_{i',j',k'} - I_{i,j,k}}{h},$$

where (i', j', k') is the closest sample to the boundary along the normal. For example, for the boundary point $(i, 0, k)$, the closest point is $(i, 1, k)$. The boundary condition is thus satisfied if the boundary is updated after each relaxation step:

$$I_{i,j,k} = \frac{2\kappa_{i,j,k} I_{i',j',k'} - 2h \, \mathbf{n} \cdot \mathbf{Q}_{i,j,k}}{h + 2\kappa_{i,j,k}},$$

where $\mathbf{Q}_{i,j,k}$ is the sampled version of the function $\sigma_s/\sigma_{tr} \mathbf{Q}_{ri}^1$.

A major drawback of relaxation schemes is their slow convergence. A powerful technique to speed up the convergence rate is to relax the system on grids with different spacings h. Following we will briefly review this method, known as the *multi-grid method* (for more details see [4]). The efficiency of the multi-grid method is due to both the fact that it can produce a good initial estimate of the solution and that it removes the high frequencies from the error by relaxing on coarser grids. These are achieved by considering a hierarchy of grids of spacings $h = 2^p$, $p = p_{coarse}, \ldots, p_{fine}$. The equation is first relaxed on the finest grid for a fixed number of iterations and then projected onto the next coarsest grid. This projection is likewise relaxed for a fixed number of iterations. These two steps are repeated until the coarsest level has been reached. The whole process is then reversed: each approximation is interpolated and relaxed on to the next finer grid. This process is repeated until the finest grid is reached. The above procedure corresponds to a complete "v-cycle" as illustrated in Figure 2. An approximation of the solution is attained by going through a fixed number of such v-cycles until convergence. In practice, the multi-grid is an order of magnitude faster then straightforward relaxation. However, this method is very memory intensive for large three-dimensional domains. Therefore, we propose an alternative method of solution corresponding to a finite element scheme.

4.2 Blob Finite Element Method

We obtain an alternate finite representation of the diffuse intensity by expanding it into a set of basis functions. We have chosen to experiment with a "blob representation" of the intensity field [18]:

$$I_d^0(\mathbf{x}) = 1/\rho(\mathbf{x}) \sum_{i=1}^{N} I_i m_i G(\mathbf{x} - \mathbf{x}_i, \sigma_i),$$

where m_i, $\mathbf{x}_i$ and σ_i model the mass, center and size of the blob, respectively. The *smoothing kernel* depends usually on distance alone and is taken here to be a Gaussian "bell" function. By inserting this representation into Eq. 6 and setting $\mathbf{x} = \mathbf{x}_j$ ($j = 1, \cdots, N$) we obtain a set of N equations:

$$\sum_{i=1}^{N} m_i I_i (\nabla \kappa(\mathbf{x}_j) \nabla G_{ij} - \alpha(\mathbf{x}_j) G_{ij}) + S(\mathbf{x}_j) = 0,$$

where $G_{ij} = G(\mathbf{x}_j - \mathbf{x}_i, \sigma_i)/\rho(\mathbf{x}_j)$. This method is actually a *collocation method* [10]. Care should be taken that the centers of the blobs are not too proximate, to avoid numerical instabilities. The system can be solved by LU decomposition when the number of blobs is below 200 or so [12].

5 Applications and Results

5.1 Light Beam in a Constant Density Atmosphere

In the first application we show the effects of the various parameters of the diffusion equation for a simple case of a constant density ρ_0 illuminated by a beam of light. For simplicity, the propagation is limited to a two-dimensional domain. We assume that the initial intensity S_0 of the beam is concentrated on the lower part of the plane corresponding to the x-axis. Then the source term of the diffusion equation can be computed analytically [6]:

$$S(x, y) = \rho_0 \left(\sigma_s + \sigma_s \sigma_t / \sigma_{tr} \bar{\mu} \right) S_0(x) \exp(-\rho_0 \sigma_t y).$$

The flux $Q_{i,j}$ appearing in the boundary conditions can be computed likewise to be:

$$Q_{i,j} = \frac{\sigma_s \bar{\mu}}{\sigma_{tr}} S^0(hi) \exp(-\sigma_t \rho_0 hj)(0, 1).$$

We have implemented the multi-grid finite difference scheme on a grid of size 512×512 with a "v"-cycle of depth 5. Only three relaxation steps were performed on each level. The solution of the diffusion equation took approximately 30 seconds on an SGI Indigo with an RS4000 processor. The following pictures depict both the diffuse intensity and the sources. Figure 3 shows the effects of the following parameters on the diffusion process: albedo Ω, extinction cross-section σ_t and the first moment of the phase function $\bar{\mu}$. As predicted, the diffusion is strongest for forward scattering in high albedo media.

5.2 Non-Constant Densities

Now we apply the diffusion approximation to a participating medium with a non-constant density distribution lit by a directional light source from above. We assume that the density is modelled as a superposition of the N Gaussian blobs [18]. In this case, the diffuse intensity drops off to zero at the edge of the density and the boundary conditions are satisfied naturally by the blob finite elements [10]. As in the previous example we used a two-dimensional domain. Each picture was rendered by assuming that the domain has a certain thickness l. The final intensity for each pixel (x, y) is then calculated by:

$$I(x, y) = \tau(x, y)I_{back} + (1 - \tau(x, y))I_{i,j} \quad \text{where} \quad \tau(x, y) = \exp\left(-\sigma_t \rho(x, y)l\right),$$

where $x = ih$ and $y = hj$. In our pictures we have set $l = 100$ and the background colour I_{back} to blue. We have computed solutions for two different numbers of blobs. The results are shown in Figure 4 and are compared to a multi-grid finite difference solution. The top pictures display the source term for each method. The source term is sampled at the center of each blob in the finite element method. The pictures at the bottom show the result after diffusion. The results demonstrate that the diffusion approximation does a fairly good job at approximating the solution given by the multi-grid scheme. This is achieved by using a discretization, which is an order of magnitude more efficient both in terms of storage (76 versus $512^2 = 262144$ elements) and computation time (0.2 versus 30 seconds). The blob solution could be used in an interactive graphics package.

5.3 Other Applications

Another potential application is the calculation of diffuse light from surfaces due to subsurface scattering. Hanrahan and Krueger calculated the effect of multiple scattering in the sub-surface layer using a Monte-Carlo simulation technique [5]. The multi-grid diffusion scheme could be used on a thin slice corresponding to one of the subsurface layers. The source intensity driving the diffusion process is equal to the refracted light incident on the surface. However, because boundary conditions are only approximate in the diffusion approximation, the results of such a simulation might not be sufficiently accurate.

6 Conclusions and Future Research

In this paper we have presented and explored applications of the diffusion approximation from transport theory to computer graphics. We have introduced a multi-grid solution to this equation that is efficient for nearly two-dimensional (thin slice) domains. In three-dimensions, this method suffers from the problems associated with grid-based methods: high computation costs and high storage requirements. To alleviate this problem, we have proposed an efficient finite element method based on Gaussian blobs to calculate the effects of multiple scattering in media with non-constant densities. The blob method gives a fairly good approximation, using far less memory and computation time. The accuracy of the diffusion approximation itself has not been tested rigorously. We intend to compare our results with the solutions obtained via Discrete Ordinates [8].

Acknowledgements

Thanks to Eugene Fiume for supervising this work, to Eric Languénou for many stimulating discussions and to Pamela Jackson for proofreading the paper.

A Proof of Angular Smoothing Due to Multiple Scattering

Both the phase function and the angular component of the intensity field can be expanded into spherical harmonics [16, 2]:

$$p(\mathbf{s} \cdot \mathbf{s}') = \sum_{l=0}^{\infty} \sum_{m=-l}^{l} p_l Y_{l,m}^*(\mathbf{s}') Y_{l,m}(\mathbf{s}),$$

$$I(\mathbf{x}, \mathbf{s}) = \sum_{l'=0}^{\infty} \sum_{m'=-l'}^{l'} I_{l',m'}(\mathbf{x}) Y_{l',m'}(\mathbf{s}),$$

in particular $p_0 = 4\pi$ and $p_1 = 2\pi\bar{\mu}/3$. We are not concerned with the exact form of the harmonics. However, we do use the property that they form an orthonormal basis of the functions defined on the unit sphere:

$$\int_{4\pi} Y_{l',m'}^*(\mathbf{s}) Y_{l,m}(\mathbf{s}) \, d\mathbf{s} = \delta_{l',l}\delta_{m',m}.$$

Consequently, a single scatter event becomes a simple multiplication by the coefficients of the phase function:

$$\mathcal{S}\{I\}(\mathbf{x}, \mathbf{s}) = \sum_{l',m'} \sum_{l,m} p_l I_{l',m'}(\mathbf{x}) Y_{l,m}(\mathbf{s}) \frac{1}{4\pi} \int_{4\pi} Y_{l,m}^*(\mathbf{s}') Y_{l',m'}(\mathbf{s}') \, d\mathbf{s}'$$

49

$$= \sum_{l,m} \frac{p_l}{4\pi} I_{l,m}(\mathbf{x}) Y_{l,m}(\mathbf{s}).$$

The accumulative effect on the intensity field of n scattering events at a location $\mathbf{x}$ can be expressed through the scattering functional S (see Eq. 2) as

$$S^n\{I\}(\mathbf{x},\mathbf{s}) = S^{n-1}\{S\{I\}\}(\mathbf{x},\mathbf{s}) = \sum_{l=0}^{\infty} \sum_{m=-l}^{l} \left(\frac{p_l}{4\pi}\right)^n I_{l,m}(\mathbf{x}) Y_{l,m}(\mathbf{s}).$$

This last expression tends towards $I_{0,0}(\mathbf{x})$ as n tends towards infinity. This is a consequence of the fact that each coefficient p_l is strictly smaller than 4π in absolute value, with the exception of the first one. This demonstrates that the dependence of the intensity field diminishes as the number of scatter events n increases.

References

1. P. Blasi, B. Le Saec, and C. Schlick. "A Rendering Algorithm for Discrete Volume Density Objects". *Computer Graphics Forum*, 12(3):201–210, 1993.

2. J. J. Duderstadt and W. R. Martin. *Transport Theory*. John Wiley and Sons, New York, 1979.

3. D. S. Ebert and R. E. Parent. "Rendering and Animation of Gaseous Phenomena by Combining Fast Volume and Scanline A-buffer Techniques". *ACM Computer Graphics (SIGGRAPH '90)*, 24(4):357–366, August 1990.

4. W. Hackbusch. *Multi-grid Methods and Applications*. Springer Verlag, Berlin, 1985.

5. P. Hanrahan and W. Krueger. "Reflection from Layered Surfaces due to Subsurface Scattering". In *Proceedings of SIGGRAPH '93*, pages 165–174. Addison-Wesley Publishing Company, August 1993.

6. A. Ishimaru. *VOLUME 1. Wave Propagation and Scattering in Random Media. Single Scattering and Transport Theory*. Academic Press, New York, 1978.

7. J. T. Kajiya and B. P. von Herzen. "Ray Tracing Volume Densities". *ACM Computer Graphics (SIGGRAPH '84)*, 18(3):165–174, July 1984.

8. E. Languénou, K.Bouatouch, and M.Chelle. Global illumination in presence of participating media with general properties. In *Proceedings of the 5th Eurographics Workshop on Rendering*, pages 69–85, Darmstadt, Germany, June 1994.

9. N. Max. Efficient light propagation for multiple anisotropic volume scattering. In *Proceedings of the 5th Eurographics Workshop on Rendering*, pages 87–104, Darmstadt, Germany, June 1994.

10. D. H. Norrie and G. de Vries. *The Finite Element Method. Fundamentals and Applications*. Academic Press, New York, 1973.

11. S. N. Pattanaik and S. P. Mudur. Computation of global illumination in a participating medium by monte carlo simulation. *The Journal of Visualization and Computer Animation*, 4(3):133–152, July–September 1993.

12. W. H. Press, B. P. Flannery, S. A. Teukolsky, and W. T. Vetterling. *Numerical Recipes in C. The Art of Scientific Computing*. Cambridge University Press, Cambridge, 1988.

13. H. E. Rushmeier and K. E. Torrance. "The Zonal Method for Calculating Light Intensities in the Presence of a Participating Medium". *ACM Computer Graphics (SIGGRAPH '87)*, 21(4):293–302, July 1987.

14. G. Sakas. "Fast Rendering of Arbitrary Distributed Volume Densities". In F. H. Post and W. Barth, editors, *Proceedings of EUROGRAPHICS '90*, pages 519–530. Elsevier Science Publishers B.V. (North-Holland), September 1990.

15. R. Siegel and J. R. Howell. *Thermal Radiation Heat Transfer*. Hemisphere Publishing Corp., Washington DC, 1981.

16. F. X. Sillion, J. R. Arvo, S. H. Westin, and D. P. Greenberg. "A Global Illumination Solution for General Reflectance Distributions". *ACM Computer Graphics (SIGGRAPH '91)*, 25(4):187–196, July 1991.

17. J. Stam and E. Fiume. "Turbulent Wind Fields for Gaseous Phenomena". In *Proceedings of SIGGRAPH '93*, pages 369–376. Addison-Wesley Publishing Company, August 1993.

18. J. Stam and E. Fiume. "Depicting Fire and Other Gaseous Phenomena Using Diffusion Processes". To appear in SIGGRAPH'95, 1995.

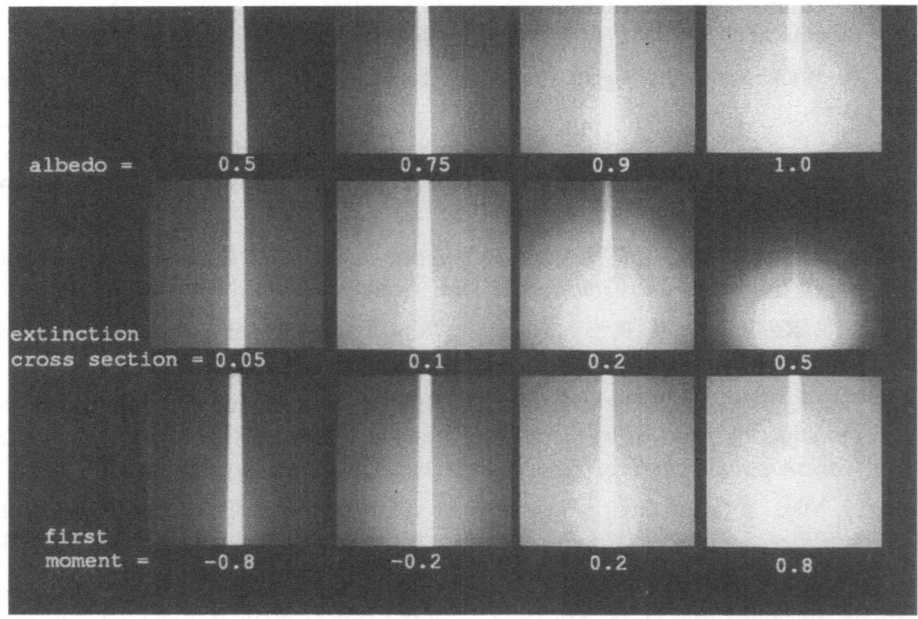

Fig. 3. Effect of Varying Ω, σ_t and $\bar{\mu}$

Editors' Note: see Appendix, p. 358 for colored figure of this paper

Optimized Maximum Intensity Projection (MIP)

Georgios Sakas, Marcus Grimm, Alexandros Savopoulos
Fraunhofer Institute for Computer Graphics
Wilhelminenstr. 7, 64283 Darmstadt, Germany
email: {gsakas,mgrimm}@igd.fhg.de

Abstract We present an improved version of the MIP algorithm that requires roughly 2%-10% of the computational effort of the brute-force, straightforward version. The algorithm conserves the image quality and requires no pre-processing. We propose four different quality levels: a fast line-traversing nearest neighbour algorithm for previewing, two efficient approximation algorithms that are sufficient for most applications, and an analytical method for images of highest quality. Additionally we present an improved cache memory access scheme. The employed 'sub-cube' volume data representation provides an additional speed up of at least 50% compared to the classical linear memory access. This is of particular interest for (but not restricted to) parallel volume rendering on shared memory multiprocessor systems.

1 Motivation

Maximum Intensity Projection (MIP) is widely accepted as a volumetric visualization method capable of improving the perception of the location, shape, and topology of vessels, and therefore is supported by all major industrial vendors of MRA devices [Vand91]. The main idea is surprisingly simple: due to the acquisition conditions, vessels result in a 'brighter' spot than their surroundings on a slice. Thus, the maximum value detected along a straight line through the volume will most probably belong to a vessel rather than to other tissue. If the maxima of all rays going through all pixels are projected on the screen, the all-around shape of vessels becomes visible. Although 'stronger' vessels may superpose thin ones and it is not possible to say which vessel is in front and which is in the back, the impression for the global vessel shape is improved significantly.

The disadvantage of the method is that the search for the maximum along a ray can become a very time consuming process. A typical MRA dataset has a resolution of $256^2 \cdot 128$, that is 8 MVoxels. If an image has the size of 256^2 pixels, assuming that on average about 80% of the rays will hit the data, approximately 50,000 rays need to be calculated. If each of these rays traverses on average 200 voxels, a total number of $50,000 \cdot 200 = 10$ million locations within the volume have to be processed, resulting in 10 million voxel accesses and evaluations even in the simplest case (nearest neighbour, no interpolation, one access per voxel, no super sampling). If tri-linear interpolation is employed, the above mentioned complexity increases by a factor of at least 4. Due to the lack of depth information in a MIP image, a small animation loop is usually appreciated, which means that 5-20 such images have to be computed. Obviously, without significant optimization such a straight-forward, brute-force method can only be implemented on large expensive computers that are not available to most users.

2 Problem Analysis

The most striking fact in the above mentioned calculation is that most of the computational effort does not conclude to the final result: Since only one maximum value is projected per ray, all other computed values are overwritten. Thus, less than 1% of the calculated values are indeed represented on the screen, a fact indicating significant potential for optimizations.

As analyzed in [Saka93d], the volume rendering process can be divided into four stages: traversing, sampling, illumination, and accumulation. Due to the nature of MIP, illumination is trivial and accumulation does not take place. Thus, optimizations have to be performed on the remaining stages that are traversing and sampling.

The task in the 'traversing' stage is to find all voxels contributing to a ray effectively. In the case of nearest neighbour access, those are all voxels hit by the 3D line that are found by using a fast 6-connected DDA algorithm ([ClWy88], [Slat92], [YaCK92]). However, due to the trilinear interpolation, voxels not directly hit by the line may also contribute to the pixel as well, see fig. 1. Finding these additional voxels requires extra work. The first optimization is to develop a fast line traversing method addressing only the voxels that contribute to the ray density.

With regard to 'sampling', an important observation mentioned above is that except for one, all other calculated values along the ray are overwritten. Since sampling employs trilinear interpolation – a very computational demanding operation –, the data could be pre-selected using an inexpensive, fast filter and sampled only at locations with promising success. In order to maintain interactivity, pre-processing of the data must be either avoided completely, or become very fast.

The implication of an improved sampling speed is that the access to the voxels stored in the main memory must be accelerated as well. Maximizing the cache coherency is becoming increasingly important when the average computations per voxel decrease.

A final observation deals with the method used to identify the exact position and value of a maximum candidate. Due to the employed trilinear interpolation, density values are not constant, but vary within the 3D space between voxel midpoints. Thus, the exact position and value of the maximum within 3D space is unknown and has to be computed. The straight-forward idea to oversample the complete ray requires prohibitive much computation time. A possible improvement is to first identify locations of interest and then to oversample these locations using either a uniform sampling or a binary search adaptively. In both cases oversampling remains computational demanding and the calculated value still is an approximation. Instead, a method is needed that provides good results while avoiding 'unsmart' oversampling with the corresponding interpolations.

In summary, four possible optimizations have been identified:

1. Addressing all voxels contributing to a ray, i.e. affected by trilinear interpolation. Effective ray-traversing by exploiting coherency, integer arithmetic etc.

2. Avoid unnecessary interpolations along the ray, evaluate only at locations promising success.

3. Find the accurate position and value of the maximum without oversampling for these selected locations.

4. Minimize the voxel access time by maximizing the cache coherency.

3 Line Traversing in Voxel Space

Gapless traversing is achieved by either ray-casting or line-drawing. In the first case the parametric equation of the ray is intersected with the analytical equations of the voxel boundaries. The results are very accurate, but also very slow. In the second case, traversing is executed in the discrete voxel space, and line coherence as well as integer arithmetic are exploited to speed-up computations. A Bresenham-like line algorithm is edge-connected, and thus, will skip several 'touched' voxels ([SaGe91b], see fig. 1). Therefore, a face-connected line algorithm is needed, see [Slat92] and [EnSo94] for a detailed discussion. The algorithms presented in [ClWy88] and [YaCK92] both fulfill this requirement. [YaCK92] is faster, but provides only integer voxel coordinates; therefore [ClWy88] is used. In addition, the coordinates of the ray intersection with the voxel boundaries at entry and exit position as real numbers are needed for the computation of the maximum as explained below in more detail (see fig. 2). The [ClWy88] algorithm fulfils this requirement without any analytical computations by exploiting the coherency.

However, two extensions that are important for MIP applications are necessary: first, in the original version, the termination criterion is based on a numerical comparison of the accumulated and the end-point coordinates. Such a termination can easily fail because of error accumulations, especially if it is implemented in fix point arithmetic and for long ray-paths. Additional tolerance criteria significantly slow down the all-round performance. We modified the termination criterion by calculating the total number of steps along each ray in advance just by comparing the total ray length to the voxel edge divided by the cosine of the ray angle. With this new termination criterion we were able to implement the algorithm in fix point arithmetic while avoiding error accumulations.

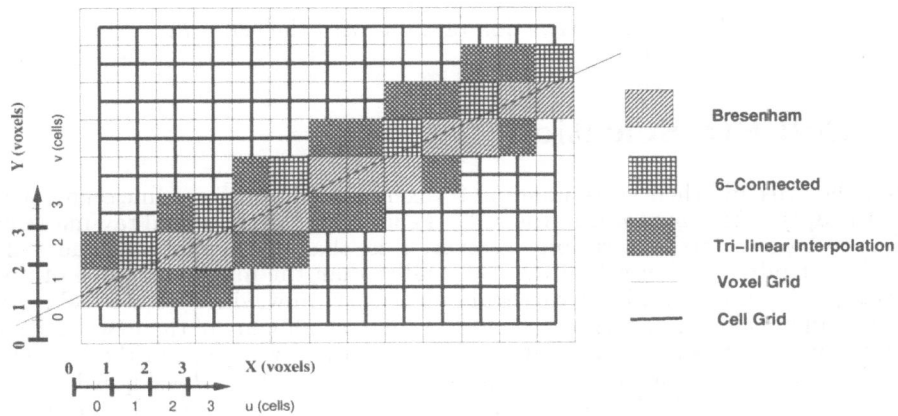

Figure 1: Voxels selected by different line-traversing methods

Even using the [ClWy88] algorithm, a comparison of the voxels selected by the face-connected line in fig. 1 and the voxels contributing to the ray shows that even this method will not select all required voxels. The reason is that the trilinear interpolation addresses all 8 voxels around the position selected on the ray. We refer to the cube defined by the midpoints of 8 neighbouring voxels an 'interpolation cell', or simply 'cell'. Within such a cell the value varies in space, but the expression of the interpolation function remains unchanged. It can easily be seen in fig. 1 that the cell grid is simply translated by a half voxel along the u,v,w directions of the voxel grid. Its resolution equals the voxel resolution minus one.

In order to address all contributing voxels in an effective way, we decided to traverse the ray on the cell grid instead on the voxel grid. Thus, with each step the line penetrates boundaries of interpolation domains instead of voxel boundaries. If a cell is selected, all of its 8 contributing voxels are selected. The complete ray-path is divided into a chain of individual segments, each of them is defined by the intersection with the ray with the cell boundaries. The density within each segment is given by a polynomial of third degree with coefficients differing between cells as expressed in eq. 7. Due to the usage of a face-connected line, each new step has 4 voxels in common with the previous one and addresses only 4 new additional voxels. Buffering the voxels helps decreasing access time.

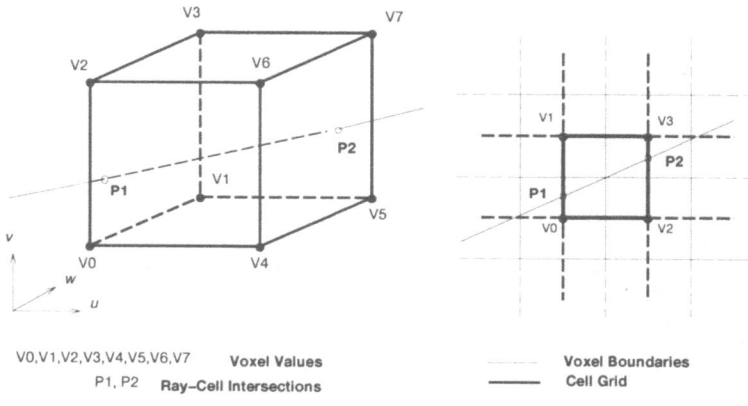

V0,V1,V2,V3,V4,V5,V6,V7   Voxel Values
P1, P2   Ray–Cell Intersections

Voxel Boundaries
Cell Grid

Figure 2: Intersection of a ray with the cell-grid

4   Cell Pre-Selection

Once the cells and their corresponding 8 voxels contributing to a line segment are identified, the maximum within the cell – a candidate for the global ray-maximum – has to be calculated. A simple observation is, that the maximum value within a cell after interpolation will always be smaller than the maximum value of the 8 voxels (or equal to that, if all voxels are identical). Now, since we are looking for the maximum along a ray, the maximum of the 8 neighbours of the newly selected cell is compared to the intermediate maximum of the ray. If none of the 8 voxels is greater than the current ray value, the cell (i.e., 8 voxels) can be skipped without further processing. Finding the maximum of a cell requires 8 voxel accesses and 7 integer comparisons. As an alternative, the maximum of each cell can be found during pre-processing and can be stored together with the data. In this case, the cell-grid is traversed using a 6-connected line. For each new cell the corresponding maximum from the pre-processed field is selected, and is compared with the current ray maximum. Thus, a single nearest neighbour integer comparison is performed instead of 7 at a single step for the cost of additional memory space. Note, that for storing the cell maximum only a pointer to the corresponding voxel is needed, i.e. a number between 0 and 7. Such a pointer requires only additional 3 bits per cell. Since MR and CT datasets usually have 12 significant bits and a voxel is typically allocated as a short integer (16 bits), these 3 pointer bits can be stored in the remaining 4 bits, and therefore, require no additional space at all.

Tests with two dozen different datasets (CT, MR, 3D-ultrasound, nuclear medicine etc.) using the comparison criterion mentioned above showed that roughly 85%-95% of the cells can be skipped without any further processing. Due to the specific characteristics of MRA datasets, the savings in this particular case are even higher and are between 90% and 99%, so that only 1% – 10% of the total cell evaluations have to be performed.

5 Maximum Value Calculation

Once an interesting cell has been selected, i.e., a cell with one of the 8 voxels higher than the current ray maximum, the maximum within this cell has to be found. Neither uniform or adaptive oversampling nor binary search are appropriate approaches since they both require several trilinear interpolations, that is by far the most expensive operation of the complete MIP process. To overcome this difficulty, we developed two different methods to find the maximum without any oversampling. For better discrimination between the voxels and cells, voxel coordinates will be refered to as (x,y,z) and the cell coordinates as (u,v,w).

The first method is based on the idea that the maximum voxel of the cell will most probably have the most significant influence on the value of the interpolation, i.e., the desired maximum value will most probably be on a ray location close to the value of the maximum of the 8 cell voxels. The point on the ray closest to this maximum voxel can be found at the intersection of the ray and the perpendicular going through the corresponding voxel midpoint, see fig. 3. C is the voxel midpoint. AB the ray segment and CK the perpendicular. The (x,y,z) coordinates of the point K can be calculated by exploiting coherence along the ray as stated below.

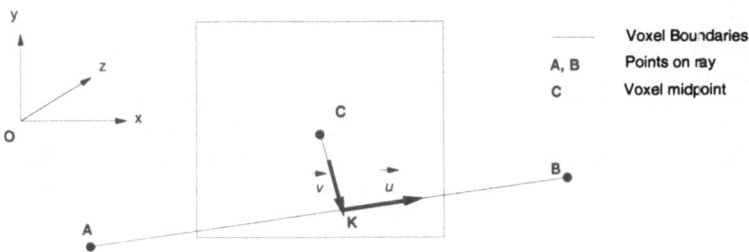

Figure 3: Estimating the perpendicular from the voxel midpoint C on the ray AB

We investigate the points $A(a_1, a_2, a_3)$, $B(b_1, b_2, b_3)$, $C(c_1, c_2, c_3)$, and $K(x_k, y_k, z_k)$. O is the origin of the coordinate system. For $\vec{u}$ perpendicular on $\vec{v}$, their scalar product has to be $\vec{u} \cdot \vec{v} = 0$. From fig. 3, $\vec{u} = \vec{OB} - \vec{OA}$ and $\vec{v} = \vec{OK} - \vec{OC}$. For $\vec{OK}$ we have:

$$\vec{OK} = \vec{OA} + \lambda \cdot (\vec{OB} - \vec{OA}) \tag{1}$$

The scalar product $\vec{u} \cdot \vec{v} = 0$ can be written as

$$(\vec{OB} - \vec{OA}) * (\vec{OA} + \lambda \cdot (\vec{OB} - \vec{OA}) - \vec{OC}) = 0 \tag{2}$$

and after substitution of the coordinates:

$$
\begin{aligned}
(b_1 - a_1) \cdot (a_1 + \lambda \cdot (b_1 - a_1) - c_1) \quad &+ \\
(b_2 - a_2) \cdot (a_2 + \lambda \cdot (b_2 - a_2) - c_2) \quad &+ \\
(b_3 - a_3) \cdot (a_3 + \lambda \cdot (b_3 - a_3) - c_3) \quad &= \quad 0
\end{aligned}
\tag{3}
$$

As a result from solving the above parametric equation, λ is

$$
\lambda = \frac{(c_1 - a_1) \cdot (b_1 - a_1) + (c_2 - a_2) \cdot (b_2 - a_2) + (c_3 - a_3) \cdot (b_3 - a_3)}{(b_1 - a_1)^2 + (b_2 - a_2)^2 + (b_3 - a_3)^2}
\tag{4}
$$

and the coordinates of K are:

$$
\begin{aligned}
x_k &= a_1 + \lambda \cdot (b_1 - a_1) \\
y_k &= a_2 + \lambda \cdot (b_2 - a_2) \\
z_k &= a_3 + \lambda \cdot (b_3 - a_3)
\end{aligned}
\tag{5}
$$

For finding the coordinates of K only the current value of λ has to be calculated. The values of $(b_1 - a_1)/((b_1 - a_1)^2 + (b_2 - a_2)^2 + (b_3 - a_3)^2)$, $(b_2 - a_2)/((b_1 - a_1)^2 + (b_2 - a_2)^2 + (b_3 - a_3)^2)$, and $(b_3 - a_3)/((b_1 - a_1)^2 + (b_2 - a_2)^2 + (b_3 - a_3)^2)$ have to be calculated only once per ray, exploiting coherence. In parallel projections these values have to be calculated once per image. For each selected cell the maximum among its 8 voxels is identified and the position of point K is calculated from eq. 4 and eq. 5. The density value $\rho(K)$ is found by trilinear interpolation. As a result, only a single interpolation is required per cell. Although an approximation, the images calculated by this method provide results sufficient for most applications (see section 7).

The second method calculates position and value of the maximum analytically, thus, involves no approximation at all. We first calculate the interpolation function giving the density along the ray segment within each cell. We used the package *Mathematica* to compute the corresponding expressions. The 8 voxels on the corners of the cell have the values $V_0, ..., V_7$. By writing the ray-equation in parametric form and substituting in the equation of trilinear interpolation, the equation for the density along the ray becomes a polynomial of third degree $\rho(t^3, t^2, t, V_0, V_1, ..., V_7)$. The value of t varies from 0.0 to 1.0 along the ray segment $P_1 P_2$[1]. The coordinates (u_1, v_1, w_1) for the entry and (u_2, v_2, w_2) for the exit point in the cell are normalized ($[0.0, 1.0]$) relative to the lower left corner of the cell, i.e., $u = x - \lfloor x \rfloor + 0.5$, see also fig. 1. We first define the following values:

$$
\begin{aligned}
s_1 &= -V_0 + V_1, \quad s_2 = -V_0 + V_2, \quad s_3 = V_0 - V_1 - V_2 + V_3 \\
s_4 &= -V_0 + V_4, \quad s_5 = V_0 - V_1 - V_4 + V_5 \\
s_6 &= V_0 - V_2 - V_4 + V_6 \\
s_7 &= -V_0 + V_1 + V_2 - V_3 + V_4 - V_5 - V_6 + V_7 \\
\Delta u &= u_2 - u_1, \quad \Delta v = v_2 - v_1, \quad \Delta w = w_2 - w_1 \\
\Delta uv &= \Delta u \cdot \Delta v, \quad \Delta vw = \Delta v \cdot \Delta w, \quad \Delta uw = \Delta u \cdot \Delta w \\
A &= \Delta u \cdot \Delta v \cdot \Delta w \cdot s_7 \\
B &= \Delta uv \cdot (s_6 + s_7 \cdot w_1) + \Delta uw \cdot (s_5 + s_7 \cdot v_1) + \\
  &\quad \Delta vw \cdot (s_3 + s_7 \cdot u_1) \\
C &= s_7 \cdot (u_1 \cdot v_1 \cdot \Delta w + u_1 \cdot \Delta v \cdot w_1 + \Delta u \cdot v_1 \cdot w_1)
\end{aligned}
$$

---

[1] Note that the value of t varies always between 0.0 and 1.0, independent of the length of the segment $P_1 P_2$

$$+s_6 \cdot (u_1 \cdot \Delta v + \Delta u \cdot v_1) + s_5 \cdot (u_1 \cdot \Delta w + \Delta u \cdot w_1)$$
$$+s_3 \cdot (v_1 \cdot \Delta w + \Delta v \cdot w_1) + s_4 \cdot \Delta u$$
$$+s_2 \cdot \Delta v + s_1 \cdot \Delta w$$
$$D = u_1 \cdot v_1 \cdot w_1 \cdot s_7 + u_1 \cdot v_1 \cdot s_6 + u_1 \cdot w_1 \cdot s_5 +$$
$$v_1 \cdot w_1 \cdot s_3 + u_1 \cdot s_4 + v_1 \cdot s_2 + w_1 \cdot s_1 + V_0$$

Using the above quantities, the equation for the trilinear interpolation and its first and second derivatives yields to:

$$\rho(t^3, t^2, t, V_0, V_1, ..., V_7) = A \cdot t^3 + B \cdot t^2 + C \cdot t + D \tag{6}$$
$$\rho'(t^2, t, V_0, V_1, ..., V_7) = 3 \cdot A \cdot t^2 + 2 \cdot B \cdot t + C \tag{7}$$
$$\rho''(t, V_0, V_1, ..., V_7) = 6 \cdot A \cdot t + 2 \cdot B \tag{8}$$

Within each cell the density function has a local maximum either at the location t where the first derivative $\rho'(t)$ is equal to zero and the second derivative $\rho''(t)$ is negative, or at the cell boundaries $t = 0$ or $t = 1$. In order to optimize the process and avoid unnecessary calculations, the calculations are organized in a hierarchy of growing complexity as explained below. First we calculate the determinant of eq. 7

$$4 \cdot B^2 - 4 \cdot 3 \cdot A \cdot C = 4 \cdot (B^2 - 3 \cdot A \cdot C) = 4 \cdot \Delta \tag{9}$$

If the determinant is less than zero ($\Delta < 0$), a real valued solution does not exist for eq. 7, thus, the maximum has to be one of the two boundary values. After substituting the values $t = 0$ and $t = 1$ in eq. 7 we find $\rho(0) = D$ and $\rho(1) = A + B + C + D$. Therefore, the cell maximum is $\rho(0)$, if $A + B + C < 0$ and $\rho(1)$ otherwise.

If $\Delta \geq 0$, real valued solutions of eq. 7 are possible. Solving the quadratic equation we get two possible values:

$$t_{1,2} = \frac{-2 \cdot B \pm \sqrt{4 \cdot \Delta}}{2 \cdot 3 \cdot A} = \frac{-B \pm \sqrt{\Delta}}{3 \cdot A} \tag{10}$$

Substituting $t_{1,2}$ in eq. 8 and solving for $\rho''(t) < 0$ we get:

$$\rho''(t_1) < 0 \Rightarrow 6 \cdot A \cdot \frac{-B + \sqrt{\Delta}}{3 \cdot A} + 2 \cdot B < 0 \quad \Rightarrow \quad \sqrt{\Delta} < 0 \tag{11}$$
$$\rho''(t_2) < 0 \Rightarrow 6 \cdot A \cdot \frac{-B - \sqrt{\Delta}}{3 \cdot A} + 2 \cdot B < 0 \quad \Rightarrow \quad -\sqrt{\Delta} < 0$$

Obviously, the first requirement is always false and the second always true. Thus, a local maximum exists only for t_2. We further discriminate three different cases as illustrated in fig. 4. In the first case t_2 is outside the interval [0,1], i.e., the maximum is not located within the section $P_1 P_2$. In this case cell maximum is calculated on one of the boundaries as in the previous case.

In the second case a true local maximum exists, in the third case a boundary value is larger than the local maximum. For discriminating between cases two and three, we further calculate t_1. If $t_2 \in [0, 1]$ and $t_1 \notin [0, 1]$, case two applies and the desired maximum is $\rho(t_2)$. In the opposite case where $t_2 \in [0, 1]$ and $t_1 \in [0, 1]$, the local maximum must be compared to the maximum of the boundary values. In this case, we first calculate the maximum boundary value as stated above and then compare it to $\rho(t_2)$.

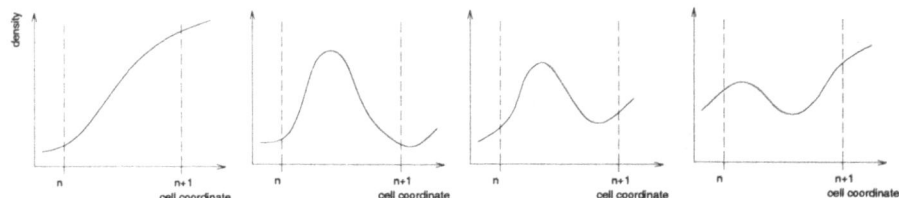

Figure 4: From left to right: no local maximum within the cell; true local maximum; boundary value may be smaller or larger than the local maximum

6 Improving Cache Coherency

After the number of interpolations for a single ray is reduced to a minimum, most of the remaining computation time during traversing is spend for the calculation of the coordinate of the next step and the memory access of the voxel values. Since for preview and approximat methods the traversing is a simple (and fast) Bresenham-like Fixpoint-DDA, the memory access time becomes an extremely important issue.

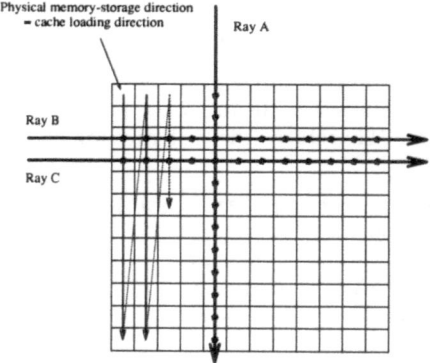

Figure 5: Cache problems - Ray A: Best case Ray B: worst case

The main observation from the evaluation of runtime results is that the rendering time depends strongly on the traversing direction even if the total number of voxel-accesses remains constant. Fig. 5 shows two typical situations (in 2D) when a ray traverses the volume. Ray A traverses the volume in direction of the physical memory allocation, i.e. in the direction of increasing addresses. For each access to the memory the operating system initially trys to load the data from the cache[2] memory, and then, if the required data is missed, from the main memory. In the case of a cache-fault the system will load additional bytes into the cache assuming that the next memory access will most likely be close to the first request. For Ray A this works fine, but it fails for Ray B, because the next traversing step does not access a pre-loaded cache-line. In this case, the system will always reload the cache memory resulting in heavy bus-traffic resulting in increasing rendering times.

---

[2] For shortness, the term 'cache' refers to the first & second level cache

It is important to note that the systems cache-loading mechanism typically works like a LRU-list: new cache-lines will remove the least recently used cache-line in the cache memory. Therefore, it depends on the viewing direction, volume resolution and cache-size whether or not a neighbour ray (Ray C) will traverse pre-loaded cache-memory. However, the typical situation for large volumes ($> 128^3$) is that the rays loaded into the cache will be replaced by new ones before a neighbour ray accesses these lines again. This increases the number of cache-faults and, therefore, the bus-traffic, that is a serious performance degradation factor on shared memory multi-processor platforms.

One possibility to work around this problem is to change the traversing method from the image to the object space (splatting). This can be done in (linear) voxel-space and guarantees a maximum cache coherence. However, this advantage of the splatting method is usually wasted since the evaluation of voxel-influences for the covered pixels - even for a 'preview like' MIP - is very computational demanding.

A better solution of this problem surprisingly is as simple as effective: the linear volume-allocation is changed to a sub-cube representation (see fig. 6) in order to increase the locality of the address-voxelspace. The volume is still allocated in one piece; this method requires only changes in the voxel memory-address calculation.

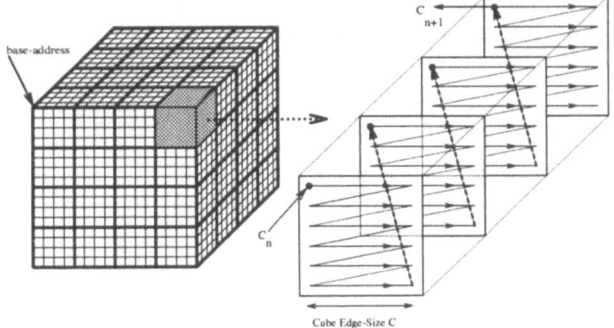

Figure 6: Sub-cube Memory Organization

Let C be the edge-size of one sub-cube, (u,v,w) the voxel-coordinate and (U_{res}, V_{res}, W_{res}) the total resolution of the volume. We first compute the resulting address-offset C_n relative to the starting address (*base-address*):

$$C_n(u, v, w) = \begin{aligned} &((w\ DIV\ C) * (U_{res}\ DIV\ C) * (V_{res}\ DIV\ C) + \\ &(v\ DIV\ C) * (U_{res}\ DIV\ C) + (u\ DIV\ C)) * C^3 \end{aligned} \qquad (12)$$

With C_n and the allocated base address the physical memory address of a voxel becomes

$$\begin{aligned} Address(u, v, w) = \ &base\text{-}address + C_n(u, v, w) + (w\ MOD\ C) * C^2 \\ &+ (v\ MOD\ C) * C + (u\ MOD\ C) \end{aligned} \qquad (13)$$

If all constant values are fractions of 2, these calculations can be done with (fast) SHIFT and AND operations, but for arbitrary volume-sizes and/or cube-sizes a complete calculation, including modulo, multiplications and divisions, is necessary - obviously to time-consuming for our purpose. In order to speed up the address calculation a 'Look Up Table' (LUT) mechanism is implemented. With Eq. 12 and Eq. 13 the address-calculation can be rewritten as

$$Address(u, v, w) = G(u) + H(v) + I(w)$$

with

$$
\begin{aligned}
G(u) &= (u \ DIV \ C) * C^3 + (u \ MOD \ C) \\
H(v) &= (v \ DIV \ C) * (U_{res} \ DIV \ C) * C^3 + (v \ MOD \ C) * C \\
I(w) &= (w \ DIV \ C) * (U_{res} \ DIV \ C) * (V_{res} \ DIV \ C) * C^3 + \\
&\quad (w \ MOD \ C) * C^2 + base\text{-}address \\
base\text{-}address &= MALLOC(sizeof(char) * U_{res} * V_{res} * W_{res})
\end{aligned}
$$

These values can be precalculated and stored in three look-up tables, thus, the memory access appears in 'C'-code like

```
value = *((unsigned char *)(G[u] + H[v] + I[w]));
```

The size of the LUT's depends on the resolution of the allocated volume. For example, a resolution of 256^3 results in $3 * 256 * 4 = 3072$ bytes of additional memory space. Since this is very small - compared to typical cache sizes (e.g. 256k byte) - will not affect the cache load-balance.

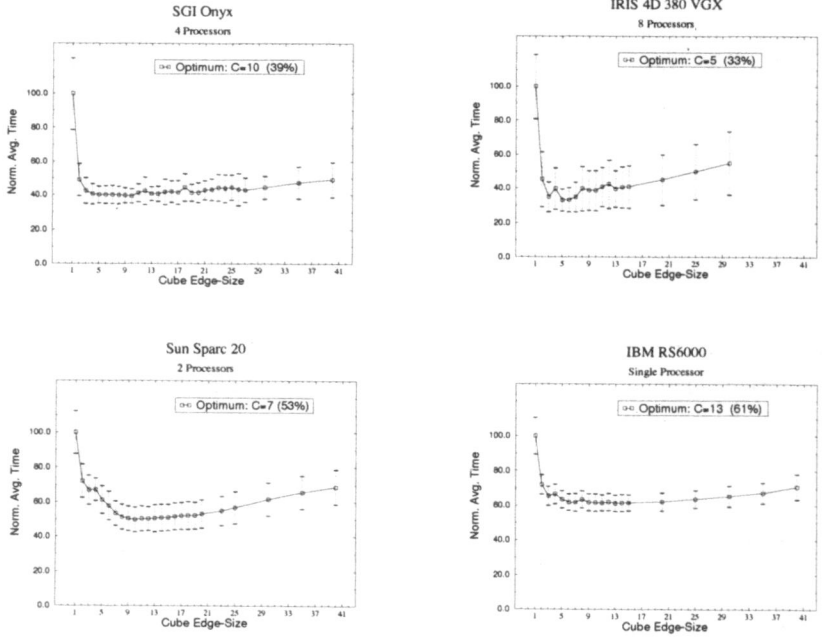

Figure 7: Average rendering times as a function of the cube edge-size

In fig. 7 we present the results of different machines of this cache-optimized memory organization. All measured rendering times are averaged over 100 different viewing directions using preview quality (Bresenham Fixpoint DDA, one nearest neighbour access step). For clarity, all times are normalized with respect to the average rendering time that is achieved if the linear memory organization is employed (cube-size = 1). For all tested platforms there is a different optimal cube-size that provides the best cache coherency. Additionally, the direction-dependency of rendering times is minimized as well for this particular cache size. The achieved speed-up varies between 2 and 3.

7 Results

The following table presents some runtimes for four different datasets and varying methods and image qualities. The image resolution is 512^2 and the volume covers approximately 70% of the pixels. The datasets represent different applications: the first dataset is a nuclear medicine examination, the second and third are MRA's, and the fourth is a 3D ultrasonic dataset.

	64^3	$256^2 \cdot 63$	$256^2 \cdot 165$	256^3
Nearest Neighbour	4.78	9.3	11.2	15.3
DDA & max. approximation	16.2	29	32.6	39.2
Cell traversing & approximation	38.3	95.7	79.5	94.6
Cell traversing & analytic	61.1	154.9	105.4	124.7

Table 1: Runtimes in CPU seconds on a SGI R4000 for four different datasets and varying image qualities

The second table presents some statistics about the various methods measured with the third dataset. The 1st row shows the fastest method (26-connected line, one access for a single step, no interpolation). The 2nd row is a 6-connected line with the maximum approximation of eq. 5. The 3rd and 4th rows are calculated with cell-traversing where the maximum is either approximated or analytically computed. Clearly, it shows that only 3%-10% of the addressed locations are evaluated; the rest is skipped without further processing.

	Nearest Neighbour	DDA traversing & approx.	Cell traversing &approx.	Cell traversing & analytic
# steps	3,580,000	6,800,000	6,800,000	6,800,000
Steps/ray	127.4	242	242	242
Voxel accesses	3,580,000	8,950,000	54,400,000	54,400,000
MIP evaluations	78,730	195,600	787,500	732,670
	(2.2%)	(2.9%)	(11.6%)	(10.7%)
MIP/ray	2.8	7.0	28.0	26.1

Table 2: Statistics measured on the third dataset for varying image quality

The following images illustrate the results of this paper. In fig. 8, we rendered a 'phantom volume' containing straight lines of the thickness of one voxel. Fig. 9 shows an MRA example (the 2nd dataset). The approximation of the maximum value using the perpendicular gives remarkably good results. In fact, differences between the accurate and the approximation methods can be shown clearly only on the specially generated phantom dataset, indicating the efficiency of the approximation.

8 Conclusion

The impetus for this research was the observation that usually over 90% of the computation during MIP calculations is wasted. We speeded up this process significantly by applying three different optimizations.

First, we introduced a cell-traversing scheme for gapless and effective selection of all voxels contributing to a ray. We further extended the algorithm published in [ClWy88] to operate with fix point arithmetic while avoiding the accumulation of numerical errors.

Second, by comparing the newly accessed voxel values with the current maximum of the ray, we avoided further processing for more than 90% of the traversed cells.

Third, we developed two different methods for calculating the maximum value within a selected cell. The first employs a simple, but very effective, approximation for the estimation of the position and value of the maximum with an accuracy sufficient for most applications, the second utilizes an accurate analytical solution. Both methods avoid oversampling and require only a single interpolation for a single selected cell.

Literature

ClWy88   Cleary, J., Wyvill, G.: *Analysis of an Algorithm for Fast Ray-Tracing Using Uniform Space Subdivision*, "The Visual Computer", Vol. 4, pp. 65-83, 1988

EnSo94   Endl, R., Sommer, M.: *Classification of Ray-Generators in Uniform Subdivisions and Octrees for Ray Tracing*, Computer Graphics Forum, Vol. 13, No. 1, pp. 3-19, March 1994

Rouf91   Roufchaie, V. (Edt.): *Power Series Perormance Guide*, Technical Report Power Series, Silicon Graphics, 1991

SaGe91b   Sakas, G., Gerth, M.: *Sampling and Anti-Aliasing Discrete 3D Volume Density Textures*, EUROGRAPHICS'91 Award Paper, Computer and Graphics, Vol. 16, No. 1, pp. 121-134, Pergamon Press, 1992

Saka93d   Sakas, G.: *Interactive Volume Rendering of Large Fields*, "The Visual Computer", Vol. 9, No. 8, pp. 425-438, August 1993

Slat92   Slater, M.: *Tracing a Ray Through Uniformly Subdivided n-Dimensional Space*, "The Visual Computer", Vol. 9, pp. 39-46, 1992

Vand91   Vandermeulen, D.: *Methods for Registration, Interpolation and Interpretation of 3D Medical Image Data for use in 3-D Display, 3-D Modeling and Therapy Planning*, Ph.D. Thesis, Katholieke Universiteit Leuven, Faculteit Toegepaste Wetenschappen, ESAT/MI2, U.D.C. 681.3 I4:616-089, April 1991

YaCK92   Yagel, R., Cohen, D., Kaufman, A.: *Discrete Ray Tracing*, IEEE Computer Graphics & Applications, September 1992

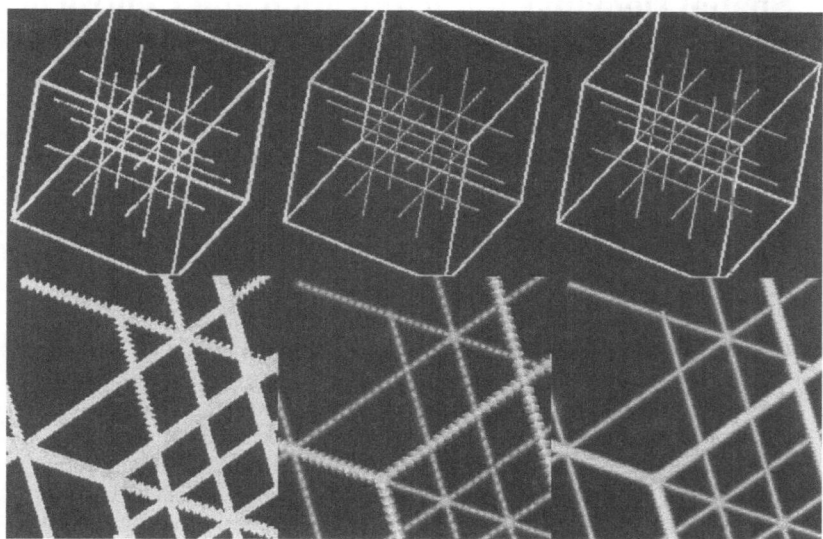

Figure 8: Rendering a phantom volume with preview, approximation, and accurate methods. Magnifications are shown in the lower row.

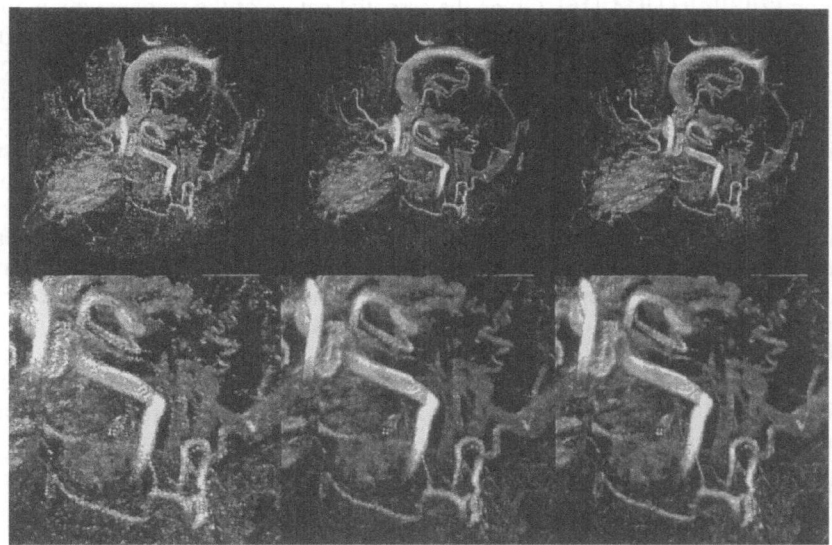

Figure 9: Rendering an MRA set ($256^2 \cdot 63$) with preview, approximation, and accurate method. Magnifications are shown in the lower row. Courtesy of Dr. Meindl, DKD-Wiesbaden

Spatial Domain Characterization and Control of Reconstruction Errors

Raghu Machiraju, Edward Swan, and Roni Yagel

Department of Computer and Information Science
The Advanced Computing Center for the Arts and Design
The Ohio State University

Abstract: Reconstruction is imperative whenever an image or a volume needs to be resampled as a result of an affine or perspective transformation, texture mapping, or volume rendering. We present a new method for the characterization and measurement of reconstruction error. Our method, based on *spatial domain* error analysis, uses approximation theory to develop error bounds. We provide, for the first time, an efficient way to guarantee an error bound at *every point* by varying the filter size. We go further to support position-adaptive and data-adaptive reconstruction which adjust filter size to the location of reconstruction and the data in its vicinity. We demonstrate the effectiveness of our methods with suitable 2D and 3D examples.

1. Introduction

A fundamental operation of many graphics and image processing algorithms is reconstruction [2][3][4][11][14][16]. Given the essential nature of the reconstruction operation it is surprising that although much work has been expended in the design of reconstruction filters, not much attention has been paid to characterize and control its numerical accuracy. In this paper we characterize the errors that arise in an interpolation method of reconstruction. The work described here is aimed to give the user, for the first time, the ability to set a point-wise numerical error bound. Unlike existing methods, which use frequency domain analysis to guarantee some global error bound, we use spatial domain error analysis to guarantee that, for a given threshold ε, the difference between the reconstructed function and the real function is not more than ε, at *any point* in the source space. Our spatial domain analysis culminates in a formal expression for the error bound at every point. Examining this expression, we observe a dependency between error magnitude and the location of reconstruction and data values. Unlike existing methods we can, therefore, adapt filter size to both reconstruction location and data complexity, using rigorous estimates. In Section 2 we introduce the terminology and describe our spatial domain error metrics. In Section 3 we quantify the error metrics and finally in Section 4 we present examples.

2. Background

Although the terminology in the following discussion is pertinent to 1D signals, it is also applicable to 2D (images) and 3D (volumes) signals. We denote by $f(x)$ a bandlimited continuous analytic function (*the signal*), which is sampled above the Nyquist frequency into the discrete dataset $f_s(kh)$, $k=1,...,S$, where h is an equidistant gap between samples, and S is the number of samples. Prior to resampling one must reconstruct from f_s the continuous function, which we denote by $f_R(x)$. The assumption of bandlimitedness is not too restrictive and holds for many images and volumes used in computer graphics and scientific visualization. During the process of acquiring digital images (e.g., cameras, scanners, numerical simulation) a filtering operation is included thus bandlimiting the image. Also, synthetic and procedural methods in order to provide antialiased images, typically employ a filtering step which bandlimits the function.

The Whitaker-Shannon-Koletnikov (WKS) theorem, known commonly as *Shannon's Sampling Theorem*, allows for the perfect reconstruction of a signal from its samples. It states that any bandlimited continuous signal $f(x)$, if sampled at or above its Nyquist frequency (yielding discrete dataset f_s) can be reconstructed as shown in Equation 1 (yielding the continuous function f_R) [9][18]. Thus, we reconstruct with the formula

$$f_R(x, h) = \sum_{k = -\infty}^{\infty} S(x, k, h) f_s(kh) \tag{1}$$

where

$$S(x, k, h) = \begin{cases} 1 & x = kh \\ \dfrac{sin\dfrac{\pi}{h}(x - kh)}{\dfrac{\pi}{h}(x - kh)} & x \neq kh \end{cases} \tag{2}$$

The function $S(x,k,h)$ is called the *Sinc* or the *Cardinal* function. We can extend this discussion to multiple dimensions through the use of *separable filters*, which sample the data successively along each axis. For 2D images, the reconstruction requires the product of two *Sinc* functions, and similarly we can use three *Sinc* functions in 3D. Thus, the image reconstruction equation becomes:

$$f_R\left(x, y, h_x, h_y\right) = \sum_{j = -\infty}^{\infty} \sum_{i = -\infty}^{\infty} S\left(x, i, h_x\right) S\left(y, j, h_y\right) f_s\left(ih_x, jh_y\right) \tag{3}$$

The quantities h_x and h_y are the sampling periods along each of the principal axes.

2.1 Practical Reconstruction Methods and Errors

The ideal reconstruction process from Equation 1, although realizable, is rarely used in practice, since it requires the contribution from all elements of the dataset. An obvious solution is to truncate the function to include only $2M+1$ integer valued points:

$$f_{Rt}(x, M, h) = \sum_{k = -M}^{M} S(x, k, h) f_s(kh) \tag{4}$$

The resulting interpolation filter is called a *finite impulse-response* (FIR) filter of order $2M+1$ and *zero phase*. The quantity M is usually referred to as the half-filter length. We call the ensuing error *truncation error* and is denoted by e_t (Equation 5). Elsewhere in the literature, this error is often referred to as post-aliasing [6][7]. Truncation error manifests itself as *blurring*, *aliasing (jaggies)*, and ringing in an image.

$$e_t\left(f_s, x, M, h\right) = \left|f_R(x, h) - f_{Rt}(x, M, h)\right|$$

$$e_t\left(f_s, x, M, h\right) = \left|\sum_{|k| > M}^{\infty} S(x, k, h) f_s(kh)\right| \tag{5}$$

In practice, the function is never reconstructed with a truncated *Sinc*. Truncation is tantamount to multiplying the infinite filter with a spatially limited *rectangular window*. As a result the frequency spectrum of the truncated *Sinc* filter suffers from distortions in the form of aliasing and oscillations. The oscillations, a consequence of *Gibbs phenomenon* in the frequency domain manifest visually as an annoying artifact, namely ringing. A common solution is to use a *window function* besides a rectangle [6][9]. These functions further alter the characteristics of the truncated frequency spectrum and the choice of one window function over another is a trade-off between blurring and aliasing. Other solutions include using trilinear interpolation (cone filter) and the cubic convolution filters [2][7]. If *NS* is a filter different from the *Sinc* function, then the reconstructed function is now given by:

$$\tilde{f}_{Rt}(x, M, h) = \sum_{k = -M}^{M} NS(x, k, h) f_s(kh) \tag{6}$$

Thus the total reconstruction error, denoted by e_R, is equal to:

$$e_R\left(f_s, x, M, h\right) = \left|f_R(x, h) - \tilde{f}_{Rt}(x, M, h)\right| \tag{7}$$

The total error can be divided into two components:

$$e_R\left(f_s, x, M, h\right) = \left|f_R(x, h) - f_{Rt}(x, M, h) + f_{Rt}(x, M, h) - \tilde{f}_{Rt}(x, M, h)\right| \tag{8}$$

$$e_R\left(f_s, x, M, h\right) \leq \left|f_R(x, h) - f_{Rt}(x, M, h)\right| + \left|f_{Rt}(x, M, h) - \tilde{f}_{Rt}(x, M, h)\right|$$

The first component is the truncation error e_t while the second error arises from the use of a filter besides a *Sinc* function. We call the latter *non-Sinc error* denoted by e_{ns}. Thus, the total reconstruction error:

$$e_R\left(f_s, x, M, h\right) \leq e_t\left(f_s, x, M, h\right) + e_{ns}\left(f_s, x, M, h\right) \tag{9}$$

An application of this error characterization leads to the conclusion that reconstruction with functions different from a truncated *Sinc* lead to lower quality images. It is well known that the truncated *Sinc* filter actually possess a lower mean square error from the ideal frequency response than filters obtained through the use of a non-rectangular window [9]. Therefore it is important to note that this characterization of the reconstruction error is purely numerical and is not based on perceptual considerations which address the issue of the suitability of an image to a human observer. Although there is a positive correlation between numerical error and image quality, not much is known about their relationship [12]. A perceptual model will assign a larger error to truncated *Sinc* filters. We do not even attempt to address these very complex questions here.

The study of reconstruction errors has received only modest attention in the graphics and image processing literature [2][7][6][10]. However, none of the earlier proposed measures are well suited for determining the accuracy of a reconstruction scheme on a sampled dataset in the spatial domain and do not allow error control on a point-wise basis. Also, the reported characterizations are not conducive to the idea of adapting the filter size to the resampling location and to local data characteristics. Adaptive filtering methods reported in the literature are cumbersome and can be used only in the frequency domain [8][13]. Our method, on the other hand, operates in the spatial domain. It can estimate with minimum computational burden the filter size for a given resampling location so that we can efficiently interpolate to a desired level of accuracy. In addition, we also determine the filter size from the complexity of the data at the resampling point. This gives us an efficient yet accurate resampling method. In the following section we provide the necessary theory and develop adaptive, spatial-domain methods.

3. Reconstruction Error Estimates

In this section we provide estimates of *truncation* error and the *non-Sinc* error. A more comprehensive treatment is available in [5].

3.1 Truncation Error Estimates

Let the resampling point x lie in cell n, i.e., between data points $f_s(nh)$ and $f_s((n+1)h)$. Also, let τ be the distance of x from data point $f_s(nh)$, i.e., $x=nh+\tau$. The truncation error was defined in Equation 5 (Section 2.1). After replacing x and the *Sinc* function $S(x,k,h)$ with appropriate expressions we get:

$$e_t\left(f_s, n, \tau, M, h\right) = \left| \sum_{|k| > M}^{\infty} \frac{sin\frac{\pi}{h}(nh + \tau - kh)}{\frac{\pi}{h}(nh + \tau - kh)} f_s(kh) \right| \qquad (10)$$

Expanding the sine term in Equation 10 as the sum of sines and cosines, replacing $n-k$ with m, and after some simplification we get Equation 11.

$$e_t\left(f_s, n, \tau, M, h\right) = \left| \frac{sin\frac{\pi\tau}{h}}{\frac{\pi}{h}} \sum_{|m| > 0}^{\infty} \frac{(-1)^m}{(mh + \tau)} f_s((n-m)h) \right| \qquad (11)$$

We now make two important observations from Equation 11.

Observation 1: The truncation error depends on the location of the resampling point within a grid cell. An important implication is that one can use filters of different lengths depending on the location of the resampling point.

Observation 2: For large values of m, the contribution from consecutive terms in the alternating infinite sum is insignificant especially if the function is smooth in small neighborhoods. The implication of this observation is that we can effectively limit ourselves to reasonably sized neighborhoods and hence smaller sized filters.

We now list some error bounds for the truncation error that can be used in practice. The error bound for this infinite sum in Equation 11 can be found by resorting to com-

68

plex analysis [17]. Before we state the relevant results we discuss an important idea of *frequency guards*. A frequency guard of width r, $0<r<1$ implies that there exists no frequency in the signal beyond $r\omega_c$, where ω_c is the cut-off frequency. The cut-off frequency is defined by the sampling grid distance h. This is a stricter requirement than just bandlimitedness, but not too restrictive. The frequency guard band can be found by determining the ratio of the maximum significant frequency of the spectrum and the cutoff frequency. A crude estimate usually suffices.

The error bound can be obtained in terms of either the maximum of the function value Max_f or the spectral energy of the function, E_f. The quantity E_f can be simply determined by Equation 12 [18]. All the sampled data points are included in the summation of Equation 12.

$$E_f = \sqrt{\frac{h \sum_k |f_s(kh)|^2}{2\pi}} \tag{12}$$

The truncation error $e_t(f_s,x,k,h,M)$ in terms of the total energy of the signal is bounded from above by the quantity

$$e_t\left(f_s, x, M, h\right) \le \frac{2E_f \sqrt{\frac{r}{h}} \left| sin\frac{\pi x}{h} \right|}{\pi^2(1-r)M} \tag{13}$$

Thus, we are able to express the truncation error bound in terms of the energy of a function and the frequency guard r. We now express the error bound in terms of the maximum of a function. The truncation error $e_t(f_s,x,M,h)$ in terms of the maximum value of a function, Max_f is bounded from above by the quantity

$$e_t\left(f_s, x, M, h\right) \le \frac{Max_f \left| sin\frac{\pi x}{h} \right|}{\pi M cos\frac{r\pi}{2}} \tag{14}$$

We now characterize the error that arises from the use of a function different from a *Sinc* function.

3.2 Non-Sinc Error

Once again we can either use the spectral energy or the maximum value of the function. The bound which includes the spectral energy is listed in Equation 15. The integral computes the difference between the two functions in the L^2 norm space. The quantity $E_f(M)$ is the energy of the signal in a $2M+1$ sized neighborhood around the resampling point. Since the filters are space invariant one can evaluate the filters when placed at $k=0$ for sake of convenience.

$$e_{ns}\left(f_s, x, M, h\right) \le E_f(M) \sqrt{\frac{1}{2\pi} \int_{-M}^{M} |S(t, 0, h) - NS(t, 0, h)|^2 dt} \tag{15}$$

One can similarly define a bound including the maximum value of the function (Equation 16).The quantity $Max_f(M)$ is the maximum of the function values in a $2M+1$ neighborhood. Once again we are determining the difference in the areas of the two filter functions.

$$e_{ns}\left(f_s, n, h, M\right) \leq Max_f(M) \int_{-Mh}^{Mh} |S(t, 0, h) - NS(t, 0, h)|\,dt \qquad (16)$$

The function *NS* can be any realizable filter. We however use windowed *Sinc* filters given their ability to lend themselves to adaptive use. In [6] it was shown that windowed *Sinc* filters compare favorably with other filters in terms of the smoothing and post-aliasing metrics defined therein. We employ the *Hamming window* in our interpolation schemes [9]. For multiple dimensions one can use a product of two or three 1D window functions.

In this section we described the errors that arise from filtering operations. Detailed explanations and derivations that were not provided here can be found in [5]. In Section 4 we use these measures to predict reconstruction errors that arise from representative resampling operations and then show how they can be used to perform adaptive reconstruction.

4. Results

In this section we first test the validity of the bounds on 1D signals. We then show how these bounds can be employed in adaptive filtering schemes. In the latter part of this section we implement our schemes for 2D and 3D examples.

4.1 Accurate and Adaptive Reconstruction of 1D Signals

We consider a representative resampling scheme that frequently arises in computer graphics. In this section we distinguish between resampling schemes and reconstruction operations. Resampling schemes provide the points where the functions are reconstructed. The resampling scheme under consideration occurs when a 2D image or a 3D volume is subjected to an affine transformation (including scaling), or during texture mapping, or during ray-casting of 3D volumes.

In Figure 1a we consider a 1D signal obtained from a row of a scanned image. It is worth noting that the signal under consideration has a very small energy content. It was observed that the value of the guard was usually less than 0.1 for all scanlines considered for this work. One can estimate the value of the frequency guard, r, by simply computing the first few Fourier coefficients above a user defined threshold. The actual error from Equation 11, the error estimates from Equation 13 (using energy) and Equation 14 (using maximum values) are determined, when the signal is resampled onto a new grid (Figure 1b). The locations of resampling points are defined by the function $x_k = x_0 + 0.99*k$ (resampling scheme), where x_0 is the location of the first row pixel and k is an integer. The estimates from Equation 14 are looser and we found the energy estimates closer to the actual error for many 1-D signals and resampling schemes. The estimates were computed for a half-filter length of $M=9$.

Here we can actually see evidence for **Observation 1** made in Section 3.1. The error behaves in a sinusoidal manner for the representative resampling scheme. One can readily conclude that the filters of the same length need not be used everywhere during the resampling operation. To use different filters at different resampling positions, one can use the error estimates of Equation 13 and Equation 14. For instance one can set the point wise error to ε for all x along the length of the signal. The required filter length at resampling point x can be determined from the computation listed in Equation 17.

$$M(x) = \frac{2E_f \sqrt{\frac{r}{h}} \left| sin\frac{\pi x}{h} \right|}{\pi^2 (1-r) \varepsilon} \tag{17}$$

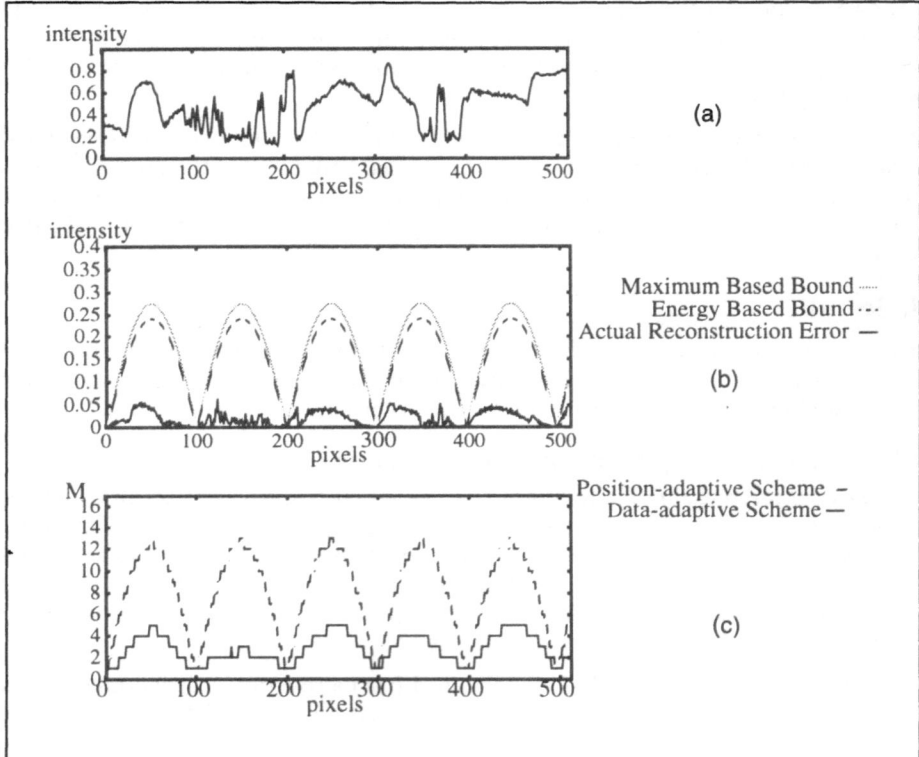

Fig. 1. Comparison of Error Estimates. (a) 1D signal obtained from a row of an image. (b) The actual error and the estimates from Equation 13 (energy) and Equation 14 (maximum). Both estimates bound the actual error well, the energy estimate being closer. (c) Filter sizes for the position- and data-adaptive schemes.

Figure 1c shows the minimum filter length at all points required to obtain an user defined accuracy of ε=0.02. We call this filtering scheme *position-adaptive*, since the size of the filter is influenced only by the position of the resampling point. The estimated bounds in Figure 1b are conservative. Taking into account the rapid decay of the *Sinc* function as one moves away from the resampling point, it might be useful to consider the energy or maximum of a function over a neighborhood of somewhat significant size as stated in **Observation 2** of Section 3.1. The problem is now reduced to determining a window of appropriate size which is suitable for a given signal. This can be determined easily from the estimates of the bounds itself. One can set the minimum error of resampling ε_{min} that can possibly arise during resampling. Then one can simply calculate the neighborhood size M_e by using Equation 17. A pre-processing step is now required which computes the energy or the maximum of the function value over neighborhoods. Figure 1c also shows the sizes of the filters used when a local neighborhood of size *25* is used. The use of smaller neighborhoods yields smaller filters and hence savings in reconstruction time We call this filtering scheme *data-adaptive*. We now consider 2D and 3D examples.

4.2 Multidimensional Examples

We consider 2D images first. The expression for the truncation error expressed in terms of spectral energy is given by Equation 18. We found that for 2D images the error bound involving the maximum was larger and therefore we did not employ that bound in our adaptive methods.

$$e\left(f, x, k, h, M\right) \leq \frac{16 E_f \sqrt{\left|\frac{r_x r_y}{h_x h_y}\right|} \left|\sin\frac{\pi\tau_x}{h}\right| \left|\sin\frac{\pi\tau_y}{h}\right|}{\pi^4 N^2 \left(1 - r_x\right)\left(1 - r_y\right)} \tag{18}$$

By specifying the minimum desired error, one can use a derivative of Equation 18 to determine the size of the neighborhood required to achieve the desired error of ε_{min}. At each resampling point, filter size is then determined by using the error estimates and the filter is applied in the neighborhood. Our results are shown in Figure 2 (see Appendix). Figure 2a shows an image obtained from a fluid dynamics simulation rotated by an angle of 30° and scaled uniformly by a factor of 0.75. The values of the frequency guards r_x and r_y were measured to be at 0.34 and 0.10. Figure 2b shows the position-adaptive filter sizes, while Figure 2c shows the data-adaptive. As evidenced from Figure 2b the filter size changes in a periodic sinusoidal fashion in the position-adaptive scheme. On the other hand, the filter size adapts to the data complexity in the data-adaptive scheme. A minimum error of 0.001 was used to determine the neighborhood size for the data-adaptive scheme. The average half-filter size for the position-adaptive scheme was measured at 7.15, while the average filter size for the data-adaptive scheme was measured at 1.96. The data-adaptive scheme thus is better than a cubic convolution scheme, which has a filter size of 5 (or half-filter size of 2.5).

In the case of 3D volumes we found that the error bound using the maximum value was more useful for data-adaptive methods. Given the sparse spectral energy content of 3D datasets, this bound reported a larger variance of filter sizes than the other bound. In Equation 19 we list the bound for the 3D reconstruction error.

$$e\left(f_s, x, y, z, h_x, h_y, h_z, M\right) \leq \frac{Max_f \left|\sin\pi\frac{x}{h_x}\right| \left|\sin\pi\frac{y}{h_y}\right| \left|\sin\pi\frac{z}{h_z}\right|}{\pi^3 M^3 \cos\frac{\pi r_x}{2} \cos\frac{\pi r_y}{2} \cos\frac{\pi r_z}{2}} \tag{19}$$

We also implemented our adaptive methods in a slicing algorithm for volumes. The reported implementation projects the desired slicing plane (described by a direction

72

vector and an offset from the origin) onto the XY-plane thus defining an implicit affine transformation. As before in the 2D example, resampling points on the XY-plane are transformed to points inside the 3D volume. The results are presented in Figure 3 (see Appendix). Figure 3a and Figure 3b show two different slices of a 256^3 volume MRI head dataset. The values of frequency guards r_x, r_y and r_z were found to be 0.086, 0.055, 0.031 respectively. Figure 3c and Figure 3d show the filter sizes used in the position- and data-adaptive schemes respectively. The error threshold is 0.01, while the minimum error used to determine the optimal neighborhood size is 10^{-5}. This minimum error threshold translates to a neighborhood size of 31 for the data-adaptive scheme. The average half filter size for position-adaptive filtering scheme were measured close to 2 (Figure 3c), while the same quantity was measured at 1 for the data-adaptive scheme (Figure 3d). As evinced in Figure 3d, higher order filters are used only at some resampling points. The savings are especially useful in volume raycasting [4]. To obtain accuracy it is common to step along the ray using small increments and thus increase the number of resampling points. A data-adaptive scheme similar to the one presented here would be very useful to guide the reconstruction process.

5. Conclusions

We developed a new approach to the characterization and measurement of reconstruction error. Our method, based on spatial domain error analysis, uses approximation theory to develop error bounds for reconstruction. We provide an efficient way to guarantee an error bound at every point by varying filter size. In addition, we support position-adaptive and data-adaptive reconstruction which adjust filter size to the reconstruction location and the data complexity. Our methods provide the user with a powerful tool for achieving any desired image quality while incurring space and computation costs that are comparable to existing methods. Future work includes an efficient implementation through the use of pre-computed table look-ups, extensions to irregular grids and signals with singularities.

6. Acknowledgments

This work was partially supported by National Science Foundation Grant CCR-9211288, and by the Advanced Research Projects Agency Contract DABT63-C-0056. We would like to thank the following individuals at The Ohio State University for supporting our efforts: Prof. Ashok Krishnamurthy, Prof. Bhavik Bhakshi, Prof. Wayne Carlson, Don Stredney, Steve May and Torsten Moeller. Also thanks go to Dr. Tom Malzbander of Hewlett Packard Labs for his comments on a version of this paper. Finally one of the authors (Raghu Machiraju) would like to thank Steve Collins of Trinity College, Dublin and Sun Microsystems for generous financial assistance enabling him to present the paper at this Workshop.

References

1.　Carlbom I., "Optimal Filter Design for Volume Reconstruction and Visualization", *Proceedings of Visualization '93*, IEEE CS Press, pp. 54-61, 1993.

2.　Glassner A.,"*Principles of Digital Image Synthesis*", Morgan Kaufmann, 1995.

3.　Hanrahan P., "Three-Pass Affine Transforms for Volume Rendering", *Computer Graphics,* 24(5):71-77, November 1990.

4.	Levoy M., "Display of Surfaces from Volume Data", *IEEE Computer Graphics and Applications,* 8(5):29-37, May 1988.

5.	Machiraju, R., Swan, E., Yagel, R., "Error Bounded and Adaptive Image Reconstruction," *Technical Research Report*, Department of Computer and Information Science, The Ohio State University, OSU-CISRC-1/95-TR03, January 1995.

6.	Marschner S.R. and Lobb R.J., "An Evaluation of Reconstruction Filters for Volume Rendering", *Proceedings of Visualization '94*, IEEE CS Press, pp. 100-107, October 1994.

7.	Mitchell D.P. and Netravali A.N., "Reconstruction Filters in Computer Graphics", *Computer Graphics, 22(4):221-228,* August 1988.

8.	Norton A., Rockwood A. P., Skolmoski P.T., "Clamping: A Method of Antialiasing Textured Surfaces by Bandwidth Limiting in Object Space", *Computer Graphics Proceedings SIGGRAPH '82,* 16, (3):1-8, July 1992.

9.	Oppenheim A.V. and Schafer R.W., *"Digital Signal Processing",* Prentice Hall Inc., Englewoods Cliffs, NJ, 1975.

10.	Parker J.A., Kenyon R.V. and Troxel D.E., "Comparison of Interpolation Methods for Image Resampling", *IEEE Transactions on Medical Imaging,* MI-2(1):31-39, March 1983.

11.	Rhodes M., Glenn W., Azzawi Y., "Extracting Oblique Planes from Serial CT Sections", *Journal of Computer Assisted Tomography,* 4(5): 649-657, October 1980.

12.	Schreiber, W., Troxel, D., "Transformation Between Continuous and Discrete Representations of Images: A Perceptual Approach", *IEEE Transactions on Pattern Analysis and Machine Intelligence,* PAMI-7(2): 178-186, March 1985.

13.	Totsuka T. and Levoy M., "Frequency Domain Volume Rendering", *Computer Graphics Proceedings SIGGRAPH '93,* pp. 271-278, August 1993.

14.	Westover L.,"Footprint Evaluation for Volume Rendering", *Computer Graphics,* 24(4):367-376, August 1990.

15.	Wolberg G., *"Digital Image Warping",* IEEE Computer Society Press, 1990.

16.	Yagel R. and Kaufman A.E., "Template-Based Volume Viewing", *Computer Graphics Forum*, 11(3): 153-157, September 1992.

17.	Yao K. and Thomas J.B., "On Truncation Error Bounds for Sampling Representations of Band-Limited Signals", *IEEE Transactions on Aerospace and Electronic Systems,* AES-2(6):640-647, November 1966

18.	Zayed A.I.,*"Advances in Shannon's Sampling Theory",* CRC Press, Boca Raton, FL, 1993.

Editors' Note: see Appendix, p. 358 for colored figure of this paper

Rendering Trees from Precomputed Z-Buffer Views

Nelson Max

University of California, Davis, CA, 95616, USA

Keiichi Ohsaki

Hokkaido Industrial Research Institute, Sapporo, Japan

Abstract. Parallel projection z-buffer images are precomputed for a number of preset viewing directions on the unit sphere. Using the depth information, we can reconstruct a 3-D point from each image pixel. Then parallel or perspective views can be found from any other viewpoint by rotating the 3-D points from the nearest three or four precomputed views into the proper position and projecting them onto an output z-buffer. A temporary z-buffer image, constructed in the same way for a viewpoint at the light source, is used for a z-buffer shadow algorithm. The rendering algorithm is applied to broad leaf and needle leaf trees, and tested in animation. Our rendering algorithm is similar to that in Chen and Williams [1], with differences listed below.

1 Introduction

Rendering complex objects like trees from a polygonal model often takes a long time, because many polygons are required. This paper presents a method, similar to that of Chen and Williams [1], for reconstructing an image from precomputed z-buffer views. Our method is different from that in [1] in four respects. First, our precomputed images store multiple z levels at each pixel, allowing hidden objects to be reconstructed from even a single view. Second, we store encoded normal and color information, so that the shading can be done as a post process. Next, we use parallel rather than perspective projection for our precomputed views. Finally, since we are dealing with fractal-like objects with high depth complexity instead of smooth textured surfaces, the morphing techniques of [1] are not applicable, and we must reproject pixel by pixel. As in [1], we also reconstruct a z-buffer from the point of view of the light source, and then apply a z-buffer shadow algorithm during the shading step.

2 Previous work

Many people have tried reprojection of pixels, dots, or texture maps as a way of reconstructing complex objects, surfaces, or scenes. The Cloudvu system of Bishop and Austin [2] takes a collection of randomly ordered 3-D points, with associated normals and colors, and shades and projects as many as possible during the frame update time. This gives a scattered version of the object during viewpoint motion and a smoother version when the motion stops. Adelson and Hodges [3] show how reprojection of earlier frames in an animation can speed up ray-tracing. Pixels not guaranteed to be correct are ray traced from scratch, so this is not a real-time technique. On the other hand, Maciel and Shirley [4] have developed a system for guaranteed real-time performance, using "imposters" formed from one or a few texture mapped polygons, for objects, or even clusters of objects, which are too complex to render in 3-D detail. The imposter chosen may depend on the viewing direction as well as the distance, so the image may visibly jump when the choice switches.

An extreme example of an imposter is a "billboard tree", a single polygon with color/transparency texture which is always turned to face the viewer (see Rohlf and Helman [5]). This technique has been applied to training simulators and video games, and is quite effective in still images. However, in animated motion, the 2-D nature of the texture is obvious, because the expected motion parallax between branches at different depths is absent. In addition, the textures are only appropriate for a single lighting direction.

Purely polygon-based level-of-detail transitions have also been used. (See [4] and Crow [6]). The long-term goal of this work is a level-of-detail system for complex organic hierarchical objects like trees, based on raster views instead of polygons. This paper discusses the preliminary work on the reprojection, without the hierarchies. Our reprojection scheme should work on more general scenes, but the hierarchical version will be specialized for trees, so we will discuss the current algorithm in that context.

3. Trees

Trees are particularly difficult to render because of the tremendous detail they contain. We wished to provide full 3-D animation, with changing illumination, at speeds greater than those possible with full polygon rendering. Therefore we decided to use the z-buffer reconstruction algorithm, based on a small number of precomputed images. The computational cost of this algorithm is proportional to the number of pixels in one of the precomputed images, and does not depend on the complexity of the polygonal model, making it practical to animate complex rigid objects like trees.

The trees were constructed from two growth models, one for *Abies sachalinensis* Masters, a needle leaf tree [7], [8], and one for *Magnolia obavata* Thunberg, a broad leaf tree [9]. The magnolia leaves have two different colors, one for the top surface, and one for the bottom. The correct color is chosen by testing whether the polygon normal is pointing towards or away from the viewer. The output of the tree growth model is an array of vertex coordinates, and an array of triangles, specified by their vertex and color table indices. The triangle normal is computed as a cross product of triangle edges, and the vertex indices are ordered to make this cross product point to the top surface of the magnolia leaves.

4. Reconstruction

The basic algorithm uses precomputed parellel projection z-buffer views as input. Each pixel in an input view is used to reconstruct a 3-D point, using the x and y pixel indices and the z-buffer depth in the inverse of the projection function. The 3-D point is then transformed into a new viewing position, and projected onto the output z-buffer for the new viewpoint.

Our eventual goal, the addition of standard prerendered trees to exterior architectural or landscape renderings, is different from the interior walkthroughs of Chen and Williams [1]. They use multiple image morphing to transform from each of the precomputed views to the output image. This is appropriate for the painted plane surfaces in their virtual museum application, but is less useful for finely divided objects like trees, where the depth coherence at adjacent pixels is much more limited. Therefore we transform each z-buffer pixel separately.

In addition, for their virtual museum, they use multiple perspective views from a collection of viewpoints near eye level, while we want to be able to move the viewpoint arbitrarily, and to composite multiple trees into a single image. Therefore in our implementation, we use parallel views as input. We can thus use precomputed images for a small collection of viewing directions on the unit sphere, instead of for a larger collection of viewpoints in 3-D space. We can also use the true z coordinate in the z-buffers for the precomputed views, while for planar polygon scan conversion in perspective projection, a non-linearly distorted $z' = -1./z$ is necessary to give the correct visible surfaces. (See [10].) In the z-buffer for the output view, the true z can also be used even in perspective projection, because we project single 3-D reconstructed points instead of polygons. Thus the following arithmetical steps are involved. (See [11] for the basic concepts.)

1) From the pixel coordinates (i, j) construct the window coordinates (x, y) using the inverse of the window-to-viewport transformation, and fetch z from z-buffer(i, j).

2) Multiply $(x, y, z, 1)$ by the 4 x 4 matrix which transforms the 3-D coordinates of the stored view into the coordinates $(x', y', z', 1)$ for the desired view.

3) If desired, revise the x' and y' coordinates to account for perspective. Determine the new pixel coordinates (i', j') from x' and y' using the window-to-viewport transformation. Use z' in the z-buffer comparison to determine whether to overwrite the z and shading data at pixel (i', j').

A problem with this reconstruction and reprojection algorithm is that pixels may be absent in the final output image. A pixel may be missed either 1) because it lies between transformed and reprojected pixels from a surface in the input image, or 2) because it lies on a surface which is hidden in the input image. The resampling problem 1) also occurs in Chen and Williams [1], where it is partially solved by color interpolation from adjacent pixels, but more sophisticated texture interpolation is also proposed. With the high depth complexity in our images, there is little coherence in the pixel displacements, so texture interpolation is not an alternative. We chose instead to leave undefined pixels transparent, so that the background shows through as between gaps in the leaves. Problem 1) can also be partially solved by using a higher resolution input image, but this will not help problem 2).

Problem 2) can be partially solved by precomputing more input images, so that one can be found closer to the desired viewing direction. As shown in [1], it also helps to use more than one input image at a time. In the computation for the output image, reconstructed points from several nearby input images can be combined into the same output z-buffer. With more input images, the likelihood that a visible surface will be hidden in all of them decreases. The larger number of 3-D samples also helps solve problem 1), so that lower resolution will suffice.

5. Multiple-Layered Z-Buffers

Another partial solution to problem 2) is to use multiple-layered z-buffers for the pre-computed images. Each layer contains both a z value and the color and normal infor-mation necessary for the shading post-process. The layers at each pixel are sorted from front to back in z. When a polygon is scan converted for a precomputed view, the z value at each pixel is compared to the z values stored in the different layers. If the new z is closer than the farthest layer, the new data is inserted at the appropriate position, perhaps forcing the data at the farthest position to be discarded. A threshold specifies the minimum z separation between layers, so that nearby leaves or needles on the same branch can occupy the same layer, with the shading data chosen from the front-most one. Because we use these multiple z layers, our algorithm cannot take advantage of current z-buffer hardware, and is implemented in software.

6. Precomputed Directions

In our system, we use three or four precomputed input images for each output image. The preset directions are chosen along the latitude circles of a unit sphere, with the north-south axis along the up-down axis of the tree trunk. The user specifies the num-ber n of latitude bands. The latitude positions are then at the north pole, the south pole, and on $n - 1$ equally spaced latitude circles separated by π / n radians. On each latitude circle, the smallest possible number of equally spaced points is chosen so that the spac-ing is less than π / n. This divides the sphere into triangles, as shown in figure 1 for $n = 4$. If a desired viewing direction lies inside one of the triangles meeting at the north or south poles, three precomputed images are used as input, otherwise four are used.

The vertical axis along the tree trunk is used as the "camera up vector" in the viewing transformation for the precomputed images. (See [11].) Thus the tree appears vertical in each view, allowing a rectangular image to efficiently contain it. The lati-tude and longitude of the desired output viewing direction are used to choose the input images, and to compute the rotation necessary to transform their reconstructed 3-D points into the final viewing coordinate system.

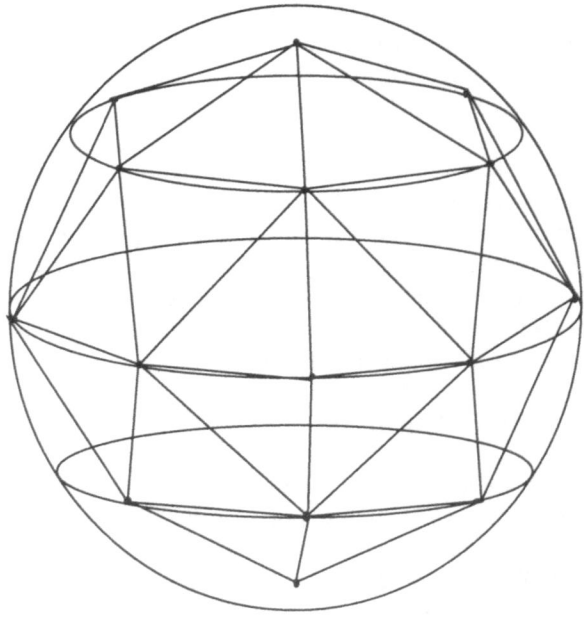

Fig. 1. Some viewing positions on latitude circles on the unit sphere.

7. Normals, Shading, and Shadows

The flat shading normals of the input polygons are coded into two bytes, one for the latitude, and one for the longitude. There is a third byte for a color table index, specifying whether the polygon belongs to the trunk, a branch, or a leaf. The normals are not transformed during the reprojection. Instead, all three bytes are copied into the final z-buffer image. During the shading post-process, tables of sines and cosines, indexed by the two normal bytes, are used to find the normal in the original coordinate system. The dot product of this normal with the untransformed lighting direction is then used to compute Lambert law diffuse shading. Phong shading could also be easily included.

Shadows can be found, as in Williams [12] and Reeves *et al.* [13], using a z-buffer from the point of view of the light source, reconstructed as described above from the same precomputed views. Currently we have only implemented an infinite light source for the sun, using parallel projection in the reconstruction, but for other applications, a finite light source could easily be implemented using perspective projection.

During the final shading step, the x and y pixel indices and the z-buffer depth value at each output pixel are again used to reconstruct a 3-D surface point. This point is then rotated into the light source viewing coordinates, and its z value is compared to the light source z-buffer depth value. If the 3-D point is farther from the light source by an amount larger than a preset error threshold, it is in shadow, and only ambient shading is used; otherwise diffuse shading is added.

Since the normal and color index information is available, the shadow and shading computations can be done as a post-process, only once per pixel, instead of each time pixel data is deposited into the final z-buffer, as was necessary for Williams [12].

8. Results

Figures 2, 3, and 4 show a 10 year old *Abies* tree, from three precomputed directions, at latitudes 90, 45 and 0 degrees, respectively, and at longitude 0. The value of n was set at 4, resulting in 23 precomputed images. Figure 5 is a perspective view, reconstructed from four of the precomputed images. Figure 6 shows the same tree at age 15 years.

Figure 7 shows a reconstructed 14 year old *Magnolia* tree in parallel projection, without shadows. Figure 8 shows the same tree in perspective with shadows. Figure 9 shows the same view, with the sun in a different position. For figures 7, 8, and 9, n was three, resulting in 14 precomputed images. For all these cases, the precomputed images were at 300 by 600 resolution, with two z-buffer layers, requiring 2,520,000 bytes each, and the output images were at 256 by 512 resolution. The output resolution must be somewhat less than that of the precomputed images, in order to make sure that there are no holes from pixels missed in the reconstruction. Figure 10 shows a grove of 7 rotated and translated copies of the same *Magnolia* tree, reconstructed from the same 14 two layer z-buffer views. This 500 by 350 image took 73 seconds to reconstruct.

The first segment in the videotape shows a 360 frame rotation cycle of the 15 year old *Abies* tree, rendered in parallel projection by software polygon scan conversion, at 6.5 seconds a frame at 400 by 400 resolution, on an SGI 4D/35 with a Mips 3000 processor. The scintillation comes from the non-antialiased rendering of many small needles. The second sequence shows a similar rotation cycle in perspective with shadows, reconstructed from 23 views, each with three z layers. It took 207 seconds to precompute the 23 views, and then 12.3 seconds a frame for the reconstruction at 400 by 400 resolution. Aside from the same scintillation, there are no glitches when the selection of images used for reconstruction changes at several points during the rotation.

The third segment of the videotape shows the *Magnolia* tree reconstructed from 14 views, using only one z layer. Here the leaves are broad, and the scintillation and glitches come from incomplete pixel coverage, rather than aliasing problems. The preprocessing took 68 seconds, and the reconstruction took 2.3 seconds a frame at 300 by 300 resolution. The fourth segment shows the same tree reconstructed from the same 14 views, but with 3 layers in the z buffers. The preprocessing took 82 seconds, and the reconstruction took 6.9 seconds a frame. The scintillation and glitches have disappeared.

9. Conclusions and future work

The technique of pixel by pixel reconstruction from prerendered multiple-layer z-buffers is useful for complex objects like trees, defined by many small polygons. It should similarly be useful for contour surfaces of complex objects constructed by the marching cubes algorithm [14].

For fractal objects, a hierarchy of z-buffer images of varying pixel sizes could be used, with higher level objects built by reprojecting multiple lower level objects at lower resolution. Then a final output image could be produced by combining objects chosen from different levels in the hierarchy, according to the proximity of the various objects to the viewpoint. Thus a tree could be built from standard branches, branches from subbranches, and a subbranch from twigs and leaves, all represented in multiple-layer z-buffers, built by reprojecting their children in the hierarchy. As the viewpoint moved closer, the tree could be replaced by its trunk and branches, and a branch could be replaced by its subbranches or twigs. We also hope to apply the level-of-detail transitions in Becker and Max [15] to the bump-mapped bark of Bloomenthal [16].

One of the Eurographics reviewers suggested precomputing a radiosity solution for the trees. This could possibly be done by the techniques of Patmore [17, 18]. However, we wanted to use the same tree in various different orientations to disguise the repetition when representing a forest, and to make renderings at different times of the day, so precomputing the effects of the sun's illumination would not be useful. On the other hand, both Patmore [18] and Greene and Kass [19] give efficient methods for finding the sky illumination within complex geometries like foliage, and a uniformly radiating sky hemisphere would be appropriate for any of the uses mentioned above.

10. Acknowledgments

This work was performed at the Hokkaido Industrial Research Institute where the first author was funded by the Hokkaido Overseas Guest Researchers Invitation Program. We wish to thank Isao Omura, Atsushi Okuda, and Shiichi Nagao for setting up an environment for efficient work during a short visit, and Michitaka Nami, Shinichi Maruyama, and Tsuyoshi Yamamoto for arranging the invitation. Jan Nunes helped record the videotape.

References

1. Chen, S. E., Williams, L.: View Interpolation for Image Synthesis. Siggraph '93 Conference Proceedings, 279-288 (1993).

2. Bishop, T., Austin J: Method and Apparatus for Fractional Double Buffering. U S Patent 4,910,683 (March 20, 1990). See also: TAAC-1 User's Manual, Sun Microsystems, Inc., Mountain View, CA

3. Adelson, S., Hodges, L.: Generating Exact Ray-Traced Animation Frames by Reprojection. IEEE Computer Graphics and Applications 15, 43-52 (May 1995).

4. Maciel P., Shirley, P.: Visual Navigation of Large Environments Using Textured Clusters. Proceedings of the ACM Siggraph Symposium on Interactive 3D Graphics, 95-102 (April 1995).

5. Rohlf, J., Helman, J.: IRIS Performer: A High Performance Multiprocessing Toolkit for Real-Time 3D Graphics. Siggraph '94 Conference Proceedings, 381-394 (1994).

6. Crow, F.: A More Flexible Image Generation Environment. Siggraph '82 Conference Proceedings, 9-18 (1982).

7. Ohsaki, K., Yamamoto, Y., Suzuki, T., Sato, H.: A Representation Method for Needle-Leaf-Trees Based on Growth Models (Japanese with English abstract). Graphics and CAD 52-4, 19-26 (August 16, 1991).

8. Suzuki, T., Ohsaki, K., Saito, H., Yamamoto,Y.: A Representation Method for Todo-Fir Shapes using Computer Graphics (Japanese). Journal of the Japanese Forestry Society 74, 504-508 (November 1992).

9. Ohsaki, K., Suzuki, T.: A Growth Model of Botanical Trees Having Abilities to Interact with the Light Environment (Japanese with English abstract). Graphics and CAD 65-6, 37-44 (October 22, 1993).

10. Newmann, W., Sproull, S.: Principles of Interactive Computer Graphics, first edition. New York: McGraw Hill (1979).

11. Foley, J., van Dam, A., Feiner, S., Hughes, J.: Computer Graphics, Principles and Practice, 2nd Edition. Reading Massachusetts: Addison Wesley (1992)

12. Williams, L.: Casting Curved Shadows on Curved Surfaces. Siggraph '78 Conference Proceedings, 270-274 (1978).

13. Reeves, W., Salesin, D., Cook, R.: Rendering Antialiased Shadows with Depth Maps. Siggraph '87 Conference Proceedings, 283-291 (1987).

14. Lorensen W., Cline, H.: Marching Cubes: A High Resolution 3D Surface Reconstruction Algorithm. Siggraph '87 Conference Proceedings, 163-169 (1987).

15. Becker B., Max, N.: Smooth Transitions between Bump Rendering Algorithms. Siggraph '93 Conference Proceedings, 183-190 (1993).

16. Bloomenthal, J.: Modeling the Mighty Maple. Siggraph '85 Conference Proceedings, 305 - 311 (1985).

17. Patmore, C.: Simulated Multiple Scattering for Cloud Rendering. In: Mudur S., Pattniak, S. (eds.): Graphics, Design, and Visualization: Proceedings of the International Conference in Computer Graphics, ICC93. Elsevier Science Publishers 1993 (pp. 29-40).

18. Patmore, C.: Illumination in Dense Foliage Models. Proceedings of the Fourth Eurographics Workshop on Rendering, 63-71 (1993).

19. Greene N., Kass, M.: Approximating Visibility with Environment Maps. Apple Computer Technical Report #41 (November 1994).

Editors' Note: see Appendix, p. 359 for colored figure of this paper

Comparing Real and Synthetic Images:
Some Ideas About Metrics [*]

H. Rushmeier[1] and G. Ward[2] and C. Piatko[1] and P. Sanders[3] and B. Rust[1]

[1] National Institute of Standards and Technology, Gaithersburg MD 20899, USA
[2] Lawrence Berkeley Laboratory, Berkeley CA 94720, USA
[3] GE NELA Park, Cleveland OH 44112, USA

Abstract. This paper explores numerical techniques for comparing real and synthetic luminance images. We introduce components of a perceptually based metric using ideas from the image compression literature. We apply a series of metrics to a set of real and synthetic images, and discuss their performance. Finally, we conclude with suggestions for future work in formulating image metrics and incorporating them into new image synthesis methods.

1 Introduction and Data from Physical Experiments

Research in realistic image synthesis suffers from a very basic gap in knowledge: no one knows how to evaluate a visual simulation. We need good image metrics to compare simulation methods, to validate simulations against measurements, and to guide progressive image synthesis calculations more efficiently. In this paper, we develop measures based on appearance rather than photometric accuracy. These perceptual metrics can be used to compare and to validate different rendering methods. Furthermore, they can be used to identify appropriate error quantities and error bounds for developing more efficient rendering algorithms. The goal of this paper is not to examine the accuracy of the particular program used to generate the synthetic images, but to consider how metrics for image comparison should be constructed.

There is bound to be some argument over which perceptual metric to use, since agreeing on one is so important to comparing rendering algorithms. Our goal in this paper is to get the conversation started, in hopes that one day we can settle on a satisfactory basis for comparing our visual simulation results. We intend to test these perceptual metrics on more complicated environments under more varied lighting conditions, and propose that others do the same before passing final judgement.

1.1 Input Data and Captured Images

We begin with the physical measurements performed to obtain the input for the synthetic images and to capture the "real" images. Understanding the limitations in the

---

[*] Certain commercial equipment and instruments are identified in this paper in order to specify the experimental procedures adequately. Such identification is not intented to imply recommendation or endorsement by the National Institute of Standards and Technology or by the Lawrence Berkeley Laboratory, nor is it intended to imply that the materials or equipment identified are necessarily the best available for the purpose.

measurement process is important to understanding the construction of a comparison metric.

In our study we use captured and synthetic images obtained in the course of a study of metrics for lighting design. The goal of that study, which is still in progress, is to relate subjective impressions of an environment to values computed from measured luminance images, along the lines suggested by Flynn [5]. A secondary goal is to determine if current lighting simulations are capable of predicting luminance images that are accurate enough to use the new metrics in lighting design. This study required an experimental setup with a room whose lighting systems could be changed to present different qualities of illumination to human observers and to a calibrated electronic camera. The geometry, materials and light sources were also measured so that lighting simulations (renderings) of the space could be produced. The test space was a conference room, shown in Fig. 1,

Fig. 1. These three images, obtained with a calibrated CCD camera, show left, middle and right views of the conference room with indirect fluorescent lighting.

at the National Institute of Standards and Technology. The room was modified to install downlights, wall washers, and to make adjustments in the direct and indirect lighting effects of the existing fluorescent fixtures. The room was deliberately uncluttered to isolate the effects of lighting changes on occupant impressions. As a real architectural space however, some complexity remained, such as the vent in the corner and seams in the walls.

For input into the synthetic imaging process the following data were taken:

Geometry: The room geometry was measured with a simple tape measure. In general, length measurements were made with an accuracy on the order of millimeters. Measurements were not made of the squareness of the room. The tilt of the vent blades and the angular position of the light fixtures were measured, but the data are accurate only to within a few degrees. The position of the table in the room was not measured precisely at the time luminance images were taken, so the table position is accurate only within a few centimeters.

Light Fixtures: No equipment was available for taking near-field photometry on the specific bulbs and light fixtures used in the experiment. Manufacturers' data were used for both goniometric and spectral data of the light bulbs. Since the fluorescent fixtures were modified, manufacturers' data were available for the tubes only, with the egg crate fixtures modeled as scene geometry. In general, variations on the order of 30%

can be expected between the manufacturers' data and actual performance depending on supplied voltage, operating temperature and bulb to bulb variations.

Reflectances: As many of the surfaces as could be sampled and carried to a measurement device (i.e. wall paint, carpet and table covering) were measured with the goniophotometer described in [9] and were found to be nearly Lambertian. The spectral reflectances for these surfaces were measured using a Minolta CM-2002 spectrophotometer. Other surfaces' reflectances – such as the baseboards, ceiling, table legs and fluorescent fixture components were estimated. The baseboards and table legs were estimated by comparing colorimeter output for these surfaces to output for a white diffuse standard under the same lighting conditions. The ceiling and lighting fixture surface reflectances were estimated visually by comparing with a card painted with a white diffuse paint which had been measured to have a reflectance of 90%.

The reflectances measured with the goniophotometer and spectrophotometer are quite accurate for the small samples on which they were made. However, as this is a room in daily use significant variations exist in all of the surfaces due to texture, aging and dirt.

Luminance images of the room under various lighting conditions were captured using the CapCalc imaging system described in ref. [8]. CapCalc is a CCD based system developed several years ago at RPI. The system is no longer state-of-the-art, but was adequate for this initial study. A major limitation is that it stores only 8 bits per pixel. The luminance range for any particular image is adjusted by changing the camera aperture. Images requiring larger dynamic ranges can be obtained by carefully combining images. All of the images captured for this study were captured at a resolution of 512 x 480 with a pixel aspect ratio of .75 and a field of view of 35°. These images were resampled to 512 x 360 images with pixel aspect ratio of 1 for applying the various metrics being examined.

An obvious limitation of a luminance imaging system is that all of our comparisons are restricted to grey scale images. However, spectral data were used in the simulations to account for the impact of spectral variations in emission and reflectance on the measured luminances.

1.2   Impact of Measurement Uncertainty on Image Metrics

There are clearly very high levels of uncertainty in the measurements made in this experiment. The combination of uncertainties results in even larger uncertainties in the final simulated luminances. For example, the uncertainty in the directional distribution coming from one of the light bulbs aimed at the wall, coupled with a few degrees uncertainty in the orientation of the bulb and small uncertainties in the surface reflectance can easily result in uncertainties on the order of a factor of 10 for the luminance at any specific point. However, the data we obtained are typical of what can be expected to be available in many (although not all) applications. Furthermore, the uncertainty in the data is typical of an environment in daily use. If appearance were closely dependent on precise photometry, the use of synthetic images for most design and training applications would be doomed. Fortunately, while appearance does depend on photometry, it is not a detailed linear dependence. Even with the data with high uncertainty obtained in this experiment, it is possible to synthesize images that look "more or less" like the real physical space. The purpose of the metrics we are looking for in this paper is to quantify "more or less".

2   How Should We Build an Image Metric?

One reason we want to compare real and synthetic images for specific applications is to validate software and measurement systems for input data. The level of "matching" required and the specific measurement accuracy required will always depend to some extent on the application. Another reason we want these metrics is to incorporate them into our global illumination calculations. We can compute images most effectively if we only compute image features that are visible in the final image.

A simple approach to comparing a synthetic and a captured luminance image of the same scene is to require that the luminances match at every pixel. If it were possible to obtain such a match, the resulting synthetic and captured images would appear identical to a human observer. However, matching exact luminances is sufficient, but not necessary. The human visual system is not a photometer. Ideally, we want a metric that measures how much alike two images *appear*.

How can we quantify the performance of such a metric? Here are some simple initial ideas for the properties of a metric $M(A;B)$ measuring the distance between images A and B. First, $M(A;A) = 0$. Second, $M(A;B) = M(B;A)$. Third, if images A and B appear similar, and A and C appear different, $M(A;C)/M(A;B) \gg 1$. Fourth, if images A, B, and C all look similar to one another, $M(A;B)/M(A;C) \simeq 1$. Fifth, if the differences between image A and image B are similar to the differences between image C and image D, $M(A;B)/M(C;D) \simeq 1$.

In our study, all of the metrics we use meet the first two criteria. To examine the third and fourth criteria we use "random" images – i.e. images in which pixel values are assigned randomly with the same mean and standard deviation as the measured images – as images that are "obviously" different. We will use "flat" images – i.e. images with surfaces rendered assuming an arbitrary uniform ambient light – as an image that looks more like the measured image than the random image. Images rendered with the *Radiance* system [10] with varying levels of quality specified will be used as images which clearly look more like the measured images than the random or flat ones. Examples of the random, flat, and simulated images are shown in Figure 2.

To examine the fifth criterion on the list we will look at the distance between two captured luminance images for two different lighting configurations, and the distance between two synthetic images for the same two lighting configurations.

The literature on human perception is voluminous, and deals with many aspects of vision outside of our area of interest. Most vision research in the area of imaging deals with detecting thresholds, that is, looking at image A and image B can you see any difference at all? For our metric, we are interested in suprathreshold effects, that is, a measure that is large when A and B are very different, and small when they are nearly the same. The vision research which would provide the basis for an entirely psychophysical model of this type does not yet exist. We have to rely on modeling a few basic characteristics of the human visual system to construct a practical system.

Fig. 2. Random, flat, and simulated images for the left view of the conference room with indirect fluorescent lighting.

To get a start, we will look at how human vision models have been used in a discipline that deals specifically with images – digital image compression. Similar to the synthesis problem in which we want to save time by only computing what will be visible in the image, in image compression the goal is to save space by saving only what will be visible in the image.

For static, grey scale images, there are several basic characteristics of human vision described in the compression literature that should be included in a metric. First, within a broad band of luminances, relative luminances rather than absolute luminances are sensed by the eye. A model should account for luminance variations, not absolute values. Second, the response of the eye is non-linear. The "brightness" perceived is a non-linear function of luminance. The particular non-linear relationship is not well established. Third, the sensitivity of the eye depends on the spatial frequency of luminance variations. At least for isolated sine grating patterns, the sensitivity is low for very low spatial frequencies, increases to a maximum for a frequency on the order of a few cycles per visual degree, and then decreases again for high spatial frequencies [3].

There are many ways these three effects can be modeled and combined. To test how sensitive a metric is to the specific model used we compare three metrics "inspired" by the compression and vision literature. We use the term "inspired" because while we are using models from these other papers, our application is different, and we are not using them in the same way as in the original papers.

Each model has slightly different features. Each uses a different CSF (contrast sensitivity function) to model the sensitivity to spatial frequencies. We use the combinations of transformations as found in the literature, rather than using the same CSF for each model, since the transformations have been found successful by others only in combination.

Model 1: After Mannos and Sakrison: Following ideas presented in [7], we begin by normalizing all of the luminance values L_{ij} in the matrix $\|L\|$ by the mean luminance L_m. Next, the nonlinearity in perception is accounted for by taking the cube root of the normalized luminance. A fast Fourier transform (FFT) is computed of the resulting values, and the magnitude of the resulting transform at frequencies in the horizontal and vertical directions (u, v), (where u and v are expressed in terms of cycles per visual degree) is denoted $f_{uv}(\|(L/L_m)^{.333}\|)$. The magnitudes f_{uv} are then filtered with the contrast sensitivity function $A_M(u, v) = A_M(r)$, where $r = u^2 + v^2$ to account for spatial frequency sensitivity to produce the array of values g_{uv}:

$$A_M(r(u,v)) = 2.6 * [0.0192 + 0.144\sqrt{r}] \exp[-(0.144\sqrt{r})^{1.1}]$$

$$g_{uv} = f_{uv}(\|(\frac{L}{L_m})^{.333}\|) * A_M(r(u,v)) \tag{1}$$

Finally, the distance between the two images is computed by finding the MSE (mean squared error) of the values of g_{uv} for the two images X and Y:

$$M(X;Y) = \frac{1}{N} \sum_{all\ u,v} (g_{X,uv} - g_{Y,uv})^2 \tag{2}$$

Model 2: After Gervais et al.: In our second model, we adapt ideas from a study of confusion between letters of the alphabet [6]. Although our problem is quite different, we selected this model because it includes the effects of phase as well as magnitude in the frequency space representation of the image. Once again the luminances are normalized by dividing by the mean luminance. An FFT is computed for this normalized image, producing an array of magnitudes $f_{uv}(\|L/L_m\|)$ and phases $p_{uv}(\|L/L_m\|)$. The magnitudes are then filtered with an anisotropic contrast sensitivity filter function constructed by fitting splines to psychophysical data presented by Campbell et al. [2], producing the filtered values $g_{uv}(\|L/L_m\|)$ The distance between images X and Y is then computed using:

$$M(X;Y) = \frac{1}{N} \sum_{all\ u,v} (((\log g_{X,uv} + 1) - (\log g_{Y,uv} + 1))(1 + p_{X,uv} - p_{Y,uv}))^2 \tag{3}$$

Model 3: After Daly: In the third model, we use ideas from a paper on visible difference prediction [4]. Because we are only interested in suprathreshold comparisons, we only use the first part of the algorithm described in the paper, and omit the components modeling detection mechanisms. In this model, the effects of adaptation and non-linearity are combined in one transformation which acts on each pixel individually. In the first two models each pixel has significant global effect in the normalization by contributing to the image mean. In this model, each luminance is transformed to an "amplitude non-linearity value" b_{ij} defined by: $b_{ij} = L_{ij}/(L_{ij} + 12.6L_{ij}^{0.63})$ where the constants 12.6 and 0.63 apply when luminance is expressed in cd/m^2.

An FFT is then applied to the values b_{ij}. The resulting magnitudes, $f_{uv}(b)$ are filtered by a CSF which is a function of the image size in degrees and light adaptation level L_m. The dependence on the light adaptation level is very weak, and for this study the CSF was computed for a level of 50 cd/m^2. The resulting contrast sensitivity filter $A_D(r(u,v))$ for our particular images is given by:

$$A_D(r(u,v)) = (.008/r^{1.5} + 1)^{-.2}1.42\sqrt{r}\exp(-.3\sqrt{r})\sqrt{1 + .06\exp(.3\sqrt{r})} \tag{4}$$

The distance between the two images is then computed as the MSE for the filtered magnitudes of the amplitude nonlinearity values as in Eq. 2 for Model 1.

3   Results and Conclusions

In all of the tests we conducted, comparisons are made on luminance images – not on 0–255 images for which a tone reproduction operator has been used to transform the image to display. We want to find luminance images that match, with the assumption that whatever tone reproduction operator is used to represent the image in the final display medium will preserve the appearance of the luminance image. Also, comparing images before tone mapping allows us to say something about how well the simulation matches the measurements assuming an "ideal" display device.

3.1   Comparisons to Pixel by Pixel MSE

The first issue we want to address is that the three models we have proposed really do perform better with respect to our requirements for a metric than a MSE measure computed on untransformed images. Table 1 shows a comparison of the results of pixel by pixel MSE for two test cases – the left view of the room with down lights, and the left view of the room with wall washers. The results in Table 1 are typical for all of the various room configurations in our study.

In particular, we look at the ratio of the distance between the random image and the measured image (R) to the distance between a good simulation and the measured image (S), and at the ratio of the distance between a flat image and the measured image (F) to the distance between a good simulation and the measured image. Our goal is to have the first ratio be very large, since the simulation clearly looks much more like the measured image than the random image does. We also want the ratio for the flat image to be much smaller than the ratio for the random image, since the flat image does capture features of the measured image. In Table 1 we show the results of adding each of the transformations in Model 1 for the left image of the downlight and wall washer lighting configurations. First, the pixel by pixel MSE is clearly very poor – it essentially gives the random image as being as close to the measured image as the simulation, and closer than the flat image. As various transformations are added in – normalizing by average luminance (NORM), comparing cube roots (CUBE ROOT), comparing the magnitudes of the FFT of the cube root luminances (FFT), and comparing filtered magnitudes (Filt FFT, Eq. 2) the measure of the relative distance to the random image increases, while the relative distance to the flat image goes to a value above one, but much less than the distance to the random image.

3.2   Considering Image Registration

One reason the MSE comparison is so poor for the measured and synthetic images is simple geometric misalignments. To test this effect, we used the "ip warp" module in AVS [1] to warp the synthetic images so that geometric features such as the vent and the table matched in the two images. The distance comparisons for the warped versus simulated images are shown in the rightmost column of Table 1 for the wall washer lighting configuration. Aligning the geometries has minimal effect on improving pixel by pixel comparisons. This is because geometric misalignment of objects in the final image is only one type of misalignment problem. Another problem is small errors in the directionality of the light source orientation, which can cause registration problems in the light patterns. We conclude that rather than introduce more assumptions and alter images to compensate for geometric factors, it is better to compare images with metrics that measure appearance rather than point by point photometry.

3.3 Comparing the Three Perceptual Models

Given that we want to use metrics that incorporate vision models, we now test the three models using the criteria we outlined. We use three different types of comparisons.

First we look at the performance of the three models in comparing the relative distances to random and flat images, as discussed in the first subsection. Again we show results for the down lights and wall washers, with the results for other lighting configurations we studied showing similar trends. These results are presented in Table 2. The most striking feature of this comparison is that Model 2 does a much poorer job at measuring the relative distances for random and simulated images. A second observation is that Model 3 reports greater relative distances between the flat and simulated images. This is desirable performance in the metric, particularly in the case of the wall washers in which the bright spots on the walls are features that clearly differentiate the measured image from a flat rendering.

Next we look at the performance of the models at detecting more subtle effects. For this test we use the measured image, flat rendering, and the three increasingly better approximations of the images of the room with indirect fluorescent lighting. Ideally the metrics should detect the slight improvements in the decreasing spatial artifacts in the three simulations. In Table 3 we show results for the three models comparing the distances for the flat, very bad, and a little better rendering relative to the distance for the best rendering. In this case again, the most noticeable feature is that Model 2 does a poor job measuring improvements in the approximation.

Finally, we look at how well the models predict similar changes in pairs of images. We look at how consistently the models give similar results when the distance between a pair of measured images for two different lighting configurations is compared to the distance between a pair of synthetic images for the same two lighting configurations. These results are presented in Table 4. In this case Model 2 does a slightly better job. Since in this test there are no geometric misalignments, the phase data that is included in Model 2 does not detect any registration problems, which mask other parts of the comparisons.

3.4 Conclusions

We have demonstrated how perceptual metrics adapted from vision and image compression research may be used to numerically compare renderings and captured images in a way that roughly corresponds to our own subjective, human impressions. In particular, the model inspired by Daly [4] tested very well against our criteria for a good perceptual metric. The Daly model was also the only one we examined that considers human limits in dark adaptation, and we expect it to outperform the other models in low light situations which we have not yet tested. The Gervais model [6] was the only one that included phase (i.e. pixel position) information, and its performance thereby suffered

Table 1. Comparing the Performance of Several Metrics

	R/S		F/S		W/S
IDEAL	a big number		$R/S > F/S > 1$		about 1
	Downlights	Wall Washers	Downlights	Wall Washers	Wall Washers
MSE	1.2	1.0	1.8	1.2	0.98
NORM	1.8	4.5	0.8	2.4	0.93
CUBE ROOT	1.8	13.8	1.1	2.6	1.09
FFT	7.1	31.6	1.4	2.4	1.19
Filt FFT	44.6	599.4	1.7	1.9	0.77

R = M(measured; random), S = M(measured; simulated)
F = M(measured; flat), W =M(measured; warped)
All comparisons are for the left view of the room.

Table 2. Comparing models' sensitivities to similar and dissimilar images.

Model #	1		2		3	
	R/S	F/S	R/S	F/S	R/S	F/S
Downlights -left view	44.6	1.7	2.5	0.7	46.2	2.9
Downlights -middle view	78.7	1.5	2.7	0.8	98.4	2.6
Downlights -right view	67.1	0.9	2.0	1.5	84.3	4.1
Wall Washers -left view	599.4	1.9	7.1	1.2	768.3	3.5
Wall Washers -middle view	338.5	1.4	4.2	1.1	468.7	1.9
Wall Washers -right view	705.1	1.9	5.7	2.3	1041.3	4.4

Table 3. Comparing models' abilities to detect progressive rendering improvements.

Model #	1			2			3		
	F/S	VB/S	B/S	F/S	VB/S	B/S	F/S	VB/S	B/S
Indirect Fluorescents -left	1.41	0.99	1.00	0.8	0.95	0.95	4.6	1.05	1.02
Indirect Fluorescents -middle	1.55	1.03	1.02	0.9	0.96	0.98	3.7	1.05	1.02
Indirect Fluorescents -right	1.22	1.02	1.01	1.6	0.93	0.98	12.7	1.14	1.06

VB = M(measured; very bad simulation), B = M(measured; bad simulation)

Table 4. Comparing models with different lighting, but no geometric misalignments.

	$\dfrac{M(SDL;SWW)}{M(MDL;MWW)}$		
Model #	1	2	3
left view	.86	.97	1.41
middle view	1.05	1.08	0.84
right view	0.79	1.13	1.42

SDL = Simulated downlights, SWW = Simulated wall washers
MDL = Measured downlights, MWW = Measured wall washers

due to subjectively minor registration problems between captured and simulated images in our tests. In situations where geometric alignment is not a problem, or is of critical importance for some other reason, this model may actually outperform the others.

Ultimately, the biggest challenge is to take insights into human perception and apply them to visual simulation directly, computing only as much as is needed to satisfy the observer. Recasting a perceptual model into a progressive calculation is not an easy task, and it is essential to start with the right model. The more reliable the model of human perception used in image synthesis, the more efficient and accurate rendering engines will be.

References

1. Advanced Visual Systems. *AVS User's Guide* AVS Inc., 300 Fifth Ave., Waltham, MA 02154, 1992.
2. F. W. Campbell, J. J. Kulikowski, and J. Levinson. The effect of orientation on the visual resolution of gratings. *Journal of Physiology*, 187:427–436, 1966.
3. T. N. Cornsweet. *Visual Perception*, Academic Press, New York, NY, 1970.
4. S. Daly. The visible difference predictor: an algorithm for the assessment of image fidelity. In A. B. Watson, editor, *Digital Images and Human Vision*, pages 179–206. MIT Press, 1993.
5. J. E. Flynn. A study of subjective responses to low energy and nonuniform lighting systems. *Lighting Design and Application*, pages 6–15, 1977.
6. M. J. Gervais, L. O. Harvey, Jr., and J. O. Roberts. Identification confusions among letters of the alphabet. *Journal of Experimental Psychology: Human Perception and Performance*, 10(5):655–666, 1984.
7. J. L. Mannos and D. J. Sakrison. The effects of a visual fidelity criterion on the encoding of images. *IEEE Transactions on Information Theory*, IT-20(4):525–536, 1974.
8. M. S. Rea and I. G. Jeffrey. A new luminance and image analysis system for lighting and vision I. Equipment and calibration. *Journal of the Illuminating Engineering Society*, pages 64–72, Winter 1990.
9. G. J. Ward. Measuring and modeling anisotropic reflection. *Computer Graphics*, 26(2), 1992.
10. G. J. Ward. The RADIANCE lighting simulation and rendering system. *Computer Graphics*, July, 1994.

A Framework for Global Illumination
in Animated Environments

Jeffry Nimeroff[1]   Julie Dorsey[2]   Holly Rushmeier[3]

[1] University of Pennsylvania, Philadelphia PA 19104, USA
[2] Massachusetts Institute of Technology, Cambridge MA 02139, USA
[3] National Institute of Standards and Technology, Gaithersburg MD 20899, USA

Abstract. We describe a new framework for efficiently computing and storing global illumination effects for complex, animated environments. The new framework allows the rapid generation of sequences representing any arbitrary path in a "view space" within an environment in which both the viewer and objects move. The global illumination is stored as time sequences of range-images at base locations that span the view space. We present algorithms for determining locations for these base images and the time steps required to adequately capture the effects of object motion. We also present algorithms for computing the global illumination in the base images that exploit spatial and temporal coherence by considering direct and indirect illumination separately. We discuss an initial implementation using the new framework. Results from our implementation demonstrate the efficient generation of multiple tours through a complex space and a tour of an environment in which objects move.

1   Introduction

The ultimate goal of global illumination algorithms for computer image generation is to allow users to interact with accurately rendered, animated, geometrically complex environments. While many useful methods have been proposed for computing global illumination, the generation of physically accurate images of animated, complex scenes still requires an inordinate number of CPU hours on state of the art computer hardware. Since accurate, detailed images must be precomputed, very little user interaction with complex scenes is allowed.

In this paper, we present a range-image based approach to computing and storing the results of global illumination for an animated, complex environment. Range-image based systems have been used previously in flight simulators [3] and in computer graphics [7]. Range-images store the distance to the visible object for each pixel, as well as the radiance. While previous research has demonstrated the potential of range-image systems to allow a user to tour a complex scene at interactive rates, the problem of efficiently rendering animated, globally illuminated environments within the context of such a system has not been considered. In this paper, we present a new framework that addresses this problem.

The contributions of this paper are several. We build on previous work by considering how animated environments (i.e. environments in which objects as well as the user can move) can be represented as time sequences of range-images. We explore how to select a set of base views for the range-images as well as the time steps required to capture the effects of object motion. Further, we consider how global illumination can be efficiently computed to generate each of the range-images. Previous global illumination methods have successfully exploited spatial coherence by separating the calculation of direct and indirect illumination [6, 21]. We build on this idea and exploit temporal coherence as well by separating the calculation of temporal variations in direct and indirect illumination. These innovations form the basis of a new framework that allows the rapid generation of views along arbitrary paths within a "view space," which is a subspace of the full environment.

2 Background

Our approach builds on work in two areas – the traversal of complex, realistically shaded synthetic environments, and the calculation of global illumination in animated environments.

2.1 Traversal of Complex, Realistic Environments

The ultimate visualization system for interacting with synthetic environments would render perfectly accurate images in real time, with no restrictions on user movement or the movement of objects in the environment. A number of different approaches have been developed for attempting to build such a system.

Polygons with Hardware Lighting. One approach is to use hardware lighting effects to render sequences of images with heuristic, *local* illumination models. In this scheme, the illumination of a surface depends only on its own characteristics and that of the parallel or non-physical point (i.e. no $1/r^2$ drop off) light sources. While hundreds of thousands, or millions of polygons can be rendered per second, for complex scenes this means that individual objects must have simplified geometries to achieve real time speeds. Hardware rendering effects can be very useful for giving a sense of traversing a space for some applications. However, they are far from realistic because of the non-physical lighting models used and the limitations on numbers of polygons that can be used to model the environment.

Radiosity. In contrast, radiosity techniques explicitly model the physical interreflection of light in a scene to compute the radiance L (energy per unit time, projected area and solid angle) leaving each object [12, 18]. A radiosity solution is a set of radiance values at locations distributed over surfaces in an environment. Given a solution, walkthroughs can be performed by converting the radiances to RGB values, which can be used in place of hardware lighting. Thus, radiosity approaches represent an improvement in both the ability to interact with a scene as well as in the accuracy of the illumination effects.

The primary limitation of the radiosity method as originally introduced, however, was that it was restricted to ideal diffuse reflectors – that is to surfaces for which L is independent of the direction of view (θ, ϕ) from the surface normal. Since the human visual system is very good at detecting and interpreting highlights that result from the directional variation of L, this representation is restrictive. Extensions of the radiosity method have been developed to account for the full range of bidirectional reflectance distribution functions (BRDF's) that occur in real life [17]. Such methods however substantially increase the pre-computation time, storage requirements, and time to traverse the complex scene.

Pre-Recorded Animations. To date, the most realistic animations are created by using algorithms which are capable of taking diffuse interreflection and nondiffuse reflection into account [20]. These algorithms are often termed photorealistic. While these algorithms are capable of depicting very accurate illumination effects, it is at the cost of interactivity. Creating an animated sequence with these algorithms is very time consuming when compared to the algorithms discussed above. Further, animated image sequences may only be generated if the viewer paths and object motions are specified *a priori*. Once a sequence is computed, the user is restricted to viewing a fixed set of frames as they were computed. A small amount of freedom of movement can be allowed by recording a network or tree of paths for the viewer to tour.

Range-Image Interpolation. Range-image interpolation has been employed in flight simulators [3] and has been applied to more general graphics applications by Chen and Williams [7]. In this approach, the three dimensional scene is replaced by a set of images for which the view point and the radiances and ranges (i.e. the distance to nearest visible object) for each pixel are stored. As a user traverses the environment, appropriate views are synthesized by morphing the base range images. Chen and Williams focus on how to perform this morphing and suggest how the images can be obtained – examples cited include physical image capture and using images from a radiosity solution.

A major advantage of the range-image approach is that storing and traversing the scene are only weakly dependent on object space complexity. In general, range-image interpolation sacrifices some of the freedom of movement possible in a radiosity walk-through for increased accuracy in geometric detail and lighting accuracy. Note, however, that unlike pre-recorded animations, the user can move freely in a subspace of the environment rather than moving only along predefined paths. The number of base images required to represent an environment for a given subspace of possible views is an open research problem.

2.2 Global Illumination of Animated Environments

We wish to tour complex environments in which objects move. Systems that produce animations with simple local shading can easily exploit image coherence. If local shading only is considered new frames can be produced rapidly by only changing the portions of the image in which there are moving objects. For images generated using complete global illumination solutions, the problem is more difficult. When one object moves it changes the illumination of all of the other objects in the scene to some extent.

There are essentially three possible ways to compute global illumination: object space, image space, and hybrid object/image space methods. In general, relatively little work has been done to develop efficient methods for animated environments.

Object Space. The radiosity method, described in the previous subsection, is an object space method. Radiance distributions $L(x, y, z, \theta, \phi)$ are computed for objects without reference to the images in which the object will appear. The object space approach has the advantage that no interreflection calculation has to be performed as images are finally computed. It has the disadvantage that many radiances have to be computed that never appear in any images. The exception to this is the importance driven radiosity algorithm proposed by Smits et al. [19].

Another major drawback of the original radiosity method was that although it allowed walkthroughs of static environments, a costly new radiosity solution was required for each frame if any object moved. Considerable effort has been put in to develop radiosity methods that exploit temporal coherence in lighting. Baum et al. [2] developed a method for identifying geometric form factors that would not need to be recomputed for a full matrix radiosity solution as an object moved through a prescribed path. Chen [5], George et al. [10], Müller and Schöffel [15] and Forsyth et al. [9] have developed progressive refinement radiosity solutions that are updated incrementally for temporal changes in object locations. Each method essentially starts with the solution for the previous time step, "undoes" the effect of the object that has moved, and then computes the effect of the object in its new position. Since most objects have a limited spatial effect, such incremental approaches converge quickly. Generally, the shadows are recomputed, and interreflected light is only propagated to a small extent before it falls below the acceptable threshold of "unshot radiosity." These methods effectively exploit the temporal coherence in the radiosity solution.

In all of the temporal radiosity methods, full illumination, rather than just direct or indirect, is computed. None of the methods have examined whether the temporal sampling rate for new radiosity solutions can be different from the frame generation rate.

Image Space. Monte Carlo path tracing (MCPT) [14] is an image space method. In MCPT stochastic methods are used to compute the radiance $L(i, j)$ which will be seen through a pixel at location (i, j) on the screen. MCPT has the advantage that if an object in the environment does not appear in a particular image, its radiance does not have to be computed. This is an advantage for environments that have many more objects than the image representing it has pixels. MCPT has the disadvantage that it does not exploit spatial coherence – each pixel is computed independently. In general, this failure to exploit spatial coherence has kept MCPT from becoming a widely used technique. No work has been done to accelerate MCPT for animated sequences.

Hybrid Object/Image Space. Hybrid methods for global illumination combine the advantages of object and image approaches. Detailed radiance is only computed for objects which appear in the image. Spatial coherence is exploited by calculating multiple reflections in object space. Examples of hybrid methods are the *Radiance* system and the multi-pass progressive refinement methods [6, 16].

Specifically, in hybrid methods, visibility and direct illumination calculations, for which the level of detail is limited by the pixel resolution, are computed in image space. Indirect illumination is computed in object space. In general, illumination is a continuous field, with sharp discontinuities occurring only when point light sources are instantaneously obscured [1]. Since indirect illumination is the result of multiple reflections, giving rise to many extended "secondary" light sources, indirect illumination is generally a smoother function than direct illumination. As a result, indirect illumination can be sampled relatively sparsely in space, and intermediate values found by interpolation. In the *Radiance* system, indirect illumination is saved as a set of "cached" values in object space. In the multi-pass progressive refinement method, indirect illumination is found by a radiosity solution for a crude discretization of the environment. To the authors' knowledge no work has been published on efficiently updating hybrid object/image space global illumination solutions for moving objects.

3 A New Framework

In this section we describe a new framework for computing global illumination for a system for traversing complex animated scenes. This framework is based on the techniques outlined in the previous section that are most able to achieve real-life freedom of movement and rendering accuracy. The new framework 1) is a range-image based system and 2) exploits coherence by computing direct and indirect illumination separately in both space and in time.

3.1 An Image Based System

As mentioned in Section 2, range-image based systems have the advantage of very efficiently representing geometrically complex environments. This advantage over polygon based systems is compounded when we wish to represent a photometrically accurate version of the environment.

The advantage of the image-based approach over radiosity for photometrically accurate scenes extends even further when allowable error in the solution is considered. For any global illumination solution, the computation time can be drastically reduced by allowing some known error level in the results, rather than attempting to compute results to machine precision [13]. *But what is an allowable error level?* The allowable error depends on viewer perception, not on the characteristics of the object. In a radiosity solution, a high degree of accuracy is required, because the view of the object is unknown. The "worst case" must be assumed. Perceptual error metrics are inherently image based, since the accuracy required for a particular radiance depends on the radiance distribution in the visual field [4]. In an image-based system, much better estimates can be made of allowable error in the radiance solution, and the solution can be computed much more efficiently.

In our new framework then, the global illumination solution will be computed in the form of a set of base range-images, which will be interpolated to produce a frame at each time step. A user will then be able to move freely within the space spanned by the base range-images.

3.2 Exploiting Temporal Coherence in Global Illumination

As discussed earlier, several researchers have proposed radiosity solutions that efficiently exploit the temporal coherence in global illumination variations as objects move. In these approaches, the location and radiance distribution is stored for each object. As the observer moves through the scene, objects are projected in to the view with the appropriate radiance. The advantage of this approach is that the global illumination for each time step has been incrementally computed by exploiting object space coherence. That is, a completely new global illumination solution is not needed for every frame. The disadvantages are the precomputation time and storage space required as the number of objects becomes very large.

In a temporally varying range-image based system, we move through time by interpolating between images in a time series for each base view. In this case, we are producing frames that represent a full global illumination solution—taking into account both diffuse and non-diffuse illumination. Radiances do not need to be stored for every object for every time.

Direct Illumination and Visibility. Relatively standard techniques for ray tracing animations can be used to exploit the coherence of direct visibility and shadowing in the base range-images. Rather than computing images for every 1/30 sec, the time steps for these base images can be determined by detecting the amount of geometry or shadowing change over longer lengths of time.

Even with this reduced number of base time-images, how can we avoid a pixel by pixel recalculation of the global illumination for each time step? As in the temporal radiosity methods we seek to exploit the temporal coherence in the full global solution to reduce the calculations.

Indirect Illumination. As noted Section 2, hybrid approaches exploit spatial coherence by computing indirect illumination effects using relatively sparse spacing in object space. We can use the same sparse sampling of object space to exploit temporal coherence.

Figure 1 illustrates the relationship between sampling indirect illumination in time and in space. Consider Figure 1a. For a static environment, we can sample indirect illumination at points A and B and interpolate between them, because the effect of object O on diffuse (or near-diffuse) reflection varies continuously between A and B. The amount of light from O that is reflected from A is slightly higher than the amount reflected from B because O subtends a larger solid angle from A, and because the angle of O to the surface normal is slightly lower at A.

If object O is moving, indirect illumination at point A at times **time 1** and **time 2** varies in the same manner that the indirect illumination varied with position between A and B in the static case. At **time 2** the light A reflects from O is a bit less because the solid angle subtended by O is smaller, and the angle of O to the surface normal has increased.

Because the changes in indirect illumination resulting from object motion are equivalent to the changes in indirect illumination as a function of distance in the static case, we can sparsely sample indirect illumination in time as well as in space.

Our approach then is to compute indirect illumination for sparsely separated points for very large time steps. Interpolation between these solutions will then be used to compute the indirect illumination for the time series of images at each base view point.

3.3 The Whole System

The overall framework of our approach is shown in Figure 2. The indirect illumination is sampled sparsely in time and space in object space (top row). The indirect illumination solution is then interpolated and used as the basis to produce the full global illumination for each of the base images (middle row). Finally, for any path in the view space, images are generated for each frame by interpolating the base images.

To build the system diagrammed in Figure 2 we need the following: 1) Rules for selecting the base view positions so that the entire space a user may wish to tour is spanned,

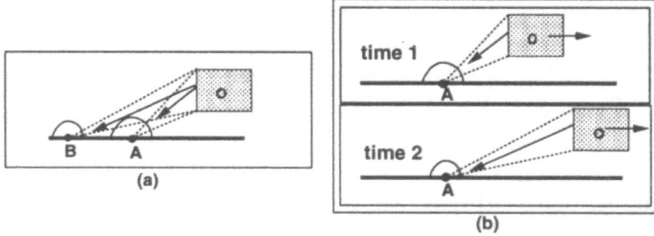

Fig. 1. Figure (a) illustrates that the indirect illumination of point A by object O is only slightly different than the indirect illumination of point B by object O. Figure (b) illustrates that the difference in indirect illumination of point A caused by the movement of object O from time 1 to time 2 is the same as the difference in indirect illumination between A and B in the static case.

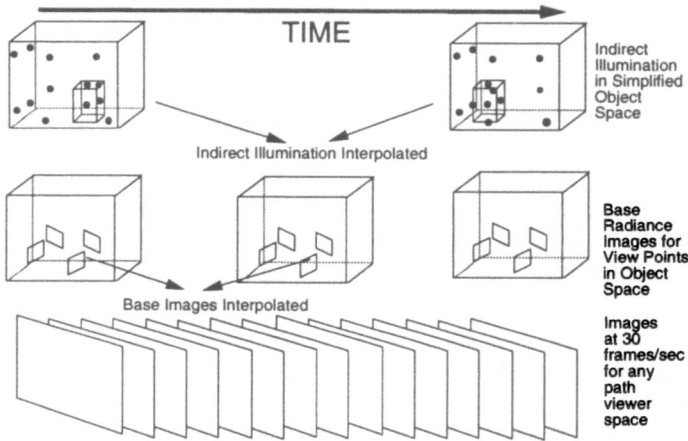

Fig. 2. Indirect illumination is sampled sparsely in time and space in a simplified, animated object space. Radiance images are computed more frequently in time for selected base views, using interpolated values from the indirect illumination solution. One image per frame is computed for any path in the view space by interpolating base images.

2) Rules for selecting the time steps at which base views are computed so that motions are adequately represented, and 3) Rules for selecting the points and times for which indirect illumination is to be computed. We also need to choose a particular method for computing the indirect illumination, the base images, and for efficiently performing the various interpolations. In the next section we describe an initial implementation of the system we have just outlined.

4 Implementation

As input to our initial implementation, we have the environment description, the specification of objects and a *view space*. The view space defines the portion of the environment that can be toured. Locations for the base views are found by adaptive subdivision. The initial time discretization is estimated by accounting for direct lighting effects. The time discretization for each view is then further refined. In parallel to the establishment of base views, the sparsely sampled indirect illumination solutions are calculated. The indirect illumination solutions are then used to compute the base images. We now consider each of the elements of the implementation in more detail.

4.1 Selecting Base Views

The view space S is a set of view locations that is some subset of the full environment. The view space may be 1-D, 2-D, or 3-D, allowing the user to move along a line, within a plane, or through a volume respectively. In our initial implementation we consider a 2-D space, although the methodology can easily be applied to the 1-D or 3-D cases.

Ideally, to allow the user to have a free range of movement within S, the view for the entire sphere of directions should be stored. In our initial implementation, however, we consider only a hemispherical fish-eye view, restricting the directions and fields of view available to the viewer. To extend our method, we would simply need to define a scheme for sampling the sphere of directions nearly uniformly (i.e. avoiding concentrations of samples at the "poles.")

The base view locations in S are determined by adaptive subdivision. The subdivision level is controlled by a preselected quality parameter q, which ranges from zero to one. A value of q equal to zero will result in no subdivision, a value of q equal to one will result in a very dense population of view locations.

The subdivision begins by defining synthetic cameras at the corners of the space. A P by Q resolution *id-image* is formed for each camera. In an id-image the pixel values are unique numerical identifiers for the objects visible at the pixel. Depending on the geometry of the objects, the id-image could be formed by a variety of techniques (scan-line, ray tracing, etc.). In our implementation we use the SGI display hardware to form the image, by assigning a unique 32-bit color to each polygon in place of its physical color. The number of pixels N that have the same id for all of the cameras is counted. The "fitness" f of this set of locations is computed as N/PQ. If f is less than the quality parameter q, the space is subdivided, and the test is applied recursively.

4.2 Time Steps for Base Views

The frequency of time sampling for each base view is determined first by checking the general variability in direct illumination and then by refining the time sequence according to a visibility test for each view point.

To check the general variability in direct illumination, we place a camera at the position of each light source and project all objects in the scene onto the camera using a fish-eye projection. Initially, this is performed for the beginning and endpoints of the animation, and a comparison of the result id-images is used to compute a value of f for the two points in time. The time interval is subdivided recursively until the value of f for all pairs of successive times exceeds q for each of the light sources.

The approach assumes point light sources. These points may be the centers of mass of clusters of small light sources, or they may be sample points chosen on area light sources.

Note that no illumination calculations are being performed with this process; we are simply estimating the time frequency for which highlights and shadows will need to be updated.

Next, for each of the base views, we wish to refine the time sequence further by using visibility tests for each of the view points. Each view point could have its own time sequence – i.e. there may be relatively little motion in some views relative to others. In our initial implementation, just one master time sequence is generated. To do the base view time refinement, the procedure is the same as just described, but the list of base view locations is used in place of the light source locations.

4.3 Indirect Illumination

To compute indirect illumination, we use a hierarchical radiosity solver [13] on a simplified environment [16]. The time steps used for recomputing the indirect illumination are found by recursive subdivision. Alternatively, a static set of points could have been chosen to compute indirect illumination with the *Radiance* package [20]. The points could have been chosen by doing a set of "overture" calculations for random views within the view space. The advantage of the radiosity preprocess however is that the resulting values are associated with objects. For large moving objects, both the value of the illumination and the position at which that illumination is valid can be interpolated in time.

A number of methods could be used to simplify the full mega-object environment to a relatively small number of polygons for the radiosity solution. In this initial implementation, we use a simple criterion based on visibility from the view constraint space. For each of some number of trials, a random time is chosen. For the environment at that time, random viewpoints in the constraint space are chosen. For each view, a large number of rays are shot through a wide viewing angle. A record is kept of how many times each object is hit in this process. Based on the number of hits, an object may be ignored (a very small number of hits), simplified (somewhat larger number of hits), or restricted in subdivision (large number of hits) in the radiosity solution.

In the indirect solution, the objects move and the radiosities change. However, once the simplified geometry has been defined, the list structure storing the indirect illumination does not change. This makes it easy to perform an object space "fitness" test. In the indirect case, f is defined as the number of vertices in the solution that have changed less than some small percentage ϵ. Once again, the time sequence is subdivided recursively based on a comparison of f and q. Note that the list of times for which each indirect illumination solution is computed is determined completely apart from the times for which each new base view is computed.

4.4 Computing and Using the Base Images

To compute the base images, we use *Radiance*, substituting the indirect illumination values we computed with the radiosity solver, interpolated for the appropriate time, for the cached values usually used in *Radiance*.

Once all the base images are computed for the selected locations and times, animations for arbitrary paths through the view space can be generated by interpolating between the images closest in time and space. The view interpolation, which is essentially the image morphing described by Chen and Williams, is performed with the *pinterp* function, which comes with the *Radiance* distribution. Time interpolation is performed using the *pcomb* function.

5 Results

To demonstrate the effectiveness of the new framework, we have applied it to two different environments – a geometrically complex architectural space and a simple "Cornell box." The complex architectural environment consisted of approximately 75,000 surfaces. These surfaces exhibited a full range of reflectance properties.

Table 1 summarizes execution times for processing a small view space in the complex scene, which we simplified to 5000 surfaces. A quality parameter q of .7 was used, and all times are for a single R4400 processor. The total time for processing the environment and generating one 30-frame animation was 3664 minutes. The power of the new framework, however, is the *small marginal cost to compute additional sequences*. For example, to produce two additional walkthroughs required only 60 cpu minutes.

Building			
Algorithm	Time (minutes)	Number of Executions	Total Time (minutes)
Visibility Coherence	23	1	23
Direct Coherence	0	0	0
Indirect Illumination	220	1	221
Base Image Generation	420	8	3360
Image Interpolation	2	30	60
Time Interpolation	0	0	0
Total			3664

Table 1. Execution times for the building environment.

To demonstrate the application to an animated environment, we used a simple "Cornell box" that contained two moving cubes. This simple scene highlights the variation of indirect illumination with object movement. The two cubes are red and blue and have rough specular surfaces. Table 2 summarizes the execution times for each stage in the processing of this environment and for computing a 30-frame walkthrough. For this animation, we used a quality q of .95, which is very high. The total time required was 2363.5 minutes. For an animated environment, the additional cost per frame is higher than the static environment, since the time interpolation of base images is required. The walkthrough sequence demonstrates that the user can walk through the moving environment and observe changes in the shiny surfaces and the indirect illumination as well as the overall object motion.

Plate 1 shows the fish-eye base views (a, b) for the complex scene and an interpolated view (c). Plate 2 shows the indirect solutions for two timesteps of the Cornell box environment (a, b) and an interpolated solution (c).

The results for these two environments demonstrate the feasibility and potential of the new framework. They do not by any means constitute a proof of robustness of the current

Cornell Box			
Algorithm	Time (minutes)	Number of Executions	Total Time (minutes)
Visibility Coherence	1	1	1
Direct Coherence	20	1	20
Indirect Illumination	5	2	10
Base Image Generation	12	$2 \times 25 = 50$	600
Image Interpolation	1.5	$45 \times 25 = 1125$	1687.5
Time Interpolation	1	45	45
Total			2363.5

Table 2. Execution times for the Cornell box environment.

implementation. Additional testing is required to understand the impact of the quality setting q, to determine appropriate initial discretizations in space and time to insure the adaptive procedures converge, and to measure performance for complex, animated environments.

6 Summary and Discussion

We have presented a new framework for efficiently computing and storing global illumination effects in complex, animated environments. Our approach is a range-image based system, which exploits coherence by computing direct and indirect illumination separately in both space and time. Indirect illumination is computed for sparsely separated points for very large time steps. Interpolation between these solutions is used to compute the indirect illumination for the time series of images at each base view point. We demonstrate that the range-image approach allows the rapid generation of the views along arbitrary paths within a view space, which is a subset of the whole environment. The framework represents a major step toward the ultimate goal of allowing users to interact with accurately rendered, animated, geometrically complex environments, as it allows for a user to tour a view space rendered with full global illumination effects in which objects move.

Within the context of the framework, there are several areas that require future research. First, we would like to devise a scheme to define and quantify an acceptable error for a given animation. Second, we would like to address the notion of freedom of movement in greater detail. For instance, many tradeoffs are possible between user interactivity and the quality of the animated sequence. Third, the problem of automatically determining the base views for a three dimensional environment is an open research topic, which could involve research in computational geometry. Last, there is a potential for real time walk-throughs using specialized hardware for the view and time interpolations.

Acknowledgements

We are grateful to Greg Ward for many helpful comments. This research was supported by a grant from the MIT Cabot Fund and an equipment grant from Silicon Graphics.

References

1. J. Arvo. The irradiance jacobian for partially occluded polyhedral sources. *Computer Graphics (SIGGRAPH '94 Proceedings)*, 28(4):343–350, July 1994.

2. D. Baum, J. Wallace, and M. Cohen. The back-buffer algorithm: an extension of the radiosity method to dynamic environments. *The Visual Computer*, 2(5):298–306, 1986.

3. K. Blanton. A new approach for flight simulator visual systems. In *Simulators IV, Proceedings of the SCCS Simulators Conference*, pages 229–233, 1987.

4. K.R. Boff and J.E. Lincoln. *Engineering Data Compendium: Human Perception and Performance, Vol. 1*. Wright-Patterson Air Force Base, 1988.

5. S. E. Chen. Incremental radiosity: An extension of progressive radiosity to an interactive image synthesis system. *Computer Graphics (SIGGRAPH '90 Proceedings)*, 24(4):135–144, August 1990.

6. S. E. Chen, H. Rushmeier, G. Miller, and D. Turner. A progressive multi-pass method for global illumination. *Computer Graphics (SIGGRAPH '91 Proceedings)*, 25(4):165–174, July 1991.

7. S. E. Chen and L. Williams. View interpolation for image synthesis. *Computer Graphics (SIGGRAPH '93 Proceedings)*, 27(4):279–288, August 1993.

8. J. Dorsey, J. Arvo, and D. Greenberg. Interactive design of complex time-dependent lighting. *IEEE Computer Graphics and Applications*, 15(2):26–36, March 1995.

9. D. Forsyth, C. Yang, and K. Teo. Efficient radiosity in dynamic environments. *Fifth Eurographics Workshop on Rendering*, pages 313–324, June 1994.

10. D. George, F. Sillion, and D. Greenberg. Radiosity redistribution for dynamic environments. *IEEE Computer Graphics and Applications*, 10(4):26–34, July 1990.

11. A. Glassner. Spacetime ray tracing for animation. *IEEE Computer Graphics and Applications*, 8(2):60–70, March 1988.

12. C. Goral, K. Torrance, D. Greenberg, and B. Battaile. Modelling the interaction of light between diffuse surfaces. *Computer Graphics (SIGGRAPH '84 Proceedings)*, 18(3):212–22, July 1984.

13. P. Hanrahan, D. Salzman, and L. Aupperle. A rapid hierarchical radiosity algorithm. *Computer Graphics (SIGGRAPH '91 Proceedings)*, 25(4):197–206, July 1991.

14. J. Kajiya. The rendering equation. *Computer Graphics (SIGGRAPH '85 Proceedings)*, 20(4):143–150, August 1986.

15. Stefan Müller and Frank Schöffel. Fast radiosity repropagation for interactive virtual environments using a shadow-form-factor list. In *5th Annual Eurographics Workshop on Rendering*, pages 325–342, June 13–15 1994.

16. H. Rushmeier, C. Patterson, and A. Veerasamy. Geometric simplification for indirect illumination calculations. In *Proceedings of Graphics Interface '93*. Canadian Information Processing Society, May 1993.

17. F. Sillion, J. Arvo, S. Westin, and D. Greenberg. A global illumination solution for general reflectance distributions. *Computer Graphics (SIGGRAPH '91 Proceedings)*, 25(4):187–196, July 1991.

18. F. Sillion and C. Puech. *Radiosity and Global Illumination.* Morgan Kaufmann Publishers, Inc., San Francisco, CA, 1994.

19. B. Smits, J. Arvo, and D. Salesin. An importance-driven radiosity algorithm. *Computer Graphics (SIGGRAPH '92 Proceedings)*, 26(4):273–282, July 1992.

20. G. Ward. The radiance lighting simulation and rendering system. *Computer Graphics (SIGGRAPH '94 Proceedings)*, 28(4), July 1994.

21. G. Ward, F. Rubinstein, and R. Clear. A ray tracing solution for diffuse interreflection. *Computer Graphics (SIGGRAPH '88 Proceedings)*, 22(4):85–92, August 1988.

Editors' Note: see Appendix, p. 361 for colored figures of this paper

Making global illumination user-friendly

Gregory J. Ward

Lawrence Berkeley Laboratory
1 Cyclotron Rd., 90-3111
Berkeley, CA   94720 USA

ABSTRACT

Global illumination researchers tend to think in terms of mesh density and sampling frequency, and their software reflects this in its user interface. Advanced rendering systems are rife with long command lines and parameters for tuning the sample densities, thresholds and other algorithm-specific variables, and the novice user is quickly lost in a sea of possibilities. This paper details a successful effort of making one such global illumination system usable by people who understand their problems, even if they do not understand the methods needed to solve them, through an assisted oracle approach. A single program is introduced to map a small set of intuitive control variables to the rendering commands and parameter settings needed to produce the desired output in a reasonable time. This new executive program then serves as the basis for a graphical user interface that is both friendly in its appearance and reliable in its performance. Finally, we conclude with some future directions for improving this interface.

1. Introduction

As rendering and especially global illumination techniques advance, the number of user-settable rendering parameters tends to increase. This is because most algorithms have associated sampling rates that are not determined by any basic property of the rendering equation, but are rather a function of the modeled environment and user requirements for output quality. Therefore, the programmer provides the user with parameters to control the calculations so that the best trade-off between time and accuracy can be achieved for a given application.

Such flexibility may be perceived as unwanted complexity by the novice user, and setting the parameters correctly to obtain the best result often requires an intimate understanding of the underlying algorithms. It is little wonder that program authors and their close associates have the most success with advanced rendering software, since they are the only ones who can make it behave properly.

The real difficulty in global illumination is mapping a given set of algorithms to a given problem in an efficient way. Current rendering software is a lot like a box of tools, and if it is not accompanied by the requisite expertise, nothing good can be built from it. What we need to do as system designers is empower the user by supplying the needed expertise along with the tools so that they can build their own house, or museum, or space station, or whatever. Other researchers have suggested this in previous papers and the notion of an *oracle* has been introduced, which is a computational agent that decides what to sample and where in a global illumination calculation [Drettakis91].

Creating robust oracles is a very difficult problem, however, and requires that some limited subset of "common sense" be programmed into these agents. For example, the user may know the geometric detail contained in a model, but a simple count of polygons is usually a poor measure, since it can be thrown off by a relatively smooth surface that is finely tesselated or a small number of polygons all intersecting each other. If the geometric detail is important to the setting of calculation parameters, an oracle will have trouble deciding what to do if it does not have common sense enough to determine the real detail level.

An alternate approach is to analyze what is being computed, and find ways to adjust the calculation automatically to some goal. In the case of synthetic images, we must find an accuracy metric that tells us how far we have to go in our progressive calculation. This can perhaps be done for a Monte Carlo path-tracing simulation, but we still do not have a good handle on what does and does not matter to the user in the resulting image. The metrics we can compute, such as RMS error, have been shown to have little correspondence to quality or correctness as perceived by a human observer. Other metrics, such as those described in [Rushmeier95], are still in the experimental stages. Even if we find and accept a good metric for image quality, we are still left with the problem of mapping our algorithms to progressive approaches that work well with this metric. For example, we may find that geometric shape is very important to human observers. If we are using progressive refinement radiosity, the geometry displayed remains constant, while the illumination changes. No amount of iteration will improve our polygonal model, so we end up refining along the wrong axis for a metric that is sensitive to geometry.

In this paper, we demonstrate an assisted oracle approach, which leans on the user to find out certain common-sense things about the model, then employs a simple set of rules to arrive at the appropriate calculation parameters from this information. The user is allowed general control over things such as "image quality", which loosely translates to visual accuracy, and output resolution, but is freed from having to understand the details of algorithms employed in the calculation. And by relying on the user's common sense, the oracle is freed from having to understand basic things about the real world.

2. Basic Concepts

Although we restrict ourselves in this paper to the context of a specific rendering system, we introduce the following concepts that may be applied readily to other global illumination calculations.

Executive Control Program

> Although toolbox systems provide the greatest flexibility, they are difficult to learn and can be difficult to run even for the experienced user. By introducing an executive program, we simplify the most frequently used

operations by combining them into a single rendering command. Doing the job well, however, requires setting the many parameters of the constituent programs very carefully. Freeing the user of this burden is at least as important as simplifying the running of the software.

Intuitive Control Variables

In order to free the user from having to think in terms of global illumination algorithms and procedures, we must distill a set of intuitive control variables that are both comprehensive and comprehensible. This actually turns out to be much easier than it sounds, though we can offer no foolproof method for mapping common-sense parameters to algorithmic ones. Such mapping requires an expert in the particular rendering software who can code this knowledge into a working program.

Simulation Zones

The simulation zone is a concept we introduce to isolate a specific set of rendering parameters. A zone is a set of simulation conditions that includes a complete scene description, a single lighting condition, and a region of interest (usually a room or an object). Within a zone there may be multiple views specified, but the illumination and other gross scene conditions remain constant. (Small objects may be animated, so long as it does not have a large effect on the lighting.) By focusing on one zone at a time, it is possible to derive a set of reliable rendering parameters.

Graphical User Interface for Rendering

The concept of a GUI for rendering is nothing new, but the design of such an interface usually requires much attention and many trials. We show in this paper how a GUI can be placed on top of an executive control program with very little thought or effort, yielding excellent results. This is because there is a very natural correspondence between the intuitive control variables and the controls of a GUI.

The specific example we explore in this paper is a program called rad, which is a recent addition to the *Radiance* lighting simulation and rendering system [Ward94]. Rad takes a small number of intuitive values and combines this information with some gleanings from the compiled scene description to assign all of the various parameters that control the simulation. We start by enumerating some of these algorithmic parameters and illustrating how difficult they are for the common user to set, then show how we extracted a more intuitive set of control variables. Next, we show how easily these variables can be attached to a GUI. Finally, we discuss the need for a diagnostic tool to troubleshoot problem images, which we leave for future exploration.

3. RADIANCE Calculation Parameters

Table 1 shows an abbreviated list of the program parameters that control the rendering process in *Radiance,* and their default values. The primary author of this software can look at these parameters and understand what they mean and why they are there, and by experience how to set them for various rendering situations. However, the average user looks at these with a very puzzled expression and says, "Well, I guess I could try changing this one or that one to see what happens," and off they go.

Table 1. Rendering algorithm parameters and default values.

Rendering Parameter	Interpretation	Default Value
-pj	pixel jitter	0.67
-ps	pixel sample	4
-pt	pixel threshold	0.05
-dt	direct threshold	0.05
-dc	direct certainty	0.5
-dj	direct jitter	0.0
-ds	direct sampling	0.25
-dr	direct relays	1
-dp	direct pretest density	512
-sj	specular jitter	1.0
-st	specular threshold	0.15
-av	ambient value	0.0 0.0 0.0
-ab	ambient bounces	0
-aa	ambient accuracy	0.2
-ar	ambient resolution	32
-ad	ambient divisions	128
-as	ambient super-samples	0
-lr	limit reflection	6
-lw	limit weight	0.005

Through no fault of their own, the users take what from the programmer's perspective seems like a carefully crafted set of tools, and they start banging on things with them. How could we expect anything different? No one has taught them what these things mean. The manual pages are long and difficult to follow, and the research papers explaining what is behind the command line are even worse. People have been given the tools, but no real guidance in their application. Even the author had to experiment at one time to learn what settings were reasonable and which ones produced good results under specific circumstances; this knowledge is very difficult to impart.

Another stumbling block for new *Radiance* users is that the software is broken into many independent modules, following the UNIX toolbox paradigm. There is no single user interface even on the command line, and users must learn about many different programs before seeing their first image. There are several CAD translators and object generator programs to assist in scene creation. There is a program to compile the scene description, and one to render the scene into an unfiltered image, and one to reduce the image and perform anti-aliasing, and conversion and display programs to put the image in a common format or display it on the monitor. Unless the user's mind works like the programmer's, mastering the intricacies of *Radiance* seems more tedious and painful than intuitive.

Our first goal in developing a user interface to this software is to replace the tedium and confusion with simplicity and clarity. We do this by unifying the operation of the software and replacing the nasty algorithm-derived parameters with more intuitive variables based on common sense. A single command taking a short input file (less than 1K, typically) can control the core rendering modules of *Radiance* and put them into a consistent, logical interface. Next, we can put a GUI on top of this new executive program so that the user does not even have to think about what to type, and we can hook in other functionality that is difficult to handle in a single command line program.

4. RAD Control Variables

The key to designing a good user-assisted oracle is finding a minimal set of intuitive control variables that tells us exactly what we need to know from the user in order to run the software efficiently. The purpose is to minimize the number of decisions the user has to make for the majority of cases. The number of control variables must be small, and the possible values for these variables must also be small or arbitrary. (I.e. if a value is irrelevant to the calculation, such as the output file name, the user is given freedom to make arbitrary assignments. If a value affects the calculation, however, the user may be restricted to a choice of "high," "medium" or "low" rather than some numeric value.) We may keep the idea of default values around, but we want the user to feel comfortable changing these settings at will. To arrive at appropriate variables for a good user-assisted oracle, we must ask ourselves two questions:

1. What does the user wish to control?

2. What additional information do we require from the user to perform the simulation?

In answer to the first question, most users want to control the time versus quality tradeoff. They also want to control the views from which the renderings take place, and probably the size and resolution of the output. After that, the typical user is just not very interested in the rendering process.

Unfortunately, the oracle in rad is not smart enough to figure out the rest on its own, so we still need the user to give us some additional clues to enable us to do a good job rendering the scene in a reasonable time. Obviously, we need to know input file name(s). Rad also asks for intermediate and output file names, though these will be assigned default values if none are given. Since we are going to maintain a compiled version of the scene, we also need to know what other files the scene depends on, similar to the information required by the UNIX make facility.

Once the file information is settled, rad needs to know a little bit about the scene geometry and lighting for the specific area being rendered, which we call a *zone*. It was decided early on that a given set of variable settings should apply to just one zone, since the geometry and lighting could vary too much from inside to outside or even one room to another in a large model. Dividing the rendering task into zones greatly simplifies the job of setting rendering parameters in *Radiance,* which depend on geometric complexity and lighting variability.

A zone is specified by type, interior or exterior, and dimensions. Rad uses a 3-dimensional, axis-aligned box in its zone specification, though the precise boundaries are of little importance. The primary information derived from the zone is a relative "scale" for rendering parameters. The scale simply tells us the distance at which lighting ceases much to matter. This information is extracted from the overall size of the zone plus the geometric detail as specified in a separate variable. Secondarily, a zone provides a convenient mechanism for establishing default viewpoints to get the user started looking at their environment.

Table 2. Rad control variables and default values.

Variable	Interpretation	Type	Default Value
materials	materials file(s)	string	-
scene	scene file(s)	string	-
illum	illum object file(s)	string	-
objects	requisite file(s)	string	-
view	image view(s)	string	X (from maximum X)
UP	view up vector	string	- (effectively +Z)
QUALITY	target image quality	qualitative	Low
RESOLUTION	output image resolution	integer	512
PICTURE	output file root	string	input file root
OCTREE	octree (compiled scene) file	string	input file root + .oct
AMBFILE	ambient value file	string	-
OPTFILE	options file	string	-
REPORT	report interval and file	string	-
ZONE	region of interest	string	bounding cube, ext.
EXPOSURE	image exposure	real	- (automatic)
PENUMBRAS	penumbras important?	boolean	False
DETAIL	geometric detail	qualitative	Medium
INDIRECT	# important interreflections	integer	0
VARIABILITY	variation in illumination	qualitative	Low
oconv	oconv options	string	-
mkillum	mkillum options	string	-
render	rendering options	string	-
pfilt	pfilt options	string	-

Four additional variables are used to assess the difficulty of the lighting calculation for the given zone. These are the lighting variability, the number of indirect reflections, and the image exposure. Variability is a qualitative setting that indicates how much light levels vary in the zone, i.e. the dynamic range of light landing on surfaces. This is important for controlling the number of rays used in sampling indirect lighting. A second variable tells rad how many diffuse reflections are critical to the lighting of a space. If a direct lighting system is used, this is set to 0. For an indirect fluorescent system, it is set to 1. For some daylight shelf systems, the setting may be 2. A third variable tells rad what multiplier to use for exposing the final images. This can be done automatically, but the results are usually not as good, and rad uses this value also to set the "ambient level" for the zone, which is a function of the final light levels and therefore cannot be determined in advance except for very simple, closed environments. Finally, a fourth variable indicates whether or not rendering penumbras is important in this zone. Turning penumbras off does not mean that area sources are treated as points; it only means that the quality of soft shadows is less important than rendering time in this model.

You might at this point be wondering why *rad* could not somehow figure out all this additional stuff and not bother the user about it? In principle, it could. This is the idea behind an "oracle" as recalled in the introduction. Unfortunately, writing omniscient oracles requires the kind of common sense reasoning that is easy for people familiar with a given environment, but difficult for computers. By the nature of the situation being modeled, the user *knows* whether to expect a high degree of variability in the lighting or a low one. Figuring this out automatically requires actually rendering the space at some level of detail, and thus solving the problem in order to begin. It may be possible to do this iteratively, but it is more complicated, takes longer and the result is no more reliable than asking the user. The question we have to ask when designing an interface is, "What can be done for the user in a way that is more pleasant than it is aggravating?" An interface that takes twenty minutes to come up with a default parameter setting is just plain annoying. As it is, rad already derives some information from the scene files, which may take several seconds to process if the scene has not already been compiled.

Table 2 shows a list of the rad variables, interpretation, type and default values. Lower case variables may have multiple settings, which are usually just concatenated together. Upper case variables may have only one valid setting.

Variables above the horizontal division are considered user control settings. In addition to the control of input files, views, image quality and output resolution, the user may set intermediate and output file names.

Variables below the horizontal division are considered program help settings, i.e. things that rad asks the user in order to determine what rendering parameters will work for this environment. These are the zone, detail, variability, indirect, exposure and penumbra settings we spoke of earlier. As a back door for expert users, variables are also provided for adding or overriding options to specific *Radiance* modules.

5. What Does RAD Do?

Once rad gets all this information, what does it do, exactly? Well, it depends on how it is invoked, but the usual action is as follows:

1. Compute default values for unspecified variables.

2. Derive rendering and filtering module parameters.

3. Recompile scene if necessary.

4. Render and filter each view.

Steps 1 and 2 are always carried out. Step 3 usually follows, unless "no action" is specified. Step 4 includes such subtleties as recovering aborted renderings, and may be replaced by an interactive or batch rendering of a single view if desired. Other options control what is printed on the standard output, if anything. (The default is to print each command as it is executed.) There is also a "touch" option for bringing file times up to date without actually doing anything, which is sometimes handy for avoiding overreactions to small changes.

To give an example of using rad on a real rendering problem, Listing 1a shows a typical rad input file, and Listing 1b shows the default values for unassigned variables as computed in Step 1. Listing 2 shows the commands executed by rad with their parameters.

How was the transformation of Listing 1 into Listing 2 accomplished by rad? Without going into detail, there are three separate procedures for Step 2, corresponding to the three possible settings of the *QUALITY* variable, Low, Medium and High. The Low procedure makes every possible compromise in

```
mat= iesroom.mat
scene= iesroom.rad extras.rad
scene= ceilingA.rad taskC.rad windows.rad
obj= terminal.rad typeA.rad typeA_cross.rad
ZONE= I  0 15  0 20  0 10
AMB= ver1.amb
VAR= Low
EXP= 1
QUA= Med
PEN= True
RES= 640 480
view= west -vf west.vp
view= efish -vf efish.vp
```

Listing 1a. Example <u>rad</u> input file, "ver1.rif".

```
OCTREE= ver1.oct
PICTURE= ver1
INDIRECT= 0
DETAIL= Medium
```

Listing 1b. Computed default values for unassigned <u>rad</u> variables.

```
oconv iesroom.mat iesroom.rad extras.rad ceilingA.rad taskC.rad
    windows.rad > ver1.oct
rpict -vf west.vp -x 1280 -y 960 -ps 3 -pt .08 -dp 512 -ar 22 -ds .2 -dj .5
    -dt .1 -dc .5 -dr 1 -sj .7 -st .1 -af ver1.amb -aa .25 -ad 196
    -as 0 -av 0.5 0.5 0.5 -lr 6 -lw .002 ver1.oct > ver1_west.raw
pfilt -1 -e 1 -r 1 -x /2 -y /2 ver1_west.raw > ver1_west.pic
rm -f ver1_west.raw
rpict -vf efish.vp -x 1280 -y 960 -ps 3 -pt .08 -dp 512 -ar 22 -ds .2 -dj .5
    -dt .1 -dc .5 -dr 1 -sj .7 -st .1 -af ver1.amb -aa .25 -ad 196
    -as 0 -av 0.5 0.5 0.5 -lr 6 -lw .002 ver1.oct > ver1_efish.raw
pfilt -1 -e 1 -r 1 -x /2 -y /2 ver1_efish.raw > ver1_efish.pic
rm -f ver1_efish.raw
```

Listing 2. *Radiance* commands executed by <u>rad</u>.

quality to achieve the fastest rendering times. This setting is best used for looking at geometry and picking views. The Medium procedure tries to do a reasonable job without taking too long. This setting is OK for work in progress where accuracy is not critical. The High procedure turns up parameters as necessary to achieve good quality results, even if the calculation will be slow. This setting is appropriate for presentation or publication images.

There is very little point in describing these routines in any detail, since they are specific to this system and these algorithms. What is significant is that these three short routines embody much of the author's knowledge about *Radiance* rendering and what works best in a given situation. As awkward as they may look, they are a form of expert knowledge, and it would have been impossible to write them without years of experience using this software. Initially, it seemed that coding this knowledge would be impossible, but it turned out instead to be cathartic.

```
rpict -vf west.vp -x 1280 -y 960 -ps 2 -pt .08 -dp 1024 -ar 45 -ds .2 -dj .5
    -dt .1 -dc .5 -dr 1 -sj .7 -st .1 -af ver1.amb -aa .25 -ad 196
    -as 0 -av 0.5 0.5 0.5 -lr 6 -lw .002 ver1.oct > ver1_west.raw
```

Listing 3. Rendering command after increasing *DETAIL* to "High".

It is fun to change one of the rad variables to see how it affects the rendering parameters. Since entirely different procedures are used for the three quality settings, changing this variable obviously has the biggest effect. Let us look instead at what happens when we change a minor variable such as the *DETAIL* setting. We will take it from the default setting of "Medium" to "High". Listing 3 shows the first rpict command with its new options. Note how only a few of the parameters change: the pixel sampling density (-ps), the direct presampling density (-dp), and the ambient resolution (-ar). It would have taken a *Radiance* expert to figure out which options to change and which to leave alone, but with rad, we only had to know that our scene is now more detailed.

Through this kind of experimentation, it is even possible for the user to gain some knowledge about the *Radiance* parameters without having to waste hours on bad renderings.

6. Putting a Graphical User Interface on RAD

Now that we have a user-friendly command line interface, we would like to take it one step further and provide a GUI for *Radiance* rendering. This turns out to be both easy and hard. It is easy in the sense that there are nice tools for building GUI's such as Tcl/Tk [Ousterhout94], which do most of the work for you. It is hard in the sense that takes about 50 Kbytes of interface code and another 50 Kbytes of help screens for an interface that manipulates about 1 Kbyte of rad control data. Fortunately, developing a GUI also allows us to add some functionality that we could not include in a single command line, such as image display and conversion. In the future, we may hook other tools to the interface as well; thus it may serve as a central point for running the entire software suite.

The current rad interface, called trad, is broken into seven interactive screens, which group functions into convenient categories. Table 3 lists the screen names, their functions, and which rad variables they may modify. Figure 1 shows a typical trad screen. The mode buttons are arranged in a constant area of the interface along the right hand side, together with HELP and QUIT buttons. A second constant area along the bottom is used for messages. The rest of the interface will change depending on which mode (screen) is selected. In the screen shown, the user has the option of changing the *ZONE* type and limits, the *DETAIL, INDIRECT,* and *VARIABILITY* settings, and the *EXPOSURE* value. All of these variables give details needed by rad to efficiently render a particular zone, thus they are logically grouped together. The "Copy" and "Revert" buttons in the lower right of the Zone screen may be used to selectively load the variables on this screen from another rad input file, or to return to the original settings from this file, respectively. These buttons are quite useful, and they appear on all of the trad screens that affect rad variables.

Table 3. <u>Trad</u> screens and functions.

Screen	Function	Modifies
File	Load/save Rad Input Files	All
Scene	Specify input files	OCTREE, materials, illum, scene, objects
Zone	Edit zone-related variables	ZONE, DETAIL, INDIRECT, VARIABILITY, EXPOSURE
Views	Edit views	view, UP, PICTURE, RESOLUTION
Options	Edit rendering options	QUALITY, PENUMBRAS, AMBFILE, OPTFILE, REPORT, oconv, mkillum, render, pfilt
Action	Start interactive or batch rendering	None
Results	Display/convert/print images	None

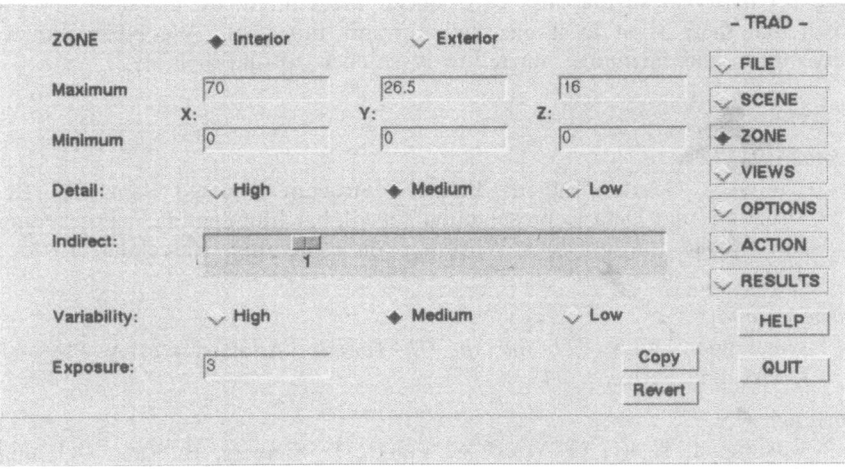

Figure 1. <u>Trad</u> Zone screen, one of seven such screens determined by the mode button selected on the right.

Context-sensitive help is provided through a help facility by control-clicking on any of the <u>trad</u> buttons or windows. It is assumed that the user has a working knowledge of *Radiance* and especially <u>rad,</u> but the GUI itself can be learned very quickly by calling on help whenever something is not understood.

7. Conclusion and Future Work

We have presented a user-friendly approach to rendering with advanced global illumination algorithms, and demonstrated the concept of a user-assisted oracle for setting calculation parameters. The system described works well and is accepted by even the most skeptical users once they give it a try. Even the author of the *Radiance* package prefers the new control program to the old manual method of rendering via pipes and monster command lines.

Future work shall continue in two areas. First, the GUI shall be linked to additional tools, such as CAD programs and translators on the input side and analysis tools on the output side. Second, a picture diagnostic tool shall be created to provide additional expertise in correcting problem renderings.

Even with the user-assisted oracle in rad, there are occasions when the rendering output is less than satisfactory, and the average user may have difficulty correcting such problems without deeper understanding of what can go wrong. A diagnostic tool would help the user to identify the nature of the problem with comparisons to other pictures with the same artifacts. The tool would then suggest or implement changes to the rad input file to correct these problems. This returns us to the iterative, trial and error approach we sought to avoid with our interface in the first place, but it should only be needed in exceptional cases, and rerendering with some intelligent changes is better than giving up or living with bad output.

Designing a good user interface to advanced rendering algorithms is not as simple as deciding what color buttons look best. It really requires an expert to sit down and codify the knowledge that permits him or her to create beautiful output with a given set of tools, so that less experienced users might do the same. We have shown that there is at least one path towards this goal. We believe there are many others, and encourage our fellow researchers to find them.

References

[Drettakis91]
>
> Drettakis, George, Eugene Fiume, "Structure-Directed Sampling, Reconstruction, and Data Representation for Global Illumination," Proceedings of the Second Eurographics Workshop on Rendering, Barcelona, 13-15 May 1991.

[Ousterhout94]
>
> Ousterhout, John, *Tcl and the Tk Toolkit*, Addison-Wesley Professional Computing Series, 1994.

[Rushmeier95]
>
> Rushmeier, Holly, G. Ward, C. Piatko, P. Sanders, B. Rust, "Comparing Real and Synthetic Images: Some Ideas About Metrics," submitted to the Sixth Eurographics Workshop on Rendering, Dublin, Ireland, June 1995.

[Ward94]
>
> Ward, Gregory, "The RADIANCE Lighting Simulation and Rendering System," *Computer Graphics*, July 1994.

The Role of Functional Analysis in Global Illumination

James Arvo

Program of Computer Graphics
Cornell University
Ithaca, NY 14853

Abstract: The problem of global illumination is virtually synonymous with solving the rendering equation. Although a great deal of research has been directed toward Monte Carlo and finite element methods for solving the rendering equation, little is known about the continuous equation beyond the existence and uniqueness of its solution. The continuous problem may be posed in terms of linear operators acting on infinite-dimensional function spaces. Such operators are fundamentally different from their finite-dimensional counterparts, and are properly studied using the methods of functional analysis. This paper summarizes some of the basic concepts of functional analysis and shows how these concepts may be applied to a linear operator formulation of the rendering equation. In particular, operator norms are obtained from thermodynamic principles, and a number of common function spaces are shown to be closed under global illumination. Finally, several fundamental operators that arise in global illumination are shown to be nearly finite-dimensional in that they can be uniformly approximated by matrices.

1 Introduction

The rendering equation has served to codify the study of global illumination since its introduction by Kajiya in 1986 [12]. Methods for the construction and solution of discrete versions of the rendering equation have been studied extensively; however, the continuous equation and its solution have received relatively little attention. This emphasis is somewhat justified given that digital computation rests upon finite representations; even though a solution exists within an infinite-dimensional function space, its approximation must be representable by a finite machine in finite time. Nevertheless, the fidelity of the finite-dimensional approximation can only be fully understood in the context of the infinite-dimensional problem.

A natural way to approach the infinite-dimensional problem is through the formalism of functional analysis. Functional analysis is the study of algebraic and topological properties of abstract spaces, particularly infinite-dimensional spaces of functions and operators that transform them. This level of abstraction can provide valuable insight by characterizing both the operators and the solutions of operator equations, and is particularly well-suited to the study of integral equations.

The techniques of functional analysis draw upon measure theory and topology. Measure theory provides the basis for integration while topology formalizes the notions of "closeness" and "convergence" that underlie all of analysis. These concepts are extremely general and extend to infinite-dimensional spaces, where familiar notions of Euclidean space often break down. For example, a linear operator on an infinite-dimensional space may be discontinuous, which is impossible in $\mathbb{R}^n$. Also, different norms on these spaces need not be equivalent; that is, a sequence may converge with respect to one norm, but not another. In more abstract terms, this means that different norms can induce different topologies. As a final example, the spectrum of an infinite-dimensional linear operator is generally more complex than that of a matrix.

The remainder of the paper is a brief exploration of these concepts and a set of guideposts for applying them in the context of global illumination. Pointers into the relevant literature are provided for those who wish to learn more.

2 The Classical Transport Equation

Equations governing the transport of radiant energy have appeared in astrophysics [5], thermal engineering [22], and illumination engineering [16]. For global illumination the governing equation may be expressed in terms of an unknown *surface radiance* function f resulting from a source term f_0. In continuous form, the governing equation is

$$f(\mathbf{r}, \mathbf{u}) = f_0(\mathbf{r}, \mathbf{u}) + \int_{\Omega_i} k(\mathbf{r}; \mathbf{u}' \to \mathbf{u}) \, f(\mathbf{r}', \mathbf{u}') \, d\mu(\mathbf{u}'), \tag{1}$$

where Ω_i denotes the hemisphere of incoming directions with respect to the surface point $\mathbf{r}$, and $d\mu$ denotes cosine-weighted integration over directions. The kernel k is the bidirectional reflectance distribution function expressed in terms of global coordinates, and $\mathbf{r}'$ is the point that is visible to $\mathbf{r}$ in the direction $-\mathbf{u}'$. Equation (1) is essentially the formulation posed by Polyak [17] in thermal engineering, which can be used to derive Kajiya's rendering equation by a change of variables.

Equation (1) is often referred to as a Fredholm integral equation of the second kind although it has several features that do not conform to the standard definition. First, the integral for a given point $\mathbf{r}$ does not depend on the entire domain of f, but only a vanishingly small subset; a difference that disappears when one considers only radiosity. Secondly, $\mathbf{r}'$ is an implicit function that depends on the argument $\mathbf{r}$ and the dummy variable $\mathbf{u}'$. This seemingly minor difference is responsible for the most important distinguishing feature of radiative transfer problems; the non-localness of the interactions. However, this property is difficult to work with as it appears above.

To precisely define the implicit function $\mathbf{r}'$ we introduce two intermediate functions. First, let $\mathcal{M}$ denote the collection of all surfaces in an environment, and define the *visible-surface function* $\nu(\mathbf{r}, \mathbf{u})$ by

$$\nu(\mathbf{r}, \mathbf{u}) \equiv \inf \{x > 0 : \mathbf{r} + x\mathbf{u} \in \mathcal{M}\},$$

where "inf" means greatest lower bound. This function returns the distance from $\mathbf{r}$ to the nearest point on $\mathcal{M}$ in the direction of $\mathbf{u}$ (Glassner [9] gives a similar definition). If no such point exists, we define $\nu(\mathbf{r}, \mathbf{u}) = \infty$. We then define the *ray casting function* by

$$\mathbf{p}(\mathbf{r}, \mathbf{u}) \equiv \mathbf{r} + \nu(\mathbf{r}, \mathbf{u})\mathbf{u},$$

which is the point of intersection with $\mathcal{M}$ when one exists; the function is undefined otherwise. It follows that $\mathbf{r}'(\mathbf{r}, \mathbf{u}) \equiv \mathbf{p}(\mathbf{r}, -\mathbf{u})$. This function will also be useful in recasting equation (1) into operator form.

3 Function Spaces

The formal study of equation (1) must include a characterization of the class of admissible functions for f_0. Let X denote a vector space of real-valued surface radiance functions defined on $\mathcal{M} \times S^2$, where S^2 is the unit sphere. For purposes of analysis, the space X must have additional structure; minimally, it must have a *topology*, which defines open sets or *neighborhoods* of functions [20]. Here we shall only consider the *metric topologies* that are an automatic consequence of a norm defined on the space. Infinitely many norms can be defined on the space of radiance functions, each inducing a different topology and each providing a different notion of size, distance, and convergence.

A second useful feature for the space X is that of *completeness*. For a normed space, completeness means that all *Cauchy sequences* converge. That is, if $f_1, f_2, \ldots$ is a sequence of functions in X such that

$$\lim_{n,m \to \infty} \| f_n - f_m \| = 0,$$

then there exists a function $f \in X$ that the sequence converges to. Since the Cauchy sequence makes no reference to the limit point itself, this definition is an intrinsic property of the space X; it ensures that every function that can be approximated by elements of the space is itself in the space. A vector space that is complete with respect to a given norm is called a *Banach space* [25, 15].

3.1 Measures and Lebesgue Integration

A *measure* is mechanism for generalizing the notion of area or volume to abstract sets. A measure is a countably additive positive set function; that is, if m is a measure over a set S, then $0 \leq m(A_1 \cup A_2 \cup \cdots) = m(A_1) + m(A_2) + \cdots$ whenever the sets $A_1, A_2, \ldots$ are mutually disjoint subsets of S. We shall let σ denote the canonical measure on the sphere [3, p. 276]; that is, $\sigma(A)$ is the surface area of any (measurable) subset $A \subset S^2$.

The Lebesgue integral is based upon the concept of measure and is commonly denoted as in equation (1), where $d\mu(\mathbf{u}')$[1] signifies both the measure μ and the dummy variable $\mathbf{u}'$ The Lebesgue integral is an appropriate abstraction for functional analysis, where the emphasis is on integrals as transformations rather than the numerical aspects of integration. While the simpler concept of the Riemann integral is equivalent when it exists, the Lebesgue integral is more robust with respect to limiting operations, which makes it a valuable tool for defining abstract spaces such as Banach spaces [21].

The measure-theoretic notation used in (1) also allows us to introduce the convenient measure μ that incorporates a cosine weighting. Formally, the measure μ is defined by

$$\mu(E) \equiv \int_E |\mathbf{u} \cdot \mathbf{n}(\mathbf{r})| \, d\sigma(\mathbf{u}), \tag{2}$$

where $E \subset S^2$ and $\mathbf{n}(\mathbf{r})$ is the surface normal at the point $\mathbf{r} \in \mathcal{M}$; thus, μ implicitly depends on $\mathbf{r}$. Equation (2) shows how one measure may be defined in terms of another. The new measure μ eliminates the proliferation of cosine factors that appear in radiative

---

[1] This notation differs among authors. Alternatives include $d\mu$ [20, p. 20] and $\mu(d\mathbf{u}')$ [7, p. 95].

transfer computations, but more importantly, it emphasizes that the cosine is an artifact of surface integration. This observation is vital in defining appropriate norms and inner products for radiance functions.

3.2 The L_p Spaces

The Lebesgue integral provides a mechanism for defining a family of fundamental function spaces called *Lebesgue spaces* or L_p-spaces [20, p. 66]. These spaces are defined in terms of the L_p-norms, which for radiance functions are given by

$$\| f \|_p \equiv \left[\int_{\mathcal{M}} \int_{\mathcal{S}^2} | f(\mathbf{r}, \mathbf{u}) |^p \, d\mu(\mathbf{u}) \, dm(\mathbf{r}) \right]^{1/p}, \qquad (3)$$

where m denotes area measure over $\mathcal{M}$, and $1 \leq p \leq \infty$ is a real number[2]. The collection of functions with finite L_p-norm is denoted by $L_p(\mu \times m)$, or simply by L_p is the measure is clear from context. Each L_p-space is a Banach space because the limit of L_p functions is again in L_p. The L_1-norm of a radiance function f is its power, and therefore carries the corresponding units [watts].

As p approaches infinity, the L_p-norm places greater emphasis on the largest values attained by the function. In the limit, when $p = \infty$, the L_p-norm becomes

$$\| f \|_\infty \equiv \operatorname*{ess\,sup}_{\mathbf{r} \in \mathcal{M}} \ \operatorname*{ess\,sup}_{\mathbf{u} \in \mathcal{S}^2} \ | f(\mathbf{r}, \mathbf{u}) |, \qquad (4)$$

where "ess sup" is the *essential supremum*, the least upper bound obtainable by ignoring a subset of measure zero. More formally, if h is a real function defined on a set A, then

$$\operatorname*{ess\,sup}_{x \in A} h(x) \equiv \inf \{ m \mid h(x) \leq m \ \text{for almost every} \ x \in A \}, \qquad (5)$$

where "almost" means to within a set of measure zero [25]. The essential supremum corresponds to the notion of maximum, but with two important differences. First, it is the *least upper bound*, or *infimum*, which exists for all bounded subsets of $\mathbb{R}$. Secondly, it is unaffected by values that cannot contribute to the integral of the function; this includes values assumed at isolated points or over sets of measure zero, such as curves in $\mathbb{R}^2$.

The L_∞-norm also has a direct interpretation; it is the maximum radiance attained or approached over all surfaces and directions; it follows that its units are those of radiance [watts/m^{2}sr]. Finally, the L_2-norm is important since it has additional algebraic properties that make it a Hilbert space, as described in the next section.

3.3 The Hilbert Space L_2

A *Hilbert space* $\mathcal{H}$ is a Banach space whose norm is defined in terms of an inner product $\langle \cdot \mid \cdot \rangle$ defined on $\mathcal{H} \times \mathcal{H}$ [15]. More precisely, the norm $\| \cdot \|$ is defined by

$$\| x \| \equiv \sqrt{\langle x \mid x \rangle}, \qquad (6)$$

---

[2] The definition is also meaningful for $p < 1$, but these norms are not *strictly convex* and are often excluded [14].

where $x \in \mathcal{H}$. Not every Banach space is a Hilbert space. Equation (6) imbues the norm and the entire space with many useful properties that a general Banach space does not enjoy: for example, the concept of orthogonality is given meaning, and every continuous linear functional (scalar-valued function) h defined on $\mathcal{H}$ can be represented by an inner product; that is, $h(x) = \langle x \mid y \rangle$ for some $y \in \mathcal{H}$.

While L_1 and L_∞ are useful Banach spaces, their norms are not compatible with any inner product, and therefore they are not Hilbert spaces. This fact is easily demonstrated using a clever observation attributed to John von Neumann. The observation is that the *parallelogram law*

$$\| f - g \|^2 + \| f + g \|^2 \;=\; 2 \| f \|^2 \;+\; 2 \| g \|^2 \qquad (7)$$

is satisfied for all f and g in a Banach space if and only if it is also a Hilbert space [18, p. 27]. This is easy to verify using equation (6) and the bilinearity of inner products. However, equation (7) is violated by both the L_1-norm and the L_∞-norm; for instance, simply let f and g be disjoint unit step-functions.

The space L_2, on the other hand, is a Hilbert space with the inner product

$$\langle f \mid g \rangle \equiv \int_{\mathcal{M}} \int_{\mathcal{S}^2} f(\mathbf{r}, \mathbf{u}) \, g(\mathbf{r}, \mathbf{u}) \, d\mu(\mathbf{u}) \, dm(\mathbf{r}). \qquad (8)$$

In fact, the space L_2 is the only L_p-space that is also a Hilbert space. This can be shown by observing that L_p is isomorphic to its own *dual space* [15, p. 106] only when $p = 2$; this is a feature of all Hilbert spaces.

The distinction between a Banach space and a Hilbert space can be important in global illumination; for example, Galerkin-based methods [26] depend in orthogonal projections, which are only meaningful in a Hilbert space.

4 Linear Operators

A function whose domain is a function space such as L_p is commonly referred to as *operator*. Since all of the L_p-spaces are infinite-dimensional for typical measures, we often speak of the operators defined on them as being infinite-dimensional as well. Common infinite-dimensional linear operators include *integral* or *differential* operators, *projection* operators, and the *multiplication* operator defined by

$$(\mathbf{M}_g f)(x) \;\equiv\; f(x)\, g(x), \qquad (9)$$

where g is some function. An operator is finite-dimensional, or *degenerate*, only if its range is finite-dimensional. An important type of degenerate operator is one that projects onto a subspace spanned by a finite number of basis functions.

The collection of linear operators that map one function space into another is itself a vector space under pointwise addition and scalar multiplication. Such a vector space can be made into a Banach space by imposing a norm. For instance, the standard *operator norm* corresponding to a given function norm $\| \cdot \|$ is defined by

$$\| \mathbf{A} \| \equiv \inf \{ m \;:\; \| \mathbf{A} h \| \leq m \| h \| \text{ for all } h \}. \qquad (10)$$

Operator equations are a generalization of integral equations in which the essential algebraic properties such as linearity and associativity are preserved, while less important details of the operators are hidden. Operator equations were first applied in global illumination by Kajiya [12], where they were used to show the existence and uniqueness of solutions to the rendering equation.

4.1 Features of Infinite-Dimensional Operators

Linear operators can possess properties that do not occur in their finite-dimensional counterparts, which correspond to matrices. For example, a linear operator may be *unbounded*; that is, it may have infinite norm. The simplest example of such an operator is the point-evaluation functional $\phi_x(f) = f(x)$, which is unbounded on all L_p-spaces. Also, most differential operators are unbounded on spaces of differentiable functions. For linear operators, unboundedness is synonymous with being discontinuous.

Another fundamental difference appears in the *spectrum* of an infinite-dimensional operator. Although spectral analysis has not yet been applied to global illumination, it illustrates another way in which infinite-dimensional operators differ from matrices. For any scalar value λ, we define the *resolvent operator* of $\mathbf{T}$ by

$$\mathbf{R}_\lambda(\mathbf{T}) \equiv (\mathbf{T} - \lambda\mathbf{I})^{-1}. \tag{11}$$

The *spectrum* of $\mathbf{T}$ consists of all the points λ in the complex plane for which $\mathbf{R}_\lambda$ fails to be a bounded linear operator [14]. For instance, $\mathbf{T} - \lambda\mathbf{I}$ may have a non-trivial *nullspace*, which means that there exists a vector $x \neq 0$ such that

$$(\mathbf{T} - \lambda\mathbf{I}) x = 0. \tag{12}$$

In this case the resolvent operator $\mathbf{R}_\lambda$ does not exist since $\mathbf{T} - \lambda\mathbf{I}$ cannot be inverted. The value λ is called an *eigenvalue* of $\mathbf{T}$ and the corresponding x is called an *eigenvector*, or an *eigenfunction* when x is a function. In a finite-dimensional space the eigenvalues are the only values at which the resolvent operator $\mathbf{R}_\lambda$ goes awry. In infinite-dimensional spaces, however, there are other possibilities. For example, the resolvent operator may exist but fail to be bounded. The collection of all values at which this occurs is called the *continuous spectrum* of $\mathbf{T}$. As we shall see, many operators associated with global illumination cannot exhibit this feature, which gives them a greater resemblance to matrices.

4.2 Linear Operators for Global Illumination

The classical governing equation can be concisely expressed as a linear operator equation [12, 11, 6, 1]. We shall use a very general formulation [1] similar to that proposed by Gershbein et al. [8]. We first define the *local reflection operator* $\mathbf{K}$ by

$$(\mathbf{K}h)(\mathbf{r}, \mathbf{u}) \equiv \int_{\Omega_i} k(\mathbf{r}; \mathbf{u}' \to \mathbf{u}) \, h(\mathbf{r}, \mathbf{u}') \, d\mu(\mathbf{u}'). \tag{13}$$

which accounts for the scattering of incident radiant energy. Here h is a *field radiance function*, that is, a radiance function corresponding to all incident light, which is distinct from irradiance. The **K** operator maps the field radiance function h to the corresponding surface radiance function after one *local* reflection. The symbol for this operator is a mnemonic for "kernel".

Next, we define the *field radiance operator* **G** that expresses the field radiance at each point of $\mathcal{M}$ in terms of the surface radiance of surrounding visible surfaces. Thus,

$$(\mathbf{G}h)(\mathbf{r}, \mathbf{u}) \equiv \begin{cases} h(\mathbf{p}(\mathbf{r}, -\mathbf{u}), \mathbf{u}) & \text{when } \nu(\mathbf{r}, \mathbf{u}) < \infty \\ 0 & \text{otherwise,} \end{cases} \tag{14}$$

where h is a surface radiance function. The **G** operator expresses the transport of radiant energy from surface to surface as a linear transformation on the space of surface radiance functions. The symbol chosen for this operator is intended as a mnemonic for "global" or "geometry". Defining **G** in this way allows us to factor out the implicit function $\mathbf{r}'(\mathbf{r}, \mathbf{u})$ from the integral in equation (1). In terms of these operators, we may write

$$f = f_0 + \mathbf{KG} f. \tag{15}$$

This formulation retains the full generality of equation (1), but is frequently more amenable to analysis. Since the operators express the process of energy transfer, they are subject to various thermodynamic constraints. We next show how these constraints allow us to compute the operator norms.

4.3 The L_1-norm of K

We compute the operator norm $\|\mathbf{K}\|_1$ in two steps: first, we produce an upper bound, and then show that the bound is attained. We begin by considering the function norm $\|\mathbf{K}f\|_1$ for an arbitrary function $f \in L_1(\mu \times m)$ and obtain a bound in terms of $\|f\|_1$ and a new expression, which will be shown to be $\|\mathbf{K}\|_1$. Since all quantities are positive, absolute value signs may be dropped. If f is a field radiance function, then

$$\|\mathbf{K}f\|_1 = \int_{\mathcal{M}} \int_{\Omega_o} \int_{\Omega_i} k(\mathbf{r}; \mathbf{u}' \to \mathbf{u}) \, f(\mathbf{r}, \mathbf{u}') \, d\mu(\mathbf{u}') \, d\mu(\mathbf{u}) \, dm(\mathbf{r})$$

$$= \int_{\mathcal{M}} \int_{\Omega_i} \int_{\Omega_o} k(\mathbf{r}; \mathbf{u}' \to \mathbf{u}) \, f(\mathbf{r}, \mathbf{u}') \, d\mu(\mathbf{u}) \, d\mu(\mathbf{u}') \, dm(\mathbf{r})$$

$$= \int_{\mathcal{M}} \int_{\Omega_i} f(\mathbf{r}, \mathbf{u}') \left[\int_{\Omega_o} k(\mathbf{r}; \mathbf{u}' \to \mathbf{u}) \, d\mu(\mathbf{u}) \right] d\mu(\mathbf{u}') \, dm(\mathbf{r}),$$

where the first equality follows from the definitions of **K** and the L_1-norm. The second equality holds by Fubini's theorem [20, p. 164], which states that the order of integration can be changed when the integral exists and is finite. In the final equality, we have isolated the kernel of the integral operator **K** to the extent possible. Next, we define the constant ω by

$$\omega \equiv \operatorname*{ess\,sup}_{\mathbf{r} \in \mathcal{M}} \operatorname*{ess\,sup}_{\mathbf{u}' \in \Omega_i} \int_{\Omega_o} k(\mathbf{r}; \mathbf{u}' \to \mathbf{u}) \, d\mu(\mathbf{u}), \tag{16}$$

which is independent of the function f. Since this quantity bounds the effect of the bracketed expression on the outer double integral above, we have

$$\| \mathbf{K}f \|_1 \leq \omega \int_\mathcal{M} \int_{\Omega_i} f(\mathbf{r}, \mathbf{u}') \, d\mu(\mathbf{u}') \, dm(\mathbf{r}) = \omega \| f \|_1, \qquad (17)$$

which shows that ω is an *upper bound* on $\| \mathbf{K} \|_1$. To show that it is a lower bound as well we must demonstrate that this bound is either attained by some function f, or approached from below by a sequence of functions. We can accomplish the latter by a sequence of beams that approach perfect collimation about the incident direction $\mathbf{u}'$ in which

$$\int_{\Omega_o} k(\mathbf{r}; \mathbf{u}' \to \mathbf{u}) \, d\mu(\mathbf{u}) \qquad (18)$$

is maximal. If this maximum is not attained, but rather approached as the incident beam approaches grazing, for example, then we let the sequence $f_1, f_2, \ldots$ approach perfect collimation while simultaneously approaching grazing. From this it follows that ω is also a *lower bound* on $\| \mathbf{K} \|_1$. Therefore,

$$\| \mathbf{K} \|_1 = \operatorname*{ess\,sup}_{\mathbf{r} \in \mathcal{M}} \ \operatorname*{ess\,sup}_{\mathbf{u}' \in \Omega_i} \int_{\Omega_o} k(\mathbf{r}; \mathbf{u}' \to \mathbf{u}) \, d\mu(\mathbf{u}). \qquad (19)$$

But the integral in this expression is the directional-hemispherical reflectivity at $\mathbf{r}$ with respect to the incoming direction $\mathbf{u}'$. This quantity is necessarily positive and bounded above by one by the first law of thermodynamics, conservation of energy. Hence, $\omega \leq 1$.

4.4 The L_∞-norm of K

Computing the L_∞-norm proceeds similarly. For any $f \in L_\infty$ we have

$$\| \mathbf{K}f \|_\infty = \operatorname*{ess\,sup}_{\mathbf{r} \in \mathcal{M}} \ \operatorname*{ess\,sup}_{\mathbf{u} \in \Omega_o} \int_{\Omega_i} k(\mathbf{r}; \mathbf{u}' \to \mathbf{u}) f(\mathbf{r}, \mathbf{u}') \, d\mu(\mathbf{u}')$$

$$\leq \left[\operatorname*{ess\,sup}_{\mathbf{r} \in \mathcal{M}} \ \operatorname*{ess\,sup}_{\mathbf{u} \in \Omega_o} \int_{\Omega_i} k(\mathbf{r}; \mathbf{u}' \to \mathbf{u}) \, d\mu(\mathbf{u}') \right] \| f \|_\infty,$$

so the expression in brackets is an upper bound on $\| \mathbf{K} \|_\infty$. Again, this bound can be approached from below by considering a sequence of increasingly collimated beams about a direction of maximal reflectance. Therefore, we have

$$\| \mathbf{K} \|_\infty = \operatorname*{ess\,sup}_{\mathbf{r} \in \mathcal{M}} \ \operatorname*{ess\,sup}_{\mathbf{u} \in \Omega_o} \int_{\Omega_i} k(\mathbf{r}; \mathbf{u}' \to \mathbf{u}) \, d\mu(\mathbf{u}'), \qquad (20)$$

which differs from the L_1 norm by exchanging the arguments of the kernel. The integral in this expression is the hemispherical-directional reflectivity at $\mathbf{r}$ with respect to the outgoing direction $\mathbf{u}$. This quantity is necessarily equal to $\| \mathbf{K} \|_1$ because of the reciprocity relation $k(\mathbf{r}; \mathbf{u}' \to \mathbf{u}) = k(\mathbf{r}; \mathbf{u} \to \mathbf{u}')$, which is a consequence of the second law of thermodynamics.

4.5 Other Bounds and their Consequences

The L_1 and L_∞ norms for $\mathbf{K}$ extend immediately to all L_p-norms by means of a useful inequality for integral operators, which states that

$$\| \mathbf{K} \|_p \leq \| \mathbf{K} \|_\infty^{(p-1)/p} \| \mathbf{K} \|_1^{1/p}. \tag{21}$$

Thus, $\| \mathbf{K} \|_p \leq \omega$. See Kato [13, p. 144] or Dunford and Schwartz [7, p. 518].

The $\mathbf{G}$ operator is the easiest to bound since it merely redistributes radiance along straight lines. It follows that $\| \mathbf{G} \|_p = 1$ if any two subsets of $\mathcal{M}$ with non-zero areas can see each other, and $\| \mathbf{G} \|_p = 0$ otherwise. Thus, $\| \mathbf{KG} \|_p \leq \| \mathbf{K} \|_p \| \mathbf{G} \|_p \leq \omega$. It is interesting to note that if the L_p-norms were based upon the measure σ rather than μ, the $\mathbf{G}$ operator would be unbounded for most geometries.

Given bounds on both $\mathbf{K}$ and $\mathbf{G}$, we next consider the operator

$$\mathbf{M} \equiv \mathbf{I} - \mathbf{KG}. \tag{22}$$

If $\| \mathbf{K} \|_p < 1$, it follows that $\mathbf{M}^{-1}$ can be expanded into the Neumann series[3]

$$\mathbf{M}^{-1} = \mathbf{I} + \mathbf{KG} + (\mathbf{KG})^2 + \cdots, \tag{23}$$

which converges with respect to all L_p-norms. Since $\| (\mathbf{KG})^n \|_p \leq \omega^n$, we have

$$\| \mathbf{M}^{-1} \|_p \leq 1 + \omega + \omega^2 + \ldots = \frac{1}{1 - \omega} \tag{24}$$

for all $1 \leq p \leq \infty$. Note that this fails when $\omega = 1$, which is true when perfect reflection occurs at grazing or because of total internal reflection. We therefore ignore these effects and assume that $\omega < 1$. From this bound it follows that $L_p(\mu \times \dot{m})$ is *closed* under global illumination. To see this, suppose that $f = \mathbf{M}^{-1} f_0$, where $f_0 \in L_p$. Then the bound on $\mathbf{M}^{-1}$ implies that $\| f \|_p \leq \| \mathbf{M}^{-1} \|_p \| f_0 \|_p < \infty$. Therefore the equilibrium solution f is also in L_p, so we have $\mathbf{M}^{-1} : L_p \to L_p$ for all $1 \leq p \leq \infty$.

Another conclusion that we can draw is that a surface radiance function over $\mathcal{M} \times \mathcal{S}^2$ will decrease in *all* L_p-norms as a result of each interreflection, which follows immediately from the bound $\| \mathbf{KG} \|_p < 1$.

4.6 Adjoint Operators

The natural generalization of "transpose" for a linear operator is the *adjoint*, which has been applied to importance-driven global illumination [24, 2]. While adjoints can be defined in a general Banach space, the symmetry between a Hilbert space and its dual leads to a simple definition of the adjoint. Given a linear operator $\mathbf{M} : \mathcal{H} \to \mathcal{H}$, the so called *Hilbert-adjoint* $\mathbf{M}^*$ is the operator that satisfies

$$\langle \mathbf{M} f \mid g \rangle = \langle f \mid \mathbf{M}^* g \rangle \tag{25}$$

---

[3] Although this series is frequently attributed to John von Neumann, it is actually due to Carl Gottfried Neumann (1832-1925).

for all f and g in $\mathcal{H}$. In order to define the Hilbert-adjoints of **K** and **G**, we equate surface and field radiance functions so that both operators map $\mathcal{H}$ into itself. To make the necessary identification, we note that the space of field radiance functions is naturally isomorphic to the space of surface radiance functions under the mapping

$$(\mathbf{H}f)(\mathbf{r}, \mathbf{u}) \equiv f(\mathbf{r}, -\mathbf{u}). \tag{26}$$

By virtue of this identification, the distinction between surface and field radiance functions can be removed, although it serves as a reminder of the physical process. Treating **K** and **G** as operators that map L_2 into itself, it is easy to see from definition (25) that both are self-adjoint. This fact hinges on associating the cosine factor with the measure μ and not with the kernel k; doing so preserves the symmetry of k and makes the corresponding **K** operator self-adjoint; that is, $\mathbf{K} = \mathbf{K}^*$. It follows that

$$\mathbf{M}^* = (\mathbf{I} - \mathbf{KG})^* = \mathbf{I} - \mathbf{GK}.$$

Thus, the same operators **K** and **G** are sufficient to form both **M** and its adjoint. This fact and the connection with the space L_2 are clarified by the operator formulation.

4.7 Compact Operators

As a final topic, we briefly explore the concept of *compactness* [15, p. 40]. A subset S of a Banach space is compact if every infinite sequence of points $x_1, x_2, \ldots$ in S has a limit point in S; that is, some point in S is attained or approached arbitrarily closely (with respect to the norm) infinitely many times by elements of the sequence. In $\mathbb{R}^n$ every closed and bounded subset is compact, but this is not so in infinite dimensions.

A *compact operator* is one that maps bounded sets to compact sets [25, p. 293]. Thus, compact operators remove one of the oddities of infinite-dimensional spaces, which frequently simplifies things. Note that the identity operator **I** is compact if and only if the space it is defined on is finite. An important property of compact operators is that they may be uniformly approximated by degenerate operators; that is, given any compact operator **T** and $\epsilon > 0$, there exists a finite-dimensional operator $\mathbf{T}_n$ such that

$$\| \mathbf{T} - \mathbf{T}_n \|_\infty < \epsilon. \tag{27}$$

Compact operators also have a simple *point spectrum*; that is, they have an empty continuous spectrum, as does a finite matrix. As an example of a compact operator, let k be a kernel function such that

$$\int_{\mathcal{M}} \int_{S^2} \int_{S^2} | k(\mathbf{r}, \mathbf{u}' \to \mathbf{u}) |^2 \, d\mu(\mathbf{u}') \, d\mu(\mathbf{u}) \, dm(\mathbf{r}) < \infty, \tag{28}$$

which means that $k \in L_2(\mu \times \mu \times m)$. Then k is called a *Hilbert-Schmidt kernel* and the corresponding integral operator acting on L_2 is compact [10, p. 17]. Thus, **K** is compact when the reflectance function is a Hilbert-Schmidt function.

As an example of a linear operator that appears in global illumination that is not compact, consider the *specular reflection operator* **S**, defined by

$$(\mathbf{S}f)(\mathbf{r}, \mathbf{u}) \equiv k_s(\mathbf{r}; \mathbf{u}' \to \mathbf{u}) \, f(\mathbf{r}, \mathbf{u}'), \tag{29}$$

where k_s is the specular kernel, a dimensionless function that is bounded away from one, and $\mathbf{u}'$ denotes the mirror reflection of $\mathbf{u}$. It is easy to see that $\| \mathbf{S} \|_p \leq 1$. The operator $\mathbf{S}$ can be factored into a product of a reflection operator (similar to $\mathbf{H}$) and a multiplication operator (similar to $\mathbf{M}_g$). But multiplication operators are not compact, and this property is inherited by $\mathbf{S}$.

To see how these facts affect the process of global illumination, consider the two-pass solution process proposed by Sillion and Puech [23]. We replace equation (15) by $f = f_0 + (\mathbf{K} + \mathbf{S})\mathbf{G}$, which includes specular reflection, and write it as

$$(\mathbf{I} - \mathbf{S}\mathbf{G})f = f_0 + \mathbf{K}\mathbf{G}f.$$

Since $\| \mathbf{S} \| < 1$, it follows that $\widehat{\mathbf{S}} \equiv (\mathbf{I} - \mathbf{S}\mathbf{G})^{-1}$ exists. Letting $g \equiv (\mathbf{I} - \mathbf{S}\mathbf{G})f$ we obtain the two-stage method

$$g = f_0 + \mathbf{K}\mathbf{G}\widehat{\mathbf{S}}g$$
$$f = \widehat{\mathbf{S}}g,$$

where the second equation accounts for specular transport chains reaching the eye. Then solving for g in the "first pass" is equivalent to inverting a new operator that includes specular reflections, $\widehat{\mathbf{M}} \equiv \mathbf{I} - \mathbf{K}\mathbf{G}\widehat{\mathbf{S}}$. The Neumann series is

$$\widehat{\mathbf{M}}^{-1} = \mathbf{I} + \mathbf{K}\mathbf{G}\widehat{\mathbf{S}} + (\mathbf{K}\mathbf{G}\widehat{\mathbf{S}})^2 + \cdots. \tag{30}$$

The products of a compact operators with a bounded operator is compact, and a convergent sequence of compact operators is again a compact operator. It follows that $\widehat{\mathbf{M}}^{-1} - \mathbf{I}$ is compact, so the function $g - f_0$, which accounts for all transport chains ending in a non-specular scatter, is the image of a compact operator. Hence, the mapping from f_0 to $g - f_0$ can be approximated to any degree by finite-dimensional operators. This is not true, however, of the mapping from g to f, which does not correspond to a compact operator. This observation provides an abstract view of the difference between specular and non-specular transfers.

5 Further Reading

Functional analysis is a very rich subject that can provide a better theoretical foundation for global illumination. For more complete discussions of the concepts touched upon in this paper, see Glassner [9], Kreyszig [14], Taylor and Lay [25], or Boccara [4]. See Luenberger [15] for a very readable account of Hilbert spaces. For more advanced treatments, see Rudin [19], Kato [13], or Dunford and Schwartz [7].

Acknowledgments

Many thanks to Peter Shirley and Erin Shaw for their helpful comments. This research was supported by the NSF/ARPA Science and Technology Center for Computer Graphics and Scientific Visualization (ASC-8920219) and the Hewlett-Packard Corporation.

References

1. James Arvo, Kenneth Torrance, and Brian Smits. A framework for the analysis of error in global illumination algorithms. In *Computer Graphics* Proceedings, Annual Conference Series, ACM SIGGRAPH, pages 75–84, 1994.

2. Larry Aupperle and Pat Hanrahan. Importance and discrete three point transport. In *Proceedings of Eurographics 93*, pages 85–94, 1993.

3. Marcel Berger. *Geometry, Volume II*. Springer-Verlag, New York, 1987. Translated by M. Cole and S. Levy.

4. Nino Boccara. *Functional Analysis, an Introduction for Physicists*. Academic Press, New York, 1990.

5. S. Chandrasekar. *Radiative Transfer*. Dover Publications, New York, 1960.

6. Michael F. Cohen and John R. Wallace. *Radiosity and Realistic Image Synthesis*. Academic Press, New York, 1993.

7. Nelson Dunford and Jacob T. Schwartz. *Linear Operators. Part I: General Theory*. John Wiley & Sons, New York, 1967.

8. Reid Gershbein, Peter Schröder, and Pat Hanrahan. Textures and radiosity: Controlling emission and reflection with texture maps. In *Computer Graphics* Proceedings, Annual Conference Series, ACM SIGGRAPH, pages 51–58, 1994.

9. Andew Glassner. *Principles of Digital Image Synthesis*. Morgan Kaufmann, New York, 1995.

10. Paul R. Halmos and V. S. Sunder. *Bounded Integral Operators on L^2 Spaces*. Springer-Verlag, New York, 1978.

11. Paul S. Heckbert. *Simulating Global Illumination Using Adaptive Meshing*. PhD thesis, University of California, Berkeley, June 1991.

12. James T. Kajiya. The rendering equation. *Computer Graphics*, 20(4):143–150, August 1986.

13. Tosio Kato. *Perturbation Theory for Linear Operators*. Springer-Verlag, New York, 1966.

14. Erwin Kreyszig. *Introductory Functional Analysis with Applications*. John Wiley & Sons, New York, 1978.

15. David G. Luenberger. *Optimization by Vector Space Methods*. John Wiley & Sons, New York, 1969.

16. Parry Moon. *The Scientific Basis of Illuminating Engineering*. McGraw-Hill, New York, 1936.

17. G. L. Polyak. Radiative transfer between surfaces of arbitrary spatial distribution of reflection. In *Convective and Radiative Heat Transfer*. Publishing House of the Academy of Sciences of the USSR, Moscow, 1960.

18. J. R. Retherford. *Hilbert Space: Compact Operators and the Trace Theorem*. Cambridge University Press, New York, 1993.

19. Walter Rudin. *Functional Analysis*. McGraw-Hill, New York, 1973.

20. Walter Rudin. *Real and Complex Analysis*. McGraw-Hill, New York, second edition, 1974.

21. Irving E. Segal and Ray A. Kunze. *Integrals and Operators*. Springer-Verlag, New York, second edition, 1978.

22. Robert Siegel and John R. Howell. *Thermal Radiation Heat Transfer*. Hemisphere Publishing Corp., New York, second edition, 1981.

23. François Sillion and Claude Puech. A general two-pass method integrating specular and diffuse reflection. *Computer Graphics*, 23(4), August 1989.

24. Brian Smits, James Arvo, and David Salesin. An importance-driven radiosity algorithm. *Computer Graphics*, 26(4):273–282, July 1992.

25. Angus E. Taylor and David C. Lay. *Introduction to Functional Analysis*. John Wiley & Sons, New York, second edition, 1980.

26. Harold Zatz. Galerkin radiosity: A higher order solution method for global illumination. In *Computer Graphics* Proceedings, Annual Conference Series, ACM SIGGRAPH, pages 213–220, 1993.

From Local to Global Illumination and Back

ALAIN FOURNIER

Department of Computer Science, University of British Columbia
Vancouver, BC, V6T 1Z4, Canada. fournier@cs.ubc.ca

Abstract: The following being musings about illumination problems and illumination answers, more particularly about the evolution and the interplay between local and global illumination concerns.

Keywords: global illumination, local illumination.

1. Introduction

Alchemists[1] had a saying "*What is above is like what is below, and what is below is like what is above*". It could be interpreted as a general statement about the self-similarity of the universe, but I prefer for now to see it as an affirmation that one can and should not separate global and local illumination too much, because they are not that different (note I do not claim that they are identical).

Let's first look at some hierarchy of things rendered (Figures 1 and 2). There are many other ways to describe and arrange this, but the basic message is that we build global behaviour from basic elements (*primitives*). So at first glance there is not much difference between computing the *bidirectional reflectance distribution function* (BRDF) of a surface from basic elements or computing the global illumination in a room to extract a view-independent light distribution. In fact one can easily conceive of a *bidirectional room reflectance distribution function* (BRRDF) which for any directional light source gives the reflected light towards an eye at infinity (either for every visible point in that direction, or just an average radiance)[2]. A lot has already been said about these hierarchies, either explicitly or implicitly, but I will mention first some general issues, and then discuss some specifics related to the work I am currently involved with.

1.1. Tight and Loose Coupling

A big difference (maybe the only valid one considering local vs global illumination) is the amount of coupling between elements contributing to the illumination. In local cases, one generally assumes that they don't move with respect to each other, and therefore a pre-computation of the results (again often in the form of a BRDF) is quite

---

1. Alchemists, at least the serious ones, were interested in the secrets of life and achieving immortality. Turning base metals into gold was only a side effect. Serious scientists still feel the same.

2. You could object that the reflected light could come out far from its point of incidence. But I would ask: what do you think the r is for in the $f_r()$ notation for the BRDF? Many references forget about that. Glassner, in his wonderful (if heavy) new book [9] gets it right.

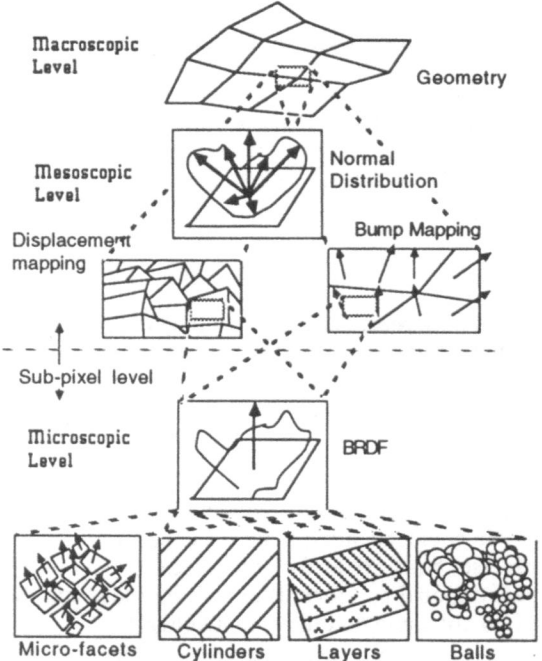

Figure 1. The main hierarchy of local illumination

reasonable. The reason BRRDF are not too popular so far is that it is not worth the investment in most applications, especially if one often rearranges the furniture. The unfortunate (and challenging) situation is with these "local" cases where the elements indeed move with respect to each other (leaves in a tree, hair in a fur, small scale waves on water, etc..). Some work in that direction has been done (the paper by Krueger [14] was an excellent start, though time was not a parameter) but more is needed (see below).

1.2. Is It Linear?

Linear in this context means that all the operators $O(I)$ on light intensity (or any quantities proportional to the light power) are linear:

$$O(\, a\, I_1 + b\, I_2) = a\, O(I_1) + b\, O(I_2)$$

This is a basic (and not always stated) assumption of every illumination computation so far, in particular *ray-tracing* and *radiosity*. Examples of real non-linear light effects range from the universal (but usually negligible) such as the variation of BRDF as a function of temperature (which is itself a function of the amount of light absorbed) to the more exotic, such as the photo-cell on my TV set which adjusts the brightness of

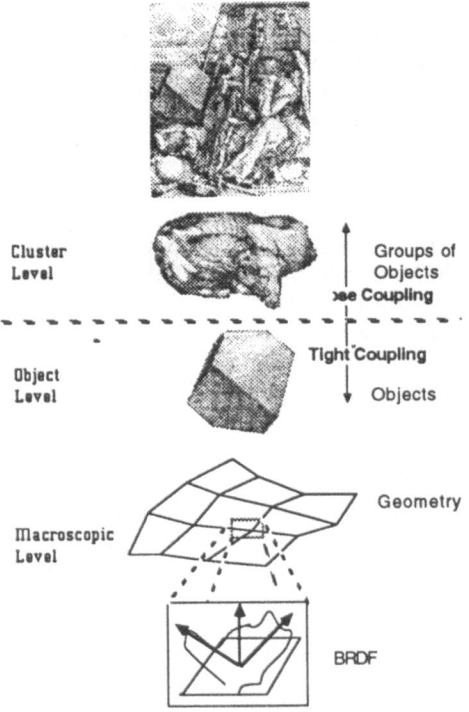

Cluster
Level

Groups of
Objects

>se Coupling

Object
Level

Tight Coupling

Objects

Macroscopic
Level

Geometry

BRDF

Figure 2.   The main hierarchy of global illumination

the CRT as a function of the ambient light (fortunately for my eyes it is not a linear feed-back). If reflectance were not generally linear, we of course would be in deep trouble to compute most of anything.

1.3. Does It Scale

If the subtext is to use global illumination techniques to compute local illumination effects or the other way around, we have to make sure that our models and computations are independent of scale (or that we know how to scale them) in spatial terms. Let's have a quick glance at the *rendering equation*, here given in the notation of Cohen and Wallace [4]:

$$L(\mathbf{x}', \omega') = L_e(\mathbf{x}', \omega') + \int_S f_r(\mathbf{x}', \omega, \omega') L(\mathbf{x}, \omega) G(\mathbf{x}, \mathbf{x}') V(\mathbf{x}, \mathbf{x}') \, dA$$

where $G()$ is a geometric factor and $V()$ the visibility factor.

The radiances are *intensive* quantities, that is they are scaleless (not dimensionless, of course), and the BRDF has a dimension of sr^{-1}, so the only spatial extensive quantities are in $G()$ and $V()$. For $V()$ it is clear that any reasonable definition of visibility should be scaleless. For $G()$ one has to look a little more closely at the integral, but lengths appear only explicitly square in dA and square in the denominator of $G()$, so they do cancel out. In the classic radiosity simplification, this is obvious, since the *form factors* are scaleless and dimensionless.

1.4. Compared to What

A relatively recent trend in illumination computation is to obtain formal error bounds on the results or to assess the images by experimental comparisons. The work of James Arvo, Dani Lischinski, Gershbein/Schröder/Hanrahan for the former, and Holly Rushmeyer and Greg Ward for the latter is especially notable, and show a degree of rigour and sophistication unequaled in any other area of computer graphics (of course IMHO).

There is a *caveat*, though. Since most illumination algorithms are based either on diffuse reflectors, which in reality are few and far between (see remark and reference "[18]" in [11]) or on "un-natural" specular reflection, since the models of luminaires used are far the real ones, and since the real ones are rarely measured with any accuracy (see for example Ashdown [1]) a bound on the error for the computation does not mean much in terms of difference between the result and real scenes. Of course we have to start somewhere, but it's good not to lose sight of the goal. As an exercise, consider what is farther from the truth: a rendering with inter-reflection but only diffuse reflectors, or a scene with realistic reflectors but no inter-reflection? Assume three exterior scene: Andrew Wyeth's "Christina's World", Claude Monet's "Cathédrale de Rouen" (any one) and Hiroshige's "Kanbara" (from *Fifty-three stages of the Tokaido*). Now repeat for three interior scenes: Hopper's "The Night Hawks", Vincent Van Gogh's "Bedroom in Arles" and Rembrandt's "The Night Watch".

2. Act Locally

Indeed the only way the light acts (at our rendering level, anyway) is locally. For this discussion I will largely ignore participating media, but even for these it all starts locally.

2.1. Models of Microstructure

A lot of reflection models, starting with Bouguer and Lambert, continuing with the Torrance/Sparrow model, or in more recent work by Hanrahan and Krueger[11], Gondek *et al*[10] or Oren and Nayar[19] was developed by considering a simple (or not so simple) assemblage of primitives[3]. Similarly to improve the generality of illumination models, Xiao *et al* [12] started from Kirchhoff equation for the light reflected at a surface (approximated by its tangent plane at the point considered) and added interreflection and self-shadowing/masking factors derived from statistical techniques (the surface height is assumed to follow a Gaussian distribution). In [20] we used a "hidden" level of geometry made of cylinders to allow the computation of anisotropic reflection. A similar approach is effective for modelling cloth, since the

---

3. Pat Hanrahan and Julie Dorsey recently devised models simulating corrosion and aging processes with layers, inverting the alchemists' dream and turning gold into base metal.

the geometry of the weave (or even the thread) is well known and available.

While all these techniques are effective within their intented scale, a major unsolved problem is to allow their simultaneous use, and in particular ensure smooth transition between models when the scale changes. Another way to formulate the same problem is that one should be able to find a way to represent the average effect of one level in terms of the level above. As it turns out, one very constraining, though unnecessary, assumption made in all the local models is that a single normal at each sampled point or area has to account for all the reflection effects.

2.2. Local or Parochial[4]

Most fractal objects are easy to render if we assume their surface is fully realized. Let us take as a simple example a fractal surface as a sample of two-variable fractional Brownian motion $fBm(x, y) = z$. For any point P on the surface to be visible from the eye (or from a point on a light source), a line segment from that point to the eye cannot intersect the surface. (see Figure 3).

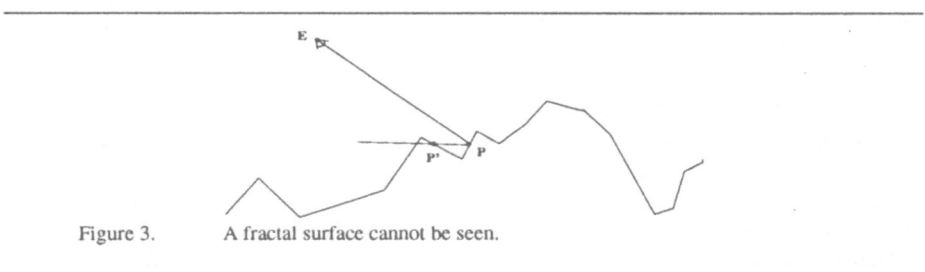

Figure 3. A fractal surface cannot be seen.

It means that for any point P' on the surface the segment PP' has a slope less than the slope of PE. As P' gets closer to P, however, that means that there is a limit to the slope of PP', which contradicts the property of fBm that the limit slope goes to ∞ with probability 1 [15]. Therefore no point on the surface can be seen from the eye or from the lights (exercise left to the reader, what if the line PE is parallel to the Z axis?). This frees us from the worry of designing an illumination model for such surfaces[5]. Also note that it is not in contradiction with the fact that one standing on the surface would see a finite horizon, as long as the observer is a finite height above the surface. I convinced John Hart of the above (I think) but he said: "What about non-random fractals, like Koch island?". I leave that as an exercise to the reader.

2.3. Bump Maps and Filtering

Bump maps is the traditional (if inelegant) name given to texture maps when the values (discrete values of texture maps are often called *texels*) are used to define or modify the normal to the surface prior to shading computations. They were originally

---

4. I have said that before, but I can't resist.

5. Should you think it does not apply to the real world, recall that one can make approximations of a black-body by stacking tightly together several old-fashioned double-edged razor blades.

introduced by Blinn [2] and have been widely used since. Unfortunately the traditional filtering techniques do not apply and they have not been successfully filtered yet. The reason is straightforward. All the pre-filtering techniques developed so far rely on the fact that they filter some quantity that can be factored out of the shading computation when the result is averaged over an area or discrete samples. The rendering equation for such surfaces over some finite area A becomes, if A_i is an element of A with a given normal direction (assuming for now they do not emit light):

$$L(\mathbf{x}', \omega') = \frac{1}{\sum_i A_i} \sum_i \int\limits_{all\ A_i} dA_i \int\limits_S f_r(\mathbf{x}', \omega, \omega') L(\mathbf{x}, \omega) G(\mathbf{x}, \mathbf{x}') V(\mathbf{x}, \mathbf{x}')\ dA$$

Any quantity that enters only linearly in the integrals can be brought out and integrated separately. For each element A_i, unfortunately, there is a different normal, and therefore nothing can be brought out of the second integral since every term is a function of the local frame, and therefore of the normal direction.

As a trivial counter-example, consider the case where the normals over the area considered are of two kinds, symmetric with respect to the average normal and equally distributed. The average of the normals will be the normal of the average plane, and this will cause highlights where the real surface has none, and not show highlights where the real surface has strong ones.

2.4. Reconstructing a Distribution of Normals

The simple example above suggests a solution. If we somehow knew that the surface has only two values of normal vectors equally distributed, these two normals alone are enough to compute the reflected light at any scale. In general, we can look at the normals over the area as defining an underlying distribution of normals $N(\theta, \phi)$ defined for each direction (θ, ϕ) on the hemisphere . The problem is to approximate this distribution by a weighted linear sum of a small number of discrete functions, each function being used then to compute their contribution to the total reflected light. One could use a variety of techniques to accomplish this. The method chosen and implemented is to represent the reconstructed distribution of normals as a weighted sum of a small number of *Phong peaks*, that is of functions of the form:

$$N(\theta, \phi) = U(\theta, \phi) \sum_{i=0}^{n-1} a_i \cos^{n_i}(\alpha_i)$$

where $U(\theta, \phi)$ is the unit vector in the direction (θ, ϕ), α_i is the angle between the direction (θ, ϕ) and the direction of peak i: (θ_i, ϕ_i). Each peak has therefore 4 variables to fit, and non-linear least squares are used to compute the fit.

The original function N () is computed by *spreading* the normals given by the initial bump map, or the relevant section of it. Spreading consists in computing for every point on the hemisphere the sum of the density of normals given by the Phong $\cos^n(\alpha)$ formula. In effect the Phong function serves as a reconstruction filter for the definition of N (). This process is carried at various levels to achieve filtering, in a manner now familiar from *MIP maps* [21] and *NIL maps* [7].

2.5. Multiple Surfaces

The building of the pyramid has a not totally unexpected side benefit: at each texel of each level of the pyramid one gets a local illumination model, and at the top level one gets a model valid when all of the original bump map is comprised within the local "sample". The model is expressed simply as a surface with more than one normal per sample, which we can call a *multiple surface*. The description of the multiple surface implies a new BDRF extracted from the bump map. The BDRF can be obtained by computing the reflected intensity for every direction of incoming and reflected light. It is not as general as an arbitrary BDRF but it has the advantages of being very compact and made of simple elements, namely Phong peaks. This makes the shading computation with this model a trivial modification of the computation normally done with a single Phong peak. Of course values for multiple surfaces do not have to be extracted from bump maps. One can deduce them in simple cases, such as a sphere or a cylinder, or invent them for "special effects".

2.6. Shadowing, Masking and Other Bothers

When the surface structure is really three-dimensional some of the details block other from the light (*self-shadowing*) or from the view (*masking*, or *self-blocking*). It is important to model these effects for convincing rendering. Textures simulating hair or fur can be geometrically adequate, for example, but not very realistic if masking and shadowing are missing. Such problems, and solutions, has been addressed notably by Max and his collaborators [17][3]. I don't have the space here to describe our solution, but it is simple, slightly sleazy and effective.

We have in all obtained an effective technique to filter bump maps, bridging the gap between bump maps and local illumination models. It lead us to a simple local illumination model where each point on a surface can have multiple normal vectors. We have also developed a technique to compute and filter the effect of self-shadowing and masking, again from basic and compact information extracted from the geometric model of the microstructure.

The relationship between BDRF and the distributions of normals we compute are also to explore. One issue is to characterize the BDRF which cannot be effectively represented that way, another is to try to extract automatically multiple surface characteristics from experimentally measured BDRF. Work on this and in general efficient representation of BRDF for direct use in renderers is being pursued by Paul Lalonde and me. Again, most surfaces are not static. The surface of water, as an important example, moves constantly. Statistical approaches to the computation of the light reflected by water exist [14] but are not well suited to animation. As another example, my initial interest in the problem of filtering surfaces arose in the context of stochastic modelling [6] where a partially evolved surface "stands in" for the fully subdivided one. In this case the shading of each polygon should be the average of the shade of all the surface details not yet produced. These two problems have similar elements and are shimmering targets above the horizon.

3. Think Globally

3.1. Whither Fredholm?

Let's look again at the rendering equation:

$$L(\mathbf{x}', \omega') = L_e(\mathbf{x}', \omega') + \int_S f_r(\mathbf{x}', \omega, \omega') L(\mathbf{x}, \omega) G(\mathbf{x}, \mathbf{x}') V(\mathbf{x}, \mathbf{x}') \, dA$$

Do we really have a Fredholm's equation of the second kind? Even since my initiation to recursive procedures, I have been mildly upset at the fact that the most commonly given first example is the computation of the factorial, which can be immediately seen as your basic iteration. Indeed in general *tail recursion* can be unrolled to be replaced by iteration. The rendering equation in a sense can be unrolled. The radiance of an element of surface we want to compute (the left hand side of the redering equation) appears within the integral only "hardly", and in fact the light it receives "from itself" can be decoupled by just storing it on the way to and from all other surfaces. This is the basic approach of *Lucifer* (more below), and it is why we can solve the equation without having to invert the integral operator applied to the radiance.

In his initial paper discussing the rendering equation [13] Jim Kajiya mentioned Neumann series as a method to solve integral equations, and indeed there is a beautiful correspondence between the terms in the series and common illumination algorithms. Fredholm himself also has a series solution (using the *resolvant kernel*[16]). The question is, what is the "physical" meaning of the terms in this kernel. I hope Jim Arvo can answer this, because I can't now.

3.2. Lucifer

Most of the drawbacks of radiosity come from the fact that it is *element-driven*, that is consider specifically pair-wise exchanges of light between elements, and from the fact it really works only for separable sources and reflectors (one can indeed go a long way with that, see my paper in these proceedings on separable BRDFs). It is at heart a global illumination solution which critically depends on a limiting assumption about the local behaviour of light. Hybrid solutions also invariably have problems because there is no neat dichotomy between specular and diffuse reflection, and real reflection/refraction is a continuum between these two extremes. That does not mean of course that there is no hope in that direction. L. Neumann and A. Neumann have a very interesting paper surveying the situation in this respect [18].

An alternative is a *light-driven* approach, where the global illumination problem is solved by propagating the light from sources (we use "source" in the broadest sense of anything radiating light) to other parts of the environment to the eye. Another important criterion is that the amount of effort spent on each part of the scene is somehow related to how much light will come from it. There is no need to compute much about the whole content of a closet whose door remains closed, even less need to compute anything if all the lights are off. What I am advocating, therefore, is a *light-driven, volume-oriented* approach.

To summarize the paradigm, consider a volume V within the environment to render, with a boundary surface S. If we know for every point of S the flux of light crossing it in any direction, then we can study separately the illumination inside and outside of V. Furthermore, even if we do not know the true situation at the boundary, but only some amount of light emitted inside V and the amount of light coming into V, and if we know how to solve the global illumination problem inside V, then we can assign to points of S the correct amounts of outgoing light. The outside of V can then be treated without considering V unless it is found that more light comes into V from outside. In this case we can solve the global illumination problem inside V again *independently* of the previous solution if we assume (and it is the only serious restriction) the *linearity* of the light effects. If we cannot solve the global illumination problem for V, we can partition it into two or more sub-volumes, and so on recursively until each section is simple enough so that we can deal with it.

3.3. So What?

Given this paradigm, one has to chose the modalities of implementation. The choices concern the volumes to use, the representation of light flux at the volume boundaries, the rendering techniques, etc.. The choice of volumes is the easiest. Octree cells give simple shapes, hierarchical decomposition of space (nothing much to do if there is nothing there), and adaptability (one is free to do anything reasonable at the level of a leaf of the octree (of course one decides when it *is* a leaf). To represent the light flux is trickier. The original implementation [8][5] used a total discretization of the walls of the *cells* (the cubes of the octree) and the directions. This was quite ugly, but that's a start and a straw-person against which to compare.

Now *wavelets* came to the rescue, and that what we are using (in current work by Bob lewis and myself) for the light flux. They have most of the qualities needed, compactness, respect of discontinuities (important for shadows, in particular) and the "natural" ability to "cluster" the light flux automatically (that is part and parcel of their use in image compression). In this application we need four-variable wavelet transforms.

We have developed the algorithms necessary to compute the propagation through empty cells, the blocking and the reflection while using only a number of operations of the order of the number of wavelet coefficients in the incoming and reflected/transmitted light flux. We hope to be able soon to convince a reluctant world that this approach is not only valid, but actually will eventually perform better than most others, because it is adaptable, accept any reflecting behaviour, is easily parallelizable, and has the asymptotic complexity of the Z-buffer (that is linear in the number of elements in the scene). So what if the constant is *very* large.

Finally, it ties everything back together, because of course the same transform used for the light flux on the cell walls can be used to represent BRDF (which again is done with Paul Lalonde) and we are right back to local illumination.

4. Conclusion

When it seems that it finally all comes together, maybe it is because we are standing too close to a black hole. Nevertheless that is how it feels. Thanks you.

Acknowledgements

I am very thankful and truly honoured to have been invited to address this workshop. I gratefully acknowledge the support of NSERC through operating grants and graduate scholarships. IBM and Silicon Graphics were generous with donations of workstations to keep graduate students happy. Many people helped me and inspired me in my research,but one pontificates alone.

References

1. I. Ashdown, "Near-Field Photometry: A New Approach," *Journal of the Illuminating Engineering Society of North America*, vol. 22, no. 1, pp. 163-180, 1993.

2. J.F. Blinn, "Simulation of Wrinkled Surfaces," *Computer Graphics*, vol. 12, no. 3, pp. 286-292, August 1978.

3. B. Cabral, N. Max, and R. Springmeyer, "Bidirectional Reflection Functions from Surface Bump Maps," *Computer Graphics*, vol. 21, no. 4, pp. 273-281, July 1987.

4.   M.F. Cohen and J.R. Wallace, *Radiosity and Realistic Image Synthesis,* Academic Press, 1993.

5.   G. Drettakis, E. Fiume, and A. Fournier, *Tightly-Coupled Multiprocessing for a Global Illumination Algorithm,* pp. 387-398, Eurographics '90, September 1990.

6.   A. Fournier, D. Fussell, and L. Carpenter, "Computer Rendering of Stochastic Models," *Comm. of the ACM,* vol. 25, no. 6, pp. 371-384, June 1982.

7.   A. Fournier and E.L. Fiume, "Constant-Time Filtering with Space-Variant Kernels," *Computer Graphics,* vol. 22, no. 4, pp. 229-238, August 1988.

8.   A. Fournier, E. Fiume, M. Ouellette, and C. K. Chee, "FIAT LUX: Light Driven Global Illumination," DGP Technical Memo DGP89-1, 1989.

9.   A.S. Glassner, in *Principles of Digital Image Synthesis,* Morgan Kaufmann, 1995.

10. J. S. Gondek, G. W. Meyer, and J. G. Newman, "Wavelength Dependent Reflectance Function," *Computer Graphics Proceedings (Siggraph '94),* pp. 213-220, 1994.

11. P. Hanrahan and W. Krueger, "Reflection from Layered Surfaces due to Subsurface Scattering," *Computer Graphics Proceedings (Siggraph '93),* pp. 165-174, 1993.

12. Xiao D. He, Kenneth E. Torrance, Francois X. Sillion, and Donald P. Greenberg, "A comprehensive physical model for light reflection," *Computer Graphics (SIGGRAPH '91 Proceedings),* vol. 25, no. 4, pp. 175-186, 1991.

13. J.T. Kajiya, "The Rendering Equation," *Computer Graphics,* vol. 20, no. 4, pp. 143-150, August 1986.

14. W. Krueger, "Intensity fluctuations and natural texturing," *Computer Graphics,* vol. 22, no. 4, August 1988.

15. B. B. Mandelbrot and J. W. Van Ness, "Fractional Brownian Motion, Fractional Noises and Applications," *SIAM Review,* vol. 10, no. 4, pp. 422-437, October 1968.

16. J. Mathews and R. L. Walker, *Mathematical Methods of Physics,* W. A. Benjamin, 1970.

17. N.L. Max, "Horizon mapping: shadows for bump-mapped surfaces," *The Visual Computer,* vol. 4, 1988.

18. L. Neumann and A. Neumann, "Radiosity and Hybrid Methods," *ACM Transactions on Graphics (to appear),* 1995.

19. M. Oren and S. K. Nayar, "Generalization of Lambert's Reflectance Model," *Computer Graphics Proceedings (Siggraph '94),* pp. 239-246, 1994.

20. P. Poulin and A. Fournier, "A Model for Anisotropic Reflection," *Computer Graphics (SIGGRAPH '90 Proceedings),* vol. 24, no. 4, pp. 273-282, held in Dallas, Texas; 6-10 August 1990, July 1990.

21. L. Williams, "Pyramidal Parametrics," *Computer Graphics,* vol. 17, no. 3, pp. 1-11, July 1983.

A radiosity approach for the simulation of daylight

S. Müller[†], W. Kresse[†], N. Gatenby[†‡], F. Schöffel[†]

[†]Fraunhofer Institute for Computer Graphics
Wilhelminenstraße 7, 64283 Darmstadt, Germany
[‡]Computer Graphics Unit, University of Manchester

Abstract. In this paper, an extension to the radiosity method, for the simulation of daylight, is presented. The sky hemisphere around the scene is subdivided into a set of *sky patches*. By defining a location on the earth, a time of day and the weather conditions (e.g., clear sky, overcast, partly cloudy) a sky model (e.g., CIE or Perez) is applied to compute the radiosity values for each sky patch. In a radiosity preprocess, the sky patches are regarded as shooting patches and are treated first. By storing the form factors within this preprocess, all parameters of the sky model can be modified and updated very quickly. Thus, a designer can see the lighting variation throughout a typical day by calling the costly form factor computation only once.

1 Introduction

The radiosity method has become very important for the simulation of lighting conditions. Several lighting simulation programs exploit the method, and are used by lighting designers and illumination engineers as planning and visualization tools, whilst accounting for the light sources of different manufacturers.

Daylight is obviously the most economical and ecological light source available. Unfortunately, its dynamic variation over time and its dependence on natural conditions (e.g., cloud cover) make its integration, into illumination planning, very difficult for illumination engineers. Conventional simulators do not support daylight modelling sufficiently well, hence its integration into a radiosity process is proposed in this paper. Representing the sun by a simple point light source is not sufficient, since atmospheric influences are non-negligible, especially for clouded skies. A better solution is to place a hemisphere, with a large radius, around the scene and apply a sky model, which simulates the luminance for each sample point of the sky dome (see Sec. 2). The integration of a hemispherical sky light source into a lighting system can be categorized in two ways:

1. *Gathering*: the sky hemisphere is treated as one big light source. For each sample point in the environment (in the context of radiosity; for each receiving patch), the visible part of the sky dome must be determined and then, integration of the illuminance values over this visible part, yields the requested sky contribution.

2. *Shooting*: the sky dome is subdivided into small emitter patches. For each sky patch, its luminance is computed and it acts as a light source in the illumination simulation process.

All daylight simulation publications, known to the authors, use the gathering approach. Nishita & Nakamae [11] describe an extension of the ray tracing approach, where they subdivide the sky dome into regular band sources. The luminance is assumed to be transversely uniform and longitudinally non-uniform within each band source. Each sample point P of the scene (in the context of ray tracing; each intersection point to be illuminated) is handled as the effective center of the sky dome because of the dome´s very large radius. The visibility between P and the sky is only determined for the sample lines (the center lines of each sky band). The contour lines of the scene objects are projected onto the hemisphere and intersected with these sample lines. As a result, the visible sections of each sample line are given in intervals of angle α (e.g., α_1-α_2, α_3-α_4, etc.). The authors used the CIE sky model and stored the pre-calculated orthogonal illuminance in a look-up table. The final illuminance of P is obtained by linear interpolation of look-up table entries, for each visible section of each sample line.

Dobashi *et al.* [5] argue that a regular subdivision of the sky dome [11] results in inaccurate illuminance calculation because the method does not take into account the luminous intensity distribution of skylight. Therefore, they propose to subdivide the sky hemisphere into band sources with almost the same illuminance contributions. Even if the band sources are subdivided in this manner, the visibility determination on the sample lines might cause errors because of missing obstacles or aliasing artifacts of the sampling method. Dobashi *et al.* address this problem by adaptively inserting subsample lines between the sample lines, if the illuminance difference between adjacent band sources is too large, or if the visible sections change drastically. By defining thresholds, the user can control the accuracy of the skylight illuminance. However, this approach still cannot guarantee to catch all shadow borders.

Tadamura *et al.* [13] note that the calculation cost of the band source method is very high: especially the intersection detection between objects and sample lines, which accounts for more than 60% of the illumination process. They suggest an efficient visibility determination algorithm which is similar to the hemi-cube approach [3], and integrate this method into their ray-tracing system. A parallelepiped is placed around each sample point of the scene, so that the top surface is facing the direction of the largest sky luminance. Each face of the parallelepiped is adaptively subdivided into a number of elements, and the contribution of skylight luminance for every element is calculated. In order to determine whether or not each element is obscured by objects in the scene, all objects are perspective-transformed onto each surface of the parallelepiped, using graphics hardware. Sky luminance is calculated by summing up contributions assigned to each unoccluded element. The results presented by Tadamura *et al.* prove the efficiency and accuracy of their method compared to the band source method. The greater the number of objects, the more favourable the application of their method becomes.

All of the methods described thus far could be directly integrated in a radiosity system. In a preprocess, the skylight contribution for each receiving patch could be computed, resulting in an increased patch emission for the final radiosity process. Because of its efficiency, the parallelepiped approach seems better suited for the visibility determination. Imagine a scene consisting of n patches (with a range between 10,000 and 50,000 in our examples): in terms of radiosity, n gathering iterations are needed by this process, but this is still too time consuming for an interactive planning system. A second disadvantage, is that the whole preprocess has to be repeated, if any parameters of the sky model are changed (e.g., time of day or cloud cover).

In this paper, a shooting method is proposed, which subdivides the sky into a number of m shooting patches, with $m \ll n$. This method can be directly integrated in a radiosity system and only m shooting iterations are needed for the simulation of the direct daylight contribution. By saving the $m \times n$ receiving-patch-to-sky-patch form factors, modifications of the sky model parameters can be updated very quickly. Thus, a designer can see the lighting variation throughout a typical day by calling the costly form factor computation only once.

Another remarkable idea for previewing the interaction of daylight with architectural scenes, over the duration of a typical day, was presented by Nimeroff *et al.* [10]. They achieve efficient re-rendering of scenes illuminated by skylight via a linear combination of pre-rendered images. The theory of steerable functions provides the machinery to derive a set of basis images which can be combined to generate an image of the scene with the illumination function at any orientation. For several sun positions, the authors rendered images using a combined progressive radiosity and stochastic ray tracing algorithm. Once the initial rendering phase is performed, images for other sun positions are rendered in negligible time. Unfortunately, the authors did not give any more details about their multi-pass global illumination algorithm, which was used to render the initial images.

2 Sky models

Several sky models can be applied which simulate the luminance for each sample point of the sky dome around a scene ([2], [12]). Each point of interest in the scene is handled as the effective centre of the hemisphere, because of the dome's very large radius. Two sky models, and the integration of measured data sets, are discussed in this section.

2.1 CIE overcast sky

The most common empirical formula for simulating the skylight distribution have been determined by the CIE, taking overcast skies and clear skies into account [2]. The distribution is defined as the luminance relative to the zenith luminance (L_z), and depends on sun position.

For cloudy skies, the zenith luminance L_z and the luminance $L(\theta)$ for each sky element (defined by θ, the angle from the zenith to the sky element) is given by the following equations.

$$L_z = \frac{1}{0.203} \cdot (8.6 \cdot \cos\theta + 0.123) \tag{1}$$

$$L(\theta) = L_z \cdot \frac{1}{3} \cdot (1 + 2\cos\theta) \tag{2}$$

2.2 CIE clear sky

For the computation of the zenith luminance L_z of a clear sky, a *turbidity* factor can be defined.

$$L_z = \frac{1}{0.203} \cdot \left((1.367 \cdot turbidity - 1.81) \cdot \tan\left(\frac{\pi}{2} - \theta_s\right) + 0.38 \right) \tag{3}$$

For each point (θ, φ) of the sky dome, its luminance is obtained by:

$$L(\theta, \varphi) = L_z \cdot \frac{(0.91 + 10e^{-3\gamma} + 0.45 \cdot \cos^2\gamma)\,(1 - e^{-0.32/\cos\theta})}{0.27385 \cdot \left(0.91 + 10e^{-3\theta_s} + 0.45 \cdot \cos^2\theta_s \right)} \tag{4}$$

γ, the angle subtended at the dome centre by the sun and the sky element, is given by:

$$\cos\gamma = \cos\theta_s \cdot \cos\theta + \sin\theta_s \cdot \sin\theta \cdot \cos(\varphi - \varphi_s) . \tag{5}$$

where θ_s defines the angle from the zenith to the sun.

2.3 Perez model

A sky model which is better suited for natural conditions, was introduced by Perez *et al.* [12]. The luminance of each point (θ, φ) of the sky dome is computed using:

$$L(\theta, \varphi) = L_z \cdot [1 + a \cdot e^{b/\cos\theta}] \cdot [1 + c \cdot e^{d \cdot \gamma} + e \cdot \cos^2\gamma] \tag{6}$$

Different insolation conditions may be specified by adjusting the coefficients a (sign and magnitude of the horizon-zenith gradient), b (the luminance gradient near the horizon), c (relative intensity of the circumsolar region, or solar aureole), d (width of the circumsolar region) and e (relative intensity of backscattered light received at the earth's surface). For further information about the Perez-parameters, see [12]. Parameter sets of the Perez sky exist to adopt the CIE standard sky.

2.4 Measured data sets

The described sky models define a luminance value for any sample point on the sky dome, depending on time of day, time of year, and location. Usually, these models are not accurate enough for light engineers, and measured data sets from sky scanners are used. Thus, a radiosity approach for the simulation of daylight should also take into account these measured data sets. At present, there are only a few sites in the world for which systematic records of daylight exist. Conventions about the measurement specifics (e.g., the sky sample points used by sky scanners and the specification of their output format) are established within Technical Committee 3.07 of the CIE.

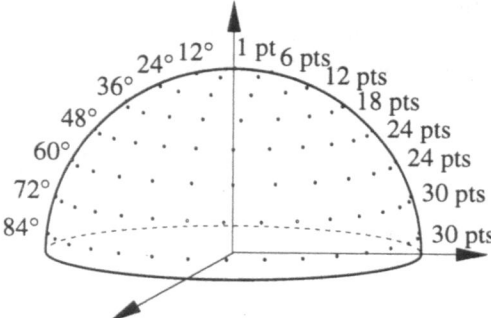

Fig. 1. Distribution of the 145 sky sample points of sky scanners (Tregenza).

The position of the sky sample points of sky scanners is not yet standardized. The most convenient sky subdivision consists of 145 sample points and is described by Tregenza [14]. The hemisphere is divided into bands, parallel with the horizon, which subtend a vertical angle of 12° (Fig. 1).

2.5 Explicit sun representation

Using the CIE or Perez sky models, the sun needs to be represented explicitly in cloudless conditions. The sun subtends a solid angle of 6.79×10^{-5} *sr* at the earth's surface.

3 Radiosity approach for daylight simulation

For a radiosity simulation of daylight, a hemisphere representing the sky is centred around the scene centre. The radius of the hemisphere depends on the size of the scene and is computed so that the computation error can be controlled by a user defined threshold ε. The hemisphere is initially subdivided into a set of patches, and a radiosity value for each sky patch is assigned according to the luminance value of the sky model. Next, all sky patches shoot their direct radiosity into the scene and the form factors are stored in a cache. By re-using these form factors, the direct daylight contribution can be updated very quickly after any change in the sky model parameters. The sun is represented explicitly and results in an extra iteration after the shooting of the sky patches.

3.1 Settings of the sky dome

For a radiosity simulation, Lambertian emission is assumed. In order for this to correspond to the true situation, it must be guaranteed that the sky dome is large enough to ensure that the direction of any one sky patch, viewed from any point of interest, is all but invariant. A hemisphere with radius r is placed around the midpoint of the scene so that the height axis, through the midpoint, points towards the zenith (Fig. 2).

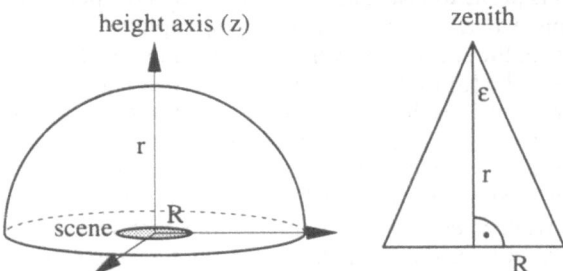

Fig. 2. Definition of the sky dome.

For the whole scene, the radius R of the surrounding circle is computed first. The biggest angle difference, found by observing a point on the sky dome from different scene positions, arises when looking towards the zenith from two ends of a diagonal of the scene-surrounding circle. If an angle ε is accepted as "all but invariant", then the radius r of the sky dome is given by:

$$r = \frac{R}{\tan \varepsilon} \tag{7}$$

For example, if the threshold angle ε is defined as one degree, the radius of the sky dome must be 60 times bigger than the radius of the scene.

For the subdivision of the sky, the 145 sample point locations of sky scanners are used (see Sec. 2.4). Thus, measured data sets can be integrated in the system in the same way as the simulated data from sky models. Sky patches are generated by placing quadrilaterals around the described sample points. The patch around the zenith has 6 vertices. By assuming the luminance to be constant within each patch around the sample point (θ, φ), the patch radiosity $B(\theta, \varphi)$ can be derived from the luminance of the sample point:

$$B(\theta, \varphi) = \pi \cdot L(\theta, \varphi) \qquad (8)$$

The basic assumption of Eq. 8, is that any sky patch is observed from each point of the scene along roughly the same direction. Therefore, the threshold ε of Eq. 7 should be chosen to be suitably small.

3.2 Radiosity approach

The simulation of the direct radiosity propagation of the sky dome is implemented as a preprocess within our radiosity system. Like the original progressive refinement approach, all sky patches are regarded as shooting patches and 145 shooting iterations are performed to compute the direct light due to the sky dome. Within each iteration, the form factors from the sky patch to all receiving patches are computed and stored in a form factor list. No sorting of maximum unshot radiosity is needed in this preprocess; all 145 patches are forced to shoot, since all form factors are needed to update arbitrary skylight conditions. The form factor lists are integrated into the data structure of the sky patches.

Each object of the scene is subdivided into a user-controlled regular mesh. Such a meshing approach is prone to visual artifacts, because of the poor radiosity approximation in those regions where the radiosity is varying rapidly. However, such a mesh is used for good reason; the specifics of which are given in Sec. 5.1.

Applying the hemi-cube [3] to the computation of scene-patch-to-sky-patch form factors would yield very bad results, and cannot be used in this context. Since the whole scene covers only a very small part (defined by the angle threshold ε of Eq. 7) of a hemi-cube placed around a sky patch, aliasing artifacts would be the norm. In our implementation, an adaptive ray-casting based form factor evaluation method (similar to that described Wallace et al. [15]) is used. From each receiving patch, 4 rays are shot towards the vertices of the sky patch and 1 ray towards its midpoint (level 0). If the visibility of the 5 rays differs, the sampling domain of the sky patch is recursively subdivided into 4 regions and the process is repeated with the subdomains. Note: instead of shooting 20 rays for the adapted sky patch, the existing ray information can be re-used and only 8 new rays need to be shot. The result of this approach is a visibility term $V \in [0,1]$, and the final form factor is obtained by multiplying the scene-patch-to-sky-patch form factor with V (as per Hanrahan et al. [7]). The area-weighted average of the delta form factors assigned to each ray might be used in an alternative approach. However, since the sky patches are so distant, the delta form factors vary very little over each sky patch and the results obtained by the multiplication with the visibility term are accurate enough.

The transparency coefficients of window glass play an important role in daylight modelling design and cannot be neglected by a daylight modelling simulation program. Therefore, a transmission colour $\vec{k}_t = (1, 1, 1)$ is assigned to each ray. If the ray intersects a transparent object, this vector is diminished by the transparency coefficient and colour of the intersected object. The process is repeated until the sky patch is reached or an intersection with an opaque object is detected. The result of each single shadow feeler is a visibility term of 1 (visible) or 0 (obstructed) and its transmission colour. The sum of all visibility terms and transmission colours divided by the number of rays within one adaptive iteration finally yields the desired values for V and $\vec{k}_t$. The radiosity contribution of a sky patch s at position (θ, φ) to a receiver r is given by:

$$\dot{B}_s(\theta, \varphi) \cdot \left(F_{rs} \cdot \vec{k}_t \cdot V_{rs} \cdot \dot{\rho}_r \right),$$

(9)

where the components of each vector cover the colour bands used by the system (usually r, g and b). Since form factor, transmission colour, visibility and reflection coefficient remain invariant if sky light conditions are changed, all values can be stored in the form factor list. In our implementation, the form factor is multiplied by these values and instead of one value, a three-component value is stored in the list. If n is the number of patches in a scene, then the additional memory needed by our approach would be $145 \cdot n \cdot 12$ bytes, while each component of the form factor is represented by 4 Bytes (e.g., for a scene consisting of 10000 patches, 17 MBytes additional main memory would be needed for the "coloured" form factors). In real scenes, a high percentage of form factors are zero. Therefore, the entries of the form factor list are run-length encoded in our implementation and the memory requirements are reduced drastically.

For sunny skies, the sun contribution is evaluated explicitly after computing the sky dome contribution. The sun, represented by a quadrilateral patch covering the solid angle described in Sec. 2.5, is placed directly under the sky dome. The radiosity exchange is computed in a similar manner as described for sky patches. However, less shadow rays need to be considered, because of the very small diameter of the sun patch. The form factors between the sun and the scene patches are not stored in the form factor list.

Direct illumination by the sky is already seen as being very important by lighting engineers, since it can be used to calculate the daylight factor [11]. The illumination of nearby buildings is discussed in Sec. 5.3. Of course, the resulting radiosity data can be integrated into any radiosity system, if a converged solution is needed, or artificial light sources need to be considered as well. Since the main primary effects are already updated by the preprocess, a hierarchical radiosity approach as proposed by Hanrahan *et al.* [7] should be used, which solves the indirect illumination fastest.

4 Results

Several tests were conducted to determine the effectiveness and the quality of the proposed algorithm. All of the timing data were obtained from performing the computation on a Silicon Graphics Onyx Reality Engine 2 with 512 MByte main memory. As a test scene, the model of the planned cafeteria of the new institute building of Fraunhofer-IGD was used. In order to represent the shadow borders on the textured floor with a regular mesh, the patch resolution of the floor was set very high. Therefore, the whole scene consists of 47500 regular patches and is rendered by the hardware at a rate of 5 frames/sec.

In Fig. 4.a-f, the same scene, under different skylight conditions, is shown. Only direct illumination by the sky is taken into account. For the initial form factor calculation, the maximum recursion level for the adaptive form factor calculation was set to 1. No more than 13 rays have been generated between any sky and receiving patch. In total, 70 million rays have been shot.

The initial form factor calculation needs about 3 hours for this scene and around 9.6 Mbytes of main memory are needed for storing the run-length encoded form factor lists. Once the initial computation phase is performed, 34 seconds are needed for updating the illumination after changing any parameter of the sky models. For the extra iteration of the sun patch (see Fig. 4.c-d), additional 24 seconds are needed.

Fig. 4.a,b show a sunny sky on a summer day (without the explicit sun representation) at noon (b) and late afternoon (c). Fig. 4.c,d displays the same simulation with the explicit sun representation. Fig. 4.e: CIE overcast sky. All images are rendered at a rate of 5 frames/sec. The reader should perhaps note that the floor has been texture mapped. Fig. 4.f shows a pseudo-colour representation of the daylight factor on a working plane positioned 85 cm above the floor.

5 Discussion

The results demonstrated in this paper summarize ongoing work in simulating daylight with a radiosity-based system. The main focus of the system is to support a simulation tool which helps light engineers, and lighting designers, to plan illumination in architectural scenes. For this kind of application, interactive response times of the simulation tools are more important than accurately rendered images, as long as the results are physically correct. Nevertheless, several points pertaining to how the accuracy of the presented method could be improved, are discussed in this section.

5.1 Scene patch subdivision

As has already been briefly mentioned in Sec. 3.2, the use of a regular (uniform) patch subdivision scheme, is not without its problems. The inability of such a mesh to adapt to regions where the radiosity is varying rapidly (such as around shadow regions) results in such regions being poorly represented in any rendered image. However, this disadvantage must be weighed against the fact that in order to be practical in real applications, the sky-patch-to-scene-patch form factors must be stored and re-used when sky conditions change. If the scene patches were allowed to adapt to 9am lighting conditions, and then were re-used for a 6pm sky, the stored scene patches would be completely unsuitable for the new shadow locations. It is for this reason that scene patches are not allowed to adapt when illuminated by the sky patches. A further justification for this approach is that the scene patches don't actually need to adapt to the sky dome illumination - the resulting shadows are invariably very 'soft'; the rapid radiosity variations are caused by direct sunlight, and other important emittors in the scene.

A meshing method for the scene patches is needed which not only allows re-use of a useful set of stored form factors, but which is also capable of adapting to the rapid radiosity variations which will arise as soon as direct sunlight, and other important emittors, are allowed to contribute. A consequence of such a scheme, where a 'basic' mesh is repeatedly adapted, is that one must be able to quickly recover the basic mesh as soon as sky/sun conditions change.

One meshing strategy considered was to use a conventional, quadtree-based, subdivision scheme, where any adaptive meshing was deferred until the after the sky dome contribution. Unfortunately, such a mesh is difficult to apply to arbitrarily-shaped polygons, presents little choice in the number of patches in the 'basic' mesh, and will tend to allow direct sunlight to 'leak' into shadowed patches.

The meshing strategy currently under development utilises a BSP-tree [8] , rather than a quadtree. Not only does a binary-subdivision approach allow one to more easily handle arbitrarily-shaped polygons, but the strategy also allows one to choose the 'best' split for optimally-shaped patches [6]. Once a basic mesh, containing a user-specified number of patches, has been created, the sky patch preprocess can take place and the re-usable form factors stored. Leaf nodes in the scene polygon meshes can now be tagged as such, and the direct sunlight pass can take place. The mesh can be refined to coincide with (direct sunlight) shadow boundaries, and the solution can proceed to convergence. When sky/sun conditions change, the mesh BSP-tree is returned to its basic, unrefined, state by deleting any branches below our previously tagged nodes. The mesh refinement process can now be repeated for the new sun location, and the solution allowed to converge once more.

A number of methods could be used to refine the basic mesh so that it coincides with the direct sunlight shadow boundaries. A simple radiosity gradient approach [4] could be used, or full discontinuity meshing [9] - with the sun modelled as a small triangle, say. The most favoured method, however, is for the only discontinuity meshing to take place during the direct sunlight pass, with the sun regarded as a point source for the mesh generation [1] and as an area source for mesh illumination. In this way, the sky dome pass will result in soft shadows, the direct sunlight will add sharp shadows, and the binary nature of the mesh will make a converged solution using a hierarchical approach [7] tractable.

5.2 Form factor computation

For the partial visibility test between a sender and a receiver patch, an adaptive ray-casting method is used in our implementation (see Sec. 3.2). This method is very expensive and causes aliasing problems, even if the recursion level is set very high. Ideally, a visibility test which can quickly establish whether two polygons are wholly intervisible, partially intervisible, or wholly occluded, is needed. The provision of such a test is very important for the efficiency of our method, and is suggested as a topic for future research.

5.3 Nearby buildings

The illumination due to nearby buildings is very important for a daylight simulation. Therefore, the facades of these buildings need to be modelled and the sky/sun illumination is handled as decribed previously (including the patches of these facades). After computing the direct sky contribution, typical progressive refinement iterations are started. If the form factor list of the current shooting patch is empty, new form factors are computed and stored. Thus, the radiosity distribution of the scene after any change of daylight parameters can be updated very efficiently, taking nearby buildings into account.

5.4 Colour information of the sun

The colour of the sun was set to bright yellow and each sky patch was set to light blue in our implementation. Of course, the colour of skylight is not uniform and its spectral distribution varies significantly depending on solar altitude. Further information about the spectral distribution of skylight can be found in Tadamura *et al.* [13] and will shortly be included into our implementation.

References

1. Campbell A.T., Fussell D.S., "Adaptive Mesh Generation for Global Diffuse Illumination", *ACM Computer Graphics (SIGGRAPH '90 Proceedings)*, Vol. 24, No. 3, August 1990, pp. 155-164.
2. CIE Technical Committee 4.2. Standardization of luminance on clear skies. CIE Publication No. 22, Commission International de l'Eclairaze, Paris, 1973.
3. Cohen M.F., Greenberg D.P.: "The Hemi-Cube: A Radiosity Solution for Complex Environments", *ACM Computer Graphics (SIGGRAPH '85 Proceedings)*, Vol. 19, No. 3, July 1985, pp. 31-40.
4. Cohen M.F., Greenberg D.P., Immel D.S., Brock P.J.: "An Efficient Radiosity Approach for Realisitic Image Synthesis", *IEEE CG&A*, Vol. 6, No. 2, March 1986, pp. 26-35.
5. Dobashi Y., Kaneda K., Nakashima T., Yamashita H., Nishita T., Tadamura K.: "Skylight for Interior Lighting Design", *Computer Graphics Forum (EUROGRAPHICS '94)*, Vol. 13, No. 3, 1994, pp. C-85 - C-96.
6. Gatenby N.: *Optimising Discontinuity Meshing Radiosity*, ph.d thesis at the University of Manchester, 1995.
7. Hanrahan P., D. Salzman, L. Aupperle: "A Rapid Hierarchical Radiosity Algorithm", *ACM Computer Graphics (SIGGRAPH '91 Proceedings)*, Vol. 25, No. 4, July 1991, pp. 197 - 206.
8. Lischinski D., Tampieri F., Greenberg D.P.: "Combining Hierarchical Radiosity and Discontinuity Meshing", *ACM Computer Graphics (SIGGRAPH '93 Proceedings)*, Vol. 24, No. 3, August 1993, pp. 199 - 208.
9. Lischinski D., Tampieri F., Greenberg D.P.: "Discontinuity Meshing for Accurate Radiosity", *IEEE CG&A*, Vol. 12, No. 6, November 1993, pp. 25- 39.
10. Nimeroff J.S., Simoncelli E., Dorsey J.: "Efficient Re-rendering of Naturally Illuminated Environments", in *Fifth Eurographics Workshop on Rendering* (Darmstadt, Germany, June 1995), pp. 359 - 373.
11. Nishita T., Nakamae E.: "Continuous Tone Representation of Three-Dimensional Objects Illuminated by Sky Light", *ACM Computer Graphics (SIGGRAPH '86 Proceedings)*, Vol. 20, No. 4, August 1986, pp. 125 - 132.
12. Perez R., Seals R., Michalsky J.: "All-Weather Model for Sky Luminance Distribution - Preliminary Configuration and Validation", *Solar Energy*, Vol. 50, No. 3, 1993, pp. 235 - 245.
13. Tadamura K., Nakamae E., Kaneda K., Baba M., Yamashita H., Nishita T.: "Modeling of Skylight and Rendering of Outdoor Scenes", *Computer Graphics Forum (EUROGRAPHICS '93)*, Vol. 12, No. 3, 1993, pp. C-189 - C-200.
14. Tregenza P.R.: "Subdivision of the sky hemisphere for luminance measurements", *Lighting Research and Technology*, Vol. 19, 1987, pp. 13-14.
15. Wallace, John R., Kells A. Elmquist, Eric A. Haines: "A Ray Tracing Algorithm For Progressive Radiosity," *ACM Computer Graphics (SIGGRAPH '89 Proceedings)*, Vol. 23, No. 3, July 1989, pp. 315-324.
16. Ward G.J.: "The radiance lighting simulation system", *SIGGRAPH '92 Global Illumination Course Notes*, ACM Press, July 1992.

Editors' Note: see Appendix, p. 362 for colored figures of this paper

Modeling the Spatial Energy Distribution of Complex Light Sources for Lighting Engineering

P.M. Deville and J.C. Paul

INRIA CRIN CNRS URA 262 Université de Nancy 1 B.P. 239
54506 Vandœuvre les Nancy cedex

June 9, 1995

Abstract

In lighting engineering the precise simulation of a lighting project requires a light source model which has the ability to reproduce real light sources. The models which assume the spatial energy is diffused over the light source, are not sufficiently precise, since real light sources do not have uniform spatial energy distributions. Other models based upon gonio-photometric diagrams provided by manufacturers have been developed, but they introduce an important error in the computation of the illumination of surfaces close to the light sources. We propose a new method which considers a light source as a domain giving off energy in the scene using an interface zone. Thus, the spatial energy distribution is computed over the interface using a projection method. This model can be used to help designers. Moreover, as the spatial energy distribution is pre-calculate, our light source model can be used as a sub-domain of the scene in a radiosity global illumination simulation.

Keywords

Image Synthesis, spatial energy distribution of Light source, High Quality rendering, Lighting Engineering.

1   Introduction

In lighting engineering as in image synthesis, realism of generated images is partially conditioned by the ability to reproduce real light sources (i.e. light sources with non-uniform spectral and spatial energy distributions). Modeling of the spectral characteristics of light sources is generally based upon a sampling of the visible wavelength domain [1], however these methods do not permit discontinuous spectral characteristics to be taken into account. This problem has led us to develop a method which allows us to take into account any type of spectral characteristics [2].

Modeling of the spatial energy distribution of non-point light sources has been the basis of much research. Nishita et al. [3] proposed a method which enables us to take into account linear light sources with a diffuse spatial energy distribution and point light sources with a non-uniform spatial energy distribution. However, this does not deal with extended light sources. In order to take into account extended light sources, other models based upon gonio-photometric diagrams were designed [4, 5, 9]. However these kinds of models cannot take into account precisely the effect of an extended light source on a given scene, as the area of usage of gonio-photometric curves (i.e. the distance between the light source and the surfaces of the scene) must be restricted around a certain distance. Notably, when close to the light source the use of these curves causes important errors in the computation of the illumination of a surface.

Houle [6] proposed a method that can treat extended light sources. Their method uses a mesh of the emitive surface of the light source where, at each point of the mesh, a spatial energy distribution is assigned. This approach gives good result but up until now manufacturers can only give gonio-photometric curves for source considered punctual (due to the dispositive of measurement). Since manufacturers can not give the spatial energy distribution at several points of the light source, there is an important error in the calculation of the illumination on a surface with this method.

In order to model extended light sources corresponding to a given shape, and thus calculate and visualize their effect on an environment, we suggest the following method. We consider the light source as a sub-domain made up of a set of surfaces giving off energy in another environment using an interface zone. The method then consists of pre-computing the spatial energy distribution on the interface (which is, in fact, the outgoing surface of the light source). This computation is then used to calculate the illumination of the scene. This spatial energy distribution is computed by modeling entirely the light source (reflectors, bulbs...) and by calculating precisely the energy exchanges between the surfaces of this sub-environment using a projection method.

In this paper we shall start by presenting the equation which enables the effect of a light source on a scene to be computed(section 2). Then we will briefly introduce the various methods proposed to compute numerically this equation(section 2.1), as well as the inherent problems in these methods (section 2.2). We will present our method which allows the distribution of radiance on the outgoing surface of the source to be pre-calculated precisely (section 3), and we will discuss the results obtained (section 5). Finally we will draw our conclusions and introduce our future work (section 6).

2 The theoretical illumination model

The computation of the effect of a light source in a given environment assumes that we know the spatial energy distribution of the light source. By knowing

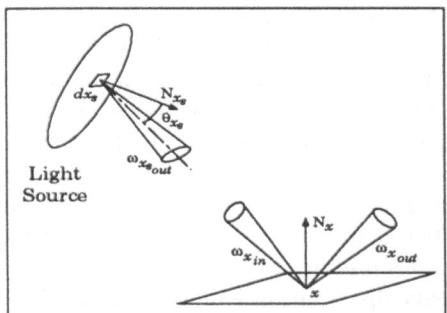

Figure 1: Computation of the effect of a light source on a surface

the spatial energy distribution at each point of the light source, we can describe the behaviour of a surface lit by this light source (see figure 1) :

$$L_\lambda(x, \omega_{x_{out}}) = \int_S \rho_\lambda(x, \omega_{x_{in}}, \omega_{x_{out}}) I_\lambda(x_s, \omega_{s_{out}}) \frac{cos\theta_{x_{in}}}{(x - x_s)^2} H(x_s, x) dx_s \qquad (1)$$

In this equation $L_\lambda(x, \omega_{x_{out}})$ represents the spectral radiance reflected in the $\omega_{x_{out}}$ direction by a surface with a bidirectional reflection function (*BRDF*) $\rho_\lambda(x, \omega_{x_{in}}, \omega_{x_{out}})$. This surface is lit by a light source S whose light intensity emitted from a point x_s in the direction $\omega_{x_{s_{out}}}$ is denoted by $I_\lambda(x_s, \omega_{s_{out}})$. $H(x_s, x)$ is the visibility function that takes the value of : 1 if x_s sees the point x and 0 otherwise.

2.1 Numerical methods to solve this equation

In order to compute the solution of equation 1 we can use several hypotheses which allow us to compute an approximate solution to this equation.

Nishita and Nakamae [3] developed a method to compute the radiance at each point of a surface lit by point or linear light sources. In this method only the point light sources have a non-uniform spatial energy distribution, while the linear light sources have a diffused spatial energy distribution. Shadow detection and penumbra detection are based upon a shadow volume computation algorithm. Although this method gives good results, it does not treat extended light sources.

A method for modeling extended light sources may involve meshing the surface of the light sources and, under certain hypotheses, approximating the equation 1 by a simple sum over the set of patches, as in the solution proposed by Verbeck et al. [5], Tellier et al. [4], Poulin et al. [9]. These methods suppose the spatial energy distribution is constant over the surface of the light source and therefore constant for each patch of the surfaces. This allows us to write :

$$L_\lambda(x) = \sum_i \rho_\lambda(x) cos\theta_{x_{in}} S_i I_\lambda(x_{s_i}, \theta_i^{out}, \phi_i^{out}) \qquad (2)$$

In this equation $I_\lambda(x_{s_i}, \theta_i^{out}, \phi_i^{out})$ represent the spatial energy distribution of the patch i of the light source for wavelength λ. This kind of approach deal with the data provided by manufacturers, however these data assume that internal reflections do not modify the spectral distribution (i.e the spectral distribution at each point of the outgoing surface of the light is the same as that from the lamp).

Using this kind of approach to model extended light sources, we suppose that the spatial intensity distribution is the same for each point of the light source. Although this hypothesis simplifies the computation of equation 1, we can be sure that the spatial intensity distribution is not constant over the outgoing surface of the light source. To define the variation of the spatial intensity distribution over the surface of the light source, Houle et al. proposed [6] meshing the surface of the extended light source. Knowing the spatial intensity distribution at some points of this mesh, they can compute the spatial intensity distribution at each point of the mesh using an interpolation method. Although this approach can treat extended light sources, they cannot be precisely modeled by this method since the spatial intensity distribution provided by a standard photo-goniometer is given for the center of the outgoing surface of light source.

2.2   Error due to this kind of model

The models that use gonio-photometric curves do not give good results since spatial intensity distributions are measured in a specific position relative to the light source (i.e. the distance between the light source and the photo-electric cell which measures the intensity of the light in a given direction is approximately $10m$ away).

This kind of model is nevertheless correct in an area of usage close to the distance where the measurement was carried out. In lighting engineering, the distance between the light sources and the surfaces is not always close to the distance of measurement of gonio-photometric curves and therefore the error in the calculation becomes significant, as shown in figure 2.

The horizontal axis of this graph represents the distance between the light source and the surface, and the vertical axis represents the relative error on the computation of the irradiance. To calculate this graph we assumed that the light source is a surfacic one (diameter equal to $30cm$) and has been emitted with a uniform flux in a conic beam (having an angle at the tip equal to 30 degree).

The error on the computed irradiance due to the models using gonio-photometric diagram (like in [5, 4]) is represented with the dashed and the continuous curve (one sample point on the surface of the light source for the dashed curves and 10 sample points on the surface of the light source for the continuous curve). The dotted curve represents the error due to the use of the Houle et al. to model the light source.

Moreover, all the models up to this point assume that the spectral energy distribution is constant at each point of the lighting system and corresponds to the spectrum of the lamp of the lighting system. Since there are internal reflections and transmissions, the spectral energy distribution also depends on

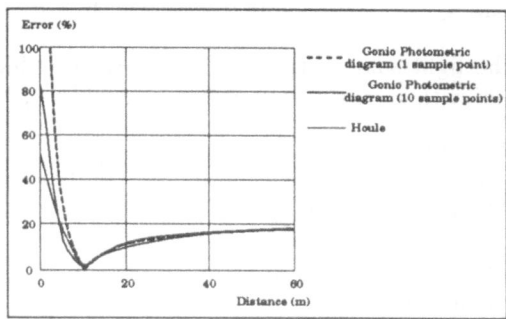

Figure 2: Error on the computation of irradiance on a surface perpendicular to the axis of the light source.

the position and the direction of the light leaving the outgoing surface of the light source.

3 Accurate modeling of light sources

In order to remedy these problems we model the geometry of the light source precisely and simulate the internal physical phenomenon in order to obtain a correct simulation (from the physical point of view) of the effect of this light source on the scene.

A light source can be considered as a sub-environment Γ_s of the scene which can spread energy in a global environment by an interface zone μ_s (see figure 3). For this reason we only have to calculate spatial and spectral energy distributions that leave the sub-environment constituted by the elements of the lighting system (i.e. reflectors, lamps corrective glass strips...) to simulate the effects of this light source on the scene. Moreover, as the computation of the spectral and spatial energy distribution is independent of the method used to compute the illumination of the scene, we will be able to pre-compute these distributions.

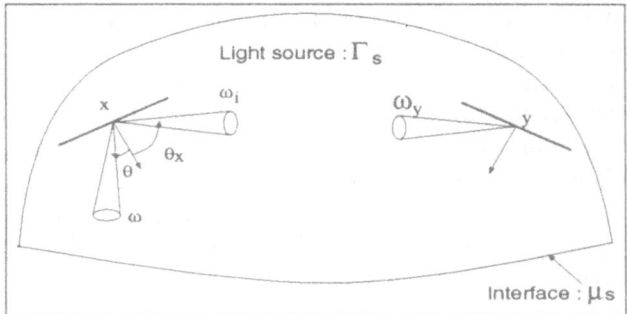

Figure 3: Computation of energy exchange between the surface of the sub-environment constituted by the light source.

The interface zone μ_s (see figure 3) is constituted by :

- a surface of the light source (the outgoing surface) which is inevitably a transparent one with a known transmittance and/or reflectance function.

- a virtual surface only used for the calculation. This surface will only have the property of transmittance. The value of the transmittance function denoted by $F(x, \omega_i, \omega)$ is given by :

$$F(x, \omega_i, \omega) = \begin{cases} 1 & \text{if } \omega_{in} = -\omega_{out} \\ 0 & \text{otherwise} \end{cases}$$

Locally to a light source, we must find the solution of Kajyia's equation [7] which allows us to calculate the radiance $L(x, \omega)$ emitted from the point x in the direction ω using the self emitted radiance $L^0(x, \omega)$ of this point, the radiance $L(y, \omega_y)$ of other points of the environment, and the bidirectional reflection or transmission function $F(x, \omega_i, \omega)$ of the point x (for an incident direction ω_i and for a reflection and/or a transmission direction ω) :

$$L(x, \omega) = L^0(x, \omega) + \int_\Omega F(x, \omega_i, \omega) L(y, \omega_y) \cos \theta_x d\omega \tag{3}$$

If we assume the environment is constituated by a set of surfaces, we can rewrite this equation by indexing L and F to a surface number :

$$L_i(x, \omega) = L_i^0(x, \omega) + \sum_n \int_{S_n} F_i(\omega_i, \omega) L_n(y, \omega_y) g(x, y) dS_n \tag{4}$$

In this formulation, F_i does not depend on x since, for a given surface, a given incident direction (ω_i), and a given reflection and/or transmission direction (ω) F_i is constant at each point of the surface S_n. The geometrical factor is $g(x, y) = (\cos \theta_x \cos \theta_y)/(x - y)^2$.

3.1 Use of the projection method

In order to solve equation 4, we propose the use of a projection method. In this case we are led to define a set of basis functions on which $L_i(x, \omega)$ will be projected, then, thanks to this representation, the resolution of the equation 4 simply consists of finding a solution to a system of linear equations. The radiance at each point of a given surface is given by : $\sum_j \beta_j^i(\omega) \gamma_j(x)$, where $\beta_j^i(\omega)$ corresponds to the projection of $L_i(x, \omega)$ on the basis function $\gamma_j(x)$ (which only depends on the position on the mesh). By using the same process, we can write $\beta_j^i(\omega) = \sum_k \alpha_{jk} \psi_k(\omega)$, where $\psi_k(\omega)$ depends only on the direction. This enables us to write :

$$L_i(x, \omega) = \sum_j \sum_k \alpha_{jk} \gamma_j(\omega) \psi_k(\omega) \tag{5}$$

From a physical point of view, this equation expresses the fact that the radiance at each point of a surface is a distribution.

In order to obtain the system of linear equations we first have to rewrite the equation 4 as a global energy balance relation by using :

$$e(L(x,\omega)) = \sum_m \int_{S_m} \int_\omega L(x,\omega) \cos \theta dS_n d\omega$$

By projecting the energy balance equation on the basis functions $\gamma_j(x)\,\psi_k(\omega)$, we have :

$$e_{jk}(g) = e_{jk}(d1) + e_{jk}(d2)$$

with :

$$e_{jk}(g) = \sum_m \int_{S_m,\omega} L_m(x,\omega)\gamma_j(x)\psi_k(\omega)\cos\theta dS_m d\omega$$

$$e_{jk}(d1) = \sum_m \int_{S_m,\omega} L_m^0(x,\omega)\gamma_j(x)\psi_k(\omega)\cos\theta dS_m d\omega \qquad (6)$$

$$e_{jk}(d2) = \sum_{m,n} \int_{S_m,\omega,S_n} F_i(\omega_i,\omega)L_n(y,\omega_y)g(x,y)\gamma_j(x)\psi_k(\omega)cos\theta dS_m d\omega dS_n$$

In this equation the quantity indexed by j,k corresponds to their projection on the basis functions $\gamma_j(x)$ and $\psi_k(\omega)$.

We replace $L_m(x,\omega)$ $L_m^0(x,\omega)$ $L_n(y,\omega_y)$ by their projections (see equation 5) to obtain :

$$e_{jk}(g) = \sum_{m,l,p} \alpha_{lp} \int_{S_m,\omega} \gamma_j(x)\psi_k(\omega)\gamma_l(x)\psi_p(\omega) \cos \theta dS_m d\omega$$

$$e_{jk}(d1) = \sum_{m,l,p} \alpha 0_{lp} \int_{S_m,\omega} \gamma_j(x)\psi_k(\omega)\gamma_l(x)\psi_p(\omega) \cos \theta dS_m d\omega \qquad (7)$$

$$e_{jk}(d2) = \sum_{m,n,l,p} \alpha_{lp} \int_{S_m,\omega,S_n} K(x,y)\gamma_j(x)\psi_k(\omega)\gamma_l(y)\psi_p(\omega_y)dS_m cos\theta d\omega dS_n$$

with $K(x,y,\omega) = F_i(\omega_i,\omega)g(x,y)$.

From this equation we can obtain the system of linear equations to solve by choosing the set of basis functions $\gamma_j(x)$ and $\psi_k(\omega)$.

3.2 Choice of the basis functions

We propose to use the finite elements method to compute the radiance L over the mesh. Using this method $\gamma_j(x)$ will be expressed as polynomials whose validity domain (denoted by $S(\gamma_j)$) will be the set of surfaces sharing the point of meshing associated to that basis function (see figure 4a). We have fixed the degree of the polynomials defining the set of basis functions $\gamma_j(x)$ as equal to 2, which means that the elements of the mesh will be triangles with 4 sample

154

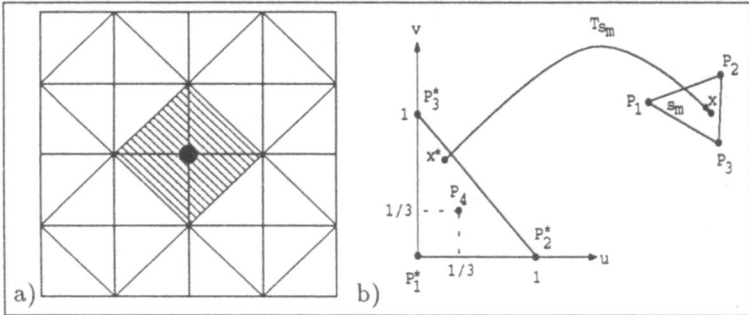

Figure 4: a) validity domain (filled zone) of the basis functions associated to the boxed point. b) Reference triangle on which the calculations are made

points (the three vertices and the geometrical centre of the triangle (see figure 4b).

With this method the computation of the elements S_m of the mesh are made on a reference triangle S^*, and thanks to a linear transformation T_{S_m} we obtain the result of the calculation on all the elements S_m of the meshing (see figure 4b). Thanks to that transformation, a point $x^* = (u, v)$ of the reference triangle can be transformed to a point $x = (x_m, y_m, z_m)$ belonging to the triangle S_m:

$$T_{S_m}(x^*) = b_{S_m} * x_m^* + a_{S_m}$$

$$\text{where}: \quad b_{S_m} = \begin{bmatrix} P_{1,x} - P_{3,x} & P_{2,x} - P_{3,x} \\ P_{1,y} - P_{3,y} & P_{2,y} - P_{3,y} \\ P_{1,z} - P_{3,z} & P_{2,z} - P_{3,z} \end{bmatrix} \quad \text{and} \quad a_{S_m} = \begin{bmatrix} P_{3,x} \\ P_{3,y} \\ P_{3,z} \end{bmatrix} \quad (8)$$

Since the computations are made in the reference triangle, the basis functions associated to each sample point can be pre-computed because they only depend on the geometry of this triangle. The basis functions associated with the sample points of the reference triangle are given by :

$$
\begin{aligned}
\gamma_1(u, v) &= 1 - u - v \\
\gamma_2(u, v) &= u - 2uv \\
\gamma_3(u, v) &= v - 2uv \\
\gamma_4(u, v) &= 4uv
\end{aligned}
\qquad (9)
$$

$\gamma_1..\gamma_4$ are the basis functions associated to the sample points $P_1^*..P_4^*$ of our reference triangle. By using the transformation given by equation 8, all integral equations over a surface of the mesh can be rewritten in a similar equation for the reference triangle :

$$\int_{S_m} f(x)dx = det(b_{S_m}) \int_{S^*} f(T_{S_m}(x))dS^* \qquad (10)$$

where : $det(b_{S_m})$ is the determinant of the matrix b_{S_m}

by applying this principle to equation 7 we obtain :

$$e_{jk}(g) \quad = \quad \sum_{m,l,p} \alpha_{lp} E^{kp}_{m,jl}$$

$$e_{jk}(d1) \quad = \quad \sum_{m,l,p} \alpha 0_{lp} E^{kp}_{m,jl} \tag{11}$$

$$e_{jk}(d2) \quad = \quad \sum_{m,n,l,p} \alpha_{lp} A^{kp}_{mn,jl}$$

with :

$$E^{kp}_{m,jl} = det(b_{S_m}) \int_\omega \int_{S^*_m} \gamma_j(x^*_m)\gamma_l(x^*_m)\psi_p(\omega)\psi_k(\omega)\cos\theta dS^*_m d\omega$$

$$A^{kp}_{mn,jl} = det(b_{S_m})det(b_{S_n})\tau^{kp}_{mn,jl}$$

$$\tau^{kp}_{mn,jl} = \int_{S^*_m,S^*_n} F_m(\omega_i,\omega)\gamma_j(x^*_m)\gamma_l(x^*_n)g(T_{S_m}(x^*_m),T_{S_n}(x^*_n))\psi_p(\omega_y)\psi_k(\omega)\cos\theta$$
$$dS^*_m dS^*_n d\omega$$

The choice of the set of basis functions depending on the direction (ψ_k) will be the last step to obtain the system of linear equations. For a given point of the light source we know that the intensity distribution could be discontinuous. We then choose the family of basis functions $\psi_k(\omega)$ piecewise constant[1] (i.e. $\psi_k(\omega) = 1$ if and only if $\omega \in [\phi_{k,1}, \phi_{k,2}] \times [\theta_{k,1}, \theta_{k,2}])$. We also assume $F_n(\omega_i, \omega)$ constant on $[\phi_{k,1}, \phi_{k,2}] \times [\theta_{k,1}, \theta_{k,2}]$. Thanks to these hypotheses in the equations $e_{jk}(g)$ and $e_{jk}(d1)$, $\psi_p(\omega)\psi_k(\omega) = 1$ if and only if $k = p$, so that the sum over the variable p is reduced to one term. The sum over the variable m is reduced to the element of the mesh such that $S_m \in S(\gamma_j)$, moreover, $\gamma_l(x^*_m)\gamma_j(x^*_m) = 1$ if and only if $S(\gamma_j) \cap S(\gamma_l) \neq \varnothing$. In the equation $e_{jk}(d2)$ the sum over the variables m is reduced to the elements of the mesh such that $S_m \in S(\gamma_i)$. It follows :

$$E^{kp}_{m,jl} = det(b_{S_m})C_k G_{m,jl}$$
$$A^{kp}_{mn,jl} = det(b_{S_m})det(b_{S_n})C_k F^k_{mn,jl} \tag{12}$$

With :

$$C_k = \int_{\omega_k} \psi_k(\omega)\psi_k(\omega)\cos\theta d\omega = \tfrac{1}{2}(\phi_{k,2} - \phi_{k,1})(\sin^2\theta_{k,2}\sin^2\theta_{k,1})$$

$$G_{m,jl} = \int_{S^*_m} \gamma_j(x^*_m)\gamma_l(x^*_m)dS^*_m$$

$$F^k_{mn,jl} = \int_{S^*_m} \int_{S^*_n} F_m(\omega_i,\omega_K)\gamma_j(x^*_m)\gamma_l(x^*_n)g(T_{S_m}(x^*_m),T_{S_n}(x^*_n))dS^*_m dS^*_n$$

the computation of the integral over ω gives :

$$\sum_{m,l} \alpha_{lk}E^{kp}_{m,jl} - \sum_{m,n,l',p} \alpha_{l'p}A^{kp}_{mn,jl'} = \sum_{m,l} \alpha 0_{lk}E^{kp}_{m,jl} \tag{13}$$

---

[1] We have thought to use others sets of basis functions (like orthogonal polynomials, spherical harmonics ...) but the complexity of the system of equations is such that the solution computed to this system is very time consuming (since the coefficients of the matrix are very complex). The use of higher order basis functions will be devellopped in our future work

Where :

m : such that $S_m \in S(\gamma_j)$

l : such that $S(\gamma_j) \cap S(\gamma_l) \neq \oslash$

l' : such that $S_n \in S(\gamma_{l'})$

p : $p \in [1..q]$ where q is the number of basis fonctions ψ

To obtain the system of linear equations we just have to rewrite this equation for all the sample points of the mesh.

3.3   Solving the system of linear equations

In order to solve the system of linear equations several methods can be used(like Gauss Siedel, Southwell,Jacoby...). We propose to use the numerical method of Southwell which converges quickly. The algorithm can be found in [8]. To calculate the coefficient C_{il} we have to integrate a polynomial over the reference triangle since $\gamma_j(x_m^*)$ and $\gamma_l(x_m^*)$ are polynomials. This integration is made in a symbolic way. The coeficient F_{jlp}^{mn} represents the portion of energy leaving the surface S_m received by the surface S_n. This term is calculated by using the Gaussian quadratures method with 4 sample points per surface.

4   Computation of the effect of the light source

After we have computed the energy leaving the sub-environment (constituted by the light source) by the interface zone, we have to take into account the effect of this energy on the calculation of the illumination of the scene. For this we merely have to compute the integral equation 1 in which we will replace $L(x, \omega_{x_{out}})$ by its decomposition (see equation 5). If we assume that the interface is constituted of a set of surfaces S_m we have to compute :

$$
L(x, \omega_{x_{out}}) = \sum_{n,j,k} \int_{S_n} \frac{\rho(x, \omega_{x_{in}}, \omega_{x_{out}}) \alpha_{jk} \gamma_j(x) \psi_k(\omega)}{\frac{\cos\theta_{x_{in}} \cos\theta_{X_s}}{(x-x_s)^2}} H(x_s, x) dS_n \tag{14}
$$

To calculate this integral we discretise the surface S_m to a set of surfaces S_n^m, and by assuming these surfaces are sufficiently small. We can write :

$$
L_\lambda(x, \omega_{x_{out}}) = \sum_{n,j,k,m} \frac{\rho_\lambda(x, \omega_{x_{in}^m}, \omega_{x_{out}}) \alpha_{jk} \gamma_j(x^m) \psi_k(\omega^m)}{\frac{\cos\theta_{x_{in}} \cos\theta_{x_s^m}}{(x-x_s^m)^2}} H(x_s^m, x) \Delta S_n^m \tag{15}
$$

Thanks to this equation we can use our method of light source modeling in the algorithm used to compute the illumination of a scene in image synthesis.

5   Results

Our method gives good results as shown by the graph (figure 5). To compute this graph we have used a light source made up by a parabolic reflector with a mercury vapour bulb. The horizontal axis of this graph represents the distance between a surface perpendicular to the axis of the light source, and the vertical axis represents the relative error calulated by :

$$error = \frac{(\sum_j | E_j^c - E_j^m |)}{\sum_j E_j^m} \tag{16}$$

In this equation E_j^c represent the irradiance computed by our method on a set of sample points, E_j^m represent the irradiance measured on the same sample points for the real light source. To calculate the spatial energy distribution on the interface zone of the light source (used to compute graph 5), we meshed its surfaces with 978 patches. The calculations took 35 minutes on a Silicon Graphics work station having a R4600 processor with $128Mo$ of ram.

Figure 6a and figure 6b were obtained by calculating the effect of a neon light source with anti reflecting diffuse light surfaces on a surface of concrete situated $1m$ from the light source. Figure 6a used the spatial energy distribution calculated by our method. This spatial energy distribution was calculated in 45 minutes on a Silicon Graphics work station having a R4600 processor with $128Mo$ of ram (there were 1534 patches after the meshing of this light source). Figure 6b was calculated for the same light sources using gonio-photometric curves. We can see in figure 6b that irradiance on the surface is uniform, whereas the result obtain by our method is not continuous (as shown in figure 6a). This is more close to reality than the result given in Figure 6a. The discontinuities in the figure 6a are not due to the choice of piecewise constant basis functions (ψ_k). This are the result that reflects the real effect produced by this combination of lamp and surface.

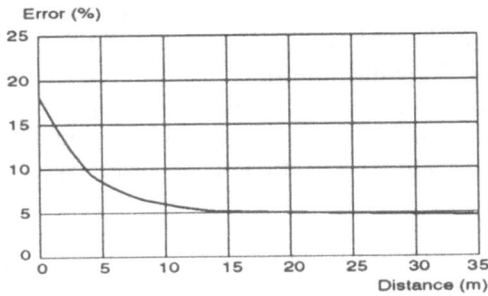

Figure 5: Relative error due to our method on the calculation of the irradiance on a surface.

The figure in the appendix is a house design by "Le Corbusier", this house is illuminated by two wall-mounted halogen light sources, these light source are protected by a metallic grid which explain the irregularities close to these light sources whereas the irregularities do not exist further away on the ceiling. If we were to use a classical model we would not simulate the subtle lighting effects close to the lamp. This image was computed on a Silicon Graphic worstation

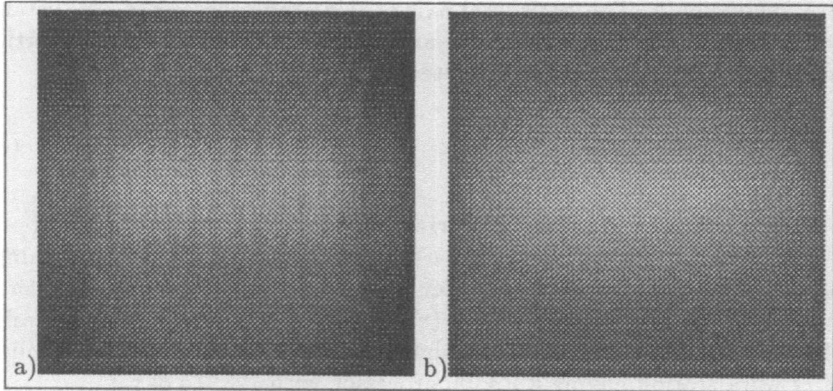

Figure 6: computation of the effect of a light source on a surface using our method (a), computation of the effect of a light source on a surface using gonio-photometric curves(b).

having a R4600 processor with $128Mo$ of ram using a radiosity algorithm, where the calculation takes 40 minutes.

6   Conclusion and future works

The method we propose gives good results since we remove the hypotheses of constant spectral and spatial energy distributions over the light sources. Nevertheless we want verify the hypotheses of piecewise constant basis functions for the set of basis fonction ψ_k and try to test other sets of basis functions such as spherical harmonics or orthogonal polynomial. This method is being implemented in an industrial application which will be used to calculate the reflectors form for light sources. Thanks to our method designers will be able to specify the geometry of their lighting systems (visualisation of the spatial energy distribution and eventualy modification of the geometry of the light source).

References

[1] G. W. Meyer. Wavelength selection for synthetic image generation. *Computer Vision Graphics and Image Processing*, pages 57–79, 1988.

[2] P. M. Deville, S. Merzouk, D. Cazier, and J. C. Paul. Spectral data modeling for lighting applications. *Proceeding of the International Conference Eurographics'94*, 13(3):97–106, September 1994. Oslo, Norway.

[3] T. Nishita, I. Okamura, and E. Nakamae. Shading models for point and linear sources. *ACM Transaction on Graphics*, 4(2):124–146, April 1985.

[4] E. Languénou and P. Tellier. Including physical light sources and daylight in global illumination model. *Proceeding of the International Conference Eurographics Workshop'92*, 1992.

[5] C. P. Verbeck and D. P. Greenberg. A comprehensive light-source description for computer graphics. *IEEE CG&A*, pages 66–75, July 1984.

[6] C. Houle and E. Fiume. Light-source modeling using pyramidal light maps. *CVGIP:Graphical Models And Image Processing*, 55(5):346–358, 1993.

[7] J. Kajiya and B. P. Von Herzen. Ray tracing volume densities. *Computer Graphics (Siggraph'84 proc.)*, 18(3):165–175, July 1984.

[8] S. Gortler, M. F. Cohen and P. Slusalle Radiosity and Relaxation Method *Princeton University Febrary 1993*.

[9] P. Poulin and J. Amantides Shading and Shadowing With Linear Light Sources *Proceeding of the International Conference Eurographics'90, 1990*

Painting surface characteristics

Pierre Poulin
Dept. I.R.O.
Université de Montréal

Alain Fournier
Dept. of Computer Science
University of British Columbia

Abstract. Surface illumination proceeds according to the strict rules of the reflection model, the light characteristics and the geometry of the scene. To get a given illumination effect on a surface in a fixed geometry, a user must determine the surface characteristics that will produce this effect. This process is part of what is called *inverse illumination*. In most current modeling systems, the user must rely only on intuition to perform this inverse illumination, which can lead to many modeling/rendering cycles to achieve a satisfactory result.

In this paper, we are concerned with the case where lighting effects are not merely a consequence of the geometry, but rather part of the design. We therefore concentrate our efforts on controlling the surface characteristics and present a tool which can reduce considerably the problem of inverse illumination by using a *painting* paradigm. An interactive system is provided where the user simply applies color points on a surface. The system then attempts in near real time to find the *best values* for the surface characteristics such that the points will retain their assigned color in the final rendering. Depending on the number of constraints (color points) given by the user, the solution is presented as a non-linear constrained optimization and a constrained weighted least-square fitting. We apply our solution to a simple illumination model using ambient, diffuse and specular components to illustrate our approach.

1 Introduction

When designing a scene to be rendered, a user generally first defines the geometry of the scene and the placement and characteristics of the light sources. Once satisfied with the model, the user then fixes the parameters determining the surface characteristics. All of these values determine the appearance of the surface in the final rendering. The surface characteristics can include surface color, quantity of ambient, diffuse and specular reflection, surface glossiness, degree of anisotropy, ratio of dielectric versus conductor properties, transparency, index of refraction, sub-surface scattering, and many others, depending on the illumination model used. Typically, as the illumination model captures more of the behavior of real surfaces, more parameters are required to control the illumination. Moreover, these parameters are often dependent on each other, making it impossible to assign each parameter individually.

In most current modeling systems, very little information is provided to help the user predict what the resulting illumination will be. The user must then rely on intuition and experience to compute mentally the *inverse illumination*: for a given surface and a given geometry of the scene, which set of values for the radiance of the light sources and surface characteristics will produce the desired illumination. A typical session then consists of estimating these values and then rendering the result, which, depending on the scene complexity, the rendering technique and the level of accuracy needed, can take anywhere from a fraction of a second to hours. With the picture as feedback, the user can return to the modeler and tune the parameters to create the desired illumination effects. This process is repeated until the image corresponds to what is wanted or until the user finally decides, after many frustrating attempts, that this is "as good as it is going to get!"

This paper describes an attempt to provide the user with a tool to directly manipulate the illumination effects. More precisely, we present a system that allows a user to control in near real time the surface parameters by simply painting color points on a surface. Each color point is governed by an equation, the variables of which are the surface property parameters. A system of equations arises from all the color points on the surface. So while the user adds and moves color points on a surface, the modeler attempts to determine values for the surface characteristics such that the color points will retain their assigned values (within a certain acceptable range) when the picture is rendered. Each color point introduces a constraint (or two constraints when a range of colors is provided) in a system of equations. When there are less color points than variables, the resulting under-constrained system is solved via non-linear constrained optimization. When there are more color points than variables, the over-constrained system is solved via a weighted least-square approximation with penalty functions to constrain the values of surface parameters. Surface characteristics can therefore be automatically determined as the user adds color points and interactively moves them on the surface.

The system deals only with *local illumination*, that is direct illumination from lights, and therefore each surface can be treated independently of the others. This restriction allows us to deal with complex illumination models by solving non-linear systems of equations. The solution can be computed and displayed in real time on current graphics workstations, providing direct feedback to the user.

This approach reduces the number of inverse illumination tasks (or more exactly *guesses*) that a user must perform, and should lead to an important reduction in the number of modeling/rendering iterations necessary to achieve a given result. It also does not require the user to know all the specifics of an illumination model and prevents the use of *magic* numbers. Since this approach can be used in conjunction with traditional systems, any user, whether experienced or not, should benefit from the extra help provided by this type of modeler.

In the next sections we will first review other work dealing with inverse illumination, then describe the scenario for using our system, and explain how we solve the inverse illumination problem by formulating it as an optimization problem or a fitting problem. Finally we discuss possible extensions of our technique and conclude.

2 Previous work

In most current modeling systems, the user is given a set of valuators to select a value for each available illumination parameter. For almost all renderers assigning a value to a parameter does not result in a prompt update of the image. This approach is typical of the *direct illumination* paradigm commonly used today. Inverse illumination consists of finding automatically values for these parameters. It has been considered a few times before in some different contexts. We summarize here the three systems we know of.

Poulin and Fournier [1] present a system where a user can control the definition and position of a light source by manipulating highlights and/or shadow volumes produced it. Their system uses simple geometric constraints which lead to a unique solution in real time. The only surface characteristic used is the surface glossiness (the exponent in *Phong-type* illumination model) defining the size of a highlight, but it provides no information about the gradient of color in the highlight.

Schoeneman *et al.* [2] address the problem of selecting lights and surface reflectances in the context of a global illumination computation with diffuse reflectors. They use inverse illumination to determine the emitted radiances of the lights. In their system a reflectance must first be associated with each surface. The user then paints colors on surfaces in the scene with a tool simulating spray paint. They assume ideal diffuse surfaces and the light radiances are determined only accounting for direct illumination.

Kawai *et al.* [3] also use inverse illumination for global illumination in a diffuse environment. They use unconstrained non-linear optimization to find a local minimum of a possibly complex objective function. The function includes physical terms (emission, directionality and distribution of the light sources and element reflectance) and terms based on human perception (impression of clearness, pleasantness, and privacy based on the scene brightness). In order to reduce the number of free variables, the user must select the active variables and impose constraints on them.

Inverse illumination problems are of course part and parcel of computer vision. The specific problems investigated include *shape from shading* direction of illuminants from images and identifying surface characteristics from a single or a series of images. The degree of difficulty of these problems is mostly due to the lack of knowledge about both the geometry and the illumination of the scene, but many of the methods are relevant to the problems we deal with here. Fortunately for us, in a modeler for computer graphics the viewing parameters and the exact scene geometry are known and therefore many problems become easier to solve. Our situation is also different from the one found in computer vision since we want the user to control interactively the illumination of a surface. As such we expect the user to provide options and feedback to the system and thus resolve ambiguities when they arise.

3 Painting scenario

Our painting system is built within a traditional modeler. The user can create and position objects and lights, and can set the viewing parameters. The user can set the surface characteristics and light radiances directly. The modeler also provides direct access to the scene geometry. When the user picks on screen a pixel corresponding to a point on an object, geometric information such as its surface normal, and illumination information such as the number and location of lights illuminating that point are available.

The interface to the painting system is simple. A user selects colors and applies them to any visible point in the 3D scene. Each time a color point is applied on the surface, the illumination parameters are recomputed given its color points and the resulting illumination is displayed. A color point is represented on the surface by a small disk. The disk is painted with the selected color but is not shaded. These color points can be added, moved and deleted, their color can be changed and each disk can be scaled up or down. Figure 1 shows some color points and their associated disks on a surface. One can see how the color on each disk is consistent with the color gradient on the surface.

The painted color points thus control the illumination of the surface, providing a high level basis (the illumination model itself) for the interpolation of the surface colors. This is to be contrasted with a traditional 2D painting system where the user can assign a different color to each pixel, or a pattern of colors to a region of pixels. Thus the user has complete control over the final look of the image, but has also full responsibility for illumination *coherence*, which can require the skills of a master painter. To facilitate that task, Hanrahan and Haeberli [4] developed a 3D painting system where a user can paint specific values of surface characteristics directly on points or regions of a 3D model. Our painting system goes further, while making things easier for the user, since it deals with a higher level abstraction than the parameters (color or other surface characteristics) at a given pixel. When the painting is done, the system tries to establish the *best* values for the illumination parameters of each surface. By *best* we mean that the system attempts to optimize certain functions (in the under-constrained case) or to fit values (in the over-constrained case) so the color points will remain as close as possible to their assigned colors when the full rendering is completed. This will be explained in more detail in the following sections. It is important to note that the user does not have to be aware of either the illumination model or the numerical methods used to provide the answers, but has only to judge if the result is acceptable.

If for some combination of painted color points no value for the surface characteristics will satisfy all the constraints, the user can then ask the system to provide colors for a set of given color points for which a solution exists. To do so, the system first relaxes a little the constraints around the latest color point given. If this does not lead to any solution, the constraints are relaxed even more. Colors for which a converging solution can be found are indicated in the color tool.

Now that we have described the general behavior of the system, we describe in the next sections the numerical algorithms used to find the best values for the surface parameters as determined by the painted color points. We will see how each color point can be interpreted as an entry in a system of equations, a constraint in an optimization problem or a sample in a fitting problem.

4 Painting: solving a system of equations

Recall we assume that the geometry of the 3D scene is known and that all the light sources are positioned with known emitted radiance. When a surface element is illuminated, the radiance directly reflected towards the viewer is a function of the illuminants, the scene geometry and the surface parameters. Consider the following popular reflection model [5] applied to a surface element illuminated by m lights:

$$L_{pixel} = k_a(\lambda)L_a(\lambda) +$$
$$k_d(\lambda)\sum_{i=1}^{m}\int_{\omega_i}(\mathbf{N}\cdot\mathbf{L}_i)L_i(\lambda)\,d\omega_i + \tag{1}$$
$$k_s(\lambda)\sum_{i=1}^{m}\int_{\omega_i}F_s(\lambda)(\mathbf{N}\cdot\mathbf{H}_i)^n L_i(\lambda)\,d\omega_i$$

where $k_a(\lambda)$ is the quantity of ambient reflection,
$\quad k_d(\lambda)$ is the quantity of diffuse reflection,
$\quad k_s(\lambda)$ is the quantity of specular reflection,
$\quad L_i(\lambda)$ is the radiance of light i,
$\quad L_a(\lambda)$ is the ambient radiance,
$\quad \mathbf{N}\quad$ is the surface normal (unit vector),
$\quad \mathbf{L}_i\quad$ is the direction towards light i (unit vector),
$\quad \mathbf{H}_i\quad$ is the bisector direction between $\mathbf{N}$ and $\mathbf{L}_i$ (unit vector),
$\quad n\quad$ is the glossiness factor (surface roughness),
$\quad F_s(\lambda)$ is the specular reflection function,
$\quad \omega_i\quad$ is the solid angle formed by light i.

$F_s(\lambda)$ is a function introduced in the specular term to adapt both to traditional models such as Phong or Blinn, or to more complex models.

If we consider $k_a(\lambda)$, $L_a(\lambda)$ and $F_s(\lambda)$ as being constant, then we have an illumination model similar to most software and hardware renderers in current use. This is important in order to control the illumination while displaying in real time the results on a given machine.

For a given color point, the light due to diffuse reflection can be summed for all m lights as:

$$L_d(\lambda) = \sum_{i=1}^{m}\int_{\omega_i}(\mathbf{N}\cdot\mathbf{L}_i)L_i(\lambda)\,d\omega_i \qquad \text{for } \mathbf{N}\cdot\mathbf{L}_i > 0.$$

And similarly for the specular reflection:

$$L_s(\lambda) = \sum_{i=1}^{m}\int_{\omega_i}(\mathbf{N}\cdot\mathbf{H}_i)^n L_i(\lambda)\,d\omega_i \qquad \text{for } \begin{cases} \mathbf{N}\cdot\mathbf{L}_i > 0 \text{ and} \\ \mathbf{N}\cdot\mathbf{H}_i > 0. \end{cases}$$

Generally speaking, $L_d(\lambda)$ and $L_s(\lambda)$ can be computed for any type of light source, whether it is a point light, a linear light or an area light. It is also possible to compute it while accounting for shadows.

Each color point contributes to a new equation at each wavelength. If there are as many independent equations as variables, the system of equations can be solved and a unique value identified for each surface attribute. Looking at Equation (1) when $F_s(\lambda)$ is constant, we can subsume it into $k_s(\lambda)$ and therefore have three terms $(k_a(\lambda), k_d(\lambda), k_s(\lambda))$ which capture the surface color and the proportion of ambient, diffuse and specular reflection, respectively. With the illumination model of Equation (1), a system of three variables can be determined with only three color points in the following form

$$\begin{bmatrix} 1 & L_{d1} & L_{s1} \\ 1 & L_{d2} & L_{s2} \\ 1 & L_{d3} & L_{s3} \end{bmatrix} \cdot \begin{bmatrix} k_a \\ k_d \\ k_s \end{bmatrix} = \begin{bmatrix} L_1 \\ L_2 \\ L_3 \end{bmatrix},$$

where L_{dj} and L_{sj} represent the computed values for the diffuse and specular reflections for the jth color point. If a solution to this system exists, a unique value for k_a, k_d and k_s can be computed. Unfortunately it is unlikely a user will be able to provide the exact colors that would lead to a solution. The next two sections present two interpretations of this problem and their respective solutions.

5 Painting: an optimization problem

We can look at this problem as an optimization problem when there are less equations than unknowns. In this scheme, each color point (its range) is given as a volume in the 3D color space of acceptable colors, thus introducing two inequality constraints in each dimension. Additional constraints are associated with the semantics of the parameters in the illumination model. For instance, no parameter in Equation (1) should be negative. Moreover, some illumination models can put an upper limit on the values of some of their parameters. The combination of all the constraints on a surface can lead to no feasible solution (over-constrained), a unique solution (rare) or an infinity of solutions (under-constrained). In the latter case, to provide the user with a unique solution, we need to minimize or maximize an objective function.

5.1 Objective function

Several objective functions are possible and each can lead to a different behavior for the system. In our current implementation, the choice of objective functions is based on the number of color points and their location. Generally, we proceed as follows. We first minimize the ambient term. Surfaces lit only with ambient light appear flat. So by minimizing this term, we ensure that the surface will not appear flat unless constrained so by the user. Once a solution is found, we bound this minimum on k_a within a narrow band to ensure that k_a remains close to its minimum and then maximize the diffuse term. We thus provide more control of the diffuse reflection which often has the most impact on the appearance of a surface.

We found that this combination of objectives leads to a behavior that is intuitive and simple to understand. However it would be possible to *personalize* the behavior of the system by providing the user with a library of objective functions. The user can then interactively select the objectives and combine them.

A series of frames are given in Figure 1 to illustrate the behavior of our system. We chose a simple elongated ellipsoid because of the wide range of possible color gradients due to the continuous changes of its surface normals. The top left image of Figure 1 shows the solution computed for a single color point applied at the bottom part of the ellipse. The ambient component is zero and a dark shade is computed from the diffuse illumination. When the second color point is added in the region in shadow in the top right image of Figure 1, the surface is reshaded with both ambient and diffuse illumination. A third color point is added in the center left image. It then specifies a value for the specular coefficient. Because this color point is added near the boundary of the highlight, it creates a very bright highlight. By moving it closer to the center of the highlight, this color gradient is reduced and therefore the intensity of the highlight is lower. This is shown in the center right image of Figure 1.

The illumination model of Equation (1) can be solved by a simple constrained linear optimization algorithm. These algorithms have the advantage of converging to the global minimum if such a minimum exists. However most of the even slightly more sophisticated illumination models often introduce non-linear constraints. Consider the following illumination model:

$$L_{pixel}(\lambda) = k_a S(\lambda) + \\ k_d S(\lambda) L_d(\lambda) + \\ k_s L_s(\lambda) [M S(\lambda) + (1 - M)].$$
(2)

This model includes a surface color S and simulates a linear dielectric-conductor ratio ($M \in [0, 1]$) for the specular reflection. It is more complex than the previous reflection model. Also notice that the coefficients of ambient, diffuse and specular reflections (k_a, k_d, k_s) are the same for all wavelengths. Therefore we cannot treat the solution independently in each wavelength. The constraints in this model are non-linear. We input these constraints and their gradients into CFSQP [6], a general algorithm to solve constrained non-linear optimization problems.

5.2 Initial guess

The specular reflection can generate a solution within a very narrow domain (spike). If the initial guess is infeasible for some constraints, CFSQP will attempt to find a feasible starting value but can fail to identify one. If this happens, no optimization can be performed even if a solution exists. To avoid this situation, we developed careful initial guesses based on our knowledge of the domains of each variable and the region in which each color point resides.

Another strategy involves enlarging the domain of certain variables and studying the gradient of the converging solutions to determine an initial guess. For instance, a large value for the glossiness factor n produces sharp and small highlights. For a color point to contribute to the highlight, it must reside within the highlight such that $((\mathbf{N} \cdot \mathbf{H})^n > t)$ for a small threshold t. Outside this highlight, the function $(\mathbf{N} \cdot \mathbf{H})^n$ has a very small gradient. If we start with a small value for the glossiness which produces a larger domain and a stronger gradient, we can use the converged solution as an initial guess to the same system of equations but with a slightly larger glossiness value. Adaptively changing the value of the glossiness can then be done automatically. This approach is more expensive computationally but offers an alternative when no other initial guess seems to lead to a solution.

6 Painting: a fitting problem

As the user adds more and more color points to control the illumination, there comes a time when the color points define more constraints than there are free variables. In this case, the problem can be interpreted as fitting the best approximation for each variable subjected to non-linear constraints. We use a non-linear least-square fitting algorithm, *lmder*, taken from MINPACK and available on netlib. *lmder* is based on the Levenberg-Marquardt algorithm.

In a typical least-square fitting, each variable is free. However in our illumination models, each variable is constrained within a certain domain. To retain this concept of boundaries we use penalty functions to represent these constraints. Let $f_p(x)$ be the penalyzed function of $f(x)$:

$$
f_p(x) = \begin{cases} f(x) \cdot e^{bl-x} & \text{if } x < bl \\ f(x) & \text{if } bl \leq x \leq bu \\ f(x) \cdot e^{x-bu} & \text{if } bu < x \end{cases}
$$

where bl and bu are the lower and upper boundaries on x, respectively. Any steep function could replace the exponential here. The steeper the function, the higher the penalty will be if a variable goes beyond its domain, but also the stiffer the system will be.

We also modify our system in order to provide different weights depending on the location of the color points. In general least-square problems, a wrong value will have a tendency to drag all the previous values in one direction. Weights can reduce this effect. From illumination Equations (1) and (2), one can observe that a color point within a shadow region on a surface can directly influence very few variables. Therefore we can increase by a large factor (100 in our system) the weight of these points. This ensures that the points in the other regions do not push the ambient term outside its limits. Similarly, the diffuse reflection is usually well controlled by one or two color points. A smaller factor (10 in our system) keeps their contributions important, although less than the ambient ones. Finally, in most cases, the designer uses more color points to finely tune the variation of colors within the highlights. Each such color point will keep a unit contribution. By choosing appropriate weights, it is possible to approximate the behavior of the objective functions in the optimization approach. If done properly, a user will not notice the passage from an optimization problem to a least-square fitting one.

However, unlike the optimization algorithm, the least-square fitting does not guarantee that every color point will retain its color in the final rendering. The weights and penalties do help to keep the final colors as close as possible to the painted ones. This technique offers a nice alternative to the optimization when the user is not able to find an initial feasible guess or when the objective function does not produce exactly the expected illumination.

In the bottom left and right images of Figure 1, two darker color points are added to the previous ones, creating a fitting problem instead of an optimization one. The darker color points positioned near the highlight contour reduce the diffuse illumination while producing a highlight with a sharper gradient.

7 Results and extensions

The main advantage of this combination of optimization and least-square fitting is that their use is mostly invisible to the user. The user does not need to know how many variables there are in the illumination model and what are their contributions to the final illumination. In fact, several illumination models could be used within the modeler and the user would never have to request one over another. The system could adapt itself to the demands of the user when he insists on certain color points to be placed at specific locations, providing a more sophisticated illumination model only when necessary.

We found that for the functions and weights we used, the behavior of our system appeared intuitive, predictable and lead quickly to the desired illumination. If the first painted color points are placed mainly in the shadowed and diffuse regions of a surface, the user gets high control on the final illumination with only a few points. Once these aspects of the illumination are satisfactory, the user can finely tune the look of the highlights with more color points. In many of our test scenes, we found that three to four color points often provide enough control to quickly produce a satisfactory result.

It is important to provide the user with adequate feedback when color points are added or moved. The real-time hardware rendering with the machine illumination model allows one to see directly the surface change as the color points are added or moved on the surface.

From our experience and as Kawai et al. [3] indicated, adding more variables to a system usually has the effect of enlarging the domain of possible solutions which makes it easier to converge to a solution. Unfortunately, depending on the contribution of the new variables, they can introduce more local minima. By starting the searches at various locations, the alternative solutions could be presented to the user only when he is not fully satisfied with the current illumination.

We believe that some additional variables could be added to extend the simple illumination models we used here. The first one is the glossiness. We did not consider it because we used the technique in [1] to define the highlights. As previously discussed, a low glossiness value can provide a larger range for initial guesses. It then becomes possible to try to maximize the glossiness in an objective function and therefore to control this variable.

Other parameters from more sophisticated illumination models could be investigated. Some examples include transparency, anisotropy, diffraction, polarization, layered surfaces, etc. However each of these new variables must be studied with respect to the inverse illumination problem which in some cases become quite difficult.

8 Conclusion

Inverse illumination is too difficult a problem to expect the user to solve mentally. In this paper, we presented a system that solves some inverse illumination tasks for the user by using a painting paradigm. Color points are painted on a surface and these points are used to find the best values for the illumination parameters so the painted colors will keep their colors during the final rendering. The color points therefore control the illumination of a surface.

With this technique, it also becomes easier to make small illumination corrections. This technique can also be used to approximate the illumination of real surfaces in the context of mixing real images with computer graphics images by taking sampled colors on a real image of the modeled surface under similar illumination.

When the system is under-constrained we use a non-linear constrained optimization algorithm to find a unique solution for all constraints. The solution guarantees all color points will be within their user-specified boundaries. The objective function defines the behavior of the system. We proposed some combinations of objective functions and techniques to find a feasible initial guess.

When the system is over-constrained we use non-linear least-square fitting to find a solution. The constraints are enforced by penalty functions, weights control the behavior of the system, depending upon the location of the color points. The results are not guaranteed to be within the constraints but are usually very close. A good choice of objective functions and weights and penalty functions provides a smooth transition between the optimization algorithm and the least-square fitting.

Our painting system deals only with direct illumination. By doing so, it provides high control of the full illumination while keeping the number of constraints and variables relatively low. This allows the system to return solutions almost in real time, which used in conjunction with hardware real-time rendering provides a direct feedback to the user adding and moving color points on the surface. Our solution with simple illumination models is a first step that we hope can be tailored to different and more sophisticated illumination models.

Our system can easily be merged with a traditional modeler where the user has to choose directly all the illumination parameters. We offer an alternative so one simply needs to fix or tightly constrain the values of the assigned parameters and let the system find values for the rest.

Our goal in this particular work was to design and implement the tools that will make inverse illumination a practical option for scene modeling. To determine whether and when this approach allows to obtain better results faster is a task that is quite different and remains to be addressed.

References

[1] Pierre Poulin and Alain Fournier. "Lights from highlights and shadows". *Computer Graphics (1992 Symposium on Interactive 3D Graphics)*, volume 25, pp. 31–38, March 1992.

[2] Chris Schoeneman, Julie Dorsey, Brian Smits, James Arvo, and Donald P. Greenberg. "Painting With Light". *Computer Graphics (SIGGRAPH '93 Proceedings)*, volume 27, pp. 143–146, August 1993.

[3] John K. Kawai, James S. Painter, and Michael F. Cohen. "Radioptimization – Goal-based Rendering". *Computer Graphics (SIGGRAPH '93 Proceedings)*, volume 27, pp. 147–154, August 1993.

[4] Pat Hanrahan and Paul E. Haeberli. "Direct WYSIWYG Painting and Texturing on 3D Shapes". *Computer Graphics (SIGGRAPH '90 Proceedings)*, volume 24, pp. 215–223, August 1990.

[5] R. Hall. "A Characterization of Illumination Models and Shading Techniques". *Visual Computer*, Vol. 2, No. 5, pp. 268–77, 1986.

[6] Craig Lawrence, Jian L. Zhou, and André L. Tits. "User's guide for CFSQP Version 2.1: A C code for solving (large scale) constrained nonlinear (minimax) optimization problems, generating iterates satisfying all inequality constraints". Technical Report TR-94-16r1, Electrical Engineering Dept. and Institute for Systems Research; University of Maryland, College Park, 1994.

Editors' Note: see Appendix, p. 363 for colored figures of this paper

Linear Radiosity with Error Estimation

Sumanta N. Pattanaik and Kadi Bouatouch

IRISA, Campus Universitaire de Beaulieu, 35042 RENNES CEDEX, France

Abstract. We present a simple and inexpensive method for computing the estimates of error in a hierarchical linear radiosity method. Similar to the approach used in [1] for constant radiosity method, we compute lower and upper linear bounds of the actual radiosity function over the surface elements. We carry out this by computing linear upper and lower bounds of the kernel of the radiosity equation. Also we compute these bounds in a form which makes trivial the effort of projecting the integral equation involving such kernels. We provide the hierarchical algorithm for computing the radiosity bounds. We derive the expression for computing error-estimates from these bounds. Finally we propose a refinement indicator for carrying out the link refinement.

1 Introduction

Radiosity in an environment is governed by an integral equation of the following form [2]:

$$B^{(i)}(s,t) = E^{(i)}(s,t) + \rho^{(i)} \sum_{j=1}^{n} \int \int K^{(i \leftarrow j)}(s,t,u,v)B^{(j)}(u,v)dudv \quad (1)$$

where i and j are the indices of the surface elements, n is the total number of surface elements in the environment, (u,v) and (s,t) are respectively the *parametric* coordinates of a point on i and a point on j, and $K^{(i \leftarrow j)}(s,t,u,v)$, the kernel of the integral equation, gives the radiosity contribution of the differential area around (u,v) on element j towards the differential area around (s,t) on element i, and has an expression as given below.

$$K^{(i \leftarrow j)}(s,t,u,v) = \frac{\cos \theta_{x_{s,t}} \cos \theta_{x_{u,v}}}{[r(\bar{x}_{s,t}, \bar{x}_{u,v})]^2} Vis(\bar{x}_{s,t}, \bar{x}_{u,v})A_j(u,v).$$

where $\bar{x}_{s,t}$ and $\bar{x}_{u,v}$ are the points on the surface element i and j, $\theta_{x_{s,t}}$ and $\theta_{-\bar{x}_{u,v}}$ are respectively the angles made by the surface normals at the above points with the line joining them, $r(.,.)$ is distance and $Vis(.,.)$ is the visibility between the points $\bar{x}_{s,t}$ and $\bar{x}_{u,v}$, and $A_j(u,v)$ is the area function of the surface j and has the following expression:

$$A_j(u,v) = \left\| \frac{\delta \bar{x}_{u,v}}{\delta u} \times \frac{\delta \bar{x}_{u,v}}{\delta v} \right\|$$

One of the widely followed approach of solving this integral equation is the projection of the continuous equation onto a finite set of basis functions. This projection gives rise to a discrete system of linear equations which can be solved to compute an approximation of the unknown radiosity function. As in any numerical method, there is bound to be a difference between the computed solution and actual solution. One wants that this difference (or *error*) remains smaller than a predefined amount, called *threshold*. If under the given setup the error is not under this threshold then one has to refine the setup and incrementally recompute the solution. However, error computation requires the knowledge of the actual solution which in general does not exist. Hence, instead of trying to compute the actual error, one aims to compute an estimate of its upper bound. Though theoretical expressions of error estimates for integral equation solution methods exist [3], they do not lend themselves to practical use. That is why the adaptive refinement of radiosity via error estimation has not been a common practice. More recently we have come across the interesting work of Lischinski *et al* [1] where they have proposed a practical method of estimating this error. They have applied this to the constant radiosity computation method, and have demonstrated that the error estimation approach can lead to an improved method for computing radiosity solution. Our effort in this paper has been to extend such error estimation work to linear radiosity computation.

We shall here briefly discuss the implication of the terms constant or linear radiosity. As said earlier, radiosity solution proceeds by projection onto a set of basis functions. Piecewise polynomial functions are oftenly used for this projection. Among the various polynomials, piecewise constants, the lowest degree polynomials, have been the widely used basis functions[4] for radiosity computations. Use of piecewise constants leads to constant radiosity solution over surface elements. Radiosity functions are in general continuous and it is well known that piecewise constants make poor approximations to a continuous function. In general, higher the degree of polynomial the better is the approximation. However, the expenses involved in the projection and in subsequent solution also grow with the degree of polynomial. Though there have been various attempts with piecewise polynomials of different degrees [5, 6, 7, 8, 2], it is not very clear what is the most optimal degree of choice for radiosity computation. In this paper we have preferred to use a piecewise linear basis set. A piecewise linear basis set leads to linear (more correctly, bi-linear) radiosity over surface elements. Thus, in this paper we describe a method for efficiently estimating the error between this computed linear function and the actual radiosity function and using this error estimate we propose an adaptive refinement strategy for improving the solution.

The key to estimation of error is the computation of the lower and the upper bound of the radiosity function over the elements. Lischinski *et al* [1] have chosen to use the lower and upper bounds of the form-factor between the elements, *i.e.* the double integral of the kernel function of the integral equation, to compute the bounds of the radiosity function. In this paper we have chosen, instead, to use the lower and upper bounds of the kernel function itself for the computation of the radiosity bounds. Particularly, we use the linear (perhaps better called *tetra-linear*) upper and lower bounds of the kernel function. Approaching in this fashion, we reduce the subsequent complexity of the projection process. In fact, in our method the effort involved in the bound computation process is very much compensated by the gain during the projection process. Our initial findings show that the resulting linear radiosity method promises to outperform the constant radiosity method in the overall cost and quality measure.

The organisation of the paper is as follows. We first briefly describe the basis functions and the projection method. Then we describe the method of computing the kernel bounds. We follow it with the algorithm for computing radiosity bounds from the kernel bounds. We then derive the expression for the estimation of error from the bounded radiosity values and the expression of a refinement indicator to carry out error-driven refinement in the context of hierarchical radiosity. Finally we show some results of the application of our algorithm to two simple environments. We compare the results of the linear radiosity method with that of the constant radiosity to emphasize the improvements.

2 Basis Functions and Projection

The work presented in this paper is based on the use of Legendre polynomials (polynomials of degree 0 and 1) as the piecewise linear basis set. That means we use two 1D basis functions

$$N_0(u) = \frac{1}{\sqrt{2}} \quad \text{and} \quad N_1(u) = \sqrt{\frac{3}{2}} u,$$

which are only defined over the parametric domain $-1 \leq u \leq +1$ and undefined outside.

These functions are orthonormal and the 2D function set

$$\left\{ \mathbf{N}_k(u,v) \mid k = 1 \ldots 2^2, \ \mathbf{N}_1(u,v) = N_0(u)N_0(v), \ldots, \mathbf{N}_4(u,v) = N_1(u)N_1(v) \right\} \quad (2)$$

formed by combining these functions, is also orthonormal. If we assume that u, v in the range $[-1, +1]$, are the parameters defined over a surface element, then we can construct the following orthonormal basis set for the whole environment:

$$\left\{ \mathbf{N}_k^{(i)}(u,v) \mid k = 1 \ldots 2^2 \ i = 1 \ldots n \right\} \quad (3)$$

where $\left\{ \mathbf{N}_k^{(i)}(u,v) \mid k = 1 \ldots 2^2 \right\}$ is the basis set over the surface element i, and n is the total number of elements.

Projecting the radiosity equation given in equation 1 on this basis we will get the following linear equations:

$$B_k^{(i)} = E_k^{(i)} + \rho^{(i)} \sum_{j=1}^{n} \sum_{l=1}^{2^2} K_{k,l}^{(i \leftarrow j)} B_l^{(j)} \quad \text{for} \quad k = 1 \ldots 2^2 \text{ and } i = 1 \ldots n \tag{4}$$

$$\text{where} \quad E_k^{(i)} = \int_{-1,-1}^{1,1} E^{(i)}(s,t) \mathbf{N}_k^{(i)}(s,t) ds dt$$

$$\text{and} \quad K_{k,l}^{(i \leftarrow j)} = \int_{-1,-1}^{1,1} \int_{-1,-1}^{1,1} K^{(i \leftarrow j)}(s,t,u,v) \mathbf{N}_l^{(j)}(u,v) \mathbf{N}_k^{(i)}(s,t) du dv ds dt.$$

The equations can be set up by evaluating $E_k^{(i)}$ and $K_{k,l}^{(i \leftarrow j)}$ values. From the solution of these equations, *i.e.* $B_k^{(i)}$'s, one can construct an approximation to the unknown radiosity function as

$$B^{(i)}(s,t) \approx B_{computed}^{(i)}(s,t) = \sum_k B_k^{(i)} \mathbf{N}_k^{(i)}(s,t).$$

As the basis functions are polynomials of degree ≤ 1 the resulting approximation $B_{computed}^{(i)}()$ will be a bilinear function over the surface element i.

Using the coefficients $K_{k,l}^{(i \leftarrow j)}$ and the basis functions we can also set up an approximation to the kernel function.

$$K^{(i \leftarrow j)}(s,t,u,v) \approx \sum_k \sum_l K_{k,l}^{(i \leftarrow j)} \mathbf{N}_k^{(i)}(s,t) \mathbf{N}_l^{(j)}(u,v) \tag{5}$$

Better is this approximation, more accurate is the radiosity solution. In the limit if the approximation can be made exact then we can have the exact radiosity function. The kernel functions defined between a pair of surfaces of the environment is so complicated that to get its exact expansion as given in equation 5, we may have to breakup the surfaces in the environment to infinitesimal elements. This will lead to a infinite linear system and hence will give rise to an impracticable solution method.

3 Computation of Linear Kernel Bounds

We have said in the beginning that the key to the error computation is the computation of the radiosity bounds and we propose to compute these bounds using the bounds of the kernel function. In this section we describe the method for computing the bounds of the kernel function, *i.e.* we wish to compute two tetra-linear functions which will completely bound the kernel function.

In the above paragraph we indicated that if we had an integral equation whose kernel can have an exact expansion using a finite set of basis function then the resulting the solution of the resulting linear system will be exact value for the unknown function. Here we shall find two such kernels and using them we shall compute the exact solution of the integral equation.

These two functions are $\underline{K}(s,t)$ and $\overline{K}(s,t)$, and are defined as follows:

$$\underline{K}^{(i\leftarrow j)}(s,t) = \sum_{k=1}^{2^2} \sum_{l=1}^{2^2} \underline{K}_{k,l}^{(i\leftarrow j)} \mathbf{N}_k^{(i)}(s,t) \mathbf{N}_l^{(j)}(u,v)$$

and $\quad \overline{K}^{(i\leftarrow j)}(s,t) = \sum_{k=1}^{2^2} \sum_{l=1}^{2^2} \overline{K}_{k,l}^{(i\leftarrow j)} \mathbf{N}_k^{(i)}(s,t) \mathbf{N}_l^{(j)}(u,v)$ \hfill (6)

where $\quad \underline{K}^{(i\leftarrow j)}(s,t) \leq K(s,t)$ and $\overline{K}^{(i\leftarrow j)}(s,t) \geq K(s,t) \quad \forall(s,t)$.

If we substitute them in the equation 1 and the resulting integral equation will be as follows:

$$\underline{B}^{(i)}(s,t) = E^{(i)}(s,t) + \rho^{(i)} \sum_{j=1}^{n} \int \int \underline{K}^{(i\leftarrow j)}(s,t,u,v)\underline{B}^{(j)}(u,v)dudv,$$

$$\overline{B}^{(i)}(s,t) = E^{(i)}(s,t) + \rho^{(i)} \sum_{j=1}^{n} \int \int \overline{K}^{(i\leftarrow j)}(s,t,u,v)\overline{B}^{(j)}(u,v)dudv. \quad (7)$$

If solution exist for each of these integral equations then we can solve them by the projection method. The solution will give us two functions $\underline{B}^{(i)}(s,t)$ and $\overline{B}^{(i)}(s,t)$. They will be bilinear and because of the definitions in equations 6 and 7 they will have the following property:

$$\underline{B}^{(i)}(s,t) \leq B^{(i)}(s,t) \text{ and } \overline{B}^{(i)}(s,t) \geq B^{(i)}(s,t).$$

Or in other words they will be the linear bounds of the actual radiosity solution.

The important factor now is that we can compute the bounds only if solutions to the substituted integral equations exist. As $\underline{K}^{(i\leftarrow j)}(s,t,u,v) \leq K^{(i\leftarrow j)}(s,t,u,v)$, if there is a solution to the integral equation with K as kernel then there will be a solution to the integral equation with $\underline{K}$ as kernel. But same cannot be true for the integral equation with $\overline{K}$ as kernel. In the later section we shall bring in some transformation to the projected linear system of this integral equation to arrive at a solution.

4 Computation of $\underline{K}$ and $\overline{K}$

We shall now proceed to compute the kernel functions given in equation 6. The method presented here has a similar flavor of the kernel approximation principle used in the *oracle* process of [7]. The *oracle* approximates the kernel between an interacting surface element pair and used the magnitude of error in this approximation to decide on whether the link can be established or not. In a similar fashion, we first find out a linear approximation of the kernel. Instead of trying to find out the error in the approximation, we go on to determine the maximum and minimum deviation of the actual kernel function from this approximation and use these deviations and the approximation to derive the kernel bounds.

The various steps of computation of kernel bounds are follows:

Step I Computation of linear approximation of the kernel:

The emphasis in this step is to find a linear approximation with minimal effort. Finding a linear approximation of a 1D function requires at least the evaluation of the function at an arbitrary pair of non-coincident points. Extending this to 4D kernel will involve the evaluation of the kernel at 2^4 points. So we evaluate the kernel at 2^4 points and set up a linear system of the following form

$$\hat{K}(s_i, t_i, u_i, v_i) = \sum_k \sum_l K_{k,l} \mathbf{N}_k(s_i, t_i) \mathbf{N}_l(u_i, v_i) \qquad \text{for } i = 1 \ldots 2^4 \quad (8)$$

Solution of this system will give the values of $K_{k,l}$.

Choosing 2^4 points amounts to choosing 2 noncoincident points each in the parametric domains of s, u, v and t. We have chosen the extremes of their parametric domain *i.e.* -1 and +1 as the required points. Thus we have the necessary 16 kernel evaluation points as:

$\{(-1,-1,-1,-1),\ldots,(1,1,1,1)\}$. Gortler *et al* [7] used Gauss quadrature points for the polynomial approximation in their oracle. This choice facilitated the subsequent Gauss quadrature for the evaluation of kernel coefficients. As we are making sure that the kernel functions are linear, we do not have to perform the Gauss quadrature for the evaluation of those coefficients. Further, choice of the extreme points of the parametric domain may prove to be better because the linear kernel function passing though them seems to be an extrema (*i.e.* either a minima or a maxima). We compute the coefficients $K_{k,l}$ by solving the linear system in equation 8.

If the kernel at any of the evaluated points is singular then its reevaluated by shifting the position of that point.

Step II Compute the maximum and minimum kernel deviation:

Using a searching technique [9] we compute the maximum and minimum deviation, respectively d_{max} and d_{min}, of the original kernel function from $\hat{K}(s, t, u, v)$.

Step III Compute the bounds of the kernel:

We define our minimal and maximal kernel functions as

$$\underline{K}(s, t, u, v) = \hat{K}(s, t, u, v) - d_{min} \ , \ \overline{K}(s, t, u, v) = \hat{K}(s, t, u, v) + d_{max}.$$

Using this definition we can derive for each of them an expansion form similar to equation 5

$$\underline{K}(s, t, u, v) = \sum_k \sum_l \underline{K}_{k,l} \mathbf{N}_k(s, t) \mathbf{N}_l(u, v)$$

$$\text{and } \overline{K}(s, t, u, v) = \sum_k \sum_l \overline{K}_{k,l} \mathbf{N}_k(s, t) \mathbf{N}_l(u, v)$$

where

$$\underline{K}_{k,l} = \begin{cases} K_{1,1} - \Delta K_{min} & \text{iff } (k = l = 1), \\ K_{k,l} & \text{otherwise.} \end{cases} \qquad \overline{K}_{k,l} = \begin{cases} K_{1,1} + \Delta K_{max} & \text{iff } (k = l = 1), \\ K_{k,l} & \text{otherwise.} \end{cases} \quad (9)$$

and $\Delta K_{min} = \dfrac{d_{min}}{N_1(s,t)N_1(u,v)} = 4 * d_{min}$ (from definition of basis function in equation 3) and similarly $\Delta K_{max} = 4 * d_{max}$.

So if these kernel bounds are used in the radiosity equation then the projection of the resulting equation now becomes trivial. Furthermore, another important consequence of the above derivation is that the difference between these two bounds of the kernel, $\Delta K(s,t,u,v) = (\Delta K_{min} + \Delta K_{max})/4 = \Delta K$, is independent of (s,t) and (u,v).

We bring to attention that such computation of bounds may give rise to a certain problem. The kernel of the radiosity equation is always nonnegative. However, the lower bound computed in the above fashion can lead to a function which is negative in some part of its domain and hence is not acceptable. Though we cannot avoid such happening we must detect it and take corrective measures. Because of the linear nature of the function one can detect this by checking the value of $K_{min}(s,t,u,v)$ at its parametric corner points. We do not at this moment know what best corrective measure must be taken. However, we take a very simple measure. It is: we redo the bound computation by switching over the degree of the kernel approximation from linear to constant at the *step I* and then we proceed as if we are dealing with linear function. We must emphasize that this event happens very infrequently, so should not cast any doubt on the usefulness of the linear approximation.

5 Radiosity Bounds

We have shown in the previous section that if we use the kernel bounds, $\underline{K}$ and $\overline{K}$, in the radiosity equation then the resulting radiosity will be the upper and lower bounds of the actual radiosity function. The form of these functions has been chosen in such a way that the projection follows without much effort. That means we can right away proceed, without any computation effort, to set up the linear systems

$$\overline{B}_k^{(i)} = E_k^{(i)} + \sum_{j=1}^{n} \sum_l \overline{B}_l^{(j)} \overline{K}_{k,l}^{(i-j)} \quad \text{and} \quad \underline{B}_k^{(i)} = E_k^{(i)} + \sum_{j=1}^{n} \sum_l \underline{B}_l^{(j)} \underline{K}_{k,l}^{(i-j)} (10)$$

The $\overline{B}_k^{(i)}$'s and $\underline{B}_k^{(i)}$'s in the above expression are the unknown expansion coefficients of $\underline{B}(s,t)$, the lower bound and $\overline{B}(s,t)$, the upper bound of the radiosity function, *i.e.*

$$\overline{B}^{(i)}(s,t) = \sum_k \overline{B}_k^{(i)} N_k^{(i)}(s,t) \quad \text{and} \quad \underline{B}^{(i)}(s,t) = \sum_k \underline{B}_k^{(i)} N_k^{(i)}(s,t)$$

All we have to do now is to write an algorithm to compute the unknown $\overline{B}_k^{(i)}$'s and $\underline{B}_k^{(i)}$'s.

5.1 Algorithm for Computing Radiosity Bounds

In [1] we have seen the adaptation of both the standard full matrix [4] and hierarchical radiosity [10] methods to the computation of the constant radiosity bounds. Here we shall extend the method of [1] to support the computation of linear radiosity bounds.

Before discussing the extension, we must see what fundamental changes are brought in by the use of *piecewise linear* basis functions in place of *piecewise constant* ones.

- Over each surface element we have 2^2 basis functions instead of 1 basis function in *constant* case and one of these 2^2, *i.e.* $N_1()$, is exactly same as the basis function used in *constant* case. Consequently there are 2^2 radiosity coefficients in the *linear* case. If we set to zero all except one (*i.e.* B_1) of the radiosity coefficients of each surface element then we shall get the piecewise constant approximation of the environment radiosity. Thus these other coefficients actually represent the linear variation of the radiosity function from this constant radiosity over an element.
- Over each interacting surface element pair, there are 2^4 basis functions instead of 1 in *constant* case. Again, as in the radiosity coefficients, one of the coefficients *i.e.* $K_{1,1}$, is exactly same as the coefficient in *constant* case. Thus all the coefficients define the various deviations of the kernel function from a constant kernel determined by the first coefficients.

From this above, we understand intuitively that as in the *constant* case the convergence of the iterative solution of the radiosity system (equation 4) depends on the fact that $\sum_j K_{1,1}^{(i \leftarrow j)} \leq 1$. As the condition $\sum_{j=1}^n \underline{K}_{1,1}^{(i \leftarrow j)} \leq 1$ is trivially satisfied, the method for full matrix constant radiosity bound computation can be used for *linear* bound computation without any modification. For the upper bound computation, a little change is required to take care of the additional kernel elements. As in [1], for each node element i we zero out all the $\overline{K}_{k,l}^{(i \leftarrow j)}$ coefficients corresponding to the dimmer elements till the condition $\left(\sum_j \overline{K}_{1,1}^{(i \leftarrow j)} \leq 1 \right)$ is satisfied. If we permute the columns such that the non-zero $\overline{K}_{k,l}^{(i \leftarrow j)}$'s are in the beginning of the row then we can write the expression for the radiosity coefficients of the i-th element during any iteration step as:

$$\overline{B}_k^{(i)} = E_k^{(i)} + \rho^{(i)} \left[\sum_{j=1}^m \sum_l \overline{K}_{k,l}^{(i \leftarrow j)} B_l^{(j)} + \frac{\left(1 - \sum_{j=1}^m \overline{K}_{1,1}^{(i \leftarrow j)} \right)}{\overline{K}_{1,1}^{(i \leftarrow (m+1))}} \sum_l \overline{K}_{k,l}^{(i \leftarrow (m+1))} B_l^{(m+1)} \right] \quad (11)$$

where m is the largest item in the permuted row of i such that $\sum_{j=1}^m \overline{K}_{1,1}^{(i \leftarrow j)} \leq 1$.

```
GatherLowerBounds(node,B̲)
{
foreach link ∈ node.links do
  for k = 1...2² do
    B̲_k += node.ρ * ∑_l K̲_{k,l} * link.source.B̲_l
if IsLeaf(node) then
  for k = 1...2² do node.B̲_k = B̲_k + node.E_k
else
  foreach child ∈ node.child do
    ConstructChildBoundFromParentBound(child, B̲, newB̲)
    GatherLowerBounds(child, newB̲)
  ConstructLowerBoundFromChildrenBounds(node.B̲, child₁.B̲, child₂.B̲, ...)
}
```

Fig. 1. Gathering Lower Bounds.

```
GatherUpperBounds(node, contribList)
{
foreach link ∈ node.links do
  add node and link to contribList
if IsLeaf(node) then
  KSum = 0
  for k = 1...2² do node.B̄_k = node.emission_k
  CreateNewSortedList(contribList, NewContribList)
  foreach pair (p_node, p_link) ∈ NewContribList do
    ConstructKernelFromParentKernel(p_node.K̄, p_link.source, node, newK̄)
    if KSum + newK̄_{1,1} ≤ 1 then
      KSum += newK̄_{1,1}
      for k = 1...2² do
        node.B̄_k += node.ρ * ∑_l newK̄_{k,l} * p_link.source.B̄_l
    else
      factor = (1−KSum)/newK̄_{1,1}
      for k = 1...2² do
        node.B̄_k += node.ρ * factor * ∑_l newK̄_{k,l} * p_link.source.B̄_l
      break
else
  foreach child ∈ node.child do
    GatherUpperBounds(child, contribList)
  ConstructUpperBoundFromChildrenBounds(node.B̄, child[1].B̄, child[2].B̄, ...)
}
```

Fig. 2. Gathering Upper Bounds.

We shall now consider the computation of linear radiosity bounds in the hierarchical framework. The two main operations in the hierarchical solution method are: gathering at nodes and *push/pull* operation. Lower bound gathering at the nodes of the hierarchy are same as that in [1]. The upper bound gathering and the associated *push/pull* operations require special attention.

We saw above, in the full matrix computation of upper bound, the convergence of the iterative solution requires ordering of contributors before any gathering is done. One must do the similar ordering while gathering at the nodes of the hierarchy. For any node element in a hierarchy, the contributors are not only the ones specified in its links but also all those specified in the links of its parent and its ancestor nodes. That is why the algorithm in [1] collects all such links in a list called *contribList*. We have to do the same thing. But it is not enough. We must take note that the kernel function between the parent/ancestor element and a source is not the same as that between the child element and the source, because there is now a change in the domain of the kernel function. We are using a parametric expression for the kernel function. A parametric expression changes with the change of the parametric domain. So we must carry out the re-parameterisation of this kernel function. We take care of this by introducing a function called *ConstructKernelFromParentKernel()*.

The *push* operation, that we know of in hierarchical radiosity, is only done in the case of lower bound computation. The pushing operation also amounts to a re-parameterisation of the radiosity function defined in parent domain, to get the function defined in child's domain. This re-parameterisation is same as applying a push filter as done in the wavelet radiosity method[7].

The *pull* operation for lower/upper bound radiosity can be viewed as constructing the minimum/maximum bound of the radiosity function resulting from the combination of the child functions. So this can be performed exactly as was done for the kernel bound computation. As the child functions are also linear, in this case finding the minimum/maximum deviation is much simpler. Here again, we check for the possibility of lower radiosity bound becoming negative at the extremities and on its detection switch over to constant bounds as the corrective measure. The routines *ConstructLowerBoundFromChildrenBounds()* and *ConstructUpperBoundFromChildrenBounds()* carry out this pulling operation.

Now we have all the modification necessary for writing a gathering algorithm for the lower and upper radiosity bound in a hierarchical framework. We have given these algorithms in figures 1 and 2.

6 Error Norms

One of the main contributions of [1] is relating the error in the computed radiosity to the upper and lower bounds of the radiosity. Assuming that we are taking out computed radiosity as the average of the lower and upper bound radiosity functions then we can use the same relationship as [1] and derive below a quantitative error estimate over each surface element.

$$\epsilon^{(i)} \leq \frac{1}{2}\left\|\overline{B}^{(i)}(s,t) - \underline{B}^{(i)}(s,t)\right\| \leq \frac{1}{2}\sum_k \left|\overline{B}_k^{(i)} - \underline{B}_k^{(i)}\right|\left\|\mathbf{N}_k^{(i)}(s,t)\right\|$$

where $\|.\|$ is a functional norm. Once we decide which norm to use, for that norm we can precalculate the $\|\mathbf{N}_k^{(i)}(s,t)\|$ values. Using them we can compute the upper bound of the error.

7 Error-Driven Refinement

The error norm computed above gives us an estimate of the error in the computed radiosity function and thus indicates if the solution is acceptable or requires further improvement. If we find that the solution is not acceptable then we must find the strategy to carry out the refinement so as to get the optimal effect. In this section we discuss such a strategy.

The radiosity over an element is the result of the gathering over the various links which connect it to other elements. So any improvement in the solution can only be carried out by refining the links. So here we must address two questions. First, which of the links need refinement ? Second, how do we refine the link ? Refining a link means subdividing one of the elements of the link. So, in this context the second question becomes: which of the two elements of a link should be subdivided?

In order to be able to decide which of the links to refine, now we must turn our attention to the error associated with each individual link. If $\epsilon^{(i \leftarrow j)}(s,t)$ is the error function over element i due to the gathering link connecting it to element j then its expression will be:

$$
\begin{aligned}
\epsilon^{(i \leftarrow j)}(s,t) \leq\ & \frac{1}{2}\left(\overline{B}^{(i \leftarrow j)}(s,t) - \underline{B}_i^{(i \leftarrow j)}(s,t)\right) \\
=\ & \frac{1}{2}\left[\int \overline{K}^{(i \leftarrow j)}(s,t,u,v)\overline{B}^{(j)}(u,v)dudv - \right.\\
& \left.\int \underline{K}^{(i \leftarrow j)}(s,t,u,v)\underline{B}^{(j)}(u,v)dudv\right]
\end{aligned}
$$

adding and subtracting $\int \underline{K}^{(i \leftarrow j)}(s,t,u,v)\overline{B}^{(j)}(u,v)dudv$ on the right we get

$$
\begin{aligned}
=\ & \frac{1}{2}\int \left[\overline{K}^{(i \leftarrow j)}(s,t,u,v) - \underline{K}^{(i \leftarrow j)}(s,t,u,v)\right]\overline{B}^{(j)}(u,v)dudv \\
& + \frac{1}{2}\int \left[\overline{B}^{(j)}(u,v) - \underline{B}^{(j)}(u,v)\right]\underline{K}^{(i \leftarrow j)}(s,t,u,v)dudv
\end{aligned}
$$

In the above we have an expression of the error due to the link $i \leftarrow j$ as a sum of two terms: the 1st term is due to the error in the kernel approximation between i and j, and the 2nd term is due to the error in the radiosity of the element j. Written in this fashion makes the following points clear:

- The link error is nonzero even when the kernel approximation is exact *i.e.* even when

$$\left(\overline{K}^{(i\leftarrow j)}(s,t,u,v) - \underline{K}^{(i\leftarrow j)}(s,t,u,v)\right) = 0.$$

- If we decide on a refinment based on the magnitude of $\epsilon^{(i\leftarrow j)}$ the subsequent solution may not at all give any reduction in the magnitude of $\epsilon^{(i\leftarrow j)}$. It is because, refinement of a link can at best improve the kernel approximation. If the kernel approximation is already correct the refinement cannot do anything better.

From these statements we infer that though the full expression of $\epsilon^{(i\leftarrow j)}$ is not a good indicator for refinement, the 1st term of its expression can serve the purpose. So here we derive a quantity $\alpha^{(i\leftarrow j)}$, which we shall call *refinement indicator* of a given link, by integrating the above 1st term over the element i, *i.e*

$$\alpha^{(i\leftarrow j)} = \frac{1}{2}\int_x \int_{u,v} \left[\overline{K}^{(i\leftarrow j)}(s,t,u,v) - \underline{K}^{(i\leftarrow j)}(s,t,u,v)\right] \overline{B}^{(j)}(u,v)dudvdx$$

$$= \frac{1}{2}\text{Area}_i \Delta K^{(i\leftarrow j)} \sum_k \overline{B}_k^{(j)} \int_{u,v} N_k^{(j)}(u,v)dudv = \text{Area}_i \Delta K^{(i\leftarrow j)}\overline{B}_1^{(j)}.$$

Thus we can refine all those links for which $\alpha^{(i\leftarrow j)}$ is more than a threshold. The solution obtained after this refinement is most likely to be an improvement over the current solution.

Now we shall address here the second question of the refinement, *i.e.* which element of the link should be subdivided so that the resulting refinement would give the maximum improvement? Intuitively, the subdivision which would reduce the magnitude of overall ΔK should be the choice. To find this we have taken a simple approach. We find the maximum variation $d^{(j)}$ of the kernel as a function of position on the element j and the variation $d^{(i)}$ as a function of position on the element i. If $d^{(i)} > d^{(j)}$ we subdivide i, otherwise we subdivide j.

8 Results

We have implemented the algorithm discussed above to compute the linear radiosity bounds. For efficiency comparison we have also implemented the error bound computation with constant basis functions. We have created various plots of the computed radiosity values along the dotted line drawn on the surfaces of the simple environments given in figure 3. We have used a very simple method of computing maximum and minimum deviation of the kernel *i.e.* d_{min} and d_{max}, by finding the minimum and maximum over the difference between the actual and approximated kernel at a finite number of random points.

In figures 4,5 we have shown the error bound computation results for the environment in figure 3(a) as a function of surface discretization. For this illustration the source dimensions have been kept very small so as to remove the source size dependent error in kernel approximation computation. In the legend

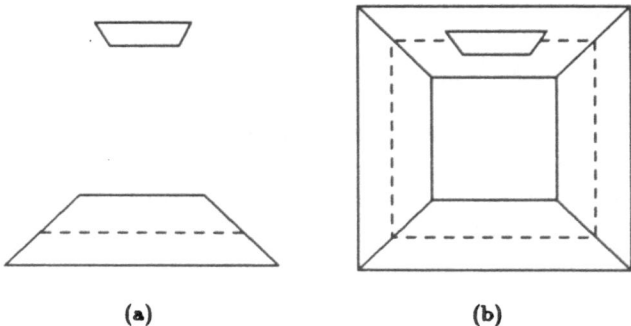

Fig. 3. Simple test environments.

of the figures, the levels indicate the discretization. Level 0 corresponds to the full surface as the element and in each subsequent level each element has been equally subdivided into 4 child elements. No attempt has been made to carry out adaptive refinement.

Figures 6 show the adaptive refinement of a similar environment but this time with a larger source, so that source also is subdivided if required. The resulting number of elements along the indicated line of the surface are: 106 for constant radiosity and 16 for linear radiosity.

Finally in figure 7 we show the results of the enclosure shown in figure 3(b). The outer most curves belong to the constant bounds, the inner most curve belongs to the actual radiosity and the curves in between belongs to linear bounds. This actual radiosity value has been obtained by carrying out a full matrix solution of the finely subdivided environment. This plot contains 5 sets of results, each set belonging to the radiosity over the dotted line on a surface, starting at the left the emitting source in the ceiling and moving along the dotted line in counterclockwise fashion. For comparison we give the execution time here. They are: 104 seconds for the constant bounds and 32 seconds for the linear bounds. The plots and the execution time respectively show that bounds computed in the linear case are tighter and the computation is faster compared to the constant case.

9 Discussion and Conclusion

We have described a hierarchical radiosity method for computing linear radiosity with tight upper and lower bounds for the actual radiosity function. We compute the radiosity bounds by creating linear upper and lower bounds to the radiosity kernel function. This computation is simple and fast. Further, we derived an *error indicator* to refine the inter-element links to reduce the error in the computed radiosity functions.

In this paper we have not brought occlusion into consideration. At the occlusion point kernel evaluates to zero. An immediate strategy to accommodate occlusion will be: for a link with occlusion (i) to switch over to constant kernel approximation, (ii) to compute the upper bound by evaluating kernel without the occlusion, and (iii) to set the lower bounds to zero. This strategy will increase the ΔK values for such links and hence force their refinement in subsequent iterations. We have to get a feel for the performance of the method based on this strategy. We believe that, for environments with sparse occlusion or for the ones prediscretised along the shadow boundaries, our method will work without any problem and give superior performance compared to the method based strictly on constant basis. However, for highly occluded environments we may have to find out some other strategy to bound the kernels.

We have only made use of non-overlaping linear basis functions. Thus the computed radiosity functions over a surface element is not likely to have any continuity with that over the neighbouring elements even if the elements belonged to the same surface. Thus prior to rendering an image, this discontinuity must be resolved by a reprojection. Because of their conflict with the hierarchical advantages, overlapping basis functions are generally not used for the projection of the radiosity equation. It may be worthwhile to reexplore with them in the error-bounding setup.

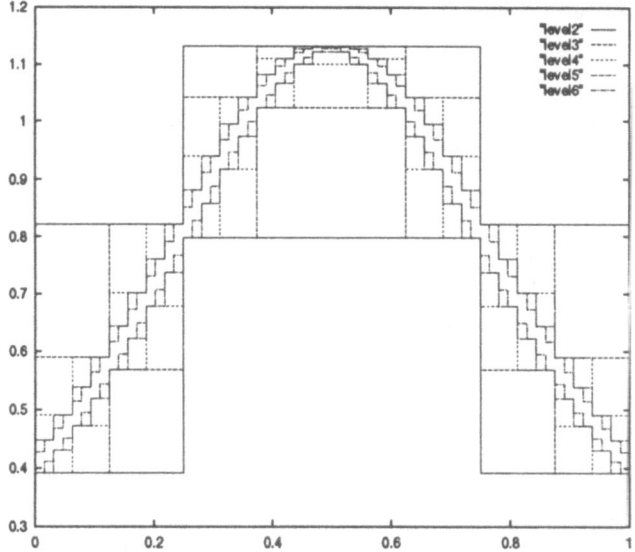

Fig. 4. Upper and lower bounds of constant radiosity for environment in figure 3(a) at various levels of subdivision.

References

1. Dani Lischinski, Brian Smits, and Don Greenberg. Bounds and error estimates

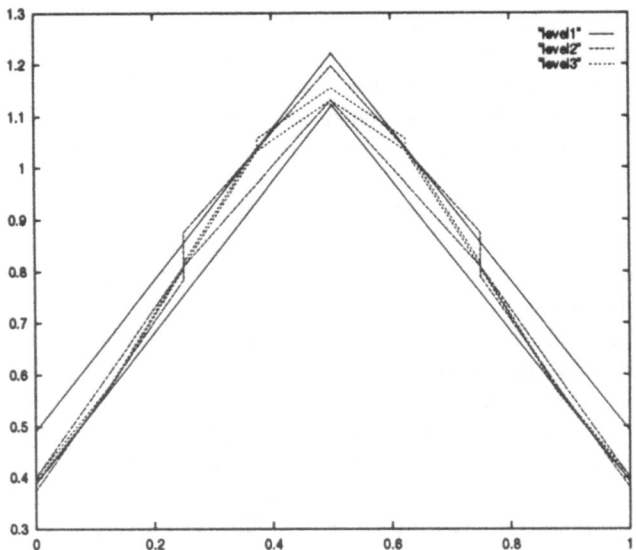

Fig. 5. Upper and Lower bounds of linear radiosity for environment in figure 3(a) at various levels of subdivision.

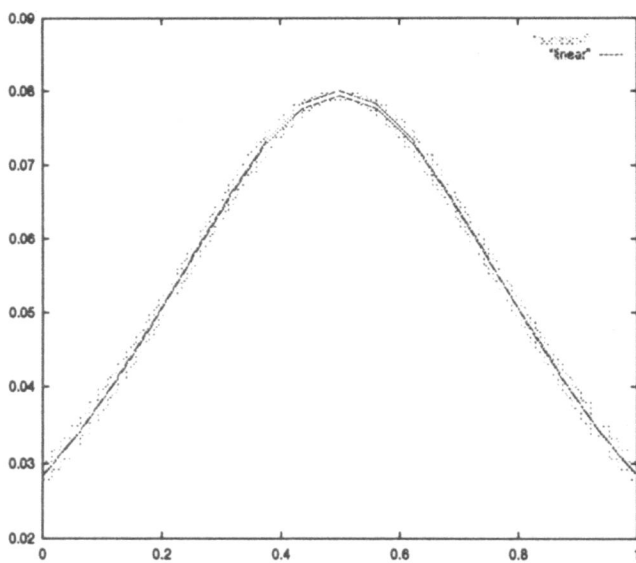

Fig. 6. Upper and Lower bounds with adaptive subdivision for figure 3(a).

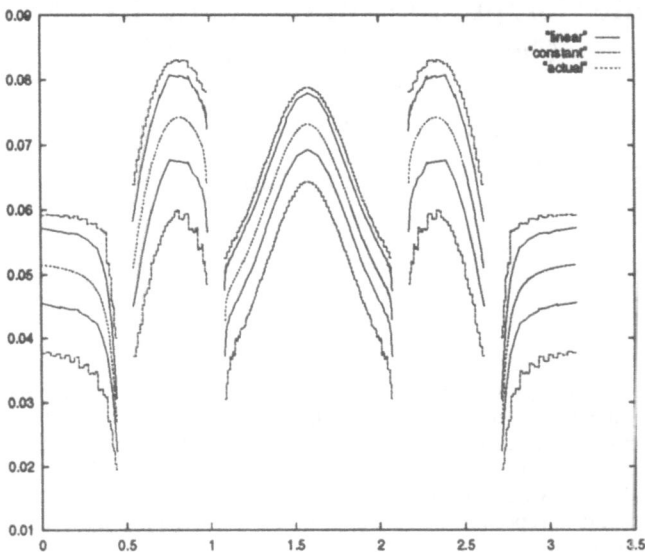

Fig. 7. Bounds in the enclosure in figure 3(b). The plot shows the actual radiosity and the bounds for constant and linear radiosity, along the dotted line of the scene.

for radiosity. *Computer Graphics (SIGGRAPH '94 Proceedings)*, 28(4):67–74, July 1994.

2. Harold R. Zatz. Galerkin radiosity. *Computer Graphics (SIGGRAPH '93 Proceedings)*, 27(4):213–220, 1993.

3. L. M. Delves and J. L. Mohamed. *Computational Methods for Integral Equations.* Cambridge University Press, 1985.

4. Cindy M. Goral, Kenneth E. Torrance, Donald P. Greenberg, and Bennett Battaile. Modelling the interaction of light between diffuse surfaces. *Computer Graphics (SIGGRAPH '84 Proceedings)*, 18(3):212–222, July 1984.

5. Nelson L. Max and Michael J. Allison. Linear radiosity approximation using vertex to vertex form-factors. In David Kirk, editor, *Graphics Gems III*, Academic Press, Inc, Boston, 1992.

6. Paul Heckbert. Discontinuity meshing for radiosity. *Third Eurographics Workshop on Rendering*, 203–216, May 1992.

7. Steven Gortler, Peter Schroder, Michel F. Cohen, and Pat Hanrahan. Wavelet radiosity. *Computer Graphics (SIGGRAPH '93 Proceedings)*, 27(4):221–230, 1993.

8. Roy Troutman and Nelson L. Max. Radiosity algorithms using higher order finite element methods. *Computer Graphics (SIGGRAPH '93 Proceedings)*, 27(4):209–212, 1993.

9. William H. Press, Brian P. Flannery, Saul A. Teukolsky, and William T. Vetterling. *Numerical Recipes in C: The Art of Scientific Computing.* Cambridge University Press, 1988.

10. Pat Hanrahan, David Salzman, and Larry Aupperle. A rapid hierarchical radiosity algorithm. *Computer Graphics (SIGGRAPH '91 Proceedings)*, 25(4):197–206, July 1991.

Accurate Computation of the Radiosity Gradient for Constant and Linear Emitters

Nicolas Holzschuch, François Sillion

iMAGIS/IMAG*

Abstract: Controlling the error incurred in a radiosity calculation is one of the most challenging issues remaining in global illumination research. In this paper we propose a new method to compute the value and the gradient of the radiosity function at any point of a receiver, with arbitrary precision. The knowledge of the gradient provides fundamental informations on the radiosity function and its behaviour. It can specially be used to control the consistency of the discretisation assumptions.

1 Introduction

Computing the effect of a given patch on the radiosity of another patch is easily done assuming the radiosity on both patches are constant. In that case, we can express the influence of the emitter on the receiver with a single number, the form-factor. However, assuming the radiosity on both patches is constant is a strong assumption, and it introduces a specific source of error in the resolution algorithm.

In 1994, Arvo et al. [2] recorded all possible sources of error in global illumination algorithms, and introduced a framework for the analysis of error. Errors can occur at several levels in the resolution process:

- During modeling: our geometry is not exactly that of the scene we want to compute, and the BRDF are not exact either.
- During discretisation: our set of basis functions is not able to represent the real solution, but only an approximated one.
- During computation: we do not compute transfer elements exactly, but only within finite precision.

Lischinski et al. [9] presented an error driven refinement strategy for hierarchical radiosity. They were able to maintain upper and lower bounds on computed radiosity, and to concentrate their work in places where the difference was too large.

However, practical tools are still lacking to measure discretisation error. The problem is to efficiently reconstruct the radiosity function, with only a small number of samples. The best position for sampling points can only be found with total knowledge of the radiosity function.

In practice, at each step, we have to intuit the behaviour of the function from our current set of samples, in order to guess if we should – or not – introduce new sampling points, and where.

---

* iMAGIS is a joint research project of CNRS/INRIA/INPG/UJF. Postal address: B.P. 53, F-38041 Grenoble Cedex 9, France. E-mail: `Nicolas.Holzschuch@imag.fr`.

Knowing the radiosity derivatives allows better sampling, and thus reduction of discretisation error. Heckbert [6] and Lischinski et al. [7] predicted an efficient surface mesh using derivatives discontinuities. Drettakis and Fiume [4, 5] used information on the structure of the function to accurately reconstruct the illumination. Vedel and Puech [11] presented a refinement criterion based on gradient values at the nodes.

However, these authors usually resorted to approximated values of the partial derivatives, using several computations of radiosity and finite differences. Computing accurate values for the gradient allows arbitrary precision on our refinement criterion.

Arvo [1] presented a method to compute the irradiance Jacobian in case of partially occluded light sources. His method is presented with constant emitters. This paper introduces a new formulation of the radiosity gradient, valid for arbitrary radiosity functions on the emitter. The derivation is presented in the case of total visibility, i.e. without occluders. However, we shall see that extending the algorithm to the case of partial visibility is easy using Arvo's technique, since the two algorithms are largely independant.

2 Reformulating the Radiosity Equation

We will consider only diffuse surfaces, characterised by their radiosity function $B(x)$, without any assumption about B.

We want to know the value of B at a point x on a given patch A_1, due to the emission of light from another polygon A_2. We will assume a reflectivity of ρ at point x.

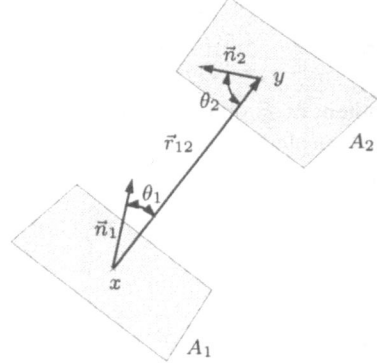

Fig. 1. Geometry of the problem

Our knowledge of radiosity at the receiving point derives from the integral equation:

$$B(x) = \frac{\rho}{\pi} \int_{A_2} \frac{B(y) \cos \theta_1 \cos \theta_2}{\|\vec{r}_{12}\|^2} dA_2 \qquad (1)$$

where $\vec{r}_{12}$ is the vector joining point x on the receiver and point y on the emitter. θ_1 is the angle between $\vec{r}_{12}$ and the normal on the receiver, θ_2 the angle between $\vec{r}_{12}$ and the normal on the emitter, and dA_2 the area element on the emitter around point y (see Fig. 1).

Should any occluders be present between point x and emitter A_2, the integral would only be over the part of A_2 visible from x.

We can reformulate Equation 1 as the expression of the flux of a vector field through surface A_2:

$$B(x) = \int_{A_2} \vec{F} \cdot d\vec{A_2} \tag{2}$$

where $\vec{F}$ is:

$$\vec{F} = -\frac{\rho B(y)(\vec{r}_{12} \cdot \vec{n}_1)\vec{r}_{12}}{\pi \|\vec{r}_{12}\|^4}$$

A classic way to deal with flux integrals as Equation 2 is to transform them into a linear integral using Stoke's theorem[2]:

$$\int_A (\nabla \times \vec{V}) \cdot d\vec{A} = \oint_{\partial A} \vec{V} \cdot d\vec{x} \tag{3}$$

These linear integrals can be easier to compute, and are also easier to estimate if there are no closed forms. However, to use Stoke's theorem (3), we need to express the vector field $\vec{F}$ as the curl of another vector field, $\vec{V}$.

A classic property is that this is equivalent to $\vec{F}$ having a null divergence ($\nabla \cdot \vec{F} = 0$). Basically, the divergence of a vector flux is a quantity that express at each point how much does the flux "radiates away" from this point, while the curl of a vector field "turns around" it at each point. The divergence of a curl is always null ($\nabla \cdot (\nabla \times \vec{V}) = 0$), and if a field has a null divergence, it can be expressed as a curl.

An easy computation shows that the divergence of $\vec{F}$ with respect to point y on surface A_2 is[3]:

$$\nabla \cdot \vec{F} = -\frac{\rho}{\pi} \frac{\vec{r}_{12} \cdot \vec{n}_1}{\|\vec{r}_{12}\|^2} (\nabla(B) \cdot \vec{r}_{12}) \tag{4}$$

and hence is null if the gradient of B on the emitting surface is null. That is to say, if the radiosity of the emitter is constant.

We can always separate $\vec{F}$ in two parts:

$$\vec{F} = \nabla \times (\vec{V}) + \vec{G}$$

Namely:

$$\vec{V} = \rho B(y) \frac{\vec{r}_{12} \times \vec{n}_1}{2\pi \|\vec{r}_{12}\|^2}$$

$$\vec{G} = -\rho \nabla(B) \times \left(\frac{(\vec{r}_{12} \times \vec{n}_1)}{2\pi \|\vec{r}_{12}\|^2} \right)$$

and thus cut Equation 2 in two integrals:

$$B(x) = \oint_{\partial A_2} \vec{V} \cdot d\vec{x}_2 + \int_{A_2} \vec{G} \cdot d\vec{A_2} \tag{5}$$

Using the properties of cross-products and dot-products, we can rewrite Equation 5 as:

$$\frac{2\pi}{\rho} B(x) = -\vec{n}_1 \cdot \oint_{\partial A_2} B(y) \frac{\vec{r}_{12} \times d\vec{x}_2}{\|\vec{r}_{12}\|^2} + \int_{A_2} \frac{\vec{r}_{12}}{\|\vec{r}_{12}\|^2} \cdot (\vec{n}_1 \times (\nabla(B) \times \vec{n}_2)) \, dA_2 \tag{6}$$

---

[2] ∂A stands for the contour of A, and $\oint$ expresses that this contour is closed.

[3] In this section, all derivative signs (∇, $\nabla\cdot$, $\nabla\times$) are relative to point y on surface A_2.

Note that this rewriting process does not make any assumption whatsoever on $B(y)$. Hence it can be used in any case. An interesting case is when $B(y)$ is constant: then $\vec{G} = \vec{0}$, and the second term is null. Another interesting case is $B(y)$ being linear: then its gradient is constant and can be carried out of the second integral, leaving only a pure geometric factor to compute. Appendix A presents a detailed study of these two cases.

This rewriting process separates the radiosity in two terms, a contour integral that we can generally compute, provided that we know the radiosity on the emitter, and a surface integral, generally harder to compute as an exact term. But, as shown later, having an integral form of this term, we can compute its value with an arbitrary precision.

3 The Radiosity Gradient

An interesting quantity to describe scalar fields, such as $B(x)$ is their gradient. Gradient is the extension of derivation for function of several variables. Basically, $\nabla(B)(x) \cdot \vec{v}$ gives the derivative of function B at point x in the direction of $\vec{v}$.

3.1 Computing the Gradient

The radiosity gradient can be computed from an equation such as Equation 1 or 6:

$$\nabla(B)(x) = \nabla\left(\int_{A_2} \vec{F} \cdot d\vec{A_2}\right) \tag{7}$$

In case the emitter A_2 does not depend on the position of the point x – that is to say, in case there are no occluder between point x and the emitting surface A_2 – this equation is equivalent to:

$$\nabla(B)(x) = \int_{A_2} \nabla\left(\vec{F} \cdot d\vec{A_2}\right)$$

Or, if we use Equation 5:

$$\nabla(B)(x) = \oint_{\partial A_2} \nabla\left(\vec{V} \cdot d\vec{x_2}\right) + \int_{A_2} \nabla(\vec{G} \cdot d\vec{A_2}) \tag{8}$$

If the emitter depends on the position of point x – that is, if there are occluders – the expression of $\nabla(B)(x)$ is the sum of two terms; the first one takes into account the variation of $\vec{F}$, and is exactly the term we are discussing, and the second one takes into account the variation of the emitter. Thus, it is easy to merge a method to compute the gradient with occluders and a constant emitter, as in Arvo [1], and our method to compute the gradient with an arbitrary emitter, but without occluders.

Note that in this section, we are taking a derivative with respect to point x on the receiving surface, not with respect to point y on the emitting surface. So for our derivating operator, the radiosity on the emitting point $B(y)$ can be regarded as constant, as well as its gradient, $\nabla(B)(y)$.

Using the properties of the gradient of a scalar product, starting from Equation 8, we can express the gradient of radiosity at the receiving point:

$$\frac{2\pi}{\rho}\nabla(B)(x) = \vec{n}_1 \times \oint_{\partial A_2} B(y)\frac{d\vec{x_2}}{\|\vec{r}_{12}\|^2} + 2\oint_{\partial A_2} B(y)\frac{\vec{n}_1 \cdot \vec{r}_{12}}{\|\vec{r}_{12}\|^4}(\vec{r}_{12} \times d\vec{x_2})$$
$$+ \int_{A_2}(\vec{n}_1 \times (\nabla(B)(y) \times \vec{n}_2))\frac{dA_2}{\|\vec{r}_{12}\|^2}$$
$$- 2\int_{A_2}\frac{(\vec{n}_1 \times (\nabla(B)(y) \times \vec{n}_2)) \cdot \vec{r}_{12}}{\|\vec{r}_{12}\|^4}\vec{r}_{12}dA_2 \tag{9}$$

This equation, like the radiosity equation (6) is divided in two parts: a contour integral which usually has a closed form, and a surface integral that we can estimate to any arbitrary precision.

As before, two interesting cases occur: if the gradient on the emitter is null, that is if we assume a constant radiosity on the emitter, all surface integrals vanish. And if the gradient on the emitter is constant, that is if we assume a linear radiosity on the emitter, it can be carried out of the surface integrals, leaving us with purely geometrical factors or vectors to compute. Please refer to Appendix A for a detailed study of these cases.

3.2 Using the gradient

Knowing the gradient at a point gives very valuable information on the function we are studying. As previous authors pointed out, the gradient may be used either to reconstruct the illumination function before display, or to check the consistency of our discretisation hypothesis.

Reconstructing the illumination function If we know the radiosity values and the gradient at our sample points, we can then reconstruct the radiosity function as, e.g. a bicubic spline.

Salesin et al. [10] and Bastos et al. [3] proposed such methods for reconstruction of radiosity using estimates of gradient. Ward and Heckbert [12] computed irradiance gradients to interpolate irradiance on receiving surfaces.

Refinement criterion Many radiosity algorithms assume a constant radiosity over patches. It may seem strange to compute the gradient of radiosity in that case, but in fact the information given by the gradient can also be used there.

Using the derivatives allows precisely to check whether our discretisation hypothesis were correct or not, and if they were not, it also gives a hint on where it would be best to refine in order to minimize the discretisation error.

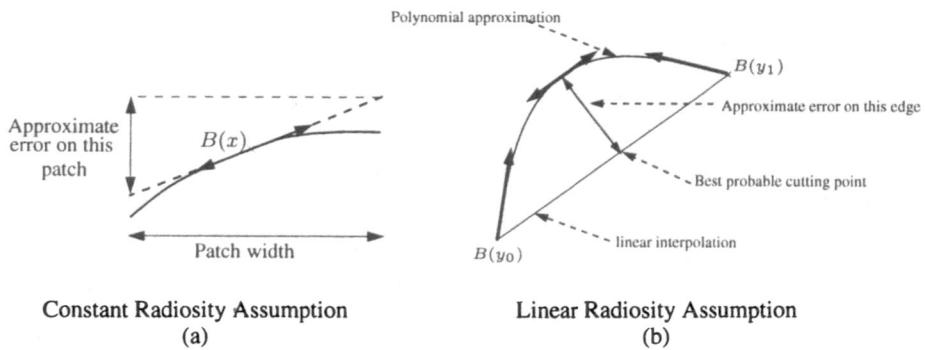

Constant Radiosity Assumption	Linear Radiosity Assumption
(a)	(b)

Fig. 2. Using the gradient to measure discretisation error

If we assume constant radiosity on our patches, the gradient gives a first estimate of how much does the function vary over the patch: $\nabla(B)(x) \cdot \vec{v}$ is approximately the difference between radiosity at point $x + \vec{v}$ and radiosity at point x. The norm of the gradient times the width of the patch gives an approximation of how much does radiosity varies over the patch (see Fig. 2a for an example in 2D). The direction of the gradient gives the best probable direction of refinement.

If we assume linear radiosity on our patches, we can compute a cubic interpolant over the patch using the radiosity and gradient values at each vertices, and then test how much this cubic interpolant differs from our linear assumption (see Fig. 2b for an example in 2D). We can even compute the difference between linear and cubic interpolant without explicitly computing the interpolants. This criterion also gives the best next sampling point, the position of the maximum difference between the two interpolants.

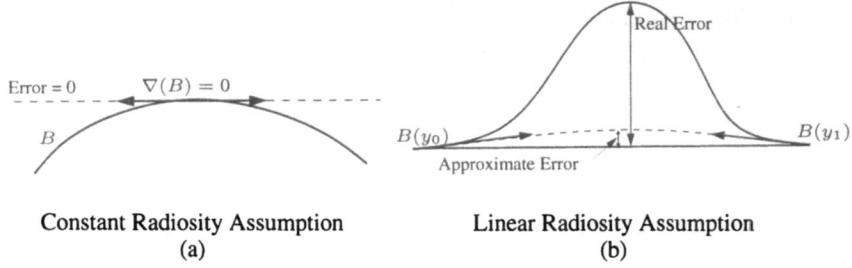

Constant Radiosity Assumption (a)   Linear Radiosity Assumption (b)

Fig. 3. Sample cases where the proposed refinement criterion fail

Although none of these refinement criterion are foolproof (see Fig. 3 for an example where these two criterion fail to detect an important discretisation error), they provide a way to measure and quantify the discretisation error.

Also, the points where these refinement criterions are more likely to be fooled are basically the extrema of the radiosity functions. We know that a single convex emitter induces only one maximum on the receiver (see, for example, Drettakis [4]).

So, to study the interaction between two patches so as to minimize discretisation error, we would, first, find the theorical position of the maximum of radiosity, then sample it, then refine the receiving patch using our gradient-based criterion.

4 Implementation and First Results

We have implemented the gradient and radiosity formulas described in appendix A, for both constant and linear emitters[4]. Using a C++ class for vectors, with definitions of cross- and dot-products makes the implementation very straightforward, being a mere recopy of the formulas. The only special attention it needs is avoiding to recompute quantities already computed at previous steps. Most of the quantities needed to express the gradient were also used for the radiosity.

In the color plates, Fig. A shows the radiosity values on a plane, due to a triangular emitter parallel to that plane (see Fig. E for the geometry of the scene). Fig. B shows the norm of the gradient of this radiosity.

Fig. C and D show the same quantities if we assume a linear emitter.

5 Conclusion and Future Work

We have provided a way to compute the gradient of radiosity at the receiving point with any distribution of illumination on the emitter. The gradient can be used in several ways, and specially to compute the discretisation error. It can also be used to find the best next refining point.

Future work will include a complete gradient computation, using the method described by Arvo in [1] to take the possible occluders into account.

---

[4] Souce code and documentation for this implementation is available at ftp://safran.imag.fr/pub/holzschu/gradient.tar.gz.

The ability to compute radiosity gradients for linear emitters is especially interesting when using linear basis functions or linear wavelets. In that case, the discretisation error can be precisely isolated.

Our next step will be a complete implementation of the refinement criterion described in section 3.2, to effectively reduce the discretisation error, within a hierarchical radiosity framework with linear radiosity.

We will then have the possible background for a complete radiosity algorithm with all possible sources of error (visibility, discretisation, computational) recorded and monitored, thus allowing to focus the computing resources at the points where this error is large.

6 Acknowledgements

Color pictures were computed by Myriam Houssay-Holzschuch using the GMT package, developped by Wessel and Smith [13].

The authors would like to thank the anonymous reviewers for useful insights and positive criticism.

References

1. Arvo, J.: The Irradiance Jacobian for Partially Occluded Polyhedral Sources. SIGGRAPH (1994) 343–350
2. Arvo, J., Torrance, K.,Smits, B.: A Framework for the Analysis of Error in Global Illumination Algorithms. SIGGRAPH (1994) 75–84
3. Bastos, R. M., de Sousa, A. A., Ferreira, F. N., Reconstruction of Illumination Functions using Bicubic Hermite Interpolation. *Fourth Eurographics Workshop on Rendering* (June 1993) 317–326
4. Drettakis, G., Fiume, E.: Concrete Computation of Global Illumination Accurate and Consistent Reconstruction of Illumination Functions Using Structured Sampling. Computer Graphics Forum (Eurographics 1993 Conf. Issue) 273–284
5. Drettakis, G., Fiume, E.: Concrete Computation of Global Illumination Using Structured Sampling. *Third Eurographics Workshop on Rendering* (May 1992) 189–201
6. Heckbert, P. S.: *Simulating Global Illumination Using Adaptative Meshing.* PhD Thesis, University of California, Berkeley, June 1991.
7. Lischinski, D., Tampieri, F., Greenberg, D. P.: Discontinuity Meshing for Accurate Radiosity. *IEEE Computer Graphics and Applications 12,6* (November 1992) 25–39
8. Lischinski, D., Tampieri, F., Greenberg, D. P.: Combining Hierarchical Radiosity and Discontinuity Meshing. SIGGRAPH (1993)
9. Lischinski, D., Smits, B., Greenberg, D. P.: Bounds and Error Estimates for Radiosity. SIGGRAPH (1994) 67–74
10. Salesin, D., Lischinski, D., DeRose, T.: Reconstructing Illumination Functions with Selected Discontinuities. *Third Eurographics Workshop on Rendering* (May 1992) 99–112
11. Vedel, C., Puech, C.: Improved Storage and Reconstruction of Light Intensities on Surfaces. *Third Eurographics Workshop on Rendering* (May 1992) 113–121
12. Ward, G. J., Heckbert, P. S.: Irradiance Gradients. *Third Eurographics Workshop on Rendering* (May 1992) 85–98
13. Wessel, P. and Smith, W. H. F.: Free Software helps Map and Display Data. *EOS Trans. Amer. Geophys. U.*, vol. 72, 441–446, 1991

A Application to Constant and Linear Emitters

A.1 Case of a constant emitter

In the case of a constant emitter the Equations 6 and 9 reduce to:

$$\frac{2\pi}{\rho}B(x) = -\vec{n}_1 \cdot \oint_{\partial A_2} B(y)\frac{\vec{r}_{12} \times d\vec{x}_2}{\|\vec{r}_{12}\|^2} \tag{10}$$

$$-\frac{2\pi}{\rho}\nabla(B)(x) = \vec{n}_1 \times \oint_{\partial A_2} B(y)\frac{d\vec{x}_2}{\|\vec{r}_{12}\|^2} + 2\oint_{\partial A_2} B(y)\frac{\vec{n}_1 \cdot \vec{r}_{12}}{\|\vec{r}_{12}\|^4}(\vec{r}_{12} \times d\vec{x}_2) \tag{11}$$

If A_2 is a polygon, these integrals have a closed form, and yield:

$$\frac{2\pi}{\rho}B(x) = -B_2\vec{n}_1 \cdot \sum_i I_1(i)\,(\vec{r}_i \times \vec{e}_i)$$

$$-\frac{2\pi}{\rho}\nabla(B)(x) = B_2\sum_i I_1(i)\,(\vec{n}_1 \times \vec{e}_i)$$

$$+ 2B_2\sum_i (\vec{r}_i \times \vec{e}_i) \cdot \vec{n}_1\,(I_2(i)\vec{r}_i + J_2(i)\vec{e}_i)$$

where the sum extends on all the edges of the polygon, and B_2 is the radiosity of the emitter. $\vec{r}_i$, $\vec{e}_i$, $I_1(i)$, $I_2(i)$ and $J_2(i)$ stand for (see also Fig. 4):

$$\vec{r}_i = \overrightarrow{xE_i}$$

$$\vec{e}_i = \overrightarrow{E_iE_{i+1}}$$

$$I_1(i) = \frac{\gamma_i}{\|\vec{r}_i \times \vec{e}_i\|}$$

$$I_2(i) = \frac{1}{2\|\vec{r}_i \times \vec{e}_i\|^2}\left(\frac{\vec{r}_{i+1} \cdot \vec{e}_i}{\|\vec{r}_{i+1}\|^2} - \frac{\vec{r}_i \cdot \vec{e}_i}{\|\vec{r}_i\|^2} + \|\vec{e}_i\|^2 I_1(i)\right)$$

$$J_2(i) = \frac{1}{2\|\vec{e}_i\|^2}\left(\frac{1}{\|\vec{r}_i\|^2} - \frac{1}{\|\vec{r}_{i+1}\|^2} - 2I_2(i)\vec{r}_i \cdot \vec{e}_i\right)$$

and γ_i is the angle sustended by edge $\vec{e}_i$ from point x.

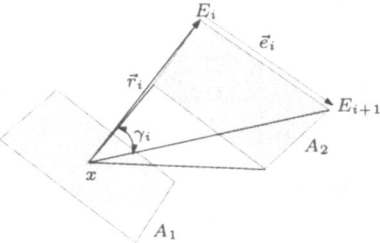

Fig. 4. Geometric Notations Used

Computing B at point x requires roughly 63 multiplications, 6 divisions, 54 additions or substractions, 6 square roots and 3 arc cosines. This equals approximately 300 additions on an SGI Indy computer, with no optimisations and the standard compiler.

Computing $\nabla(B)(x)$ requires roughly 87 multiplications more, 57 additions more and 3 divisions more. Which, with the same material, equals approximately 150 additions.

Although this computationnal cost may depend on implementation details as well as on the computer used (some compilers have very fast implementations of arc cos and square root), computing the gradient along with the radiosity does not over-increase computation time.

A.2 Case of a linear emitter

If the emitter is not constant, the gradient of radiosity on the emitter is not null, and must be used in our computations. However, if we assume the radiosity of the emitter is linear, then its gradient is constant and can be carried out of the integrals. Moreover, this gradient is orthogonal to $\vec{n}_2$, and can be expressed as:

$$\nabla(B)(y) = \vec{n}_2 \times \vec{k}$$

with $\vec{k}$ orthogonal to $\vec{n}_2$. $\vec{k} = \frac{1}{2A_2}((B_2 - B_0)\vec{e}_0 + (B_1 - B_0)\vec{e}_2)$

Using the properties of $\vec{k}$, we can express Equation 6 as:

$$\frac{2\pi}{\rho}B(x) = -\vec{n}_1 \cdot \oint_{\partial A_2} B(y)\frac{\vec{r}_{12} \times d\vec{x}_2}{\|\vec{r}_{12}\|^2} + (\vec{n}_1 \cdot \vec{n}_2)(\vec{k} \cdot (\vec{m} \times \vec{n}_2)) + (\vec{m} \cdot \vec{n}_2)(\vec{n}_2 \cdot (\vec{n}_1 \times \vec{k}))$$

with:

$$\vec{m} = \int_{A_2} \frac{\vec{r}_{12}}{\|\vec{r}_{12}\|^2}dA_2 = \int_{A_2} \nabla(\ln(r_{12}))dA_2$$

Computing the contour integrals does not induce any particular difficulties. However, computing $\vec{m}$ is harder. We can make use of Ostrogradsky's theorem, similar to Stoke's:

$$\int_A \nabla(V) \times d\vec{A} = -\oint_{\partial A} V d\vec{x}$$

to express $\vec{m} \times \vec{n}_2$.

$\vec{m} \cdot \vec{n}_2$ is null if point x is on polygon A_2. If point x is not on polygon A_2, it can be estimated with arbitrary precision.

The formula for $B(x)$ is then:

$$\frac{2\pi}{\rho}B(x) = -\vec{n}_1 \cdot \oint_{\partial A_2} B(y)\frac{\vec{r}_{12} \times d\vec{x}_2}{\|\vec{r}_{12}\|^2} - (\vec{n}_1 \cdot \vec{n}_2)\vec{k} \cdot \oint_{\partial A_2} \ln(r_{12})d\vec{x}_2$$
$$+ (\vec{m} \cdot \vec{n}_2)(\vec{n}_2 \cdot (\vec{n}_1 \times \vec{k}))$$

If we derive this formula rather than use Equation 9, we find:

$$-\frac{2\pi}{\rho}\nabla(B)(x) = \vec{n}_1 \times \oint_{\partial A_2} B(y)\frac{d\vec{x}_2}{\|\vec{r}_{12}\|^2} + 2\oint_{\partial A_2} B(y)\frac{\vec{n}_1 \cdot \vec{r}_{12}}{\|\vec{r}_{12}\|^4}(\vec{r}_{12} \times d\vec{x}_2)$$
$$- (\vec{n}_1 \cdot \vec{n}_2)\oint_{\partial A_2} \frac{\vec{r}_{12}}{\|\vec{r}_{12}\|^2}(\vec{k} \cdot d\vec{x}_2)$$
$$+ (\vec{n}_2 \cdot (\vec{n}_1 \times \vec{k}))(\vec{n}_2 X_1 - 2(\vec{n}_2 \cdot \vec{r}_0)\vec{p})$$

with:

$$\vec{p} = \int_{A_2} \frac{\vec{r}_{12}}{\|\vec{r}_{12}\|^4} dA_2$$

$$X_1 = \int_{A_2} \frac{dA_2}{\|\vec{r}_{12}\|^2}$$

Computing $\vec{p}$ is exactly like computing $\vec{m}$: we can compute $\vec{p} \times \vec{n}_2$, and we can estimate $\vec{p} \cdot \vec{n}_2$ with arbitrary precision. Then we use:

$$\vec{p} = \vec{n}_2 \times (\vec{p} \times \vec{n}_2) + (\vec{p} \cdot \vec{n}_2)\vec{n}_2$$

Hence:

$$\frac{2\pi}{\rho} B(x) = -\vec{n}_1 \cdot \sum_i (B_i I_1(i) + \delta B_i J_1(i)) (\vec{r}_i \times \vec{e}_i)$$

$$- (\vec{n}_1 \cdot \vec{n}_2) \sum_i (\vec{k} \cdot \vec{e}_i) K_1(i)$$

$$+ (\vec{r}_0 \cdot \vec{n}_2)(\vec{n}_2 \cdot (\vec{n}_1 \times \vec{k})) X_1$$

$$-\frac{2\pi}{\rho} \nabla(B)(x) = \sum_i (B_i I_1(i) + \delta B_i J_1(i)) (\vec{n}_1 \times \vec{e}_i)$$

$$+ 2 \sum_i \vec{n}_1 \cdot (\vec{r}_i \times \vec{e}_i) B_i (I_2(i)\vec{r}_i + J_2(i)\vec{e}_i)$$

$$+ 2 \sum_i \vec{n}_1 \cdot (\vec{r}_i \times \vec{e}_i) \delta B_i (J_2(i)\vec{r}_i + K_2(i)\vec{e}_i)$$

$$- (\vec{n}_1 \cdot \vec{n}_2) \sum_i (\vec{k} \cdot \vec{e}_i) (I_1(i)\vec{r}_1 + J_1(i)\vec{e}_1)$$

$$- (\vec{n}_2 \cdot (\vec{n}_1 \times \vec{k}))(\vec{n}_2 \cdot \vec{r}_0)\vec{n}_2 \times \sum_i I_1(i)\vec{e}_i$$

$$+ (\vec{n}_2 \cdot (\vec{n}_1 \times \vec{k})) (X_1\vec{n}_2 - 2(\vec{r}_0 \cdot \vec{n}_2)^2 X_2)$$

With:

$$\delta B_i = B_{i+1} - B_i$$

$$J_1(i) = \frac{1}{\|\vec{e}_i\|^2} \left[\ln \left(\frac{\|\vec{e}_{i+1}\|}{\|\vec{e}_i\|} \right) + (\vec{r}_i \cdot \vec{e}_i) I_1(i) \right]$$

$$K_1(i) = \frac{1}{2\|\vec{e}_i\|^2} (\vec{r}_{i+1} \cdot \vec{e}_i \ln(\|\vec{e}_{i+1}\|^2) - \vec{r}_i \cdot \vec{e}_i \ln(\|\vec{e}_i\|^2) + 2\|\vec{r}_i \times \vec{e}_i\|\gamma_i)$$

$$K_2(i) = \frac{1}{\|\vec{e}_i\|^2} (I_1(i) - \|\vec{r}_i\|^2 I_2(i) - 2(\vec{r}_i \cdot \vec{e}_i) J_2(i))$$

$$X_2 = \int_{A_2} \frac{dA_2}{\|\vec{r}_{12}\|^4}$$

If the the distance between point x and the emitter surface is null, $\vec{m} \cdot \vec{n}_2$ and $\vec{p} \cdot \vec{n}_2$ are both null. If it is not, we prefer to estimate X_1 and X_2. As we know bounds on the values of the function and its derivatives, we make use of a Gaussian quadrature.

Editors' Note: see Appendix, p. 364 for colored figures of this paper

A Clustering Algorithm for Radiance Calculation In General Environments

François Sillion, George Drettakis* , Cyril Soler

*i*MAGIS **

Abstract: This paper introduces an efficient hierarchical algorithm capable of simulating light transfer for complex scenes containing non-diffuse surfaces. The algorithm stems from a new formulation of hierarchical energy exchanges between object clusters, based on the explicit representation of directional radiometric distributions. This approach permits the simplified evaluation of energy transfers and error bounds between clusters. Representation and storage issues are central to this type of algorithm: we discuss the different choices for representing directional distributions, and the choice between explicit storage or immediate propagation of directional information in the hierarchy. The framework presented is well suited to a multi-resolution representation, which may in turn significantly alleviate the storage problems. Results from an implementation are presented, indicating the feasibility of the approach and its capacity to treat complex scenes.

1 Introduction

The hierarchical radiosity algorithm permits the efficient computation of radiosity solution within well-understood error-bounds. Its main limitation is the "initial-linking" step, which for scenes of diffuse polygons adds a quadratic computational cost. As a consequence the algorithm is unusable for large environments. Recently presented clustering algorithms for hierarchical solutions [10, 6], avoid the quadratic cost by first clustering the environment and then refining the clusters.

Nonetheless, little work has been performed for non-diffuse environments. Two-pass algorithms [9, 11] and a general solution using directional representations [7] have treated more general environments in the context of progressive refinement radiosity. A hierarchical solution to general environments has also been proposed [1], but in the case of that algorithm the initial linking cost becomes $\mathcal{O}(n^3)$ in the number of initial polygons, making it unusable even for moderately complex scenes.

The processing of complex environments with general reflectors is a necessity, since almost all interesting scenes contain at least some percentage of non-diffuse materials. In this paper we present a framework which provides the necessary machinery for the treatment of non-diffuse environments in the context of a hierarchical clustering algorithm. This framework is a natural extension of previous clustering methods since, as noted before [6], clusters do not behave as isotropic scatterers, even if composed solely of diffuse surfaces. It is based on the representation of radiant intensity by directional distribution functions, and extends the spirit presented in [7] to hierarchical clustering. The result is the first efficient hierarchical algorithm permitting the efficient of complex, non-diffuse environments. In addition, this representation affords a smooth transition between the representation at the level of (non-diffuse and diffuse) surfaces to the

---

* The second author performed this research with an ERCIM fellowship (funded by the EU Commission), partially at UPC, Barcelona, Spain and GMD, St. Augustin, Germany.
** *i*MAGIS is a joint research project of CNRS/INRIA/INPG/UJF. Postal address: B.P. 53, F-38041 Grenoble Cedex 9, France. Contact E-mail: `Francois.Sillion@imag.fr`.

level of clusters. Finally, the framework opens the way to an efficient multi-resolution representation of light properties for clusters.

In contrast with previous clustering approaches our new method is based on the storage of directional properties with the clusters. This approach requires the reconsideration of some of the quantities previously used since we are now dealing with directional energy exchanges between clusters. In Section 2 we characterise the directional properties of clusters which are used in our solution. In Section 3 we introduce the new algorithm which is based on the directional representation, in Section 4 we discuss the issues pertaining to possible approaches to storing directional distributions and in Section 5 we present some implementation issues and some first results. We conclude in Section 6 with a discussion of limitations and the directions for future research.

2 Characterization of directional energy transfer

As outlined above, we will be treating the light leaving and impinging on clusters as a function of direction. In particular we want to be able to store and manipulate directional functions to characterize the radiant behaviour of a cluster. In this section we discuss the physical quantities used, their representation and their relation to traditional radiosity variables.

For the most general discussion of directional light transfer, we consider light leaving the cluster, light impinging on the cluster, and light passing through the cluster. We also introduce a particular directional function useful for the expression of energy exchanges with distributions. In the remainder of this paper we will denote a direction in space by a unit vector, with the convention that $\vec{u}$ represents an outgoing direction and $\vec{v}$ an incident direction (See Fig. 1).

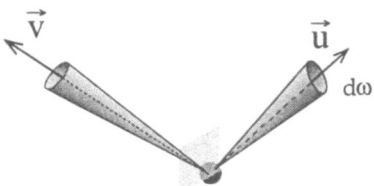

Fig. 1. Notations used for directional functions.

2.1 Outgoing Light

For the description of light leaving the cluster, we use *radiant intensity*, I, representing power per unit solid angle. At a point x on a surface, radiant intensity is related to radiance by the following formula:

$$dI(x, \vec{u}) = L(x, \vec{u}) \, dA \, (\vec{u} \cdot \vec{n}), \tag{1}$$

where $\vec{n}$ is the surface normal and dA is the differential surface area around point x. In the case of a diffuse surface with radiosity B, radiant intensity is thus given by

$$dI(x, \vec{u}) = \frac{B}{\pi} \, dA \, (\vec{u} \cdot \vec{n}).$$

2.2 Incoming Light

For light arriving on a cluster, we use the standard (incoming) *radiance* quantity, defined as the amount of power received per unit area perpendicular to the direction of incidence and per unit solid angle.

With this definition, if the distribution of incident radiance at point x is $E(x, \vec{v})$, the incoming flux density per unit solid angle on a surface placed at x with normal direction $\vec{n}$ is

$$E_s(x, \vec{v}) = E(x, \vec{v}) (\vec{v} \cdot \vec{n}) \tag{2}$$

2.3 The Tangent-sphere function

In Equations 1 and 2 above, the scalar products must be understood as being zero if the surface is not facing the right direction. For notational convenience we represent this extended scalar product as a function of $\vec{u}$. Let us define the *tangent-sphere* function $T_{\vec{n}}(\vec{u})$ for a direction $\vec{n}$ by

$$T_{\vec{n}}(\vec{u}) = \begin{cases} \vec{u} \cdot \vec{n} & \text{if } \vec{u} \cdot \vec{n} \geq 0 \\ 0 & \text{Otherwise} \end{cases} \tag{3}$$

As shown in Fig. 2 the surface given in spherical coordinates by $r = T_{\vec{n}}(\vec{u})$ has the shape of a sphere tangent to the plane orthogonal to $\vec{n}$.

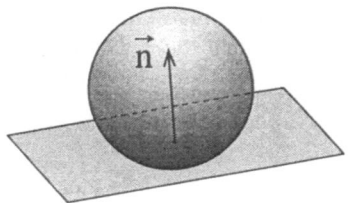

Fig. 2. Tangent-Sphere function.

Using this function, Equations 1 and 2 can be rewritten as

$$I(x, \vec{u}) = L(x, \vec{u}) \, dA \, T_{\vec{n}}(\vec{u}) \tag{4}$$

and

$$E_s(x, \vec{v}) = E(x, \vec{v}) \, T_{\vec{n}}(\vec{v}) \tag{5}$$

2.4 Extinction properties

The transmission properties of object clusters can be discussed using a fruitful analogy with semi-transparent volumes with optical extinction properties. Previous work along this line has proposed to compute equivalent isotropic extinction coefficients for object clusters based on the total area they contain [6] ($\kappa = A/4V$, where A is the total surface area of the objects in the cluster and V is its volume).

In the general approach presented here we lift the isotropic assumption and compute for each cluster a directional extinction coefficient, used to evaluate the attenuation of a light beam traversing the cluster in a given direction. The total projected area in a given direction can be precomputed and stored with each cluster. It is given by the following sum over the surfaces contained in the cluster:

$$\mathcal{A}(\vec{v}) = \sum_i A_i T_{\vec{n}_i}(\vec{v}) \tag{6}$$

A directional extinction coefficient is then obtained with the following formula:

$$\kappa(\vec{v}) = \frac{\mathcal{A}(\vec{v})}{V} \tag{7}$$

$\kappa(\vec{v})$ is used as in [6] to compute approximate transmission through a cluster, as it represents the rate of attenuation per unit length in the direction of interest. Note that the factor of 4 from the isotropic formula is no longer present, since it accounted for the averaging over all directions. Plate 1 (see Appendix) shows results obtained with directional extinction.

2.5 Light Scattering

For now we only consider the transformation of incoming light into outgoing light to take place at surfaces. We assume that a surface oriented in direction $\vec{n}$ is placed at the origin. The surface is small enough for all distributions to be safely assumed constant across its surface. One difficulty in expressing the general light scattering equation is that surface scattering is best described in a coordinate system that is local to the surface. Let us define a linear transformation $M_{\vec{n}}$ such that $\vec{u}' = M_{\vec{n}}\vec{u}$ is the unit vector representing the direction of $\vec{u}$ in a coordinate system attached to the surface. As shown in Fig. 3, both vectors are aligned, they simply have different coordinates because they are expressed in different frames of reference.

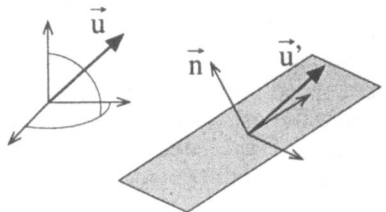

Fig. 3. Notations for the scattering equation.

Surface scattering In this paragraph we express all directions in the surface coordinate system. The radiance leaving the surface in a direction $\vec{u}'$ is given by

$$L(\vec{u}') = \int_{\vec{v}' \in \Omega_+} E_s(\vec{v}')\rho_{bd}(\vec{u}', \vec{v}')d\omega_{\vec{v}'} \tag{8}$$

where $E_s(\vec{v}')d\omega_{\vec{v}'}$ is the incident flux density on the surface from the differential solid angle $d\omega_{\vec{v}'}$ around direction $\vec{v}'$. Ω_+ is the upper hemisphere (above the surface).

Expressing radiant intensity from incident radiance We now wish to express the scattering equation using the directional quantities defined above, and in a general (world) coordinate system, not tied to any particular surface. This simply requires a number of coordinate transformations using $M_{\vec{n}}$. Combining Equations 4 and 8, we can express the radiant intensity leaving a surface in direction $\vec{u}$ as

$$I(\vec{u}) = A\, T_{\vec{n}}(\vec{u})\, L(\vec{u}) \tag{9}$$

$$= A\, T_{\vec{n}}(\vec{u})\, L(M_{\vec{n}}\vec{u}) \tag{10}$$

$$= A\, T_{\vec{n}}(\vec{u}) \int_{\vec{v}' \in \Omega_+} E_s(\vec{v}')\rho_{bd}(M_{\vec{n}}\vec{u}, \vec{v}')d\omega_{\vec{v}'} \,. \tag{11}$$

Using Equation 5 and changing the integration variable to be a unit vector in the hemisphere above the oriented surface, $\vec{v} = M_{\vec{n}}^{-1}\vec{v}'$, we have

$$I(\vec{u}) = A\, T_{\vec{n}}(\vec{u}) \int_{\vec{v} \in M^{-1}\Omega_+} E(\vec{v})T_{\vec{n}}(\vec{v})\rho_{bd}(M_{\vec{n}}\vec{u}, M_{\vec{n}}\vec{v})d\omega_{\vec{v}} \tag{12}$$

Ideal diffuse case For ideal diffuse surfaces, the BRDF is a constant, and Equation 12 reduces to

$$I(\vec{u}) = A\, T_{\vec{n}}(\vec{u})\, \frac{\rho_d}{\pi} \int_{\vec{v} \in M^{-1}\Omega_+} E(\vec{v})T_{\vec{n}}(\vec{v})d\omega_{\vec{v}} \tag{13}$$

The integral in Equation 13 represents the total incident flux density (irradiance) on the surface.

3 A Cluster-Based Illumination Algorithm for General Scenes

Existing radiosity clustering algorithms can be adapted to work with directional information, with little modification as described in this section. We assume here that the reader is familiar with hierarchical radiosity and clustering algorithms [3, 10, 6]. In these methods, a hierarchical subdivision structure of 3D space is used to collect surfaces into clusters. The main idea of the new general clustering algorithm is to associate to each cluster or surface a number of directional distributions representing its radiant properties. The scattering equation (12) must then be evaluated for each surface, using the appropriate incident radiance and radiant intensity distributions.

3.1 Form factor

Since we are using a radiant intensity distribution on the emitter, the estimation of energy transfer between a pair of objects is slightly different than with usual radiosity. Transfer estimates are needed in two stages of a hierarchical radiosity algorithm. First, a bound on the total energy transfer between two objects (or clusters) must be computed during the link refinement stage. Second, the actual energy transfer takes place in a *gathering* stage, where the incoming energy is computed across each link.

The notion of "form factor" used in our algorithm is redefined from purely algorithmic considerations: the form factor associated to each link is the scalar quantity by which the radiant intensity value of an emitter must be multiplied to obtain the incident irradiance (power per unit area perpendicular to the direction of propagation) on the receiver.

This quantity is simply derived from the expression of radiant intensity and irradiance, and is

$$F_{pq} = \int_p \int_q \frac{1}{r^2} dp \, dq \qquad (14)$$

3.2 Link refinement

For the purpose of making a refinement decision, a hierarchical subdivision criterion must be defined. Our preliminary implementation uses an estimate of the energy transferred between two objects q and p (objects can be surfaces or clusters [6]). To obtain this estimate we select two sample points in p and q, yielding a direction $\vec{u}$. Multiplying $I_q(\vec{u})$ with the "form-factor" F_{pq} we obtain an incident irradiance contribution on p from direction $\vec{v} = -\vec{u}$, denoted by $\mathcal{E}_{pq}$. Note that, in a manner similar to Lischinski *at al*'s work [5], an actual bound on this transfer can be computed, provided we store not only the average radiant intensity but also the maximum radiant intensity for each object. To obtain an energy value from incident irradiance requires a multiplication by the total projected area of the cluster's contents in direction $\vec{v}$, $\mathcal{A}(\vec{v})$, introduced in Section 2.4. Our estimate of the energy contribution of the link between q and p is thus

$$P = \mathcal{A}_p(\vec{v})\mathcal{E}_{pq} \qquad (15)$$
$$= \mathcal{A}_p(-\vec{u})I_q(\vec{u})F_{pq} \qquad (16)$$

Note that the previous discussion ignores intra-cluster visibility issues. These are not treated in this paper, although recent work shows that it is possible to integrate their effect with reasonable cost [8]. It is interesting to note the benefit of storing the radiant intensity in the form of a directional distribution, since the transfer estimate does not require the interrogation of the cluster contents. This represents a potential gain over previous hierarchical clustering algorithms [6, 10].

3.3 Gather

Due to the change in quantities used to represent and store light, the traditional process of gathering across linked clusters or surfaces must be appropriately modified.

One of the most important choices to be made when representing directional properties in a hierarchy of clusters, is which properties to store explicitly at all levels in the hierarchy and which to store implicitly by pushing them down to the level at which additional storage cost is incurred. In particular the efficient treatment of incident energy contributions requires some attention. We consider here two alternatives, and discuss their relative merits.

Storing an incident radiance distribution The simplest directional clustering algorithm is probably one where incoming radiance is stored with each cluster, together with (outgoing) radiant intensity. The main advantage of this approach is that the amount of work performed for each link in the gathering phase is fixed, and does not depend on the clusters' complexity. This "constant-time" transfer computation, combined with the linear number of links with respect to the total number of surfaces [3, 10], results in a clustering algorithm with linear asymptotic complexity.

Unfortunately, storing incoming radiance is difficult and expensive. First, in the context of our framework we want to use a continuous, directional function representation. Incoming radiance is inherently discontinuous, as for instance the contribution of a given source is non-zero only for directions reaching the source. This difficulty can be eliminated by estimating a continuous approximation to each source's contribution to the incident radiance.

Consider again the transfer from q to p. Since our refinement criterion has established the link at this level, it is reasonable to assume that the transfer is well represented by a point-to-point calculation. An estimation of the error incurred by this assumption must evidently be undertaken in the future. The incident *irradiance* on p is obtained as explained in Section 3.2. This irradiance can be spread across the solid angle subtended by q, using a simple parametric filter in the shape of a peak. We are investigating the use of rotated $\cos^n(\theta)$ distributions as convolution filters. Clearly however this operation involves a significant additional computational cost.

In addition, explicit storage implies the need for an expensive convolution operation when pushing the incoming radiance down the hierarchy of clusters. At the transition from clusters to surfaces the conversion from incident radiance to radiant intensity must be performed, as shown in Equations 12 for the general case and 13 for the diffuse case. Again this implies significant additional computation.

Immediate propagation of incoming contributions An alternative to storage of incoming radiance is to explicitly push incoming light down the hierarchy at each gather operation. To perform this we no longer consider radiance, but *irradiance*, computed as in Section 3.2. This quantity, accompanied by the incoming direction $\vec{v}$ is pushed down the cluster hierarchy by simple addition. This irradiance is the term $E(\vec{v})d\omega_{\vec{v}}$ in Equation 12. At the surface level we need only evaluate Equation 12, replacing the integral by an "impulse" from direction $\vec{v}$, with the surface irradiance value $\mathcal{E}_{pq}T_{\vec{n}}(\vec{v})$. This surface irradiance is used to scale the surface's BRDF, which reduces to a constant for diffuse surfaces.

3.4 Push/Pull

In our implementation we have chosen the option of immediate pushing of incoming radiance as opposed to storing the quantity as a directional function. Thus the traditional Push-Pull operation only needs to perform the "Pull" portion, since the "Push" occurs at the gathering stage. Since radiant intensity is a power quantity, the radiant intensity of a cluster is obtained from that of its sub-clusters by simple summation. The result is a combined directional function representing the total radiant intensity of the cluster.

4 Representation of Directional Distributions

Several storage schemes have been investigated in the context of simulating non-diffuse radiant exchanges. A major difficulty in selecting a representation is to achieve the best possible balance between the storage cost of each option and its suitability given a number of algorithmic requirements. Any finite representation of directional functions is based on the selection of a number of basis functions. The representation of a distribution then consists of its coordinate vector in the chosen basis.

Previous algorithms employ for example constant basis functions defined over the cells of a "global cube" [4], or spherical harmonics basis functions up to a prescribed order [2, 7]. The global cube approach has the advantage of simplicity, first because it is very easy to manipulate, but also because function products can be evaluated easily (since the basis functions have non-overlapping support). However it is inherently a discontinuous representation, prone to disturbing rendering artifacts.

Spherical harmonics, on the other hand, always produce continuous functions. But they are non-zero over the entire hemisphere, making the computation of function products much more expensive.

4.1 Spherical Harmonics

In our implementation we use spherical harmonics basis functions. These form an orthogonal basis of the set of distributions on the unit sphere. This infinite collection of basis functions is typically denoted by $Y_{l,m}(\theta, \phi)$ where $0 \leq l < \infty$ and $-l \leq m \leq l$. In direct analogy with a Fourier series in one dimension, any square-integrable function, $f(\theta, \phi)$, can be expressed in this basis, with a set of scalar coefficients $C_{l,m}$.

An approximate representation of a directional function is obtained by storing only the first few coefficients of this decomposition, up to a given maximum level. BRDFs can be encoded by such vectors of coefficients for use in a radiosity simulation [7].

Representation of diffuse surfaces using Tangent-Sphere functions In the diffuse case, all radiant intensity distributions are combinations of oriented Tangent-sphere functions (see Equation 13).

The decomposition of $T_{\vec{n}}(\vec{u})$ into spherical harmonics can be computed for a given direction $\vec{n}$. The simple shape of this function allows a very good approximation with only 9 coefficients ($l \leq 2$). The coefficients of this decomposition are thus functions of $\vec{n}$, and they can themselves be decomposed using spherical harmonics of $\vec{n}$. This double decomposition was already used by Westin *et al.* to represent anisotropic BRDFs [12]. In our case it is stored in a data file, since the Tangent-sphere function is always the same.

The spherical harmonics representation of $T_{\vec{n}}(\vec{u})$ is obtained by evaluating the value of each coefficient for the direction $\vec{n}$. Since this only depends on the surface orientation, it is only performed once in the program, and is then stored with the polygon (and thus shared by all hierarchical elements on the surface).

Computation of the scattering integral If incident radiance is stored with the clusters, the integral in Equation 12 must be evaluated at each cluster-surface interface. The convolution of incident radiance and the BRDF is quite costly to compute, especially since function products are difficult to express with spherical harmonics coefficients. We are currently investigating an efficient algorithm to compute such convolutions, based on the use of recurrence relations, and the observation that the integral of a function is represented by it's ($l = 0, m = 0$) coefficient.

5 Implementation and First Results

We have implemented the representation of radiant intensity and the equivalent push/pull operation in our testbed clustering system. As described above we have used spherical harmonics for the representation of directional functions. Our implementation is still preliminary in the sense that for now a limited number of orientations are allowed for non-diffuse surfaces. The color plates in the appendix demonstrate the versatility and high potential of the method.

5.1 Directional properties for clusters of diffuse surfaces

We first consider the anisotropic behaviour of clusters containing only diffuse surfaces. Plate 2 shows an example with over 6,000 surfaces. The ceiling receives no primary illumination, and is only illuminated by light reflected by the cluster. We see that the pattern of light on the ceiling is displaced with respect to the vertical direction.

As an indication to the reader of the relative cost of the storage of directional radiant intensity, comparisons are made to images generated using the algorithms presented in [6, 8], in which directional functions are not used. Since the refinement criteria are no longer the same, we set our subdivision threshold so that the two executions result in similar number of links refined for two iterations. The following table gives the computation time (in seconds) and memory cost (in Mb) for directional (dir) and traditional (trad) clustering algorithms.

Name	Polygons	Time (dir)	Time (trad)	Mem. (dir)	Mem. (trad)
Simple	13	29.6	24.0	8.5	4.7
Cubes	6000	140.0	46.1	13.4	6.9

We see that the computation time for the directional approach is between 20% to 3 times higher. This can be explained by the additional expense in combining the tangent sphere functions and the directional representations of radiant intensity. The comparisons are given only as an indication; in the resulting images for the *Cubes* scene the directional algorithm obtains a much higher quality representation of the secondary illumination on the ceiling (see Plate 2).

The memory requirements for the directional representation are approximately twice that of the traditional clustering approach. These numbers are more meaningful since they are not affected as much by the different refinement criteria. If the growth factor is close to the indicated factor of two, this implies that memory utilization does not pose a major problem for our approach, since even very complex scenes will not require unmanageable amounts of memory.

5.2 Results for general reflectors

Plates 3 and 4 show simulations performed with a cluster of glossy surfaces. Both directional reflection and directional attenuation are demonstrated, by illuminating the scene from two different directions. Plate 5 illustrates the view-dependent character of radiant intensity distributions, with two different views of the same scene. Computation times for all these images range from 17 to 103 seconds.

6 Discussion and Conclusions

We have presented a general framework for the hierarchical representation of energy exchanges taking into account the non-uniform directional behavior of surfaces and object clusters. Although conceptually simple, this approach raises a number of practical issues, which we discuss below.

Benefits and limitations of the Approach The explicit representation of directional radiant functions for object clusters has several important benefits. First, it allows a smooth integration of non-diffuse reflectors in a clustering algorithm. Second, if incoming radiance is stored explicitly, it reduces the asymptotic complexity of the clustering algorithm. Third, the consideration of directional extinction properties greatly improves the applicability of the approximate transmission calculation based on the volume analogy. Finally, the method allows the simulation of non-isotropic scattering volumes with arbitrary phase functions. In practice we consider that the most useful feature is the ability to mix diffuse and non-diffuse reflectors in a scene at a moderate additional cost. In particular the overhead costs for diffuse reflectors remain reasonable, while allowing much more accurate transfers between clusters. We tend to prefer the option of implicit storage for incident radiance, since it appears very difficult to do away completely with any traversal of the hierarchy during the gathering stage. For instance, the consideration of intra-cluster visibility is much easier when each contribution is pushed down to the surfaces [8]. The efficient representation of directional functions is a difficult issue. For general reflectors many spherical harmonics coefficients may be needed, resulting in high storage and computation costs.

Future directions A major area of research for future work is the investigation of multi-resolution representations of directional functions. It may be possible to store different levels of detail at each cluster, instead of storing a complete distribution everywhere. This would dramatically lower the storage costs, while allowing true multi-resolution visibility computation through object clusters [8]. Another interesting direction is the computation (and storage) of complete scattering functions for all clusters. These will allow the direct transformation of incoming radiance to radiant intensity, similar to a volumic phase function. However the storage costs for such bidirectional phase functions may be prohibitive.

References

1. Larry Aupperle and Pat Hanrahan. A hierarchical illumination algorithm for surfaces with glossy reflection. In *Computer Graphics Proceedings, Annual Conference Series:* SIGGRAPH '93 (Anaheim, CA, USA), pages 155–162. ACM SIGGRAPH, New York, August 1993.

2. Brian Cabral, Nelson L. Max, and Rebecca Springmayer. Bidirectional reflection functions from surface bump maps. *Computer Graphics*, 21(4):273–281, July 1987. Proceedings SIGGRAPH '87 in Anaheim (USA).

3. Pat Hanrahan, David Saltzman, and Larry Aupperle. A rapid hierarchical radiosity algorithm. *Computer Graphics*, 25(4):197–206, August 1991. Proceedings SIGGRAPH '91 in Las Vegas (USA).

4. David S. Immel, Michael F. Cohen, and Donald P. Greenberg. A radiosity method for non-diffuse environments. *Computer Graphics*, 20(4):133–142, August 1986. Proceedings SIGGRAPH '86 in Dallas (USA).

5. Dani Lischinski, Brian Smits, and Donald P. Greenberg. Bounds and error estimates for radiosity. In *Computer Graphics Proceedings, Annual Conference Series:* SIGGRAPH '94 (Orlando, FL). ACM SIGGRAPH, New York, July 1994.

6. François Sillion. A unified hierarchical algorithm for global illumination with scattering volumes and object clusters. *to appear in IEEE Transactions on Visualization and Computer Graphics*, 1(3), September 1995. (a preliminary version appeared in the fifth Eurographics workshop on rendering, Darmstadt, Germany, June 1994).

7. François Sillion, James Arvo, Stephen Westin, and Donald P. Greenberg. A global illumination solution for general reflectance distributions. *Computer Graphics*, 25(4):187–196, August 1991. Proceedings SIGGRAPH '91 in Las Vegas (USA).

8. François Sillion and George Drettakis. Feature-based control of visibility error: A multiresolution clustering algorithm for global illumination. In *Computer Graphics Proceedings, Annual Conference Series:* SIGGRAPH '95 (Los Angeles, CA). ACM SIGGRAPH, New York, August 1995.

9. François Sillion and Claude Puech. A general two-pass method integrating specular and diffuse reflection. *Computer Graphics*, 23(4), August 1989. Proceedings SIGGRAPH '89 in Boston (USA).

10. Brian Smits, James Arvo, and Donald P. Greenberg. A clustering algorithm for radiosity in complex environments. In *Computer Graphics Proceedings, Annual Conference Series:* SIGGRAPH '94 (Orlando, FL). ACM SIGGRAPH, New York, July 1994.

11. John R. Wallace, Kells A. Elmquist, and Eric A. Haines. A ray tracing algorithm for progressive radiosity. *Computer Graphics*, 23(3):315–324, July 1989. Proceedings SIGGRAPH '89 in Boston.

12. Stephen H. Westin, James R. Arvo, and Kenneth E. Torrance. Predicting reflectance functions from complex surfaces. *Computer Graphics*, 26(4):255–264, July 1992. Proceedings of SIGGRAPH '92 in Chicago (USA).

Editors' Note: see Appendix, p. 365 for colored figures of this paper

The Stochastic Ray Method for Radiosity

László Neumann[1]   Werner Purgathofer[2]   Robert F. Tobler[2]
Attila Neumann[1]   Pavol Eliás[2]   Martin Feda[2]
                     Xavier Pueyo[3]

Abstract. This paper solves the system of radiosity equations with a stochastic numerical approach. Due to the high complexity of the problem for highly complex scenes, a stochastic variation of Jacobi iteration is developed which converges stochastically to the correct solution. The new method, called the Stochastic Ray Method, is a significant improvement of Stochastic Radiosity. A large number of independent rays is chosen stochastically by importance sampling of the patches according to their power after the previous iteration step. They all carry an equal amount of power into random directions, thereby representing together the total energy interreflection of the entire environment in a stochastic manner. Assuming a correctly distributed initial solution, which can be reached easily, the iteration process converges quickly and reduces the error in the result faster than other stochastic radiosity approaches. The new algorithm can easily be extended to treat various phenomena which are normally rather costly to incorporate in radiosity environments: perfect specular reflection and specular transmittance, non-diffuse self-emission and point light sources.

1 Introduction

The original radiosity method is based on a discretization of the environment into flat polygons, called *patches*. Constant radiosity is assumed across the surface of each patch, and all surfaces are assumed to be perfect Lambertian reflectors. The resulting system of equations can be solved to obtain the radiosities of each patch [7].

This algorithm is very costly due to the computation of the form factor matrix that encodes the interactions between each two patches. Several modifications of the original method have been described (e.g. [2], [3], [17] and [6]). These "shooting" methods are still unsuitable for very complex scenes containing millions of patches, since they need to calculate a complete line of form factors in each iteration step. As each shooting step considers only the energy of a single patch, a large number of iterations are necessary to distribute all available energy in the scene. Galerkin Radiosity [26] and Wavelet Radiosity [8] are recent approaches that represent the radiosity of entire surfaces as combinations of different classes of basis functions. Depending on these classes discontinuities or ringing may appear as a problem. The computation of the radiosity function is very costly, especially for the standard Galerkin approach.

Other radiosity algorithms (e.g. [19], [20], [21], [15], and [18]) try to reduce the computational cost by using a stochastic approach based on shooting rays. This also enables the integration of non-diffuse effects into radiosity. Note, that all stochastic radiosity methods have one common weakness: they need an *a priori* mesh of the scene.

The Radiance system [24] which also solves the global illumination problem by stochastic sampling, is based on distribution ray tracing [5] and the Monte Carlo approach for raytracing [11]. Thus it is different from the radiosity based approaches which try to calculate a view independent solution. Monte Carlo approaches have been used to solve integral equations in other areas, e.g. thermal heat transfer [22].

---

[1] Maros u. 36, Budapest, Hungary, H-1122
[2] Institute of Computer Graphics, Technical University of Vienna, Karlsplatz 13/186, A-1040 Wien, Austria
[3] Universitat de Girona, Spain

The new stochastic method presented in this paper uses an approach, that is more based on numerical mathematics, to solve the system of linear equations, resulting in faster convergence to the solution. Therefore, a higher scene complexity is possible.

The first implementations of the radiosity method used Gauss-Seidel or Jacobi-iteration to solve the set of radiosity equations. Both iteration methods need to calculate the full form factor matrix to perform one iteration step. This represents a prohibitive cost for complex scenes. Most modern methods therefore use algorithms based on progressive refinement radiosity [3], which has been shown to be equivalent to Southwell iteration [9], [12]. Although very slow for solving general systems of equations, Southwell iteration is well suited for the set of radiosity equations. To solve the radiosity equations, these methods need only calculate one column of the form factor matrix per iteration step. The theoretical complexity of Southwell Iteration is $O(N^2)$, where N is the number of patches in the scene. Although for mostly directly illuminated scenes the complexity to achieve a visually satisfying result is lower, it is still considerably greater than $O(N)$.

The method presented in this paper is based on the Stochastic Radiosity Method [13], which reduces the computational complexity of a single interreflection step by approximating a full form factor matrix stochastically. Although the original stochastic radiosity method seems to be very promising, the following problems arise:

- The variance for large form factors is very high.
- Due to the use of hemicubes for form-factor computation, there are considerable aliasing artifacts.
- For the same reason perfect specular reflection cannot be handled.
- The unmodified τ_k series that was used results in very slow convergence for moderately high average values of ρ (e.g. average $\rho > 0.7$)
- The algorithm exhibits stochastic convergence instead of deterministic convergence (i.e. the expected value of the solution after k steps converges to the real solution as k goes to infinity).

The method presented in this paper will overcome all but the last of these problems.

In section 2 we will give a short summary of the Stochastic Radiosity Method upon which the new algorithm is built. Section 3 first describes the Stochastic Ray Method algorithmically, then explains the required importance sampling technique, and finally gives an introduction into the mathematical background of this stochastic family of radiosity methods. Differences to related methods are outlined in section 4 and the adaptation to special effects are described in section 5. Finally, results of our implementation and a performance analysis in section 6 preceeds the conclusions and future trends section 7.

2 Background

The Stochastic Radiosity Method

The basis of the Stochastic Radiosity Method [13], is the stochastic shooting technique. The main idea of this approach is to approximate stochastically the Neumann series[4] of the underlying system of equations.

The Stochastic Radiosity Method works with radiant power values $P_i = B_i \cdot Area_i$ (in Watt) rather than with radiosity values B_i. The radiosity equation can easily be expressed in terms of power:

$$P_i = W_i + \rho_i \cdot \sum_{j=1}^{N} F_{ji} \cdot P_j \qquad (1)$$

where $W_i = E_i \cdot Area_i$ is the self-emitted power and ρ_i is the diffuse reflection coefficient of patch i. This formulation of the radiosity equation is used to facilitate

---

[4] traditional numerical method

the following importance sampling method.

The idea of Stochastic Radiosity is to select a fixed number M of shooting patches (e.g. $M = 500$) at each iteration step. This selection is made stochastically by importance sampling, so that the probability of a patch being selected is proportional to its power. These M shooting patches shall represent the complete environment and therefore have to distribute the total available power. Due to the sampling strategy, the power shot from each of the M shooting patches has to be equal and is given by:

$$P_{patch} = \frac{1}{M} \cdot \sum_{i=1}^{N} P_i = \frac{1}{M} \cdot P_{total} \qquad (2)$$

This iteration step implicitly calculates an approximate form factor matrix, which has non-zero columns only for the M shooting patches.

Although this step is called a shooting step, there is a notable difference to progressive refinement radiosity which is based on the Southwell iteration method. Since Stochastic Radiosity, similar to the new method proposed in this paper, is based on stochastic mathematical principles which will be explained in more detail in section 3.4, there are no unshot power values. At each iteration step the total available power is shot. The M chosen patches act as representatives of the total scene, and the power value of each patch after an iteration step is calculated as a weighted average of the newly received power and the result after the previous step. The weights used for this averaging – which will also be used in the new method – are also explained in section 3.4.

3 The Stochastic Ray Method

3.1 Outline of the New Method

First, recall that we are interested in highly complex scenes. The Stochastic Radiosity Method as described up to now uses standard algorithms to calculate the form factors (e.g. Hemicube [1]) for the approximate form factor matrices. Due to the stochastic nature of the method, the following problems arise with these algorithms:

- Only a fraction of all patches are chosen in each iteration step and each chosen patch gets a large amount of power to shoot. Thus the discretization of the power may introduce a large variance in the solution of the original Stochastic Shooting Method [13].
- Due to the large number of patches, hemicube methods or other z-buffer based algorithms, exhibit aliasing problems that can only be overcome by using high resolution z-buffers, and thus increasing the computational cost.

Therefore our goal was to invent a method that allows a finer discretization of the total power in the shooting step. We achieve this by dividing the total power into a large number m of equally sized portions (e.g. $m = N \cdot k$, where $10 \leq k \leq 1000$). Each of these portions is carried by a single ray. The fraction of power carried by each ray is equal and they are chosen randomly to represent the total available power in the environment. This can be expressed similarly as in equation (2):

$$P_{ray} = \frac{1}{m} \cdot \sum_{i=1}^{N} P_i = \frac{1}{m} \cdot P_{total} \qquad (3)$$

In order to shoot the rays we do importance sampling based on the power: each patch will emit a number of rays proportional to its fraction of the total power. With this operation we implicitly calculate a stochastic approximation of the form factor matrix. Shooting a ray is a very simple operation:

- In the absence of better knowledge, select a random point V on the surface of shooting patch i,
- Select a random direction D using a probability distribution according to the diffuse reflection or emission.

- Intersect the ray $V + t \cdot D$ with the scene and determine the patch j that contains the closest intersection point.
- Deposit the power carried by the ray on patch j.

The form factor computation is performed implicitly: the form factor corresponds to the expected value of the fraction of rays that are received at patch j of those emitted at patch i (for details see [18]).

3.2 The Algorithm

The new stochastic ray algorithm is illustrated in figure 1 using a pseudo-code description. The new power values for each patch are calculated as weighted averages of the previous approximation and the newly calculated power values. The weights that are used for this approximation are different for each iteration step and form a series denoted $\{\tau_k\}$. The rationale behind this equation is explained in section 3.4.

```
for all patches i: { P_i = W_i }
while not converged:
{   compute P_total
    P_ray = P_total / m                                              // see equation (3)
    for all patches i: { set r_i , the number of received rays of patch i, to 0 }
    for all patches i:
    {   compute m_i , the number of rays to shoot from patch i       // see equation (5)
        for each ray to shoot from patch i:
        {   choose a point V on the surface of patch i
            choose a direction D according to the reflection law
            determine the closest patch j intersected by the ray V + t · D
            increment r_j
        }
    }
    for all patches i: { P_i := (1 - τ_k) · P_i + τ_k · [ ρ_i · r_i · P_ray + W_i ] }   // see equation (14)
}
```

Figure 1: Pseudo-code description of stochastic ray radiosity.

3.3 Importance Sampling

Each patch holds a fraction of the total power in the environment. Since each ray carries an equal amount of power, we employ an importance sampling scheme based on the patch power P_i, in order to compute the number of rays that have to be shot from each patch i. This can be implemented in linear time as follows: a discrete cumulative distribution function G is defined by:

$$G_j = \frac{\sum_{i=1}^{j} P_i}{\sum_{i=1}^{N} P_i} \qquad (4)$$

The number of rays m_i of equal energy that have to be shot from patch i can then be calculated as follows:

$$m_i = \lfloor G_i \cdot m + rnd \rfloor - \lfloor G_{i-1} \cdot m + rnd \rfloor \qquad (5)$$

where m is the total number of rays to be shot and rnd is a single random value of uniform distribution in the interval $[0,1)$ which is the same for all patches, but different at each new iteration.

Figure 2 shows a graphical representation of this importance sampling technique which is also used in the Stochastic Radiosity Method [13].

Note that usually there is significant coherence between the geometry of the scene and the sequence of the data structure, i.e. a number of successive patches in the data structure cover the area of a hypothetical "superpatch". Therefore, the stratified importance sampling strategy also produces correct results for the larger areas of these superpatches with high probability.

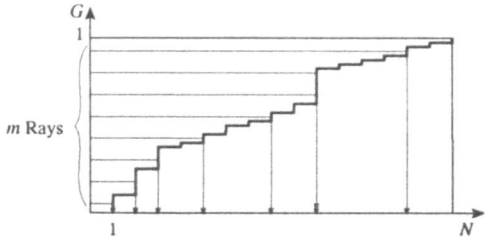

Figure 2: Importance sampling using a discrete cumulative distribution function.

For generating colour images, the sum of the power in all colour bands[5] is used for the computation of P_{total} and the power values in each colour band are used to calculate the proportions of powers in the respective bands that have to be carried by each ray. Since the fraction of the power in each colour band does not exactly represent the importance, the resulting sampling scheme can only be viewed as an approximation of importance sampling. In order to implement this, the rays need to be modified to carry fractional powers of all colour bands.

If more than one ray needs to be shot from one patch, randomly chosen starting points can lead to undesired clustering. To avoid this, jittered sampling in a grid can be used, making use of the knowledge of the number of rays to be shot from a patch in one iteration step.

For choosing the direction to shoot a ray, importance sampling has to be applied to the diffuse part of the reflection function. If pure lambertian reflectors are used the number of rays must be proportional to the cosine of the angle with respect to the surface normal.

3.4 Mathematical Background of the Stochastic Ray Method for Radiosity

Following [13], the system of radiosity equations (1) can be rewritten in the following, simpler form:

$$x = A \cdot x + b \tag{6}$$

where x denotes the solution vector, A the matrix of form factors multiplied with the ρ_i's, and b the vector of self emissions.

The solution to this equation can be expressed in the form of a Neumann series:

$$x = b + A \cdot b + A^2 \cdot b + A^3 \cdot b + ... \tag{7}$$

In the context of radiosity, b corresponds to self-emission, $A \cdot b$ to direct illumination, $A^2 \cdot b$ to indirect illumination via one intermediate reflector, and so on.

Jacobi iteration is the simplest method to calculate this series. At each iteration step, the approximation of the solution is improved by the following formula:

$$x^{(k)} = A \cdot x^{(k-1)} + b \tag{8}$$

With an initial vector $x^{(0)} = b$, this iterative formula leads exactly to the partial sums of the Neumann series. Without modifications, this method would be too costly for complex scenes, since the full matrix A is required to perform one iteration step.

Stochastic Radiosity as described in [13] overcomes this problem by using stochastic convergence instead of deterministic convergence: the intermediate solution vectors $x^{(k)}$ of an iteration method converge stochastically to vector x, if for arbitrary positive ε:

$$\lim_{k \to \infty} \left[P\left(\left\| x^{(k)} - x \right\| \geq \varepsilon \right) \right] = 0 \tag{9}$$

where P denotes probability and $\|...\|$ is an arbitrary vector norm.

---

5   This simple formula is surely suboptimal. A more precise investigation of this topic is subject to future work.

To reduce the computational cost of Jacobi iteration, the full interreflection matrix A is replaced by a different approximate matrix A_k at each iteration step. The only necessary condition is that the expected value E of each approximate interreflection step $A_k \cdot x$ is identical to the exact interreflection step $A \cdot x$, i.e. A_k is chosen so that:

$$E[A_k \cdot x] = A \cdot x \qquad (10)$$

Note that $E[A_k] = A$ is not required to meet criterion (10). The approximate matrices A_k contain elements fulfilling equation (10). These elements are generated implicitly with the importance sampling strategy in the Stochastic Ray algorithm and are a very sparse collection of equal values P_{ray} (or multiples thereof) according to equation (3). However, if A_k is used instead of A for Jacobi iteration in formula (8), $x^{(k)}$ does not converge stochastically, because different approximate matrices A_k are used at each iteration step k. This becomes clear by expanding the first iterations of iteration formula (8) with A_k instead of A:

$$x^{(1)} = b + A_1 \cdot b$$
$$x^{(2)} = b + A_2 \cdot b + A_2 \cdot A_1 \cdot b \qquad (11)$$
$$x^{(3)} = b + A_3 \cdot b + A_3 \cdot A_2 \cdot b + A_3 \cdot A_2 \cdot A_1 \cdot b$$

...

The first solution $x^{(1)}$ contains the first-order term $A_1 \cdot b$, while $x^{(2)}$ and $x^{(3)}$ contain first-order terms $A_2 \cdot b$ and $A_3 \cdot b$,. In the same way, $x^{(2)}$ and $x^{(3)}$ contain different second-order terms, and so on. Therefore, the iteration results $x^{(k)}$ are not converging.

Stochastic convergence can be achieved only if all terms of the partial sum $x^{(k-1)}$ are contained in the new partial sum $x^{(k)}$. This means that new terms of any order n must not replace the nth order terms of the previous partial sums, but they have to be combined, e.g. by averaging:

$$x^{(1)} = b + A_1 \cdot b$$
$$x^{(2)} = b + \tfrac{1}{2} \cdot (A_1 + A_2) \cdot b + A_2 \cdot A_1 \cdot b$$
$$x^{(3)} = b + \tfrac{1}{3} \cdot (A_1 + A_2 + A_3) \cdot b + \tfrac{1}{3} \cdot (A_2 \cdot A_1 + A_3 \cdot A_1 + A_3 \cdot A_2) \cdot b + \qquad (12)$$
$$+ A_3 \cdot A_2 \cdot A_1 \cdot b$$

Since all $A_k \cdot x$ have the same expected value $A \cdot x$, the iteration is guaranteed to converge stochastically to the correct solution. It is important to note that each iteration k improves the accuracy of the solution in two ways: the variance of terms already contained in $x^{(k-1)}$ is improved in $x^{(k)}$, and a new term of order k is added.

Reducing the variance of an nth order term means in the radiosity context, that the nth order interreflection corresponding to this term is simulated more accurately than in the previous intermediate solution $x^{(k-1)}$. The reduction of the variance by averaging approximate matrices A_k of identical expected value $E[A_k \cdot x] = A \cdot x$ becomes clear by the following fact (which is a basic property of the expectation):

$$\lim_{n \to \infty} \tfrac{1}{n} \cdot \sum_{k=1}^{n} A_k \cdot x = A \cdot x \qquad (13)$$

Equation (13) can be generalized for n^{th} order terms. By that it can be shown that the iteration converges stochastically to the correct solution [14].

In addition to the variance reduction, each iteration k adds a new term of order k, which represents one additional diffuse interreflection step in the radiosity context: while $x^{(1)}$ accounts for self-emission and direct illumination only, an approximation of indirect illumination via one intermediate reflector is contained in $x^{(2)}$, an approximation via two intermediate reflectors is contained in $x^{(3)}$, etc.

Unfortunately, it is impossible to compute the average terms with the correct weighting factors as in equation (12) by an iteration method. The numerical result $x^{(k)}$

cannot be split up into separated terms, and therefore the different terms of order n generated in subsequent iterations cannot be averaged with correct weighting factors. So other averaging methods have to be found which do not require the single terms of the partial sums to be manipulated.

In [14] the following iteration formula is proposed, which is simple to handle and memory efficient, because it does not require any storage for averaging:

$$x^{(k)} = (1 - \tau_k) \cdot x^{(k-1)} + \tau_k \cdot \left[A_k \cdot x^{(k-1)} + b \right] \tag{14}$$

where $\{\tau_k\}$ is an appropriate series which converges to 0. For example, the harmonic series can be used for $\{\tau_k\}$:

$$\tau_k = \frac{1}{k} \tag{15}$$

Using equations (14) and (15), the partial sums of the first three iterations are:

$$x^{(1)} = b + A_1 \cdot b$$

$$x^{(2)} = b + \tfrac{1}{2} \cdot (A_1 + A_2) \cdot b + \tfrac{1}{2} \cdot A_2 \cdot A_1 \cdot b$$

$$x^{(3)} = b + \tfrac{1}{3} \cdot (A_1 + A_2 + A_3) \cdot b + (\tfrac{1}{3} \cdot A_2 \cdot A_1 + \tfrac{1}{6} \cdot A_3 \cdot A_1 + \tfrac{1}{6} \cdot A_3 \cdot A_2) \cdot b + \tag{16}$$

$$+ \tfrac{1}{6} \cdot A_3 \cdot A_2 \cdot A_1 \cdot b$$

The low-order terms in (16) contain the average of matrices, just as in (12). However, higher order terms are not averaged correctly, because the weighting factors of matrices or of products of matrices do not sum up to one. The sum of the weighting factors can be used to analyze the progress of the iteration in (16). Calculating these sums for the first few steps yields the following table:

$$
\begin{aligned}
w^{(1)} &= (1 \quad 1 \quad 0 \quad 0 \quad 0 \quad 0 \quad 0 \quad ...) \\
w^{(2)} &= (1 \quad 1 \quad .50 \quad 0 \quad 0 \quad 0 \quad 0 \quad ...) \\
w^{(3)} &= (1 \quad 1 \quad .67 \quad .16 \quad 0 \quad 0 \quad 0 \quad ...) \\
w^{(4)} &= (1 \quad 1 \quad .75 \quad .29 \quad .04 \quad 0 \quad 0 \quad ...) \\
&\ \ \vdots \\
w^{(10)} &= (1 \quad 1 \quad .90 \quad .62 \quad .29 \quad .09 \quad .02 \quad ...) \\
&\ \ \vdots \\
w^{(50)} &= (1 \quad 1 \quad .98 \quad .89 \quad .71 \quad .47 \quad .26 \quad ...)
\end{aligned}
\tag{17}
$$

Obviously the sum of the weighting factors for each term converges to one, as the iteration progresses. Therefore, the iteration process based on formulas (14) and (15) is guaranteed to converge stochastically to the correct solution. Nevertheless, none of these coefficients will ever reach the value 1, except for the first two. In order to represent more than the 1st order term exactly, additional elements with value 1 can be prepended to the τ_k series. Inserting one element with value 1 at the beginning will insert a column of 1's at the left side of the table of the summed weighting factors, thereby shifting all others one column to the right. Unfortunately, in this way the result of this first iteration will not contribute to variance reduction. More details of the theoretical background of this method will be given in [14].

The convergence speed of the summed weighting factors is rather slow. For scenes with a high average reflection coefficient (e.g. 0.7, this is very common!) using the original τ_k series (15) would result in a noticeable lack of total power. Assuming a scene with the same reflection coefficient ρ for all patches, the total power in the solution can be estimated using a geometric series. Comparing this result with the total power obtained using the summed weighting factors (17) will give an estimate for the missing power. Table 1 gives the fraction of the total power that is missing after 1000 iteration steps for different values of average ρ and different numbers of 1's inserted into the original τ_k series.

Table 1

average ρ	original τ_k	one 1 inserted
0.5	0.00892	0.00446
0.6	0.02542	0.01526
0.7	0.06788	0.04753
0.8	0.17259	0.13810

From table 1 can be seen that – using b as starting vector for the iteration – the fraction of the total power still missing after 1000 iteration steps (each with a high number of rays) depends heavily on the average ρ of the scene. For $\rho = 0.5$ only a little less than 1% of the converged power will be missing, but for $\rho = 0.8$ about 17% is still not generated. By adding one additional 1 at the beginning of the τ_k series the figures are improved.

This problem can be overcome by choosing a better starting vector for the iteration. Theoretically it can be proven that our iteration method converges with any starting vector. In practice, however, if the starting vector has the following characteristics, then the convergence speed is enhanced drastically, and the problem of missing power is removed:

* the total power in the starting vector is reasonably close to the total power in the solution;
* the distribution of the power is a rough approximation of the solution; and,
* the variance in the elements of the starting vector does not need to be low, i.e. it is acceptable that neighbouring patches which will have similar power in the final solution have drastically different powers in the starting vector

Such a starting vector can be calculated using the Random Walk Method [15] with a low number of rays or – to stay consistent with the overall strategy – with the Stochastic Ray Method itself using a τ_k series of only 1's and a low number of rays per iteration. The latter approach is equivalent to prepending a certain number of 1's to the used τ_k series . Table 2 shows the missing power fractions for different numbers of 1's added to the τ_k series after the corresponding iteration steps and after 1000 iteration steps using equation (15) for the other τ's. It can be seen that for average scenes, 30 iteration steps with a low number of rays will lead to a starting vector fulfilling our demands. This starting vector has a very high variance (see figure 14, appendix), but is much better than the trivial starting vector b. Additionally, its calculation is marginal in terms of computational cost.

Table 2

avg. ρ	steps	n = number of 1's added to the τ_k series				
		0	1	10	30	50
0.5	n	0.25000	0.12500	0.00025	0.00000	0.00000
	1000	0.00892	0.00446	0.00001	0.00000	0.00000
0.6	n	0.36000	0.21600	0.00218	0.00000	0.00000
	1000	0.02542	0.01526	0.00016	0.00000	0.00000
0.7	n	0.49000	0.34300	0.01384	0.00001	0.00000
	1000	0.06788	0.04753	0.00192	0.00000	0.00000
0.8	n	0.64000	0.51200	0.06872	0.00079	0.00001
	1000	0.17259	0.13810	0.01857	0.00021	0.00000

4 Differences to Other Methods

4.1 Differences to Progressive Refinement Radiosity

Progressive Refinement Radiosity [3] is based on Southwell iteration. It keeps track of unshot radiosities (or powers) and distributes the unshot power of the patch which has the most.

Stochastic Ray Radiosity does not use unshot radiosity values. At each iteration step the total power of the scene is distributed using an importance sampling scheme. A new estimate for the power of each patch is calculated and combined with the current estimate to improve the solution.

Thus Progressive Refinement Radiosity will need at least as many iteration steps as there are light sources to distribute primarily all emitted power into the scene. This corresponds to the first order term $x^{(1)}$ of equation (11). Stochastic Ray Radiosity on the other hand distributes all available power at each iteration step, independent of the number of light sources at the cost of higher variance. Shirley's method [19] starts with spending much effort on computing direct illumination with little variance, while indirect illumination is ignored at the beginning, causing significant inaccuracy. When finally no patch has enough energy to emit a ray, this energy is either lost, distributed with excessive effort, or included as an ambient term.

4.2 Differences to the Random Walk Method

Pattanaik and Mudur [15] introduced a simulation method for solving global illumination: single rays are emitted at the light sources and are reflected or absorbed on each surface with probabilities according to its surface properties.

The new Stochastic Ray Method seems to be very similar to the Random Walk Method, but the similarities are only superficial. The theoretical concepts on which these two methods are based, are completely different.

First of all, the Random Walk Method is not really an iteration method: each of the shot rays is completely independent of all others. In the Stochastic Ray Method on the other hand, real iteration steps are performed, and each one of these steps consists of shooting a complete set of rays (e.g. 10^6).

In the Random Walk Method the rays that are shot later on do not know anything about earlier rays. This method converges only because of the law of the large numbers, and therefore the variance is proportional to the squareroot of the number of rays. The variance of higher-order interreflections grows very fast, like in distribution ray tracing[6] [5], [16]: if a single ray is traced through the scene, reflected or absorbed at the surfaces according to a reflectance probability, the higher-order terms are represented by a very small part of all rays. If partial higher-order rays are traced, single rays contribute less and less to the final image.

The new method presented in this paper on the other hand is self-correcting. All the information obtained in earlier iteration steps is fully exploited later on. The rays shot in the kth iteration simultaneously improve the partial images of the 1st through k^{th} order. In addition to that, the approximation obtained in the kth iteration step is used to guide the importance sampling for the next iteration.

4.3 Differences to the Original Stochastic Radiosity

The original Stochastic Radiosity method [13] used the hemicube to calculate all form factors from a few selected patches in each iteration step. These form factors were then used to calculate the approximate matrices A_k for that iteration step. For this reason a very high variance in the power of patches with large form factors was introduced. In addition to this, the hemicube algorithm caused aliasing problems and prevented the method from coping with perfect specular reflection. All of these problems are avoided in the new method, since all form factors are implicitly

---

6   originally called *distributed* ray tracing

calculated using ray tracing. Additionally, the convergence speed of the new algorithm for high average values of ρ is increased significantly since a different τ_k series is used (as described in section 3).

5 Special Effects

Similar to other ray based Monte Carlo methods for radiosity [19], [15], [18], the Stochastic Ray Method can be adapted easily to render some effects which are normally outside the scope of radiosity methods. The following "special effects" are easy to implement and significantly increase the range of images which can be generated by this method. The effects of such modifications on the variance of the solution have not been studied yet. In order to display these effects a raytracer has to be used in the final rendering step.

5.1 Specular Reflection and Specular Transmittance

The propagation of power in the Stochastic Ray Radiosity is solved entirely by shooting rays which carry a known portion of the total power. Since ray tracing is used for this operation, it is easy to handle objects with specular reflection or specular transmittance using one of the standard reflection models [25], [4], [10]: a portion of the power of the ray is bounced off the surface or sent through the surface. Thus, it is only necessary to handle rays with fractional powers and to implement a recursive ray tracer which traces reflected and transmitted rays.

Alternatively, the ray can be reflected (transmitted) or absorbed with a probability proportional to the reflection (resp. transmittance) coefficient. In this case a constant computation time per transported power is achieved, since no rays carrying partial powers are traced, but the variance in the solution increases.

Figure 6 (see appendix) shows a scene that contains a mirror with perfect specular reflection.

5.2 Non-diffuse Emission and Point Light Sources

The new method uses rays to distribute power into the scene. Therefore it can be extended easily to handle light sources with non-diffuse emission characteristics: it is only necessary to adjust the probability of emitting a ray into a certain direction according to the desired emission distribution function.

The Stochastic Ray Method uses the radiosity equation in terms of power, as shown in equation (1). These powers are finite values even for point light sources which would have infinite radiosity values. None of the operations performed during an iteration step explicitly depends on the area of any patch. The form factor computation, which implicitly incorporates the area of the patches, uses the probability of a ray hitting a patch as an approximation of its form factor. Therefore it is trivial to introduce special singular "patches" with no area at all.

If these two possible effects are combined, point light sources, slide projectors, and general spot lights can be modeled.

Figure 7 (see appendix) shows a scene that contains a point light source.

6 Results and Performance Analysis

In order to evaluate the performance of the new method we used the Random Walk Method and Shirley's method for comparison. For the Random Walk Method we define a single ray to carry power from one surface to the next. A photon, as defined in their method, will be propagated using a number of single rays. Since shooting a ray will now have nearly the same cost for all these methods, they can be easily compared using the number of rays that need to be shot as a measure for computational effort. Our testbed implementation, written in C++, performs about 2600 rays per second on an SGI R4000 workstation for the following test scene.

Figure 4 and 5 (see appendix) show two images of a fully converged solution calculated with stochastic ray radiosity.

Figure 8 (see appendix) shows the geometry and meshing of the test scene with 86000 triangles and an average reflectance coefficient of 0.7. Figure 9 (see appendix) shows a reference solution which can be computed with either method by shooting about 10^9 rays. The "shadows" behind the fireplace and the dark spots on the arms of the chairs in the images are due to "shadow leaks" due to bad modeling. No Gouraud shading is performed to enable a better comparison of the results.

The convergence of the methods was estimated using the RMS error of intermediate solutions when compared to the reference solution. Table 3 and figure 3 show the RMS error[7] versus the number of rays for all three methods. The new method was used with a starting vector calculated with 30 ones prepended to the τ_k series and 10^4 rays per iteration and the following real iterations with 10^6 rays per iteration with the τ_k series given in equation (15).

Table 3

	millions of rays					
	5	10	20	40	80	160
Shirley	0.0488	0.0330	0.0224	0.0165	0.0128	0.0107
Random Walk	0.0368	0.0269	0.0202	0.0149	0.0107	0.0086
Stochastic Ray	0.0299	0.0223	0.0159	0.0115	0.0084	0.0066

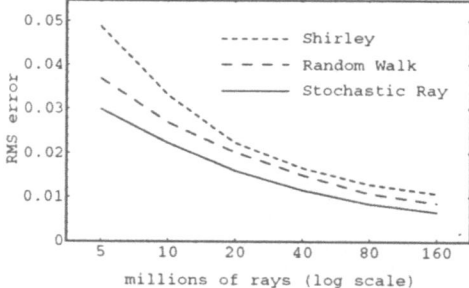

Figure 3: A graphical representation of table 3.

The new method is faster than both the Random Walk Method and Shirley's method. This is due to the utilization of all available information in later iteration steps.

Figures 10 and 11 (see appendix) show the intermediate solutions of the Random Walk Method and the new method after shooting $10 \cdot 10^6$ rays. The variance in the power values calculated by the new method is visibly lower.

Figures 12 and 13 (see appendix) show the same scene after shooting $20 \cdot 10^6$ rays, again for both methods. At this point the variance of the image calculated with the Random Walk method is similar to the variance in the image calculated with the new method in half the time (compare figure 11, appendix), and the new method has reduced the variance even further.

As previously explained, it is necessary to obtain a good starting vector to represent the total power in the scene correctly. This preprocessing step is only needed to "pump" energy into the scene and obtain a rough approximation of the final energy distribution. Figure 14 (see appendix) shows the intermediate solution after this preprocessing step with 30 iterations and 10^4 rays per iteration. The first real

---

[7] RMS error is probably not an optimal error measure for stochastic methods, since the variance in neighbouring patches is not adequately measured. This is a topic for future investigation. Nevertheless, RMS was used here for simplicity and comparability with previous results in literature.

iteration step with 10^6 rays per iteration will reduce the variance in the elements of the solution vector drastically. Figure 15 (see appendix) shows the image after this first iteration step.

Although the previous results are derived from only a few scenes, there are some general observations which can be made: If the object coherence in the scene is high, a constant number of iteration steps (e.g. 100 using the proposed preprocessing step to obtain a starting vector) will approximate the correct solution to the radiosity problem adequately. However, the variance in the solution will be dependent on the number of rays. If the patches are very small, the power values of neighbouring patches may differ due to the variance introduced by stochastically shooting rays. For this reason, the number of rays shot in each step should be directly proportional to the number of patches in the scene. Thus the computational complexity of the algorithm is about $O(N \log N)$. This is based on the assumption that a single ray can be traced with a cost of $O(\log N)$.

For scenes with little object coherence, e.g. a maze, this argument does not apply, since in this case the number of iteration steps needed to get an adequate solution depends on the number of patches. Therefore, the computational complexity for these scenes will be larger.

7 Conclusion and Future Trends

A powerful new radiosity evaluation method called Stochastic Ray Method has been presented, which is applicable to highly complex scenes. The new method uses stochastic iteration steps to improve all power values in a scene successively. It solves a number of problems that have not been addressed adequately for radiosity methods previously. Comparisons with the Random Walk Method show about 50% reduction in cost for comparable image quality. Nevertheless, there are a number of problems, which have not been solved completely yet:

Due to the stochastic nature of the method, scenes with little object coherence will result exhibit very poor convergence. For this reason, new variance reduction methods have to be considered in order to increase the quality of the solution.

Variance could be reduced by depositing the power carried by rays not on individual patches, but on clustered patches, depending on the distance traveled.

Various schemes to refine adaptively the mesh in places with high energy transfer or high gradient in the illumination function will also be investigated. This could be extended to avoid the need for an *a priori* mesh.

Another possible improvement is the introduction of importance driven methods [23]: Due to the high complexity of the scenes, it can be very time consuming to calculate view-independent solutions to the global illumination problem. It might be possible to reduce computation time by limiting the calculations to parts of the scene that will have some effect on the chosen view.

Acknowledgements

This paper was partly funded by "Fonds zur Förderung der wissenschaftl. Forschung" (FWF, project P09639-PHY). Special thanks go to Kresimir Matkovic, Mateu Sbert, Manfred Kopp, Eduard Gröller, Peter Stieglecker, and Michael Gervautz.

References

1. M. Cohen, D. Greenberg: The Hemi-Cube - A Radiosity Solution for Complex Environments. *Computer Graphics*, 19(3), 1985
2. M. Cohen, D. Greenberg, D. Immel, P. Brock: An Efficient Radiosity Approach for Realistic Image Synthesis. *IEEE Computer Graphics & Applications*, 6(2), 1986

218

3. M. Cohen, S. Chen, J. Wallace, D. Greenberg: A Progressive Refinement Approach for Fast Radiosity Image Generation. *Computer Graphics*, 22(4), 1988

4. R. L. Cook, K. Torrance: A Reflectance Model for Computer Graphics. *ACM Transactions on Graphics*, 1(1), pp 7-24, January 1982

5. R. L. Cook, T. Porter, L. Carpenter: Distributed Ray Tracing. *Computer Graphics*, 18(3), pp. 137-145, 1984

6. M. Feda, W. Purgathofer: Accelerating Radiosity by Overshooting. *Proceedings of the 3rd Eurographics Workshop on Rendering*, Bristol, UK, 1992

7. C. Goral, K. Torrance, D. Greenberg, B. Battaile: Modeling the Interaction of Light Between Diffuse Surfaces. *Computer Graphics*, 18(3), pp. 213-222, 1984

8. S. J. Gortler, P. Schröder, M. F. Cohen, P. Hanrahan: Wavelet Radiosity. *Computer Graphics* Proceedings of SIGGRAPH '93, pp. 221-230, August 1993

9. S. Gortler, M. Cohen: Solving the Radiosity Linear System. Communicating with Virtual Worlds, *Proceedings of Computer Graphics International '93*, N. & D. Thalmann (Editors), Springer, 1993

10. R. A. Hall, D. P. Greenberg: A Testbed for Realistic Image Synthesis. *IEEE Computer Graphics and Applications*, 3(8), pp. 10-20, November 1983

11. J. Kajiya: The Rendering Equation. *Computer Graphics*, 20(4), 1986

12. L. Neumann, A. Neumann: Radiosity and Hybrid Methods. Accepted for *Transactions on Graphics*, 1994

13. L. Neumann, M. Feda, M. Kopp, W. Purgathofer: A New Stochastic Radiosity Method for Highly Complex Scenes. *Proceedings of the 5th Eurographics Workshop on Rendering*, Darmstadt, BRD, 1994

14. L. Neumann: Monte Carlo Radiosity. *Computing*, 55(1), pp. 23-42, 1995

15. S. N. Pattanaik, S. P. Mudur: Computation of Global Illumination by Monte Carlo Simulation of the Particle Model of Light. *Proceedings of the 3rd Eurographics Workshop on Rendering*, Bristol, UK, 1992

16. W. Purgathofer: A Statistical Method for Adaptive Stochastic Sampling. *Computers & Graphics*, Vol. 11, N° 2, pp. 157-162, 1987 and in *Proceedings of Eurographics'86*, A. A. G. Requicha (Editor), North-Holland, 1986

17. R. Recker, D. George, D. Greenberg: Acceleration Techniques for Progressive Refinement Radiosity. *Computer Graphics*, 24(2), 1990

18. M. Sbert: An Integral Geometry Based Method for Fast Form-Factor Computation. *Computer Graphics Forum*, 12(3), (*Procceedings of the Eurographics '93*), pp. (c-409)-(c-420), 1993

19. P. Shirley: A Ray Tracing Method for Illumination Calculation in Diffuse-Specular Scenes. *Proceedings of Graphics Interface '90*, pp. 205-212, Halifax, Nova Scotia, May 1990

20. P. Shirley: A Ray Tracing Framework for Global Illumination Systems. Proc. GI'91, pp. 117-128, 1991

21. P. Shirley: Radiosity via Ray Tracing, in Graphics Gems II (editor: J. Avro), Academic Press, pp. 306-310, 1991

22. R. Siegel, J. Howell: Thermal Radiation Heat Transfer. McGraw-Hill, New York, 1981

23. B. Smits, J. Arvo, D. Salesin: An Importance-Driven Radiosity Algorithm. *Computer Graphics*, 26(2), 1992

24. G. Ward: An Improved Illumination Model for Shaded Display. *Computer Graphics* Proceedings of SIGGRAPH '94, pp. 459-472, July 1994

25. T. Whitted: An Improved Illumination Model for Shaded Display. *Communications of the ACM*, 23(6), pp 343-349, June 1980

26. H. R. Zatz: Galerkin Radiosity: A higher Order Solution Method for Global Illumination. *Computer Graphics* Proceedings of SIGGRAPH '93, pp. 213-220, August 1993

Editors' Note: see Appendix, p. 367 for colored figures of this paper

Global Illumination via Density-Estimation

Peter Shirley   Bretton Wade   Philip M. Hubbard   David Zareski   Bruce Walter
Donald P. Greenberg

Program of Computer Graphics, Cornell University, Ithaca, NY, USA.

1 Introduction

This paper presents a new method for the production of view-independent global illumination solutions of complex static environments. A key innovation of this new approach is its decomposition of the problem into a loosely coupled sequence of simple modules. This approach decouples the global energy transport computation from the construction of the displayable shaded representation of the environment. This decoupling eliminates many constraints of previous global illumination approaches, yielding accurate solutions for environments with non-diffuse surfaces and high geometric complexity.

Our algorithm produces a view-independent *display mesh* that represents the irradiances on surfaces in a form that allows direct display of the shaded surface. Most traditional radiosity algorithms also use a *computational mesh* to represent intermediate results in the light transport calculation (*e.g.*, the piecewise-constant global solution of Smits *et al.* [17]). Typically, a single representation is used for both the computational and display meshes (*e.g.* the static mesh used by Neumann *et al.* [11] and the adaptive mesh used by Teller *et al.* [18]).

Very few display mesh solutions have been produced for environments with more than a few thousand initial surfaces. The only implementation we are aware of that has produced a display mesh for more than 10,000 initial surfaces is the system by Teller *et al.* [18], which was run on a model with approximately 40,000 initial surfaces. Teller *et al.* argue that the reason for these surprisingly small limits is the high memory overhead of the data structures associated with the computational mesh.

To solve this problem, we draw on an observation by Lischinski *et al.* [10], that the computational mesh and the display mesh have different purposes and characteristics and therefore should be decoupled. Our method is based on the idea that once the display mesh and computational mesh are decoupled, the computational mesh can be replaced with a simpler data structure based on particle tracing. This replacement allows for the solution of larger models with more general reflectance properties.

Our method is composed of three phases which operate without a computational mesh. The first phase uses particle tracing to record a list of particle "hit points" for each surface. The second phase uses these lists to generate a view-independent functional representation of surface irradiance. This process is called *density-estimation* because the representation is an approximation of the underlying density function that generated the hit point locations. The third phase converts the functional representation into a view-independent display mesh. A novel aspect of the third phase is its use of a geometric mesh-decimation algorithm to reduce the size of the display mesh.

In our method all diffuse surfaces will be portrayed accurately regardless of display method. In addition, the contribution of non-diffuse surfaces to the appearance of diffuse surfaces will be accounted for correctly. Non-diffuse surfaces in this mesh will be portrayed accurately if displayed in a view-dependent second pass.

2 Background

Previous global illumination techniques have one or more of the following significant limitations:

- **High intermediate complexity (memory overhead)**. Current radiosity methods use large data structures to accelerate visibility computations. These data structures are usually the limiting factor in performing large radiosity simulations [18]. In practice, an algorithm that stores more than a few hundred bytes per polygon in physical memory will not be practical.

- **Difficulty with local complexity**. In cases where the model has a very high "global complexity" (large numbers of surfaces), but a limited "local complexity" (only small subsets of surfaces are mutually visible), partitioning can be used to decompose the model into subsets which can be solved separately [18]. But if any subset has a high local complexity, then partitioning may not reduce the subproblems to a solvable size. This is a problem in an environment such as a hotel atrium.

- **Quadratic time complexity**. Any algorithm that computes interactions between all pairs of N objects will require at least $O(N^2)$ time. This limits their utility in dealing with large models.

- **"Ideal" specular effects**. Many radiosity algorithms can only use the "virtual image method" [13], which is practical for solving models with only a limited number of ideal, planar, specular objects. Real models have windows, gloss paint, and metal luminaire-reflectors, and in general, non-diffuse surfaces.

- **Lack of parallelism**. Most existing radiosity methods were designed as serial algorithms, and cannot be easily adapted for parallel computation. This limits their ability to take full advantage of one of today's typical computing environments: a local area network of high-speed workstations sharing a common file system.

These limitations need to be overcome in a single system if the use of view independent global illumination solutions are to become widespread. Keeping the memory overhead low favors a Monte Carlo particle-shooting approach [12], which only requires a ray-tracing acceleration structure. Handling local complexity in sub-quadratic time suggests either a clustering approach [17] or a Monte Carlo shooting approach[1]. A Monte

---

[1] No global illumination algorithm has been proven to be sub-quadratic, but there is empirical evidence that both Monte Carlo shooting algorithms [15] and clustering algorithms [17] are sub-quadratic for reasonably "well-behaved" environments.

Carlo shooting approach also allows for more general specular transport, and possesses inherent parallelism, as each shot can be processed independently. Because specular transport through glass is important in many applications, we have chosen to pursue the Monte Carlo approach.

Although Monte Carlo radiosity schemes have been applied with great success using *a priori* computational meshes [11], there has been little success generating adaptive computational meshes. Appel [1] traced particles from the source to estimate direct lighting. Arvo [2] extended this idea to include illumination reflecting from mirrors before striking surfaces. Heckbert [8] extended Arvo's work to include adaptive meshing, and was the first to observe that this was a form of density-estimation. Chen *et al.* [3] used a *kernel-based* density-estimation technique to deal with *caustic maps*, and our density-estimation work can be considered an extension of their caustic map techniques to account for all illumination effects in a scene. Collins has one of the most sophisticated density-estimation techniques for global illumination [5], but his method does not account for multiple diffuse reflections.

Our strategy is similar to Heckbert's and Collins', but differs in that the meshing is delayed until all Monte Carlo particle tracing has been completed. This allows us to use all the information collected while estimating surface irradiances to generate a good display mesh. The additional storage due to stored hit-points can be processed sequentially and therefore need not be simultaneously resident in real memory.

3 Description of Density-Estimation Algorithm

The algorithm is composed of three basic phases:

1. **Particle-tracing phase:** Power carrying particles are emitted from each luminaire using an appropriate radiant intensity distribution, and are then tracked through the environment until they are probabilistically absorbed. A list of all particle "hit points" is generated and saved.

2. **Density-estimation phase:** The stored hit points are used to construct an approximate irradiance function $H(u, v)$ for each receiving surface.

3. **Meshing phase:** The approximate irradiance function $H(u, v)$ is further approximated to a more compact form $\bar{H}(u, v)$ that can be used for efficient hardware rendering or ray tracing display. If the desired output is a set of Gouraud-shaded polygonal elements for interactive display and walk-through on a conventional graphics workstation, then $\bar{H}(u, v)$ will be piecewise linear.

The algorithm is outlined in figure 1. Note that although the environment is right-left symmetrical, the solution is not. This is because of the randomness introduced by the particle tracing.

3.1 Particle-Tracing Phase

We begin the particle-tracing phase by totaling the power emitted by all luminaires Φ. We then generate approximately n "particles", each carrying power $\phi = \Phi/n$. We use the

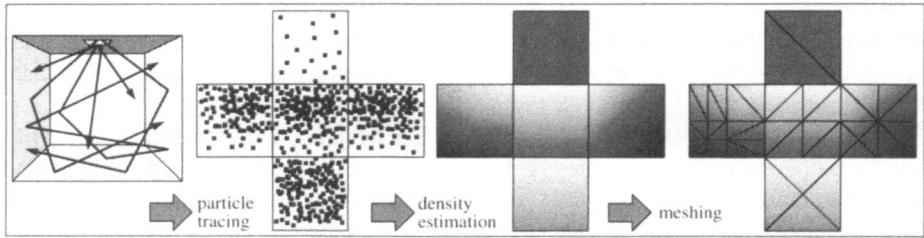

Fig. 1. Overview of the density estimation algorithm. The surfaces in the room are depicted "unfolded" in the three figures on the right.

traditional particle approximation where the particles obey geometric optics, and have an associated color.

For each luminaire ℓ_i with emitted power Φ_i, we trace an expected $N_i = n\Phi_i/\Phi$ rays. Since N_i is not necessarily an integer, we trace at least $\lfloor N_i \rfloor$ rays, and sometimes trace an additional ray with probability $N_i - \lfloor N_i \rfloor$. Each of these rays is sent with a probability density function that is determined by the emission characteristics of the luminaire:

$$p(x,\omega) = \frac{L_e(x,\omega)\cos\theta}{\int_X \int_\Omega L_e(x,\omega)\cos\theta d\omega dx}$$

where p is a probability density function for ray generation, x is a point on the luminaire, ω is a direction, L_e is the emitted surface radiance, θ is the angle between ω and the surface normal at x, X is the set of points on the luminaire, and Ω is the set of outgoing directions on the hemisphere oriented with the surface normal.

At each surface the particle is probabilistically reflected, transmitted, or absorbed based on $\rho(x,\omega,\omega')$, the surface's bidirectional reflectance distribution function (BRDF).

3.2 Density-Estimation Phase

After completing the particle-tracing phase, we have associated with each surface a set of hit points with incoming power ϕ. It seems logical to guess a reasonable irradiance from the local denseness or sparseness of these hit points. For example, where the density of these points is high, we expect a high irradiance. As pointed out by Heckbert [8], this is a classic *density estimation* problem, where we attempt to guess a plausible density function given a set of non-uniform random samples[2]. Before getting to the details of how we apply density estimation, we first establish that the radiometric quantity we wish to estimate is the irradiance.

A Lambertian surface has a BRDF that is a constant R/π for all incoming/outgoing direction pairs, where R is the reflectance (ratio of outgoing to incoming power). This

---

[2] Note that this density estimation problem has a set of sample locations, but does not have function values at these locations. This is different from the problem of reconstructing a signal from a sampled function. It is easy to get these two problems confused. Ironically, the strategy of placing kernels at the hit points is very similar, but in density-estimation the kernels are *not* scaled.

implies that a Lambertian surface will have a constant surface radiance for all incoming/outgoing direction pairs. Ultimately, we wish to approximate this surface radiance for all Lambertian points.

For a particular parametric Lambertian surface with reflectance $R(u,v)$ and irradiance $H(u,v)$ (incident power per unit area at (u,v)), the radiant exitance $M(u,v)$ (outgoing power per unit area at (u,v)) is $R(u,v)H(u,v)$. Because the radiance of a Lambertian surface is $L(u,v) = M(u,v)/\pi$, the relationship between irradiance H and radiance L can be expressed by the following equation [3]: $L(u,v) = R(u,v)H(u,v)/\pi$. This equation implies that we can store the irradiance and reflectance at each point and later reconstruct the radiance. This is convenient because the reflectance may change quickly, while the irradiance may change slowly, allowing the irradiance to be stored in a coarse mesh. These ideas are based upon the "patch-element" radiosity work of Cohen et al.[4].

For a given surface, a list of hit point locations (u_j, v_j) is stored. Each of these points has the same power, ϕ. The irradiance function represented by this list is a set of "delta" functions where a finite amount of power strikes an infinitely small area. In one dimension, this is essentially taking a set of n samples x_i and noting that a possible density function f is:

$$f(x) = \frac{1}{n} \sum_{i=1}^{n} \delta\left(x - x_i\right)$$

This sum of spikes would be a bad guess if we know f is smooth. Instead we could replace the δ functions with smooth "kernel" functions $k_1(x - x_i)$, where k_1 has unit volume. This generates a smoother estimate for f. An example kernel estimate is shown in Figure 2.

Using kernel functions on the hit points is analogous to the idea of "splatting" in volume rendering [20], and is similar to the illumination ray tracing of Collins [5]. Silverman [16] notes that whatever properties the derivatives of k_1 have will be shared by f, so we can ensure a smooth estimate for f by choosing a smooth k_1.

Good choices for k_1 are similar to the choices used for splatting or pixel filtering. As in those applications the kernels should be centered at the origin, have limited support (non-zero region), and should be roughly "lump" shaped. If the volume of the function we are approximating, A, is not unity (so the function is not a probability density function), we can compensate by multiplying the sum by A.

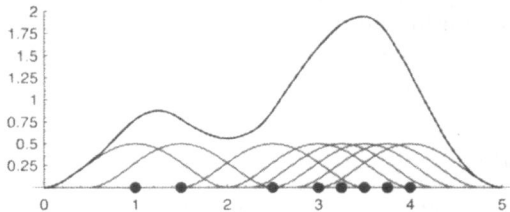

Fig. 2. Kernel estimate showing individual kernels.

---

[3] See the recent texturing work of Gershbein et al. [6] for a more detailed analysis.

In two dimensions, the irradiance function can be estimated as:

$$H_i(\mathbf{x}) = \frac{\Phi}{n} \sum_{j=1}^{n_i} \delta(\mathbf{x} - \mathbf{x}_j)$$

Where $\mathbf{x}_j$ is the position of the jth hit point. We can replace the delta functions with n_i "kernel" functions k_j, and note that $\Phi/n = \phi$:

$$H_i(\mathbf{x}) = \phi \sum_{j=1}^{n_i} k_j(\mathbf{x}_j) \tag{1}$$

The kernel functions have the conflicting requirements of being narrow enough to capture detail, and being wide enough to eliminate the random mottling caused by the irregular pattern of the hit points. We can use a scaling parameter h to widen or narrow the filter. Because narrowing the filter will decrease its volume, we also increase the height of the kernel to keep its volume constant:

$$H_i(\mathbf{x}) = \frac{\phi}{h^2} \sum_{j=1}^{n_i} k\left(\frac{\mathbf{x} - \mathbf{x}_j}{h}\right) \tag{2}$$

Note that for Equation 2 to represent irradiance, k must have unit volume. On a locally planar surface with orthogonal length parameters (u, v), this is straightforward to guarantee. A more complex form would be needed to conserve energy on more complex surfaces.

3.3 Meshing Phase

At first it seems logical to render the approximate $H(u, v)$ directly, but the number of sample points is large enough that any method that attempts to randomly access all the points in the environment will not be practical for large environments. Instead, we need to reduce the amount of information needed to specify an approximate irradiance function.

The most obvious strategy is to sample $H(u, v)$ at a finite set of locations and use some type of polynomial elements to interpolate between these values. Ideally, the sample points should be chosen so that they are dense only where the irradiance function has many features.

Once we have a more compact representation of $H(u, v)$ we can display an image of the illuminated surfaces using either 3-D graphics hardware or ray tracing. For Gouraud shading we should approximate $H(u, v)$ with piecewise-linear elements, but for ray tracing we can use higher-order elements.

3.4 Parallel Execution

Each of the three phases above are ideally suited to take advantage of parallelism. In the particle-tracing phase, particle paths can be computed independently, and once the particle hit points for each surface are grouped together, the density-estimation and meshing phases can compute the shading of each surface independently.

4 Implementation

We have implemented the algorithm in C++ as three separate serial programs that communicate using files. The first program reads the input geometry, performs the particle-tracing phase, and writes out the hit points. The second program reads the hit points and geometry, performs the density-estimation phase, and then performs the initial pass of the meshing phase by generating a finely-tessellated display mesh. The third program reads this display mesh and performs the final pass of the meshing phase by decimating the mesh so that it can be displayed more quickly without significant loss of image quality.

We have also implemented a parallel version of the algorithm in C++ as two separate parallel programs [21]. The first is a parallel version of the serial particle tracer, and the second is a combined, parallel version of the both the serial density-estimation and mesh-decimation programs. The second parallel program also performs the hit point sorting.

The three serial programs mentioned above are described in the remainder of this section. Our goal has been to implement each component of the density-estimation framework as simply and conservatively as possible. This strategy has allowed us to explore the basic strengths and weaknesses of density-estimation without getting bogged down with low-level issues. Our implementation should therefore be considered a proof-of-concept which leaves open many avenues of investigation that will improve on our results.

4.1 The Particle-Tracing Program

This program implements the particle-tracing phase exactly as described in Section 3.1. Rays are emitted from random locations on each luminaire in a directional-distribution determined from the emitted surface radiance of the luminaire.

Each time a ray hits a diffuse surface, the surface id (4 bytes) and fixed-point representations of the uv coordinates (2 bytes each) are written to a file. This means we can store approximately 125 million hit points on a one gigabyte disk. This code is run once for each of the red, green, and blue channels.

The only memory overhead in the particle-tracing phase is the uniform-subdivision ray-tracing efficiency structure (approximately 140 bytes per patch in our implementation, or about 7 million patches per gigabyte).

An alternative way to store hit points would be with surface normal information in a 3D data structure, as is done by Ward [19] and by Jensen and Christensen [9]. This would raise memory usage, but would eliminate some problems associated with models that are hard to parameterize.

4.2 The Density-Estimation and Initial-Meshing Program

Ideally we would like to make a density-estimation of the irradiance function of the ith surface $H_i(\mathbf{x})$, and then output a piecewise linear approximation with as few linear elements as are needed to accurately represent $H_i(\mathbf{x})$. However, because generating a concise, piecewise-linear approximation is a hard problem, and because we wanted to determine the potential accuracy of density-estimation techniques before attempting to solve the most difficult problems suggested by the technique, we adopted a strategy of over-meshing the solution, and then decimating this mesh.

The density-estimation program begins by sorting all hit points by surface id in each of the red, green, and blue channel files produced by the particle-tracing program. Each surface is then processed in series by examining all its hit points, calculating a density estimate of its irradiance function $H_i(\mathbf{x})$, and then outputting an "over-meshed" point-sampled approximation to $H_i(\mathbf{x})$.

The current implementation is restricted to rectangular surfaces only. It samples each rectangle on a n_u by n_v lattice, and outputs this approximation as a triangular mesh with $2(n_u - 1)(n_v - 1)$ elements and $n_u n_v$ vertices, with irradiance values at each vertex. We use triangles as mesh elements instead of rectangles because it simplifies the mesh-decimation algorithm.

We have chosen to use Silverman's K_2 kernel function [16]:

$$K_2(u, v) = \frac{3}{\pi} \max \left(0, (1 - ||\mathbf{x} - \mathbf{x}_j||^2)^2\right) \tag{3}$$

The width of the kernel function, h, is chosen to relate it to the average distance between sample points on the ith surface. This is approximated by $C_1 \sqrt{A_i/n}$, where A_i is the area of surface i, n is the number of sample points, and C_1 is a positive constant that controls the width of the kernel. The desired spacing between adjacent grid points is chosen as $C_2 \sqrt{A_i/n}$, where C_2 is typically less than C_1. Since each polygon can be meshed independent of other polygons, we only need keep this grid in memory for one polygon at a time, and paging has not been a problem on any of our runs. Near the boundary we use the *reflection method* [16] to avoid darkening near the edge of polygons.

The trade-off between noise and blurring as controlled by C_1 is shown in Figure 3. In this figure C_2 has been set to 8, which is small enough to not affect the images. We have found useful values of C_1 range from 10 to 40, and useful values of C_2 to range from $C_1/10$ to $C_1/2$. It is important to note that surfaces that receive fewer particles will get wider kernels and coarser meshes. This avoids the under-sampling problems of traditional illumination ray tracing [2] in a manner similar to Collins [5]. Unlike Collins, we do not require any coherence between adjacent particle paths, so we can choose appropriate kernel sizes for data that includes diffuse interreflection.

Fig. 3. Different noise/blur effects for $C_1 = 10, 30, 100$.

4.3 Irradiance-Mesh-Decimation Program

The final program decimates the triangulated mesh produced by the density-estimation program. Its goal is to eliminate as many mesh elements as possible without compromising mesh accuracy.

In order to take advantage of the rich literature in geometric mesh decimation, we transform our 2-D surface mesh, which we call an *illumination mesh*, into a 3-D mesh. The X and Y axes correspond to the surface's parametric space, and the Z axis corresponds to "brightness." This mesh is a height field because there are no "ledges" that overhang other parts of the mesh.

To this 3-D mesh we apply geometric decimation techniques. As long as the result is still a height field, it converts to a decimated illumination mesh by simply ignoring the Z coordinate. To decimate the 3-D mesh, we use the algorithm of Schroeder *et al.*[14]. It uses two heuristics to approximate curvature at a mesh vertex. If curvature is low enough, it removes the vertex and re-triangulates the resulting "hole" in the mesh.

This decimation algorithm does not necessarily produce a height field, so we added a simple enhancement. When re-triangulating a hole, the enhanced algorithm checks for triangles on "overhanging ledges"; if it finds any, it does not remove the vertex.

Another disadvantage of Schroeder's algorithm is that it does not consider the decimation to be an optimization task. It uses a fixed threshold on curvature, decimating all vertices which cause curvature changes below the threshold. We turned the algorithm into an optimization task by using a *priority queue*. The queue holds all vertices ranked by the change in curvature their decimation would cause. The new algorithm decimates vertices in the order they come off the queue, thus minimizing the change in curvature with each decimation. Maintaining the queue is efficient, since each access takes only $O(\log n)$ time for a mesh of n vertices.

The main challenge in using the Schroeder *et al.* algorithm is picking the exact mapping from the illumination mesh to a purely geometric, 3-D mesh. The geometric mesh has one set of units (spatial, *e.g.*, meters) but the illumination mesh has two: spatial for the surface's two parametric dimensions (X and Y), and "brightness" for the third (Z). The mapping must balance the two sets of units, since the decimation algorithm cannot distinguish between them.

We map the two sets of units to a common scale, and choose a single maximum-allowable error, ϵ, in this scale. We scale the spatial dimensions so that the smallest important feature has width ϵ. We scale the "brightness" dimension by using

$$z = \left(\frac{R(x,y)H(x,y)/\pi}{w_0} \right)^{1/3},$$

where $R(x,y)$ is photometric reflectance, $H(x,y)$ is illuminance, w_0 is the white-point, and the exponent is due to Stevens Law [7]. We clamp z to 1.0, and choose w_0 so that $z = \epsilon$ corresponds to the largest allowable "brightness" error. In practice, determining the scaling parameters requires some trial and error. Fortunately, in our experience we found useful parameter values after only two or three attempts.

Decimation works well in practice. Figure 4 shows an example in which decimation removed 90% of the triangles produced by the density-estimation program. We achieved similar decimation rates in our other tests.

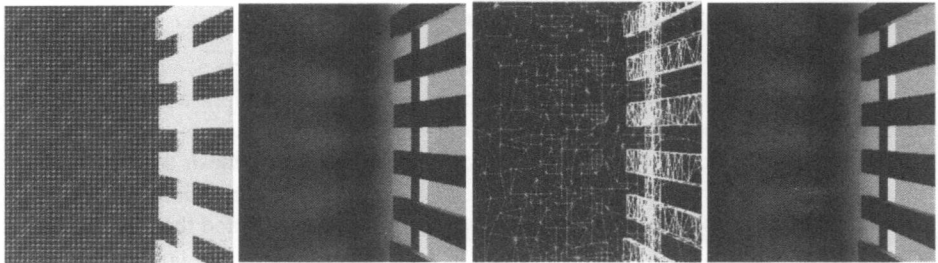

Fig. 4. Left: undecimated mesh. Right: 90% decimated mesh.

4.4 Sample results

Figure 5 shows a ray-traced image of a view-independent density-estimation solution. The environment depicted has sixteen light sources forming a compact lattice to the left of the image. This image illustrates how we correctly handle transport chains that include glass and specular reflection from metals.

Notice how light passes through the glass and then through the fence, reflects from the steel, and casts a green streak on the floor. The shadowing is stored in the illumination mesh, so only the colors of the metal and glass need to be calculated during ray tracing.

One characteristic of the error in our solutions is that the red, green, and blue channels of our images have uncorrelated oscillations, which causes a visible colored texture if the kernels are too narrow. Eliminating this colored texture increases the blurring of desired features such as shadow boundaries.

Figure 6 (left) shows a hardware-rendered decimated version of a model with approximately 10,000 initial surfaces. The decimated mesh has approximately 12% of the triangles in the original mesh.

Figure 6 (right) shows the solution of a model with approximately 150,000 original polygonal surfaces. This solution is roughly four times larger than the largest previous solution produced by radiosity methods which compute a display mesh *a posteriori*. The undecimated display mesh contained about 4.2 million triangles and the decimated mesh had approximately 400,000 triangles. In all, the solution took approximately 37 hours to compute on an HP model 755 100MHz PA-Risc 7100 workstation. A total of 96 million particles were traced (32 million in each of the red, green, and blue channels).

Preliminary investigations indicate time can be reduced by more than one order of magnitude by using our parallel workstation cluster [21].

The proportion of time spent in each of the three programs was: particle-tracing: 49%; density-estimation and initial-meshing: 29%; mesh-decimation: 22%.

5 Conclusion

We have presented a new global illumination method based on density estimation. The method is straightforward to implement, can attack much larger problems than previous techniques, accounts for specular transport, and is designed to use parallelism efficiently in each of its sequential phases. In addition to these new capabilities, this method also

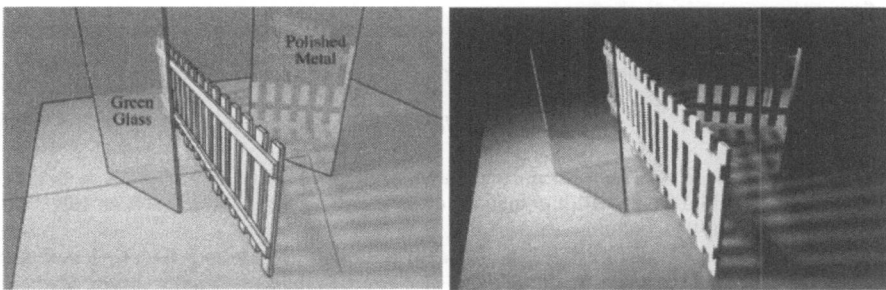

Fig. 5. Fence with green glass filter and polished metal reflector (ray-traced).

Fig. 6. Left: Room with 10,000 initial polygons. Right: Room with 150,000 initial polygons.

retains many of the historical advantages of radiosity methods, including view indepen-dence of diffuse components, physical accuracy, and capability for progressive refine-ment. Future work should include investigating other methods for density estimation that do a better job of reconstructing shadows and other details in the illumination function, and better methods of decimation or mesh optimization.

Acknowledgments

Thanks to Jim Arvo for his many helpful suggestions. Special thanks to Gene Greger who created all of the models depicted in the paper. This work was supported by the NSF/ARPA Science and Technology Center for Computer Graphics and Scientific Visualization (ASC-8920219) and by NSF CCR-9401961 and performed on workstations generously provided by the Hewlett-Packard Corporation.

230

References

1. A. Appel. Some techniques for shading machine renderings of solids. In *AFIPS 1968 Spring Joint Computing Conference*, pages 37–49, 1968.
2. James Arvo. Backward ray tracing. *Developments in Ray Tracing*, pages 259–263, 1986. ACM Siggraph '86 Course Notes.
3. Shenchang Eric Chen, Holly Rushmeier, Gavin Miller, and Douglass Turner. A progressive multi-pass method for global illumination. *Computer Graphics*, 25(4):165–174, July 1991. ACM Siggraph '91 Conference Proceedings.
4. Micheal F. Cohen, Donald P. Greenberg, David S. Immel, and Philip J. Brock. An efficient radiosity approach for realistic image synthesis. *IEEE Computer Graphics & Applications*, 6(2):26–35, 1986.
5. Steven Collins. Adaptive splatting for specular to diffuse light transport. In *Proceedings of the Fifth Eurographics Workshop on Rendering*, pages 119–135, June 1994.
6. Reid Gershbein, Peter Schröder, and Pat Hanrahan. Textures and radiosity: Controlling emission and reflection with texture maps. *Computer Graphics*, pages 51–58, July 1994. ACM Siggraph '94 Conference Proceedings.
7. E. Bruce Goldstein. *Sensation and Perception*. Wadsworth Publishing Co., Belmont, California, 1980.
8. Paul S. Heckbert. Adaptive radiosity textures for bidirectional ray tracing. *Computer Graphics*, 24(3):145–154, August 1990. ACM Siggraph '90 Conference Proceedings.
9. Henrik Wann Jensen and Niels Jorgen Christensen. Bidirectional monte carlo ray tracing of complex objects using photon maps. *Computers & Graphics*, 19(2), 1995.
10. Dani Lischinski, Filippo Tampieri, and Donald P. Greenberg. Combining hierarchical radiosity and discontinuity meshing. *Computer Graphics*, pages 199–208, August 1993. ACM Siggraph '93 Conference Proceedings.
11. László Neumann, Martin Feda, Manfred Kopp, and Werner Purgathofer. A new stochastic radiosity method for highly complex scenes. In *Proceedings of the Fifth Eurographics Workshop on Rendering*, pages 195–206, June 1994.
12. S. N. Pattanaik. *Computational Methods for Global Illumination and Visualization of Complex 3D Environments*. PhD thesis, Birla Institute of Technology & Science, February 1993.
13. Holly E. Rushmeier. *Realistic Image Synthesis for Scenes with Radiatively Participating Media*. PhD thesis, Cornell University, May 1988.
14. William J. Schroeder, Jonathan A. Zarge, and William E. Lorensen. Decimation of triangle meshes. In Edwin E. Catmull, editor, *Computer Graphics (SIGGRAPH '92 Proceedings)*, volume 26, pages 65–70, July 1992.
15. Peter Shirley. Time complexity of monte carlo radiosity. In *Eurographics '91*, pages 459–466, September 1991.
16. B. W. Silverman. *Density Estimation for Statistics and Data Analysis*. Chapman and Hall, London, 1985.
17. Brian E. Smits, James R. Arvo, and Donald P. Greenberg. A clustering algorithm for radiosity in complex environments. *Computer Graphics*, 28(3):435–442, July 1994. ACM Siggraph '94 Conference Proceedings.
18. Seth Teller, Celeste Fowler, Thomas Funkhouser, and Pat Hanrahan. Partitioning and ordering large radiosity calculations. *Computer Graphics*, 28(3):443–450, July 1994. ACM Siggraph '94 Conference Proceedings.
19. Gregory J. Ward. The radiance lighting simulation and rendering system. *Computer Graphics*, 28(2):459–472, July 1994. ACM Siggraph '94 Conference Proceedings.
20. Lee Westover. Footprint evaluation for volume randering. *Computer Graphics*, 24(4):367–376, August 1990. ACM Siggraph '90 Conference Proceedings.
21. David Zareski, Bretton Wade, Philip Hubbard, and Peter Shirley. Efficient parallel global illumination using density estimation. In *Proceedings of the 1995 Parallel Rendering Symposium*, 1995.

Editors' Note: see Appendix, p. 369 for colored figures of this paper

Global Monte Carlo. A Progressive Solution

Mateu Sbert, Frederic Pérez, Xavier Pueyo

Departament d'Informàtica i Matemàtica Aplicada
Universitat de Girona

Lluis Santaló s/n, E 17003 Girona.
phone +34 (72) 418419/47
fax +34 (72) 418399
e-mail {mateu|frederic|xavier}@ima.udg.es

Abstract. In this paper we review global Monte Carlo techniques for radiosity. A technique for progressively refining the solution in global Monte Carlo is presented, based in the classical statistical results on the expected value and variance of a weighted sum of independent random variables. The method is shown to work well also for the classic Monte Carlo methods. We finally show its usefulness in distributing the work over a workstations network.

1 Introduction

Particle transport techniques were first used in Radiative Heat Transfer [Siegel92] and introduced afterwards in the Radiosity field by Shirley [Shirley90], Pattanaik [Pattanaik92] and Feda [Feda93]. These techniques are known as Monte Carlo Radiosity algorithms and may or may not include the concept of progressive refinement. The basic Monte Carlo algorithm sends rays from the sources, and follows them through their interactions with the surfaces in the environment. We are going to call the methods using this strategy, *local Monte Carlo algorithms*.

On the other hand, other Monte Carlo algorithms embed the scene in a field of lines; i.e. trace lines that cross the scene [Sbert93][Neumann94]. These algorithms use Monte Carlo principles as well but the selection of rays is not based in a local region of the scene (i.e., a patch) as in the methods presented in the previous paragraph. For this reason we call them *global Monte Carlo algorithms*.

Progressive solutions may be presented in Monte Carlo methods through the use of some techniques such as the described in [Feda93], or computing form factors from the shooting patch as in the classic progressive radiosity [Cohen88].

From Monte Carlo techniques features, we may derive that combining results in an optimal way, we could obtain a succession of radiosity solutions, each one more accurated than the previous one, and we would have progressive solutions towards the converged one.

In section 2 will be analysed the features of global Monte Carlo methods. In section 3 an efficient progressive technique will be established for the global Monte Carlo algorithms. In section 4 results are presented which show the behaviour of global Monte Carlo methods. Conclusions are presented in section 5.

2 Global Monte Carlo methods

2.1 Global Monte Carlo and local Monte Carlo

By global Monte Carlo methods in Radiosity we understand the use of global random directions (that is, not tied or cast from any particular patch) to intersect or project the scene. The directions may be used to compute form-factors, or to transport energy. To each direction there may correspond one line, many parallel lines in a bundle or lattice, or they may be simply used as directions of projections for a z-buffer or other projection algorithms. The theoretical justification for those methods arise from different basis. From the pure heuristics of Buckalew et al. [Buckalew89], passing through Integral Geometry considerations by Sbert et al. [Sbert93] [Sbert95a] and Pellegrini [Pellegrini95], till the stochastic radiosity methods by Neumann [Neumann94]. We will give here some intuitive reasons why it may work, and for what scenes those methods may work best. Also, we give in table 1 a classification of those methods. We include for completness the work by Buckalew, although it is not a random technique.

Table 1. The different techniques considered in global Monte Carlo.

Strategy vs Implementation	Form-Factor	Energy transport
one line per direction	[Sbert93]	[Sbert95a]
bundle or lattice of parallel lines		[Sbert95a] [Buckalew89]
z-buffer		[Neumann94]
area projection	[Pellegrini95]	

By local Monte Carlo we understand those techniques that are based in the casting of lines tied to or beginning from some particular patch, so that those lines are only of use to that particular patch. Here we may consider all classic Monte Carlo techniques, such as random walk techniques, including the work by Shirley [Shirley90], Pattanaik [Pattanaik92], and also of distributed ray tracing [Cook84][Ward88][Ward94] and path tracing [Kajiya86]. Also, we consider here the techniques to compute form factors from one patch based in the casting of lines from that same patch, that is, solving by Monte Carlo integration the form factor integral.

2.2 Integral Geometry based method

In [Sbert93] a global Monte Carlo method was presented which is based on the fact that the form factor F_{ij} between patch i and patch j may be interpreted as the probability of a line that exits patch i, according to a given probability density function (pdf), lands in patch j.

Integral Geometry [Rey-Pastor51][Santaló76] shows that taking a uniform global density of lines in the scene and focusing only on those lines that intersect patch i, we are provided with lines that fulfill the same pdf as above for patch i. From that we have that the form factor F_{ij} may be estimated as the relation given by $\frac{r_{ij}}{r_i}$, where r_i is the number of lines that intersect patch i and r_{ij} is the number of these lines which also intersect patch j.

Then, to compute the form factors, lines could be cast from each patch according to the above given pdf, and counted how many of them land on each other patch. But most work made in intersecting lines with the environment is wasted, because only the intersection with the closest patch is used for each line. An alternative which avoids this inefficiency is to define a global density of lines, and to use *every* intersection of each line with the environment. Now N_r lines are cast randomly and each is intersected with the scene. The intersections of each line are sorted along the line defining pairs of mutually visible intersections. From this one can derive the relations $\frac{r_{ij}}{r_i}$.

The global Monte Carlo Integral Geometry based algorithm can be shown to be, for a structured in bounding boxes scene, $\mathcal{O}(N_r(\log n_s + n_i \log n_i))$ [Sbert95b], where n_s is the number of surfaces in the scene and n_i is the average number of intersections a random line makes with the scene. For a non-structured scene, we have $\mathcal{O}(N_r(n_s + n_i \log n_i))$. The term $n_i \log n_i$ represents the average cost of sorting an intersection list, and for 'normal' scenes, such as a room with a lot of furniture, the value of n_i is less than 5, so the cost is dominated by the term n_s or $\log n_s$, which represents the cost of intersecting the scene. Once fixed an error bound and a minimum area for any surface the value of N_r remains unchanged. That means that you can increment the surfaces in the scene with no need of incrementing the number of lines cast. That is, you have

> **Rule 1:** *In the global Monte Carlo Integral Geometry method, under certain constraints, you can increase the number of objects in scene without having to increase the number of global directions, to a same accuracy.*

Now we will compare this technique with a similar local Monte Carlo technique. Suppose we want to compute the form factors between n_p patches with the technique of casting lines from a patch, counting how many intersect every other patch and dividing by the total of lines cast. In the global technique we cast N_r global lines. If we suppose an average probability p that a global line crosses a patch, then an average of $N_r p$ lines will have crossed a patch. Now, if we want to compute the form factors from a local Monte Carlo perspective, keeping the same accuracy, we should cast $N_r p$ per patch. As we have n_p patches, that makes $N_r p n_p$ lines. But $p n_p$ is the average number of intersections per line, n_i. So, we have $N_r n_i$ as the cost of a local Monte Carlo technique, and then we can conclude for the technique just considered:

> **Rule 2:** *The relative efficiency of the global Monte Carlo technique— for computing all form factors—relative to the local Monte Carlo one is equal to the average number of intersections a random line has with the scene.*

Then, if n_i represents roughly the complexity of scene, the higher the complexity, the higher the relative efficiency.

2.3 Multi-path method

In the method just exposed we compute form factors, to later solve the radiosity equations system. In the multi-path method, exposed in [Sbert95a], we do not compute form factors, we only compute radiosities. That is, the global lines, which were used in the previous method to obtain visibility lists will now be used to transfer energy between patches.

We are going to cast globally a predetermined number of randomly oriented lines. Each line will produce an intersection list, and we follow this list taking into account successive pairs of patches. Each patch has two quantities. One records the energy accumulated, the other one is the unshot energy. For every pair of patches along the intersection list, the first patch of the pair will transmit its unsent energy to the second patch of the pair. Given the number of lines we are going to cast, we compute for any light source beforehand the forecasted lines passing through it. This can be done with Integral Geometry methods as in [Sbert93]. The division of the total source energy by this number gives the energy per line exiting an emitter patch. In figure 1 the principle of this method is synthesized. Every global line has the effect of advancing many simultaneous random paths, and starting a new path when crossing a source.

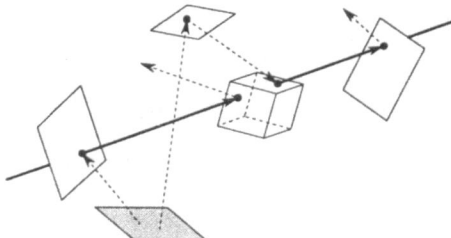

Fig. 1. Simultaneous random paths from the source (gray patch). A global line (the thick continuous one) makes many (two in this case) paths advance at once.

It is clear that the more the sources, the higher the efficiency of the algorithm, because almost each line will be used to advance paths. The effect of having many sources can be obtained by shooting the energy from the sources, and converting the receivers in sources. If the primitive source sees many patches, the expected effect will be obtained, and we can put to work the multi-path algorithm. So,

> **Rule 3:** *If you are going to use a global technique, try first to "smooth" the scene with a non-global technique.*

Although it may seem that rule 3 defeats the spirit of global Monte Carlo, it is only a way of "starting the engine" so it works in the best conditions. This rule can also be applied to the integral geometry method, in the sense of computing the form factors from the source to a higher level of accuracy with some local technique, such as sending lines from the source.

Now we want to see if rules 1 and 2 apply also to the multi-path technique. In an ideally "smoothed" scene N_r global lines in the multi-path method would originate from each patch n_{rave} paths of average length $\frac{n_{rave}}{2}$, where n_{raver} is the average number of intersections per patch, making a total length of $n_p \frac{n_{raver}^2}{2}$. As $n_{raver} = N_r\, p$ and $n_p\, p = n_i$ (see previous section 2.2) we have a total length of $n_i\, N_r\, n_{rave}$ generated with N_r global lines. So each global line would be equivalent to $n_i\,n_{rave}$ local lines. Trying to obtain the same total length with a random walk method leads us to the rule 2', not as precise as rule 2:

> **Rule 2':** *The efficiency of the global Monte Carlo multi-path technique respective to a classic random walk technique is proportional to the product of the average number of intersections per line, n_i, and the average number of lines per patch, n_{rave}.*

In what respects rule 1, we remark here that, fixing a minimum area per surface, and adding surfaces with that constraint, n_{rave} remains the same. Then, if the accuracy depends on the hits per surface, it should not be affected. However, if we add a few surfaces so they occlude most of the source, the visibility conditions from the source to the scene would change radically, and the efficiency of the global method may be affected considerably. So we can state rule 1':

> **Rule 1':** *Assuming that the accuracy depends strongly on the number of hits per patch, the effect of adding surfaces to a scene so that the visibility from the source is not radically changed, will not affect the accuracy of the solution obtained with the multi-path method.*

Experimental results for the multi-path technique are presented in figures 2 and 6, corresponding to a scene with increasing number of surfaces and casting in each case the same number of lines.

We finish this section with a general rule for using global Monte Carlo:

> **General Rule for using global Monte Carlo:** *Use it for complex scenes with many objects and many intersections per line, and put it to work through some "local starter".*

3 Merging Solutions

It is well known in elemental Statistics that the expected value of a weighted sum of independent random variables is the weighted sum of expected values, and the variance is the square weighted sum of the variances. That is, if B_1 and B_2 are random variables with expected value B and variance V_1 and V_2 respectively, and $a + b = 1$, we have, where E stands for expected value and Var for variance: $E((aB_1 + bB_2)) = aE(B_1) + bE(B_2) = aB + bB = (a + b)B = B$ and $Var((aB_1 + bB_2)) = a^2Var(B_1) + b^2Var(B_2) = a^2V_1 + b^2V_2$.

The variances V_1 and V_2 would be equal in case we used the same parameters, but changing for instance the number of lines cast in a Monte Carlo algorithm, that is no more the case. The minimum variance of the weighted sum of two independent estimators, $aB_1 + bB_2$, is achieved when $a = \frac{V_2}{V_1+V_2}$ and $b = \frac{V_1}{V_1+V_2}$, where $Var(B_1) = V_1$ and $Var(B_2) = V_2$.

To know the weights a and b we should know a priori the variances. But in the case where we know a priori that both are equal, because we have used the same parameters, we get simply $a = \frac{1}{2}$, $b = \frac{1}{2}$, which corresponds to the intuitive result of taking the average of both results of sampling the estimators.

To further combine a third estimator B_3 we should look for an optimal combination of $a(\frac{1}{2}B_1 + \frac{1}{2}B_2) + bB_3$, with $a + b = 1$. The optimal values are $a = \frac{2}{3}$,

$b = \frac{1}{3}$, as it intuitively should be, because we have merged one result with the result of merging two ones, and so the weight of the last one is double. That simple rule is valid again and again, that is, if we combine the $n + 1$ result with the result of incrementally combining the n first ones, the weights would be proportional to n and 1. And the variance is always the variance of one simple result divided by the number of results merged. With two results it would be $\frac{V}{2}$, with n results $\frac{V}{n}$.

3.1 The algorithm

As in global Monte Carlo algorithms the variance is inversely proportional to the number of lines or rays cast (changing line by trial, this can be asserted also of any Monte Carlo method), instead of casting at once N_r lines to obtain a solution, we may divide the problem into smaller ones, and obtain incrementally the solution with n results of $\frac{N_r}{n}$ lines each (strictly speaking, to do that we must have unbiased estimators, but see section 3.2) using the results developed in the first paragraphs of this section. So, in that technique, the only additional work done is that of merging or combining the radiosity vectors (and also the work of solving n times an equation system for a full matrix technique, such as the Integral Geometry technique). This technique may also be used in classic Monte Carlo random path technique, because a random path technique with N paths is nothing but merging N independent estimators of the radiosities.

The technique presented here may be considered a generalisation of the technique presented in [Feda93]. The main difference lies in the fact that in Feda's method each progressive step uses the results of the previous step, and so the steps are not independent and the concepts developed in the beginning of this section can not be directly applied.

Also, suppose that we do not always cast the same number of lines. As the variances are inversely proportional to the number of lines, that is, $V_1 = \frac{k}{N_{r1}}$ and $V_2 = \frac{k}{N_{r2}}$, we have the optimal weights:

$$a = \frac{V_2}{V_1 + V_2} = \frac{N_{r1}}{N_{r1} + N_{r2}} \qquad b = \frac{V_1}{V_1 + V_2} = \frac{N_{r2}}{N_{r1} + N_{r2}}$$

where N_{r1} and N_{r2} are the lines cast respectively.

The progressive solutions obtained in this way are not constrained to cast at each iteration the same number of lines, as shown above.

We can also distribute the work between different workstations, with a number of lines to be cast in each workstation proportional to its computing power, communicate the results and merge them. Or we can have each workstation computing and merging results of its own, and later communicate to a resuming workstation the merged results, which in turn would be sum-weighted to obtain the final solution. That would permit an optimal dynamic load balancing. That is, for a given time t, every workstation i will have computed and merged m_i solutions with N_r lines each. If B_i are the result of merging the m_i partial solutions in the workstation i, the optimal result would be to merge all the B_is with the weights m_i.

3.2   Biased solutions

When the solutions can not be guaranteed to be unbiased, we can try to look for a non-biased estimator, or we can go ahead and do the merging of solutions, in the confidence that the bias decreases rapidly as a function of N_r. Anyway, some care must be taken in selecting a minimum N_r. At this effect, a knowledge of the bias as a function of N_r may help. The Integral Geometry method has an exponential negative bias, due to the fact that the probability of a patch not being intersected is not null, the multi-path method has a bias due to the fact that the paths have finite length. Those biases can be dealt with imposing a minimum number of intersections per patch.

Classic Monte Carlo random walk techniques may also be biased, for instance when we follow paths from the source till a predetermined length. If we follow paths of length k, we get a *biased* estimation of B, because we are estimating $B^{(k)}$, not B, where $B^{(k)}$ would be the solution obtained with k Gauss Seidel iterations. Then, merging solutions we obtain a better estimation of $B^{(k)}$, not of B.

4   Results

Results are presented of the progressive approach based on the two global techniques described in sections 2.2 and 2.3. We have a test scene with 2200 patches for the first technique. In figure 4 we present for the Integral Geometry technique three solutions of the same scene incrementally obtained from the progressive merging of the results of independent executions of the program with the same number of lines each, N_r, being $N_r = 3.8 \times 10^5$. This is equivalent to having independent solutions with N_r, $4N_r$ and $10N_r$ lines. We present also the solution with $10N_r$ lines (figure 4d). Also a second scene is taken with 66000 patches for the second global Monte Carlo technique (multi-path algorithm). In figure 5 (see Appendix) we present three solutions of the same scene incrementally obtained from the progressive merging of the results of independent executions of the program with the same number of lines each, N_r, being $N_r = 1.4 \times 10^7$. In the lower right part of the same figure we present a solution obtained by merging 10 independent solutions and a solution with $10N_r$ lines.

Error graphs for MSE errors for the first global technique for the 2200 patches scene and for the second global technique for the 66000 patches scene are given in figure 3.

5   Conclusions

A new technique has been presented that consists in merging solutions of diferents computations of the radiosities of the same scene by global Monte Carlo algorithms. This technique may be extended to other Monte Carlo algorithms, such as the classic random walk technique or particle tracing. The new technique permits us to present to the user progressive radiosity solutions, and also distribute the computational work over several workstations.

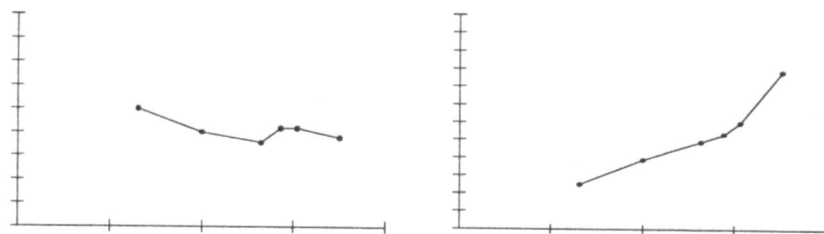

Fig. 2. Behaviour of MSE (vertical axis; axis step $= 0,00001$) and time (vertical axis; axis step $= 10000$ s) in the global multi-path method against the increasing number of surfaces (in logarithmic scale: $1, 10, 100\dots$)

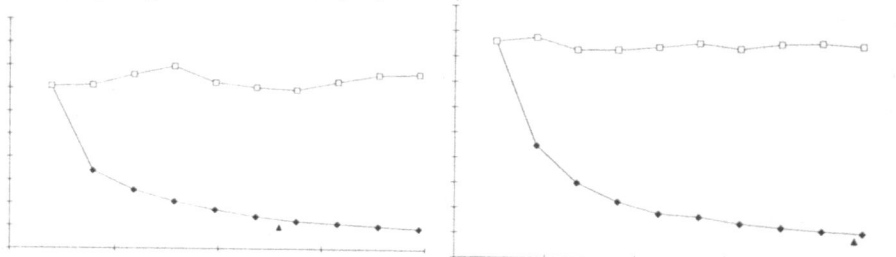

Fig. 3. MSE errors (vertical axis) against time for ten progressive merged solutions (black squares) and the equivalent solution (black triangle): using the Integral Geometry method for a scene with 2200 patches (left; axis step $= 0,00002$); using the multi-path method for a scene with 66000 patches (right; axis step $= 0,00004$). The top curve shows each of the independent solutions (white squares).

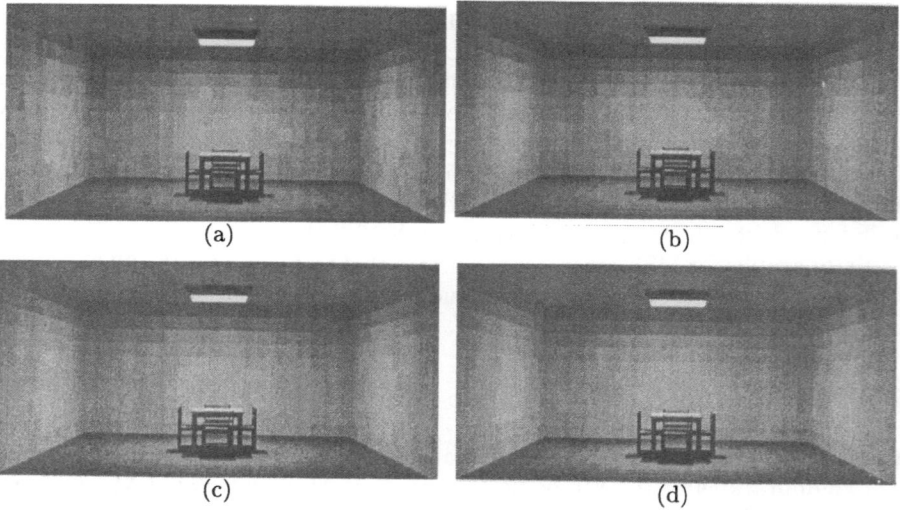

Fig. 4. Merging radiosities with the Integral Geometry method ($N_r = 3.8 \times 10^5$): a radiosity solution with N_r lines (a); merging of four (b) and ten (c) independent radiosity solutions, each one generated with N_r lines; solution generated with $10N_r$ lines (d).

6 Acknowledgements

Many thanks to Georges Drettakis, Gonzalo Besueivski, Joaquim Gelabertó and Carles Barceló for their useful comments, and to P. Shirley for providing the scenes database. This project has been funded in part with grant number TIC 92-1031-C02-01 of the CICYT. Frederic Pérez is also supported by a FPI grant from the Ministerio de Educación y Ciencia.

References

[Buckalew89] Chris Buckalew, Donald Fussell, "Illumination Networks: Fast Realistic Rendering with General Reflectance Functions", Computer Graphics (SIGGRAPH '89 Proceedings), 23(3), July 1989, pp. 89-98.

[Cohen88] Michael Cohen, Shenchang Eric Chen, John R. Wallace, Donald P. Greenberg, "A Progressive Refinement Approach to Fast Radiosity Image Generation", Computer Graphics (SIGGRAPH '88 Proceedings), 22(4), August 1988, pp. 75-84.

[Cook84] Robert L. Cook, Thomas Porter, Loren Carpenter, "Distributed Ray Tracing", Computer Graphics (SIGGRAPH '84 Proceedings), 18(3), July 1984, pp. 137-145.

[Feda93] Martin Feda, Werner Purgathofer, "Progressive Ray Refinement for Monte Carlo Radiosity", Fourth Eurographics Workshop on Rendering, Eurographics Technical Report Series EG 93 RW, Paris, France, June 1993, pp. 15-26.

[Kajiya86] James T. Kajiya, "The Rendering Equation", Computer Graphics (SIGGRAPH '86 Proceedings), 20(4), August 1986, pp. 143-150.

[Neumann94] L. Neumann, "Monte Carlo Radiosity". Submitted to Computing. (Invited speech to the Fourth Eurographics Workshop on Rendering, Paris, 1993)

[Pattanaik92] S.N. Pattanaik, S.P. Mudur, "Computation of Global Illumination by Monte Carlo Simulation of the Particle Model of Light", Third Eurographics Workshop on Rendering, Bristol, UK, May 1992, pp. 71-83.

[Pellegrini95] M. Pellegrini, "Monte Carlo Approximation of Form Factors with Error Bounded a Priori", 11th ACM Symposium on Computational Geometry, June 1995, Vancouver.

[Rey-Pastor51] J. Rey Pastor, L.A. Santaló Sors, Geometría Integral, Espasa-Calpe, 1951.

[Santaló76] L.A. Santaló, Integral Geometry and Geometric Probability, Addison-Wesley, 1976.

[Sbert93] M. Sbert, "An Integral Geometry Based Method for Fast Form Factor Computation", Computer Graphics Forum (Eurographics '93), 13(3), Barcelona, Spain, Sept. 1993, pp. 409-420.

[Sbert95a] M. Sbert, X. Pueyo, L. Neumann, W. Purgathofer, "Global Multi-Path Monte Carlo Algorithms for Radiosity". To appear in The Visual Computer.

[Sbert95b] M. Sbert, X. Pueyo, "Integral Geometry Methods for Form-Factor Computation", Encuentros de Geometría Computacional, Barcelona, July 1995. (& Research Report Universitat de Girona IMA-94-04, 1994)

[Siegel92] Robert Siegel, John R. Howel, Thermal Radiation Heat Transfer, Third Edition, Hemisphere Publishing Corporation, Washington, 1992.

[Shirley90] Peter Shirley, "A Ray Tracing Method for Illumination Calculation in Diffuse-Specular Scenes", Proceedings of Graphics Interface '90, Canadian Information Processing Society, Toronto, Ontario, May 1990, pp. 205-212.

[Ward88] G.J. Ward, F.M. Rubinstein, R.D. Clear, "A Ray Tracing Solution for Diffuse Interreflection", Computer Graphics (SIGGRAPH '88 Proceedings), 22(4), August 1988, pp. 85-92.

[Ward94] G.J. Ward, "The RADIANCE lighting simulation and rendering system", Computer Graphics Proceedings, Annual Conference Series, July 1994, pp. 459-472.

Editors' Note: see Appendix, p. 370 for colored figures of this paper

Smart Links and Efficient Reconstruction for Wavelet Radiosity

Philipp Slusallek   Michael Schröder   Marc Stamminger   Hans-Peter Seidel

Computer Graphics Group, University of Erlangen

Abstract

Wavelet radiosity is the unification of two important methods to solve the radiosity equation: hierarchical radiosity and Galerkin radiosity. Although wavelet radiosity can reap the benefits of both methods, there is still a lot of overhead and in practice several problems occur. For example, using Haar wavelets the traditional push-pull scheme leads to obviously wrong results near common patch boundaries. Moreover, interaction between partially visible patches leads to unnecessarily fine subdivisions, and higher order wavelets introduce a significant overhead for low-power links. In this article we propose a set of *smart links* that cope with these problems and can increase both the efficiency of the algorithm and the quality of the solution.

Additionally, we show how the expensive traditional reconstruction step that is required for piecewise constant basis functions can be avoided in the case of flatlets.

1   Introduction

Although wavelet radiosity (WR) is an efficient means for radiosity calculations, in practice several problems occur. In this paper we address some of these problems and propose new links—called *smart links*—that manage these difficulties. We restrict ourselves to wavelet radiosity with tree wavelets (namely multiwavelets and flatlets), because the wavelet radiosity algorithm simplifies significantly for this wavelet type.

In Section 2 we give a brief overview of the radiosity method with tree wavelets as proposed by Gortler et al. [5], before we describe the use of *double links* to eliminate obviously wrong results near common patch boundaries in Section 3. In Section 4 we introduce a new integration method (*boundary interpolation*) and the *shadow mask link* type to address problems in the case of partial visibility. An easy way to reduce the number of numerical integrations by replacing low-power links by cheap *quick links* is proposed in Section 5. Finally, we present a very efficient reconstruction technique to obtain smoother results with the discontinuous flatlet basis in Section 6.

2 Wavelet Radiosity

The aim of all radiosity algorithms is to find an approximate solution to the radiosity integral equation (1). This equation is a special case of the Rendering Equation [7] and describes light transport in environments with diffuse surfaces.

$$B^p(\underline{s}) = E^p(\underline{s}) + \sum_q \int_q K^{p\leftarrow q}(\underline{s},\underline{t})\, B^q(\underline{t})d\underline{t} \qquad (1)$$

$$\text{with} \quad K^{p\leftarrow q}(\underline{s},\underline{t}) = \rho^p(\underline{s})\, G^{p\leftarrow q}(\underline{s},\underline{t})\, V^{p\leftarrow q}(\underline{s},\underline{t}), \qquad (2)$$

where p and q are surfaces in the scene. Every surface is parameterized by a two dimensional parameter $\underline{s}$ or $\underline{t} \in R^2$. $B^p(\underline{s})$ is the radiosity solution of surface p as a function of the surface parameter $\underline{s}$. $E^p(\underline{s})$ represents the emission of patch p, and $K^{p\leftarrow q}$ is the kernel of the integral equation containing a geometry term G, describing the relative geometry of the two patches, a visibility term V that describes the visibility between points on p and q, and the receiver's reflectance ρ^p.

In Galerkin radiosity (GR) [12] $B^p(\underline{s})$ is approximated by a function from a function space spanned by a finite set of basis functions $\{N_i(\underline{s})\}$: $B^p(\underline{s}) \approx \sum_i b_i^p N_i(\underline{s})$. This approximated radiosity is described by the finite set of coefficients b_i^p. Substituting the approximation in Equation (1) results in a system of linear equations (3) in the coefficients b_i^p, which can be determined with iteration methods like Gauss-Seidel.

$$\forall p,i : b_i^p = e_i^p + \sum_{q,j} I_{i,j}^{p\leftarrow q} b_j^q \qquad (3)$$

The interaction coefficients $I_{i,j}^{p\leftarrow q}$ are a kind of "form factors" for higher order basis functions. For piecewise constant basis functions they are identical to the well known form factors of classical radiosity [4]. In general, the interaction coefficients are defined as

$$I_{i,j}^{p\leftarrow q} = \int_p \int_q K^{p\leftarrow q}(\underline{s},\underline{t})\tilde{N}_i(\underline{s})N_j(\underline{t})\, d\underline{s}\, d\underline{t}, \qquad (4)$$

where $\tilde{N}_i(\underline{s})$ are the dual basis functions to $N_i(\underline{s})$. The dual functions $\{\tilde{N}_i(\underline{s})\}$ are spanning the same space as the $\{N_i(\underline{s})\}$ and are defined by $\int \tilde{N}_i(\underline{s})N_j(\underline{s})d\underline{s} = \delta_{ij}$ (δ_{ij} = Kronecker delta).

Wavelet Radiosity is Galerkin Radiosity using a wavelet basis. The general wavelet algorithm can be simplified by using tree wavelets and the non-standard decomposition operator ([9]) for kernel and radiosity. In this tree wavelet algorithm the radiosity of a patch is stored in a quadtree representing a uniform subdivision of the patch. Every node in the tree contains Galerkin coefficients with respect to the wavelet scaling functions translated and scaled to fit on the corresponding subpatch. This is a simple multi-resolution representation, where the actual wavelet functions are not used at all. To determine the interaction of two patches an oracle ([9]) decides, whether the power transport between the two patches can be described sufficiently on the current resolution level. If this is true, the two patches are linked with a bundle of normal Galerkin coefficients (Equation (4)). Otherwise one patch is refined and the four new pairs of patches are considered recursively.

This algorithm is very similar to hierarchical Radiosity (HR). As in HR after each gathering step it is necessary to consolidate the radiosity gathered at different levels of the multi-resolution hierarchy (push-pull procedure). A more detailed description of the algorithm can be found in [5] or [9].

3 Double Links for Hierarchical Radiosity Near Singularities

One problem of the hierarchical radiosity algorithm arises near the singularities of adjacent patches. Depending on the subdivision threshold the algorithm can force subdivision along the common edge until the area threshold is reached. In this case the small patches near the edge become far too bright (see Figure 1).

Figure 2(a) illustrates this problem for a simple two-dimensional scene of perpendicular patches a and b of unit length. If the oracle considers the form factor $F_{a \to b}$ to be too large, the patches are subdivided. Furthermore, the form factors $F_{a_2 \to b_2} =: F_1$ and $F_{a_1 \to b_2} = F_{a_2 \to b_1} =: F_2$ may be small enough to be accepted. Because of similarity $F_{a_1 \to b_1}$ is the same as $F_{a \to b}$ and further subdivision with additional links is required. Note that this is also true if the oracle measures the variation of the form factor, as described in [6].

Figure 1: Bright border between two perpendicular patches of size 1×5 obtained with Haar wavelets.

The radiosity received from patch a at the finest level is:

$$B(b_{1\dots1}) = F_2 B(a_2) + F_2 B(a_{12}) + \dots + F_2 B(a_{1\dots12}) + F_3 B(a_{1\dots1})$$

If patch a has constant radiosity B_a, the radiosity gathered in b is $(nF_2 + F_3)B_a$, where n is the number of subdivisions. This value diverges with growing n, which is obviously wrong.

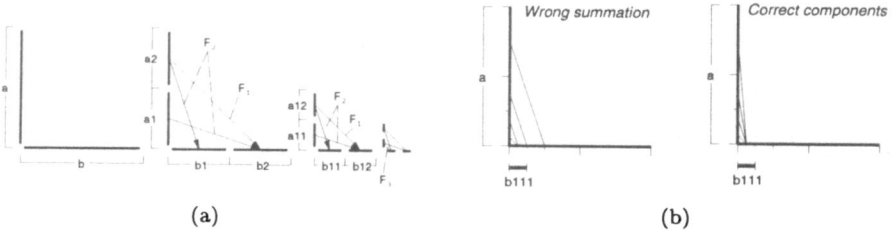

(a)   (b)

Figure 2: Summation of form factors for a simple 2D scene

The reason for this can be seen in Figure 2(b). It shows the form factors added for patch b_{111} by the normal push-pull algorithm (left) and the form factors that should have been added to obtain the correct result (right). The problem is that the form factors summed up are independent of $\cos(\theta_a)$, which converges to zero near the edge. The problem can be solved with a modified push-pull algorithm and a new *double link* type.

The key idea is to include $\cos(\theta_a)$ in the form factor computation. Of course, it is unreasonable to keep track of every patch used in the push procedure. Instead, we split the form factor into two parts: one independent and one dependent on $\cos(\theta_a)$. Figure 3 shows the configuration for the form factor F between two patches a and b.

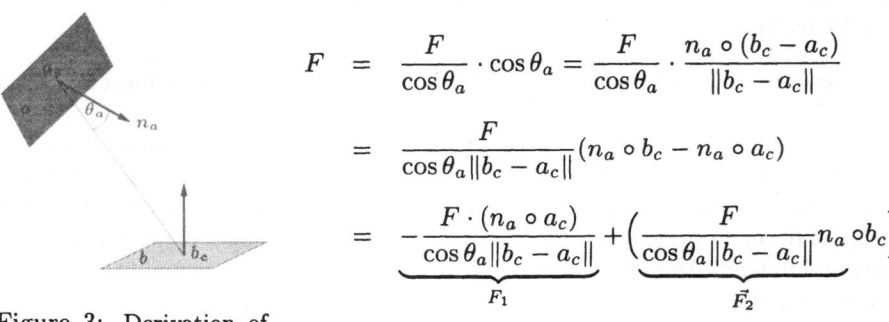

$$F = \frac{F}{\cos\theta_a} \cdot \cos\theta_a = \frac{F}{\cos\theta_a} \cdot \frac{n_a \circ (b_c - a_c)}{\|b_c - a_c\|}$$

$$= \frac{F}{\cos\theta_a \|b_c - a_c\|}(n_a \circ b_c - n_a \circ a_c)$$

$$= \underbrace{-\frac{F \cdot (n_a \circ a_c)}{\cos\theta_a \|b_c - a_c\|}}_{F_1} + \underbrace{\left(\frac{F}{\cos\theta_a \|b_c - a_c\|} n_a \circ b_c\right)}_{\vec{F}_2}$$

Figure 3: Derivation of the modified push

$$= F_1 + \vec{F}_2 \circ b_c$$

If the gathering algorithm is changed to use a double link which stores both F_1 and $\vec{F}_2$, two different radiosities are maintained. The first one, B_1, is calculated using F_1 and the second one, $\vec{B}_2$, is a vector of radiosities and depends on $\vec{F}_2$. During the push algorithm the radiosity of a subpatch with center b_c is then calculated as

$$B(b_c) = B_1 + \vec{B}_2 \circ b_c$$

For the two-dimensional case of two perpendicular patches of unit length the differential form factor $F(x_b)$ from patch a to patch b can be calculated analytically as $F(x_b) = \frac{1}{2}(1 - x_b(1 + x_b^2)^{-1/2})$. Figure 4 compares this analytical from factor (solid line) with the form factor calculated by the standard push algorithm and the result of the modified push algorithm.

One can see that the curve calculated with double links does not diverge near the singularity. The drawback is that slightly more time is spent in the gathering algorithm, which can be neglected compared to visibility calculations, and that the memory occupied by each link is increased.

4 Shadow Links

Links with partial visibility introduce two kinds of problems in WR: Radiosity discontinuities at patch boundaries, due to improper sampling and the use of

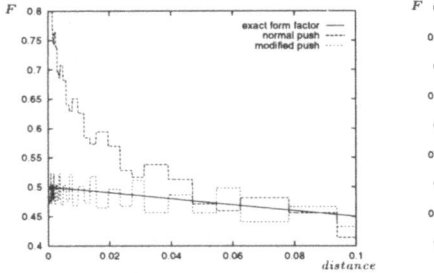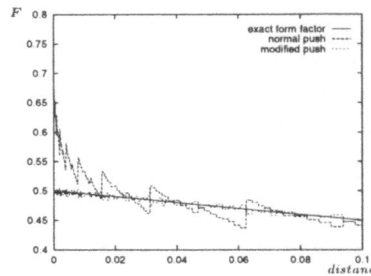

Figure 4: Differential form factor for the configuration from Figure 2 as a function of the distance to the singularity, computed with the normal and the modified push-pull algorithm. The figures are calculated with a subdivision threshold F_ϵ of 0.05 (left) and 0.01 (right).

tree wavelets, and a large number of links to properly approximate a sharp shadow boundary.

The first problem can be addressed by calculating such partial visibility links with another integration method, which we called *boundary interpolation*. This method smoothes discontinuities, but it cannot decrease the number of links. Another approach are *shadow mask links*, which also lead to smoother solutions, but additionally avoid deep refinement of partial visibility links due to discontinuities in the kernel caused by shadow boundaries.

4.1 Boundary Interpolation

The kernel function in Equation (2) contains a visibility term which exhibits discontinuities at shadow boundaries. Especially with multiwavelets these edges result in unpleasant effects near shadow boundaries in the final radiosity solution. A new integration method for multiwavelets and partially visible interactions can cope with this situation and delivers smoother and more continuous shadow boundaries.

For multiwavelets the computation of the interaction coefficients $I_{i,j}^{p \leftarrow q}$ requires numerical integration of the kernel function. The standard numerical integration schemes (e.g. Gauss-Legendre) interpolate the kernel by polynomials through sample points. Figure 5 shows two interpolations through the Gauss-Legendre sample points over a discontinuity edge of a simple one-dimensional function.

While linear interpolation produces large gaps at the patch boundary, the interpolation with a polynomial of degree six exhibits additional ripples near the discontinuity. Although the interpolated kernel function is integrated, the gaps and ripples are not completely smoothed out and can still be noticed in the resulting radiosity solution. One reason for this unpleasant behavior is that in the case of tree wavelets the basis functions for adjacent patches do not overlap. As a result a continuous solution cannot be guaranteed.

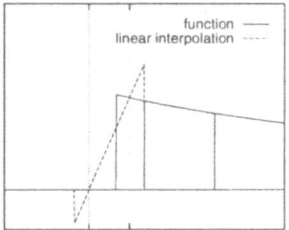
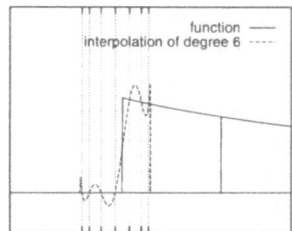

Figure 5: Interpolation of a discontinuous function with polynomials of degree 1 (left) and 6 (right). The vertical lines denote the sample positions for Gauss-Legendre integration.

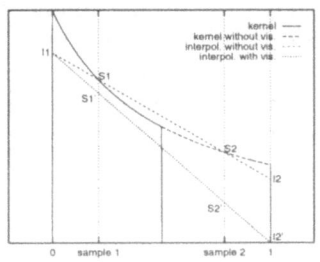

Figure 6: The boundary interpolation method

To produce smoother shadow boundaries we propose a special numerical integration scheme for interactions with discontinuous kernel functions. This boundary interpolation method is illustrated in Figure 6 for a one dimensional function. In a first step, the kernel function without the visibility factor is sampled at the usual sample points (S_1, S_2). These points are interpolated by a polynomial, which itself is sampled at a new set of sample points which contains the boundary points (I_1, I_2). These samples are set to zero if the corresponding visibility factor is zero, leading to (I_1, I_2'). Finally, the function is re-interpolated at the sample points (S_1', S_2') required for the numerical integration.

This method guarantees that the kernel interpolation returns useful values at the boundary of adjacent sub-patches. Because the visibility term is sampled at the patch boundaries, adjacent patches use the same visibility information along their common edge or point. Thus, our method diminishes gaps at the patch boundaries and leads to smoother solutions, although, from a numerical point of view, the overall error of the interpolation is not necessarily decreased. Situations can be constructed, where the normal integration method is better than boundary interpolation and vice versa.

Figure 7 shows a simple shadow boundary in linear multiwavelets rendered with and without boundary interpolation.

Although the algorithm consists of several transformations, most of them can be combined. In a first step only the visible boundary samples are determined from the wavelet coefficients by linear combination, whereas the in-

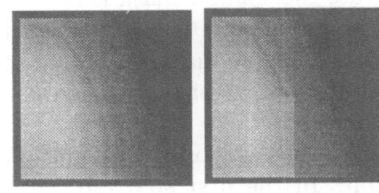

Figure 7: Shadow boundary with (left) and without (right) boundary interpolation

visible samples are simply set to zero. From these samples the interaction coefficients can be obtained by a single linear transformation. This integration
takes less than twice the time of a standard integration.

The boundary interpolation method is only used if a link is created for the
interaction of two patches with partial visibility. It is especially useful for linear
multiwavelets, but it also works with higher order multiwavelets. However,
for higher orders the interpolation starts to exhibit ripples near the shadow
boundary again.

4.2 Shadow masks

In [12] Zatz introduced shadow masks to improve Galerkin radiosity calculations in the presence of shadow boundaries. Although the idea is simple, the
implementation in Galerkin radiosity is quite tricky. As shown in this section,
wavelet radiosity allows a simpler implementation of shadow masks.

A shadow mask is an approximation to the visibility term of the kernel
function. It is a function $M^{p \leftarrow q}(\underline{s})$ which approximates $V^{p \leftarrow q}(\underline{s}, \underline{t})$ by averaging
it over the source patch:

$$M^{p \leftarrow q}(\underline{s}) = \int_q V^{p \leftarrow q}(\underline{s}, \underline{t}) d\underline{t}$$

$M^{p \leftarrow q}(\underline{s})$ is the portion of patch q that can be seen at point $\underline{s}$ on patch
p. It can be considered a shadow texture map representing the shadow on the
receiving patch. Since the shadow mask $M^{p \leftarrow q}(\underline{s})$ does not depend on $\underline{t}$ it can
be moved out of the integral in the radiosity equation (1):

$$B^p(\underline{s}) \approx E^p(\underline{s}) + \sum_q M^{p \leftarrow q}(\underline{s}) \int_q \tilde{K}^{p \leftarrow q}(\underline{s}, \underline{t}) B^q(\underline{t}) d\underline{t},$$

where $\tilde{K}^{p \leftarrow q}$ is the kernel without the visibility term $V^{p \leftarrow q}$.

With this approximation the light transport between two patches can be
divided into two steps. In the first step radiosity is gathered as if there were no
shadow boundaries. Then the gathered radiosity is multiplied with the shadow
mask function in a second step. The quality of the shadows depends on how
accurate the shadow mask is calculated.

The problem in Galerkin radiosity is how to multiply the gathered radiosity
with the shadow mask. If the multiplication is done within the normal basis
most information of the shadow mask is lost, so other ways have to be found
[12].

In wavelet radiosity the multiplication can be performed using a finer resolution: In the first step radiosity is gathered with interactions that do not
consider visibility. Then this radiosity is pushed down in the radiosity tree to
the desired resolution. In this finer resolution the radiosity can be multiplied
with the shadow mask, so no information of the shadow mask is lost by the
multiplication. Figure 8 illustrates this algorithm.

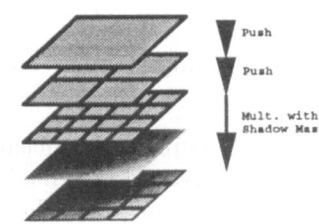

Figure 8: Shadow masking in wavelet radiosity

In our implementation the wavelet oracle tests the smoothness of the kernel function neglecting the visibility factor. If a link is considered smooth but links two partial visible patches, a shadow mask link is established. This link carries the link coefficients for total visibility and the shadow mask function, sampled on an equally-sized grid of an appropriate resolution on the gathering patch. The shadow mask samples are calculated by a number of visibility tests to jittered points on the sender, where the number of tests is chosen depending on the transported radiosity. The grid contains M^2 points on any of the leaf subpatches, where M is the order of the used wavelets.

If radiosity is gathered over this link, it is gathered into a separate radiosity representation, from where it is pushed down to the desired resolution. In this higher resolution the radiosity is multiplied with the shadow mask function and then added to the normal radiosity tree of the patch.

For flatlets, the radiosity coefficients can directly be multiplied with the shadow mask value at the center of their support. When multiwavelets are used, more effort is required. As a first step, on every leaf subpatch the function of gathered radiosity is sampled at the points of the shadow mask grid. These M^2 sample values are an equivalent representation of the subpatch's radiosity. They are multiplied with the corresponding shadow mask values and transformed back to multiwavelet coefficients.

To decrease the memory consumption we combine shadow masks with the idea of final gathering [1]. In all but the last iteration step, radiosity is gathered by a simple link that approximately considers visibility. Just in the last step the complete gathering procedure as described above is performed. As the shadow mask is only needed in this final high resolution gathering step, it is calculated "just in time", multiplied with the gathered radiosity, and deleted again. This avoids the storage of shadow masks — in fact only one shadow mask has to be stored at any time. On the other hand, the intermediate solutions contain a relatively large error due to the approximative links used in the non-final steps, but the resulting error in the final solution of our test scenes was neglectable.

An analysis of the error produced by the use of shadow masks and by the final gathering simplification is difficult, because for both methods, cases can be constructed that result in an arbitrarily large error. It is also possible that energy is produced. In practice, however, no problems occurred.

Furthermore it must be clearly stated that with the described implementation of shadow mask links the computation time cannot be decreased dramatically, although the number of links to be calculated is significantly smaller. The reason is that in most scenes the calculation of visibility dominates the time needed to compute the links. So it seems that shadow mask links optimize an anyway not crucial part.

Nevertheless, shadow mask links have two great advantages:

- With the number of calculated links, the memory consumption is lowered enormously.

- Radiosity transport and visibility calculations are decoupled, so efficient visibility methods can easily be introduced. Even adaptive meshing methods could be used to efficiently calculate the shadow mask function. Thus, two apparently not matching methods as wavelet radiosity with its inherently uniform subdivisions and adaptive meshing can be combined.

Figure 9 shows the shadow of a rotated rectangle between two parallel squares — one emitter and one receiver. In all images only one link between the root nodes is used. The first image is calculated without a shadow mask, the other three solutions are obtained with increasing resolution, resulting in radiosity trees of depth one, two and three. All images are rendered using third order multiwavelets.

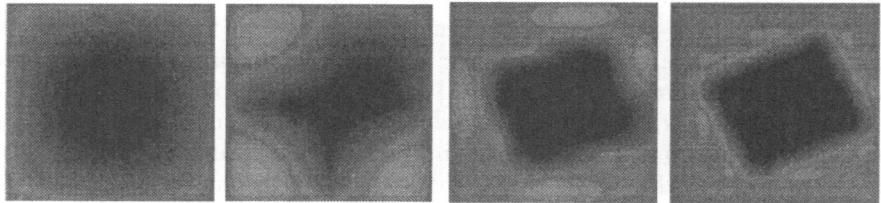

Figure 9: Shadow rendered with shadow masks of different resolutions

5 Quick Links for Multiwavelets

Using wavelets of order M, every link contains M^4 interaction coefficients. For $M = 4$ this requires 256 numerical integrations. When multiwavelets are used many of these coefficients between distant patches are small and can be neglected. Time can be saved if low-power links are restricted to the few interactions with relevant contributions.

In general, an approach would be desirable that determines the orders needed to approximate the different dimensions of the integrand and that creates only interactions between the relevant pairs. This is possible, but we made the experience that the time needed to determine the orders of the kernel exceeds the time saved due to lower-order integrations. In [3] Gershbein uses a similar idea to reduce the order of the quadrature rule by considering the order of the radiosity of the sending patch and not of the kernel function.

Another approach is to replace multiwavelet links which transport few power by the single interaction of the constant basis functions (this is a form factor). This approach is fast, but not satisfactory. If one patch receives radiosity from numerous other patches via such form factor links, the small errors accumulate and lead to discontinuous "blocky" solutions, due to neglecting the non-constant basis functions.

A better solution, which we call *quick links*, is illustrated in Figure 10. Quick links are restricted to the four interactions between the constant basis function of the sender and the four constant and linear basis functions of the receiver. This idea is similar to substructuring in [2]. Radiosity is gathered by these quick links as a bilinear function. This avoids the occurrence of discontinuous blocks in the radiosity solution.

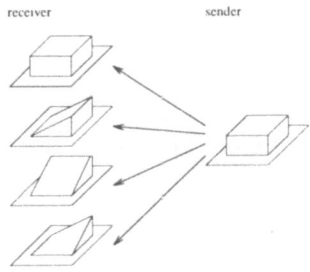

Figure 10: Illustration of Quick Links

In our implementation quick links are used if the transported power between two patches is below a certain threshold. Generally, between 10 and 20 percent of the multiwavelet links can be replaced by quick links without a noticeable loss of quality.

6 Efficient Reconstruction with Flatlets

Flatlets are piecewise constant functions. This results in a blocky radiosity solution, which requires an additional reconstruction or interpolation step before the radiosity can be used for rendering. A very good and general, but expensive reconstruction technique is final gathering [1]. In this chapter we propose a cheap alternative for flatlets.

In the case of flatlets the calculation of the interaction integral (4) is very expensive, because the dual basis functions are difficult to handle. Therefore, Schröder et al. [9] suggested a basis change. If gathered radiosity is represented in the dual base, the dual basis function $\tilde{N}_i(\underline{s})$ in (4) is replaced by $\tilde{\tilde{N}}_i(\underline{s}) = N_i(\underline{s})$:

$$\hat{I}_{i,j}^{p\leftarrow q} = \int_p \int_q K^{p\leftarrow q}(\underline{s},\underline{t}) N_i(\underline{s}) N_j(\underline{t}) \, d\underline{s} \, d\underline{t} \tag{5}$$

In this case, the numerical integration of the integral is much easier and the interaction coefficients $\hat{I}_{i,j}^{p\leftarrow q}$ are the standard form factors between subpatches of p and q. For these form factors good approximations or even closed-form solutions [10] are available.

However, with this "symmetric" formula radiosity is gathered in the dual flatlet basis. The dual coefficients can be transformed back to the standard basis using the dual version of the push operation. After pushing the coefficients no transformation is necessary anymore, because in the highest resolution the dual basis is equal to the original one (Figure 11).

The algorithm with flatlets is quite similar to hierarchical radiosity, but it has two advantages: The usage of the dual push procedure allows to push higher order components of the gathered radiosity in contrast to the HR push, which can only push the constant parts. Secondly, the oracle of flatlet radiosity is in general not as stringent as the HR oracle.

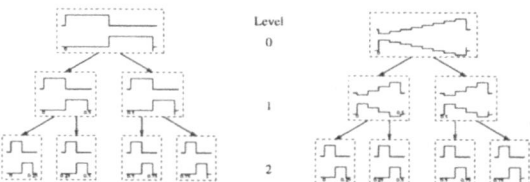

Figure 11: Normal (left) and dual (right) linear flatlet bases for a depth of two.

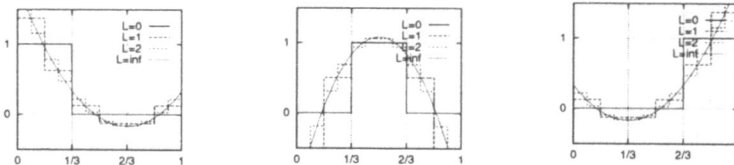

Figure 12: Dual third order flatlet basis functions of the coarsest level for different depths of the radiosity tree.

An example for a one dimensional flatlet basis and its dual counterpart is shown in Figure 11. The construction of the basis is described in [9]. Radiosity in a tree is represented in the normal flatlet basis on the left. If light is transmitted by a symmetric interaction, the coefficients are calculated for the dual basis functions on the right.

Figure 12 shows the dual basis functions of the coarsest resolution for different maximal resolution levels. It can be seen that a deep hierarchy results in smoother basis functions, which converge against polynomials p_i^M of degree $M - 1$, where M is the wavelet order. One way to take advantage of this effect would be to make the trees deeper as necessary. This approach leads to smoother solutions but is costly in time and memory usage.

A much better approach is to simulate an infinitely deep radiosity tree mathematically. In this case the dual basis functions are the limit polynomials p_i^M. They can be determined as the fixpoint of the dual push relation. For linear and quadratic flatlets these polynomials are

$$\mathcal{F}_2 : p_1^2(x) = \frac{3}{2} - 2x, \quad p_2^2(x) = p_1^2(1 - x)$$

$$\mathcal{F}_3 : p_1^3(x) = \frac{9}{2}(x - \frac{2}{3})^2 - \frac{1}{6}, \quad p_2^3(x) = -9(x - \frac{1}{2})^2 + \frac{13}{12}, \quad p_3^3(x) = p_1^3(1 - x)$$

It can be shown that again no transformation is necessary to get the coefficients of the normal flatlet basis from the coefficient of this continuous dual basis, so within the iteration loop no changes in the algorithm are necessary.

However, it is a good idea to consider the coefficients in the tree at the end of the algorithm as dual basis coefficients. This means that for reconstruction the radiosity is not calculated with the normal basis functions but with the polynomials p_i^M: $B^p(\underline{s}) = \sum_i b_i^p p_i^M(\underline{s})$.

Figure 13 shows the reconstructed (one dimensional) radiosity for three coefficients b_1, b_2 and b_3 with the flatlet basis and with the polynomials p_i^3.

It is important to note that for $M > 2$ this polynomial solution is not just an interpolation of the piecewise constant reconstruction.

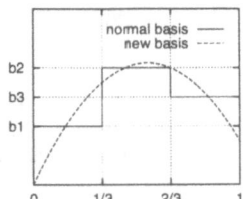

Figure 13: Reconstruction of third order flatlets

7 Conclusion

In this paper we introduced several extensions to the wavelet radiosity algorithm, which allow to generate better solutions in less time (also see example images in Appendix).

However, still much effort has to be made to reach reasonable computation times for complex scenes, possibly containing non-diffuse reflectors. Several approaches as clustering and wavelet radiance have been examined recently. Our future goal will be to include the ideas of this paper into these more sophisticated algorithms.

References

[1] Per H. Christensen, Eric J. Stollnitz, David H. Salesin, and Tony D. DeRose. Wavelet radiance. In *Fifth Eurographics Workshop on Rendering*, pages 287–302, Darmstadt, Germany, June 1994.

[2] Michael Cohen, Shenchang E. Chen, John R. Wallace, and Donald P. Greenberg. A progressive refinement approach to fast radiosity image generation. In *Computer Graphics (SIGGRAPH '88 Proceedings)*, pages 75–84, August 1988.

[3] Reid Gershbein. An adaptive gauss method for computing irradiance coefficients of galerkin radiosity systems. Technical report, Department of Computer Science, Princeton University, 1995.

[4] Cindy M. Goral, Kenneth E. Torrance, Donald P. Greenberg, and Bennett Battaile. Modelling the interaction of light between diffuse surfaces. In *Computer Graphics (SIGGRAPH '84 Proceedings)*, pages 212–22, July 1984.

[5] Steven J. Gortler, Peter Schröder, Michael F. Cohen, and Pat Hanrahan. Wavelet radiosity. In *Computer Graphics (SIGGRAPH '93 Proceedings)*, pages 221–230, 1993.

[6] Nicolas Holzschuch, Françoise Sillion, and George Drettakis. An efficient progressive refinement strategie for hierarchical radiosity. In *Fifth Eurographics Workshop on Rendering*, pages 343–357, Darmstadt, Germany, June 1994.

[7] James T. Kajiya. The rendering equation. In *Computer Graphics (SIGGRAPH '86 Proceedings)*, pages 143–150, August 1986.

[8] Michael Schröder. Implementierung des Hierarchical Radiosity Algorithmus im Vision System. Master's thesis, Universität Erlangen, 1994.

[9] Peter Schröder, Steven J. Gortler, Michael F. Cohen, and Pat Hanrahan. Wavelet projections for radiosity. In *Fourth Eurographics Workshop on Rendering*, pages 177–184, 1993.

[10] Peter Schröder and Pat Hanrahan. On the form factor between two polygons. In *Computer Graphics (SIGGRAPH '93 Proceedings)*, pages 163–164, 1993.

[11] Marc Stamminger. Wavelet radiosity. Master's thesis, Universität Erlangen, 1994.

[12] Harold R. Zatz. Galerkin radiosity: A higher order solution method for global illumination. In *Computer Graphics (SIGGRAPH '93 Proceedings)*, pages 213–220, 1993.

Editors' Note: see Appendix, p. 370 for colored figures of this paper

Spherical Wavelets: Texture Processing

Peter Schröder[*][†] and Wim Sweldens[*][‡]

[*] Department of Mathematics   [†] Department of Computer Science
University of South Carolina, USA

[‡] Department of Computer Science
Katholieke Universiteit Leuven, Belgium

Abstract: Wavelets are a powerful tool for planar image processing. The resulting algorithms are straightforward, fast, and efficient. With the recently developed spherical wavelets this framework can be transposed to spherical textures. We describe a class of processing operators which are diagonal in the wavelet basis and which can be used for smoothing and enhancement. Since the wavelets (filters) are local in space and frequency, complex localized constraints and spatially varying characteristics can be incorporated easily. Examples from environment mapping and the manipulation of topography/bathymetry data are given.

1 Introduction

Over the last few years, wavelets have proven themselves as a versatile tool for (planar) image processing [13]. They have been used for applications such as image compression [4], image enhancement, feature detection [12], and noise removal [5]. Wavelets are computationally attractive as the associated transform is linear in the number of pixels. In the signal processing context the transform is often referred to as subband filtering. The resulting coefficients describe the features of the underlying image in a *local* fashion in both frequency and space. Once in the wavelet domain, operators such as smoothing, enhancement, edge finding, and noise removal can be performed in a straightforward fashion.

Recently, the authors introduced a construction of wavelets on the sphere [15]. Having a fast wavelet transform on the sphere and a family of wavelets with various properties to choose from, the present paper considers their use in the processing of spherical texture maps.

Examples of such textures in computer graphics include environment maps[1] and textures on spheres. While the former are defined over the set of directions, which forms the sphere S^2 in R^3, the latter applies to the sphere as a geometric modeling primitive. In this paper we consider examples of texture processing from both of these domains, and show how spherical wavelets can be applied to these tasks.

We begin with an introduction to spherical wavelets including a description of the resulting transform and its implementation. This is followed by a discussion of diagonal operators in the wavelet domain and how they relate to the common tasks of smoothing and sharpening of images. We then give concrete examples of processing environment maps and a spherical texture subject to complex localized constraints. The paper concludes with a discussion and outlook to further applications.

---

[1] Thanks to Paul Haeberli for suggesting this application domain.

2 Spherical Wavelets

In this section we first give the basic subdivision of a sphere which induces the hierarchy needed as a foundation for multiresolution analysis. Next we explain the construction of spherical wavelets. We limit ourselves to the construction of bases arising from interpolating subdivision schemes. Other constructions are described in [15]. We present the fast spherical wavelet transform and its implementation.

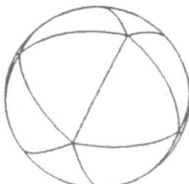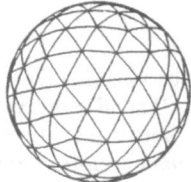

Figure 1 The geodesic sphere construction starting with the icosahedron on the left (subdivision level 0) and the next 2 subdivision levels. Successive levels are generated cutting each triangle into four children. This is accomplished by adding vertices at the midpoint of edges and connecting them with geodetics.

2.1 Subdividing a Sphere

The construction of spherical wavelets in [15] relies on a recursive partitioning of the sphere into spherical triangles. This is done starting from a Platonic solid of triangles and recursive subdivision of the triangles (see Figure 1) and is known as the geodesic sphere construction [6].

Denote the set of all vertices obtained after j subdivisions with $S_j = \{s_{j,k} \in S^2 \mid k \in K(j)\}$, where $K(j)$ is an index set. The vertices of the original Platonic solid are in S_0; S_1 contains those vertices and all new vertices on the edge midpoints (see Figure 1 left and middle). Since $S_j \subset S_{j+1}$ we also let $K(j) \subset K(j+1)$, so that $s_{j,k} = s_{j+1,k}$. The index k of a vertex in S_0 is retained when indexing the same vertex as a member of S_1 and so on. All new members of S_1, the edge midpoints, get indices m different from the ones already taken by the vertices inherited from S_0. Let $M(j) = K(j+1) \setminus K(j)$ be the indices of the vertices added when going from level j to $j+1$. The vertices on level $j+1$ thus consist of two groups: the "old" ones inherited from S_j ($s_{j+1,k}$ with $k \in K(j)$) and the "new" ones ($s_{j+1,m}$ with $m \in M(j)$). Indices will be used consistently in the sense that $k \in K(j), l \in K(j+1)$, and $m \in M(j)$.

Figure 1 shows this subdivision scheme for several levels, beginning with the icosahedron. Choosing the icosahedron as the starting point, the resulting triangulation has the least imbalance in area between its constituent triangles. Such imbalances, most pronounced in the subdivision starting from the tetrahedron, can lead to visible artifacts. Here we will consider only the icosahedral geodesic subdivision for which $\#K(j) = 10 \cdot 4^j + 2$.

2.2 Multiresolution Analysis

We begin by defining the notion of multiresolution analysis on the sphere S^2. Consider the function space $L_2 = L_2(S^2)$ with the area measure $d\omega$, i.e., all functions of finite energy. We define a multiresolution analysis as a sequence of closed subspaces $V_j \subset L_2$, with $j \geqslant 0$, so that

1. $V_j \subset V_{j+1}$,
2. $\bigcup_{j=0}^{\infty} V_j$ is dense in L_2,
3. for each j, scaling functions $\varphi_{j,k}$ with $k \in K(j)$ exist so that $\{\varphi_{j,k} \mid k \in K(j)\}$ is a Riesz basis[2] of V_j.

In this paper we only consider interpolating scaling functions, i.e., scaling functions for which

$$\varphi_{j,k}(s_{j,k'}) = \delta_{k-k'} \quad \text{for} \quad k, k' \in K(j).$$

This can be visualized as a function centered around a given vertex where its value is 1 while it is 0 at all other vertices. Since $\varphi_{j,k} \in V_j \subset V_{j+1}$ we can write $\varphi_{j,k}$ in the basis of V_{j+1}. Because of the interpolation property this linear combination, also known as the *refinement relation*, takes the form

$$\varphi_{j,k} = \varphi_{j+1,k} + \sum_{m \in M(j)} h_{j,k,m}\, \varphi_{j+1,m}. \tag{1}$$

Note that the coefficients $h_{j,k,m}$ of this linear combination can be different for every $k \in K(j)$ at a given level $j \geqslant 0$. The index m in the sum ranges over bases at new vertices $M(j) = K(j+1) \setminus K(j)$.

The easiest example of interpolating scaling functions are the hat functions; a hat function $\varphi_{j,k}$ is 1 at $s_{j,k}$ and dies of linearly towards its immediate neighbors.

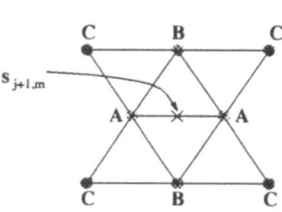 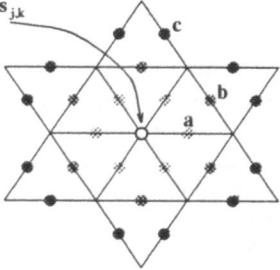

Figure 2 Local neighborhoods for the Butterfly scheme. On the left are the vertex index sets A, B, and C, whose values are used in determining the new value at the central edge midpoint. On the right are the vertex index sets a, b, and c, of all new edge midpoints to which the value of the central "old" vertex makes a contribution.

2.3 Subdivision Schemes

Interpolating scaling functions can be constructed using interpolating subdivision schemes. The idea of an interpolating subdivision scheme is the following: given the "old"

---

[2] A Riesz basis of a Hilbert space is a countable subset $\{f_k\}$ so that every element f of the space can be written uniquely as $f = \sum_k c_k f_k$, and positive constants A and B exist with $A\|f\|^2 \leqslant \sum_k |c_k|^2 \leqslant B\|f\|^2$.

values $\lambda_{j,k}$ of a function on S_j, find the "new" values on $T_j = S_{j+1} \backslash S_j$ (while preserving the values at the vertices of S_j). A simple example of this is a linear subdivision, which assigns each new edge midpoint the average of the values at the end points of its parent edge. To make matters concrete we define the following two neighborhoods:

- $n(j,k) \subset M(j)$: indices of the new values affected by the old value $\lambda_{j,k}$,
- $N(j,m) \subset K(j)$: indices of the old values who determine a new value $\lambda_{j+1,m}$.

These two sets are related through $n(j,k) = \{m \in M(j) \mid k \in N(j,m)\}$. The subdivision scheme can now be written as

$$\lambda_{j+1,m} = \sum_{k \in N(j,m)} h_{j,k,m} \lambda_{j,k}.$$

The scaling function $\varphi_{j,k}$ itself can be generated by starting on level j, setting the value $\lambda_{j,k'}$ of all vertices $\mathbf{s}_{j,k'}$ to zero except for $\mathbf{s}_{j,k}$ whose value $\lambda_{j,k}$ is set to 1, followed by an application of the subdivision scheme ad infinitum. The resulting scaling function satisfies $\varphi_{j,k}(\mathbf{s}_{j+i,l}) = \lambda_{j+i,l}$, and the following refinement relation:

$$\varphi_{j,k} = \varphi_{j+1,k} + \sum_{m \in n(j,k)} h_{j,k,m} \varphi_{j+1,m}. \tag{2}$$

Note that the set $N(j,m)$ defines the summation over the *coefficients* λ while the set $n(j,k)$ defines the summation over the *functions* φ. We may think of this as defining an adjoint relationship between N and n: $N(j,m) = n^T(j,k)$. This property is useful when changing the order of quantifiers since $[\forall k \in K(j) : \forall m \in n(j,k)]$ is equivalent to $[\forall m \in M(j) : \forall k \in N(j,m)]$.

Let us discuss two examples of interpolating subdivision schemes. Define for a vertex $\mathbf{s}_{j+1,m}$ the local neighborhoods $A(j,m)$, $B(j,m)$ and $C(j,m)$, each of them subsets of $K(j)$, and for a vertex $\mathbf{s}_{j,k}$ the neighborhoods $a(j,k)$, $b(j,k)$ and $c(j,k)$, each of them subsets of $M(j)$ as in Figure 2. The upper and lower case notations for the neighborhoods are each others adjoints (like n and N). The uppercase sets have the property that they are easier to implement than the lowercase ones. The chief reason being that they are smaller and have a fixed size ($\#A = 2$, $\#B = 2$, $\#C = 4$), while the size of the lowercase ones depends on the connectivity of $\mathbf{s}_{j,k}$. The latter becomes particularly relevant around the vertices of the original icosahedron, whose valence is 5 as opposed to 6 for all other vertices.

In a linear scheme $\lambda_{j+1,m}$ gets as value the average of the values of the two neighboring vertices in S_j.

$$\lambda_{j+1,m} = 1/2 \sum_{k \in A(j,m)} \lambda_{j,k}.$$

This results in the hat function referred to earlier. In the Butterfly scheme [7] a new value is found as:

$$\lambda_{j+1,m} = 1/2 \sum_{k \in A(j,m)} \lambda_{j,k} + 1/8 \sum_{k \in B(j,m)} \lambda_{j,k} - 1/16 \sum_{k \in C(j,m)} \lambda_{j,k}.$$

The hat functions are continuous, but not differentiable. The Butterfly scheme can lead to differentiable functions if a smooth map from the sphere to a regular planar triangulation exists. This map is determined by the partitioning of the sphere. The geodesic sphere construction presented here does not everywhere lead to such a smooth map. However, visually the basis functions are quite smooth (see the left image in row 3 of the color plate 5 for the corresponding wavelet). It is possible to build more elaborate partitionings of the sphere which ensure the differentiability of the basis functions.

2.4 Wavelets

The basic idea of wavelets is that they form a basis for a space complementing V_j in V_{j+1}. Such a space is denoted W_j so that $V_{j+1} = V_j \oplus W_j$. Note that we do not require W_j to be orthogonal to V_j as in the classical wavelet case. A basis of W_j is given by wavelet functions $\{\psi_{j,m} \mid m \in M(j)\}$ and we get

$$L_2 = V_0 \oplus \bigoplus_{j=0}^{\infty} W_j \,,$$

thus constructing a basis for L_2 with

$$\{\varphi_{0,k} \mid k \in K(0)\} \cup \{\psi_{j,m} \mid j \geqslant 0, \, m \in M(j)\} \,.$$

A very simple construction for a complement space is given by $\psi_{j,m} = \varphi_{j+1,m}$ for $m \in M(j)$. However, this does not lead to a stable (Riesz) basis for L_2. Part of the problem is that the wavelets do not have a vanishing integral. Instead we propose wavelets of the form

$$\psi_{j,m} = \varphi_{j+1,m} - \sum_{k \in A(j,m)} s_{j,k,m} \, \varphi_{j,k}. \tag{3}$$

In words, we define the wavelet at the midpoint of an edge as a linear combination of the scaling function at the midpoint $(j+1, m)$ and two scaling functions on the *coarser level* at the two endpoints of the parent edge $(j, k_{1,2})$. The weights $s_{j,k,m}$ are chosen so that the resulting wavelet has a vanishing integral

$$s_{j,k,m} = I_{j+1,m}/2\, I_{j,k} \quad \text{with} \quad I_{j,k} = \int \varphi_{j,k} \, d\omega \,.$$

This construction of wavelets is a particular instance of a more general scheme called the "lifting scheme" [18, 17]. To facilitate notation we define for the coarsest level $M(-1) := K(0)$, $\psi_{-1,k} := \varphi_{0,k}$, and $\gamma_{-1,k} := \lambda_{0,k}$. With this notation a function $f \in L_2$ can be realized as

$$f = \sum_{-1 \leqslant j} \sum_{m \in M(j)} \gamma_{j,m} \, \psi_{j,m} \,.$$

2.5 Fast Wavelet Transform

Consider a function $f \in V_{j+1}$ given by its scaling function coefficients:

$$f = \sum_{l \in K(j+1)} \lambda_{j+1,l} \, \varphi_{j+1,l} \,. \tag{4}$$

Note that because of the interpolating property it holds that $\lambda_{j+1,l} = f(s_{j+1,l})$. We can also write this function as:

$$f = \sum_{k \in K(j)} \lambda_{j+1,k} \, \varphi_{j,k} + \sum_{m \in M(j)} \gamma_{j,m} \, \varphi_{j+1,m} \,. \tag{5}$$

Evaluating both expressions at $s_{j,k}$ confirms that we use the same $\lambda_{j+1,k}$ coefficients. The coefficients $\gamma_{j,m}$ can be found by evaluating (4) and (5) at a vertex $s_{j+1,m}$:

$$\lambda_{j+1,m} = \gamma_{j,m} + \sum_k \lambda_{j+1,k} \, \varphi_{j,k}(s_{j+1,m}) = \gamma_{j,m} + \sum_{k \in N(j,m)} \lambda_{j+1,k} \, h_{j,k,m} \,. \tag{6}$$

The latter follows from the refinement relation (2). We can also write this function as

$$f = \sum_{k \in K(j)} \lambda_{j,k} \, \varphi_{j,k} + \sum_{m \in M(j)} \gamma_{j,m} \, \psi_{j,m} \,. \tag{7}$$

This can be seen by substituting the lifting equation (3) in (7) and identifying components with (5). This results in:

$$\lambda_{j+1,k} = \lambda_{j,k} - \sum_{m \in a(j,k)} s_{j,k,m} \gamma_{j,m} . \tag{8}$$

One step in the analysis (decomposition) goes from the $\{\lambda_{j+1,l}\}$ on one hand to the $\{\lambda_{j,k}\}$ and $\{\gamma_{j,k}\}$ on the other hand, while one step in the synthesis (reconstruction) does exactly the opposite. A complete transform from some finest level $j = n$ to $j = 0$ now follows from recursing on j.

The implementation of the Synthesis and Analysis is now straightforward and consists of two phases. Note that it only uses the the neighborhoods A, B, and C, which are the easier ones to implement.

Analysis_Stage_I: Calculate the $\gamma_{j,m}$ as follows (using (6)):

$$\forall m \in M(j) : \gamma_{j,m} := \lambda_{j+1,m} - 1/2 \sum_{k \in A(j,m)} \lambda_{j+1,k} -$$
$$1/8 \sum_{k \in B(j,m)} \lambda_{j+1,k} + 1/16 \sum_{k \in C(j,m)} \lambda_{j+1,k} .$$

Analysis_Stage_II: Calculate the $\lambda_{j,k}$ using the $\gamma_{j,m}$ from Stage I (using (8)):

$$\forall k \in K(j) : \lambda_{j,k} = \lambda_{j+1,k}$$
$$\forall m \in M(j) : \forall k \in A(j,m) : \lambda_{j,k} += s_{j,k,m} \gamma_{j,m} .$$

Synthesis_Stage_I: Calculate the $\lambda_{j+1,k}$:

$$\forall k \in K(j) : \lambda_{j+1,k} = \lambda_{j,k}$$
$$\forall m \in M(j) : \forall k \in A(j,m) : \lambda_{j+1,k} -= s_{j,k,m} \gamma_{j,m} .$$

Synthesis_Stage_II: Calculate the $\lambda_{j+1,m}$ using the $\lambda_{j+1,k}$ from Stage I:

$$\forall m \in M(j) : \lambda_{j+1,m} := \gamma_{j,m} + 1/2 \sum_{k \in A(j,m)} \lambda_{j+1,k} +$$
$$1/8 \sum_{k \in B(j,m)} \lambda_{j+1,k} - 1/16 \sum_{k \in C(j,m)} \lambda_{j+1,k} .$$

It it immediately clear that Synthesis is the inverse of Analysis. This is one of the advantages of the lifting scheme. The wavelets constructed here fall in the class of biorthogonal wavelets. If so wanted, one can use the lifting scheme to construct the dual scaling functions and wavelets. For the analysis in this paper, the dual functions are not needed and one can derive the transform by simply making use of the interpolating properties of the scaling functions.

2.6 Calculation of the Integrals

In order to find the coefficients $s_{j,k,m}$, one needs to calculate the integrals $I_{j,k}$ of the scaling functions. This again can be done in a recursive fashion. At the finest level they are approximated with a quadrature formula. Usually, a simple one point quadrature is sufficient. Going from level $j + 1$ to level j is accomplished with the following algorithm:

```
Calculate_Integrals:
```
$$\forall k \in K(j) \,:\, I_{j,k} := I_{j+1,k}$$

$$\forall m \in M(j) \,:\, \begin{cases} \forall k \in A(j,m) \,:\, I_{j,k} \mathrel{+}= 1/2\,I_{j+1,m} \\ \forall k \in B(j,m) \,:\, I_{j,k} \mathrel{+}= 1/8\,I_{j+1,m} \\ \forall k \in C(j,m) \,:\, I_{j,k} \mathrel{-}= 1/16\,I_{j+1,m} \end{cases}$$

This construction ensures that for all levels j the integral of $\sum_{k \in K(j)} \lambda_{j,k}\,\varphi_{j,k}$ is the same.

3 Operators in Wavelet Bases

Consider the computational aspect of applying some linear operator $\mathcal{T}$ to a given function. This is easiest when we can find the eigenfunctions of the operator. For in the basis formed by the eigenfunctions the operator itself becomes diagonal. The cost lies mostly in the transformation back and forth to the eigenfunctions.

The typical example of an operator which is diagonal in space is multiplication with a function. Examples of operators which are diagonal in frequency are convolution (multiplication in the frequency domain), integration and differentiation (multiplication with or division by a monomial), fractional integration and differentiation (multiplication with an algebraic function). The latter relies on the fact that exponentials are eigenfunctions of a differential operator. These operators are used frequently for image processing. One can think of fractional integration as a smoothing operator and of fractional differentiation as an enhancement operator.

Obviously spatially local operators do not need a basis transform. They can be applied directly in the spatial domain. On the other hand, operators which are local in the frequency domain are calculated using the Fourier transform. This picture changes for more general operators. In that case it becomes computationally too expensive to find the eigenfunctions (typically this requires an $O(n^3)$ algorithm).

Wavelets with their support being local in both space and frequency can provide a straightforward and rapidly computable, but at times crude, approximation of more general operators. Localization in space arises from their compact support, while localization in frequency is due to vanishing moments and smoothness. This means that, roughly speaking, wavelets are *approximate eigenfunctions* to operators which exhibit some locality in both space and frequency. A typical example are integral operators whose kernels die off at a particular rate, so-called Calderón-Zygmund operators.

An example from the area of image processing might be an operator which does smoothing or enhancement in different spatial locations. Those operators are typically almost diagonal in the wavelet basis. By only considering the diagonal elements after transformation to the wavelet basis, one can rapidly find a crude approximation to the operator. In many cases, e.g., image processing, this is good enough. Indeed, in those cases the issue is not so much the perfect computation of, for example, the derivative of the given function. Rather, differentiation is pursued since it leads to enhancement. In such cases an approximation of differentiation suffices.

More generally, in numerical analysis applications, one can often use approximate inverses of operators in iterative schemes that converge to the true inverse or one can use them to build inexpensive preconditioners. For historical reasons, it is interesting to point out that people working in abstract mathematics and harmonic analysis already realized some of this in the sixties and at the same time anticipated wavelet-like basis functions. When wavelets came about in the eighties, they provided the perfect computational framework for these ideas. This accounts for part of their immediate success.

Let us go into a little more detail for the case of differentiation. To begin with, consider the classical case where the wavelets are formed by translates and dilates of one "mother" wavelet $\psi(x)$, $\psi_{j,m}(x) = \psi(2^j x - m)$. Now assume that $D\,\psi(x) \approx \psi(x)$. Note that this approximation has to be thought of as very crude. It says nothing more than that a wavelet is a smooth, local "wiggle", and so is its derivative. This now implies that the derivative of a function in the wavelet basis can be approximated as

$$D \sum_{j,m} \gamma_{j,m}\,\psi_{j,m} \approx \sum_{j,m} 2^j\,\gamma_{j,m}\,\psi_{j,m}\,.$$

The approximate derivative in the wavelet basis is thus simply a multiplication with powers of two. Conversely, approximate integration is a multiplication with 2^{-j}. Fractional differentiation and integration would be multiplication with $2^{\pm j\alpha}$. Now assume that we would like to calculate an operator which smoothes in one particular area while performing an enhancement in another area. This would simply result in multiplying the coefficients of the wavelets, whose center of support lies in the former area with a negative power, and the ones whose support lies in the latter area with a positive power. Any number of hybrid schemes can be derived depending on the application.

Spherical wavelets are not formed as translates and dilates of one particular function. In fact they are a typical example of so-called "second generation wavelets" [17]. The idea behind this development is precisely to give up the translation and dilation structure of wavelets, without compromising on the desirable aspects such as localization and fast transforms. This allows construction of wavelets in much more general settings.

For the approximate calculation of operators in this more general context a similar reasoning can be applied. Therefore we consider operators $\mathcal{T}_\beta$ of the form

$$\mathcal{T}_\beta \left(\sum_{j,m} \gamma_{j,m}\,\psi_{j,m} \right) = \sum_{j,m} \beta^{j+1}\,\gamma_{j,m}\,\psi_{j,m}\,.$$

These smooth out if $\beta < 1$ and enhance if $\beta > 1$, and always leave the scaling functions on the coarsest level ($\varphi_{0,k} = \psi_{-1,k}$) untouched. More advanced operators with space and frequency localization can be built by letting β be space dependent. Since the wavelets with $j \geqslant 0$ are constructed to have a vanishing moment, it immediately follows that

$$\int_{S^2} \mathcal{T}_\beta\, f\, d\omega = \int_{S^2} f\, d\omega\,.$$

This insures a desirable property in image processing: the overall brightness of an image is invariant under enhancement and smoothing.

4 Spherical Textures

In this section we consider concrete examples of spherical texture processing and present results achieved with our implementation applying some of the ideas described above. All computations were performed with the lifted Butterfly basis on a spherical icosahedral base mesh subdivided $n = 8$ levels, yielding $10 \cdot 4^8 + 2$ vertices on $20 \cdot 4^8$ triangles. Environment mapping images were ray traced while the texture mapping images were rendered with RenderMan.

4.1 Environment Mapping

A common technique employed in the rendering of highly reflective objects is the use of an environment map [2]. In this technique the radiance reflected across a mirror like surface in the direction of the viewer is approximated by a table lookup in a texture map. The texture map corresponds to a sphere at infinity, giving the incoming radiance as a function of direction. While being only an approximation, which for example, fails with respect to objects close to the reflecting object, impressive effects can be achieved with it. The use of environment maps exhibits the classical tradeoff between computation time and fidelity. Efficiency is bought at the expense of sometimes gross simplification which is deemed acceptable so long as the results are still plausible.

An environment map is typically given as a cubic map, i.e., as six faces of a cube. Since the reflection vector is used as an index into these maps they are effectively point sampled. As with all point sampling techniques care must be taken to avoid aliasing artifacts. Greene [9] suggested the use of MIP maps [19] on each face of the cubic map. The basic idea of a MIP map is to build an image pyramid by recursive averaging over 4 neighboring pixels. Readers familiar with wavelets can think of it as a Haar transform (with only the low pass and not the high pass filters). Filtering each face of the cube separately, however, leads to obvious artifacts at the cube face boundaries. The problems are exacerbated by the fact that proper filtering of a cubic map implies spatially variant filtering, since the desired filter is a function of the distortion between the sphere of directions and its cubic projection. To address this problem, Greene and Heckbert [10] proposed the use of weighted elliptical average filters. They did not, however, use prefiltered environment maps but instead computed each convolution directly. For small filter kernels this is acceptable, but for large filter geometries the performance can degrade quickly and one of the goals of using environment maps, speed, is compromised.

Another application of appropriately filtered environment maps is the approximation of glossy (or mixed diffuse and directional) reflection as pointed out by Greene [9]. Assume a BRDF which is centered around the mirror direction with a symmetric fall-off away from it. Integrating such a BRDF against the environment map is equivalent to the convolution of the map with an appropriately shaped filter. For simple reflection models these convolutions can be precomputed, in effect resulting in an appropriately smoothed environment map. Greene [9, Figure 8] demonstrated this idea for smooth transitions between mirror reflection and diffuse reflection.

The basic task of prefiltering texture maps has received much attention in computer graphics. Examples include MIP mapping [19], filtering by repeated integration [11], summed area tables [3], and decomposition into basis functions [8]. All of these techniques were designed for the processing of *planar* textures.

The main difficulty in applying these techniques to environment maps is that we seek to filter a spherical map, not a planar one. Any mapping from the sphere onto the plane will yield large distortions, e.g., at the poles. Consequently correct filtering implies grossly distorted filter footprints. What is needed instead is a preprocess which filters the original spherical map on a sphere. Typically, this is done for a sequence of increasingly larger filter sizes, not unlike a MIP map. For convenience these filtered maps can then be resampled onto cubic environment maps at appropriate resolution yielding the desired successively smoothed versions of the original map without artifacts introduced by the mapping onto the faces of a cube.

One way to compute these successively smoothed versions is through the use of spherical harmonics. Given an expansion of the texture in terms of spherical harmonics smoothing and enhancement can be applied by proper scaling of the coefficients. However, a number of difficulties are associated with the use of spherical harmonics. Due to their global spatial support they require many high order coefficients to adequately represent sharp features. This also accounts for the high cost of computing expansions of functions in spherical harmonics. Specifically, every sample contributes to every basis function, requiring work which is approximately quadratic in the number of samples. Furthermore application of spatially varying operators would be very difficult.

We have processed an environment map using the ideas of Section 3. In order to visualize the entire environment map we have computed images of the environment reflected in a sphere. This in effect shows the entire map including extreme distortion around the silhouette of the reflective sphere. The original map is shown on the left of the top row in Figure 5. To its right is an enhanced version with $\beta = 1.5$. Note the increased contrast overall and the enhancement of detail in the floor and ceiling. On the right of the top row is an extreme enhancement of $\beta = 2.0$, which brings out much of the noise in the original texture, as one would expect. All images in the top row reflect the processed environment off a perfectly specular sphere. The images in the second row show the simulation of the transition from mirror reflection to diffuse. The model is a mixed model of diffuse plus blurred specular, $(1 - \beta)T_0 + \beta T_\beta$, with $\beta = 0.75$, $\beta = 0.5, \beta = 0$ (left to right).

4.2 Localized Processing of Textures

To demonstrate the ideas of the local processing of spherical textures we chose a topography/bathymetry data set (ETOPO5) obtained from the NOAA. It gives the height/depth in meters from 0 for the earth. The resolution of the original data set is 5 arc minutes. Due to its large size we first resampled it to 10 arc minutes. A piecewise linear pseudo coloring of the data set is shown on the bottom left of the color plate 5. Note that the height displacements are grossly exaggerated for visualization purposes.

Now consider the following task: Smooth the texture but insure that all coastlines are perfectly reconstructed. This implies that smoothing can only occur away from coastlines. High spatial frequencies can be attenuated already a small distance from a coastline, while low spatial frequencies can only be attenuated at further distances. Coastlines were defined as the zero level set of the original texture ± 20m (each triangle at level $n = 8$ has an approximate edge length of 26km).

The basic idea is to split the set of indices $\{(j, m) \mid -1 \leqslant j \leqslant n, \, m \in M(j)\}$ into two disjoint sets: U for the ones that stay untouched and T for the ones that can be touched. The operator we use is diagonal in the wavelet basis and looks like

$$\mathcal{T}_\beta \left(\sum_{(j,m) \in T \cup U} \gamma_{j,m} \, \psi_{j,m} \right) = \sum_{(j,m) \in U} \gamma_{j,m} \, \psi_{j,m} + \sum_{(j,m) \in T} \beta^{j+\frac{1}{2}} \, \gamma_{j,m} \, \psi_{j,m}.$$

The question now is how to find the sets T and U. The idea is the following: first flag all finest level vertices which are close to the coastlines. Call this set $\{s_{n,k} \mid k \in K(n), (n, k) \in F\}$. We use the following rule to find F: if for a certain vertex $s_{n,k}$ the sign of the given data is different at any of its immediate neighbors, or if the absolute value of the data is below 20 meters, then $(n, k) \in F$. The set U now can be found by a recursive algorithm just like Analysis, observing that a coarser level basis is in U if any of the bases in its refinement relation are in U. This construction assures that

$$\forall (n, k) \in F \, : \, \mathcal{T}_\beta f(s_{n,k}) = f(s_{n,k}),$$

meaning none of the coastlines will have been altered after processing.

The middle image of the third row in Figure 5 shows all triangles at the finest level (green and blue) which intersect the zero contour, i.e., all triangles whose vertices $s_{n,k}$ have $(n, k) \in F$. Approximately $40,000$ of the vertices (6.1%) fall into this category. Next we determine all wavelets at all levels whose support overlaps the coastline. Their centers, i.e., the $s_{j,m}$ with $(j, m) \in U$, are shown on the right of the third row in Figure 5. The image demonstrates how the density of basis functions which overlap the coastlines decreases with distance from the coastline. Approximately $142\,000$ (22%) of all basis functions have support which overlaps some coastline. Note for example that in the Mediterranean most basis functions overlap some coastline. In fact all basis functions at levels $0 - 3$ overlap coastlines somewhere in their respective supports. Any processing must leave these basis functions unchanged to ensure perfect reconstruction of the coastlines.

The fourth row of Figure 5 shows the unprocessed texture (left) followed by a smoothed version ($\beta = 0.75$). Note how the interior of continents and the bottom of the Atlantic are smoothed out while coastlines are preserved in all their details. This kind of processing would be very difficult to achieve in any non-local scheme. The last image on the fourth row is a rendering of a "soccer-trophy" put (appropriately) in a bar scene. It is a metal sphere that represents the earth; the continents are perfect mirrors and the oceans are mate.

5 Summary and Discussion

We have shown how spherical wavelets can be used to facilitate common texture processing tasks such as smoothing and sharpening for textures which are inherently defined on the sphere. The examples considered the case of a texture defined over a set of directions (environment mapping) and a texture defined over a spherical body (earth topography/bathymetry). Transforming a texture from its nodal representation to the wavelet basis is a linear operation in the resolution of the texture. After this step both smoothing and sharpening operators can be efficiently applied pointwise. The inverse transform then yields the desired result. The local support property of wavelets allows us to apply smoothing or enhancement operators in complex, spatially varying ways.

We have only scratched the surface of the possible texture processing tasks one might perform. It is hoped that the availability of this basic spherical technology will lead to many other applications. Possible future work includes more accurate approximations of BRDFs such as those proposed by Schlick [14] by a sequence of preprocessed environment maps, in effect expressing them as small linear combinations of appropriately shaped filters. Another direction would be segmentation based on wavelet probing [1] as might be useful in satellite based remote sensing.

Acknowledgment

Special thanks to Paul Haeberli of SGI for suggesting environment map processing as an application area of spherical wavelets. Paul Haeberli also provided environment maps and ray tracing software which were used to produce some of the examples described.

The first author was supported by DEPSCoR grant N00014-94-1-1163. The second author was supported by NSF EPSCoR grant OSR-9108 772-004 and ARPA grant AFOSR F49620-93-1-0083. He is also Senior Research Assistant of the National Fund of Scientific Research Belgium (NFWO). Other support came from Pixar Inc. and

DURIP/ONR grant N00014-94-1-0299.

References

1. ANDERSSON, L., HALL, N., JAWERTH, B., AND PETERS, G. Wavelets on closed subsets of the real line. In [16]. pp. 1-61.
2. BLINN, J., AND NEWELL, M. Texture and Reflection in Computer Generated Images. *Communications of the ACM 19*, 10 (October 1976), 542-547.
3. CROW, F. Summed-Area Tables for Texture Mapping. *Computer Graphics (SIG-GRAPH '84 Proceedings)*, Vol. 18, No. 3, pp. 207-212, July 1984.
4. DEVORE, R. A., JAWERTH, B., AND LUCIER, B. J. Image compression through wavelet transform coding. *IEEE Trans. Inform. Theory 38*, 2 (1992), 719-746.
5. DONOHO, D. L., AND JOHNSTONE, I. M. Ideal spatial adaptation via wavelet shrinkage. *Biometrika to appear* (1994).
6. DUTTON, G. Locational Properties of Quaternary Triangular Meshes. In *Proceedings of the Fourth International Symposium on Spatial Data Handling*, 901-910, July 1990.
7. DYN, N., LEVIN, D., AND GREGORY, J. A Butterfly Subdivision Scheme for Surface Interpolation with Tension Control. *Transactions on Graphics 9*, 2 (April 1990), 160-169.
8. FOURNIER, A., AND FIUME, E. Constant-Time Filtering with Space-Variant Kernels. *Computer Graphics (SIGGRAPH '88 Proceedings)*, Vol. 22, No. 4, pp. 229-238, August 1988.
9. GREENE, N. Environment Mapping and Other Applications of World Projections. *IEEE Computer Graphics and Applications 6*, 11 (November 1986), 21-29.
10. GREENE, N., AND HECKBERT, P. S. Creating Raster Omnimax Images from Multiple Perspectives Views using the Elliptical Weighted Average Filter. *IEEE Computer Graphics and Applications 6*, 6 (June 1986), 21-27.
11. HECKBERT, P. Filtering by Repeated Integration. *Computer Graphics (SIGGRAPH '86 Proceedings)*, Vol. 20, No. 4, pp. 315-321, August 1986.
12. MALLAT, S., AND ZHONG, S. Characterization of Signals from Multiscale Edges. *IEEE Trans. Patt. Anal. Mach. Intell. 14* (1992), 710-732.
13. MALLAT, S. G. Multifrequency Channel Decompositions of Images and Wavelet Models. *IEEE Trans. Acoust. Speech Signal Process. 37*, 12 (1989), 2091-2110.
14. SCHLICK, C. A customizable reflectance model for everyday rendering. In *Fourth Eurographics Workshop on Rendering*, 73-83, June 1993.
15. SCHRÖDER, P., AND SWELDENS, W. Spherical wavelets: Efficiently representing functions on the sphere. *Computer Graphics, (SIGGRAPH '95 Proceedings)* (1995).
16. SCHUMAKER, L. L., AND WEBB, G., Eds. *Recent Advances in Wavelet Analysis*. Academic Press, New York, 1993.
17. SWELDENS, W. The lifting scheme: A construction of second generation wavelets. Department of Mathematics, University of South Carolina.
18. SWELDENS, W. The lifting scheme: A custom-design construction of biorthogonal wavelets. Tech. Rep. 1994:7, Industrial Mathematics Initiative, Department of Mathematics, University of South Carolina, 1994. (ftp://ftp.math.scarolina.edu/pub/imi_94/imi94_7.ps).
19. WILLIAMS, L. Pyramidal Parametrics. *Computer Graphics (SIGGRAPH '83 Proceedings)*, Vol. 17, No. 3, pp. 1-11, July 1983.

Editors' Note: see Appendix, p. 371 for colored figures of this paper

Integration Methods for Galerkin Radiosity Couplings

Reid Gershbein

Department of Computer Science, Princeton University

Abstract

Computing energy transfer between objects is the most expensive operation in radiosity systems. This energy transfer operation, known as the irradiance operator, is an integral that, in general, must be calculated numerically. We perform a study of numerical integration techniques to increase the speed of this computation without severely compromising fidelity. A theoretical discussion of numerical integration is presented followed by details of the studied methods. The results of our study give us insight into greatly reducing the cost of the irradiance operator while maintaining accuracy. An adaptive method for choosing Gauss quadrature rules is presented, and our performance analysis of the new adaptive algorithm shows that it can be up to 10 times faster than previous methods.

1 Introduction

The radiosity equation can be written as a simplification of the rendering equation, introduced by Kajiya [8], by assuming that all surfaces are perfectly diffuse (Lambertian):

$$B(x) = B^e(x) + \rho(x) \int dA_{x'} G(x, x') \pi^{-1} B(x')$$

$B(x)$ is the radiosity at point x, consisting of emitted and reflected radiosity, $\rho(x)$ is the reflectance, and $G(x, x') = \frac{cos\theta_x cos\theta_{x'}}{\|x-x'\|^2} V(x, x')$ characterizes the radiant coupling between points x and x'. G accounts for relative surface orientation, distance, and visibility ($V = 0$ or $V = 1$, depending on whether x can or cannot see x'). The integral is taken over the hemisphere about x and represents the amount of energy per unit area received from other surfaces, thus computing irradiance.

Radiosity algorithms are usually based on finite element methods. It is assumed that all functions will be represented in the chosen orthonormal basis $\{M_i\}_{i=1,\ldots,n}$. The linear system is

$$B_i = B_i^e + \sum_{j=1}^{n} K_{ij} B_j$$

$$K_{ij} = \int dA_x \int dA_{x'} \rho(x) G(x, x') \pi^{-1} M_i(x) M_j(x') \tag{1}$$

B_i is coefficient of the radiosity projection onto the basis, B_i^e is the emission function's projection, and K_{ij} is the global irradiance projection. Here, we consider $\rho(x)$ to be constant since it can be removed from the global irradiance integral K_{ij} and applied locally as shown by Gershbein et al. [3]. The computation of K_{ij} is by far the most expensive operation of any radiosity system.

There have been many studies of finite-element methods for radiosity [4, 1, 6, 7, 19, 20, 5, 12, 15], and the irradiance projection. A survey of methods for computing the irradiance integral for a constant basis (called the form factor) is discussed by Cohen and Wallace [2]. For non-constant bases, the methods of choice have been Gauss quadrature product rules, except when there are singularities in the kernel [20, 19, 5, 13, 11].

In a hierarchical Galerkin radiosity system, a subdivision strategy is invoked so that each K_{ij} has the same amount of error. When a degree N basis is used, this strategy tries to make the kernel $G(x, x')$ close to a degree N polynomial and the integrand in (1) is at most a degree $2N$ polynomial along each axis since it is simply the product of a basis function and G. This assumption about $G(x, x')$ is not valid when there is a change in visibility, but the subdivision tries to resolve this problem. Previously, the computation of K_{ij} for an order N basis used $(N+1)^4$ kernel evaluations. The locations and weights of these evaluations were derived from Gauss quadrature rules.

We explore the efficiency of the computation of the irradiance integral by studying a number of quadrature methods. First, we establish a framework for our study through a brief discussion of numerical integration theory. The theoretical merits of different methods are presented and a number of tests are conducted to evaluate their performance on the irradiance integral. Based on these results we construct an adaptive method for choosing Gauss-Legendre quadrature rules and discuss its performance, which can result in a factor of ten speedup.

2 Numerical Integration Theory

2.1 Numerical Integration With One Variable

A quadrature rule is any numerical method that approximates the integration of a single variable function, $f(x)$. We look at quadrature rules that evaluate the function at a finite set of points. These quadrature rules have the following form

$$\int dx\, w(x) f(x) = \sum_{i=1}^{N} C_i f(x_i) + Error \qquad (2)$$

where $w(x)$ is a weight function, the points $\{x_i\}_{i=0,\dots,N}$ are the quadrature points at which we evaluate the function, $\{C_i\}_{i=0,\dots,N}$ are the quadrature weights, and error value necessary for to get the correct value of the integral.

If we look at deterministically generated points and weights, a criteria for judging the methods is needed. Typically, this criteria is given in terms of the maximum-degree polynomial the quadrature rule will exactly integrate. We are looking for the cheapest way of evaluating these integrals. Based on this, Gauss integration rules are the best. An N point Gauss rule will exactly integrate polynomials of up to degree $2N - 1$. As stated in [16], Gauss quadrature rules compared to methods such as Newton-Cotes and extrapolation yield the most accurate results for the same amount of computation.

When generating points and weights stochastically the error term for a given $f(x)$ and $w(x)$ will be in a range of values, occuring with some probability distribution. In designing Monte Carlo quadratures, most effort is spent reducing the error through techniques such as stratified sampling and importance sampling to reduce variance [9].

2.2 Multi-Variate Numerical Integration

The multiple variable version of a quadrature rule is a cubature rule. For a function of M variables

$$\int \ldots \int dx_1 \ldots dx_m w(x_1, \ldots, x_m) f(x_1, \ldots, x_m) = \sum_{i=1}^{N} C_i f(x_1, \ldots, x_m) + Error$$
(3)

For deterministic cubature rules we can require a maximum-degree polynomial exactness criteria to judge our rules as we did with quadratures. A detailed account of such rules can be found in [17] and we now present an abridged discussion of the topic.

A cubature rule in the form (3) has degree d if it is exact for all polynomials in $x_1, \ldots, x_m$ whose exponents sum to $\leq d$. If a cubature rule is of degree d there exists a monomial of degree $d + 1$ for which the rule is not exact. This definition has a subtlety that will be important when we look at *product* and *non-product* rules in the following discussion. A cubature rule may be of degree d and additionally be exact for all polynomials that have exponents whose sum is greater than d but has no single exponent greater than d.

Usually, the first step is to take the tensor product of single variable rules. These define a class of cubature rules called product rules. It is not necessary to use the same rule for each variable of the domain and if we choose to do this we reduce the degree of exactness of the formula to that of the lowest degree rule. If we know that the degree of the function in certain variables will be less than others then this is exactly what we want to do. This will be the main property we exploit in our adaptive quadrature approach.

Non-product cubature rules also exist. It is possible to create a rule of degree N that has the advantage of not being exponential in the number of variables being integrated. For example if we look at the 4-D radiosity case, there exists a degree 3 non-product rule that has 8 points versus the degree 3 Gauss product rule which has 16.

Monte Carlo methods can also be extended to multiple integrals in a straightforward manner. We simply define a probability distribution function (PDF) $p(x_1, \ldots, x_m)$ over multiple variables. Once again this error term is a random variable. If the choice of a value for each variable is independent of all other variables, our PDF $p(x_1, \ldots, x_m)$ is the product of the set of single variable PDFs. This is a useful property because it simplifies the process of probabilistically chosing the values of the variables.

3 Intergration Methods Study

All of the methods described in the paper have positive weights and points in the integration domain. These methods typically have less error than methods that have some negative weights and/or have points outside the integration domain [17]. The numerical integration methods we have studied can be broken down into three main categories: Gauss product rules, non-product Rules, and Monte Carlo methods. The goal was integration methods with fewer quadrature points than Gaussian product rules.

3.1 Gauss Product Rules

Univariate Gaussian quadrature rules can integrate degree $\leq 2N - 1$ functions with N function evaluations, which is fewer evaluations than other methods. Multivariate

Gauss product rules are constructed through the tensor product of univariate rules. We exclusively studied Gauss-Legendre quadrature rules since they have been the most commonly used method when determining the non-singular irradiance integral we are studying, though other Gauss rules can be considered. The irradiance integral is 4-dimensional, two variables on the source surface and two on the receiver, so we may construct a product rule from four different univariate rules.

Previously, when a degree N basis was used a degree $2N - 1$ Gauss rule, $N + 1$ quadrature points, was used for each variable resulting in $(N+1)^4$ total points. We call this the $FullGauss$ method. Noting that often the source's higher order basis functions have small coefficients, we test Gauss product rules that assume that their contribution is negligible. The rule $ConstSrcGauss$ (constant source) uses 1-point rules on the source and $N+1$ point rules on the receiver resulting in $(N+1)^2$ total points. This rule exactly integrates polynomials of degree $2N - 1$ over each of the receiver's variables. The second is $LinSrcGauss$ (linear source) which uses an 2-point rule for each variable on the source and an $N+1$ rule for each variable on the receiver: $(4*(N+1)^2)$ total points. Similar to $ConstSrcGauss$, this method exactly integrates polynomials up to degree $2N - 1$ on the receiver. We always use an $N + 1$ point rule on the receiver because we assume that all the coefficients of receiver's basis functions are significant. This assumption is made because, essentially, these are the coefficients we are computing.

3.2 Non-Product Rules

There exist fixed point cubature rules that can be classified as degree N and not be exponential in the dimension of the integral. For a given basis, we test a number of these rules that are of the same degree as the $FullGauss$ rule and have fewer function evaluations.

The non-products methods tested are presented by Stroud [17] and our experiments used linear and quadratic bases. In the linear case, $FullGauss$ is degree 3 and uses 16 function evaluations ($N = 2$, 2^4). The non-product methods that had the least error were $StroudN + 1$, a degree 2 rule that had 5 kernel evaluations (Stroud's C_n 2-1), and $Stroud2N$, a degree 3 rule that had 8 kernel evaluations (Stroud's C_n 3-1). In the quadratic case, $FullGauss$ is degree 5 and used 81 function evaluations (3^4). The best performing non-product rules were $Stroud65$, a degree 5 rule with 65 function evaluations (Stroud's C_n 5-7), and $HierStroud$, which is created by stratifying the receiver's domain into 4 regions, applying $Stroud2N$ to each, and taking the sum.

3.3 Monte Carlo Methods

Monte Carlo integration techniques' error and performance can not be classified in the same way as fixed point rules because they are stochastic. We tested Monte Carlo methods with the same number of samples as the $FullGauss$ rules with uniform, N-Rook [14], and Stratified PDFs. We only show the results of the stratified sampling method, $Stratified$, because it reduces variance most and generally has the smallest error. The $Stratified$ methods for an degree N basis breaks each variable domain into $N + 1$ regions and perform one function evaluation in each of the $(N + 1)^4$ regions from randomly chosen point.

4 Experiments

4.1 Error Metric

We compute the irradiance integral in a variety of situations with linear and quadrative multiwavelets and measure the amount of error. Since, in general, no closed form solution of this integral exists for non-constant bases, we compute our estimate of the "true" answer through a stratified Monte Carlo method. We measure the amount of error of a numerical integration method, I, by computing an upper bound on the L_1 norm of the difference error of the radiosity computed by the "true" solution and I. This upper bound is derived as follows. First, we have an approximation of the radiosity function in terms of our orthonormal multiwavelet basis of degree $n+1$. We expand the L_1 norm and derive an upper bound. This upper bound can be computed by taking the differences of the coefficients of the individual basis functions and is defined as follows:

$$\int dx \mid (b_1 B_1(x) + \ldots b_n B_n(x)) - (\hat{b}_1 B_1(x) + \ldots + \hat{b}_n B_n(x)) \mid$$

$$\leq \mid b_1 - \hat{b}_n \mid (\int dx \mid B_1(x) \mid) + \ldots + \mid b_n - \hat{b}_n \mid (\int dx \mid B_n(x) \mid) \qquad (4)$$

We call this error metric "Abs L1 error".

4.2 Experiment Description

We perform our tests with the Legendre polynomials as our basis, these are a multiwavelet basis. In all of our experiments, we separately measure the contribution from the source's constant, linear, and (when we use a quadratic basis) quadratic Legendre polynomials to the error and assume that their coefficients are 1. In the figures, each method has a cost less than or equal to those to the left. Consult Section 3 for the number of quadrature points used in each rule. Each figure's bar's total height represents the total amount of error. The bar's subsections represent the partial contribution of the source's basis functions.

The methods in the first 8 figures are compared against a 160,000 sample stratified Monte Carlo method. Figures 1 and 2 measure the error with two parallel unit area quadrilaterals that are a unit apart. Figures 3 and 4 show two perpendicular unit quadrilaterals that are .25 units away from each other (they were placed .25 units away from each other in order to avoid the singularity). To test partial occlusion, Figures 5 and 6, depict the parallel scenario with an occluding parallel quadrilateral with area .25 square units .25 units away from the source. Figures 7 and 8 have the occluder halfway.

Figures 9 through 12 compare a number of methods in a scenario where subdivision occurs. This scenario uses a BF refinement [6] oracle with visibility criteria based on the Teller-Hanrahan visibility classification [18] and a quadtree subdivison. A unit quadrilateral source is 10 units above a parallel 400 unit receiver. There is a unit occluder halfway between them and it is oriented 45 degree around it's normal in order to go against the quadtree meshing. Figures 9 through 12 show the sum Abs L_1 error in all of the unoccluded or partially occluded links where each link is compared against a 10,000 point stratified Monte Carlo method.

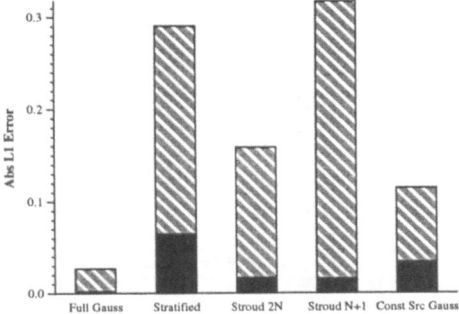

Figure 1: Abs L1 Error: Unoccluded Parallel Quads: Linear Multiwavelets, Solid Grey = Constant Source, Striped Grey = Linear Source

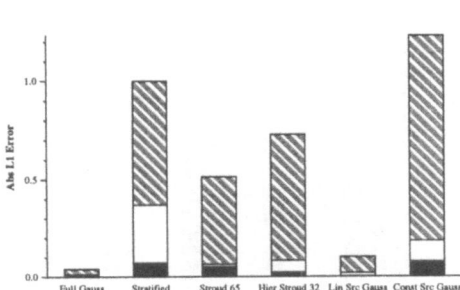

Figure 2: Abs L1 Error: Unoccluded Parallel Quads: Quadratic Multiwavelets, Solid Grey = Constant Source, Solid White = Linear, Striped Grey = Quadratic

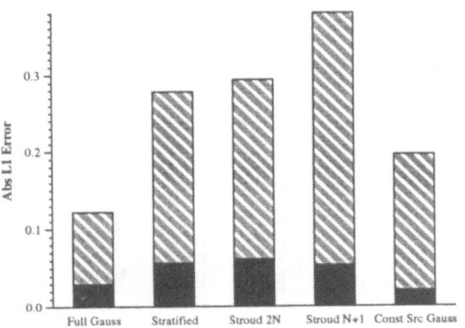

Figure 3: Abs L1 Error: Unoccluded Perpendicular Quads: Linear Multiwavelets

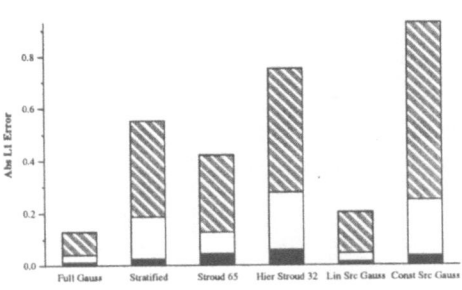

Figure 4: Abs L1 Error: Unoccluded Perpendicular Quads: Quadratic Multiwavelets.

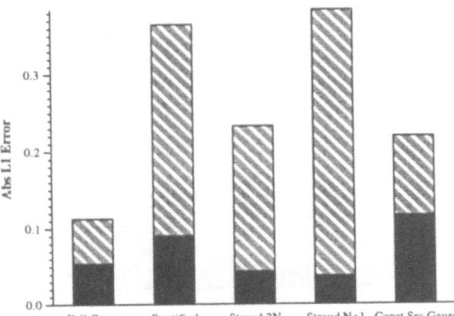

Figure 5: Abs L1 Error: Partially Occluded Parallel Quads, Blocker .25 From Source: Linear Multiwavelets

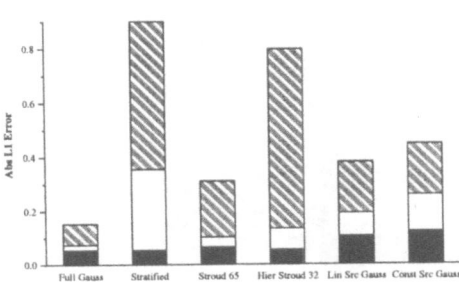

Figure 6: Abs L1 Error: Partially Occluded Parallel Quads, Blocker .25 From Source: Quadratic Multiwavelets

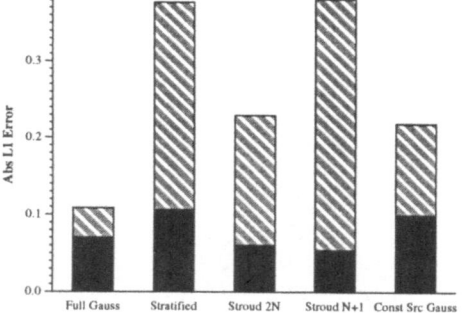

Figure 7: Abs L1 Error: Partially Occluded Parallel Quads, Blocker .5 From Source: Linear Multiwavelets

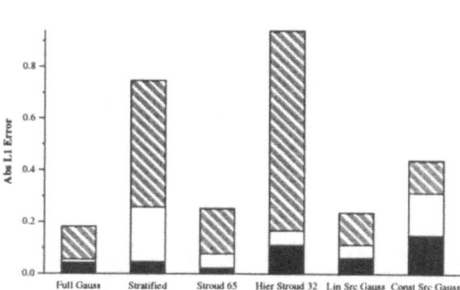

Figure 8: Abs L1 Error: Partially Occluded Parallel Quads, Blocker .5 From Source: Quadratic Multiwavelets

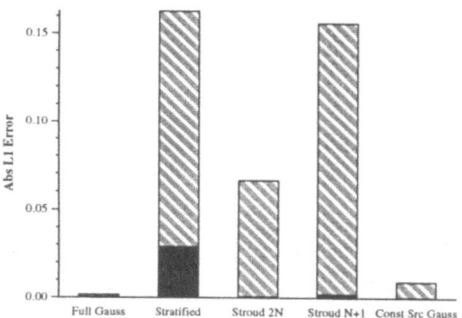

Figure 9: Abs L1 Error - Unoccluded Links: Subdivision Around Occluder : Linear Multiwavelets

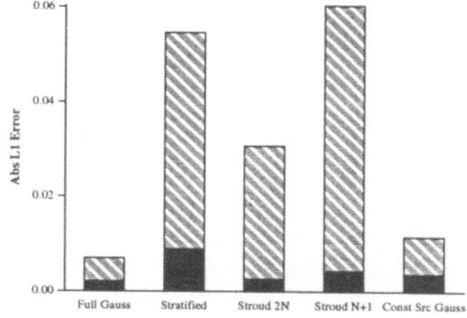

Figure 10: Abs L1 Error - Partially Occluded Links: Subdivision Around Occluder : Linear Multiwavelets

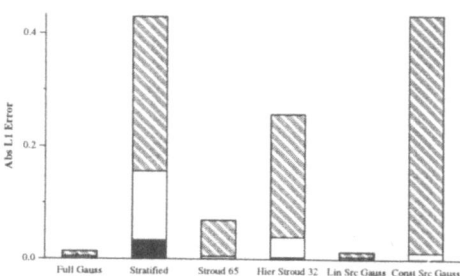

Figure 11: Abs L1 Error - Unoccluded Links: Subdivision Around Occluder : Quadratic Multiwavelets

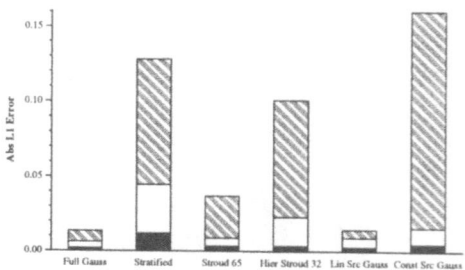

Figure 12: Abs L1 Error - Partially Occluded Links: Subdivision Around Occluder : Linear Multiwavelets

4.3 Experiment Result

Our results show the overall strength of Gauss methods. Predictably, the Gauss methods perform extremely well in the unoccluded scenarios often having comparable amounts of error with fewer quadrature points than other methods. In the linear case, $ConstSrcGauss$ is the least expensive method tested and always outperforms the more expensive non-Gauss rules. In the quadratic case, $LinSrcGauss$ rule has less error than the more expensive non-Gauss rules. Additionally, Gauss methods perform extremely well in the partially occluded scenarios. We find that the variance of the stratified Monte Carlo methods of 16 or 81 points causes so much error that we get better performance from the Gauss rules. The Gauss superiority during partial visibility occurs in the presence of a non-constant basis. When the coupling is partially visible and a constant basis is used the Gauss rules do not outperform the Monte Carlo.

We see more benefits of Gauss rules by looking at the breakdown of error due to the degree of the source's basis function. In the linear case, we can look at the amount of error that the $FullGauss$ methods gives in a specific scenario. By looking at the dark section of the bar we can see which methods give us the the same or less error when the source is constant. Often $ConstSrcGauss$ and the other methods fullfill that property. Similarly, the same can be done for the quadratic case. Now, we can compare error of a source's constant (low black bar) and linear (middle white bar) for a particular method with the total error of $FullGauss$. We see that the $LinSrcGauss$ rule performs quite well when the source is constant or linear. The $ConstSrcGauss$ often performs comparably when the source is constant.

5 Adaptive Algorithm

Based on the above observations, we now present an adaptive way of choosing Gauss quadrature rules that compute the irradiance coupling between basis functions in a hierarchical Galerkin wavelet radiosity system. The magnitudes of the source's basis functions' coefficients and occlusion factors will be used to choose a Gauss quadrature method. The choice of quadrature method is made after we have performed subdivision and have determined that the geometric kernel G is sufficiently smooth. The oracle that makes this decision could be, for example, BF refinement described by Hanrahan et al. [6] or Gortler et al.'s polynomial fitting approximation [5]. The subdivision strategy could be a quadtree subdivison, or discontinuity meshing as presented by Lischinski et al. [10].

Once we have determined the level at which we should compute the irradiance coupling between basis functions, we must choose a quadrature method. This can be done by noting that if M of the highest order basis functions for a variable have very small coefficients, then any integration in the presence of these functions is also small. Therefore, in that variable's domain the basis is essentially of degree $N - M$ instead of degree N and we can use an $(N - M) + 1$ point rule rather than an $N + 1$ point rule. When computing this integral we know the radiosity coefficients of the basis functions of the source. We may take advantage of this fact and use the $(N - M) + 1$ rule along each variable of the source surface (possibly with a different M for each variable, M_0 and M_1) when the coefficients are sufficiently small. This results in $(N - M_0 + 1)(N - M_1 + 1)(N + 1)^2$ kernel evaluations instead of the $(N + 1)^4$

of previous methods. Similar knowledge of the receiver's basis function is not available, so we must assume that it is a higher-frequency function.

We now construct an adaptive algorithm based on this criterion. When the basis is of degree N, we use an $N + 1$ point Gauss rule along each axis of the receiver. We then choose a rule of 1 to $N + 1$ points for each axis of the source based on an error threshold, $ErrThres$, set by the user. The coefficients of the source are checked along one of its axes and we find the highest order basis function, M, that has a coefficient above $ErrThres$. An $M + 1$ point rule is then used along that axis and this process is repeated for the other axis. Finally, tensor products of the source and receiver rules are used evaluate the integral.

There is more error in partially occluded regions and this should be accounted for when choosing a quadrature rule. To reduce this error, when the integral is partially occluded we randomly choose an axis on the source that has fewer than $N+1$ points and increase the number of points along the axis by one. After an iteration of the radiosity solver, we subdivide if necessary and check the coefficients of all couplings to see if we need a better quadrature rule due to the energy gain. This additional test is necessary because the higher order coefficients may now be above the threshold.

We have tried the adaptive algorithm in a range of scenes with linear, quadratic, and cubic multiwavelets. These tests were done with a quadtree subdivision. The subdivision oracle was BF refinement [6] and visibility was determined by Teller and Hanrahan's visibility classification [18]. We find that the speedup is half the theoretical best-case maximum of 4, 9, and 16 times for linear, quadratic, and cubic bases, respectively. This theoretical maximum occurs when you have only constant sources. The images in Plate 1 show a comparision of the fixed point method and the adaptive method using a cubic multiwavelet basis. The rightmost is the fixed point method $FullGauss$. The leftmost image used the adaptive algorithm without accounting for partial visibility and had 12 times fewer kernel evaluations. The center image is the adaptive rule accounting for partial visibility and is 8 times faster than the non-adaptive method.

6 Summary and Conclusion

We have presented a study of numerical integration methods for computing irradiance couplings in Galerkin radiosity systems. An adaptive method for choosing Gauss product rules is constructed and tested due to the fact that Gauss rules performed extremely well in our experiments. This algorithm takes advantage of the characteristics of the source's basis functions and accounts for partial visibility. Typically, our algorithm achieves a speedup of half the theoretical maximum (when all sources are constant) , which can be translate into an order of magnitude or greater speedup over non-adaptive methods.

The study and algorithm should be extended to deal with subdivision strategies and oracles other than quadtree and BF refinement. The error due to the current assumptions of the kernel should be looked at more closely, more numerical integration methods can be explored, and new basis functions tried.

We look optimistically upon extensions of the algorithm for Galerkin radiance systems. The adaptive approach's speedup is proportional to the basis degree and the dimensionality of the integral since more kernel evaluations can be avoided. This situation improves for adaptive approachs applied to the 6-dimensional angularly-dependent radiance case. This is due to the extraordinary amount of samples previously used to compute couplings, $(N + 1)^6$ for a degree N basis.

7 Acknowledgements

I would like to thank Pat Hanrahan for support, discussions, and creating a fruitful environment in which to work. Peter Schröder and Seth Teller created the wavelet radiosity infrastructure upon which this work was developed. Thanks go to Peter Schröder and Don Mitchell for many patient hours of teaching, discussing, stimulating, and befriending. Phil Lacroute saved me with LaTeXsettings. This research was supported by equipment grants from Apple and Silicon Graphics Computer Systems, and a research grant from the National Science Foundation (CCR-9208966).

References

[1] COHEN, M. F., AND GREENBERG, D. P. The hemi-cube: A radiosity solution for complex environments. *Computer Graphics 19*, 3 (July 1985), 31–40.

[2] COHEN, M. F., AND WALLACE, J. R. *Radiosity and Realistic Image Synthesis*. Academic Press Professional, Boston, 1993.

[3] GERSHBEIN, R., SCHRÖDER, P., AND HANRAHAN, P. Textures and radiosity: Controlling emission and reflection with texture maps. In *Computer Graphics 1994* (August 1994), Siggraph, pp. 51–58.

[4] GORAL, C. M., TORRANCE, K. E., GREENBERG, D. P., AND BATTAILE, B. Modelling the interaction of light between diffuse surfaces. *Computer Graphics 18*, 3 (July 1984), 212–222.

[5] GORTLER, S., SCHRÖDER, P., COHEN, M., AND HANRAHAN, P. Wavelet radiosity. In *Computer Graphics 1993* (August 1993), Siggraph, pp. 221–230.

[6] HANRAHAN, P., SALZMAN, D., AND AUPPERLE, L. A rapid hierarchical radiosity algorithm. *Computer Graphics 25*, 4 (July 1991), 197–206.

[7] HECKBERT, P. S. Radiosity in flatland. *Computer Graphics Forum 2*, 3 (1992), 181–192.

[8] KAJIYA, J. T. The rendering equation. *Computer Graphics 20*, 4 (1986), 143–150.

[9] KALOS, M. H., AND WHITLOCK, P. A. *Monte Carlo Methods Volume I: Basics*. Whiley-Interscience, New York, 1986.

[10] LISCHINSKI, D., TAMPIERI, F., AND GREENBERG, D. P. Combining hierarchical radiosity and discontinuity meshing. In *Computer Graphics 1993* (August 1993), Siggraph, pp. 199–208.

[11] SCHRÖDER, P. Numerical integration for radiosity in the presence of singularities. In *Fourth Eurographics Workshop on Rendering* (1993).

[12] SCHRÖDER, P., GORTLER, S. J., COHEN, M. F., AND HANRAHAN, P. Wavelet projections for radiosity. In *Fourth Eurographics Workshop on Rendering* (June 1993), Eurographics, pp. 105–114.

[13] SCHRÖDER, P., AND HANRAHAN, P. On the form factor between two polygons. In *Computer Graphics 1993* (August 1993), Siggraph, pp. 163–164.

[14] SHIRLEY, P. Discrepancy as a quality measure for sampling distributions. In *Eurographics '91* (September 1991), pp. 183–193.

[15] SMITS, B., ARVO, J., AND GREENBURG, D. A clustering algorithm for radiosity in complex environments. In *Computer Graphics 1994* (August 1994), Siggraph, pp. 435–442.

[16] STOER, J., AND BULIRSCH, R. *Introduction to Numerical Analysis*. Springer Verlag, New York, 1980.

[17] STROUD, A. H. *Approximate Calculation of Multiple Integrals*. Prentice-Hall, New Jersey, 1971.

[18] TELLER, S., AND HANRAHAN, P. Global visibility algorithms for illumination computations. In *Computer Graphics 1993* (August 1993), Siggraph, pp. 239–246.

[19] TROUTMAN, R., AND MAX, N. Radiosity algorithms using higher-order finite elements. In *Computer Graphics 1993* (August 1993), Siggraph, pp. 209–212.

[20] ZATZ, H. R. Galerkin radiosity: A higher-order solution method for global illumination. In *Computer Graphics 1993* (August 1993), Siggraph, pp. 213–220.

Editors' Note: see Appendix, p. 361 for colored figures of this paper

Reconstruction of Illumination from Area Luminaires

Steven Collins[1]

ISG, Trinity College Dublin, Ireland

Abstract. This paper is concerned with the efficient reconstruction of illumination from area luminaires. We outline a 2-pass scheme; a light-pass, tracing ray bundles from the luminaires followed by a general eye-pass ray trace phase. Special attention is paid during the first pass to the reconstruction of shadows, both umbral and penumbral regions, for general luminaire geometries with no practical restriction on surface reflectance distributions. In order to minimise computation times, adaptive sampling techniques are used to concentrate effort in regions of high illumination gradients and in particular regions exhibiting discontinuities. Illumination functions are reconstructed from samples in a manner related to adaptive kernel density estimation techniques.

1 Introduction

Recently the illumination from specular surfaces has been separated from other transport mechanisms and dealt with as a pre-processing stage. Arvo [Arv86] traces rays from the light sources and records these rays on surfaces in *illumination maps*. Shirley [Shi90] combines this light-pass with a low resolution zonal radiosity pass and finally a distribution ray tracing eye-pass to compute a final solution. Both approaches suffer from being limited in practise to point light sources, due to noise problems associated with sampling area sources. Heckbert [Hec90] used bidirectional ray tracing and adaptive illumination maps to handle all transport paths at the expense of large *light quad-trees*. More recently, the work of Shirley et al. [Shi95] uses density estimation techniques (in a manner similar to that proposed here) and records illumination as particle hit points with the surfaces.

The method proposed in this paper borrows from previous work; pencil tracing [STN87] and Ray Casting for Radiosity Shadows [Ase92]. We extend our earlier efforts [Col94] which tracked the wavefront from a point light source to allow for wavefront tracking from area sources. Rays are sent from the area source (initially approximating the area source as a point source), and having determined a point of intersection, the intersected object acts as a *shadow/caustic lens*. Each ray has associated with it some $\Delta\Phi_s$, a fraction of the total source power. Having intersected an object, we determine the solid angle through which this energy has arrived and distribute reflected and transmitted rays distributed within the reflected/refracted solid angle. To compute shadows we cast backwards shadow rays which carry *negative power*, $-\Delta\Phi_s$, again distributed within the solid angle. In order to deposit the power on surfaces we use adaptive Gaussian kernels to

---

[1] The author may be contacted at Steven.Collins@cs.tcd.ie or on the web at http://vangogh.cs.tcd.ie/scollins/scollins.html

preserve detail in regions of high frequency illuminance gradients and minimise noise in areas of low gradient (effectively the adaptive kernel density estimation technique [Sil86]). We present an adaptive sampling scheme which is capable of sampling finely in area of sharp shadowing/caustics and coarsely in areas of diffuse reflection and umbral/penumbral shadow regions.

The illuminance stored in the illumination maps is used during a 2nd pass (the *eye pass*), in that rays incident on a surface will extract the radiance estimation from the illumination map, and then according to the BRDF of the surface, specularly reflected/transmitted rays will be fired. Note, however, that no shadow rays are required during this phase of the simulation.

2 Problem Definition

We first define the irradiance on a surface, $E(x)$, in terms of separate transport paths; direct illumination E_d and indirect illumination E_i:

$$E(x) = E_d(x) + E_i(x) = \int_{\Omega_S} L(\omega_s) \cos\theta d\omega_s + \int_{\Omega_{\bar{s}}} L(\omega_{\bar{s}}) \cos\theta d\omega_{\bar{s}} \qquad (1)$$

Ω_S is the set of directions in which the light sources are directly visible and $\Omega_{\bar{s}}$ all other directions[2]. We can further classify E_d as the total irradiance from all light sources less the obstructed irradiance (where S' is the solid angle subtended by the sources, assuming unocclusion):

$$E_d(x) = \int_{\Omega_S'} L(\omega_s) \cos\theta d\omega_s - \int_{\Omega_S'} L(\omega_s)\overline{V(\omega_s)} \cos\theta d\omega_s \qquad (2)$$

The algorithm presented here will assume an un-occluded contribution to each dA from each light source and will then compensate by irradiating dA with negative power to compensate for the $V(\omega_s)$ term in Equation 2. In short, we cast rays from the luminaires, each ray carrying a fraction of the total source power Φ_s/n. Rays hitting surfaces contribute illuminance given by $E \equiv \frac{d\Phi}{dA}$.

Note that using the irradiance quantity in this way resolves the normal dichotomy normally associated with the treatment of point sources[3]. If the power-carrying rays hit a surface we shoot new rays distributed according to the BRDF of the surface to contribute indirect illuminance to other surfaces. However we also fire backwards shadow rays in the direction of the original ray, carrying power $\Phi_r = -\Phi_s/n$. These rays will approximate the occluded irradiance of Equation 2 on surfaces occluded by the initial surface.

The radiance at a point on a surface may now be expressed in terms of these quantities:

---

[2] This assumes that light will not be indirectly reflected from or transmitted through the light sources themselves, in general a reasonable approximation.

[3] For point sources of non-finite dA we must use *radiant intensity* which is related to power by $d\Phi \equiv I(\omega)d\omega$.

$$L(x, \omega') = L_e(x, \omega') + \int_{\Omega - \Omega_S} \rho(x, \omega, \omega') L(\omega) \cos \theta d\omega$$

$$+ \sum_{AllSources} \int_{\Omega_S} \rho(x, \omega_s, \omega') L_s(\omega_s) \cos \theta d\omega_s$$

$$- \sum_{AllSources} \int_{\Omega_S} \rho(x, \omega_s, \omega') L_s(\omega_s) \overline{V(x, \omega_s)} \cos \theta d\omega_s \qquad (3)$$

3 Illumination Storage

To record the shadow and indirect illuminance from luminaires on surfaces we use *illumination maps* in the spirit of [Arv86], in favour of *radiosity textures* [Hec90]. Essentially we represent the illuminance on a surface as a projection onto some function basis B_i:

$$E(x) \approx \hat{E}(x) = \sum_{i=0}^{n-1} e_i B_i(x) \text{ where } e_i = \sum_{x=0}^{X} E(x) B_i(x) \qquad (4)$$

This has the advantage that we can choose arbitrary bases. We currently employ a piecewise linear basis, but are investigating various wavelet bases to provide efficient storage of the illumination maps.

As rays deposit power in the illumination maps cells, the cell accumulates this power in its current total cached power: $\Phi_{old} = \Phi_{new} + \Phi_r$. During the eye-pass, the cached power in a cell of area A is converted to radiance using $L = \frac{\rho_r \Phi}{\pi A}$.

This is based on the assumption that future eye-pass rays will determine the specularly reflected/transmitted radiance and the illumination map stores only the energy that is diffusely reflected (thus $\rho_{BRDF}(\omega, \omega') = \frac{\rho_r}{\pi}$ where ρ_r is now a reflectance quantity).

3.1 Illumination Map Resolution

The resolution of the illumination map is critical, in that too coarse a resolution will filter all detail from the solution, and too fine a resolution will incur memory overheads, and introduce aliasing problems. We can guide the resolution determination either

(a) by using view dependent information and setting the resolution proportion to the projected area of the surface on the viewing plane [Hec90] or

(b) using a view independent scheme where resolution is adaptively chosen according to the illuminance gradients on the surface [Col94].

In our current implementation we adopt a view dependent approach, and choose a resolution $R_x = R_y = 2^n$ where n is chosen so that $A_{map} \approx \frac{A_{pix}}{2}$ where A_{map} is the area of an illumination map pixel projected into screen space and A_{pix} the area of a pixel in screen space.

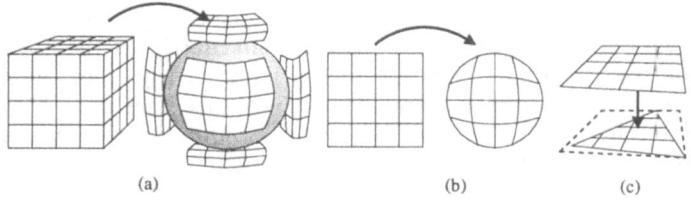

Fig. 1. Various approximately area-preserving parameter space mappings. (a) shows the cubic mapping onto a sphere, (b) an inverse radial stretch mapping a square to a disc and (c) a parallel projection for polygonal elements.

3.2 (u, v) Mapping

Illumination maps are defined with respect to parameter space (u, v) where $u \times v \subset \Re^2$. This mapping from parameter space to object space is not necessarily linear, and in fact rarely is. As a result, illumination map pixel area is not preserved and thus the radiance estimate will be skewed (for example near the poles in a spherical mapping). To counter this, primitive objects must have associated with them a mapping that is, or approximates, an area preserving mapping. To this end we use a cubic projection method for spheres, parallel projection for polygonal elements and *inverse radial stretch* of a square to a circle for discs (used as caps in solid cylinders). These mappings are shown in Figure 1. This highlights one of the main deficiencies of the approach. Ideally, we would like to store illuminance in an object independent fashion, perhaps volumetrically as in [War92]. This is currently under investigation.

4 Wavefront Tracking

Central to the algorithm is the tracking of rays from the luminaires into the environment. If the power associated with a ray is deposited as a single point in the illumination maps then, to minimise noise, we must shoot many rays or alternatively increase the size of the illumination map pixels. However, by associating each ray with a differential solid angle, $d\omega$ of the source, and through tracking the convergence/divergence of this $d\omega$ we can determine an *area of influence* for the ray when it hits a surface (ie: the area over which the power associated with the ray must be spread). Previous attempts to track the wavefront in such a way [Col94] required the use of expensive ray-tree caches, recording the intersection of each ray in the tree and correlating between neighbouring rays to determine a *spread factor*. As the ray tree increased in depth, the storage costs associated with this cache became prohibitive.

We propose a new approach to wavefront tracking which borrows much from *paraxial theory* [Hect87] of geometric optics and *pencil tracing* [STN87], a contemporary application of paraxial theory to computer graphics.

A *paraxial ray* is a ray propagating in the region of an *axial ray*. Each paraxial ray is represented by a *ray vector*, a four dimensional vector quantity $\psi = (x_1 x_2 \xi_1 \xi_2)^T$.

$(x_1 x_2)^T$ is the intersection of the paraxial ray and the plane $(\mathbf{u} \times \mathbf{v})$, where $(\mathbf{u}, \mathbf{v}, \mathbf{w})$ is an orthogonal coordinate system, with $\mathbf{w}$ co-incident with the direction of the axial ray. $(\xi_1 \xi_2)$ is the projection of the paraxial direction vector on

278

the ($\mathbf{u} \times \mathbf{v}$) plane (see Figure 2(a) for the associated geometry). We can now represent any optical interface as a 4×4 system matrix M (assuming coherent propagation media) if the deviation of the paraxial ray from the axial ray is small enough. Thus the transformed paraxial ray becomes $\psi' = M\psi$.

To derive the system matrix M^r, [STN87] approximate the surface as a paraboloid (similar to the tangent plane approximation of [Bar86]). A maximum paraxial ray spread angle is then approximated using a tolerance based on pixel width and ray sampling interval. Herein lies a difficulty with the approach. The convergence/divergence of the wavefront is a feature that we wish to adapt to and indeed exploit to reduce the number of rays required. Wavefront divergence (for example when the wavefront is incident on a convex mirror) should result in a reduced density of rays tracked, whereas focused light should result in higher sampling densities to accurately capture the illumination detail.

Rather than approximate optical interfaces as transfer matrices, we explicitly build a paraxial ray description of the differential wavefront $\Delta\omega$ being represented by the axial ray. We define a *slice* as $\psi \overset{\Delta}{=} \{(x\xi), (x_u\xi_u), (x_v\xi_v)\}$.

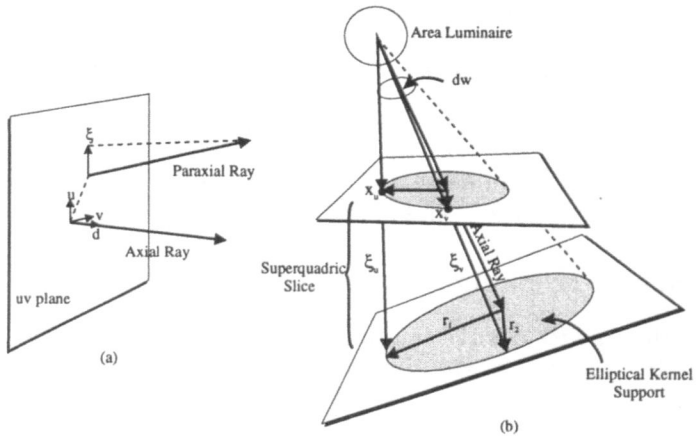

Fig. 2. (a) The geometry of pencil tracing. (b) The superquadric slice.

The 3 rays $(x\xi)$, $(x_u\xi_u)$ and $(x_v\xi_v)$ define a superquadric slice (see Figure 2(b)). By tracking the rays through the environment we track the superquadric as it experiences deformation at media interfaces. When the slice hits a surface, the slice's power is deposited over the area defined by the intersection of the slice and the surface. In order to simplify the determination of this region, we assume planarity at the interface giving an super-conical region of influence.

Effectively we are using the approach of the variable kernel method for the reconstruction of a density function [Sil86]:

$$f(t) \approx \hat{f}(t) = \frac{1}{n} \sum_{j=1}^{n} \frac{1}{hd_{j,k}} K\left(\frac{t - X_j}{hd_{j,k}}\right) \tag{5}$$

K is some kernel function such that $\int_{-\infty}^{\infty} K(x)dx = 1$, h a smoothness parameter and $d_{j,k}$ a space variant density estimator. Usually this method requires an initial density estimation to determine $d_{j,k}$. However, in determining the region of influence of the slice we have determined an effective measure of $d_{j,k}$.

For the kernel shape we use an elliptical Gaussian. Using the method proposed in [Got93] the elliptical Gaussian *splat* of energy can be computed from an appropriate set of basis kernels:

$$K(r_1, r_2, \theta)(x, y) = \sum_{i,j,k} c_{ijk}(r_1, r_2, \theta) B_{ijk}(x, y) \qquad (6)$$

$K(r_1, r_2, \theta)$ represents a canonical elliptical kernel of radii r_1, r_2, rotated by θ. The coefficients, c_{ijk} are computed using singular value decomposition techniques.

4.1 The Superquadric of Confusion

Given that all the superquadric slices have the centre of the luminaire as an apex, we can handle only point source effects. To extend the algorithm to allow area luminaires to be effectively simulated we are required to sample the surface area of the luminaire in addition to the solid angle through which the source radiates. This dramatically increases the noise level in the solution and requires significantly higher sampling rates. We now propose an extension to the superquadric slice tracing idea to cater for area luminaires.

We can observe that when a light-pass ray is cast from the luminaire with its origin at the centre of the luminaire, the point of intersection of this ray and a surface may be considered as a focal point for a bundle of rays. Behind the surface this bundle volume diffuses from the focal point. When incident on a receiving surface the bundle defines a *region of confusion*, a term borrowed from the notion of a *circle of confusion* when dealing with lens effects. The bundle of rays therefore define what we term the *superquadric of confusion*.

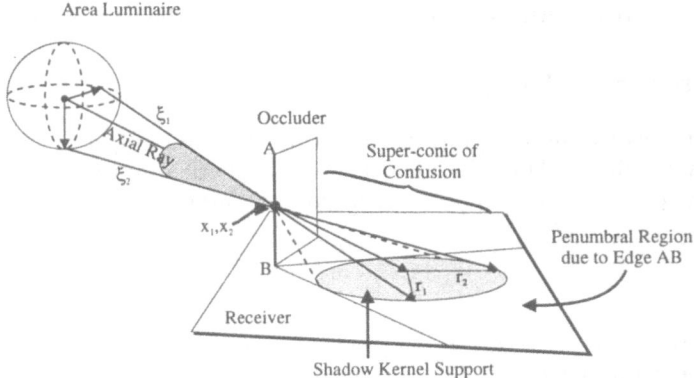

Fig. 3. (a) The superquadric of confusion resulting from a point on an occluder and a spherical light source.

This bundle of rays is no more than the rays defining the solid angle subtended by the source at the surface intersection point, as shown in Figure 3, for a spherical light source. This idea has been used in [Ase92] to partition the environment between receiver (the intersected surface) and the source according to the size of penumbral region that objects in the region will cause on the receiver, to determine how coarsely to sample those objects with a view to computing the shadows cast.

To use this we extend our definition of the slice to include 2 co-axial slices:

1. The point source superquadric slice $\psi_{ps} \triangleq \{(x\xi), (x_u^{ps}\xi_u^{ps}), (x_v^{ps}\xi_v^{ps})\}$

2. The superquadric of confusion slice $\psi_{sc} \triangleq \{(x\xi), (x_u^{sc}\xi_u^{sc}), (x_v^{sc}\xi_v^{sc})\}$

The final complete differential wavefront estimator becomes:

$$\psi = \psi_{ps} \cup \psi_{sc} = \{(x\xi), (x_u^{ps}\xi_u^{ps}), (x_v^{ps}\xi_v^{ps}), (x_u^{sc}\xi_u^{sc}), (x_v^{sc}\xi_v^{sc})\} \tag{7}$$

Approximating the solid angle subtended by the source as a super-quadric is not in general satisfactory, except for sources which are themselves superquadrics. To handle polygonal sources, the angle subtended must be represented as a collection of such slices. Our current implementation assumes spherical luminaires.

When ψ is incident on a surface the superconic within which the power is to be deposited is determined by examining both superconic topologies resulting from the point source slice and the confusion slice.

If the superquadric of confusion estimate is used exclusively for area sources, the result will be noisy illumination detail in regions approaching singularity, due to the inadequacy of the point source sampling rate. An example of this is depicted in Colour Plate 1(a). Therefore, when this estimate, $\hat{E}_{sc}$, becomes smaller than that of the point source sample estimate, $\hat{E}_{ps}$, we revert to the point source sample, which is designed to provide an effective sampling strategy when the sample rate is low: $\hat{E} = max(\hat{E}_{ps}, \hat{E}_{sc})$.

If the BRDF of the surface is complex, we can subdivide the superquadric of confusion or even extend it. For example, a point source illuminating a directional diffuse surface [HTSG91], would result in the superquadric of confusion being extended to diffuse the incident light about the directional diffuse direction. Colour Plate 1(b) illustrates the effect of increasing the light source size.

5 Adapting to Illumination Events

We shoot rays by choosing directions within the solid angle through which the light source radiates. Directions are chosen for spherical sources using a stratified sampling approach[4]. $\psi = (x, \xi)$, x =luminaire center.

$$\xi = \begin{pmatrix} \cos\theta\sin\phi \\ \sin\theta\sin\phi \\ \cos\phi \end{pmatrix}$$

$\theta = \cos^{-1}(2u - 1)$, $\phi = 2\pi v$ and $u, v = rand(0, 1)$. As with any sampling algorithm, the sampling rate is crucial. With a sampling rate that is too coarse we will miss such effects as

---

[4] We assume a diffuse distribution for the sources.

- The D^0 discontinuities[5] associated with shadows cast by point sources.
- The D^0 discontinuities associated with shadows cast by touching surfaces.
- The singularities at penumbral foci, near the D^0 discontinuities.
- Singularities caused by concave mirrored surfaces and refracting media.

We can also introduce unwanted artifacts including shadow/caustics leaks and darkened regions at shared edges. Rather than simply increase the sample rate everywhere, we look for illumination events and determine whether they represent just cause for adaptively sampling in those sampling regions. An illumination event can be signalled either by wavefront convergence indicating the possibility of a singularity or when the surface intersected by the ray differs from that of its neighbours.

When tracking the slices through the environment, we may have applied many power kernels before an event is detected. In such cases we would be required to *un-shoot* the power associated with these slices before super-sampling the slice. To cater for this, we defer the application of the kernels to the maps until the entire ray tree has been traversed, storing information regarding the required depositions in a *splat list*. If no event is detected, the splat list is used to apply the deferred illumination deposits. If an event is detected however, we throw away that part of the splat list which is to be re-evaluated at a higher resolution and supersample that sub-set of the ray tree. Figure 4 shows the results of the adaptive sampling schemes for the illumination reulting from a metal band.

To determine the resolution of the new sub-division scheme, we examine the size of the kernels being deposited at the event region, and subdivide such that the support of the kernel is approximately the size of an illumination pixel. Thus we never subdivide beyond the level of detail that the illumination map is capable of displaying. Colour Plates 2 and 3 demonstrate the improvement in image quality when using adaptive sampling techniques.

5.1 The 'Feeler Ray' Pass

Due to the expense of tracking a large number of rays through the entire spherical solid angle, we use an idea from [Shi90] where an initial low resolution pass is used to simply identify the directions in which objects are visible to the light source. We fully sample within these sample regions only.

6 Results

One of the most significant results of the algorithm is that for a given surface visible to the viewer, the number of shadow rays cast to that surface, n_s, will usually be $\ll$ number of pixels, n_p, associated with the surface on the screen. This is in contrast to the 'gather' approach monte carlo systems, which typically cast $m \times n_p$ shadow rays, where typically $m = \{4 \dots 64\}$. This is primarily due to the coherence that can be exploited by a 'shooting' monte carlo approach.

In order to increase the speed of the algorithm, we have approximated the elliptical kernels with circular kernels of radius $r = max(r_1, r_2)$. This has the

---

[5] A D^n discontinuity (after notation in [LTG92]) exists at x if the function is C^{n-1} continuous at x but not C^n.

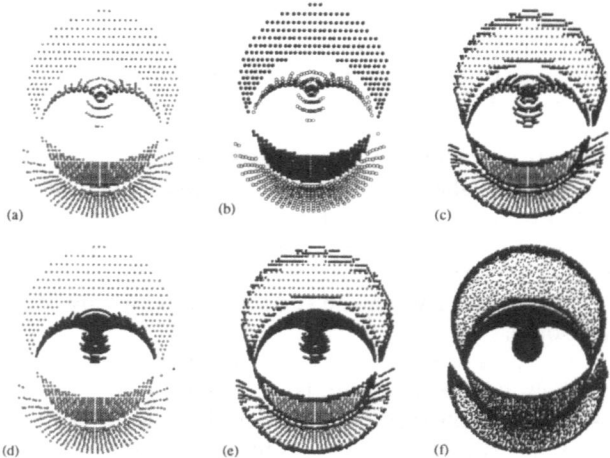

Fig. 4. Adaptive sampling schemes: (a) An initial low resolution spot diagram for the metal band in Colour Plate 4. (b) Rays classification; black spots are shadow rays, and white, the caustic rays. (c) Black spots represent rays shot as a result of adapting to illumination edges, (d) they represent rays sent to regions of illumination convergence, (e) shows the combined result and finally (f) represents a high resolution sampling, showing the concentration of samples in regions of interest.

effect of reducing slightly the illumination detail, but has the advantage that all kernels are fully symmetric, which improves the performance of the splatting process.

Colour Plate 5 demonstrates the high illumination detail that can be achieved using this algorithm. Note that the crystal object is approximated using triangular patches, and the illumination cast effectively represents a differentiation of the piecewise linear surface amplifying the edges of the patches in a manner similar to an emboss filter. The lightsource in this case has a very small radius (and is thus barely visible) and is located in the centre of the piece.

7 Conclusions

We have presented an algorithm to determine the illumination from area luminaires which captures both low and high frequency detail in the illumination using density-estimation and adpative sampling techniques, representing both the differential wavefront area around power carrying rays and the solid angle subtended by the light source as a superquadric slice, defined by an axial ray and 2 pairs of paraxial rays.

Problems remain in the current implementation. In order to be truly useful arbitrary luminaires should be allowed (our current implementation is restricted to spherical geometries). This in principle should be a straightforward extension to the system, allowing super-sampling of the superquadric of confusion. The storage of the illumination maps currently represents the major memory bottleneck in the system. The use of a wavelet basis [Chu92] to encode the illumination map is under investigation and current results are very promising.

8 Acknowledgements

Thanks to Dr. Dan McCarthy, my supervisor, Prof. John Byrne for his continued support and funding of this project and to the members of the Image Synthesis Group for helpful suggestions and critique.

References

[Arv86] Arvo J., Backward Ray Tracing, *SIGGRAPH '86 Developments in Ray Tracing seminar notes*, Vol. 12, Aug. 1986.

[Ase92] Asensio F., A Hierarchical Ray-Casting Algorithm for Radiosity Shadows, *Proceedings of the 3rd Eurographics Workshop on Rendering*, pp:179-188, May 1992.

[Bar86] Barr A.H., Ray Tracing Deformed Surfaces, *Computer Graphics*, 20(4):287-296, August 1986, ACM Siggraph '86 Conference Proceedings.

[Chu92] Chui C.K., *An Introduction to Wavelets*, Vol.1 of *Wavelet Analysis and its Applications*, Academic Press, Inc. Boston, MA, 1992.

[Col94] Collins S., Adaptive Splatting for Specular to Diffuse Light Transport, *Proceedings of the 5th Eurographics Workshop on Rendering*, pp:119-135, June 1994.

[Got93] Gotsman C., Constant Time Filtering by Singular Value Decomposition, *Proceedings of the 4th Eurographics Workshop on Rendering*, pp:145-155, June 1993.

[HTSG91] He X.D., Torrance K.E., Sillion F.X., Greenberg D.P., A Comprehensive Physical Model for Light Reflection, *Computer Graphics*, 25(4):175-186, July 1991, ACM Siggraph '91 Conference Proceedings.

[Hect87] Hecht H., *Optics 2nd Ed.*, pp:128-240, Addison Wesley, 1987.

[Hec90] Heckbert P.S., Adaptive Radiosity Textures for Bidirectional Ray Tracing, *Computer Graphics*, 24(4):145-154, August 1990, ACM Siggraph '90 Conference Proceedings.

[LTG92] Lischinski D., Tampieri F., Greenberg D.P., Discontinuity Meshing for accurate Radiosity, *IEEE Computer graphics and Applications*, 12(6):25-39, November 1992.

[STN87] Shinya M., Takahashi T., Naito S., Principles and Applications of Pencil Tracing, *Computer Graphics*, 21(4):45-54, July 1987, ACM Siggraph '87 Conference Proceedings.

[Shi90] Shirley P., A Ray Tracing Method for Illumination Calculation in Diffuse-Specular Scenes, *Proceedings of Graphics Interface*, Canadian Information Processing Society, pp:205-212, Toronto, May 1990.

[Shi95] Shirley P., Wade B., Hubbard P.M., Zareski D., Walter B., Greenberg D.P., Global Illumination via Density Estimation, *Proceedings of the 6th Eurographics Workshop on Rendering*, June 1995.

[Sil86] Silverman B.W., *Density Estimation for Statistics and Data Analysis*, Chapman and Hall, London 1986.

[War92] Ward G., The RADIANCE Lighting Simulation System, *Global Illumination*, ACM Siggraph '92 Course Notes.

Editors' Note: see Appendix, p. 372 for colored figures of this paper

A Two-Pass Solution to the Rendering Equation with a Source Visibility Preprocess

Kurt Zimmerman[1]   Peter Shirley[2]

[1] Department of Computer Science, Indiana University, Bloomington, IN 47405, USA
[2] Program of Computer Graphics, Cornell University, Ithaca, NY 14853, USA

1 Introduction

The grand challenge for the global illumination community is the successful rendering of complex scenes containing arbitrary reflectance properties and numerous light sources. Even for completely diffuse scenes, high geometric complexity and large numbers of light sources present a problem which current algorithms cannot solve in a practical amount of time. However, recent research by Rushmeier et. al. [7] utilizes geometric simplification to offer a promising solution to the problem of high geometric complexity and work by Shirley et. al. [9, 10] presents shadow ray optimization techniques for efficient handling of large numbers of luminaires. We present an approach which combines and improves upon ideas from these works. Our work adds to the growing toolbox of importance sampling techniques used in realistic image synthesis (e.g. [4, 14]).

Our approach employs a two-pass algorithm: a radiosity prepass followed by a view-dependent "gather". The algorithm differs from previous two-pass methods; it is designed for environments with tens of thousand of primitives and hundreds of luminaires. This is the first attempt to combine the ideas of geometric simplification with Monte Carlo shadow ray optimization. More than a simple composition, the algorithm employs visibility and lighting coherence both to determine and to vary in space the regions upon which explicit gathering (shadow rays) and implicit gathering (reflection rays) are performed. This allows the algorithm to restrict the number of explicit transfer calculations down to one explicit gather and one implicit gather per viewing ray. In addition, visibility estimation and visibility coherence is used to reduce the probability of querying invisible or partially visible luminaires. As rays are not being sent to every luminaire, our algorithm has the potential to run significantly faster than previous two-pass solutions, especially in scenes with many luminaires or bright secondary reflectors. The main limitation of this new method is that it is restricted to predominantly diffuse scenes.

We use "two-pass method" to mean an algorithm which uses a view-independent pass followed by a view-dependent pass. A further restriction is that the values computed in the view-independent pass are not applied directly to the final image but are used to help calculate the displayed values. Because two-pass methods that use a "gather" for diffuse surfaces are relatively recent, we will begin with a brief overview of two-pass methods and gathering strategies in Section 2. Next, in Section 3, we present our new algorithm followed by the implementation, sample images, and results in Section 4. Finally we discuss the merits of our algorithm in Section 5.

2 Background

In this section we briefly review path tracing and two-pass methods that gather at diffuse surfaces (for a more complete review please consult [17].). We begin in Section 2.1 by reviewing the rendering equation and the basis for two-pass methods. In Section 2.2 we review path tracing as it is used in practice. In Section 2.3 we review the *implicit gather* which gathers in directional space and the *explicit gather* which gathers in geometry space. In Section 2.4 we review Rushmeier et al.'s GSII algorithm. In Section 2.5 we review previous methods that can be directly applied to explicit gathers.

2.1 Rendering Equation

We now examine the rendering equation for diffuse reflectors and general emitters. We review both the explicit (area-based) form presented by Kajiya [3], and the implicit (directional) form presented by Immel [2]. The implicit form is:

$$L_s(\mathbf{x}, \hat{\omega}) = L_e(\mathbf{x}, \hat{\omega}) + \frac{R(\mathbf{x})}{\pi} \int_{\mho} L_f(\mathbf{x}, \hat{\omega}')(-\hat{\omega}' \cdot \hat{n}) d\sigma(\hat{\omega}') \qquad (1)$$

where $L_s(\mathbf{x}, \hat{\omega})$ is the surface radiance of $\mathbf{x}$ in direction $\hat{\omega}$, $L_e(\mathbf{x}, \hat{\omega})$ is the emitted surface radiance in direction $\hat{\omega}$ at $\mathbf{x}$, $\mho$ is the unit hemisphere of incoming directions oriented about $\hat{n}$, $R(\mathbf{x})$ is the reflectivity at $\mathbf{x}$, $L_f(\mathbf{x}, \hat{\omega}')$ is the field radiance from direction $\hat{\omega}'$ incident at $\mathbf{x}$, and σ is the solid angle measure. The explicit form is:

$$L_s(\mathbf{x}, \hat{\omega}) = L_e(\mathbf{x}, \hat{\omega}) + \frac{R(\mathbf{x})}{\pi} \int_{\mathcal{X}} g(\mathbf{x}, \mathbf{x}') L_s(\mathbf{x}', \hat{\omega}')(-\hat{\omega}' \cdot \hat{n}) \frac{\cdot (\hat{\omega}' \cdot \hat{n}')}{\|\mathbf{x} - \mathbf{x}'\|^2} \, dA(\mathbf{x}') \quad (2)$$

where $\mathcal{X}$ is the set of all points on surfaces and $g(\mathbf{x}, \mathbf{x}')$ is the *geometry term*, which is zero if there is an obstruction between $\mathbf{x}$ and $\mathbf{x}'$ and one otherwise, $\|\mathbf{x} - \mathbf{x}'\|$ is the distance between $\mathbf{x}$ and $\mathbf{x}'$, and A is the area measure, Figure 1.

Equations 1 and 2 are equivalent, but suggest different solution strategies. Equation 1 suggests sampling directions, and Equation 2 suggests sampling patches. Clearly we cannot sample every patch at every pixel for complex scenes, but we cannot naively sample directions because small bright surfaces will cause high errors. We want to explicitly sample a few very important surfaces, and directionally sample to estimate the contribution of all other surfaces.

2.2 Monte Carlo Path Tracing (MCPT)

A naive Monte Carlo solution to an integral $I = \int_S f(\tau) \, d\tau$, where $\tau \in S$ can be expressed as

$$I \approx \frac{1}{n} \sum_{i=1}^{n} \frac{f(\tau_i)}{p(\tau_i)}.$$

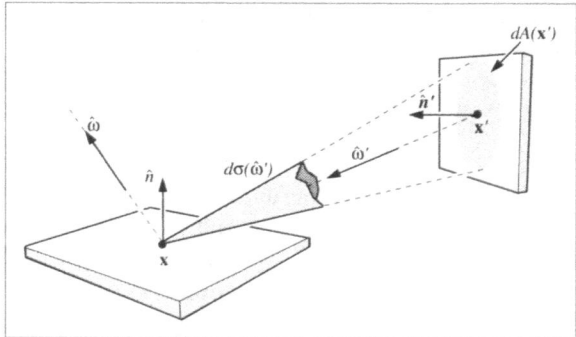

Fig. 1. Rendering equation

Here $\tau_1, \tau_2, \ldots, \tau_n$ are random variables distributed by the probability density function p, written $\tau_i \sim p$.

For an integral equation in the form of Equation 1 this suggests the approximation:

$$L_s(\mathbf{x}, \hat{\omega}) \approx L_e(\mathbf{x}, \hat{\omega}) + \frac{R(\mathbf{x})}{\pi} L_f(\mathbf{x}, \hat{\omega}') \frac{(-\hat{\omega}' \cdot \hat{n})}{q(\hat{\omega}')} \tag{3}$$

where $\hat{\omega}'$ is a random direction chosen according to the probability density function q. Because $L_f(\mathbf{x}, \hat{\omega}')$ is not known, it must be solved by tracing a ray, $\mathbf{x} + \hat{\omega}'$, to find $\mathbf{x}'$. Because this is very inefficient for scenes with small bright sources, Kajiya [3] combined Equations 1 and 2 to form the following approximation:

$$L_s(\mathbf{x}, \hat{\omega}) \approx L_e(\mathbf{x}, \hat{\omega}) + R(\mathbf{x}) \left[L_i(\mathbf{x}, \hat{\omega}') \frac{(-\hat{\omega}' \cdot \hat{n})}{q'(\hat{\omega}')} + L_e(\mathbf{x}', \hat{\omega}'') \frac{(-\hat{\omega}'' \cdot \hat{n})(\hat{\omega}'' \cdot \hat{n}')}{p'(\mathbf{x}') \|\mathbf{x} - \mathbf{x}'\|^2} \right]$$

where L_i is the indirect component of the field radiance, $\hat{\omega}'$ is distributed by q' over the hemisphere of reflectors and $\mathbf{x}'$ is distributed by p' over emitters. This equation is the basis for path tracing (see Figure 2a) where a shadow ray is sent to a random point on each luminaire.

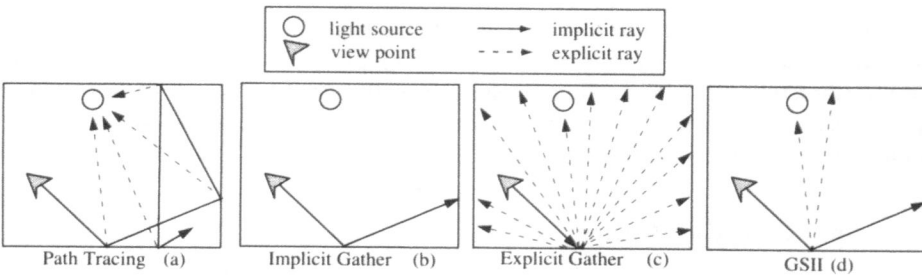

Fig. 2. Different view-dependent rendering methods.

2.3 Implicit and Explicit Gathers

One drawback with path tracing is that recursion is necessary for global effects. Rushmeier [8] noted that we could terminate this recursion by running an approximate radiosity solution, resulting in the following integral (as opposed to an integral equation):

$$L_s(\mathbf{x}, \hat{\omega}) \approx L_e(\mathbf{x}, \hat{\omega}) + \frac{R(\mathbf{x})}{\pi} \int_{\bar{\mho}} \bar{L}(x, \hat{\omega}')(-\hat{\omega}' \cdot \hat{n}) \, d\bar{\sigma}(\hat{\omega}') \tag{4}$$

where $\bar{L}$ is the radiance from the radiosity solution. Solving the integral above is easier than solving the full rendering equation, and is the basic idea behind the two-pass methods discussed in this paper. Because solving Equation 4 can be thought of as calculating the light that $\mathbf{x}$ gets from the patches in the radiosity solution, it is often called a *gather* or an *implicit gather*, Figure 2b. Because it is a calculation for only a single point $\mathbf{x}$ it is also called a "local pass" (as opposed to a "global pass" which calculates radiances for all surfaces).

Alternatively, Equation 4 can be solved by sending a shadow ray to every patch in the radiosity solution [6]. We call this an *explicit gather*. This method is very expensive for large environments, but will be relatively noise free. Figure 2c.

2.4 Geometric Simplification for Indirect Illumination (GSII)

Rushmeier et al. [7] observed that a two pass method could be more efficient if bright reflectors could be reclassified as light sources and the implicit gather was from a geometrically simplified environment, Figure 2d. One drawback with this approach is that gathering from nearby objects will cause obvious artifacts. Even if only the illumination is simplified this proximity bug will occur (simplifying the geometry is just an extreme way of simplifying the field radiance function). To get around this problem a user defined parameter r_thresh is introduced that determines when to use the simplified radiosity solution or when to use MCPT[3].

If it can be assumed that most renderings encounter the bulk of the computation in modeling the diffuse or nearly diffuse inter-reflection, then GSII is very effective. The simplified radiosity solution can be performed in a fraction of the time it may take for a full resolution solution and multiple levels of reflection rays required for MCPT are, in most cases, eliminated.

2.5 Efficient Explicit Gathers

The explicit gather as noted in Section 2.3 requires that rays be sent to every patch or, in the case of direct lighting, to every luminaire. Typically this is overkill because in many cases only a few light sources or patches are important to the illumination of the gather point. For direct lighting, Ward [15] suggested sorting the luminaires according to their contribution in descending order, sample the sources in order until the sum of the contributions is above some threshold, and then estimate the remaining contribution. This

---

[3] This is a greatly simplified discussion. GSII also uses r_thresh to determine how much the radiosity environment is simplified.

can be thought of as ranking the importance of each luminaire, then sampling the most important sources. Shirley and Wang [9] observed that one luminaire sample per viewing ray could be used if they could assure that important luminaires were more likely to be sampled than unimportant luminaires. This requires careful design of the probability density function p used in the single sample Monte Carlo estimate for the rendering equation in the form of Equation 2:

$$L_s(\mathbf{x}, \hat{\omega}) \approx L_e(\mathbf{x}, \hat{\omega}) + \frac{R(\mathbf{x})}{\pi} L_s(\mathbf{x}', \hat{\omega}') \frac{(-\hat{\omega}' \cdot \hat{n})(\hat{\omega}' \cdot \hat{n}')}{p(\mathbf{x}') \|\mathbf{x} - \mathbf{x}'\|^2} \tag{5}$$

Here $\mathbf{x}'$ is a random point on a selected surface and $\mathbf{x}' \sim p$. As an example, assume two luminaires l_1 and l_2 are sampled according to the probability density functions $p_1(\mathbf{x}')$ and $p_2(\mathbf{x}')$. These functions can be combined into one *mixture density* by applying the weighted average, $p(\mathbf{x}') = \alpha p_1(\mathbf{x}') + (1 - \alpha)p_2(\mathbf{x}')$, where $\alpha \in [0, 1)$. This function can then be applied in Equation 5. The function p is indeed a probability density because its integral over the two luminaires is one and it is strictly positive over all points on the luminaires. The coefficients α and $(1 - \alpha)$ are called mixing weights.

This idea can be extended to N luminaires if one can determine the mixing weights $\alpha_1, \ldots, \alpha_N$. If each luminaire's estimated contribution to the gather point can be determined then we can use these estimates to determine the mixing weights. If L_i' is the estimated contribution for light l_i then we can define $\alpha_i = L_i'/(L_1' + \cdots + L_N')$. The mixture density is then $p(\mathbf{x}') = \alpha_1 p_1(\mathbf{x}') + + \cdots + \alpha_N p_N(\mathbf{x}')$ where the α_i sum to one.

The important point to notice about this process is that the values $\alpha_1, \alpha_2, \ldots, \alpha_N$ must be generated for each direct lighting calculation. While generating these estimates is much faster than generating an equivalent number of shadow rays, even this amount of computation can be crippling when the number of luminaires becomes hundreds or thousands. For this reason, the use of spatial subdivision of light sources has been suggested [10]. The reasoning for this is that seldom are all lights important to every region in the environment. Therefore the list of important lights should vary in space. This can be done by attaching an important light list to the cells of a conventional subdivision structure such as a regular grid. To determine which light sources are entered into which cells an influence region is defined for each source. An influence box is then intersected with the subdivision structure and the light is inserted into the important list for each cell in the intersection. All sources not in the important list for a particular cell are considered unimportant to that cell. Probabilistically unimportant lights will be sampled but this should be infrequent. If it can be assumed that the unimportant luminaires contribute an equal amount of radiance to a scene, then a new probability density function can be formed with the mixing weights determined by $\alpha_i = L_i'/(L_1' + L_2' + \cdots + ML_u')$ where M is the number of unimportant luminaires and L_u' is the estimated average unimportant contribution.

3 The New Gather Algorithm

In this section we discuss the development of our algorithm. In Section 3.1 we explain why a simple combination of methods described in Section 2 is problematic. In Sec-

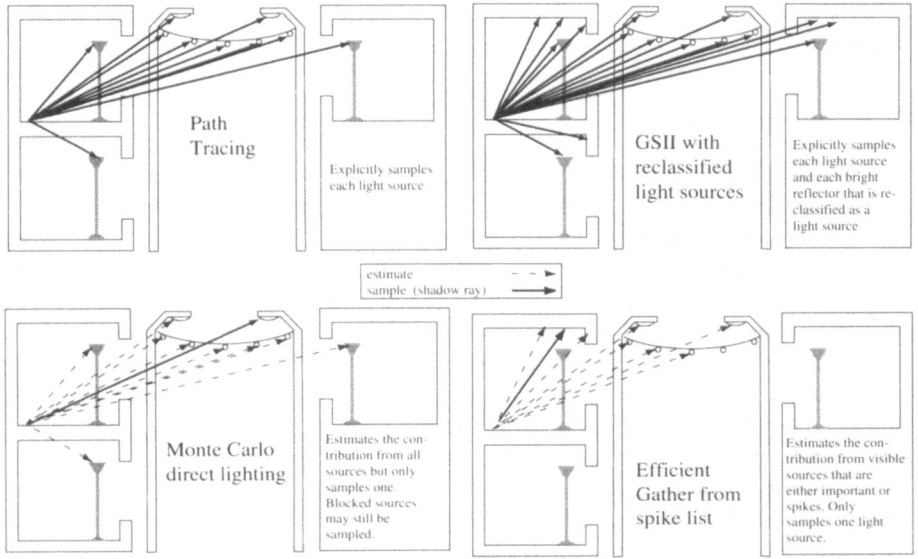

Fig. 3. How different methods send shadow rays.

tion 3.2 we propose a solution to this problem and in Section 3.3 we present the pseudocode for our algorithm.

3.1 Overestimates: Spikes

Since the explicit gather from Section 2.3 is relatively noise free, and since the spatial subdivision method of Section 2.5 makes explicit gathering more efficient, a logical progression would be to combine these with geometric simplification to create an algorithm which performs only an explicit gather. All surfaces in the simplified environment would be considered light sources and, as in GSII, the algorithm could resort to MCPT if a selected surface is less than `r_thresh` from the gather point. However, this strategy would produce very noisy images. The problem is that we cannot assume that all unimportant lights contribute equally to the illuminated point. In practice many unimportant luminaires will not contribute at all. Another problem is that it is possible for a luminaire with high radiance, a star for example, to be unimportant. Such a source would be selected infrequently, but when it is selected the combination of high power and low probability will produce a large estimate. Such an over estimate will require many extra samples to overcome.

In quantitative terms, this problem can be seen in the following way. If α_u is the probability of having to select one of M unimportant lights then $\alpha_u = ML'_u/(L'_1 + L'_2 + \cdots + ML'_u)$. Assuming that unimportant lights contribute equally, a uniform selection from the unimportant list is made with probability $1/M$. If the selected luminaire is then visible a sample point on the luminaire is then selected with $p_u(\mathbf{x}')$. The value for the probability density will be $p(\mathbf{x}') = [\alpha_u p_u(\mathbf{x}')]/M$. If $p(\mathbf{x}')$ is inserted into Equation 5, it is easy to see that a large M or small α_u and/or $p_u(\mathbf{x}')$ may give a gross overestimate or spike.

3.2 Eliminating Spikes

To eliminate this problem of large overestimates we propose that the offending high luminance but low contribution sources be sampled explicitly. This amounts to having a "spike" list (high luminance patch list) rather than an importance list at each grid or octree cell. A spike list differs from an importance list because it includes any source l_i which exceeds some user defined threshold regardless of whether or not the influence region for l_i intersects the cell. This means that many sources which would be considered unimportant by the method described at the end of Section 2.5 will be included in a spike list. In practice all bright sources are automatically included in the spike list whereas dim sources and reclassified sources (bright reflectors) are tested against their influence regions to determine membership.

A problem with maintaining any list of spikes is that a scene may contain many spikes (e.g., an office building). However, in most scenes only a few spikes are visible (non-zero geometry term) at any given point. These "invisible" spikes should not be in the list.

To accomplish this exclusion of invisible patches from a spike list, we perform a visibility preprocess in each cell. Thus sources which are not visible to a cell will not be included in the spike list and can be ignored. Of course, if many bright sources are visible, as would be true in the middle of a football stadium, then the spike list will be large. However, for most architectural scenes, including night time city scenes, the visibility preprocess will provide significant savings. In the event that the spike list is large, we will still only send one shadow ray for an explicit gather from all spikes, so even several hundred spikes should be allowable without too much degradation in performance. Because visibility calculation in complex scenes is very difficult [12], we use point sampling for visibility estimation, so we falsely exclude some spikes. This amounts to truncation, but will never occur for spikes that are completely visible.

3.3 The Algorithm

The algorithm performs the following steps, the first two are taken directly from GSII:

1. Simplify surfaces and create a coarse mesh for the radiosity solution according to user defined parameters[4].

2. Perform radiosity solution with the coarse mesh over the geometrically simplified environment.

3. Create the lighting grid by treating all surfaces in the simplified radiosity solution as luminaires.

---

[4] Automatically simplifying a scene is a difficult problem. For our algorithm the user must provide this simplified version of the scene. This is not as great a hardship for the user as one might guess. The generation of a simplified environment, a process called *massing*, is commonly employed by designers and architects [1].

4. Perform the ray tracing final pass according to the algorithm in Figure 4 where *LE* is the emitted component, *R* is the reflected component and *N* is the surface normal at *x*. The function *getSpikeList(x)* returns the spike list corresponding to the cell in which *x* resides. The function *spikeColor* uses the Monte Carlo direct lighting method shown in Section 2.5. Note that a check must be made to determine if the point *xi* resides on a surface in the spike list. If it does reside on such a surface then the radiance at *xi* is accounted for in the explicit gather on the spike list.

```
color raycolor(ray, depth, list)
    color L = 0;
    if (depth == 0)
      if (ray hits at x)
        list = getSpikeList(x);
        L += LE(x) + R(x) * spikeColor(x, N(x), list);
        if (depth < maxDepth)
          L += R(x) * raycolor(randomRay, depth+1, list);
        return L;
      else
        return background;
    else
      if ((ray hits at x) and (| x - ray_origin | < r_thresh))
        list = getSpikeList(x);
        L += R(x) * spikeColor(x, N(x), list);
        if (depth < maxDepth)
          L += R(x) * raycolor(randomRay, depth+1, list);
        return L;
      else if (ray hits at xi)
        if (xi is not in list)
          L += R(x)*radsimp_color(ray);
        return L;
      else
        return background;
```

Fig. 4. Pseudocode

4 Implementation and Results

For our implementation, we use an axis aligned regular grid to store the spike lists. This grid is of the same size and dimension as the geometry grid used to store the full resolution environment. By making the lighting grid the same size as the geometry grid we can eliminate the storage of spike lists in cells which do not contain geometry. We introduce user defined values $\underline{E}$ and $\overline{E}$ as spike thresholds. We assume that any light source l_i with emittance $E_i > \overline{E}$ can produce a spike in the image. Therefore we insert l_i into each grid cell's spike list provided that l_i is visible from the cell. If $E_i < \underline{E}$ then it is assumed that l_i cannot produce a spike and is left to be sampled implicitly. If $\underline{E} < E_i < \overline{E}$ then the influence region as in [9] is used to determine the cells in which l_i may cause a spike. Again, l_i is inserted into a cell only if it is visible from the cell.

The visibility tests are performed by sending rays through the environment from random points in a grid cell to random points on the light source. A visibility variable g_i is maintained which represents the percentage of rays which are not blocked. This is similar to the visibility estimate of Smits et al. [11]. This technique is not as accurate as the techniques presented by Teller and Hanrahan [12] but is applicable in "less well-behaved" environments. We use a self-refining method which initially sends 10 rays, if each ray reaches the light source then g_i is set to 1 and l_i is inserted into the spike list. If more than one but fewer than 10 rays reach the light source, 10 more samples are generated and $newg_i$ is stored. If $\|newg_i - g_i\| \leq 0.1$ then $g_i = (newg_i + g_i)/2$ and l_i is inserted into the spike list. If l_i is not inserted or if one or fewer rays reach the light source, this process continues until a maximum number of rays are sent. In our implementation the maximum number is 100. If $g_i = 0$ then the light source is fully occluded and can be left out of the cell's spike list.

The spike lists are sampled during the ray tracing pass according to the linear method from Shirley and Wang [9] with the geometry term included in the computation. The mixing weights are then defined by: $\alpha_i = g_i L_i /(g_1 L_1 + g_2 L_2 + \cdots + g_N L_N)$ If we choose l_i from the spike list with corresponding probability density function p_i then the probability density function for the estimate is $p(\mathbf{x}') = \alpha_i p_i(\mathbf{x}')$. Note that the visibility term g which in most Monte Carlo methods is either 1 or 0 is now worked into the density function.

To avoid variance discontinuities in screen space, we randomly choose one of the spike lists near the illuminated point $\mathbf{x}$. We do this in a distance-weighted fashion, which can be thought of as storing spike lists at grid vertices, and using trilinear coordinates as weighting probabilities. A similar method was used by Smits in his local pass to avoid the underlying mesh structure from appearing as a variance artifact[5].

The images in Figures 5 and 6 were produced with our algorithm with 64 samples per pixel. These images represent two different view points in the same test environment which contains 1666 primitives including 318 light sources. The radiosity prepass was performed on simplified version of this environment that was tessellated into 32294 triangles. A view of the radiosity solution is shown in Figure 7. For comparison, a MCPT solution with 64 samples per pixel is shown in Figure 8. For this scene, the extra storage required for the spatial data structure containing the spike lists was of the same order as the grid structure which stored the actual scene description. These two structures and their associated geometry accounted for about 20% of the total storage. The remaining 80% was due to the simplified radiosity solution and its corresponding spatial structure. We estimate that in a more streamlined implementation the storage required for the radiosity solution and its spatial structure to be about 50% of the total requirement after this improvement. While it is quite possible to construct scenes where the spike lists will require substantial storage (e.g. the stadium example), we expect requirements similar to those of our test scene on average.

Table 1 compares the performance of our algorithms with MCPT and GSII[6] These

---

[5] Brian Smits, personal communication.

[6] Our implementation of GSII is somewhat deficient because we do not reclassify bright reflectors

Fig. 5. New Gather with 64 samples per pixel (exterior)

Fig. 6. New Gather with 64 samples per pixel (interior)

Fig. 7. Solution for radiosity prepass

Fig. 8. MCPT with 64 samples per pixel

	MCPT	GSII	Our Algorithm
Viewing Rays	60,000	60,000	60,000
Implicit Rays	422,640	68,652	68,992
Explicit (shadow) Rays	147,429,560	21,973,800	69,476
Preprocessing Time	none	10 minutes	1.2 hours
Rendering Time	20 hours	1.6 hours	4 minutes

Table 1. Three algorithms run on the test environment, 300x200 images at one sample per pixel.

results are for 300 by 200 image sampled at one sample per pixel on the above mentioned environment. The small image size and sampling rate were necessary because of the computational expense of MCPT. The times are for a single processor Silicon Graphics workstation with an R4400 processor.

as light sources. Because of this, we do not provide an example of an image using this method, but we expect the image quality to similar to the view depicted in Figure 5 and slightly less noisy of the view depicted in Figure 6. It should be noted that reclassification will only increase the number of explicit samples necessary for this method.

The artificially small image size and sampling rate used to generate the values in Table 1 does not display the true power of our method. For a larger image of the same scene with a higher sampling rate per pixel, the preprocessing times for our algorithm remain unchanged and the implicit and explicit ray numbers will continue to be of the same order as the number of viewing rays. Using the above table as a guide, approximate times for a 1000x1000 image of the same scene with 64 samples per pixel would be on the order of 126 weeks for MCPT, 53 days for GSII, and 3 days for our algorithm. Note that GSII will have less noise than our algorithm in such a run, and MCPT will have more noise, so time only tells part of the story.

5 Discussion

We have presented results for only one model. This model is somewhat unusual in having so many lights that are only decorative. However, there are 24 lights that are not decorative, and many reflectors that have been reclassified. The lack of standard test scenes remains a severe impediment to the comparison of algorithms.

Our algorithm is no longer a pure Monte Carlo method (unlike [3, 13]), so our solution will have both noise and deterministic error. Note that almost all current methods are such hybrids; e.g., most visibility checks are Monte Carlo. We have not made any analytical statements about the magnitude of this error in our results. Bounding our error will be difficult. Surprisingly, almost no global illumination algorithms have known error bounds on their solutions; Lischinski et al. [5] have provided us with error bounds on piecewise-constant radiosity solutions. We are aware of no other such results. So our algorithm is not unusual in not having well-understood error properties.

Like Ward [16], we use non-diffuse transport only for the last non-specular bounce before the eye (ie. he replaces $eye\ S^{*}GG^{*}\ light$ paths with $eye\ S^{*}GD^{*}\ light$ paths, where G is a general BRDF). We will perform poorly for $eye\ S^{*}DS^{*}\ light$ paths. This type of path seems to be the "rock in the shoe" for almost all global illumination algorithms.

Recent work by Veach and Guibas [14] suggests that the integral should not be partitioned, but should instead be sampled directionally (Equation 3) using a mixture of several directional densities. Our sampling methods should still apply in such a case.

6 Conclusion

We have presented a two-pass global illumination method that has a gather that is practical for complex diffuse scenes with many luminaires. This algorithm borrows the ideas of simplified geometry and light source reclassification from GSII. It also performs visibility estimates to associate visible light sources to regions in the environment. An implementation of this method has been run on a scenes with tens of thousands of surfaces and hundreds of luminaires.

The crux of this paper is that efficiency can be gained by explicitly sampling only a few very important surfaces, and directionally sampling to estimate the contribution of the remaining surfaces. In addition, the use of visibility coherence was used to lower variance. This amounts to dividing the integral into two components, and applying different quadrature methods for each component. The techniques in this paper provide a mechanism that efficiently makes this division.

Acknowledgements

This work was supported by NSF CCR-9401961 and performed on equipment supplied by IU-RUGS and NSF CISE II grant 9303189. Thanks to Ken Chiu for providing the parallel execution framework used to speed debugging and image creation.

References

1. Donald P. Greenberg. Computers and architecture: advanced modeling and rendering algorithms allow designers and clients to walk through buildings long before construction. *Scientific American*, 264:104–109, February 1991.
2. David S. Immel, Michael F. Cohen, and Donald P. Greenberg. A radiosity method for nondiffuse environments. *Computer Graphics*, 20(4):133–142, August 1986. ACM Siggraph '86 Conference Proceedings.
3. James T. Kajiya. The rendering equation. *Computer Graphics*, 20(4):143–150, August 1986. ACM Siggraph '86 Conference Proceedings.
4. Eric P. Lafortune and Yves D. Willems. The ambient term as a variance reducing technique for monte carlo ray tracing. In *Proceedings of the Fifth Eurographics Workshop on Rendering*, pages 163–172, 1995.
5. Dani Lischinski, Brian Smits, and Donald P. Greenberg. Bounds and error estimates for radiosity. *Computer Graphics*, 28(3):67–74, July 1994. ACM Siggraph '94 Conference Proceedings.
6. Mark C. Reichert. A two-pass radiosity method driven by lights and viewer position. Master's thesis, Cornell Program of Computer Graphics, January 1992.
7. Holly Rushmeier, Charles Patterson, and Aravindan Veerasamy. Geometric simplification for indirect illumination calculations. In *Graphics Interface '93*, pages 227–236, May 1993.
8. Holly E. Rushmeier. *Realistic Image Synthesis for Scenes with Radiatively Participating Media*. PhD thesis, Cornell University, May 1988.
9. Peter Shirley and Changyaw Wang. Distribution ray tracing: Theory and practice. In *Proceedings of the Third Eurographics Workshop on Rendering*, pages 200–209, 1992.
10. Peter Shirley, Changyaw Wang, and Kurt Zimmerman. Monte carlo techniques for direct lighting calculations. *ACM Transactions on Graphics (TOG)*, 1995. accepted for publication.
11. Brian E. Smits, James R. Arvo, and David H. Salesin. A clustering algorithm for radiosity in complex environments. *Computer Graphics*, 28(3):435–442, July 1994. ACM Siggraph '94 Conference Proceedings.
12. Seth Teller and Pat Hanrahan. Global visibility algorithms for illumination computations. *Computer Graphics*, 27:239–246, August 1993. ACM Siggraph '94 Conference Proceedings.
13. Eric Veach and Leonidas Guibas. Bidirectional estimators for light transport. In *Proceedings of the Fifth Eurographics Workshop on Rendering*, pages 147–162, June 1994.
14. Eric Veach and Leonidas Guibas. Optimally combining sampling techniques for monte carlo rendering. *Computer Graphics*, 29(3), August 1995. ACM Siggraph '95 Conference Proceedings.
15. Greg Ward. Adaptive shadow testing for ray tracing. In *Proceedings of the Second Eurographics Workshop on Rendering*, 1991.
16. Gregory J. Ward. The radiance lighting simulation and rendering system. *Computer Graphics*, 28(2), July 1994. ACM Siggraph '94 Conference Proceedings.
17. Kurt Zimmerman and Peter Shirley. A two-pass realistic image synthesis method for complex scenes. Technical Report 434, Department of Computer Science, Indiana University, May 1995.

Separating Reflection Functions
for Linear Radiosity

ALAIN FOURNIER

Department of Computer Science, University of British Columbia
Vancouver, BC, V6T 1Z4, Canada. fournier@cs.ubc.ca

Abstract: Classic radiosity assumes diffuse reflectors in order to consider only pair-wise exchanges of light between elements. It has been previously shown that one can use the same system of equations with separable bi-directional reflection distribution functions (BRDFs), that is BRDFs that can be put in the form of a product of two functions, one of the incident direction and one of the reflected direction.

We show here that this can be easily extended to BRDFs that can be approximated by sums of such terms. The classic technique of Singular Value Decomposition (SVD) can be used to compute those terms given an analytical or experimental BRDF. We use the example of the traditional Phong model for specular-like reflection to extract a separable model, and show the results in term of closeness to ordinary Phong shading. We also show an example with experimental BRDF data. Further work will indicate whether the quality of linear radiosity images will be improved by this modification.

Keywords: BRDF, separable BRDF, global illumination, form factors, singular value decomposition.

1. Introduction

There is no need to repeat here the principles involved in computing global illumination through the *radiosity* method (we will use this synecdoche, since it is now well accepted and understood). We will use here the notation and terminology of Cohen & Wallace [1] whenever applicable. We will include within the class *linear pair-wise radiosity*, or *linear radiosity* for short, the methods which use an equation of the form:

$$B_i = E_i + R_i \sum_{j=1}^{N} B_j F_{ij} \qquad (1)$$

Where R_i is only a function of the element i (the reflectance ρ_i in the classic case), and F_{ij} are only geometric functions of the pairs ij, the *form factors*. Our goal in this paper is to show how one can extend considerably the class of reflective behaviours which still lead to a linear radiosity solution.

2. Separable Models and Form Factors

The starting point for the radiosity equations is the *rendering equation* as given for example in [1]. The corresponding geometry is shown in Figure (1).

$$L(\mathbf{x}', \omega') = L_e(\mathbf{x}', \omega') + \int_S f_r(\mathbf{x}', \omega, \omega') L(\mathbf{x}, \omega) G(\mathbf{x}, \mathbf{x}') V(\mathbf{x}, \mathbf{x}') \, dA \qquad (2)$$

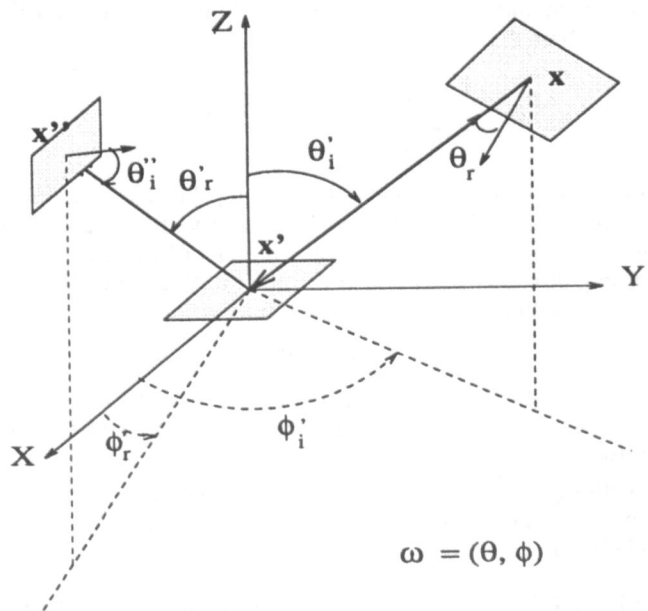

Figure (1). Geometry of 3-point transport

where $G()$ is a geometric factor:

$$G(\mathbf{x}, \mathbf{x}') = \frac{\cos\theta \ \cos\theta'}{|\mathbf{x} - \mathbf{x}'|^2} \qquad (3)$$

and $V()$ is a visibility factor (1 if the points are mutually visible, 0 if not). Noting that for Lambertian reflectors we have:

$$f_r(\mathbf{x}', \omega, \omega') = \frac{\rho(\mathbf{x}')}{\pi}$$

and that the radiosity is π times the radiance, one obtains:

$$B(\mathbf{x}') = E(\mathbf{x}') + \rho(\mathbf{x}') \int_S B(\mathbf{x}) \frac{G(\mathbf{x}, \mathbf{x}')V(\mathbf{x}, \mathbf{x}')}{\pi} \, dA \qquad (4)$$

Note that it has been implicitly assumed that the light sources are Lambertian emitters as well, which is not really necessary. To obtain equation (1), one discretizes the surfaces into elements. Integrating over A' for a finite area, one obtains an average radiosity for A':

$$\bar{B}' = \frac{1}{A'} \int_{A'} B(\mathbf{x}') dA'$$

The integration over S is an integration over A for each of the elements. Using the subscript i for primed quantities, and j for un-primed, and summing for all j elements, one obtains equation (1), if B_j can be taken to be constant over the element j, where P_i is ρ_i and where the form factors F_{ij} are:

$$F_{ij} = \frac{1}{A_i} \int\limits_{A_i} \int\limits_{A_j} \frac{G(\mathbf{x}, \mathbf{x}')V(\mathbf{x}, \mathbf{x}')}{\pi} \, dA_j \, dA_j \qquad (5)$$

It has been shown, notably by Neumann & Neumann [5] that we can still use the same system of equations if the BRDF, instead of being constant as a function of the directions, is *separable*, that is can be written as the product of two functions, one a function of the incoming direction $I(\mathbf{x}, \omega_i)$ and the other a function of the outgoing direction $O(\mathbf{x}, \omega_r)$. So that with the notation used before:

$$f_r(\mathbf{x}', \omega, \omega') = I(\mathbf{x}', \omega) \times O(\mathbf{x}', \omega')$$

One should note that if the BRDF is to obey reciprocity, $O()$ and $I()$ should be the same functions for each point within a constant, but this is not affecting any of the formulas which follow.

We start again with equation (4), and substitute the separable BRDF. Since $O(\mathbf{x}', \omega')$ is not a function of the integration variable in the integral over S, we can get it out of the integral, and obtain:

$$L(\mathbf{x}', \omega') = L_e(\mathbf{x}', \omega') + O(\mathbf{x}', \omega') \int\limits_{S} I(\mathbf{x}', \omega) \, L(\mathbf{x}, \omega)G(\mathbf{x}, \mathbf{x}')V(\mathbf{x}, \mathbf{x}') \, dA \qquad (6)$$

To transform this relation between radiances into a relation between radiosities or irradiances, one need the basic relation:

$$B = \int\limits_{\Omega} L(\omega) \cos \theta \, d\omega$$

where the integral is over the hemisphere in our case. So if we integrate both sides of equation (6), we get:

$$\int\limits_{\Omega} L(\mathbf{x}', \omega') \cos \theta_r' \, d\omega' = \int\limits_{\Omega} L_e(\mathbf{x}', \omega') \cos \theta_r' \, d\omega'$$

$$+ \int\limits_{\Omega} \cos \theta_r' \, d\omega' \, [O(\mathbf{x}', \omega') \int\limits_{S} I(\mathbf{x}', \omega) \, L(\mathbf{x}, \omega)G(\mathbf{x}, \mathbf{x}')V(\mathbf{x}, \mathbf{x}') \, dA \,]$$

One can call:

$$E(\mathbf{x}') = \int\limits_{\Omega} L_e(\mathbf{x}', \omega') \cos \theta_r' \, d\omega'$$

In other word $E(\mathbf{x}')$ is the radiosity due to light emission (note that the distribution can be anything we want which is integrable). We can also note that only $O(\mathbf{x}', \omega')$ is affected by the integral over Ω, so it all simplifies to:

$$B(\mathbf{x}') = E(\mathbf{x}') + [\int\limits_{\Omega} O(\mathbf{x}', \omega') \cos \theta_r' \, d\omega'] \times [\int\limits_{S} I(\mathbf{x}', \omega) \, L(\mathbf{x}, \omega)G(\mathbf{x}, \mathbf{x}')V(\mathbf{x}, \mathbf{x}') \, dA \,] \quad (7)$$

We can define $SO(\mathbf{x}') = \int\limits_{\Omega} O(\mathbf{x}', \omega') \cos \theta_r' \, d\omega'$, in effect a normalization of $O(\mathbf{x}', \omega')$.

In general for any $\mathbf{x}$ and ω we can write:

$$L(\mathbf{x}, \omega) = K \times O(\mathbf{x}, \omega)$$

for some positive constant K (since $O()$ is the function giving the distribution of the reflected light at $\mathbf{x}$), and multiplying both sides by $\cos \theta \, d\omega$ and integrating:

$$B(\mathbf{x}) = K \times SO(\mathbf{x})$$

The ratio of these two equations gives the relationship between $L(\mathbf{x}, \omega)$ and $B(\mathbf{x})$:

$$L(\mathbf{x}, \omega) = \frac{B(\mathbf{x}) \times O(\mathbf{x}, \omega)}{SO(\mathbf{x})}$$

We can use this to replace $L(\mathbf{x}, \omega)$ in equation (7).

All told, we then obtain:

$$B(\mathbf{x}') = E(\mathbf{x}') + SO(\mathbf{x}') \int\limits_{S} B(\mathbf{x}) I(\mathbf{x}', \omega) \, \frac{O(\mathbf{x}, \omega)}{SO(\mathbf{x})} \, G(\mathbf{x}, \mathbf{x}') V(\mathbf{x}, \mathbf{x}') \, dA \qquad (8)$$

which is the new version of equation (4).

We can now discretize (8) as we did for (4). Integrating over A for each element, averaging $B(\mathbf{x})$ over A' and summing over all elements:

$$\frac{1}{A'} \int\limits_{A'} B(\mathbf{x}') dA' = \frac{1}{A'} \int\limits_{A'} E(\mathbf{x}') dA'$$

$$+ \sum_{all\ elements} \frac{1}{A'} \int\limits_{A'} SO(\mathbf{x}') dA' \int\limits_{A} B(\mathbf{x}) \, I(\mathbf{x}', \omega) \, \frac{O(\mathbf{x}, \omega)}{SO(\mathbf{x})} \, G(\mathbf{x}, \mathbf{x}') V(\mathbf{x}, \mathbf{x}') \, dA$$

Using the same indices as before, and the same assumption about $B(\mathbf{x}) = B_j = $ constant over A, one gets:

$$B_i = E_i + SO_i \sum_{j=1}^{N} B_j \frac{1}{A_i} \int\limits_{A_i} \int\limits_{A_j} I_i(\omega) \, \frac{O_j(\omega)}{SO_j} \, G(\mathbf{x}, \mathbf{x}') V(\mathbf{x}, \mathbf{x}') \, dA_i dA_j = E_i + SO_i \sum_{j=1}^{N} B_j F_{ij}$$

where the new form factors are:

$$F_{ij} = \frac{1}{A_i} \int\limits_{A_i} \int\limits_{A_j} I_i(\omega) \, \frac{O_j(\omega)}{SO_j} \, G(\mathbf{x}, \mathbf{x}') V(\mathbf{x}, \mathbf{x}') \, dA_i dA_j \qquad (9)$$

Notice that the relation: $F_{ij} \times A_i = F_{ji} \times A_j$ always valid for diffuse reflectors, is here only true if $O_j(\omega) = I_i(\omega)$ and $SO_i = SO_j$. For different materials this is not going to be true, and even for the same material, first reciprocity has to apply, and since the same ω corresponds to different direction in i and j frames of references, this would be true only for special cases.

3. Sum of Separable Models

The basic problem with separable models is that very few real surfaces exhibit behaviour compatible with a straight separable model[1]. Neumann & Neumann presented an ingenious exception, the *lacquer* model, where a Lambertian reflector was covered by a layer of absorptant material (which obey Beer's law, but that is not necessary). This model, however, when implemented, gives a reflecting behaviour quite unsatisfactory compared to most real materials (see paper by Lewis [4]).

Let us see what happens if we represent the BRDF as a *sum* of M separable components. The equation is now at point $\mathbf{x}'$:

$$f_r(\mathbf{x}', \omega, \omega') = \sum_{m'=1}^{M'} I_{m'}(\mathbf{x}', \omega) \times O_{m'}(\mathbf{x}', \omega')$$

Similarly at point $\mathbf{x}$:

$$f_r(\mathbf{x}, \omega, \omega') = \sum_{m=1}^{M} I_m(\mathbf{x}, \omega) \times O_m(\mathbf{x}, \omega')$$

Substituting in equation (2), we have now:

$$L(\mathbf{x}', \omega') = L_e(\mathbf{x}', \omega') + \int_S [\sum_{m'=1}^{M'} I_{m'}(\mathbf{x}', \omega) \times O_{m'}(\mathbf{x}', \omega')] L(\mathbf{x}, \omega) G(\mathbf{x}, \mathbf{x}') V(\mathbf{x}, \mathbf{x}') \, dA \quad (10)$$

The integral over S can now be separated into M' integrals of the form:

$$\int_S I_{m'}(\mathbf{x}', \omega) \times O_{m'}(\mathbf{x}', \omega') L(\mathbf{x}, \omega) G(\mathbf{x}, \mathbf{x}') V(\mathbf{x}, \mathbf{x}') \, dA$$

In each of these integrals $O_{m'}(\mathbf{x}', \omega')$ is not dependent on A and therefore can be removed from the integral:

$$O_m(\mathbf{x}', \omega') \int_S I_m(\mathbf{x}', \omega) \times L(\mathbf{x}, \omega) G(\mathbf{x}, \mathbf{x}') V(\mathbf{x}, \mathbf{x}') \, dA$$

We can now as before multiply by $\cos \theta_r' d\omega'$ and integrate:

$$B(\mathbf{x}') = E(\mathbf{x}') + \sum_{m'=1}^{M'} [SO_{m'}(\mathbf{x}') \int_S I_{m'}(\mathbf{x}', \omega) \, L(\mathbf{x}, \omega) G(\mathbf{x}, \mathbf{x}') V(\mathbf{x}, \mathbf{x}') \, dA]$$

We can also replace $L(\mathbf{x}, \omega)$ by:

$$L(\mathbf{x}, \omega) = B(\mathbf{x}) \frac{\sum_{m=1}^{M} O_m(\mathbf{x}, \omega)}{\sum_{m=1}^{M} SO_m(\mathbf{x})}$$

which gives;

$$B(\mathbf{x}') = E(\mathbf{x}') + \sum_{m'=1}^{M'} [SO_{m'}(\mathbf{x}') \int_S B(\mathbf{x}) \, I_{m'}(\mathbf{x}', \omega) \frac{\sum_{m=1}^{M} O_m(\mathbf{x}, \omega)}{\sum_{m=1}^{M} SO_m(\mathbf{x})} G(\mathbf{x}, \mathbf{x}') V(\mathbf{x}, \mathbf{x}') \, dA]$$

---

1. Of course Lambertian reflectors are also rather rare, but you have to start somewhere.

Again using the indices i and j, and replacing by the element averages (we will use m and n for the indices of the separable elements for element i and j, respectively):

$$B_i = E_i + \sum_{m=1}^{M} SO_{im} \sum_j B_j \frac{1}{A_i} \int_{A_i} \int_{A_j} I_{im}(\omega) \frac{\sum_{n=1}^{N} O_{jn}(\omega)}{\sum_{n=1}^{N} SO_{jn}} G(\mathbf{x}, \mathbf{x}') V(\mathbf{x}, \mathbf{x}') \, dA_i dA_j$$

This is equivalent to having $M \times N$ pairs ij, with the pair equation:

$$B_{im} = E_{im} + SO_{im} \sum_j B_j \frac{1}{A_i} \int_{A_i} \int_{A_j} I_{im}(\omega) \frac{O_{jn}(\omega)}{\sum_{n=1}^{N} SO_{jn}} G(\mathbf{x}, \mathbf{x}') V(\mathbf{x}, \mathbf{x}') \, dA_i dA_j \quad (11)$$

or:

$$B_{im} = E_{im} + SO_{im} \sum_j B_j F_{im,jn}$$

The constraint on E_{im} is $E_i = \sum_{m=1}^{M} E_{im}$. Of course putting for example $E_{i0} = E_i$ and all others to 0 will do. We have now $M \times N$ form factors:

$$F_{im,jn} = \frac{1}{A_i} \int_{A_i} \int_{A_j} I_{im}(\omega) \frac{O_{jn}(\omega)}{\sum_{n=1}^{N} SO_{jn}} G(\mathbf{x}, \mathbf{x}') V(\mathbf{x}, \mathbf{x}') \, dA_i dA_j$$

We can modify the equations to obtain a slightly better form, by multiplying B_j by $\frac{SO_{jn}}{SO_{jn}}$ in equation (11). Denoting:

$$B_{jn} = \frac{B_j \, SO_{jn}}{\sum_{n=1}^{N} SO_{jn}}$$

we can write:

$$B_{im} = E_{im} + SO_{im} \sum_j B_{jn} F_{im,jn}$$

where the form factor is modified to be:

$$F_{im,jn} = \frac{1}{A_i} \int_{A_i} \int_{A_j} I_{im}(\omega) \frac{O_{jn}(\omega)}{SO_{jn}} G(\mathbf{x}, \mathbf{x}') V(\mathbf{x}, \mathbf{x}') \, dA_i dA_j$$

and therefore much more similar to the one given in equation (9).

Now the important practical questions are: for the BRDFs that one might actually want to use, how well can we separate them, and what is the size of M and N? In effect we multiply the size of the problem by the average of $M \times N$ for all the pairs of elements. The additional cost of computing form factors is not that bad, since the visibility function is the same for all pairs im, jn. One must however, keep in mind that the alternatives can be much worse, from considering all triples of patches in the full solution, which multiplies the number of form factors by n and the size of the solution by n^2 [3] to using various basis functions for input or output radiosity as for instance in Sillion *et al* (up to 200 coefficients) [7].

There are various ways to achieve an analytical sum of product decomposition of functions, from Taylor series expansion to spherical harmonics, but there is a numerical approach that has the advantage of being simple, almost universal, optimal under some conditions, and applicable to experimentally-measured BRDFs as well.

4. Singular Value Decomposition

Singular value decomposition (SVD) is a technique which given A a $P \times Q$ matrix[2], $P \geq Q$, decompose it into the product of three matrices:

$$A = U \ W \ V^T$$

where U is a $P \times Q$ column orthonormal matrix , V is a $Q \times Q$ column (and row) orthonormal matrix, and W is a $Q \times Q$ diagonal matrix. This decomposition is unique within row permutations. For more details see Golub [2] and for code see *Numerical Recipes in C* [6]. The result of SVD can be seen as writing each element of A as a weighted sum of the rows of U and the columns of V^T, where the weights are the diagonal elements of W:

$$A_{ij} = \sum_{k=1}^{Q} W_{kk} \times U_{ik} \times V_{jk} \qquad (12)$$

If we take the M largest elements (in magnitude) of W, we then obtain an approximation of A with M products per element. The SVD guarantees that the result will be optimal in the least-square sense for this number of terms.

The technique applies to functions in the following way. Given a function $f(x, y)$, we chose P values x_i of the abscissa and Q values y_j of the ordinate. The elements of the matrix A are:

$$A_{ij} = f(x_i, y_j)$$

Clearly each row of A corresponds to samples at constant x, and each column to samples at constant y. After applying SVD to A, equation (12) means that all the samples can be approximated by the sum of the weighted products of M elements of a row U and M elements of a row of V. These rows are only functions of x and y respectively. We can then fit a function to each relevant row of U, $g_k(x)$ such that $g_k(x_i) = U_{ik}$ and fit a function to each relevant row of V, $h_k(y)$ such that $h_k(y_j) = V_{jk}$ and we have:

$$f(x, y) = \sum_{k=1}^{M} W_k k \ g_k(x) \times h_k(y)$$

In other words we have expressed $f(x, y)$ as a sum of separated terms.

The samples have to be chosen so that more weight is given to ranges that are important for the function at hand. The error made comes from both the SVD and the fit with the basis functions used. In both cases these errors are known from their

---

2.   Usually the dimensions are noted $M \times N$, but we do not want to promote confusion with the number of separate factors in the BRDF.

respective methods. In our case we want to take a function of four variables and separate it into sum of products of two two-variable functions. Fortunately the method is very much the same. We chose P pairs $(\theta_i \phi_i)$ for the incoming direction and Q pairs $(\theta_j \phi_j)$ for the outgoing direction. direction. For each tuple of pairs, we compute:

$$A_{ij} = f_r(\theta_i, \phi_i, \theta_j, \phi_j)$$

Again the pair should be chosen according to the function at hand. In practice for functions known analytically, we picked random direction whose projections on the unit circle are uniformly distributed. The justification is that according to the Nusselt analog they represent a uniform distribution in the diffuse form factor.

For experimental data, one should obtain or extract by interpolation a $P \times Q$ array of values.

5. Decomposition of Phong Model

To test the practicality of this solution, we made a preliminary study for an analytical formulation, namely *Phong* shading. We used a reciprocal version of Phong shading [4] for which the BRDF has the simple form:

$$f_r(\omega, \omega') = k \, (\cos \alpha)^n$$

where α is the angle between the bisector of (ω, ω') and the normal to the surface (the Z axis in its local frame). Of course $\cos \alpha$ is known as N.H in the trade; this is the "Blinn" modified version of Phong. We chose this because it is popular, used by most renderers, adjustable to high glossiness through the value of n, and a difficult case. The only redeeming value here is that it is isotropic. The process was to take a user-defined number of samples in incoming and outgoing directions (the size of the matrix), an exponent n, and the number of terms t to be used in the approximation. Once the SVD was done, the first t rows of U and the first t rows of V were fitted to a bicubic equation (16 coefficients) by least square (actually using SVD again). The choice of bicubic is quite arbitrary, and we have not yet explored better basis functions. As mentioned above, each direction is chosen randomly, with projections uniformly distributed over the unit circle.

n	Size $P = Q$	Number of Terms	RMS after SVD	Max Δ	RMS after fit	Max Δ
1	40	5	0.011	0.087	0.019	0.17
1	40	10	0.00088	0.00095	0.016	0.14
4	40	5	0.029	0.27	0.032	0.27
4	40	10	0.0046	0.041	0.016	0.077
8	40	5	0.050	0.55	0.052	0.55
8	40	10	0.0091	0.096	0.019	0.12
32	40	5	0.088	0.91	0.10	0.92
32	40	10	0.039	0.40	0.073	0.34
32	40	15	0.013	0.080	0.069	0.33

The table shows the results for a range of exponents and number of terms (separate components M) kept. As expected, for small exponents the BRDF is easy to separate, and is approximated within a few percent with 5 terms. Even when $n = 8$, 10 terms give a 2% accuracy. For an exponent of 32, 15 terms are necessary to do a good job. Notice that the fit of the separated functions is sometimes responsible for most of the RMS error. As mentioned before we have not yet spent much time on this aspect of the fit. Note that the maximum difference between computed and fitted values can be alarmly high. We suspect that more weight has to be put on the direction pairs causing a specular highlight. Also the fit used here did not use isotropy of the input or force isotropy of the result.

Of course the numbers here are not telling the whole story. The symmetry, or lack thereof, of the recovered functions can be important in many cases. What we have to offer for now is some images computed with the separated BRDFs. Figure (2) shows spheres shaded by a built-in Phong shader (non-reciprocal), a reciprocal interpreted one (for sanity check), and a diffuse surface. The specular surfaces have a small ambient term added (0.1). The eye is at (0, -20, 0), the balls all around the origin, and there are two directional light sources, one at (0.4, -0.9, 1) and the other at (-0.87, 0.5, 1). One can see that the separated functions (in this case with $n = 8$ and 5 terms selected) do a decent specular surface. Remember that you can put this BRDF into your favourite radiosity-based renderer at very little added cost.

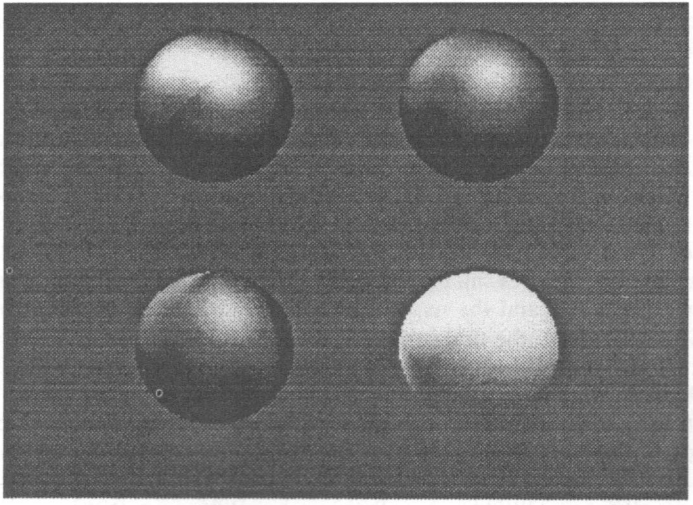

Figure (2): Phong model, original and reconstructed, with two lights. Upper left: non-reciprocal Phong, upper right: reciprocal Phong, lower left: separated reciprocal Phong, lower right: diffuse.

6. Decomposition of Experimental Data

As a quick test we used Greg Ward's experimental data [8]. It came in two flavours, a raw data file with 27330 experimental pairs of directions (file g50bw.brdf), and a "filtered" one with 2647 data pairs (file g50bw.rdu). To use this data we inserted the values into a quad tree where the node are (θ, ϕ) bins, and split the nodes when they had too many data points. At the end the nodes with enough data points (typically 40 to 50) were used. The centre pair value of each node was the sample values used for building the matrix. The reflectance values were determined by interpolation for these samples. Usually a 50×50 matrix is output. The following table show some results.

Data Points $P = Q$	Size of Terms	Number after SVD	RMS Δ	Max after fit	RMS Δ	Max
2647	50	5	0.021	0.29	0.031	0.30
2647	50	10	0.011	0.083	0.029	0.25
27330	50	5	0.033	0.35	0.18	5.2
27330	50	10	0.019	0.35	0.18	5.2

It can be noted that the filtered data works well, when the raw data fails. In fact in the latter case the situation does not improve with more terms. Better use of these experimental data is tied in with reconstruction from irregularly sampled data, a topic we are currently investigating.

7. Conclusions

We have shown that expressing BRDFs as sums of separable functions leads to a simple implementation within linear radiosity systems. We have also shown how singular value decomposition helps us produce these sums from analytical or experimental data. The experiments with Phong BRDF and Greg Ward's experimental data are promising, but there is still a lot to explore in order to fine tune the approach. The next step, obviously, is to incorporate this into a linear radiosity system, and we have done so starting with *rad*, the program from S.N. Pattanaik (images to follow).

Acknowledgements

I gratefully acknowledge the support of NSERC through operating grants and graduate scholarships. Paul Lalonde and Bob Lewis provided advice and help (also tried to mess up my commas). I thank Greg Ward for his data (and expect more).

References

1. M.F. Cohen and J.R. Wallace, *Radiosity and Realistic Image Synthesis*, Academic Press, 1993.

2. G. H. Golub and C. F. Van Loan, *Matrix Computations*, John Hopkins University Press, 1983.

3. D.S. Immel, M.F. Cohen, and D.P. Greenberg, "A Radiosity Method for Non-Diffuse Environments," *Computer Graphics*, vol. 20, no. 4, pp. 133-142, August 1986.

4. Robert Lewis, "Making Shaders More Physically Plausible," *Fourth Eurographics Workshop on Rendering*, pp. 47-62, 1993.

5. L. Neumann and A. Neumann, "Photosimulation: Interreflection with Arbitrary Reflectance Models and Illumination," *Computer Graphics Forum*, vol. 8, pp. 21-34, 1989.

6. W. H. Press, B. P. Flannery, S. A. Teukolsky, and W. T. Vetterling, *Numerical Recipes in C*, Cambridge University Press, 1994.

7. Francois X. Sillion, James R. Arvo, Stephen H. Westin, and Donald P. Greenberg, "A global illumination solution for general reflectance distributions," *Computer Graphics (SIGGRAPH '91 Proceedings)*, vol. 25, no. 4, pp. 187-196, 1991.

8. Gregory J. Ward, "Measuring and modeling anisotropic reflection," *Computer Graphics (SIGGRAPH '92 Proceedings)*, vol. 26, no. 2, pp. 265-272, 1992.

Potential-driven Monte Carlo Particle Tracing for Diffuse Environments with Adaptive Probability Functions

Philip Dutré, Yves D. Willems

Department of Computer Science, Katholieke Universiteit Leuven
Celestijnenlaan 200A, B-3001 Heverlee, Belgium
Philip.Dutre@cs.kuleuven.ac.be; Yves.Willems@cs.kuleuven.ac.be

Abstract. A possible method for solving the global illumination problem is to use a Monte Carlo model, where particles are shot from the light sources and perform a random walk through the scene. The proposed algorithm tries to optimise the sampling process by constructing probability functions that closely match the visual potential function. Importance sampling ensures us that, within the given resolution and accuracy of the probability functions, particles are used in an optimal way, thereby lowering the overall variance of the picture. Sampling based on the local potential functions is done at light sources and surface patches, and thus influences every step of the random walk of a particle.

1 Introduction

The problem of global illumination in computer graphics can basically be solved using two distinct approaches: deterministic finite element algorithms and Monte Carlo techniques (although hybrid methods are also possible). The Monte Carlo approach is usually the simplest, since it provides us with a simple algorithm to compute the various integrals, and since it ensures that the expected values of the computational results equals the correct physical values. Monte Carlo algorithms are able to solve all possible light-surface interactions, can handle all types of bidirectional reflection distribution functions, and usually require no mesh. The drawback is that in order to compute the illumination of a simple scene, a huge number of samples must be generated. Various algorithms have been proposed in order to compute the global illumination using Monte Carlo algorithms: stochastic ray tracing [1, 11, 12]; path tracing [4]; particle tracing [7, 3]; bidirectional ray tracing [13, 5].

The method presented here uses particle tracing: particles are generated at the light sources and are stochastically propagated through the scene by random walks. The sampling of new directions of travel at the light sources and at each reflecting surface is based on estimates for the potential functions. In order to store these potential functions, the surfaces are divided into a mesh. Since computation of these potential functions requires a solution of the dual global illumination problem, they cannot be computed in advance. Therefore, an incremental algorithm is used, where the probability functions are refined gradually during computation.

2 Mathematical background

The global illumination problem can be formulated by two dual sets of equations. The rendering equation with an associated expression for the flux is probably the best known set. $L(x,\Theta_{out})$, the surface radiance leaving a point x in direction Θ_{out}, is given by the sum of the initial surface radiance $L_e(x,\Theta_{out})$ (if (x,Θ) belongs to a light source) and the reflection of all incident radiance values over the hemisphere Ω_x (equation 1). $f_r(\Theta_{out},x,\Theta)$ is the bidirectional reflectance distribution function (BRDF); $cos(\Theta)$ is the cosine between Θ and the normal in x; $r(x,\Theta)$ is the raytrace function, which gives the closest surface point seen from x in direction Θ ($\tilde{\Theta}$ is the inverse direction of Θ, such that $r(r(x,\Theta),\tilde{\Theta}) = x$). The flux $\Phi(S)$ through a given set S of points and directions is a double integral over all surfaces and hemispheres, where the set is defined by means of W_e ($W_e(x,\Theta) = 1$ if $(x,\Theta) \in S$, $W_e(x,\Theta) = 0$ if $(x,\Theta) \notin S$). $d\mu$ and $d\omega$ represent differential surface areas and solid angles.

$$L(x,\Theta_{out}) = L_e(x,\Theta_{out}) + \int_{\Omega_x} L(r(x,\Theta),\tilde{\Theta})f_r(\Theta_{out},x,\Theta)|\cos\Theta|d\omega_\Theta \qquad (1)$$

$$\Phi(S) = \int_A\int_{\Omega_x} L(x,\Theta)\,W_e(x,\Theta)|\cos\Theta|d\omega_\Theta d\mu_x \qquad (2)$$

These equations are used for describing 'gathering' algorithms, where energy is accumulated at the sets of interest. Algorithms based on this approach are stochastic ray tracing (where sets are defined w.r.t. each individual pixel), and most radiosity algorithms (where sets are individual surface elements). On the other hand, the potential equation [8, 9] and the associated flux expression (equations 3 and 4) describe 'shooting' algorithms, where energy is shot from the light sources. In these algorithms, one is more interested in the contribution of $L_e(x,\Theta)$ to $\Phi(S)$. This contribution is given by the potential function $W(x,\Theta)$ which is expressed by a similar recursive integral equation.

$$W(x,\Theta_{in}) = W_e(x,\Theta_{in}) + \int_{\Omega_{r(x,\Theta_{in})}} W(r(x,\Theta_{in}),\Theta)f_r(\tilde{\Theta}_{in},r(x,\Theta),\Theta)|\cos\Theta|d\omega_\Theta \quad (3)$$

$$\Phi(S) = \int_A\int_{\Omega_x} L_e(x,\Theta)\,W(x,\Theta)|\cos\Theta|d\omega_\Theta d\mu_x \qquad (4)$$

The transport properties of $W(x,\Theta)$ behave more as an 'incoming' function, as opposed to $L(x,\Theta)$, which behaves as an 'outgoing' function (figure 1). Instead of computing $\Phi(S)$ by evaluating $L(x,\Theta)$ for points belonging to S, one now evaluates $W(x,\Theta)$ for all points belonging to the light sources. It can be proven that these two sets of equations form an adjoint set, w.r.t. to a well-defined inner product. These sets of equations describe the same problem, but formulate it from a different point of view.

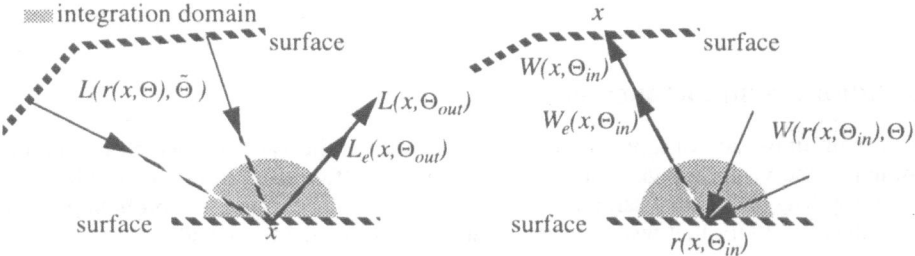

Fig. 1. Transport of surface radiance and surface potential using solid angle integration.

Our algorithm tries to compute $\Phi(S)$ for every individual pixel (towards the eye) using a Monte Carlo algorithm. In order to compute $\Phi(S)$ we have to evaluate equation 4, and use a random walk to evaluate $W(x,\Theta)$ (appendix 1). We only find contributions to $\Phi(S)$ if for a certain pair (x^i, Θ^i) of the random walk $W_e(x^i, \Theta^i) = 1$. However, it is highly unlikely that we will ever encounter such a pair. The use of next event estimation provides a way out. We apply recursive substitution in equation 3, to obtain:

$$W(x, \Theta_{in}) = W_e(x, \Theta_{in}) + W_N(x, \Theta_{in})$$
$$+ \int_{\Omega_{r(x,\Theta_{in})}} W_R(r(x, \Theta_{in}), \Theta) f_r\left(\Theta, r(x, \Theta_{in}), \tilde{\Theta}_{in}\right) |\cos\Theta| d\omega_\Theta \qquad (5)$$

where:

$$W_N(x, \Theta_{in}) = \int_{\Omega_{r(x,\Theta_{in})}} W_e(r(x, \Theta_{in}), \Theta) f_r\left(\Theta, r(x, \Theta_{in}), \tilde{\Theta}_{in}\right) |\cos\Theta| d\omega_\Theta$$
$$\qquad (6)$$
$$W_R(y, \Theta) = \int_{\Omega_{r(y,\Theta)}} W(r(y, \Theta), \Psi) f_r(\Psi, r(y, \Theta), \tilde{\Theta}) |\cos\Psi| d\omega_\Psi$$

The term $W_N(x,\Theta_{in})$ is the next event estimator. This term can be computed much more efficiently, since there is an easy way to determine whether $W_e(x,\Theta_{in}) = 1$: trace a ray from the intersection point to the eye. A complete estimator for $W(x,\Theta_{in})$ can then be computed as the sum of all next event estimators during a random walk (figure 2). This algorithm is the exact dual algorithm of path tracing, where shadowrays act as next event estimators.

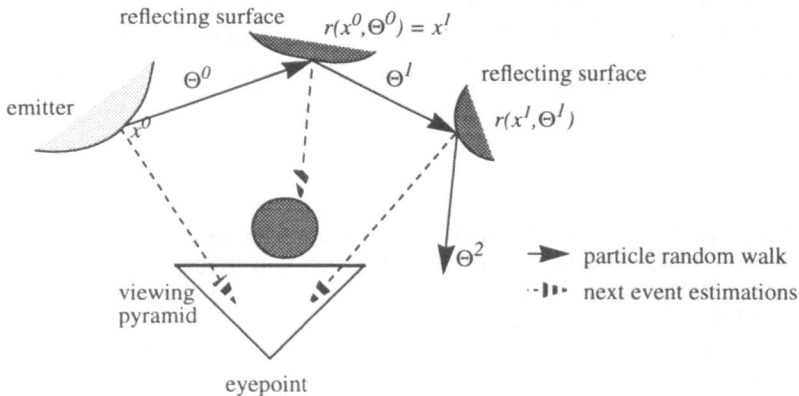

Fig. 2. Particle tracing algorithm using next event estimation

3 Adaptive importance sampling

The main drawback of any Monte Carlo algorithm is the variance, which can highly influence the visual image. Importance sampling is often used in order to reduce the variance. The idea is that samples should be generated according to a probability density function (PDF) that resembles the shape of the integrand (appendix 1).

In the above algorithm, importance sampling can be introduced in both the evaluation of $\Phi(S)$ and $W(x,\Theta)$. Both have a two-dimensional hemisphere Ω as part of their integration domain, so we shall focus on two-dimensional approximations of the integrand and store two-dimensional PDFs as piecewise constant functions. We shall write a piecewise constant approximation of a function $g(x)$ as $g(x)^*$ and the PDF derived from $g(x)^*$ as $pdf(g(x)^*)$.

For a single point x, $\Phi(S)$ (equation 4) only depends on direction Θ, the integration variable, and does not depend on any outside parameters. As such it is a two-dimensional function, fully defined over the integration domain. Since we are planning to use two-dimensional PDFs in order to sample directions, there should be no problem in computing and using $pdf(L_e(x,\Theta)\ W(x,\Theta)\ |cos\Theta|^*)$.

The expression for the potential $W(x,\Theta)$ (equation 5), is slightly more complex. The first two terms of the sum require straight evaluations. The third part requires a sampling process, because the random walk needs an outgoing direction Θ in $r(x,\Theta_{in})$. As stated earlier, the ideal PDF should be based on the product $W_R(r(x,\Theta_{in}),\Theta)$ $f_r(\Theta,r(x,\Theta_{in}),\tilde{\Theta}_{in})\ |cos\Theta|$. However, the integrand is, due to the nature of the BRDF, a four dimensional function for a given point x. There are different choices we can make in order to construct a PDF:

- We use the complete function as a basis for building up a PDF. This requires a four dimensional discretisation, which will be very memory-expensive. Moreover, it is questionable whether enough information will be available in order to build up good approximations, since the same number of samples has to be divided over more dimensions.

- We use the BRDF $f_r(\Theta,r(x,\Theta_{in}),\tilde{\Theta}_{in})$ as our PDF [2]. This would be a viable solution if we can somehow use an analytical expression for the BRDF (i.e. a Phonglike model) that can be transformed into a PDF. The results will be better if the BRDF is dominant for the overall behaviour of $W_R(r(x,\Theta_{in}),\Theta)\ f_r(\Theta,r(x,\Theta_{in}),\tilde{\Theta}_{in})\ |cos\Theta|$, as is the case with highly specular surfaces.

- We use $W_R(r(x,\Theta_{in}),\Theta)$ as the basis for our PDF. Given $r(x,\Theta_{in})$, it has the advantage of being only dependent on one direction Θ, so every particle that gets reflected in $r(x,\Theta_{in})$ contributes to W_R^* and $pdf(W_R^*)$. The results will be better if W_R dominates the integrand, which means that it will work well with diffuse-like surfaces. This is the approach we will use in our algorithm.

Thus we will store approximations of the potential, to be used both for light source sampling and reflection sampling. One remaining problem is the dependency on the surface points. In theory, every single surface point x has its own associated potential function, and thus a different optimal PDF. We have to discretise the surfaces in patches, and only use a single PDF for each patch. This applies as well to light sources as to non-emissive surfaces. The constructed mesh is not used in the final visualization, but is only used to store the different PDFs. Since a Monte Carlo algorithm works with any PDF, this mesh introduces no errors to the expected value of the computed physical values, but has an influence on the variance of the overall process.

4 Algorithm

Since our PDFs will be approximations of the potential functions W_R on each patch, they are not known at the start of the algorithm. The algorithm is split up in several iterations. During each iteration, all random walks will provide more information about W_R and the approximations W_R^* and $pdf(W_R^*)$ are adjusted accordingly. The

310

next iteration then starts with the newly updated PDFs, and should be more efficient than the previous one. All PDFs start as uniform functions.

The VEGAS method [6, 10] is a possible way of refining PDFs in order to gain more efficient importance sampling. However, the method was designed for one-dimensional integration, and is not easily extended to multidimensional non-separable functions. A previous paper [3] described the use of the VEGAS algorithm, based on k-d trees, applied to the directional sampling at light sources.

In this paper we propose another way of using adaptive PDFs. Each PDF is stored as a piecewise constant function, defined on a grid. Each grid element represents an equal solid angle on the hemisphere (figure 3). Each sample that is needed in order to compute a new direction for a particle that gets reflected, is generated using this PDF. The corresponding computed value of W_R is stored at the relevant grid element, and will at the end of the iteration be used to update W_R^* and $pdf(W_R^*)$.

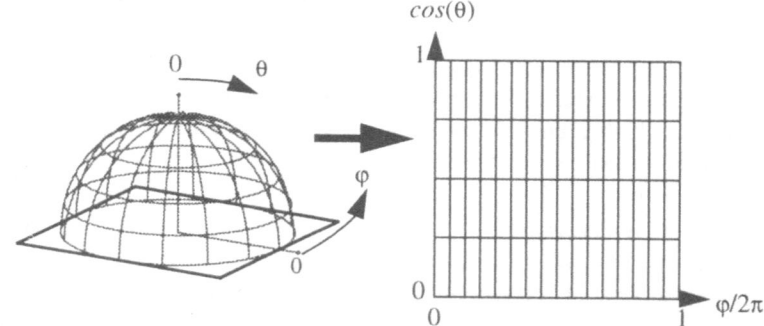

Fig. 3. Discretisation of a hemisphere in grid elements

Once an iteration has been processed, each grid element where samples were generated, provides us with an estimate W_R^* for the average value of W_R over that grid element. The accuracy is dependent on the number of samples that were used to estimate W_R over that grid element. Typically, the W_R^* values at the light sources are very accurate (because a lot of particles originate there), but the values of W_R^* at surface patches are less accurate. Some grid elements may have generated no samples at all. Since a bad importance sampling can produce much worse results than no importance sampling at all, we have to be on the safe side in constructing a new $pdf(W_R^*)$. This is controlled by a parameter S_{min}, which indicates the minimum number of samples needed in order to make a 'good guess' about the average value of W_R in that grid element. If the number of samples in a grid element exceeds S_{min}, we assume that the estimate is good enough, and the values of W_R^* in the grid element are then used to construct $pdf(W_R^*)$. If not, we take estimates from all neighboring elements in order to reach the minimal number of samples (figure 4). Once we have established all 'accurate' values, we can construct $pdf(W_R^*)$, by scaling the values such that the total probability over the hemisphere = 1. Future iterations only improve the estimates. Within the resolution of the fixed grid, the optimal situation should be reached after a certain number of iterations (depending on scene complexity and S_{min}).

One last issue to be decided is the termination of the random walks. We use an absorption probability based on the fraction of energy reflected for that particular surface and incident angle, although other methods such as Russian Roulette can be used as well.

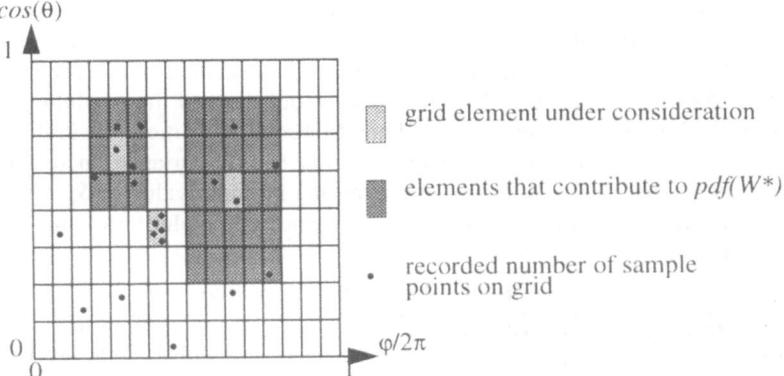

Fig. 4. Computation of $pdf(W_R*)$, with $S_{min} = 5$.

5 Results

The algorithm has been tested on different scenes. The scene shown here consists of a cornellbox with all surfaces diffuse-like and one light source, located on the ceiling just outside the viewing area. The surfaces are divided into 824 different patches. The results of the algorithm are shown in figure 5.

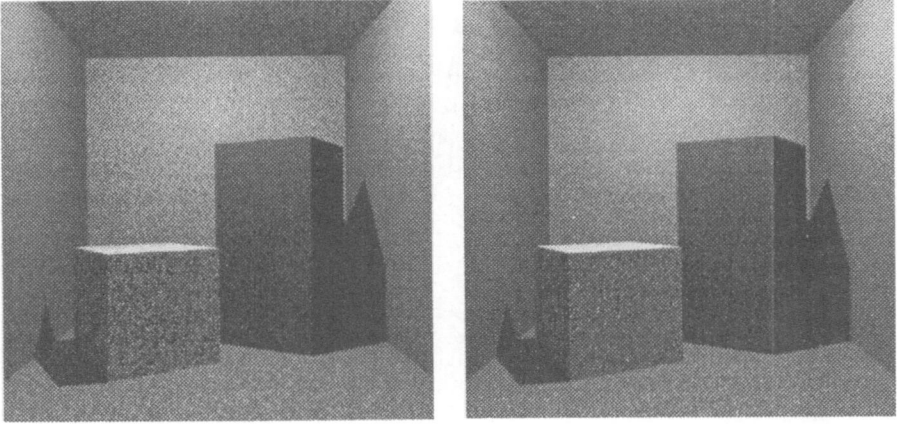

Fig. 5. Cornellbox, 10,000,000 particles. The picture on the left is rendered without adaptive PDFs, the picture on the right uses adaptive hemispherical PDFs (32x8; S_{min}=50)

The picture on the left was rendered with a standard particle tracing algorithm, without any PDF optimization. All particles are divided evenly across the scene. If we take a look at the noise present on the different surfaces, we see that the noise is fairly uniform distributed. The picture on the right was rendered using adaptive hemispherical PDFs. This picture still contains some noise, but the nature of the noise is different, resulting in some pixels that have a very high intensity value (especially noticeable in the shadows). This can be explained due to the fact that the adaptive PDFs attribute a low probability to those regions (they don't contribute significantly to the flux through the total screen). This means that very few particles will be sent to those regions, but the ones who arrive there have a rather high weight to compensate for the low probability. We experimented with several optimization schemes, which are summarized in table 1. As can be expected, the total variance decreases if the resolution of the hemispherical PDFs gets larger. Indeed, finer PDFs allow a more accurate sampling of reflected particles, and thus will result in better overall variance. Increasing S_{min} does not yield a significant advantage. However, the minimal value of S_{min} is closely connected to the total number of particles shot and the resolution of the hemispherical PDF grids.

Table 1. Results for Cornellbox scene

hemispherical grid size	final variance on flux through the screen (expected value = 4.28e-1)	fraction of surface hits that contribute to the flux through the screen
no adaptive PDFs	2.15e-4	31%
8x2; S_{min} = 50	1.94e-4	47%
32x8; S_{min} = 50	1.83e-4	54%

The plot in figure 6 represents the approximated potential W^* for the lightsource after all iterations are finished. The final PDF is a scaled version of this plot. It shows that there is indeed a significant difference with a uniform sampling process.

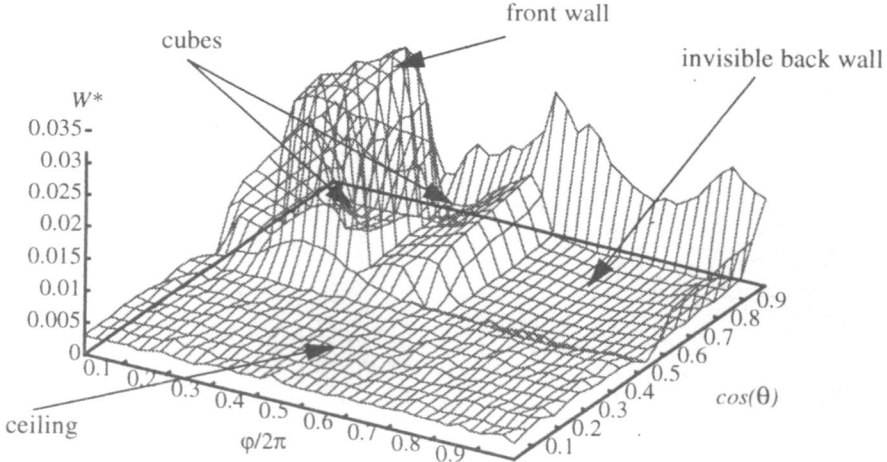

Fig. 6. W^* plot for the lightsource in figure 5.

6 Discussion

The algorithm outlined above will work well (within the limitations of a Monte Carlo method) for diffuse-like environments. In this case, the nearly constant BRDFs have little influence on the total evaluation of the potential. Specular surfaces are much harder to render, since the BRDF is not used in the reflective importance sampling. For these surfaces, a sampling procedure based on the BRDF will be more appropriate.

The grid size used for the PDFs, as well as the division of the surfaces in patches, is an important factor for efficiency. Too coarse grids will smooth out variations of the potential, while too fine grids consume a lot of memory and computation time will go up for determining workable PDFs. Hierarchical grids could provide a way out. Also, discontinuities in the potential function across surfaces or hemispheres can severely hinder good estimates. Discontinuity meshing based on the behavior of the potential function might be a good idea.

Pixels play no part in the algorithm. All functions are optimized with one goal in mind: optimise the flux going through the screen. It makes no difference whether the screen has a very small or very large resolution. Currently, experiments are being carried out where pixels are turned on or off for the evaluation of the potential functions: if a pixel is rendered with a certain degree of accuracy, it will be turned off. The overall effect should be that some areas of the screen will be rendered very fast, after which the algorithm turns its attention to other regions. The PDFs also change dynamically in order to steer more particles to the unrendered regions.

The algorithm should perform well in scenes were light sources illuminate visible surfaces indirectly, or where large parts of the directly lit surfaces are invisible to the eye. Experiments with indirectly lit scenes gave improvements of a factor 10 on the variance and the number of screen contributions. The algorithm can be extended to transparent surfaces. It would require storing two different hemispherical PDFs for a transparent patch, one for each side of its surface. However, this would add more noise to the resulting images.

7 Conclusion

We have presented a full potential-driven Monte Carlo particle tracing algorithm. During the algorithm, PDFs based on the potential functions are gradually built up, as well for light source sampling as for surface reflectance sampling. The PDFs are represented by regular piecewise constant functions. During the refinement of the PDFs, a minimum number of samples is taken into account in order to obtain more accurate values. The built-up PDFs differ significantly with the initial uniform PDFs. Noise is still present, but is manifested through some high-intensity pixels.

This kind of optimization is almost a necessity for particle tracing. Unlike stochastic ray tracing, we have initially no control over where the particles will travel and to what fluxes they will contribute most efficiently. The algorithm can also incorporated in Monte Carlo radiosity methods.

Interesting areas for future research include:
- hierarchical PDFs;
- wavelets defined on a sphere in order to generate PDFs;
- discontinuity meshing for surface patches and hemispherical PDFs.

Acknowledgments

This text presents research results of the Belgian incentive program "Information Technology" - computer science of the future, initiated by the Belgian State, Prime Minister's Service, Science Policy Office. The scientific responsibility is assumed by its authors.

References

1. Cook, R., Porter, T., Carpenter, L.: Distributed Ray Tracing. Computer Graphics (SIGGRAPH '84 Proceedings), 18(3):137-145 (1984)

2. Dutré, Ph., Willems, Y.: Proceedings of the 3rd International Conference on Computer Graphics, COMPUGRAPHICS '93, Portugal, (1993)

3. Dutré, Ph., Willems, Y.: Importance-driven Monte Carlo Light Tracing, Proceedings of the 5th Eurographics Workshop on Rendering, pp. 185-194 (1994)

4. Kajiya, J.: The Rendering Equation. Computer Graphics (SIGGRAPH '86 Proceedings), 20(4):143-150 (1986)

5. Lafortune, E., Willems, Y.: A Theoretical Framework for Physically based Rendering. Computer Graphics Forum, Vol. 13 (1994)

6. Lepage, G.: A New Algorithm for Adaptive Multidimensional Integration. Journal of Computational Physics, 27: 192-203 (1978)

7. Pattanaik, S., Mudur, S.: Computation of Global Illumination by Monte Carlo Simulation of the Particle Model of Light. Proceedings of the 3rd Eurographics Workshop on Rendering, pp.71-83 (1992)

8. Pattanaik, S., Mudur, S.: The Potential Equation and Importance in Illumination Computations, Computer Graphics Forum, 12(2) (1993)

9. Pattanaik, S.: Computational Methods for Global Illumination and Visualisation of Complex 3D Environments, PhD Thesis, Birla Institute of Technology and Science, Pilani, India (1993)

10. Press, W., Teukolsku, S., Vetterling, W., Flannery, B.: Numerical Recipes in Fortran, 2nd edition (1992) Cambridge University Press, pp. 309-314

11. Shirley, P., Wang, C.: Direct Lighting by Monte Carlo Integration. Proceedings of the 2nd Eurographics Workshop on Rendering (1991)

12. Shirley, P., Wang C.: Distribution Ray tracing: Theory and Practice, Proceedings of the 3rd Eurographics Workshop on Rendering (1991)

13. Veach, E., Guibas, L.:Bidirectional Estimators for Light Transport. Proceedings of the 5th Eurographics Workshop on Rendering, pp. 147-161 (1991)

Appendix 1: Importance sampling & random walks

Suppose we want to integrate a function $f(x)$ over a domain D:

$$I = \int_D f(x)\, dx \tag{7}$$

The value I can be estimated by generating N random points x_i, using a probability density function $p(x)$ defined over D:

$$\langle I \rangle = \frac{1}{N} \sum_{i=1}^{N} \frac{f(x_i)}{p(x_i)} \tag{8}$$

The expected value of $<I>$ equals I. The variance σ equals:

$$\sigma = \sqrt{\int_D \left(\frac{f(x)}{p(x)} - I\right)^2 p(x)\, dx} \tag{9}$$

which can be estimated by:

$$\langle \sigma \rangle = \sqrt{\frac{\frac{1}{N}\sum_{i=1}^{N}\left(\frac{f(x_i)}{p(x_i)}\right)^2 + \left(\frac{1}{N}\sum_{i=1}^{N}\frac{f(x_i)}{p(x_i)}\right)^2}{N}} \tag{10}$$

The variance will be exactly 0 if $p(x)$ is proportional to $f(x)$. It's generally not possible to construct such a $p(x)$, but $p(x)$ should approximate this as close as possible in order to reach optimal variance.

A Fredholm equation of the second kind (such as the rendering and potential equations) can be written as:

$$a(x) = b(x) + \int_D K(x,y)\, a(y)\, dy \tag{11}$$

The function a needs to be evaluated for a certain x_0. Using a Monte Carlo algorithm with a single sample:

$$\langle a(x_0) \rangle = b(x_0) + \frac{K(x_0, x_1)\, a(x_1)}{p(x_1)} \tag{12}$$

In turn, $a(x_1)$ needs to be evaluated. Thus, $a(x_0)$ can recursively be approximated by a 'random walk' over the domain D:

$$\langle a(x_0) \rangle = b(x_0) + \frac{K(x_0, x_1)\, b(x_1)}{p(x_1)} + \frac{K(x_0, x_1)\, K(x_1, x_2)\, b(x_1)}{p(x_1)\, p(x_2|x_1)} + \dots \tag{13}$$

In theory, this is an infinite sum. However, using the principle of absorption (i.e. rejection sampling or Russian Roulette), the random walk will stop. Each random walk is a primary estimator for $a(x_0)$. By averaging several random walks, a better approximation for $a(x_0)$ can be computed.

Importance-Driven Progressive Refinement Radiosity

Philippe Bekaert and Yves D. Willems

Katholieke Universiteit Leuven, Department of Computer Science
Celestijnenlaan 200 A, B-3001 Leuven, Belgium
e-mail: Philippe.Bekaert@cs.kuleuven.ac.be

Abstract: A simple way of using importance, also called visual potential, in progressive refinement radiosity and similar radiosity methods is presented. This is accomplished by taking the visual potential of the patches into account when choosing of the "next most contributing" patch. Quite faster convergence is obtained for individual views in which only a relatively small part of a scene is visible. We also show how changes of the viewing parameters can be handled efficiently by computing importance incrementally.

1 Introduction

Visual potential is a dual quantity of radiance, the quantity to be computed in global illumination computations [7]. The visual potential of a patch in a radiosity scene is a measure for how important the light being emitted and reflected by that patch is for a given view. Visual potential can be used to obtain fast, but view-dependent, approximations to the radiance (or radiosity) distribution in a scene.

The use of visual potential in radiosity algorithms was first proposed by Smits et al. [11] for hierarchical radiosity [5]. Although these methods are a very substantial improvement over previous radiosity-gathering methods, their use is limited by the cost of the initial linking step, which is quadratic in the number of initial patches. Recent research was aimed at eliminating this limitation of hierarchical radiosity algorithms by not only subdividing initial patches, but also treating clusters of patches or regions in 3D space as entities between which light transport is computed [8, 10].

Although hierarchical radiosity-gathering methods offer better means for error-control and may even converge faster when clustering is used, progressive refinement (PR) radiosity [3] is probably the only approach really being used extensively in industry today. Grouping of patches has also been studied in the context of progressive refinement radiosity [6] and PR may still be the method of first choice for handling extremely complex scenes, or for parallel implementations. These approaches will directly benefit from the extension to use importance as proposed in this paper.

It is shown in §2 how by a small change to the basic progressive refinement radiosity algorithm ("solving in sorted order" [3]) an importance-driven radiosity-shooting algorithm is obtained. The scheme is not restricted to this form of progressive refinement radiosity however.

The result of the computation is however only accurate for the view it was generated for. If the viewing parameters are changed, more work has to be done to obtain an accurate new view of the scene. An efficient solution to handle changes of the viewing parameters is to compute importance incrementally. This is explained in §3. We compare our method with Smits' method in §4. Finally, some results are presented in §5.

2 Importance-driven progressive radiosity

The equation to be solved in radiosity computations is

$$B_i = E_i + \rho_i \sum_j F_{ij} B_j \qquad (1)$$

where

- B_i is the (exitant) radiosity of patch i (to be computed);
- E_i is the self-emitted radiosity of patch i (nonzero only if patch i is a light source);
- ρ_i is the reflectivity of patch i;
- F_{ij} is the form-factor from patch i to patch j.

Algorithm 2.1 is the basic progressive refinement algorithm ("solving in sorted order" [3]) for solving this equation. ΔB_i is the unshot radiosity of patch i.

Algorithm 2.1 *Basic progressive radiosity algorithm*

1. Initialise $B_i = \Delta B_i \leftarrow E_i$;
2. Repeat until convergence is reached
   (a) choose the patch j for which $| A_j \Delta B_j |$ is largest;
   (b) for each other patch i do
        i. Δrad $\leftarrow \rho_i F_{ij} \Delta B_j$;
        ii. $B_i \leftarrow B_i + \Delta$rad;
        iii. $\Delta B_i \leftarrow \Delta B_i + \Delta$rad.
   (c) $\Delta B_j \leftarrow 0$.

Step 2a in this algorithm identifies the patch from which the next largest contribution to the radiosity solution is expected. The unshot power of a patch is chosen as a criterion here. Just like brightness-driven hierarchical radiosity methods [5], this method over-solves globally and under-solves locally [11]. In interactive systems, or when only one view of a scene is of interest, it is desired also to take into account how important the unshot radiosity of the patch is for the view being generated at each moment. This is possible when considering not only the unshot power of the patches but also their visual potential.

Visual potential is solved from the following equation (see e.g. [11]):

$$I_i = R_i + \sum_j \rho_j F_{ji} I_j \qquad (2)$$

where

- I_i is the (incident, whence the switch of indices in $\rho_j F_{ji}$) importance of patch i;
- R_i is the directly received importance of patch i.

One possible definition of R_i, the directly received importance of a patch i, is:

$$R_i = \int_{A_i} \frac{\cos \theta_x \cos \theta_{eye}}{r_{x,eye}^2} \mathrm{vis}(x, \mathrm{eye}) \mathrm{d}\mu_x \qquad (3)$$

318

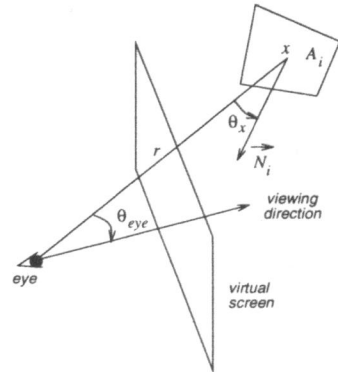

Fig. 1. Geometry for computing the directly received importance

where (see figure 1):

- $d\mu_x$ is a differential area at point x on patch i;
- θ_x is the angle between the direction from x to the observer position and the normal on patch i in point x;
- θ_{eye} is the angle between the direction from the observer position to the point x and the viewing direction;
- $r_{x,eye}$ is the distance between point x and the observer position;
- $\text{vis}(x, \text{eye})$ is 1 if point x is visible through the virtual screen from the observer position and 0 if not.

With small modifications, all familiar methods for computing point-to-patch form-factors can be applied to compute the R_i.

With directly received importance defined this way, the product $(1/\pi)B_i I_i$ of a patch's radiance and importance can be shown to be the flux Φ_i of light passing through the virtual screen observed at the viewing position caused by emission of a radiosity B_i at patch i. We therefore propose to take the product $\Delta B_i I_i$ as a criterion for selecting the next most radiosity contributing patch in step 2a of algorithm 2.1.

The importances I_i can be computed with an algorithm analogous to algorithm 2.1 for computing radiosity. We used the unshot importance ΔI_i as a criterion to select the next most importance contributing patch.

An important question is how the radiosity and importance computations should be combined. Importance clearly has to be computed at least roughly before advantage can be taken of it for radiosity propagation. A first possibility is to compute importance and radiosity in two distinct phases: first importance until a certain importance computation stop-criterion is met (e.g. all unshot importances $| \Delta I_i |$ fall below a certain threshold) and then radiosity. Another possibility is to alternate steps propagating importance and radiosity as soon as the directly received importance has been computed (algorithm 2.2). A third possibility is to first propagate importance until a given stop-criterion is met and then alternate steps propagating importance and radiosity. Yet another possibility is to interleave different numbers n and m of steps propagating importance and radiosity.

Algorithm 2.2 *Importance-driven progressive radiosity*

---

1. Initialise $B_i = \Delta B_i \leftarrow E_i$;
2. Compute R_i for each patch and initialise $I_i = \Delta I_i \leftarrow R_i$;
3. Repeat until convergence:
    (a) Propagate importance:
        i.   choose the patch j for which $|\ \Delta I_j\ |$ is largest;
        ii. for each other patch i do
             A. $\Delta\mathrm{pot} \leftarrow \rho_j F_{ji}\Delta I_j$;
             B. $I_i \leftarrow I_i + \Delta\mathrm{pot}$;
             C. $\Delta I_i \leftarrow \Delta I_i + \Delta\mathrm{pot}$.
        iii. $\Delta I_j \leftarrow 0$.
    (b) Propagate radiosity:
        i.   choose the patch j for which $I_j\ |\ \Delta B_j\ |$ is largest;
        ii. for each other patch i do
             A. $\Delta\mathrm{rad} \leftarrow \rho_i F_{ij}\Delta B_j$;
             B. $B_i \leftarrow B_i + \Delta\mathrm{rad}$;
             C. $\Delta B_i \leftarrow \Delta B_i + \Delta\mathrm{rad}$.
        iii. $\Delta B_j \leftarrow 0$.

The use of importance will be most effective when importance and radiosity are computed in two distinct phases. This means however that it takes some time before the radiosity computations start. In interactive systems where quick feedback is desired, interleaving of the importance and radiosity computation (algorithm 2.2) will be preferred. We have used this strategy to obtain the results described in §5.

3 Change of the viewing parameters

The directly received importances R_i (equation (3)) depend strongly on the viewing parameters (observer position, looking direction, field of view, ...). The methods described in §2 will therefore only render an accurate image for one particular set of viewing parameters. If the viewing parameters change (e.g. by moving the viewpoint or looking into another direction) the new image of the scene may not be accurate anymore. View-independence is however one of the main advantages of radiosity algorithms over other global illumination algorithms and it is often desired to be able to change the viewing parameters without having to do all computations over.

Smits [11] suggests some possible solutions to this problem. Equation (3) defines directly received importance from a single point-source of importance. It is possible to extend (3) to multiple point-sources or to curve-sources of importance. These approaches are however only applicable if all viewing positions and looking directions of interest are known in advance.

If the viewing parameters of interest are not known in advance, another strategy is needed. Since there is often a large coherence between successive frames in walkthroughs and animations, advantage can be taken from computing importance incrementally as proposed in [2] for radiosity recomputation after e.g. surface reflectivity changes: after a change in viewing geometry, the new directly received importances R_i' are computed according to (3) and the difference $\Delta R_i = R_i' - R_i$ between the new and old directly received importances is propagated (algorithm 3.1). If the change in viewing geometry is small, the ΔR_i will mostly also be small and their propagation will take only a short time.

Algorithm 3.1 *Incremental importance-driven progressive radiosity*

1. for each patch i
   (a) initialise $B_i = \Delta B_i \leftarrow E_i$;
   (b) initialise $R_i = I_i = \Delta I_i \leftarrow 0$.
2. first time or whenever the viewing parameters change, do
   (a) compute the new directly received importances R_i';
   (b) for each patch i
       i. $\Delta R \leftarrow R_i' - R_i$;
       ii. $\Delta I_i \leftarrow \Delta I_i + \Delta R$;
       iii. $I_i \leftarrow I_i + \Delta R$;
       iv. $R_i \leftarrow R_i'$
   (c) Until convergence is reached or the viewing parameters have changed:
       i. propagate importance (step 3a of algorithm 2.2);
       ii. propagate radiosity (step 3b of algorithm 2.2).

4 Comparison with Smits' method

- It should be stressed that importance is used in an very different way in Smits' method [11] and the methods described here: In [11] importance is used to control hierarchical subdivision of patches and refinement of the interactions between the patches. We use importance to select the next shooting patch in a radiosity method that *can* be combined with hierarchical refinement, but does not *have* to.
- Importance can be used in a hierarchical progressive refinement algorithm for both the selection of a next shooting patch and the hierarchical refinement. This should however not be done in an algorithm like algorithm 3.1 since the importance-based refinement leads to propagation of radiosity that will be accurate for a first view, but might be very inaccurate for other views. It is an advantage of radiosity-gathering methods, like Smits' method, that any radiosity distribution can be used as a starting point to obtain an accurate solution.
- The computation of directly received importance is the same in Smits' method and in our method. It should be noted that if the eye-point is the only source of importance, only patches that are visible from the eye-point have nonzero directly received importance. This implies that only those patches have to be considered for reconstruction and display of the radiosity solution. If directly received importance is computed by ID-rendering, only those patches have to be rendered twice. The overhead of having to compute directly received importance is small if only a small part of a scene is visible.
- In Smits' method, the importance and radiosity are propagated simultaneously. This elegance is lost in the methods described here. In our algorithms the propagation of importance and radiosity are essentially two distinct processes, leaving more possibilities for tuning.
- In our methods, form-factors that are used for propagation of importance will be needed for radiosity propagation later. In Smits' method, a form-factor is used for both the propagation of importance and the propagation of radiosity at the same moment. If form-factors are computed only once and are all kept in the computers' primary storage, which is the case in the system we implemented, there is no penalty. If to the contrary form-factors are not stored but recomputed whenever they are needed — e.g. because it is not possible to store all the form-factors —, our method will cause more overhead. In interactive systems shooting methods are preferred over

gathering methods however because of the faster initial convergence (see e.g. [4]). Moreover, if only a small part a the scene is visible, our method will just cause some work to be done twice to avoid a lot of other work.

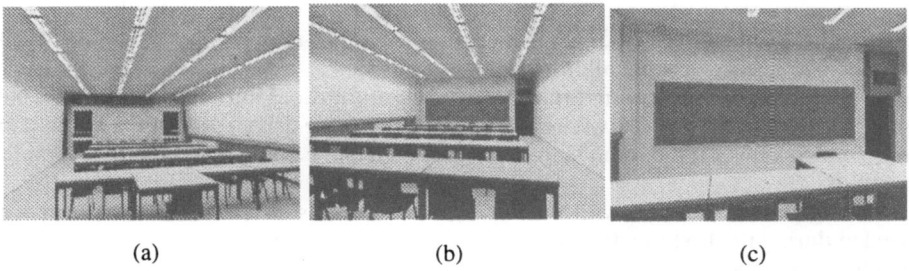

(a)   (b)   (c)

Fig. 2. Test-scene: a seminar room.

5 Results

The algorithms described in this paper, extended for hierarchical refinement based on unshot power, were tested on a SUN SPARCstation 20 ZX for a seminar-room scene consisting of 5251 patches (figure 2). The observer is placed behind the row of chairs and tables in front of the room and is looking towards the blackboard (figure 2c). The illumination of the tables, chairs, the row of pegs . . . in the back of the room contributes very little to the illumination in the front part of the room. Without using importance (algorithm 2.1 — right side of fig. 4 and fig. 5) however, no such distinction between important and less important parts of the scene is made and illumination is computed to the same degree of accuracy all over the scene. Using importance (algorithm 2.2 — left

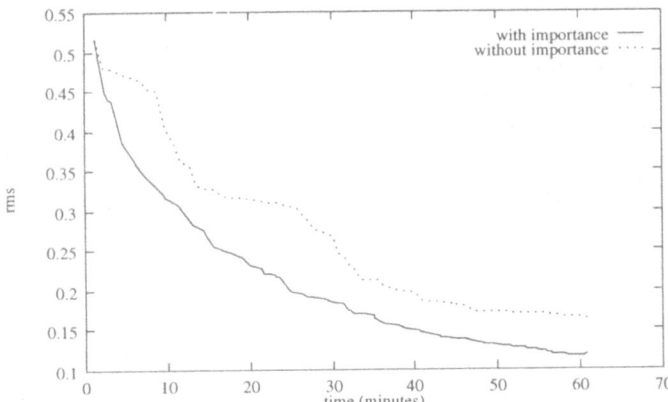

Fig. 3. RMS difference between the images obtained after each iteration and a reference image as a function of time.

side of fig. 4 and fig. 5) the computational effort is focussed to the parts of the scene that contribute more to the view being generated. The difference is clearest at the ceiling of the room, which is only indirectly lit.

In figure 3 the (normalised) RMS difference between the image obtained after each iteration of the importance-driven and non-importance driven progressive refinement radiosity algorithm and a reference, converged, image (figure 2c, obtained after a bit more than 4 hours CPU-time) is plotted as a function of time. The graph shows a significant improvement of convergence speed when importance is used. After one hour (121 iterations) refinement led to 45450 elements with 712172 interactions. About 38 MB of storage was needed to store all the data.

The convergence of the importance-driven algorithm does not depend on objects outside the room being viewed whereas the non-importance driven algorithm would converge much slower if the room being viewed would e.g. be only one room of a complex building.

Using Smits' method, with decreasing error bounds so even no refinement was needed during the first iteration, the first image where a radiosity was computed for all patches in the scene was obtained after 39 minutes. The RMS difference of that image with the reference image (26%) was significantly worse than the RMS difference of the image obtained with the importance-driven progressive refinement radiosity (13%). The computation had to be interrupted during the second iteration after more than six hours because the machine ran out of primary storage (64 MB). This worse result for Smits' method is entirely due to initial linking.

Algorithm 3.1 proves to be very effective when changing the viewing parameters. This is tested by turning and moving the camera by small angles and distances while the computations are going on. Whenever the viewing parameters are changed, the order of computation also changes immediately: the parts of the scene that were not visible in previous views typically appear darker first, but become brighter very soon.

6 Conclusion

This paper described a simple method for using importance in radiosity-shooting algorithms like progressive refinement radiosity. We have developed and applied the method for the rendering of fairly complex scenes where it still is possible to keep most of the needed form-factors in the computers' primary storage however. Quite faster convergence was obtained for individual views where only a relatively small part of the scene is visible. Incremental computation of importance proves to be an efficient way of handling changes of the viewing parameters, allowing for faster generation of animations and walktroughs.

For scenes where it is not possible to store most of the needed form-factors in the computers' main memory, the method will cause more overhead. The usefulness of the method will depend more strongly on how much of the scene is visible in each view to be generated.

The method is not restricted to the basic progressive refinement radiosity algorithm and can be applied to most of its variants. Neither is it restricted to diffuse environments: similar approaches are possible for dealing with non-diffuse reflectors [1, 9].

Acknowledgements

The first author would like to acknowledge the financial support by a grant from the Flemish 'Institute for the promotion of Scientific and Technological Research in the Industry' (IWT#941120).

References

1. Ph. Bekaert and Y. D. Willems. A progressive importance-driven rendering algorithm. In *Proceedings of the X. Spring School on Computer Graphics, Bratislava, Slovakia*, pages 58–67, June 1994.
2. S. E. Chen. Incremental radiosity: An extension of progressive radiosity to an interactive image synthesis system. *Computer Graphics*, 24(4):135–144, 1990.
3. M. F. Cohen, S. E. Chen, J. R. Wallace, and D. P. Greenberg. A progressive refinement approach to fast radiosity image generation. *Computer Graphics*, 22(4):75–84, 1988.
4. G. Greiner, W. Heidrich, and Ph. Slusallek. Bockwise refinement — a new method for solving the radiosity problem. In *Proceedings of the fourth Eurographics Workshop on Rendering, Paris, France*, pages 233–245, 1993.
5. P. Hanrahan, D. Salzman, and L. Aupperle. A rapid hierarchical radiosity algorithm. *Computer Graphics*, 25(4):197–206, 1991.
6. A. Kok. Grouping of patches in progressive radiosity. In *Fourth Eurographics Workshop on Rendering, Paris, France*, pages 221–232, June 1993.
7. S. Pattanaik and S. Mudur. The potential equation and importance in illumination computations. *Computer Graphics Forum*, 12:131–136, 1993.
8. F. Sillion. Clustering and volume scattering for hierarchical radiosity calculations. In *Proceedings of the fifth Eurographics Workshop on Rendering, Darmstadt, Germany*, pages 105–115, 1994.
9. F. X. Sillion, J. R. Arvo, S. H. Westin, and D. P. Greenberg. A global illumination solution for general reflectance distributions. *Computer Graphics*, 25(4):187–196, 1991.
10. B. Smits, J. Arvo, and D. Greenberg. A clustering algorithm for radiosity in complex environments. In *Computer Graphics (SIGGRAPH '94 Proceedings)*, pages 435–443, July 1994.
11. B. E. Smits, J. R. Arvo, and D. H. Salesin. An importance-driven radiosity algorithm. *Computer Graphics*, 26(2):273–282, 1992.

324

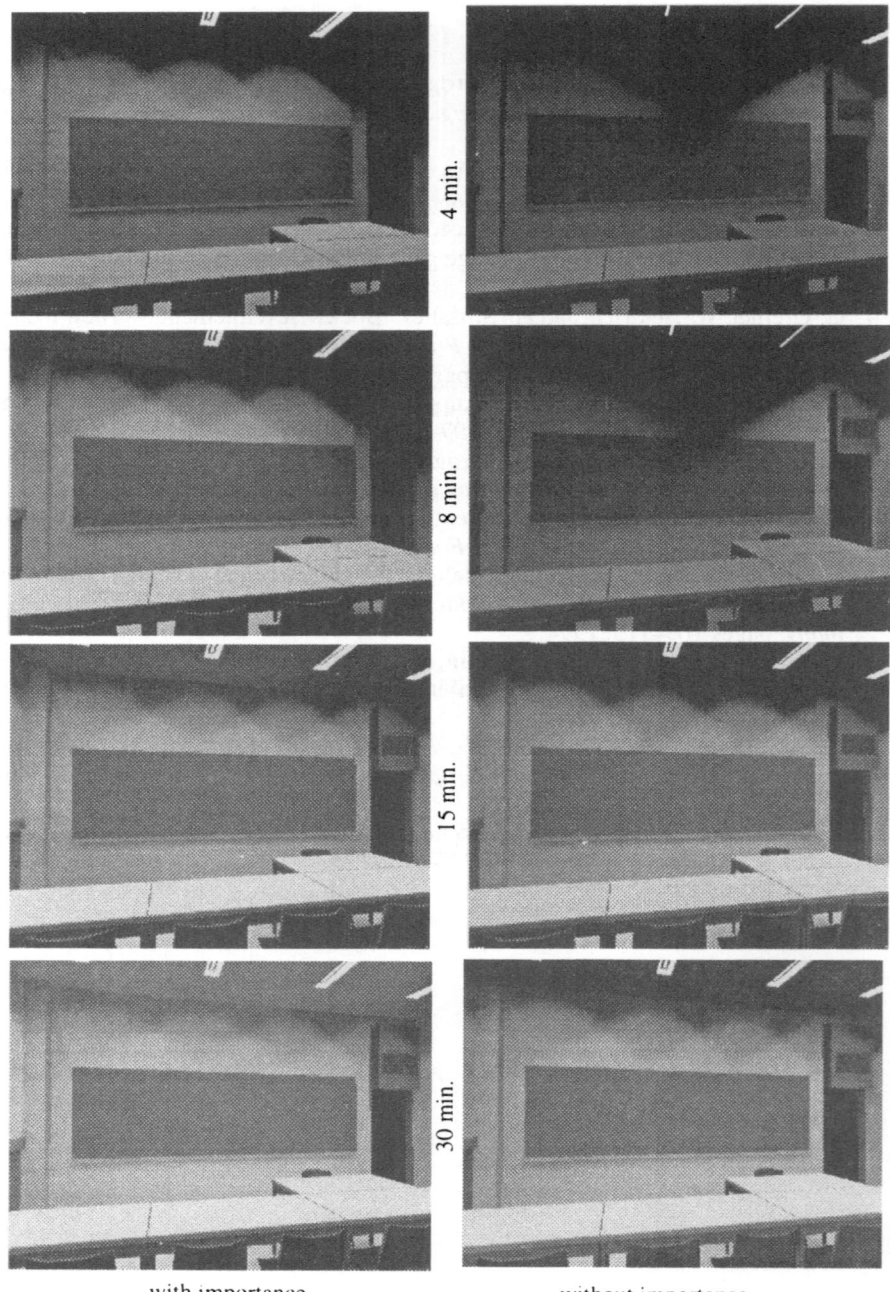

4 min.

8 min.

15 min.

30 min.

with importance   without importance

Fig. 4. Evolution of a view as a function of time.

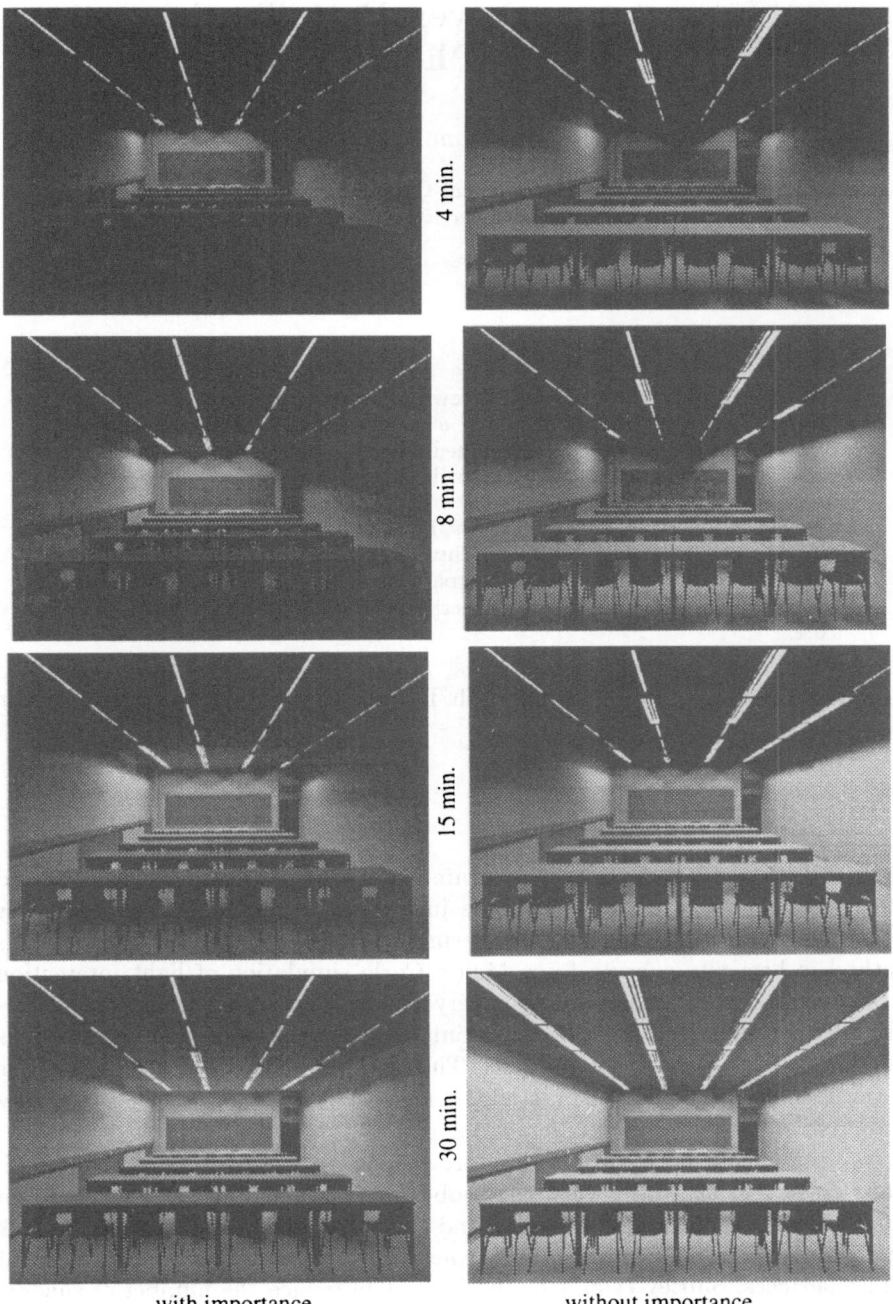

4 min.

8 min.

15 min.

30 min.

with importance   without importance

Fig. 5. Evolution as seen from a distance.

Importance Driven Path Tracing using the Photon Map

Henrik Wann Jensen*

Dept. of Graphical Communication
Technical University of Denmark

Abstract: This paper presents a new importance sampling strategy for Monte Carlo ray tracing in which a rough estimate of the irradiance based on the photon map is combined with the local reflection model to construct more efficient probability density functions that can be used in an importance sampling scheme.
The algorithm gives unbiased results, handles arbitrary reflection models and it is particularly efficient in scenes with highly non-uniform indirect illumination. Initial results and comparisons with traditional importance sampling strategies indicate a reduction in the noise level of more than 70%

Key Words: Global Illumination, Path Tracing, Importance Sampling, Photon Map

1 Introduction

Photorealistic rendering requires accurate simulation of global illumination and much work has been done in this area in the last 10 years. The problem was actually solved in 1986 by Kajiya [6] using a method called path tracing. This method is basically a brute force Monte Carlo simulation of light interaction with a given model. Path tracing is very general and it can be applied to arbitrarilly complex models. It requires only small amounts of memory and it is very applicable to parallel computers. The rendering time with path tracing is however so enormous that the method — in spite of being general — is not very attractive on current computers architectures.

Several papers have presented improvements to the path tracing method. Ward et al. [19, 22], did a very good job, by introducing a caching scheme in which indirect illumination is stored and reused at ideal diffuse surfaces. This significantly reduces the number of rays necessary in scenes with many flat, ideal diffuse surfaces. Shirley et al. [15] and Ward [20] reduce the number of shadow rays required to compute direct illumination in scenes with many light sources. Arvo et al. [1] described a technique called Russian roulette that eliminates the

---

* e-mail: igkhwj@unidhp.uni-c.dk   url: http://www.gk.dtu.dk/home/hwj/

infinite reflection of light rays without introducing bias in the final solution. Several authors [10, 4] use importance sampling where the reflection characteristics of the surface are used to guide sampling rays into those directions from where the light will contribute mostly. Another approach is adaptive sampling where samples are concentrated in the most interesting parts of the scene. Lafortune et al. [9] constructs a 5d tree representing the overall flux in the scene and uses this tree in the selection of new sampling directions. Adaptive sampling can however easily lead to biased solutions [2] and it must be used with great care. Recently bidirectional path tracing was introduced by Lafortune et al. [8] and Veach et al. [18]. It is a mixture of path tracing from the eye and path tracing from the light sources and it is particularly efficient in scenes with highly non-uniform indirect illumination.

Currently the simulation of global illumination is obtained most efficiently by the two pass methods in which a light pass (ie. radiosity) produces a solution that is visualized with a simplified path tracing algorithm [14, 17, 5, 13, 7]. Another efficient method or collection of methods is presented in the Radiance rendering program by Ward [23].

These two pass methods and the Radiance program do however degrade to pure path tracing in very complex environments where the surfaces are no longer ideal diffuse or ideal specular or where the objects are either too complex or too many to be represented by polygons. Even though some of the two pass methods can let the light pass step work on simplified scenes [13, 7] they still have to visualize the solution using path tracing in order to eliminate artifacts in the light pass step. This path tracing step does not utilize the fact that the model does contain information on the distribution of the light and the importance sampling is therefore still only using the reflection characteristics of the surface to guide new sampling rays.

This is particularly problematic in scenes with highly non-uniform indirect illumination. These situation are handled more efficiently using bidirectional path tracing, but this method does not use the irradiance stored within the model. It would be more appropriate to use the information created in the light pass to guide the path tracing algorithm. This would also permit the use of the method in two pass techniques where path tracing is used only for the first reflection seen by the eye [5, 13, 7].

In this paper we present an importance sampling scheme in which the scene is preprocessed and rough estimates of the incoming light are created everywhere in the model. These rough estimates are used to generate sampling directions based on probability density functions that more closely fits the true light contribution as opposed to standard importance sampling methods which only use the local reflection model.

In this way we concentrate the samples in the important parts of the scene. This approach does not give any bias on the final solution as opposed to some of the common adaptive strategies that also tries to put more samples into important parts of the scene.

2 Mathematical Background

Given the integral

$$I = \int g(x)\, dx \quad, \quad x \in D \subset R^n \tag{1}$$

We can evaluate this integral using a Monte Carlo technique known as the sample-mean method [12] by representing the value of the integral as the expected value of any stochastic variable X with p.d.f. $p(x)$, $x \in D$ such that $p(x) > 0$ when $g(x) \neq 0$

$$I = \int \frac{g(x)}{p(x)} p(x)\, dx = E\left\{ \frac{g(x)}{p(x)} \right\} \tag{2}$$

An estimate of the integral is obtained by taking N random sample points x_i distributed according to $p(x)$

$$I \approx \frac{1}{N} \sum_{i=1}^{N} \frac{g(x_i)}{p(x_i)} \tag{3}$$

The error on this estimate largely depends on the choice of $p(x)$ and the number of samples but as a general rule the standard deviation is proportional to $1/\sqrt{N}$. That is, in order to halve the error we have to quadruple the number of samples! Careful selection of $p(x)$ can however lower the error. $p(x)$ should be constructed so that more samples are put into those regions where $g(x)$ has the highest absolute value. It can be shown that the optimal choice for $p(x)$ is [12]

$$p(x) = \frac{g(x)}{I} \tag{4}$$

This choice gives a standard deviation of zero always! Unfortunately it also requires knowledge of I which is the value we are trying to compute. But in general we can do better by using a p.d.f. that looks like the function we are integrating instead of just using a uniform distribution.

The problem in global illumination is given in the rendering equation [6]. It expresses the radiance, L_r, reflected from position $\mathbf{x}$ as

$$L_r(\mathbf{x}, \Psi_r) = \int_{\text{all } \Psi_i} f_r(\mathbf{x}, \Psi_r, \Psi_i) L_i(\mathbf{x}, \Psi_i) \cos\theta_i\, d\omega_i = \int_{\text{all } \Psi_i} f_r(\mathbf{x}, \Psi_r, \Psi_i) \frac{d^2\Phi_i(\mathbf{x}, \Psi_i)}{dA\, d\omega_i}\, d\omega_i \tag{5}$$

where Ψ_r and Ψ_i are the direction of the reflected respectively incoming radiance/flux. f_r is the BRDF at $\mathbf{x}$, L_i is the incoming radiance and Φ_i is the incoming flux.

In order to solve this integral light is sampled from a number of discrete directions Ψ_i. Just sampling from random directions is in most situations very inefficient — for a specular surface only light from a small solid angle is important and it would be more efficient to sample within this small solid angle.

Most implementations of path tracing and similar Monte Carlo based algorithms therefore use importance sampling. These implementations use the knowledge of f_r to sample those direction from where incoming light will contribute mostly to the reflected radiance. For specular surface this approach is very efficient since the choice of sampling direction is significantly narrowed down. This is not the case with diffuse surfaces since the entire hemisphere can contribute to the reflected radiance. A p.d.f. based on the ideal diffuse BRDF is particularly inefficient when the incoming radiance L_i is highly non-uniform (ie. the incoming radiance is concentrated in small solid angles). In this situation it would be better to use the optimal p.d.f. $p(\mathbf{x}, \Psi_r, \Psi_i)$

$$p(\mathbf{x}, \Psi_r, \Psi_i) \propto f_r(\mathbf{x}, \Psi_r, \Psi_i) \frac{d^2 \Phi_i(\Psi_i)}{dA\, d\omega_i} \qquad (6)$$

Unfortunately this requires knowledge about the incoming flux, Φ_i, which is not available. However, even a crude estimate of Φ_i can be used to create a more optimal p.d.f. and in the following sections we will describe a method in which the photon map is used to obtain this estimate.

3 The Photon Map

The photon map [7] represents a distribution of photons (particles) throughout the scene and it is created by emitting a large number of photons from each light source into the scene based upon the emissive characteristics of the light source. The technique is similar to particle tracing with the exception that the intersection point of each particle is stored explicitly within the scene.

Each photon is traced through the scene using a strategy similar to path tracing. The first object that the photon hits gives rise to two events: Firstly if the surface of the object is diffuse the photon is stored at the intersection point and secondly Russian roulette is used to determine whether the photon is reflected or absorbed by the object. The new direction of a reflected photon is computed using the BRDF of the surface. We only store the photons representing indirect illumination (ie. photons that have been reflected at least once). The light sources are separated in the sampling process and they should not be part of the irradiance estimate used to compute the p.d.f.

The photon represents a small packet of energy arriving at a surface from a given direction. Since the number of photons can be quite large we have chosen a relatively compact representation that occupies only 36 bytes:

```
struct photon {
    long energy;                    // Packed energy (RGB)
    float position[3];              // Photon position
    float theta,phi;                // Photon direction
    char normal[3];                 // Surface normal
    char key;                       // kd-tree parameter
    struct photon *left, *right;    // Rest of the kd-tree
    };
```

In this structure the photon energy is packed using a method similar to Wards packed pixels [21]. The energy covers several wavelengths. In other contexts it might be relevant to store energy for individual wavelengths — this would also make the name, photon, more correct.

In the photon map we need to be able to locate the n photons that have the shortest distance to a point $\mathbf{x}$. This can be done quite efficiently using a kd-tree [3].

4 Importance Driven Path Tracing using the Photon Map

In the following discussion we assume that the intersection point $\mathbf{x}$ and the reflected direction Ψ_r are given and they are therefore omitted. As shown in section 2 the optimal choice of $p(\theta_i, \phi_i)$ to select a sampling directions is

$$p(\theta_i, \phi_i) \propto f_r(\theta_i, \phi_i) \frac{d^2\Phi_i(\theta_i, \phi_i)}{dA \, d\omega_i} \tag{7}$$

where $(\theta_i, \phi_i) = \Psi_i$.

The existing importance sampling approaches that use f_r as the p.d.f. can in most situations use standard transformation techniques to generate random numbers with the wanted distribution. In [16] it is described how to create a transformation function T that maps a uniform distribution of points (u, v) on the unit square onto a sampling direction (θ, ϕ). We use the following notation for describing the transformation of (u, v) into a direction

$$(\theta, \phi) = T(u, v) \tag{8}$$

Likewise we use the notation $(u, v) = T^{-1}(\theta, \phi)$ to denote the inverse transformation. As an example, to generate a sampling direction based on the BRDF for an ideal diffuse surface the following transformation should be used

$$(\theta, \phi) = (\text{acos}\sqrt{1 - u}, 2\pi v) \tag{9}$$

In order to take Φ_i into account we apply the information from the photon map. Like [7] we locate the N photons that have the shortest distance to $\mathbf{x}$. Each photon p carries the flux $\Delta\Phi_{i,p}$ in the direction (θ_p, ϕ_p) (note that (θ_p, ϕ_p) must be transformed from the global representation stored in the kd-tree into a direction compatible with the local coordinate system used at $\mathbf{x}$). If we assume that all n photons intersected the surface at $\mathbf{x}$ then we can compute the contribution from each photon p to the reflected flux $\Delta\Phi_r$ as

$$\Delta\Phi_r = f_r(\theta_p, \phi_p)\Delta\Phi_{i,p}(\theta_p, \phi_p) \tag{10}$$

To use this information in our generation of sampling directions we construct a discrete p.d.f. on the unit square. Each point (u, v) in this unit square corresponds to a sampling direction $T(u, v)$ and each incoming photon corresponds to

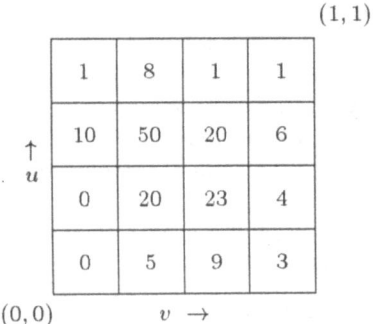

Fig. 1. The unit square is partitioned into distinct regions and the photon contributions in each region are accumulated.

a point $(u_p, v_p) = T^{-1}(\theta_p, \phi_p)$ in the unit square. For every photon we find the corresponding point in the unit square and we insert the photon energy at this position. The unit square is then partitioned into $m \times n$ regions (see fig. 1) and the energy in each region is accumulated. To avoid bias we eliminate all regions with zero energy (probability) by adding a small fraction of the overall energy stored within the unit square to these regions. The result is an estimate of the energy arriving from different sets of directions. This is our p.d.f. and it contains all of the elements found in equation 7.

To use the constructed p.d.f. we create a discrete cumulative probability density function from the information in the unit square. This is illustrated in

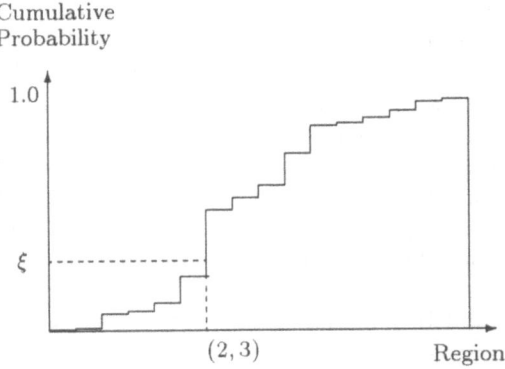

Fig. 2. The accumulated energy is used in the creation of a cumulative probability distribution function and this function is used to select the region that contains the new sampling direction. The dashed line demonstrates how a random value ξ is mapped into a specific region in unit square.

fig. 2 and as demonstrated in the graph this function is used to select a region in the unit square based upon a random value ξ. The chance that a region is selected is proportional to the energy accumulated in that region which means that it is more likely that we select a region (ie. set of incoming directions) that contributes significantly to the reflected radiance. Once a region is found we select a random point (u, v) within the region and our sampling direction becomes $(\theta, \phi) = T(u, v)$.

Due to the non-uniform sampling we have to scale the radiance returned by our sampling ray. The scaling factor s is

$$s = \frac{\text{Total energy in the square}}{(\text{Energy in region}) * (\text{number of regions})} \tag{11}$$

5 Results and Discussion

We have implemented the importance sampling algorithm in a program called MIRO on a Pentium PC with 32MB RAM running Linux. The results have been produced using a parallel implementation of the program running on the Linux machine and 31 Silicon Graphics workstations. The implementation currently supports ideal diffuse, ideal specular, rough specular and anisotropic reflection models. The photon map has only been incorporated in the importance sampling algorithm for ideal diffuse reflection.

Two test scenes have been created. Test scene 1 is an empty version of the Cornell box. The walls in the box are white with the exception of the left wall which is red and the right wall which is green. There is a small square shaped light source just below the ceiling. The light source is only illuminating the ceiling and most of the scene is therefore illuminated indirectly.

The purpose of test scene 1 is to test the convergence speed of importance sampling with and without the photon map. We initially computed a reference image using 32000 samples pr. pixel in the resolution 80x60 — we did not use importance sampling for this computation. Due to the strong indirect illumination we had to use a very large number of samples in order to remove all visible noise from the image.

The estimate from the photon map depends on several parameters: The number of photons, N, used in the estimate, the number of photons N_p stored in the kd-tree and the number of regions in the discrete p.d.f. To limit the amount of adjustable parameters we use a fixed partitioning of the p.d.f. We found that 4x16 (4 θ-intervals and 16 ϕ-intervals) gave reasonable results with the values of N and N_p that we tested. In general the number of partitions should be increased as N and N_p become larger.

We tested the different configurations by creating images using $1, 2, 3, \ldots, 500$ samples pr. pixel. We measured the variance of the difference between the computed images and the reference image — also known as the mean-square error, MSE. This value gives a good indication of the amount of noise present in the image and since we use Monte Carlo techniques it provides a good measure of the quality of our images.

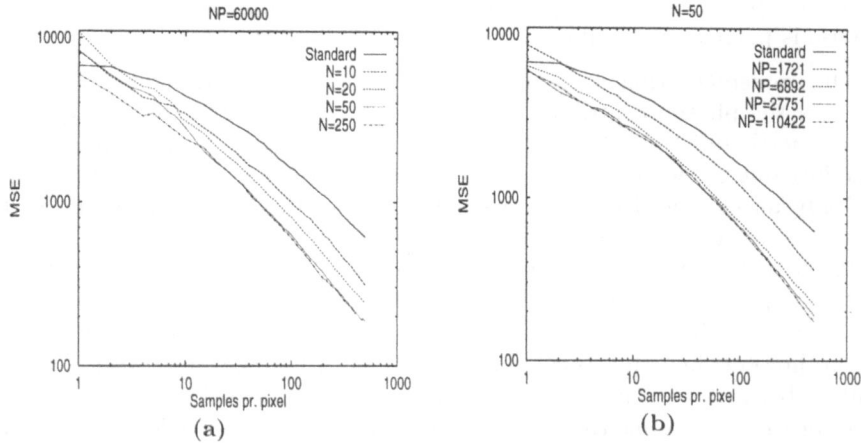

Fig. 3. The effect of N and N_p on the convergence speed

The graph in fig. 3a demonstrates how an increasing number of photons in the estimate improves the quality of the computed images. Using $N_p \approx 60000$ stored photons we were able to reduce the noise in the images by increasing N to a value of 50 photons. Increasing N beyond this value had only very little effect on the results. The graph also demonstrates how the convergence speed is improved when the information from the photon map is included in the importance sampling scheme. At 500 samples pr. pixel the standard importance sampling method gave a MSE value that was more than 3 times larger than the MSE value obtained when the photon map was used.

We also examined the effect of N_p on the quality of the computed images. Using $N = 50$ we obtained the results shown in the graph in fig. 3b. With the used parameter configuration we found that increasing N_p beyond 30000 did not improve the result.

In fig. 4 (see colour plates) we have shown the computed images corresponding to 100, 200, 300, 400 and 500 samples pr. pixel. The top row contains images computed with standard importance sampling and the bottom row contains images computed using importance sampling based on the photon map. The images demonstrates how the noise level is reduced when the information from the photon map is added.

Our second test scene was created to test the algorithm in a more realistic environment. The desk is illuminated by two light sources: One large in the ceiling and one small light bulb within the lamp shade. The light from the light bulb is scattered diffusely through the lamp shade.

We created two images of test scene 2. In fig. 5 we used standard importance sampling and in fig. 6 we used the photon map with $N_p = 33000$ and $N = 50$. We also created a reference image using 2000 samples pr. pixel and the MSE of fig. 5 was approximately 4 times larger than the value for fig. 6. The reduction in noise is particularly visible at the wall just behind the lamp shade.

The implementation of the photon map has not been optimized. The computation of the photon contribution to the reflected radiance makes heavy use of trigonometric functions. Still the computation time of fig. 6 was only increased with 20% due to the use of the photon map. The time used by the photon map was only affected noticeably by changing N and this is primarily due to the change in the number of evaluations of trigonometric functions.

We tried to reduce the effect of N on the computation time by replacing the photon map with hemicubes stored at discrete positions within the scene. During importance sampling the nearest hemicube would represent the incoming flux. We did however find that this approach suffered from aliasing problems and the results obtained were not very good. Instead we plan to limit the number of directions for a photons to perhaps 65000. In this way we would be able to use lookup tables and completely avoid trigonometric evaluations.

6 Conclusion and Future Directions

In this paper we have demonstrated how the use of photon maps in an importance sampling scheme can improve the quality of images computed using the path tracing algorithm. Based on a rough estimate of the incoming flux we concentrate our samples in those directions that contributes mostly to the reflected radiance. This improves the convergence speed without adding bias to the final solution. By using the photon map we were able to reduce the noise level in the computed images with more than 70% compared with traditional importance sampling approaches without increasing the number of sampling rays.

Future enhancements include further investigation in the parameters for the method. By increasing the number of photons used we should be able to obtain even better results. Combining this with a more efficient usage of the information in the photon map would make the method very suitable for the visualization step in the existing two pass techniques for global illumination.

Acknowledgments

The author wishes to thank GK for providing excessive computational resources and to the reviewers and Eric Lafortune for their helpful comments to the paper.

References

1. Arvo, James and David Kirk, "Particle Transport and Image Synthesis". *Computer Graphics* **24** (4), 53-66 (1990).
2. Arvo, James and David Kirk, "Unbiased Sampling Techniques for Image Synthesis". *Computer Graphics* **25** (4), 153-156 (1991).
3. Bentley, Jon Louis and Jerome H. Friedman, "Data Structures for Range Searching". *Computing Surveys* **11** (4), 397-409 (1979).

4. Blasi, Philippe; Bertrans Le Saëc and Christophe Schlick: "An Importance Driven Monte-Carlo Solution to the Global Illumination Problem". *Eurographics Workshop on Rendering* **5**, Darmstadt (1994).

5. Chen, Shenchang Eric, Holly E. Rushmeier, Gavin Miller and Douglas Turner, "A Progressive Multi-Pass Method for Global Illumination". *Computer Graphics* **25** (4), 165-174 (1991).

6. Kajiya, James T.: "The Rendering Equation". *Computer Graphics* **20** (4), 143-149 (1986).

7. Jensen, Henrik Wann and Niels Jørgen Christensen: "Photon maps in Bidirectional Monte Carlo Ray Tracing of Complex Objects". *Computers and Graphics* **19** no. 2, (1995)

8. Lafortune, Eric P.; Yves D. Willems: "Bidirectional Path Tracing". *Proceedings of CompuGraphics*, 95-104, june (1993)

9. Lafortune, Eric P.; Yves D. Willems: "A 5D Tree to Reduce the Variance of Monte Carlo Ray Tracing". *Eurographics Workshop on Rendering* **6**, Dublin (1995)

10. Lange, Brigitta: "The Simulation of Radiant Light Transfer with Stochastic Ray-Tracing". *Eurographics Workshop on Rendering* **2**, Barcelona (1991)

11. Nicodemus, F. E.; J. C. Richmond; J. J. Hsia; I. W. Ginsberg; T. Limperis: *"Geometrical Considerations and Nomenclature for Reflectance"*. National Bureau of Standards, okt. 1977

12. Rubinstein, Reuven Y.: *"Simulation af the Monte Carlo Method"*. John Wiley & Sons, (1981)

13. Rushmeier, Holly; Charles Patterson and Aravindan Veerasamy: "Geometric Simplification for Indirect Illumination Calculations". *Proceedings of Graphics Interface '93*, 227-236 (1993)

14. Shirley, Peter, "A Ray Tracing Method for Illumination Calculation in Diffuse-Specular Scenes". *Proc. Graphics Interface*, 205-212 (1990).

15. Shirley, Peter and Changyaw Wang, "Direct Lighting Calculation by Monte Carlo integration". *Eurographics Workshop on Rendering* **2**, Barcelona (1991).

16. Shirley, Peter: "Nonuniform Random Point Sets via Warping". In *Graphics Gems III*, David Kirk (ed.), Academic Press, 80-83 (1992).

17. Sillion, François X., James R. Arvo, Stephen H. Westin and Donald P. Greenberg, "A Global Illumination Solution for General Reflectance Distributions". *Computer Graphics* **25** (4), 187-196 (1991).

18. Veach, Eric and Leonidas Guibas: "Bidirectional Estimators for Light Transport". *Eurographics Workshop on Rendering* **5**, Darmstadt (1994)

19. Ward, Gregory J.; Francis M. Rubinstein and Robert D. Clear, "A Ray Tracing Solution for Diffuse Interreflection". *Computer Graphics* **22** (4), 85-92 (1988).

20. Ward, Gregory J., "Adaptive Shadow Testing for Ray Tracing". *Eurographics Workshop on Rendering* **2**, Barcelona (1991).

21. Ward, Greg: "Real pixels". In *Graphics Gems II*, James Arvo (ed.), Academic Press, 80-83 (1991).

22. Ward, Gregory J. and Paul S. Heckbert: "Irradiance Gradients". *Eurographics Workshop on Rendering* **3**, Bristol (1992).

23. Ward, Gregory J.: "The RADIANCE Lighting Simulation and Rendering System". *Computer Graphics* **28** (4), 459-472, (1994).

Editors' Note: see Appendix, p. 372 for colored figures of this paper

The Constant Radiosity Step

László Neumann[1]   Robert F. Tobler[2]   Pavol Eliás[2]

Abstract. This paper gives a detailed derivation of the constant radiosity step, a transformation of the radiosity equation system that can be used to accelerate iteration methods for solving the problem of diffuse light propagation in closed environments. This iteration step can be performed without calculating form factors and can be applied to classic and stochastic radiosity methods. It simultaneously changes each member of the current solution vector by the same amount, thereby reducing the magnitude of the residual vector. The elements of the residual vector are changed in proportion to the absorption of the corresponding patch, so that the sum of the elements of the new residual vector is zero.

1 Introduction

The radiosity method is an approximation of the global illumination problem that uses a discretisation of the environment into flat polygons, called *patches*. Constant radiosity is assumed across the surface of each patch and all surfaces are assumed to be perfect lambertian reflectors. These assumptions lead to a linear system of equations that can be solved to obtain the radiosity of each patch in the environment [5].

The first implementations of this method used Jacobi- or Gauss-Seidel-iteration to solve the system of equations [1], since both approaches can be easily proved to converge for the radiosity equation system. Several improvements on the original algorithm have been described, that try to reduce the computational complexity (e.g. [2], [3], [12], and [4]). These methods are so-called shooting methods, that are based on Southwell iteration. An alternative approach that uses a different kind of iteration method is based on the positive definite form of the radiosity equation system [8]. Recently, a number of stochastic methods have been introduced (e.g. [14], [11], and [13], [7] and [10]) that try to reduce the computational cost by using a stochastic approach based on shooting rays.

For closed environments the computational cost of these methods can be increased by an appropriate transformation of the equation system. This transformation can be viewed as an iteration step that simultaneously shifts all elements of the current solution vector, thereby reducing the magnitude of the residual vector. A transformation called *constant radiosity step* was initially introduced by Neumann [9], [8] and it was shown to speed up positive definite radiosity methods in [8].

This paper will give a motivation for introducing such a transformation in section 2, present a detailed derivation of the constant radiosity step in section 3 and show the application for variance reduction in stochastic radiosity methods in section 4. The Appendix shows the relation of the constant radiosity step to the ambient term, which has been used to improve the display of progressive refinement radiosity [3].

---

[1] Maros u. 36, Budapest, Hungary, H-1122

[2] Institute of Computer Graphics, Technical University of Vienna, Karlsplatz 13/186, A-1040 Wien, Austria

2 Motivation

The solution of the radiosity equation system consists of a vector of radiosities. These radiosities are positive values that indicate the power per unit area that is radiated by each patch in the equilibrium situation.

A way of solving a system of this type, is to split the solution into a known "average" part, which is the same for all elements of the solution vector and thus "constant", and the difference to the actual solution. This can be viewed as a shift of the whole solution by a constant term. Figure 1 shows such a shift.

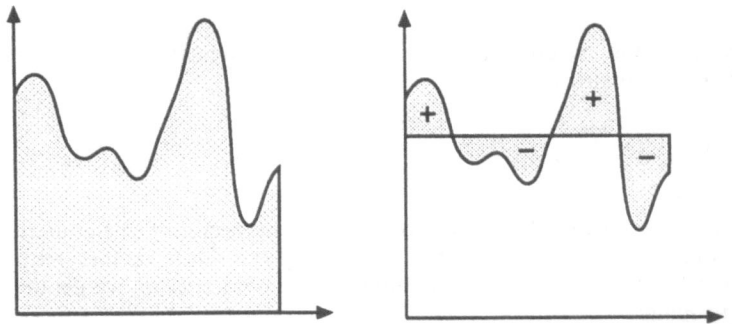

Figure 1: Magnitude of elements of a sample solution vector before and after the shift.

The motivation behind this transformation is that the "shifted" equation system, may be easier to solve: If a standard, deterministic iteration method is used, the magnitude of the residual vector of the shifted system can be reduced, and thus the speed of the algorithm can be increased. The actual amount by which an element of the residual vector is reduced is proportional to the absorption of the corresponding patch. If a Monte-Carlo method is used, the variance of the solution vector is decreased since the magnitude of the part of the system that has to be calculated by stochastic integration is reduced.

This shift can be performed at the start of the iteration method. In order to calculate the shift value, we need to define a condition for the shifted equation system. A simple choice is a shift value that reduces the sum of the self-emissions of the shifted system to 0.

For variance reduction in stochastic algorithms another type of shift can be performed in order to adapt the iteration to the currently known approximation of the solution. In this case, the shift is chosen in such a way as to reduce the sum of the elements of the currently known approximation to 0. Thus only the differences to the current average solution need to be propagated.

3 Derivation of the Deterministic Constant Radiosity Step

3.1 The Radiosity Equation System

The system of radiosity equations relates the unknown radiosity B_i of each patch i to the radiosities of all other patches j in the environment (E_i is the self emission of patch i):

$$B_i = E_i + \rho_i \cdot \sum_{j=1}^{N} F_{ij} \cdot B_j \tag{1}$$

In matrix form this systems of equations can be written like this (we will use the symbol M for the matrix):

$$M \cdot x = b \tag{2}$$

$$M = I - R \tag{3}$$

where x is the vector of unknown radiosities, b is the vector of self-emissions, I is the identity matrix, and R is a matrix containing the form factors and reflection coefficients. Solving this equation system using Jacobi iteration, we get the following iteration formula:

$$x^{(k+1)} = R \cdot x^{(k)} + b \tag{4}$$

The residual vector during iteration can then be defined as:

$$r^{(k)} = b - M \cdot x^{(k)} \tag{5}$$

or alternatively as: $r^{(k+1)} = r^{(k)} - M \cdot \left(x^{(k+1)} - x^{(k)} \right) \tag{6}$

3.2 Shifting the Radiosity Vector

Before solving the radiosity equation system using a traditional method, we can perform a constant radiosity step: we shift the system by a "constant radiosity" β in each element of the solution vector x, i.e. we set

$$x_i^{(k+1)} = x_i^{(k)} + \beta \tag{7}$$

We write the transformation in a manner similar to an iteration step, so that we can use the standard formulations for the residual as presented in equations (5) and (6). We now assume a closed environment, so that the sum of each line of form factors equals to 1, i.e.:

$$\sum_{j=1}^{N} F_{ij} = 1 \tag{8}$$

Using this fact we can combine equations (1), (3) and (6) to derive a formula for the elements of the new residual vector:

$$r_i^{(k+1)} = r_i^{(k)} - (1 - \rho_i) \cdot \beta \qquad (9)$$

This shows the nontrivial fact that the elements of the residual vector are shifted in proportion to the absorption of the corresponding patch.

3.3 Choosing an appropriate "shift value" β

In order to choose an appropriate β, we will now try to minimise the "magnitude" of the residuum vector of the shifted equation system. Since we are free to choose the desired magnitude of the new residual vector arbitrarily, we can even set it to 0. In order to do this we can define the magnitude of the residuum in any norm we like. Due to the fact that we are dealing with an energy balance we chose to use the sum-norm of the residuum expressed in powers, in order to perform a kind of area weighting, i.e. we search for a β so that:

$$\sum_{j=1}^{N} A_j \cdot r_j^{(k+1)} = 0 \qquad (10)$$

Combining this condition with equation (9) we get an explicit expression for β:

$$\beta = \frac{\sum_{j=1}^{N} A_j \cdot r_j^{(k)}}{\sum_{j=1}^{N} A_j \cdot (1 - \rho_j)} \qquad (11)$$

This equation is based on the elements of the currently known residual vector $r^{(k)}$. At the beginning of the iteration, if $x^{(0)}$ is set to (0, 0, 0,..., 0) the residual vector is equal to the vector of self-emissions:

$$r_j^{(0)} = b_j = E_j \qquad (12)$$

Thus the constant radiosity value β for the original problem can be written as follows:

$$\beta = \frac{P_{total}}{\sum_{j=1}^{N} A_j \cdot (1 - \rho_j)} \qquad (13)$$

After applying the constant radiosity step the residual vector is shifted so that the new total power in the system is equal to zero. Since this is only a necessary, but not a sufficient condition for convergence, it cannot be used to determinate if the iteration should be terminated. In subsequent iterations new power will be gathered in P_{total} that can be reduced to zero by applying the constant radiosity step again.

Since no form factors need to be calculated to obtain β, this step which has a significant potential for speeding up the iteration, can be performed at minimal cost.

3.4 Application of the Constant Radiosity Step

The constant radiosity step can be applied to Jacobi- and Gauss-Seidel-iteration as an initial step as presented. Since it reduces the magnitude of the residuum vector in the sum-norm to 0, the absolute value norm of the residual vector will also be decreased and this speeds up the computation.

For the radiosity method using the positive definite form this kind of radiosity step can be performed at any time. For this iteration method the constant radiosity step has been proven to converge, and the decision between normal iteration steps and constant radiosity steps has been solved optimally [8].

Applying the constant radiosity step to Southwell iteration leads to negative amounts of unshot radiosity. Although this can be handled empirically as demonstrated by Feda for overshooting [4], the convergence of the resulting iteration method has not been proven yet.

4 The Constant Radiosity Step for Stochastic Radiosity Methods

The initial constant radiosity step can easily be applied to stochastic methods such as [7]. This initialisation step will pump all the available power into the system, so that the remaining task is not to shoot power, but to redistribute power within the environment. However, for stochastic methods it is also possible to use a variant of the original constant radiosity step that reduces the "stochastic part" of the current solution vector (as opposed to the magnitude of the residual vector). Radiosity methods that use importance sampling (e.g. [10]) benefit from that approach, since then the importance sampling is based on the differences of the current solution to an educated guess (the constant radiosity part), thereby decreasing the variance of a stochastic radiosity method. A variance reduction method for Monte Carlo raytracing which is based on comparable ideas was developed by Lafortune and Williams [6].

To use the constant radiosity step for variance reduction we need to develop a variant. In order to derive this transformation we will use the power variant of the radiosity equations. This can be derived from equation (1) by using the fact that $A_i \cdot F_{ij} = A_j \cdot F_{ji}$ (here $P_i = A_i \cdot B_i$ is the power and $W_i = A_i \cdot E_i$ is the self-emitted power of each patch i):

$$P_i = W_i + \rho_i \cdot \sum_{j=1}^{N} F_{ji} \cdot P_j \tag{14}$$

During each iteration k of a Jacobi-type iteration (4) we normally need to calculate the product of a matrix R (which contains the form factors and reflection coefficients) with our current solution $P^{(k)}$ to obtain a better approximation:

$$P^{(k+1)} = R \cdot P^{(k)} + W \tag{15}$$

We now split the current approximation into two parts (again we introduce this as an additional iteration step):

$$P^{(k)} = P_\alpha^{(k)} + P_\beta^{(k)} \tag{16}$$

The part that is extracted is again based on "constant radiosities":

$$P_\beta^{(k)} = \left(\beta^{(k)} \cdot A_1, \beta^{(k)} \cdot A_2, ..., \beta^{(k)} \cdot A_N \right) \tag{17}$$

This vector can be exactly multiplied by the reflection matrix R:

$$R \cdot P_\beta^{(k)} = \beta^{(k)} \cdot \left(A_1 \cdot \rho_1, A_2 \cdot \rho_2, ..., A_N \cdot \rho_N \right) \tag{18}$$

We now choose $\beta^{(k)}$ in a way, such that the sum of the compnents of the $P_\alpha^{(k)}$ vector is zero (Thus we only do the $R \cdot P_\alpha^{(k)}$ operation stochastically):

$$\sum_{j=1}^{N} P_{\alpha,j}^{(k)} = \sum_{j=1}^{N} P_j^{(k)} - \beta^{(k)} \cdot \sum_{j=1}^{N} A_j \cdot \rho_j = 0 \tag{19}$$

We again obtain an explicit equation for $\beta^{(k)}$:

$$\beta^{(k)} = \frac{\sum_{j=1}^{N} P_j^{(k)}}{\sum_{j=1}^{N} A_j \cdot \rho_j} = \frac{P_{total}^{(k)}}{\sum_{j=1}^{N} A_j \cdot \rho_j} \tag{20}$$

Therefore we can perform this operation at each iteration k with negligible additional effort, since the total power $P_{total}^{(k)}$ of the current solution vector can be calculated easily on the fly (for some methods it is even needed for other reasons as well, and thus no additional effort is required) and the denominator of equation (20) can be precalculated once.

5 Discussion

The initial constant radiosity step reduces the residuals of the transformed iteration method, so that all iteration methods that are based on residuals are sped up. The amount by which the elements of the residual vector are reduced can be easily seen in equation (9).

The constant radiosity step is related to the ambient term (see Appendix) which was introduced to display intermediate results of Southwell-type iterations (e.g. progressive refinement radiosity). However, whereas the ambient term is a purely cosmetical improvement since it does not change the speed of progressive refinement radiosity itself, the constant radiosity transformation leads to faster convergence of the transformed system of equations. This is due to the fact that it changes the structure of the residual vector. In addition to that the residual vector is known throughout the iteration.

The increased speed obtained with the help of the constant radiosity step is due to the separation of the equation system into an "average" part which is solved exactly and the remaining unknown part which is smaller in magnitude, and can therefore be solved faster. This is completely different from the overshooting method [4] which increases the speed by adjusting the "step size" of a single iteration step, as known from relaxation methods in numerical mathematics.

Both the standard constant radiosity step (section 3) and the alternative constant radiosity step for stochastic methods (section 4) shift the equation system so that negative radiosities (or powers) have to be dealt with. The deterministic constant radiosity step transforms the system so that the sum-norm of the new right-hand side is zero. The stochastic constant radiosity step transforms the system so that the sum-norm of the new solution is zero. Since both transformations reduce the "magnitude" of the problem (as measured by the L_1-norm) and the matrices of the radiosity system are contracting, the transformed equation system is expected to exhibit faster convergence.

Iteration methods that are based on importance sampling, such as the stochastic radiosity method [7], benefit from this transformation, since now most rays are shot for patches with powers that differ from the constant radiosity solution. Therefore, the difference of the actual solution and an educated guess (the constant radiosity part) is determined using a Monte Carlo integration method. This is a lot less effort than Monte Carlo integrating the absolute value of the solution. The general constant radiosity step updates the guess of the current solution based on newly obtained information, so that the part of the solution which is determined by the Monte Carlo method is reduced in magnitude.

6 Results

We implemented the constant radiosity step for stochastic ray radiosity [10]. This radiosity method uses importance sampling and Monte Carlo integration to perform a new type of stochastic iteration. In each iteration step the interreflection matrix is stochastically sampled, reducing the computational complexity of a single iteration step significantly.

The constant radiosity step was evaluated using a test scene containing about 86 000 patches with an average reflectance ρ_{avg} of 0.7. The Stochastic Ray radiosity algorithm was used with 10^6 rays per iteration. The results of the intermediate solutions were compared to a reference solution that was calculated by shooting 10^9 rays. Table 1 shows the RMS error versus the number of rays for the original Stochastic Ray algorithm (SRR) and the algorithm with a constant radiosity step (CRR; the variant for stochastic methods as presented in section 4 without using the deterministic step on startup) performed after each standard iteration step.

Table 1

	millions of rays				
	10	20	40	80	160
SRR	0.0247	0.0169	0.0118	0.0088	0.0068
CRS	0.0166	0.0104	0.0065	0.0037	0.0016

This table shows that for our test scene the constant radiosity step significantly improves the speed of the Stochastic Ray method. In our test scene the RMS error is up to 75% smaller for the same number of rays. For obtaining an image with a given RMS error, the constant radiosity step reduce the computation time for our test scene by up to 400%. This confirms the results that were obtained for a deterministic method [8].

7 Conclusion and Further Trends

The constant radiosity step, a new type of iteration step for solving the system of radiosity equations with classical deterministic and stochastic iteration methods has been derived. This step can be performed with negligible additional effort and has been shown to speed up a stochastic algorithm for a concrete scene by up to 400%.

Further investigation is necessary using both the deterministic and stochastic constant radiosity step, since it is easy to see that the achievable speed-up increases extremely as the average reflectance in the scene approaches 1 and/or the variance in reflection coefficients tends to 0.

For non-diffuse, closed environments the residual vector can also be updated without any form factor computation, but it is still necessary to investigate how this affects the speed of convergence.

References

1. M. Cohen, D. Greenberg: The Hemi-Cube - A Radiosity Solution for Complex Environments. *Computer Graphics*, Vol. 19, N° 3, 1985
2. M. Cohen, D. Greenberg, D. Immel, P. Brock: An Efficient Radiosity Approach for Realistic Image Synthesis. *IEEE Computer Graphics & Applications*, Vol. 6, N° 2, 1986
3. M. Cohen, S. Chen, J. Wallace, D. Greenberg: A Progressive Refinement Approach for Fast Radiosity Image Generation. *Computer Graphics*, Vol. 22, N° 4, 1988
4. M. Feda, W. Purgathofer: Accelerating Radiosity by Overshooting. *Proceedings of the 3rd Eurographics Workshop on Rendering*, Bristol, UK, 1992
5. C. Goral, K. Torrance, D. Greenberg, B. Battaile: Modeling the Interaction of Light Between Diffuse Surfaces. *Computer Graphics*, Vol. 18, N° 3, pp. 213-222, 1984
6. E.P. Lafortune, Y.D. Williams: The Ambient Term as a Variance Reducing Technique for Monte Carlo Ray Tracing. *Proceedings of the 5th Eurographics Workshop on Rendering*, Darmstadt, BRD, 1994
7. L. Neumann, M. Feda, M. Kopp, W. Purgathofer: A New Stochastic Radiosity Method for Highly Complex Scenes. *Proceedings of the 5th Eurographics Workshop on Rendering*, Darmstadt, BRD, 1994
8. L. Neumann: New Efficient Algorithms with Positive Definite Radiosity Matrix. *Proceedings of the 5th Eurographics Workshop on Rendering*, Darmstadt, BRD, 1994
9. L. Neumann: Monte Carlo Radiosity. *Computing*, Vol. 55, N° 1, pp. 23-42, 1995
10. L. Neumann, W. Purgathofer, R.F. Tobler, A. Neumann, P. Elias, M. Feda, X. Pueyo: The Stochastic Ray Radiosity. *Proceedings of the 6th Eurographics Workshop on Rendering*, Dublin, 1995.
11. S. N. Pattanaik, S. P. Mudur: Computation of Global Illumination by Monte Carlo Simulation of the Particle Model of Light. *Proceedings of the 3rd Eurographics Workshop on Rendering*, Bristol, UK, 1992
12. R. Recker, D. George, D. Greenberg: Acceleration Techniques for Progressive Refinement Radiosity. *Computer Graphics*, Vol. 24, N° 2, 1990
13. M. Sbert: An Integral Geometry Based Method for Fast Form-Factor Computation. *Computer Graphics Forum*, Vol. 12, N° 3 (*Proceedings of the Eurographics '93*), pp. (c-409)-(c-420), 1993
14. P. Shirley: A Ray Tracing Method for Illumination Calculation in Diffuse-Specular Scenes. *Proceedings of Graphics Interface '90*, pp. 205-212, Halifax, Nova Scotia, May 1990

344

A The Ambient Term and the Constant Radiosity Step

The ambient term can be derived from the power version of the radiosity equation system (14) by using a scalar approximation of the complete system:

$$P_{total}^{amb} = W_{total} + \rho_{avg} \cdot P_{total}^{amb} \tag{21}$$

here $\rho_{avg} = \sum_{j=1}^{N} A_j \cdot \rho_j \Big/ \sum_{j=1}^{N} A_j$ is the area-weighted average of the reflection coefficients. The explicit expression for this approximation can be written as follows (W_{total} is the self-emitted term):

$$P_{total}^{amb} = W_{total} + \frac{\rho_{avg}}{1 - \rho_{avg}} \cdot W_{total} \tag{22}$$

Lacking additional information the best way of distributing the total average Power P_{total}^{amb} among the individual patches can be written like this:

$$P_i^{amb} = W_i + \frac{\rho_{avg}}{1 - \rho_{avg}} \cdot W_{total} \cdot \frac{\rho_i \cdot A_i}{\sum_{j=1}^{N} A_j \cdot \rho_j} \tag{23}$$

Extracting the constant part of equation (23):

$$\beta = \frac{\rho_{avg} \cdot W_{total}}{\left(1 - \rho_{avg}\right) \cdot \sum_{j=1}^{N} A_j \cdot \rho_j} \tag{24}$$

and using the fact that $P_{total} \equiv W_{total}$ at the beginning of the iteration, it can be shown that the constant used in the ambient term is the same as in the constant radiosity step:

$$\beta = \frac{P_{total}}{\sum_{j=1}^{N} A_j \cdot \left(1 - \rho_j\right)} \tag{25}$$

Reformulating (23) using the constant we get:

$$P_i^{amb} = W_i + \beta \cdot \rho_i \cdot A_i \tag{26}$$

or:

$$B_i^{amb} = E_i + \beta \cdot \rho_i \tag{27}$$

Thus the ambient term for a patch i, B_i^{amb} is equal to the self emission plus the constant radiosity (as calculated via the derived constant radiosity step) multiplied by the reflection coefficient of the patch.

Fast Radiosity Solutions For Environments With High Average Reflectance

Gladimir V. Guimarães Baranoski[1]   Randall Bramley[1]   Peter Shirley[2]

[1] Indiana University, Bloomington, IN, USA
[2] Cornell University, Ithaca, NY, USA

1 Introduction

In radiosity algorithms the average radiance of n Lambertian patches is approximated by solving a linear system with n unknowns. When n is small (i.e. fewer than thousands of patches), general matrix methods like Gauss-Siedel can be used where the explicit $n \times n$ matrix can be pre-computed and stored [5]. When n is large, progressive techniques are used where the matrix rows or elements are recomputed as needed [4]. When n is very large (i.e. hundreds of thousands of patches), stochastic techniques can avoid computing or storing the n^2 elements of the matrix [10].

In applications where n is small enough to store the entire matrix in main memory, general matrix techniques will be faster than progressive techniques[3]. For "massing studies" [8] the lighting can be examined on simple geometric approximations of the environment being designed, and n can be very small. When the color scheme and lighting are being designed, the computationally expensive part (form factors) of the matrix in the linear system can be reused as the material properties are changed. For these applications the fastest possible general matrix solution is desirable.

This paper examines the Chebyshev method for solving linear systems, which for environments with high average reflectance can converge faster than the methods usually used in radiosity problems. We discuss some important characteristics of the linear systems in radiosity applications. We also look for solution methods that converge in small amounts of time, as opposed to a small number of iterations. For this discussion we assume a conventional RISC architecture, where coherent memory access is vital.

1.1 Radiosity System of Linear Equations

For an environment divided into n patches, the total spectral radiant power leaving a patch depends on the spectral radiant power emitted by the patch plus the spectral radiant power that is reflected. The spectral radiant power depends in turn on the total spectral radiant power leaving the other patches in the environment. The following system of equations represents the process of spectral radiant power transfer:

$$\Phi_j = \Phi_j^E + \rho_j \sum_{i=1}^n F_{ij}\Phi_i \qquad for \ \ each \ \ j = 1, 2...n \qquad (1)$$

---

[3] Progressive techniques will initially converge faster because they can begin iterations before computing the entire matrix. If general matrix techniques are modified to gradually construct the matrix during initial iterations, then this advantage of progressive method goes away.

where:

Φ_j = total spectral radiant power leaving patch j (watts/nm).

Φ_j^E = spectral radiant power emitted by patch j (watts/nm).

ρ_j = reflectivity of patch j (dimensionless).

F_{ij} = fraction of energy leaving patch i hitting patch j (dimensionless).

Applying the mathematical derivation described in [1] we get the classical expression in terms of spectral radiant exitance, M, which holds for each patch in the environment:

$$M_j = E_j + \rho_j \sum_{i=1}^{n} F_{ji} M_i \qquad for \quad each \quad j = 1, 2 ... n \qquad (2)$$

Radiosity, B, is the term used for radiant exitance in the computer graphics literature. Determining the radiant exitance (or radiosity) of each patch involves solving the linear system $GB = E$, given by:

$$\begin{bmatrix} 1 - \rho_1 F_{11} & -\rho_1 F_{12} & \cdots & -\rho_1 F_{1n} \\ -\rho_2 F_{21} & 1 - \rho_2 F_{22} & \cdots & -\rho_2 F_{2n} \\ \vdots & \vdots & \ddots & \vdots \\ -\rho_n F_{n1} & -\rho_n F_{n2} & \cdots & 1 - \rho_n F_{nn} \end{bmatrix} \begin{bmatrix} B_1 \\ B_2 \\ \vdots \\ B_n \end{bmatrix} = \begin{bmatrix} E_1 \\ E_2 \\ \vdots \\ E_n \end{bmatrix}$$

Iterative methods used to solve the radiosity system of linear equations can be divided into general matrix methods, which update all components of the solution vector on each iteration, and radiosity-specific methods [4] such as progressive refinement and overshooting methods, which update a single component on each iteration.

1.2 Eigenvalues Estimates

The Chebyshev method depends on eigenvalues estimates (see Appendix for relationship between eigenvalues and iterative solvers). The characteristic polynomial of a square $(n \times n)$ matrix G is given by $p(\lambda) = det(G - \lambda I)$, where I represents the identity matrix.

The zeros of $p(\lambda)$ are called *eigenvalues* or characteristic values of the matrix G. If $v \neq 0$ is such that $(G - \lambda I)v = 0$ holds, then v is called an *eigenvector* or characteristic vector of G corresponding to the eigenvalue λ.

Usually calculating the eigenvalues of a matrix G requires more computation than that required to solve the corresponding linear system. However we can obtain relatively inexpensive estimates of the eigenvalues using the Gerschgorin Circle Theorem [3]. This theorem says that the eigenvalues of G are contained within the union of n circles $S_i = \{z \in C \mid |z - g_{ii}| \leq \sum_{j \neq i}^{n} |g_{ij}|\}$, where C is the complex plane. The union of any k of these circles that do not intersect the remaining (n-k) must contain precisely k (counting multiplicities) of the eigenvalues.

In an environment formed by planar or convex surfaces ($F_{ii} = 0$) the radiosity matrix has all the main diagonal entries equal to one. So the centers of the circles are also have value one. In a closed environment ($\sum_{j=1}^{n} F_{ij} = 1$), the radius of S_i is given by ρ_i.

---

[4] We use the expression *radiosity-specific methods* to group methods specifically developed to solve the radiosity problem. Although those methods can be considered variations of numerical methods such as Southwell Iteration [7] or SOR [9], they have been particularly adjusted and finetuned to the radiosity case.

2 The Chebyshev Method

Gauss-Seidel [7] is a linear stationary method, which implicitly updates solutions by
$B^{(j+1)} = TB^{(j)} + \tilde{E}$, where T is an iteration matrix. Nonstationary methods have an
implicit iteration matrix T_j which changes on each iteration. The Chebyshev method
[12] [11] [2] is a nonstationary method based on residual polynomials (see Appendix).
It is directly applicable to nonsymmetric matrices like the radiosity coefficient matrix.
However it requires estimates μ and ν of the smallest and largest eigenvalues, λ_{max} and
λ_{min}, of the corresponding coefficient matrix. The iterative process is characterized by:

$$B^{(j+1)} = B^{(j)} + \Delta D^{(j)} \qquad \Delta D^{(j)} = q_j^{-1}(\Delta B^{(j)} + p_j \Delta D^{(j-1)}) \qquad (3)$$

where $\Delta D^{(j)}$ is a correction vector, $\Delta B^{(j)} = E - G * B^{(j)}$ is the residual, and q_j and
p_j are coefficients of the residual polynomials.

To obtain fastest reduction in the residual norm a residual polynomial method needs
to select polynomials whose ordinates quickly go to zero on the spectrum of the coefficient matrix G as the degree of the polynomial increases. For radiosity problems the
eigenvalues are all real and positive, so given a knowledge of an interval $[\mu, \nu]$ containing the spectrum of G we select polynomials P_k that have their maximum absolute value
on $[\mu, \nu]$ minimal over all monic polynomials (polynomials with leading coefficient 1)
of degree k. In addition to this "minimax" property, Chebyshev polynomials can also
be computed using a three term recursion which implies that the iteration can be implemented using only three additional vectors of storage (see Appendix).

Adapting the classical Stiefel iteration [12] [11], the Chebyshev algorithm in radiosity context becomes the following:

```
1       for (each i)
2           B_i^(0) = starting guess
3       compute ΔB^(0) = E − G * B^(0)
4       α = 2/(ν − μ)
4       β = (ν + μ)/(ν − μ)
6       γ = β/α
7       for (each i)
8           B_i^(1) = B_i^(1) + γΔB_i
9       compute ΔB^(1) = E − G * B^(1)
10      ω = 4/(ν + μ).
11      j = 1
12      while (not converged)
13          ω = (γ − 1/(4α²) ω)^(−1)
14          for (each i)
15              ΔD_i = ω * ΔB_i^(j) + (γω − 1)ΔD_i
16              B_i^(j+1) = B_i^(j) + ΔD_i
17          compute ΔB^(j+1) = E − G * B^(j)
18          j = j + 1
```

In the above algorithm λ_{max} and λ_{min} have been replaced by ν and μ, where $0 <
\mu \le \lambda_{min} < \lambda_{max} \le \nu$. The rate of convergence of Chebyshev is maximal when
$\mu = \lambda_{min}$ and $\nu = \lambda_{max}$, and the method can even diverge if λ_{max} is underestimated by
ν. Therefore to implement the Chebyshev method successfully the extremal eigenval-
ues of the matrix G must be estimated. However, since the Chebyshev polynomials grow

very rapidly if we underestimate the maximal eigenvalues, we will notice very quickly the sudden increase of the error norm. This would allow us to immediately reset the estimates and proceed.

Using the Gerschgorin Disk Theorem the extremal eigenvalues may be approximated by $1.0 \pm \rho_{max}$, where ρ_{max} is the highest reflectivity in the environment, which may correspond to the reflectivity of a single patch or of a group of patches. The increase of the highest reflectivity may not significantly change the overall reflectivity, expressed in terms of ρ_{avg}, e.g. if only the reflectivity of few small patches is changed. In that case our experiments show that increasing the highest reflectivity does not significantly change the convergence. On the other hand if we increase the overall reflectivity of the environment, e.g. high albedo scenes, then slow convergence results. Our experiments show that using ρ_{avg} instead of ρ_{max} to estimate the eigenvalues gives better results for all the cases tested. Therefore our Chebyshev parameters are given by $\nu = 1.0 + \rho_{avg}$ and $\mu = 1.0 - \rho_{avg}$ in which ρ_{avg} is given by:

$$\rho_{\text{avg}} = \frac{\sum_{i=1}^{n} \rho_i A_i}{\sum_{i=1}^{i=n} A_i}, \qquad (4)$$

where A_i is the area of patch i.

In all the cases tested the use of a starting guess which takes into account the ambient component gives better results than a starting guess which uses only the vector of emittances. To use this starting guess we replace line 2 of the above algorithm by $B_i^{(0)} = E_i + \rho_i Ambient$, where the ambient term is computed replacing ΔB_i by E_i in the ambient equation presented in [4].

3 Testing Parameters

We compared five algorithms, using explicitly stored form factors: Gauss-Siedel(GS), Progressive Refinement(PR) [7], Overshooting(FEDA) [6], Conjugate Gradient(CG) [1] and Chebyshev(CHEBY). The starting guesses were chosen in order to obtain the best possible rate of convergence for each tested algorithm. Consequently the initial error norm is not the same for curves on a single graph. The starting guess used for Gauss-Siedel and Conjugate Gradient algorithms was the vector of emittances and for the radiosity-specific methods we used a vector of zeros. For the Chebyshev algorithm we used the starting guess which takes into account the *Ambient* term, i.e. $B_i = E_i + \rho_i Ambient$.

The general matrix methods check the convergence after a complete sweep of the coefficient matrix, i.e. one iteration. The radiosity-specific methods perform this check after one relaxation step, i.e. one step of iteration. To make our measurement uniform we count steps of an iteration. In this context an iteration of a general matrix method corresponds to n steps of an iteration, where n is the order of the coefficient matrix.

To measure the time we start the clock at the beginning of a cycle of k steps of an iteration and stop it after k steps of an iteration. For the general matrix methods tested we use $k = n$. We check for k at each step in order to make the timing overhead the same for all methods. In addition all the error norms are computed outside of the timing cycles. The time measurements are given by elapsed CPU time on a SGI Challenge (20-R4400). All the algorithms were implemented using the same software guidelines to avoid differences that could affect the timing.

We use as our stopping criteria the largest unshot energy, i.e. the L_∞ norm of the vector with components $r_i A_i$, in which r_i represents the residual and A_i the area of patch i, given by:

$$\xi_\infty = \max_{1 \le i \le n} |r_i A_i| \tag{5}$$

If ξ_∞ is smaller than a given tolerance we stop the iterations. The value assigned to the tolerance depends on how visually close to true solution one wants the final image be. In general it is not necessary to use very low tolerance as in most numerical applications. We used a tolerance equal to 10^{-3}, but present the full convergence histories so that the methods can be compared for larger tolerances.

The test model used in our experiments consists of a sphere in the middle of a room. The sphere was divided into 128 patches and the faces of the surrounding cube were divided into 144 patches forming a total of 992 patches. The light source corresponds to 16 patches on the center of the "ceiling" of the cube. Assigning different values for the reflectivities varies ρ_{avg} and changing the sphere radius, $r = 1.0$ and $r = 2.0$, gives different densities (δ) for the coefficient matrix, 70% and 53% respectively.

4 Testing Results

Testing was performed to compare the performance of the five algorithms which are described in detail in [1]. In particular, we examine the effect of the matrix spectrum (which depends on the reflectivities in the scene). Numerical testing is necessary because most theory about the convergence rates of these methods deals with *asymptotic* convergence. For the low accuracy solutions needed in graphics radiosity problems, oftentimes an adequate solution is available before the asymptotic convergence region is approached.

The Gauss-Seidel and CG methods are *parameter-free*, that is, there are no algorithmic parameters which must be set by the user. Chebyshev requires estimates of the smallest and largest eigenvalues, but for this application those can be set automatically as was done here, by using $1 \pm \rho_{avg}$. The Feda method [6] can be fine-tuned by different choices of the overshooting parameter, in the same way that Gauss-Seidel is generalizable to the SOR method [9]. However, like the SOR method the optimal choice of parameters is unknown except for a few special cases. The version tested here automatically selects the overshooting parameter.

4.1 Steps of Iterations *vs* Time

Usually progressive refinement or overshooting converge in fewer steps of an iteration than the other three methods. However, counting steps of an iteration does not account for the differing amounts and types of work performed on each step. So a method that converges in fewer steps of an iteration may in fact require more overall time.

The experiments show that this distinction does occur in radiosity applications. Figure 1_{Left} shows that for test case A with $\rho_{avg} = 0.24$ progressive refinement methods converge in fewer steps of an iteration for $tol = 10^{-3}$. However, Figure 1_{Right}, showing the same convergence history as in Figure 1_{Left} but plotted against elapsed CPU time, shows that Gauss-Seidel and Chebyshev methods converge in less CPU time. When the overall reflectivity of the environment is increased, the difference becomes even more noticeable, as shown in Figure 2 for test case B with $\rho_{avg} = 0.46$.

Counter-intuitively, Gauss-Seidel and Chebyshev methods require more operations than the radiosity-specific methods, but require less CPU time. The main reason is the differing amounts of pipelining and data locality the algorithms allow. Note that in progressive refinement methods, we search for the patch with largest amount of unshot radiosity, which involves traversing a potentially large amount of data without performing any operations on it that decrease the residual. The general matrix methods, by contrast, simply process each row of the matrix in order. Although this may mean processing rows whose corresponding patch has no unshot radiosity remaining, in practice performance is enhanced. By avoiding the search phase, the computations can be better pipelined by compilers, and all data which is brought into the processor is actually used in improving the solution rather than searching for the next row to handle.

Furthermore, the innermost loop of the progressive refinement and overshooting methods consists of a *saxpy* (vector update of the form $\mathbf{y} = \mathbf{y} + \alpha\mathbf{x}$, where $\mathbf{x}$ and $\mathbf{y}$ are vectors and α is a scalar) operation, which entails $4n$ memory references (n each for reading ρ_j, $\triangle B_j$, F_{ij}, and an additional n for writing $\triangle B_j$) and $3n$ floating point operations (flops). By contrast the Gauss-Seidel, Chebyshev and CG methods have an inner product as the innermost loop. For the last two methods this entails $2n$ memory references and $2n$ floating point operations, because quantities not indexed by the innermost loop are kept in registers and so do not require a memory reference. In particular, the carry-around scalar that the inner product is summed into, and the reflectivity ρ_i, are kept in registers. Hence the ratio of memory references to flops is 4/3 for the radiosity specific solvers, while the ratio is 1 for the general matrix methods. This means the general matrix methods better utilize data locality, getting more flops out of data in the cache or registers before having to read or write new cache lines. Note that the better data re-use of the general matrix methods is not *a priori* evident from examining the algorithms. It is possible that in progressive refinement, only a few patches are selected to shoot out radiosity over and over again. In that case, the data associated with those patches would likely remain in cache, potentially giving better data locality properties. Our experiments show that this is not the case in practice, however. Usually over 90% the patches are selected the same number of times, ± 1. Furthermore, the patches selected most often are only selected a few more times than the average.

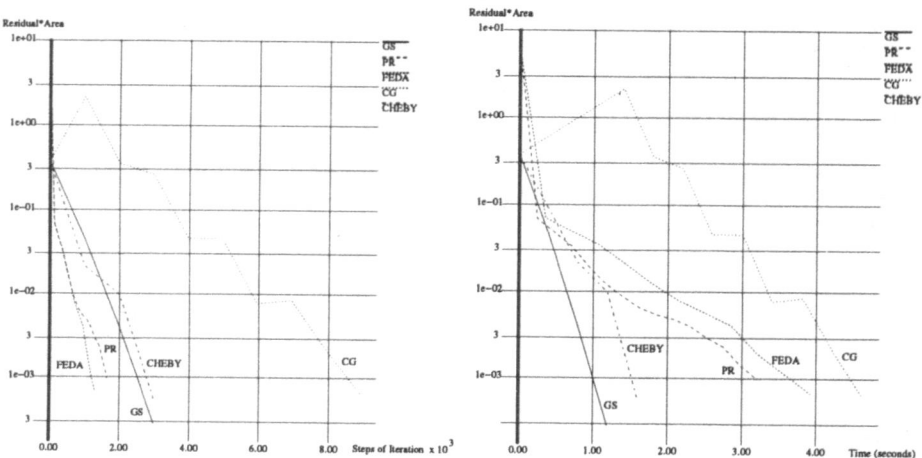

Fig. 1. Case A ($\rho_{avg} = 0.24$, $\delta = 53\%$) Left: steps of an iteration. Right: CPU time.

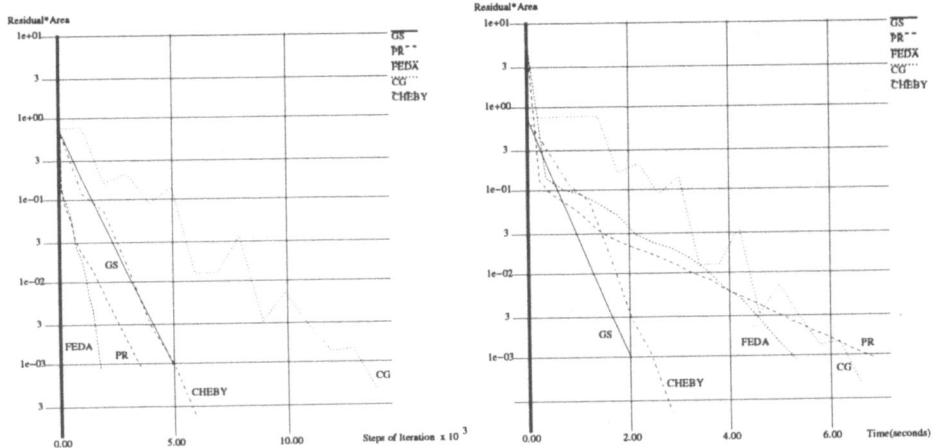

Fig. 2. Case B ($\rho_{avg} = 0.46$, $\delta = 53\%$) Left: steps of an iteration. Right: CPU time.

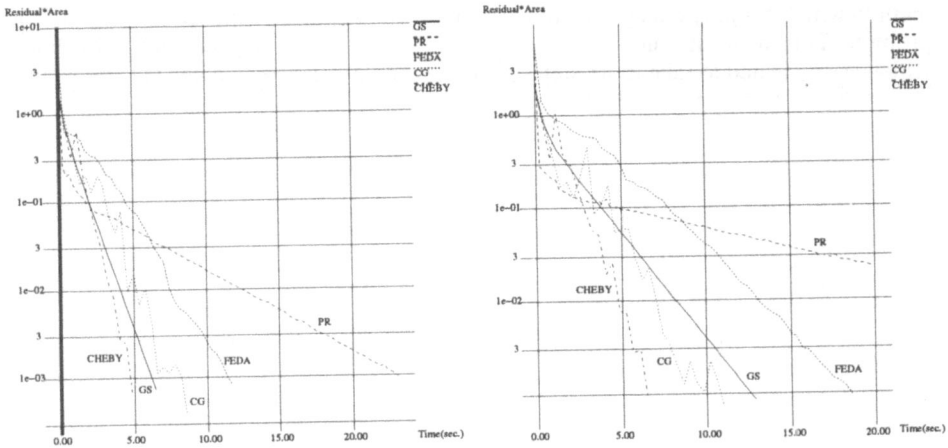

Fig. 3. Left: Case C ($\rho_{avg} = 0.77$, $\delta = 53\%$). Right: Case D ($\rho_{avg} = 0.88$, $\delta = 53\%$).

4.2 Effects of Reflectivity

Figures 2 and 3 show the performance of the various methods as matrix density (occlusion in the environment) is kept fixed at $\delta = 53\%$ and overall reflectivity is increased. Figure 4 does the same for $\delta = 70\%$. High reflectivities cause a larger number of interreflections, causing the eigenvalues to become more spread out which in turn slows

352

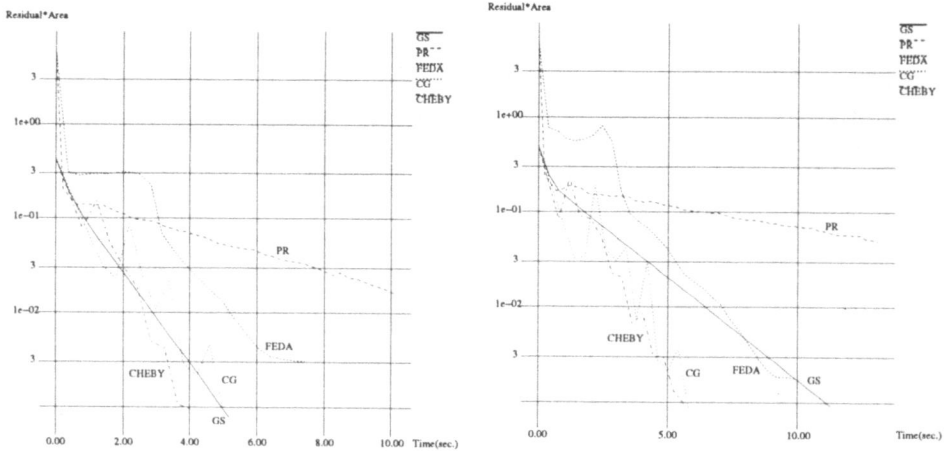

Fig. 4. Left: Case E ($\rho_{avg} = 0.78$, $\delta = 70\%$). Right: Case F ($\rho_{avg} = 0.89$, $\delta = 70\%$).

the convergence. Figure 5 shows the effects of the environment's overall reflectivity increase on the eigenvalue distribution. The increase of reflectivity is especially deleterious for PR. Because PR selects which patch to process on each step, it is a nonstationary method which actually changes its innermost loop depending on the specific data of the problem. This means it is not as amenable to analysis as the Chebyshev or CG methods, which are expected to take more steps of an iteration as the eigenvalues get spread out.

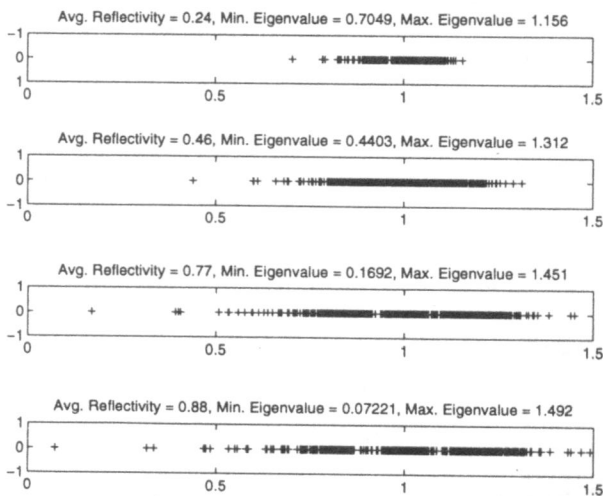

Fig. 5. Eigenvalue distribution as the overall reflectivity increases.

As reflectivity increases the spectral radius of the Gauss-Seidel iteration matrix approaches 1.0, and its relative performance decreases. The Gauss-Seidel method has a linear convergence rate that directly depends on the spectral radius of the iteration matrix. The Chebyshev method also has worsening performance, but relative to Gauss-Seidel it is not as sensitive to the increase in reflectivity. The adaptivity of the CG method makes its relative performance better as reflectivity increases; however, as Figure 4 shows only for the highest reflectivity and density levels tested did it become competitive with the Chebyshev method.

Table 1 summarizes the results for the test problems, and for each test case the time of the fastest algorithm is presented in boldface. Note that the Feda method implemented failed on test problems E and F, which have high density and reflectivity. In general, the Gauss-Seidel and Chebyshev methods are the fastest overall. These conclusions do not change when using different stopping tests or the other error norms described in [1].

Methods	Test Cases					
	A	B	C	D	E	F
CG	4.68	6.60	8.63	11.02	5.05	5.80
CHEBY	1.61	2.81	**4.81**	**6.45**	**4.05**	**5.64**
FEDA	3.92	5.32	11.73	18.47	7.45+	9.92*
GS	**1.20**	**2.01**	6.43	12.83	5.23	11.26
PR	3.21	6.85	23.03	50.56	22.53	50.43

Table 1. Algorithms performance (total time in seconds). The symbols * and + indicate failure to converge after 2478 and 3304 steps of an iteration respectively.

5 Conclusion and Future Research

Our experiments using explicitly stored form factors have shown that although radiosity-specific methods make rapid initial improvement, faster than any other method for limited tolerances (10^{-1}), they are slower than the general matrix methods for higher tolerances. Radiosity-specific methods require searching for a patch to shoot on each step, which can require traversing a large data structure. The disadvantage of general matrix methods of storing the form factors is compensated by the regularity of the computations which allows good pipelining and data locality.

The performance advantages of the general matrix methods are not as attractive when the form factors are computed on the fly, e.g. when n is large. In that case, the innermost loop consists of computing the form factors, which generally requires more flops than the matrix solving algorithms themselves. Avoiding even a few extra form factor computations by searching through rows for the most unshot radiosity may then give the edge to radiosity-specific methods such as Feda's method.

For environments with high average reflectance, which may occur in several applications, the rate of convergence is slower for all of the iterative methods used. Our experiments have also shown that the CG method and the Chebyshev method, with the estimates of the maximal eigenvalues described previously, represent the fastest approaches to handle those cases.

The experiments also show that selecting the "best" method is delicate, and no single method is superior in all cases. The relative performance depends on architectural performance features such as pipelining and data locality as well as problem character-istics. Developing practical solution strategies will likely require implementing a variety of linear solvers, with the one actually used chosen at runtime dependent on problem parameters such as reflectivity and occlusion, and figuring out the best parallel implementation for shared memory multiprocessor workstations. It will also be necessary to bring more numerical linear algebra tools to bear on the problem.

Finally we believe that the understanding of the physical meaning of the eigenvalues and eigenvectors in the radiosity context may help us to obtain even faster approximations for the radiosities vector. Our future efforts will be focused on that question.

Appendix - Residual Polynomial Methods and Eigenvalues

A Eigenvalues and Eigenvectors

A.1 Definition and Basic Properties

An *eigenvector* v of a matrix G is a nonzero vector that does not rotate when G is applied to it. In other words, there is some scalar constant λ, an *eigenvalue* of G, such that $Gv = \lambda v$. Every square matrix G of order n has n possibly nondistinct complex eigenvalues $\lambda_1, \lambda_2, ..., \lambda_n$. When G is symmetric the eigenvalues are real-valued. The set $\sigma(G)$ of eigenvalues of a matrix is called its spectrum.

A.2 Relationship with Iterative Methods

Eigenvalues determine the convergence of iterative solvers used to solve linear systems such as $GB = E$. For linear stationary methods of the form $B^{(j+1)} = TB^{(j)} + \tilde{E}$, which includes Jacobi, Gauss–Seidel, and SOR, the eigenvalues of the iteration matrix T are the relevant ones. The matrix T is derived from the coefficient matrix G; for example in the Gauss-Seidel iteration $T = (D + L)^{-1}U$ where D, L, and U are the diagonal, strictly lower triangular, and strictly upper triangular parts of G, respectively. However, no connection need hold between the eigenvalues of T and those of G. Linear stationary methods converge if and only if $\rho(T) < 1$, where $\rho(T)$ is the size of the eigenvalue with largest magnitude. Furthermore, convergence is faster for smaller $\rho(T)$.

For nonstationary methods such as conjugate gradients or Chebyshev, the eigenvalues of the coefficient matrix G are the important ones. The Chebyshev method has convergence determined by the convex hull of the spectrum of G, which is determined by the extreme eigenvalues. For a matrix with positive real eigenvalues the largest (λ_{max}) and smallest (λ_{min}) eigenvalues completely determine convergence, which is faster for larger values of $(\lambda_{max} + \lambda_{min})/(\lambda_{max} - \lambda_{min})$. The Conjugate Gradient method's convergence is determined by the overall distribution of eigenvalues, and even for a given $\sigma(G)$ it is impossible to predict the exact number of an iterations CG will require. However, CG generally requires only $s + 1$ iterations when the eigenvalues occur in only $s < n$ clusters, and has faster convergence for larger values of $(\lambda_{max} + \lambda_{min})/(\lambda_{max} - \lambda_{min})$.

B Residual Polynomial Methods

Most iterative solvers for linear systems can be analyzed using *residual polynomials*. Consider the linear system $GB = E$ with an approximate solution $B^{(j)}$. An iterative method can be seen as choosing a direction of motion $\Delta B^{(j)}$, then choosing a stepsize α to move in that direction:

$$B^{(j+1)} = B^{(j)} + \alpha_j \Delta B^{(j)}, \quad j = 0, 1, \ldots \tag{6}$$

Because of the residual vector $E - G * B^{(j)}$ corresponds to the direction of steepest descent, it is most commonly used for $\Delta B^{(j)}$. An iterative method can then be constructed by choosing the stepsizes α_j to minimize a measure of the error in $B^{(k)}$, where k is the number of iterations made. Recursively substituting (6) into the definition of residual vector gives [12]:

$$\Delta B^{(k)} = P_k(G)\Delta B^{(0)} \tag{7}$$
$$P_k(\lambda) = (1 - \alpha_{k-1}\lambda)(1 - \alpha_{k-2}\lambda)\cdots(1 - \alpha_0\lambda) \tag{8}$$

P_k is called a residual polynomial; note that $P_k(0) = 1$ necessarily holds.

If G is diagonalizable then $G = SDS^{-1}$ where S is a nonsingular matrix and D is the diagonal matrix with $\lambda_1, \lambda_2, \ldots, \lambda_n$ on its diagonal. In this case $P_k(G) = SP_k(D)S^{-1}$, and to obtain fastest reduction in the residual norm a residual polynomial method needs to select polynomials whose ordinates $P_k(\lambda_i)$ quickly go to zero as the degree of the polynomial increases. These ordinates give the reduction in the ith eigencomponent of the residual after the kth step of the iteration. In addition to this optimality property, a good residual polynomial should be computed using short recursions so that only a few of the previous residual vectors need be stored.

C Chebyshev Polynomials

The Chebyshev polynomials τ_k [3] for the interval $[-1, 1]$ are defined by $\tau_k(x) = \cosh[k \cosh^{-1}(x)]$, for each $k \geq 0$. Because they are orthogonal with respect to the weight function $w(x) = (1 - x^2)^{-1/2}$, Chebyshev polynomials can be computed using the three term recursion:

$$\tau_0(x) = 1, \quad \tau_1(x) = x, \quad \tau_{k+1}(x) = 2x\tau_k - \tau_{k-1}; \quad k \geq 1.$$

Most importantly, Chebyshev polynomials have a *minimax* property: of all k^{th}–degree polynomials with leading coefficient 1, $2^{1-k}\tau_k$ has the smallest maximum norm in $[-1, 1]$. The value of its maximum norm is 2^{1-k}. Figure 10 shows the graphs of monic Chebyshev polynomials of degree 3,4 and 5.

Given an interval $[\mu, \nu]$ containing the eigenvalues of a matrix G the Chebyshev method uses residual polynomials based on monic Chebyshev polynomials shifted from the interval [-1,1] to the interval $[\mu, \nu]$, and scaled so that $P_k(0) = 1$. This gives:

$$P_k(\lambda) = \frac{\tau_k\left(\frac{\nu+\mu-2\lambda}{\nu-\mu}\right)}{\tau_k\left(\frac{\nu+\mu}{\nu-\mu}\right)}.$$

The three term recursion can similarly be translated to the new variables, giving the Chebyshev algorithm presented in the paper.

356

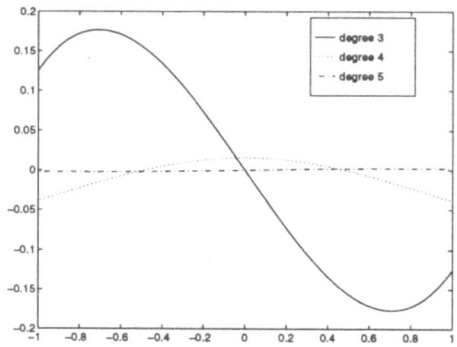

Fig. 6. Monic Chebyshev polynomials.

Acknowledgements

The work reported in this paper was supported in part by the *Conselho Nacional de Pesquisas* (CNPq, Brasil) and by *NSF* (Grant CDA 93-03189, USA).

References

1. G. V. BARANOSKI, R. BRAMLEY, AND P. SHIRLEY, *Iterative methods for fast radiosity solutions*, tech. rep., Indiana University, 1995.
2. R. BARRETT ET AL., *Templates for the Solution of Linear Systems: Building Blocks for Iterative Methods*, SIAM, Philadelphia, 1 ed., 1994.
3. R. BURDEN AND J. FAIRES, *Numerical Analysis*, PWS-KENT Publishing Company, Boston, 5 ed., 1993.
4. M. COHEN, S. CHEN, J. WALLACE, AND D. GREENBERG, *A progressive refinement approach to fast radiosity image generation*, Computer Graphics, 22 (1988), pp. 75–84.
5. M. COHEN AND D. GREENBERG, *The hemi-cube: A radiosity solution for complex environments*, Computer Graphics, 19 (1985), pp. 31–40.
6. M. FEDA AND W. PURGATHOFER, *Accelerating radiosity by overshooting*, in Proc. of the Third Eurographics Rendering Workshop, Consolidation Express, June 1992, pp. 21–32.
7. S. GOERTLER, M. COHEN, AND P. SLUSALLEK, *Radiosity and relaxation methods*, IEEE Computer Graphics and Applications, 14 (1994), pp. 48–58.
8. D. GREENBERG, *Computers and architecture*, Scientific American, 264 (1991), pp. 104–109.
9. L. HAGEMAN AND D. YOUNG, *Applied Iterative Methods*, Academic Press, New York, 1981.
10. L. NEUMANN, *New efficient algorithms with positive definite radiosity matrix*, in Proc. of the Fifth Eurographics Rendering Workshop, June 1994, pp. 219–237.
11. Y. SAAD, A. SAMEH, AND P.SAYLOR, *Solving elliptic difference equations on a linear array of processors*, SIAM Journal of Scientific and Statistical Computing, 6 (1985), pp. 1049–1063.
12. E. STIEFEL, *Kernel polynomials in linear algebra and their numerical application*, in Further Contributions to the Solutions of Simultaneous Linear Equations and the Determination of Eigenvalues, National Bureau of Standards, Applied Mathematical Series - 49, 1958.

Appendix: Color Images

Bump on the right hand face of a box (Kurzion and Yagel, Fig. 5)

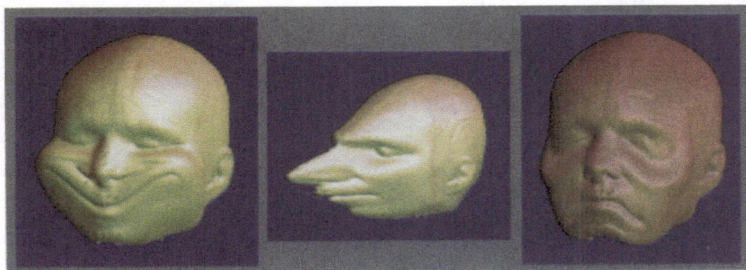

Examples of deflecting a volume from MRI with multiple deflectors (Kurzion and Yagel, Fig. 6)

A teapot modeled from a box (right) and a teapot modeled from a sphere (left), both represented by a 128^3 volume. A teapot represented by a polymesh consisting of 256 polygons being deflected (center) (Kurzion and Yagel, Fig. 7)

(Noma, Fig. 4)

(Noma, Fig. 5)

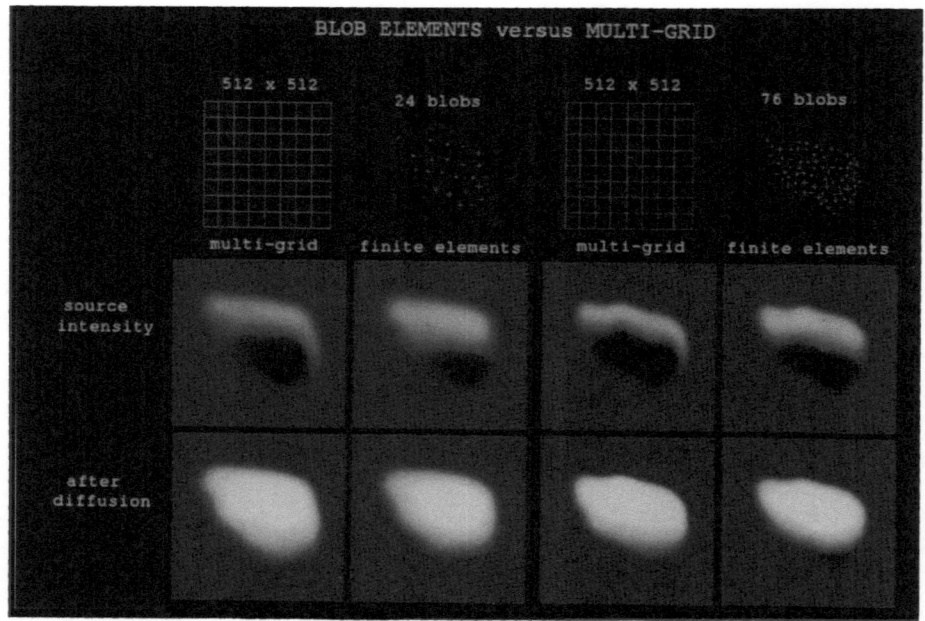

Non-constant densities (Stam, Fig. 4)

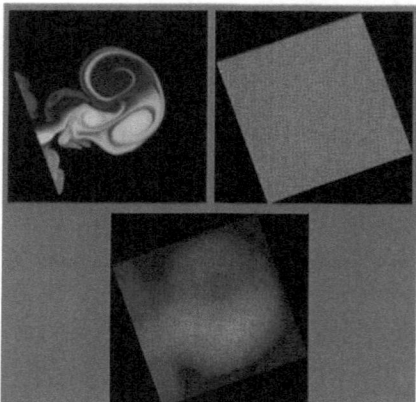

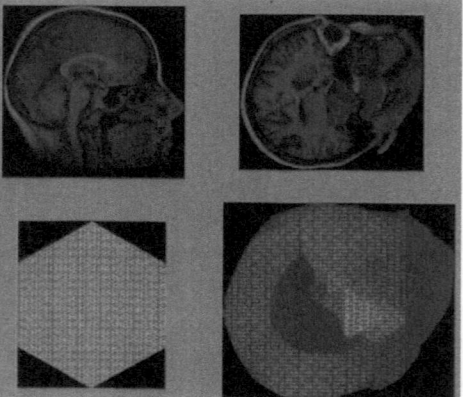

Images are ordered in clockwise fashion beginning from top left corner. (a) An image from a fluid dynamics simulation reconstructed by the data-adaptive method where ε is 0.02, rotated by 30 degrees, and scaled by a factor of 0.75. (b) Filter sizes used for the position-adaptive method. (c) Filter sizes used for the data-adaptive method. Bright values stand for larger filters sizes (Machiraju et al., Fig. 2)

Images are ordered left to right and top to bottom. (a) An almost vertical slice of a 3D MRI head volume dataset through the center. (b) A slice with directional vector (1,1,1) passing through the center. The error threshold ε is 0.01. (c) The filter sizes used in the position-adaptive scheme for (b). (d) The filter sizes used in the data-adaptive scheme for (b) (Machiraju et al., Fig. 3)

Top view of *Abies*
(Max and Ohsaki, Fig. 2)

Slant view of *Abies*
(Max and Ohsaki, Fig. 3)

Side view of *Abies*
(Max and Ohsaki, Fig. 4)

Reconstructed *Abies*
(Max and Ohsaki, Fig. 5)

Reconstructed *Abies*
(Max and Ohsaki, Fig. 6)

Reconstructed *Magnolia*
(Max and Ohsaki, Fig. 7)

360

Magnolia with shadows
(Max and Ohsaki, Fig. 8)

Magnolia with shadows
(Max and Ohsaki, Fig. 9)

A grove of seven identical rotated and translated *Magnolia* trees with shadows (Max and Ohsaki, Fig. 10)

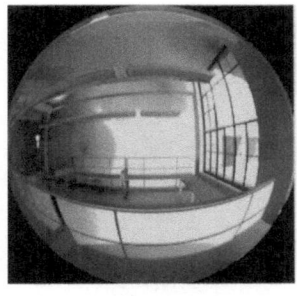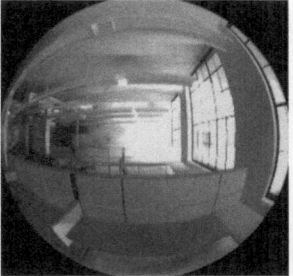

Two fisheye views (left, center) of our studio model and an interpolated view (right) (Nimeroff et al., Color Plate1)

Indirect illumination solutions calculated for two times (left, center) and an interpolated indirect solution (right) (Nimeroff et al., Color Plate 2)

Method (speedup compared to fixed): *left* adaptive, no partial (12×), *center* adaptive, partial (8×), *right* fixed (Gershbein, Plate 1)

362

(Müller et al., Fig. 4a)

(Müller et al., Fig. 4b)

(Müller et al., Fig. 4c)

(Müller et al., Fig. 4d)

(Müller et al., Fig. 4e)

(Müller et al., Fig. 4f)

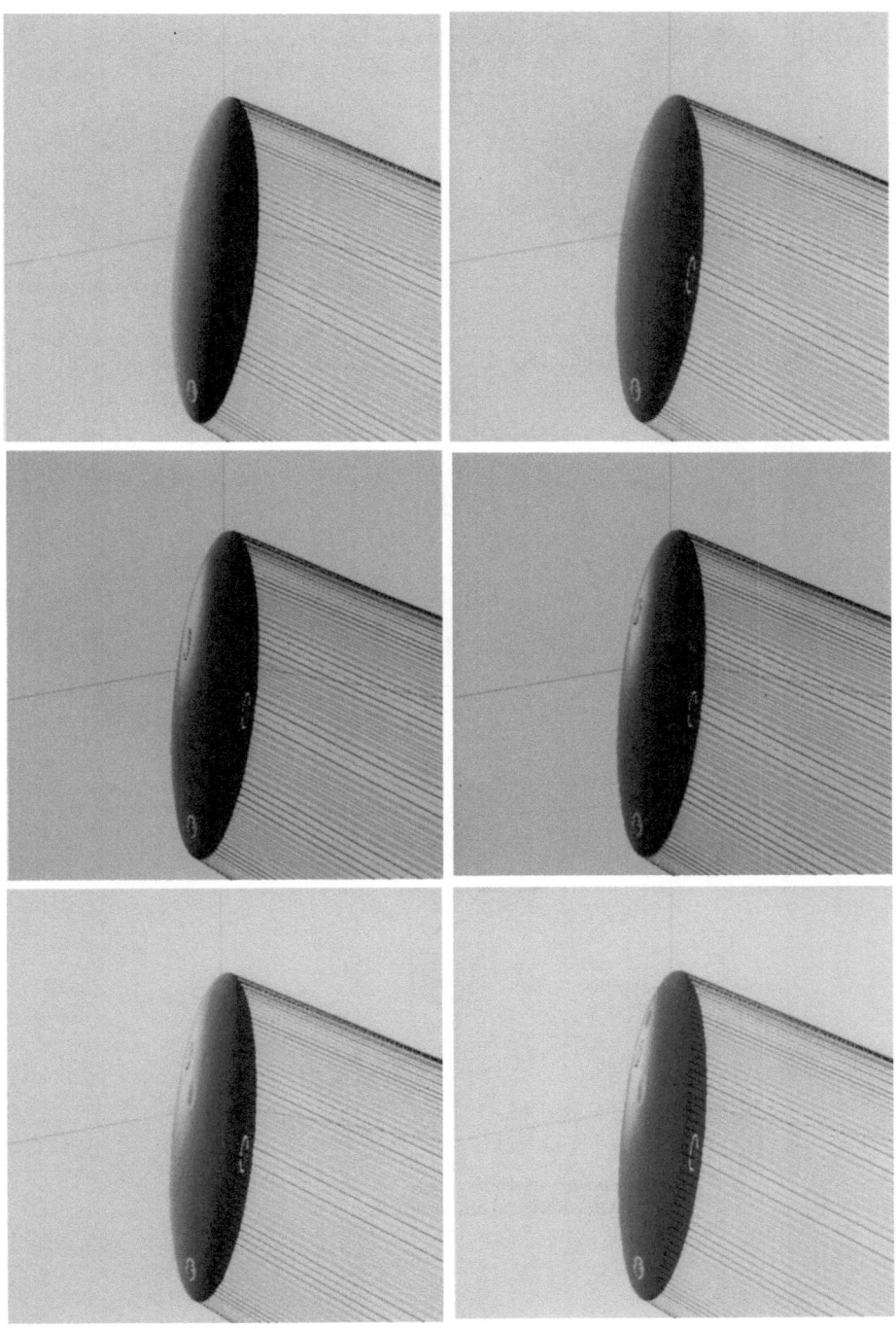

Painting colors on a surface (Poulin and Fournier, Fig. 1)

Radiosity on the receiving plane, due to a constant emitter (Holzschuch and Sillion, Fig. A)

Norm of radiosity gradient, due to a constant emitter (Holzschuch and Sillion, Fig. B)

Radiosity on the receiving plane, due to a linear emitter (Holzschuch and Sillion, Fig. C)

Norm of the radiosity gradient, due to a linear emitter (Holzschuch and Sillion, Fig. D)

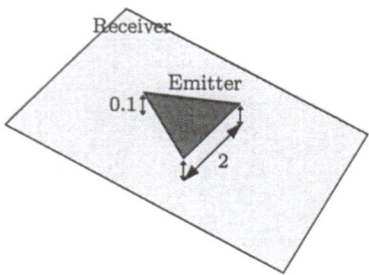

Geometry of our test scene
(Holzschuch and Sillion, Fig. E)

a

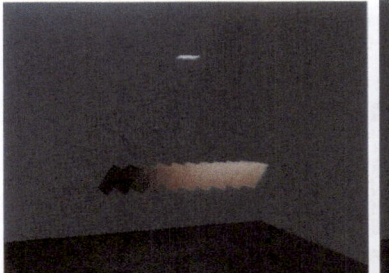

b

c

Using directional visibility information: **a** representation of the directional extinction coefficient for the cluster of slanted objects. **b** Simulation showing the varying attenuation in the shadow area. **c** Simulation using isotropic extinction: note the uniform attenuation in the shadow area (Sillion et al., Plate 1)

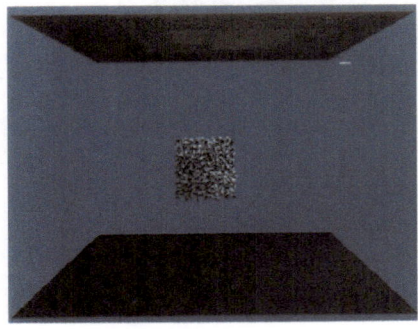

a

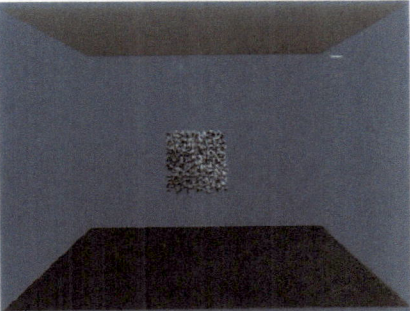

b

Solution for a scene with 6000 diffuse surfaces: **a** directional, **b** non-directional clustering (Sillion et al., Plate 2)

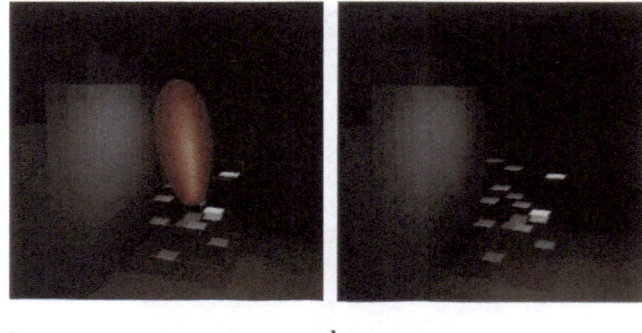

a   **b**

Simulation with a cluster of specular reflectors (overhead illumination): **a** distribution of radiant intensity for the selected cluster, **b** final image (Sillion et al., Plate 3)

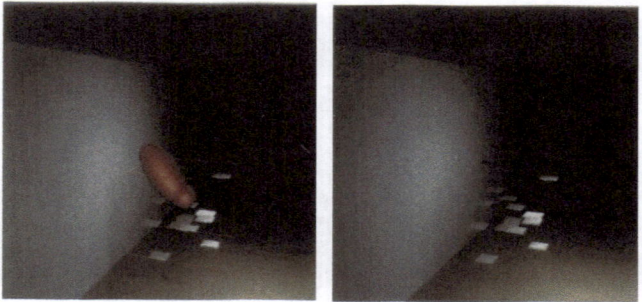

Simulation of the same scene (with illumination coming from the side). Compared to Plate 3, note the change in secondary illumination and the change in the cluster's shadow (Sillion et al., Plate 4)

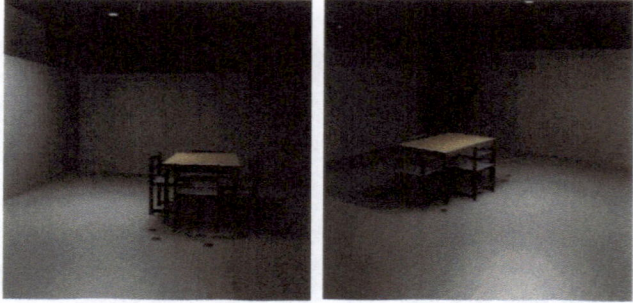

Two views of a scene with glossy surfaces (floor and table top). Note the differences in the appearance of the non-diffuse surfaces (Sillion et al., Plate 5)

A scene rendered with Stochastic Ray method
(Neumann et al., Fig. 4)

Another view of the same scene
(Neumann et al., Fig. 5)

A scene with perfect specular reflection
(Neumann et al., Fig. 6)

The same scene, containing a point light source
(Neumann et al., Fig. 7)

The scene and mesh that were used for comparisons
(Neumann et al., Fig. 8)

The reference solution for the comparisons
(Neumann et al., Fig. 9)

Random Walk Method after 10 million rays
(Neumann et al., Fig. 10)

Stochastic Ray Radiosity after 10 million rays
(Neumann et al., Fig. 11)

Random Walk Method after 20 million rays
(Neumann et al., Fig. 12)

Stochastic Ray Radiosity after 20 million rays
(Neumann et al., Fig. 13)

The starting vector (30 iterations, 10^4 rays each)
(Neumann et al., Fig. 14)

Stochastic Ray Radiosity after 1 iteration
(Neumann et al., Fig. 15)

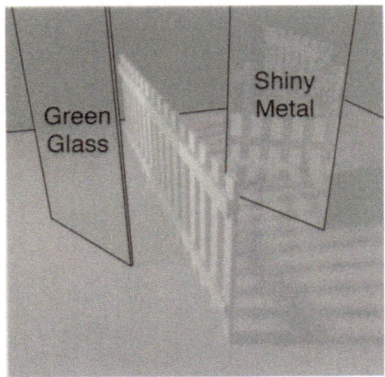

Undecimated solution of fence model showing specular reflection. This image is ray-traced (Shirley et al., Plate A)

(left) Decimated and (right) undecimated solution of room with 10.000 initial surfaces. Undecimated solution is ray-traced (Shirley et al., Plate B)

Decimated solution of model with 150.000 initial surfaces (Shirley et al., Plate C)

Undecimated solution of traditional Cornell Box (Shirley et al., Plate D)

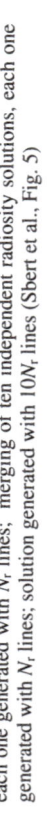

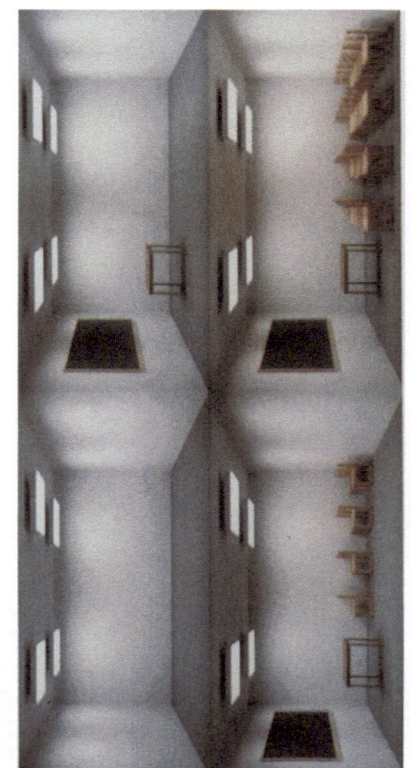

Merging radiosities with the multi-path method ($N_r = 1.4 \times 10^7$): from left to right and top to bottom: a radiosity solution with N_r lines, merging of four independent radiosity solutions, each one generated with N_r lines; merging of ten independent radiosity solutions, each one generated with N_r lines; solution generated with $10 N_r$ lines (Sbert et al., Fig. 5)

Images generated with the multi-path method, each with the same number of lines, 1.4×10^8. From left to right and top to bottom: scene with 30, 114, 1122 and 3138 surfaces (Sbert et al.,

Example scene 6 of Peter Shirley rendered with Haar Wavelets, double links and final gathering (Slussallek et al.)

Table and elevator scene rendered with third order multiwavelets, shadow masks and quick links (Slussallek et al.)

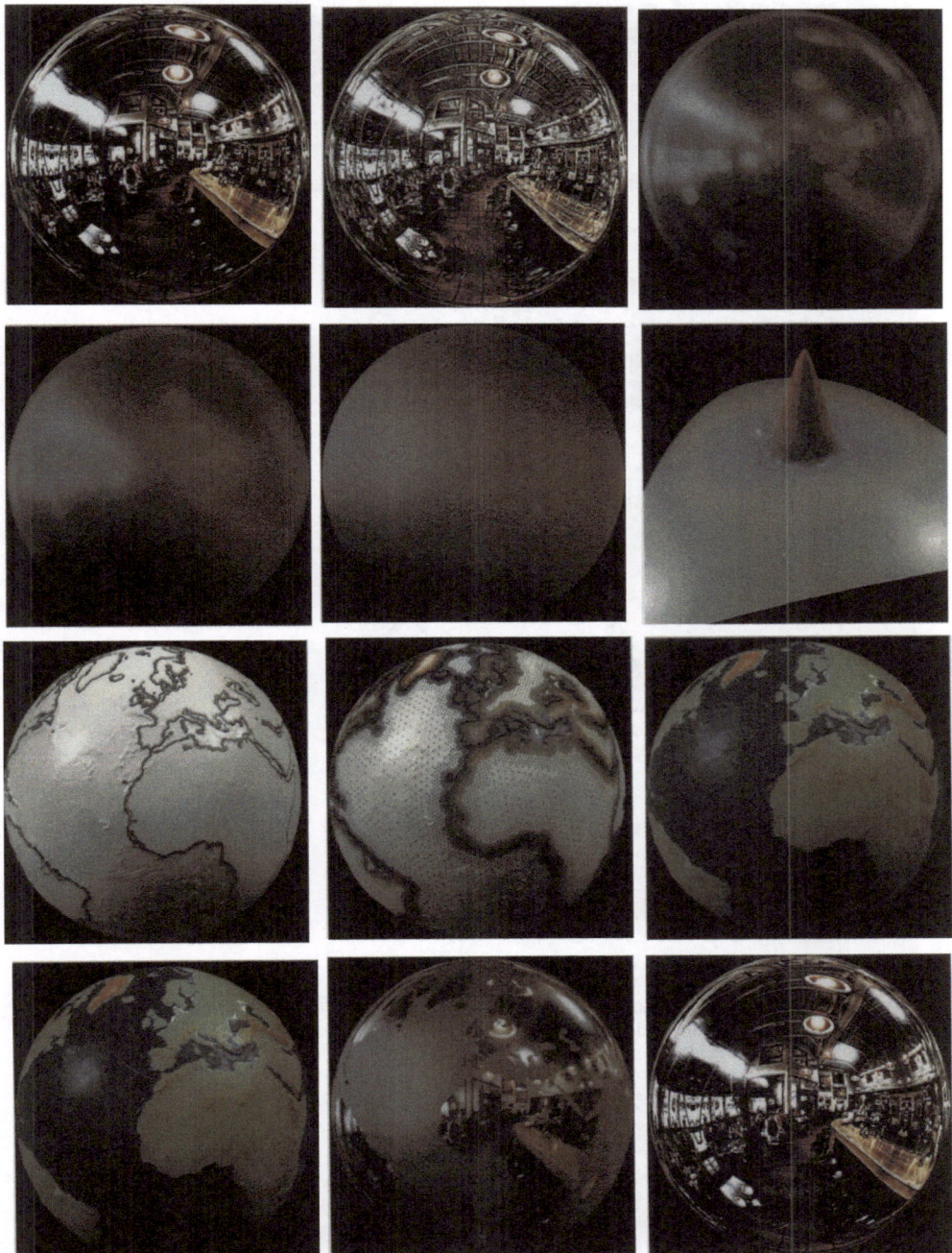

Examples of processed environment maps and spherical textures (Schröder and Sweldeus, Fig. 3)

  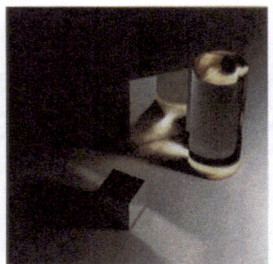

(Collins, Colour Plate 1 a)   (Collins, Colour Plate 1 b)

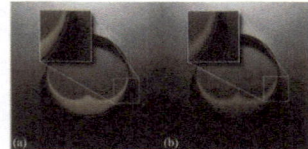 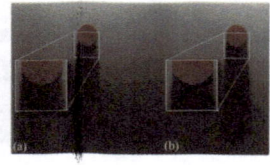

(Collins, Colour Plate 2)   (Collins, Colour Plate 3)

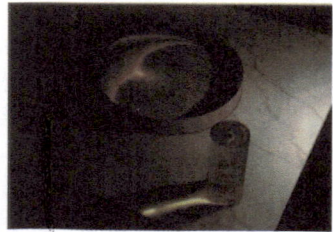 

(Collins, Colour Plate 4)   (Collins, Colour Plate 5)

Test scene 1 sampled using 10, 200, 300, 400 and 500 samples pr. pixel. The top row shows the results using standard importance sampling and the bottom row shows the results when the information from the photon map is added (Jensen, Fig. 4)

Test scene 2 sampled with 50 samples pr. pixel using standard importance sampling (Jensen, Fig. 5)

Test scene 2 sampled with 50 samples pr. pixel using importance sampling enhanced with the photon map (Jensen, Fig. 6)

Riccardo Scateni, Jarke J. van Wijk, Pietro Zanarini (eds.)

Visualization in Scientific Computing '95

Proceedings of the Eurographics Workshop in Chia, Italy, May 3–5, 1995

1995. 110 figures. VII, 161 pages.
Soft cover DM 85,–, öS 595,–
ISBN 3-211-82729-3

(Eurographics)

Prices are subject to change without notice

This book represents results in the field of Scientific Visualization which is nowadays an indispensable discipline to get insight in the huge amounts of data produced by large scale simulations or advanced measurement devices.

The readers will find a selection of state-of-the-art results and techniques in Scientific Visualization reserach, which they can use to find solutions for their visualization problems.

Springer-Verlag Wien New York

Sachsenplatz 4–6, P.O.Box 89, A-1201 Wien · 175 Fifth Avenue, New York, NY 10010, USA
Heidelberger Platz 3, D-14197 Berlin · 3-13, Hongo 3-chome, Bunkyo-ku, Tokyo 113, Japan

Martin Göbel, Heinrich Müller, Bodo Urban (eds.)

Visualization in Scientific Computing

1995. 150 figures. VIII, 238 pages. ISBN 3-211-82633-5
Soft cover DM 118,–, öS 826,–. (Eurographics)

Visualization is the most important approach to understand the huge amount of data produced in today's computational and experimental sciences. Selected contributions treat topics of particular interest in current research, for example visualization of multidimensional data and flows, time control, interaction, and volume visualization. Readers may profit in getting insight in state-of-the-art techniques which might help to solve their visualization problems.

Wolfgang Herzner, Frank Kappe (eds.)

Multimedia/Hypermedia in Open Distributed Environments

Proceedings of the Eurographics Symposium in Graz, Austria, June 6–9, 1994

1994. 105 figures. VIII, 330 pages. ISBN 3-211-82587-8
Soft cover DM 118,–, öS 826,–. (Eurographics)

This book represents the results from the Eurographics symposium on "Multimedia/Hypermedia in Open Distributed Environments", June 6–9, 1994, Graz, Austria. Its six sessions "Standards and Standards Exploitation", "Demonstrations", "Tools", "Hypermedia and Authoring", "Architectures", and "CSCW and Information Services" give a comprehensive overview about current research and development, including the future mm/hm standards MHEG and PREMO. The reader will profit in getting up-to-date information about the current trends in (the development of) mm/hm services and applications in open, distributed environments.

Prices are subject to change without notice

Springer-Verlag Wien New York

Sachsenplatz 4–6, P.O.Box 89, A-1201 Wien · 175 Fifth Avenue, New York, NY 10010, USA
Heidelberger Platz 3, D-14197 Berlin · 3-13, Hongo 3-chome, Bunkyo-ku, Tokyo 113, Japan

Springer-Verlag
and the Environment

WE AT SPRINGER-VERLAG FIRMLY BELIEVE THAT AN international science publisher has a special obligation to the environment, and our corporate policies consistently reflect this conviction.

WE ALSO EXPECT OUR BUSINESS PARTNERS – PRINTERS, paper mills, packaging manufacturers, etc. – to commit themselves to using environmentally friendly materials and production processes.

THE PAPER IN THIS BOOK IS MADE FROM NO-CHLORINE pulp and is acid free, in conformance with international standards for paper permanency.